Library of
Davidson College

VOID

THE ARMY IN BOURBON MEXICO

THE ARMY IN BOURBON MEXICO, 1760–1810

Christon I. Archer

UNIVERSITY OF NEW MEXICO PRESS
Albuquerque

Library of Congress Cataloging in Publication Data

Archer, Christon I. 1940–
　The army in Bourbon Mexico, 1760–1810.

　Bibliography: p. 347
　Includes index.
　1. Spain. Ejército—Colonial forces—History.
2. Mexico—History—Spanish colony, 1540–1810. I. Title.
UA789.A7　　　355.3'52'0946　　　76-57536
ISBN 0-8263-0442-7

© 1977 by the University of New Mexico Press. All rights reserved.
Manufactured in the United States of America
Library of Congress Catalog Card Number 76-57536
International Standard Book Number 0-8263-0442-7
First Edition

For C. A. A.

CONTENTS

Preface	xi
Introduction	1
1. The Gachupín Dilemma	8
2. Strategic Veracruz	38
3. The Port versus the Viceroys	61
4. The Perception of Danger	80
5. The Army Bureaucracy and the Bourbon Administration	106
6. The Army and the Cabildos	136
7. The Merchants and the Military	168
8. The Officer Corps	191
9. Manpower	223
10. Discipline, Punishment, and Conditions of Service	254
11. Cast Adrift	278
Conclusion	299
Appendix 1. Troops Cantoned at Córdoba, Orizaba, Perote, and Jalapa in August 1806	303
Appendix 2. List of the Viceroys of New Spain, 1760–1810	304
Glossary	305
Notes	309
Bibliography	347
Index	357

TABLES

1.	Composition of the Regular Army of New Spain in 1784	22
2.	The Regular Army Proposed by Colonel Crespo	23
3.	The Provincial Army Proposed by Colonel Crespo	25
4.	Origins of Some Prominent Veracruz Merchants, 1810	50
5.	Cost of Sending an Army of 6,000 from the Interior Cantonment to Veracruz and Maintaining It for Six Months	52
6.	Entries, Departures, and Deaths in the Military Hospital of San Carlos and the Poor Hospital of Montesclaros, Veracruz, 1787–1804	56
7.	Neutral Vessel Commerce at the Port of Veracruz, September 26, 1805, to March 31, 1807	75
8.	Militia Brigades of the Army of New Spain, 1800–1810	110
9.	Disabilities of Militiamen in the Provincial Infantry of Mexico Stationed at Córdoba, 1798	151
10.	Food and Commodity Prices Fixed by the Cabildo of Orizaba, 1797	155
11.	Ratio of Militiamen to Eligible Population in the Cavalry Regiment of the Prince and the Infantry Battalion of Guanajuato, 1796	158
12.	Donations and Expenditures for the Formation of the Cavalry Regiment of the Prince and the Battalion of Guanajuato, 1795	160
13.	Numbers of Whites, Castizos, and Mestizos Eligible for Militia Service in the Ten Jurisdictions of Michoacán, 1794	162
14.	Donations toward the Formation of the Infantry of Tres Villas, 1795	164
15.	Regular Army Majors Assigned to the Provincial Militia Units in the 1790s	192
16.	Age and Origins of Senior Officers in the Regiment of the Crown, 1788	193
17.	Senior Regular Army Officers of the Army of New Spain, 1799	195
18.	Senior Provincial Army Officers of the Army of New Spain, 1799	212
19.	The Population of Mexico City in 1790	227
20.	Origins of Enlisted Men in the Regiment of the Crown, 1788	228
21.	Ratio of Mexican and *Peninsular* Enlisted Men in the Army of New Spain, 1790	228
22.	Recruiting Teams Dispatched by the Regiment of the Crown, 1790–99	231
23.	Ratio of Mexican and *Peninsular* Enlisted Men in the Army of New Spain, 1799–1804	234

24.	Origins of Enlisted Men in the Regiment of New Spain, 1804	234
25.	Occupations of Enlisted Men in the Battalion of Oaxaca, 1796	238
26.	Occupations of Enlisted Men in the Battalion of Guanajuato, 1795	239
27.	Reserve Company Enlistment in 1797	240
28.	Deaths and Desertions in the Regiments of the Crown and New Spain, 1800–1802	268

PREFACE

When I began research on the army of New Spain over eight years ago, my primary concern was to isolate the causes of militarism and then to plunge into a study of the royalist army following the outbreak of the Hidalgo revolt. The first stage appeared to be a matter of testing the statements of the nineteenth-century historians who had examined the preindependence period illustrating precursor movements and seeking the roots of the impending struggle. On one point, these historians were almost unanimous; the recently introduced military had created a definite consciousness of martial honors and privileges. As Carlos María de Bustamante put it, Mexicans "... fell like flies into the honey."[1] Conservatives and liberals as diametrically opposed on most issues as Lucas Alamán and José María Luis Mora identified an *"espíritu militar"* or *"espíritu marcial"* evident before 1810.[2] As might be expected, the liberals condemned the defunct colonial regime for having granted legal position and special status to soldiers. Mora, a confirmed enemy of any privileged corporations and particularly of the army and the clergy, argued that such anachronisms simply could not coexist with a modern democratic republic. Until the final destruction of the *fuero militar* and any other exemptions from the laws of the nation, the army would remain *"un instrumento de persecución."*[3]

Although these views have withstood intact the test of time, I became convinced that the colonial army did not fit the description of historians who quite naturally blamed the Spanish regime for the problems of the republic. As long as the passions generated by the revolutions remained, the former enemy was a convenient target. At the same time, as María del Carmen Velázquez and Lyle N. McAlister discovered in recent studies of the colonial army, there were forces at work in New Spain which gave considerable credence to Mora's conclusions.[4] My own objective is to place the army into a broader perspective and to see how social, political, and economic factors during the second half of the eighteenth century determined the directions of policy and how external events intervened to shape the Mexican situation. To accomplish these ends, this book examines the theory and practice of defense from the imperial cabinet level at Aranjuez, Madrid, and elsewhere in Spain to the lowest level in Mexican towns such as Zimapán and Xochimilco where the local subdelegate or militia officer implemented the royal will. Here, the common people were confronted with military service and the concept of duty to the *patria*. Between these levels, the gulf might best be described in terms of the width of the Atlantic between mother country and colony. The complexity of Mexican society and the intricacies of the system which governed it confounded contemporary observers as well as later historians. Even so, the color and raw dynamism of the late colony come alive from the documents. In my own view, the army presents a useful vehicle for bringing these qualities into perspective. It had to deal with elites and commonality, almost all of the major institutions, and the full spectrum of racial mixtures produced by three centuries of miscegenation. Since the military was a latecomer, it had to struggle for position and acceptance; its confrontations with the royal jurisdiction, miners, merchants, hacendados, and other powerful groups illustrate many of the strengths and weaknesses of late Bourbon Mexico.

As in the case of most major historical watersheds, hindsight view is clear and unimpeded. Often historians have interpreted the events in such a way that when 1810 arrives and the anticipated cataclysm cracks New Spain to its foundations, the reader need not express great surprise or shock. To the contemporary witnesses, however, the preparation for what occurred was a vague premonition, incomplete, or more often nonexistent; despite warnings, Hidalgo's rebel masses caught the regime and the army brooding about a possible French invasion. Just as important, the legendary degradation, corruption, and evil of Godoy's Spain become convenient motives for attacking the viceroys and other officials who suffered the extreme misfortune of being appointed or, even worse, of being related to the favorite. The viceroys, Marqués de Branciforte, Félix Berenguer de Marquina, and José de Iturrigaray, were not the venal functionaries described by most historians. When more research on these figures has been completed, I doubt that many of the charges against them will stand up. Branciforte, certainly a conservative when compared with the more popular figures of the Spanish Enlightenment, made his career in a number of important appointments during the halcyon years of Charles III. In New Spain he was to become one of the more effective administrators. Unlike his immediate predecessor, the Conde de Revillagigedo, Branciforte demonstrated an admirable grasp of how best to satisfy *criollo* aspirations and at the same time to direct their energies for the imperial cause. Successful in playing upon the criollos' vanity and rage for position, he raised an army without even having to tap the royal exchequer. This in itself was later an embarrassment to criollo historians: obviously, he had to be corrupt. If no evidence could be found, Branciforte was married to

Preface

one of Godoy's sisters and therefore damnable as the pawn of the immoral favorite.

Traditionally, Mexican historians, in their anxiety to affirm their nationality and to give meaning to the independence movement, have tended to adopt a patriotic bias. This of course has changed; the works of Enrique Florescano, Romeo Flores Caballero,[5] and many others have altered the pattern. At the same time, however, one cannot blame the Mexicans for perpetuating a nationalist interpretation of the immediate preindependence period. Spanish historians, the natural heirs of the imperial side, until recently have not been able to generate much enthusiasm either for the reign of Charles IV or for the events leading up to the national collapse before Napoleon. Since they were convinced about the general corruption and treachery of Godoy, it was not difficult for them to accept the most negative opinions on the state of the colonial regime in Mexico. Here again, there are signs of change; in the work of Enrique Lafuente Ferrari during the 1940s and more recently in the scholarship of José Antonio Calderón Quijano, Luis Navarro García, and the students of the Escuela de Estudios Hispano-Americanos in Seville,[6] one can perceive the beginnings of an imperial interpretation.

The pall of gloom and clichés which haunts the 1790s does not extend back into the reign of Charles III. The spirit of reform and the prevailing optimism of the Spanish Enlightenment have engendered a positive attitude by historians which extends to New Spain. Herbert Priestley, for example, might have made José de Gálvez appear in a much worse light than the Marqués de Branciforte. Gálvez's cruelty in crushing the revolts of 1767, his lifelong devotion to nepotism, his refusal to listen to opposing opinions, and his mental breakdown in Sonora, during which he raved about importing an army of apes from Guatemala to put down Indian insurrection, provide material enough to destroy his reputation.[7] Whatever his faults, though, Gálvez was a reformer and thus attractive in the modern way of thinking. The same is true of the Conde de Revillagigedo (1789–1794), considered to be a great viceroy because he reflected Enlightenment themes and exhibited a dogged dedication to reform. The facts that his innovations almost ruined the army of New Spain and that he expressed a dislike for Mexico and an unconcealed contempt for its inhabitants have not injured his prestige.

Until very recently, historians of eighteenth-century New Spain have been limited by the paucity of published research on almost any subject. Those who were in the field suffered from the lack of monographs treating allied themes or institutions. The single major exception was and still is the comprehensive account left by that perceptive scientist and traveller, Alexander von Humboldt.[8] Yet for all of his powers of observation, Humboldt could not be expected to write a definitive account of all institutions and to treat every level of society. Since he was connected with the regime and dealt mostly with the elites, it is quite natural that he reflected certain of their attitudes. Moreover, local officials probably painted a rosy picture, knowing their information was for the record. Just as in their reports to the viceroys or the imperial government, some issues and problems were best not exposed to scrutiny. In today's world, concerned with environmental pollution and conditions of labor, Humboldt's descriptions of the healthy miners at Guanajuato, for example, fall flat. After talking to the local physicians, he assured his readers that part of the population of Guanajuato actually drank the water used in the amalgamation of silver ores and mercury—the *agua de lavanderos*. No ill effects were supposed to result from this practice.[9] Quite probably the Guanajuato physicians put their best face forward for the distinguished visitor. Mercury poisoning and other miners' diseases went unmentioned. Certainly the case was quite different when the army recruiters attempted to enlist the same healthy miners. Now, instead of being robust and in perfect physical condition, the mine workers were described by physicians and mineowners as anemic skeletons suffering incurable lung diseases and numerous other chronic afflictions.

In the past few years, a number of major monographs on the eighteenth century have brought truly remarkable changes to the field of Bourbon studies on New Spain. Books and articles by Enrique Florescano, Nancy Farriss, David Brading, Brian Hamnett,[10] and others have given historians some new foundations and directions. In many respects they made my own work possible and I owe them a great debt of gratitude. Like these historians, I discovered that archival research is the only key to unlocking the treasure of colonial history. Once the unfamiliarity of research in an area where guides and catalogues are incomplete at best has been overcome, hard labor, personal contacts with archivists and fellow scholars, and even luck are needed. But the challenge of the search is often rewarded by rich finds. I will never cease to be amazed at the thoroughness of the eighteenth and early nineteenth-century Bourbon administrators. The army bureaucrats filed almost every scrap of paper that crossed their desks. There have been some losses in the intervening years, but for research on the military of New Spain, the task of covering the material becomes something of an odyssey. Four research trips to Mexico and two to Spain have left me relatively satisfied although it is always difficult to know just where to draw the line. Since both the Archivo General de la Nación and the Archivo de Indias in Seville contain entire sections of uncatalogued documents, future researchers may well have more to say about the army.

Preface

I wish to express my gratitude to the many people who have assisted me in one way or another since the beginning of this project. First, at the State University of New York at Stony Brook, Guillermo Céspedes del Castillo interested me in Mexican colonial history and set me off on the course which has resulted in this book. María del Carmen Velázquez of El Colegio de México helped me to understand the eighteenth-century military of New Spain and has pointed me in the right direction on a number of occasions. Lyle N. McAlister of the University of Florida, whom I had the good fortune to meet during my doctoral research in Seville, has read much of my material and listened patiently to my ideas. Without his good guidance and suggestions, not only would my work have suffered, but I would also have missed a rich learning experience. I am especially indebted to Stanley R. Ross of the University of Texas, who directed my doctoral dissertation and who has continued to give me most useful and constructive criticism along the way. I must also mention Jack Ogelsby who introduced me to the field of Latin American history at the University of Victoria in British Columbia. Other friends and colleagues I want to mention by name are Nancy Farriss, Norman Martin, S.J., Brian Hamnett, Leon Campbell, Donald Cutter, David Trask, Niall and Jean Spears, Larry Steck, Dauril Alden, and Father Francis Guest. In Spain, the directors and staffs of the Archivo General de Indias, the Archivo General de Simancas, the Archivo Histórico Nacional, and the Museo Naval gave me a warm welcome and encouraged my research. In Mexico, I must thank the directors and staffs of the Biblioteca Nacional, El Colegio de México, and most of all of the Archivo General de la Nación. The patience and good humor of the director, Dr. J. Ignacio Rubio Mañé, and his willingness to share his vast knowledge of the eighteenth century with a foreign student of Mexican history have made my visits to the national archives memorable experiences. The State University of New York, the University of Calgary, the Foreign Area Fellowship Program, and the Canada Council assisted my research and financed travel. I must express special thanks to the Canada Council for a post-doctoral research fellowship in 1974 and 1975 to make one last visit to Spanish and Mexican archives and then to prepare the manuscript. Finally, to my wife Carol and to my children Katherine and John, I owe more than I can express in words. My wife spent many months assisting me in archives without any recognition and has provided me with the strength necessary to complete the book. To have lived for so long with a husband who more often than not has been half in the twentieth century and half in the eighteenth must have been a considerable burden.

INTRODUCTION

Following the bold work of conquest and assertion of Spanish control during the sixteenth century, New Spain fell into a fairly peaceful existence. Mineral resources were exploited, stockraising and agriculture developed, cities grew to meet the requirements of commerce and industry, and, in the process, a new society evolved. With the exception of an occasional, rather futile, plebeian rising aimed more at righting local inequities than at achieving any major change in sovereignty, there was no real tradition of unrest to cause the maintenance of a large military establishment. Even the depredations of pirates or the potential threat of expeditionary armies sent across the Atlantic by European enemies were of no immediate danger to the major population centers located far inland from the coasts. Settled regions could be defended and policed by a very few regular companies which might if necessary give aid to the law enforcement agencies. For these soldiers, army life meant little more than routine guard duty over viceroys and public buildings, and colorful holiday demonstrations of military prowess to amuse the populace. Any additional defensive needs could be met by recruiting merchants, hacendados, and artisans, who were quite capable of suppressing civil disorders such as those which occurred in Mexico City during 1692 and 1693 or from time to time in other cities.[1]

The geography and political situation of New Spain relegated defense to the frontiers and coasts. The wild northern frontier and constant warfare with unsubdued Indian tribes, reminiscent in the eyes of Spanish army officers of the struggle against the Moors in the Iberian Peninsula and North Africa, trained an exceptionally tough force of light cavalry. Fortúnately for the more settled provinces, however, the Provincias Internas formed a buffer halting most southward penetration of Indian raiders. Following the visitation of José de Gálvez in 1765–71, the creation of a semiautonomous commandancy general, headed by an army officer, recognized the special situation of the north. Except for the provinces of Nuevo Santander and Nuevo León, which came under the direct jurisdiction of Mexico City, the defense of the Provincias

Internas was a secondary if worrisome concern. Although most of the late eighteenth-century viceroys would have liked nothing better than to regain full control over the north, for our purposes this region will be examined only when soldiers of the main force of the army of New Spain were sent to the frontier or on occasions when events in and beyond the Provincias Internas appeared to threaten the security of the south.[2] The coasts, open to the attacks of enemy powers, corsairs, and the contraband traffic of both foreigners and Mexicans, demanded much more defensive attention. Since the navy could not match the British or maintain even a few adequate vessels to carry out coastal reconnaissance, the army had to form the first line of defense. The deployment of forces along the Gulf coast and the even more isolated Pacific coast was a matter dictated by unsettled open expanses, the nature of the available population, and the climate's general insalubrity. High levels of disease deterred efforts to settle unacclimatized groups on the coasts and decimated men from the interior highlands or overseas who were sent into temporary garrison duties. The main consolation in these problems was the knowledge that enemy invaders would be subject to the same difficulties experienced by the defenders. The elements of disease, supply, and communications were utilized fully by defense planners. All but the most inexperienced or foolhardy of the potential invaders viewed the viceroyalty as an impractical target. Indeed, once good intelligence information was obtained, projects against New Spain failed to materialize.

North of the province of Yucatán, Veracruz was the only major fortified position along the Gulf coast of New Spain. This city, guarded by the strong offshore fortification of San Juan de Ulúa, had to be the primary target for any invader or enemy who wished to isolate New Spain from overseas trade and communications. Veracruz was the single terminus of the roads leading from the interior—if they deserved that name. A general who aspired to defeat the army of New Spain and possibly to occupy Mexico City had to gain control over the port. To the north no other ports but New Orleans allowed easy access to the interior of the continent. As the history of Mexico has proved on a number of occasions since independence, whoever controlled Veracruz had a good chance of eventually winning the nation. The remainder of the Caribbean coast was left to a number of irregular militia companies that could man observation watchtowers and harass contrabandists and ship's crews marauding for provisions, but assuredly would prove inadequate against a concerted effort by even a small force. Fortunately for the defenders, such coastal intrusions were of limited practical use to an enemy. Impassable mountain ranges, deserts, and great distances as well as a complete lack of developed roads into the interior prevented movement inland. There was little advantage to be gained from capturing small subsistence farms or the grass huts of coastal fishermen. On the Pacific coast, isolation from potential enemy bases further reduced the danger of an enemy invasion and the small castle of San Diego at Acapulco provided adequate protection.[3]

Defense of the Spanish-American empire, based upon a strategy of a few strongly fortified ports such as Havana, Cartagena, Veracruz, and Campeche, worked well enough until the eighteenth century. Attacks upon the treasure fleets and on coastal cities and settlements by British, French, and Dutch raiders, while damaging in immediate terms, caused no significant peril to the Spanish imperial system. Despite Spain's seventeenth-century decline in naval and military power, no enemy could entertain more than fleeting notions of reducing the empire sufficiently to occupy New Spain or Peru. By the mid-eighteenth century, however, the rise of Britain to a position of overall maritime superiority altered the situation. The fortresses of Spanish America were open to siege and possible capture. It was easy to see that if a bulwark such as Havana or Veracruz fell, Britain could move expeditionary forces from Europe and, accompanied by troops and supplies raised in her own colonies, begin the conquest of the great viceroyalties. Anglo-American troops already had been used in Caribbean service at the time of the War of the Spanish Succession and, in subsequent conflicts, both Spanish and French America had felt their weight.[4] To increase the apprehension of the defenders of Mexico, Jamaica, with its well-developed contraband installations, furnished an excellent base for military operations against Veracruz.

Spain's belated entry into the Seven Years' War in 1762 offered the British a whole series of golden opportunities. The French empire lay battered and almost without further potential when Charles III joined the fray. Selecting Havana, Cuba as the single most strategic quarry and as a place which would further British commercial designs, an amphibious force managed to wrest the fortified city from Spanish control. In a single operation, Britain had brought the Spanish empire to the brink of disaster. In the aftermath, even before the recriminations over the failure had ended, new policies were being discussed by the cabinet. Havana had been considered impregnable and its ignominious surrender crushed the long-standing dependence upon a few strong fortresses. If they fell, almost nothing stood between the enemy forces and the dazzling prospect of seizing the wealth of the colonies. With Havana occupied, Veracruz was the next logical objective and if it surrendered, Britain would be able to divert the flow of silver and other exports away from the Spanish commercial system. When by good luck Havana was returned to Spain at the peace conference, it was obvious that speedy action was needed to prevent repetition of the disaster. Since the regular and militia forces had failed, military reform became an important priority.⁵

Metropolitan Spain could not afford the expense or the manpower to garrison the American empire. The demands of European wars and of the North African frontier were sufficient to spread resources very thin. Besides, if Britain was to be the enemy, her naval dominance would prevent reinforcements from being sent the moment a war broke out. The only logical solution was to station a moderate cadre of peninsular officers and troops in overseas possessions; these forces would have the great responsibility of inculcating patriotism and instructing the inhabitants of the American colonies so that they might undertake their own defense. Such a decision resulted from necessity and not desire. Members of the supreme war council in Madrid suffered no illusions about the potential hazards. Plainly, the arming of Mexicans and other Spanish Americans might possibly backfire and result in weapons being turned against the mother country. No matter how long army officers thought about the subject, the debacle at Havana proved that untrained civilians were no match for regular soldiers. The solution would have to lie in a system of checks and balances, but most of all it would be contingent upon the ability of the regime to inculcate patriotism and to draw upon men of *"actividad, aplicación, y talento."* In the view of many Spanish officers, however, the process of *mestizaje* had produced a multitude of *castas* devoted to sloth and addicted to the full range of social vices. Few Mexicans displayed the noble characteristics expected of Spaniards or the humility and diligence of Indians. Since economy was another guiding principle of the colonial military, many of the viceroys were unwilling to pay the high costs of establishing an army and then to continue the level of expenditure needed to implant martial institutions. During peacetime, when defense lost its urgency, the army suffered neglect and was often forgotten until the next international crisis. The result was a force that on more than one occasion was described as little more than "a giant paralytic, numerous but of little respect or power."⁶

The endeavor to make Spanish America capable of its own self-defense was only one of the major innovations introduced by the ministers of Charles III. Many of the archaic institutions that carried the blame for having permitted the empire to stagnate or not to fulfill its true worth to the mother country now were exposed to severe scrutiny and reform. Far-reaching changes in policy improved the commercial system, facilitating a greater exchange of goods between the peninsula and colonies and even amongst the colonies. Not only were attempts made to stimulate new commerce and industry, but Spain also began to regain at least some of the contraband trade conducted by foreign and national smugglers. These developments focused attention and debate upon the state of the administration at both the imperial and colonial levels of government. Certainly the most outstanding example of reform in this area was the introduction of the intendancies to replace the system of *corregidores* and *alcaldes mayores,* which had been characterized by extraordinary abuse and corruption. These reforms, described by David Brading as a "revolution in government,"[7] did not solve all problems and in some respects aggravated existing grievances. The army, closely connected with the administrative sector, witnessed and in many cases experienced the difficulties because military finance, recruitment, supply, and other important matters were handled by the intendants and subdelegates.

Yet, no matter what transpired within the Spanish empire, external forces transcended and altered internal events. Enlightenment philosophers stimulated thinking on matters such as liberty and republicanism as well as awakening interest in agricultural, industrial, and scientific themes welcomed by the regime. It was impossible to filter out ideas and information on news events which would lead Spanish Americans to at least an awareness of change in the world. The imperial government was thrown into a quandary when the revolt of the Anglo-Americans presented a choice of either seeking revenge for the shameful defeats of the Seven Years' War or permitting Britain to suppress a colonial uprising that if successful could not help but provide an example for Spanish America. The decision to take advantage of Britain's preoccupation with the American Revolution produced immediate gains, but the long-term risks were soon evident. A Mexican regiment served in the Caribbean theater of the war and, during the operations at Pensacola and in other engagements, Spanish Americans came into firsthand contact with the goals and aspirations of the Anglo-American republicans. From this date forward, Mexicans and Spaniards continued to express a lively curiosity about the United States. Whether stated in terms of a desire to learn about the northern neighbor or of an arrogant superiority over everything American, it mattered little; there was no escape from a new fact of life.

Important as the American Revolution was in the history of the Spanish empire, it was nothing compared to the disasters begun by the outbreak of the French Revolution. The tide of reaction following 1789 drove the Spanish reformers from positions of power or made them reject anything varying from absolute orthodoxy. As a result, many of the positive achievements accomplished by the supporters of the Spanish Enlightenment went unrecognized and some of the nonpolitical programs were abandoned. Attempts to erect a *cordón sanitario* to exclude or smother revolution, liberty, and republicanism increased censorship, harassment of French residents, and the activity of the

Inquisition, but did little to dampen interest in the French upheaval.[8] Official efforts to suppress all news and information from France changed after the trial and execution of Louis XVI. Charles IV of Spain, determined to engage in holy war against the murderers of his royal cousin, stimulated Spaniards throughout the empire to react with patriotic donations and support for the principle of monarchy. The acts of the Convention in France horrified most Spaniards and forged a temporary degree of national unity. Despite early victories, however, the crusade bogged down, and the nationalism aroused against France turned into bitterness and hatred for the favorite, Manuel Godoy, who became the scapegoat for Spain's weakness.

The conflict against France ended with the Treaty of Basle (1795) which was followed by a return to the traditional alliance against Britain. Spain was now the unwitting pawn in a struggle between the greater powers and peace remained beyond reach. War against Britain went on from 1796 to 1802 and again from 1804 to 1808. These conflicts disrupted the economy and society of the empire and once again permitted an increase in contraband trade from British and foreign sources. For a short period in 1799, the regime sanctioned the trade of neutral vessels in Spanish-American ports, but this permitted trade with the enemy since no one could tell the difference between Anglo-Americans and Englishmen. The colonial population had no alternative other than to shoulder greater and greater defensive burdens and to finance what came to be seen as a European problem. Uncertain of enemy intentions, the viceroys of New Spain reached deeper into the available reserve of manpower, breaking accepted racial guidelines and exposing the poorer sectors to social and economic dislocations. Years of service under arms damaged families, ruined businesses, and opened a new and lucrative source of income for those empowered to grant military deferments. Although the regime did what it could to prevent corrupt practices, the avarice of the subdelegates and local officials exposed nerves and pointed out the real weaknesses of the administrative reforms. For the viceroys and senior army officers of New Spain, expediency took precedence over equity. The British capture of Trinidad (1797) and then the attacks on Buenos Aires and Montevideo (1806) demonstrated the importance of the military and solid intelligence reports made it quite clear that Mexico had been designated as a primary target. To many Mexicans as well as to other Spanish Americans, European wars and the burden of supporting the empire forced a reevaluation of their situation. They were impressed by the successes of the United States and the profits to be made by playing the role of independent neutral during European conflicts.

The Napoleonic invasion of the peninsula, although it relieved the threat of an invasion of Mexico, dealt a body blow to the Spanish empire. With the colonies already cast adrift by naval blockades, the overthrow of the House of Bourbon left the colonial regime rudderless. The governing juntas which sprang up in Spain to claim the mantle of continuity aggravated rather than calmed the situation overseas. Justifying their existence through the reasoning that upon the removal of the king, sovereignty returned to the people, the juntas left the way open for Spanish Americans to follow suit. In the deepening crisis, the governing elements in New Spain, the peninsular and criollo sectors, turned against each other and in the process temporarily neglected the bulk of the population. Remarkably, the mobilized army lay paralyzed in its cantonments while small groups of civilians and irregular militiamen overthrew the legitimate regime. In the aftermath of these events, up to 1810, the irresponsible praetorian military tradition condemned by historians was conspicuously absent: rather, the army officers clung to legitimacy and supported the vestigial regime long after it became a hollow pretense. At the same time, however, the attention of the military was riveted upon the European conflagration. Signs of impending disaster within New Spain were either dismissed or misunderstood until too late.

1

THE GACHUPÍN DILEMMA

After almost two and a half centuries during which it had been Spanish policy to disarm the population of the settled Indian civilizations and to discourage all but the most essential military formations, little remained of the warlike tradition of either *conquistador* or Indian. Although the Conde de Revillagigedo expressed some shock in 1789 at seeing Indians at his court armed with bows and arrows, spears, and obsidian-edged clubs when they came to protest against ill-treatment or vexations by local officials, there was little real danger. Generally, such weapons had become ceremonial accouterments of the annual Corpus Christi holiday, Holy Week, and visits to the viceroy.[1] Yet, since the sixteenth century, the coasts of New Spain had been notoriously insecure and on several occasions the ports of Campeche and Veracruz fell to small groups of corsairs. In 1683, for example, the dispatch of militia units from the interior did not save the port. By the time they straggled down to the coast, a small pirate force commanded by Nicolás de Agrammont had pillaged the city and sailed away.[2] In wartime, it was customary for viceroys to raise temporary militia forces, but no one was enthusiastic about their fighting potential. Army officers charged with responsibility for defense against foreign invasion and the maintenance of internal tranquillity found their assignments incredibly troublesome and not a little distasteful. Nothing about Mexico gave confidence to the commanders. Great distances separated population centers from the coasts and from each other, and the eligible manpower did not fit any European concept of order. The Indians and many of the castas were alienated or semialienated from Spanish society by a multitude of social, racial, and legal barriers; even the minority of whites divided according to criollo or gachupín origins.

When in 1762 the Seven Years' War brought the first real threat of invasion, Viceroy Marqués de Cruillas encountered exceptional difficulties in raising the most rudimentary defenses. Although Havana had fallen to the British and Veracruz lay open to attack, the population manifested little concern that New Spain might be the next objective. Militiamen recruited at Alvarado and along the Veracruz coast demanded releases from service to plant their milpas of maize. Since they possessed no arms anyway, they could see no reason why they should be kept on active duty. The viceroy met with even less success when he ordered six hundred Indians from the districts of Cosamaloapan, Tuxtla, and Acayucan to rush to Veracruz with machetes and iron tools to help repair the fortifications and extend the sand dunes. Local employers opposed any effort to remove Indian laborers and the avaricious *justicias* refused to support the government. One alcalde mayor claimed to have misplaced the viceregal orders, which meant that other officials of his jurisdiction did not receive any notification of manpower requirements.[3]

In the interior, Cruillas had to resort to pleas begging the wealthy classes to present their servants and any weapons they owned for the militia. The alcalde mayor of Tlaxcala sent his *alguacil mayor* on a house-to-house canvass of all Spaniards and *"gente de razón,"* a search which eventually produced seven pistols, four shotguns, and four swords. All of these arms were old and worn—the type employed by shopkeepers to protect their premises from thieves. The officials held out little hope of increasing this arsenal since none but the Spaniards could be expected to have any defensive weapons. In the countryside around Tlaxcala, even the owners and managers of haciendas possessed no arms other than long knives which served in their work as well as for self-defense. Eligible militiamen were equally scarce: some men volunteered, but most were too young, overage, obliged to remain close to their Indian workers, or were themselves Indians or members of unacceptable castas. In nearby Huamantla, a company of fifty-three cavalrymen composed of hacienda managers proved to be of no use because the men were beyond military age or burdened by the support of large families.[4] Elsewhere, militiamen who were rounded up and marched to the coast were abandoned in Veracruz, where barracks and other essential facilities failed to meet demand. Yellow fever struck the unacclimatized militiamen, causing high death rates and making a mockery out of the defensive preparations. Even with the expenditure of 736,801 pesos on extraordinary military and defense programs in 1762, Cruillas could show little improvement.[5]

Although many officials on both sides of the Atlantic persisted in the view that colonial populations should not be armed, the occupations of Havana and Manila in 1762 forced a thorough review of defense strategy. The imperial government had to agree to permanent defensive forces stationed in the

American possessions and in 1764 a secret defense committee drafted a plan for colonial armies. These would be led by a number of regular infantry and dragoon regiments raised in the colonies and supported by the rotation of selected European units. Furthermore, a significant cadre of Spanish or European officers and soldiers was to accept permanent assignment to the Americas. Even so, the great majority of the new armies, the real pillar about which the defense system had to coalesce, consisted of colonial militia units organized in a form similar to that of the Spanish provincial militia.[6]

The crown devoted full attention to the difficulties and even the hazards of introducing an army in a province such as New Spain. Because of the importance attached to the reforms and the need to instill correct attitudes toward service and duty to the state, the new military apparatus received sufficient autonomy to implant and to administer the army. Lieutenant General Juan de Villalba y Angulo, captain general of Andalusia and a most important army officer, received the post of *comandante general* and *inspector general* of the army of New Spain. To help with his commissions, Villalba was assigned a strong Spanish cadre—4 field marshals, 6 colonels, 5 lieutenant colonels, 10 majors, 109 lieutenants, 7 adjutants, 16 cadets, 228 sergeants, 401 corporals, and 151 soldiers including drummers, fifers, a kettledrummer, and a trumpeter. Moreover, a regular infantry regiment named the "Regiment of America" was raised in part in Cádiz to be completed by Mexicans when it arrived in New Spain.[7] This European force was to motivate the regular army units to be raised in Mexico, and to provide small training cadres which would implant martial virtues in the new provincial regiments and battalions.

Stationing an officer of Villalba's stature and power in Mexico led to an immediate conflict of authority. The army did not fit well into existing administrative structures and the officials of other jurisdictions and tribunals resented any real or imagined diminution of their powers. Many of the anticipated birth pangs became chronic weaknesses. The commander general carried specific instructions to subordinate himself to the viceroy, who in turn was to acknowledge the primacy of the army chief in military matters. Both were told to be prudent and zealous and to remember the general good of the monarchy. If agreement could not be reached on specific issues, the field marshals were to form a junta with the power to make decisions through a plurality of votes.[8] Unfortunately, the relations between the viceroy as captain general and the new commandant general were so bitter that the regulatory mechanism failed to operate. From the moment he arrived at Veracruz in November 1764, Villalba began to make policy decisions without consulting the viceroy.[9] He disbanded the existing dragoon units to raise the dragoon regiments "Spain" and "Mexico," appointed officers to commands, and ordered numerous troop movements contrary to Cruillas's wishes. On numerous occasions, officers received diametrically opposing orders from their two senior commanders. If no agreement was possible on major decisions, similar disputes raged over what honors each should receive and there was constant debate over where the powers of the viceroy ended and those of the commandant general began. Villalba dismissed all of Cruillas's efforts to form an army during the Seven Years' War, stating that it was useless in constitution and lacked both powder and ammunition. He spurned the offer of a coach the viceroy presented for his entry into Mexico City and then refused to present his full credentials. Since his letters did nothing other than to heap criticism and condemnation for past failures, Cruillas suspended communications, stating that he did not have time to answer the barrage of charges. Because Villalba was not a judge of the viceroy's *residencia* or an official investigator of his policies, he saw no purpose in defending himself.[10] What had been intended by the crown to be an effective working relationship ended up in a mud-slinging match and a total impasse which retarded the implementation of the military system. Cruillas refused to accept any responsibility for the quarrels. In near total frustration, he wrote to Villalba, "... your words and your actions are very clear indication that your plan is to build a reputation upon the ruins of the viceroyalty and of all who cast a shadow on your splendor."[11]

While this struggle raged in Mexico City, the field marshals and other officers journeyed to the provinces with the purpose of enlisting infantry and cavalry units. The type of unit and whether it was to be cavalry, dragoons, or infantry depended upon the available population, geography, and varying strategic requirements. In the regions of heavy population and proximity to Veracruz, they raised six provincial infantry regiments—"Mexico," "Puebla," "Toluca," "Tlaxcala," "Córdoba-Orizaba," and "Veracruz." It was calculated that there were at least half a million families eligible for militia service in New Spain, and enlisting one man for each twenty families would result in a potential militia force of twenty-five thousand troops.[12] In their instructions on how to go about forming militia units, the officers were advised to exercise great care with the recruits and at all times to treat them as "true and beloved vassals." Mexicans deserved a full explanation of the troubled international situation so they might understand that for the security of their families and property they should sign up with the new militia. Villalba's instructions were to draw upon almost all of the castas, exempting only the Indians and Negroes, who were not to be trusted with weapons. Other than these important exceptions, the various mixtures were to be admitted without racial distinctions. The one qualification was that, except in isolated cases where population dictated otherwise, no more than a third of any company was to belong to a nonwhite racial group. If, however, the Spaniards expressed repugnance at being placed in units alongside the part-African castas of *pardos* and *morenos,* Villalba could solve the problem as he saw fit. As might be expected, there were immediate protests; in Mexico City, Puebla, and Veracruz separate battalions or companies of pardos and morenos were formed to solve this problem.[13] Some towns initiated proposals for special units. Puebla, for example, raised a provincial dragoon regiment, recruiting men and locating horses in nearby towns and villages. Querétaro, Celaya, and San Juan del Río pooled their resources to enlist a provincial cavalry regiment. In some other jurisdictions, militia units such as the Urban Regiment of Commerce in Mexico City or the Corps of Lancers of Veracruz that had existed prior to the reforms continued after thorough inspection.[14]

Villalba returned to Spain in 1766, abandoning the problem of forming an adequate army to Viceroy Carlos Francisco de Croix and two subordinate inspectors general. The Marqués de la Torre, colonel of the Regiment of Lombardía, became inspector general of infantry and Francisco Douché, colonel of the Cavalry Regiment of the Príncipe, inspector general of cavalry and dragoons. They added new militia units in Valladolid, Guadalajara, Pátzcuaro, Oaxaca, and along the coasts of Tampico and Pánuco. During the plebeian riots of 1767 in Guanajuato and San Luis Potosí, Visitador General José de Gálvez ordered the formation of two mixed legions of infantry and cavalry which he named "Príncipe" and "San Carlos."[15] The urban risings renewed fears in some circles that militia soldiers might some day turn their muskets against the mother country. Croix attempted to strengthen potential weaknesses by adding regular army units, which he considered much more trustworthy. He separated the third battalion from the Regiment of America, creating a new regular infantry unit called the Regiment of the Crown.

Despite these measures, the fear of rebellion supported by Mexican militiamen continued to haunt Spanish authorities. In 1766, a person calling himself Monsieur Guiller, a French architect, informed the Spanish government from London that while in Madrid at the beginning of 1765, he had stayed at the same inn as two disgruntled Mexicans. They were preparing to present their grievances at the royal court, but if they did not gain satisfaction, they declared their readiness to "throw off the yoke" of Spanish rule. These men laid out the traditional criollo case against the *gachupines*. Their ancestors had conquered New Spain at great cost in blood and fortune and yet they now found themselves without power or prerogatives in their own homeland. They complained against European priests who had no knowledge of the Indians or the Indian languages; even worse, Mexicans were denied the archbishoprics, bishoprics, canonships, and even the good curacies. Merchants languished under a multitude of taxes on European goods and seldom possessed sufficient currency since all silver was shipped to Spain.[16]

According to Guiller, the viceroy of New Spain refused to permit Mexican delegates to lay their case before the king. Instead, two merchants from Puebla and a criollo priest travelled under the guise of business to Madrid. There they obtained an audience with some senior official, but no sooner did the substance of their petition become clear than they were silenced and threatened with punishment as traitors. The three Mexicans were unanimous in their opinion that Spanish domination must be terminated, but they were not at all sure how to achieve independence or what sort of regime should replace the colonial administration. Monarchy did not seem to be a viable solution because there were numerous noble families and none would ever be able to dominate the others. At this point, the Mexicans were supposed to have enlisted the aid of Guiller to prepare a plan for a republican form of government and he convinced them that the support of Britain would be necessary. He proposed the cession of Veracruz and San Juan de Ulúa to Britain in return for aid and protection. At first, the Mexicans rejected the idea of close proximity to English Protestantism. After discussion, however, they accepted the British presence and agreed to a series of articles granting a commercial monopoly in exchange for recognition of the republic. With the conclusion of this business, the Mexicans returned to New Spain, departing from Coruña on September 1, 1765. Following their return, Guiller claimed to have received one letter in which they asked Britain to do nothing more than to occupy Veracruz and San Juan de Ulúa.[17]

The minister of the Indies, Julián de Arriaga, considered this entire matter to be "pure fiction," but at the same time noted that the king wanted Viceroy Croix to investigate and to exercise whatever precautions might be needed.[18] Croix could not verify any aspect of the plot, but he took the matter seriously. Whether or not the specifics of the affair were apocryphal, the charges raised by the Mexican agents documented real issues in New Spain. In his opinion, the plan was at least credible and might not be difficult to execute with British aid. This evidence bolstered Croix's arguments for additional regular army units.[19]

Quite clearly, the army plan was not progressing as well as planned or as some reports indicated. Personality and jurisdictional disputes played an important role, but more often than not the problem was New Spain itself. Senior Spanish army officers who held the inspector generalship or regimental commands had difficulty coming to grips with the Mexicans. No matter how much experience they had in Europe or even in the North African presidios, they required a lengthy period of acclimatization before they began to understand

Mexico. Even then, many officers could not escape a negative and condescending view of the country and its population. Experience in Mexico or elsewhere in the American colonies was essential before meaningful military planning might be carried out. The viceroys, responsible for the improvement of the army, blamed failures upon the inspectors general and other commanders, who in turn cursed the Mexicans or the shortage of funds which prevented Spain from stationing a large force of European regulars in the viceroyalty.

As early as 1765, Field Marshal Antonio Ricardos, one of Villalba's commanders, noted that while it was simple to enlist anyone in Mexico who could shoulder a musket, the new militiamen could not be trusted to appear at subsequent assemblies. The diversity and mobility of the population, combined with unmilitary attitudes and irreverence for the European view of good citizenship, left officers angry and frustrated.[20] The experience of the Marqués de Torre was typical. He arrived at Veracruz in June 1768, with three European battalions from the Regiments of Savoya, Ultonia, and Flandes. From the beginning, he reported a state of total confusion in the existing militia units. Discipline and levels of training were poor and many of the Spanish regulars Villalba had posted to serve as a disciplined cadre had married, fathered large numbers of children, and lost their usefulness. Others made an even more negative contribution; drawn from the dregs of Spanish regiments and even from prisons, they transmitted their bad habits to their Mexican pupils. Torre could not even inspect the Battalion of Pardos of Mexico City because the militiamen's record sheets had not been kept up. He had no information about their service records, level of training, or the state of their uniforms and weapons. The regimental records were in an equally bad state. Although he could not make any sense of the documents, he saw that one sergeant was in debt to the battalion for sixty pesos and many soldiers for as much as twenty or thirty pesos.[21]

After less than five months in New Spain, Torre presented his findings on the militias. Except for the units in the capital which were under the watchful eye of the viceroy, he called the rest of the provincial infantry regiments as "imaginary as they are useless." They were not uniformed, armed, or trained and no regular assemblies took place to instruct the militiamen. Whenever the inspector general visited units, the local authorities and officers rounded up a motley assortment of men supposed to be the regiment. He dismissed most of these as seminaked, without permanent homes, and weighed down with the responsibility of caring for large numbers of dependents. Bachelors were scarce because of the custom in the country of marrying at only fourteen to sixteen years of age. Many men seemed to suffer from bone dislocations and poorly mended fractures, hernias, hemorrhages, chest conditions, and other sundry disorders. To make matters even worse, Mexico lacked adequate numbers of the artisans and workers who in Europe would man the militias. A great number of jobs were filled by Indians, who were not even taken into account by the military. Where there were suitable men, enlistment threatened to damage family structure and the local economy. If these individuals were mobilized and their incomes reduced to the pay of a common soldier, their families would soon suffer the most miserable penury. Torre painted a grim picture of children reduced to begging for crusts and women prostituting themselves in order to survive.[22]

The regular army training cadre assigned to the provincial militia regiments failed to fulfill its mission. Scattered throughout the various units, in only four years the officers, noncommissioned officers (NCOs), and soldiers lost their military vocation if indeed they ever had one. They slipped into total inactivity—adopting the slovenliness, drunkenness, thievery, and other vices Torre ascribed to the Mexican militiamen. These individuals accomplished little other than to promote discord and dissension in the Mexican provincial towns where there was little hope of their promotion or betterment. Not only did this reverse the whole rationale of the training cadre, but the trend to negative Mexicanization also extended to the European regiments on rotation in the viceroyalty. Those sent out to inculcate martial values soon became useless to the royal service. Besides, in only four years of Mexican duty, more than half of the enlistment in the Regiment of America was drawn from the Mexican castas. In as little as seven years, desertion, death, and retirement would make these units almost totally American in composition. Torre saw long-term danger to Iberia if these regiments of castas returned to "adulterate" and "debauch" the Spanish population.[23] The solution to this bleak picture would be to enlist regular regiments in Mexico, exercising care to recruit the best men available, and then to redirect them away from their bad habits. Torre proposed a regular army of ten infantry battalions, which, when reinforced for wartime service, would present a potential total of nearly ten thousand men. The existing provincial militia regiments would be disbanded and replaced by loosely organized reserve companies. No longer would the regular cadre be needed since the new companies would be used only in emergencies to reinforce the regular battalions—serving in place of the *quintas* used in Spain.

The situation in the dragoon and cavalry regiments was no different. Inspector General Francisco Douché reported that the Cavalry Regiment of Querétaro possessed no horses and the Legion of San Carlos had a regular army cadre of only one junior officer, a sergeant, and three corporals. They had the responsibility to train and discipline 2,754 cavalry officers and men who were divided into nineteen companies and spread out over an immense region. The same officer, assisted by the sergeant and one of the corporals, had to look after the eleven companies of infantry belonging to the same legion. In total there were 3,587 officers and militiamen enlisted—a force almost independent of regular army direction. This was exactly the situation feared by the crown, and Arriaga, surprised by the weakness of controls over the militia, wrote, "... it is contrary to good politics to have such a numerous unit in America in which the commander, officers, and enlisted men are all criollos."[24] Despite the reservations of the minister of the Indies, the legion was not improved. In 1775, the alcalde mayor of San Luis Potosí, Joaquín de Llano y Villaurrutia, described it as a disorganized multitude which served as an asylum for vagabonds and the indolent. There were still far too many men enlisted for the number of regular army instructors and the constitution of the unit created constant frictions. Only the Spaniards (whites) enjoyed the *fuero criminal,* but others attempted to claim the privilege. When a militiaman who was not a Spaniard committed a crime, he claimed the *fuero;* the result invariably was an ugly dispute between the civilian magistrates and the military authorities. Often, the civilian courts simply gave up and criminals escaped punishment. The alcalde mayor identified very few real Spaniards in the legion; most were mulattoes, *Indios lobos,* or pertained to as many of the castas as he cared to identify.[25] His advice was to remove the fuero from all soldiers of the legion. He noted that unlike other cities of New Spain, where the cabildos created the militia units and then continued to exercise controls over them, the Legion of San Carlos existed as an autonomous entity. There was no census to determine how many men should serve and the cabildo of San Luis Potosí was not consulted on officer selection, recruiting, or on any other matter.

The negative view of New Spain and the attitude of contempt for the military capacity of the population expressed by European officers and administrators endured until Mexico became independent. If taken to its extreme, those who expressed loudest opposition to the use of militiamen had to propose some other system of raising or importing regular troops. Yet there were never sufficient funds to support a large regular army. Despite the wealth of the colony, the metropolis had greater priorities: the *situados,* the enormous financial subsidies paid to support the Philippines, Havana, Louisiana, and the Caribbean possessions; reconstruction or expansion of the imperial navy; and transfers of surplus revenues to support chronic shortages in Europe. There were any number of urgent expenditures which came before the Mexican army. Even so, many officers refused to compromise with Mexico. The key to success lay in taking advantage of criollo aspirations and in developing good working relationships with the cabildos. After 1776, however, when José de Gálvez became minister of the Indies, the move to appoint European Spaniards to offices formerly held by criollos tended to obscure some fairly simple solutions.[26] For many of the reformers in the army and the administration, traditional approaches had to be altered.

Through most of the 1770s, Viceroy Antonio María Bucareli, while by no means an exponent of the military potential of Mexicans, steered a course of moderation. Promoted from the governorship of Cuba, he knew enough about colonial populations to avoid extremes or radical changes in existing structures. At the same time, however, Bucareli once remarked that to be captain general of New Spain in time of war must be the greatest misfortune an officer could experience.[27] In this regard he was most fortunate for no international conflict developed to cloud the situation; Bucareli and his inspector general, Pascual de Cisneros,[28] received the first opportunity to bring a degree of continuity and stability to the Mexican army. Cisneros, who remained in his post until 1783, rejected the common view that Mexican militiamen were nothing more than a collection of naked vagabonds. In his opinion, the problem resulted from a basic lack of cooperation between different authorities responsible for recruiting. The solution lay in developing much closer working relationships with the alcaldes mayores and other justicias before militia enlistment commenced. Instead of seeking unattached bachelors, Cisneros saw a need to obtain the services of men who had a stake in their communities; to add even further stability, he saw nothing at all wrong with enlisting some married men and even those with small families.[29] Just as important, officers and NCOs must be informed of their duties and acceptable procedures in handling civilian soldiers. Whipping and beating of militiamen could not be tolerated; each regiment maintained a guardhouse for soldiers guilty of insubordination or other minor offenses. Regimental commanders were to maintain a close watch over the regular army cadre to prevent corrupt practices, laziness, and any loss of discipline and mission. Officers were to avoid unnecessary jurisdictional disputes and to make sure that the regiment respected the officials of all secular and ecclesiastical tribunals. Wherever possible, the militia was to maintain as much harmony as possible with the rest of the population. Militia captains had to attend weekly classes and the troops met for assembly every Sunday for training and exercise. To make sure that all of these regulations were followed, Cisneros and his staff endeavored to carry out regular inspections.[30]

If Cisneros convinced himself and Viceroy Bucareli about the usefulness of the provincial militias, it was not without loud opposition and constant harassment from the detractors. The fiscal of the royal treasury, José Antonio

Areche, later *visitador general* of Peru, examined Cisneros's military plans and arrived at quite different conclusions. He produced a diatribe describing New Spain as a virtual desert settled by a largely useless population. Even the Spanish immigrants had accomplished little in Mexico to make up for the population drain from the mother country. Many Europeans could be seen in the streets and plazas of Mexico City, Puebla, Guanajuato, and other cities naked, hungry, and wrapped in nothing more than a coarse blanket. These Spaniards brought shame to their kind and embarrassment to the state—particularly since there were jobs available and good agricultural land lying fallow. The hacendados, an equally parasitic class, dominated the fertile land and sought to capture a labor force by advancing food, clothing, or other items at usurious rates. Others sacrificed their estates by renting to Indian farmers who lacked method and talent in their agricultural techniques. Areche pictured the alcaldes mayores and justicias as totally rapacious, allied with wealthy merchant financiers who advanced capital to extend the evil *repartimiento* in their provinces, making enormous profits at the expense of the Indians. Anyone who attempted to engage in commerce or to open a business in competition with the alcaldes mayores provoked implacable opposition from these entrenched interests. To further confuse the picture, racial mixture produced a multitude of unidentifiable castas, such as the *tente en el aire* and the *no le entiendo,* which formed a large rootless population. Even the better classes contributed less than their potential numbers made possible. The Church drained off too many young men and women and damaged the economy even further through the ownership of enormous rural and urban properties. In sum, good laborers and artisans were almost impossible to locate. The castas and Indians were slothful, inclined to any number of excesses, and not influenced by trust or kindness. Employers needing workers went to the justicias, who, for a price, conducted a work gang to their haciendas, *obrajes,* or projects. Of course, the laborers had to be confined under guard at night to prevent their escape.[31] Such was the society asked to raise good militia forces and to guard New Spain against foreign enemies.

Areche's description of Mexican conditions left little room for optimism. The fact that he was a favorite of José de Gálvez and a strong supporter of the reform faction gave considerable weight to his opinions. Although much of the attack was designed to give support to the cause of administrative reform, Cisneros found that the invective made his own task more difficult. When the fiscal Martín Merino considered the debate over the merits of the militias, he concluded, "They are not only useless, but harmful besides, being costly to the royal treasury." When Merino went on to recommend the total abolition of the provincial forces, Cisneros felt obliged to reply. He lashed out against all who condemned without really making any effort to learn about the true nature of the army. In his opinion, the opponents of the militias damned the whole because of the faults of a few.[32] Whatever the truth of the matter, the deep division over the merits of the army was exploited by tribunals and individuals who saw their own privileges being circumscribed. Their attacks tended to confirm what Areche and others were saying to the crown.

Major Pedro de Gorostiza submitted a new report on the army to José de Gálvez in August 1776. Gorostiza had served for seven years in New Spain, and during the Gálvez visitation he was responsible for mopping up the insurrection at Guanajuato.[33] Like so many other officers, Gorostiza was convinced that in the twelve years since the introduction of the militias, no progress had been made. In his opinion, the proper establishment of provincial forces required a degree of trust and stability not common in Mexico.[34] But even if one supported the militia and managed to improve its performance so that it trained regularly and performed the annual assembly of thirteen days as did the Spanish provincial units, there was no reason for any confidence. In an open province like New Spain, part-time soldiers never could attain the degree of preparation needed to engage an enemy army. Reality must be recognized; because militias were mere lists of men and nothing more, it was futile and above all dangerous to depend upon them. Then the high costs of the regular cadres—nearly two million pesos in the past twelve years—might be avoided and, along with the expenditure, the danger of long-term idleness which ruined professional soldiers. While Gorostiza did not propose to disband the existing provincial regiments and the two mixed legions, he opposed the creation of any new units.[35]

In Gorostiza's military plan, all future militias had to be untrained reserve companies (*compañías sueltas*) formed according to a loose set of regulations and without pretensions other than to enroll men for emergency use. Each company would have a captain, lieutenant, ensign, three sergeants, and six corporals, but there would be no need to carry on an extensive training program. As for the regular army presence, an annual inspection by one officer would be sufficient to examine each company and to make replacements as needed. The real strength of Gorostiza's army depended upon expanding the number of regular units to three full infantry regiments, three battalions of pardo light infantry, the two existing dragoon regiments, a unit of lancers at Veracruz, and two companies of artillery. The peacetime total force of 7,114 could be increased from the reserve companies to 13,132 in wartime. The annual cost for this army would be 1,312,709 pesos or only about 200,000 pesos more than the sum spent in 1776 for regular troops stationed in Mexico.[36] Gorostiza justified the increased expenditure, pointing out the added level of protection, the efficiency of an expanded regular army, and the possibility of reducing dependence upon the untrustworthy militia. Furthermore, once the new system took over, the treasury and the metropolitan army could terminate the high costs in support and manpower connected with stationing European units in the viceroyalty. Though neither Gálvez nor any other important officer of the imperial regime paid heed to Gorostiza's recommendations, this plan was not doomed to obscurity. When in 1789 Gorostiza became subinspector general of the army of New Spain, his ideas received a new lease on life.

When Spain declared war on Britain in 1779 and openly aided the Anglo-American revolutionaries, the forebodings of Bucareli and other officers about commanding Mexican forces in wartime proved to be essentially correct. Although there was little danger of invasion, men of all classes resisted military duty with great tenacity. Even the regular units were weakened by desertion, chronic drunkenness, a wide range of disciplinary problems, and a resulting drain of soldiers into the presidios where they were condemned for their crimes.[37] Viceroy Martín de Mayorga, who governed New Spain from 1779 to 1783, discovered to his horror that neither the army nor the defenses could withstand a raid, let alone an invasion. Even the highly regarded Lancers of Veracruz had degenerated to such a low state that Mayorga regarded the unit as fit only to carry supplies for the port garrison.[38] The provincial militia regiments of the interior, described for so long as illusory, proved during attempts to mobilize some units that the charges had been correct. When Mayorga attached some blame to the approaches used by Inspector General Cisneros, the two commanders wasted time exchanging insults rather than seeking to improve the army. Cisneros, promoted to the rank of lieutenant general in 1779, refused to accept criticism from a viceroy who was only a field marshal.[39] The crown paid little heed to these quarrels. Since New Spain was not directly endangered, the viceroyalty was used to supply troops as well as funds needed in more exposed possessions; for the first time Mexican soldiers of the Regiment of the Crown served overseas in Havana, Santo Domingo, and in the army of operations commanded by Bernardo de Gálvez.[40]

With the restoration of peace in 1783, any pressures to improve the army were forgotten. As before, troops appeared only during festivals and Holy Week parades and many of the militia units ceased to exist. In this case, however, the weakness did not result from any peacetime relaxation as much as from a lack of direction and continuity. For the military as well as for the administration, the remainder of the 1780s were years of unmitigated confusion. At the beginning of the decade, José de Gálvez appeared to have matters well in hand. Established in the ministry of the Indies, he was in the right position to introduce his anticipated administrative reforms and to place his friends and relatives in offices from which they might smooth transitions and smother opposition. The picture changed very quickly with the sudden deaths of two viceroys, Gálvez's brother Matías de Gálvez, who was in office from 1783 to 1784, and then his nephew Bernardo de Gálvez, who succumbed in 1786 after a short term. Instead of the firm leadership anticipated from the Gálvez family, a vacuum in executive power coincided with the introduction of the intendancies in 1786 followed the next year by the death of José de Gálvez. When Manuel Antonio Flórez became viceroy in 1787, he had to sort out near chaos in many departments resulting from short periods of executive rule by the audiencia and the archbishop. Flórez's first concern was to establish or reestablish the powers of the viceroy in the new administrative structure.[41] Having done so, his effectiveness was reduced when he was stricken by severe arthritis, which crippled his hands and made the bureaucratic functions of office impossible. Flórez simply could not sign the multitude of state papers and other documents which came before him daily.[42] After only two years disease forced his early resignation.

Despite twenty years' trial and experimentation, the captains general and ranking army officers had failed to meet their own minimal expectations concerning the establishment of a stable military system. Viceroy Matías de Gálvez, impatient over the amount of time he had to spend sorting out questions connected with military matters, decided in 1783 to commission yet another study on how to improve the basic constitution of the army. To accomplish this task he appointed the interim sub-inspector general Colonel Francisco Crespo, who had the kind of experience and background necessary to avoid some of the chronic problems connected with raising and maintaining an army. Crespo, a forty-year career officer, had spent thirteen years on assignments in New Spain and as governor of the frontier province of Sonora during the war against the northern Indians. When he became acting sub-inspector general, he was *corregidor* of Mexico City and an active member of the intellectual community in the Real Academia de San Carlos.[43] Unlike so many of his predecessors, who had drafted military plans without adequate knowledge of New Spain, Crespo understood the social, economic, and political barriers confronting those responsible for raising military forces. His report and plan gave reasonable answers to many of the questions left open by the inspectors general since 1764; in the long run, the majority of his substantive recommendations were adopted by the crown.

Crespo analyzed the problem of defense and the military needs of New Spain—past, present, and future. Dividing his plan into sections, he began by outlining the risks of exposure to enemies along the coasts and frontiers. Second, he considered the environmental and physical barriers to army formation and pointed out the need for a maximum degree of flexibility in order to respond to different enemy challenges. The army must be able to cooperate with the forces of the Provincias Internas against Indian incursions as well as to guard the strategic port of Veracruz and the routes inland from the coasts. Third, he examined the best means of improving the army; he proposed a balanced force of regular regiments, provincial and urban militias, and reserve companies located in the interior and along the exposed littoral. Finally, he outlined the methods most suitable to raise manpower and to obtain financial support for the militias.

In many respects, the Crespo Plan represented a compromise among previous military plans which had placed too much emphasis upon the regular army. While Crespo agreed that one of the best ways to instill martial values in Mexicans was to garrison Spanish regiments in New Spain, the costs of transporting so many men back and forth across the Atlantic were disproportionate to the possible advantages. At best, only one soldier in three ever returned to Spain. The rest deserted to join vagabond elements, perished from diseases contracted in Veracruz, or retired in the viceroyalty when they were no longer useful to the army. To terminate the manpower drain, the subinspector proposed the formation of a regular army in Mexico consisting of four infantry regiments, an infantry battalion stationed permanently at Veracruz, the two dragoon regiments, and the two existing Companies of Catalonia[44] (see tables 1 and 2). The result would be a total peacetime force of 5,807 regulars at an annual expenditure of 1,164,512 pesos. During wartime conditions, the regular army could be expanded to a total of 9,319

TABLE 1
Composition of the Regular Army of New Spain in 1784.

Units	Number of Troops	Annual Cost (pesos)
Regiment of Zamora (from Spain)	1,377*	251,659
Regiment of the Crown	1,377	251,659
2 Companies of Catalonia	160	27,882
2 Companies of San Juan de Ulúa	240	34,769
Dragoon Regiment of Spain	521	151,444
Dragoon Regiment of Mexico	521	151,444
Totals	4,196	868,857

*Since most of these units were seldom complete, the total number of troops was much smaller.

Source: Proyecto militar de 1784, AGI, México, leg. 2418.

TABLE 2
The Regular Army Proposed by Colonel Crespo.

Units	Number of Troops	Annual Cost
Regiment of the Crown	961	175,695
Regiment of New Spain	961	175,695
Regiment of Mexico	961	175,695
Regiment of Puebla	961	175,695
Fixed Battalion of Veracruz	881	147,568
2 Companies of Catalonia	160	25,109
Dragoon Regiment of Spain	461	144,525
Dragoon Regiment of Puebla	461	144,525
Totals	5,807	1,164,507

Source: Proyecto militar de 1784, AGI, México, leg. 2418.

troops. As in previous plans, the regulars were to form an elite corps of dedicated warriors who would inspire and give an example so badly needed to improve the provincial militias.

Although Crespo shared the biases of his fellow officers against the mixed races of New Spain, the militia remained the backbone of the army. According to army statistics, there were nearly forty thousand men enrolled in the different types of militia. Some units were the ones raised by Villalba, others during the Gálvez visitation, and quite a number during the past war against Britain. All of the units lacked discipline and, upon the slightest investigation, many appeared to be nothing more than lists of men. As matters stood, the imaginary militia cost the royal treasury 269,622 pesos, 4 reales annually in addition to the 215,932 pesos, 4 reales raised by local militia taxes.[45] Before this situation might be rectified, however, the sub-inspector attempted to clarify the major difficulties involved in raising militias in New Spain. First, the population eligible for service was often small and scattered over huge territories. There was always a danger of causing harm to a local economy if too many men were withdrawn for duty. In the cities, most recruiting had been done in the lower social sectors; many of these militiamen changed domicile to escape service or simply fled if they heard any mention of regimental mobilization. Men of the better classes either joined the urban units, which never left their specific jurisdiction, or more often simply frustrated the efforts of census takers and recruiters to form an accurate picture of the eligible population. Third, enlistment could lower tax revenues and interfere with the administration of justice if fueros or other privileges were granted to militiamen. Fourth, taxes legislated to support militias generally failed to cover operating costs. If the militia was to be of any use, it had to have adequate uniforms, arms, equipment, and horses. Wear and tear on equipment was costly in any army and in New Spain, moths and chewing insects made short work of clothing and harnesses. Muskets, swords, and other hardware rusted very quickly and there were few artisans skilled in trades associated with the army. Cavalry and dragoon horses were a problem wherever these units existed for part-time mounts were as untrustworthy as their riders. Fifth, the royal treasury could not maintain an army of regular troops large enough to guarantee a meaningful defense. In other words, army planners must banish any notion of excluding Mexicans from the army and from a primary responsibility in defending their country.

Crespo's reformed provincial militia system would guarantee an assured defense force of 11,075 men in peacetime and, adding the 5,807 regulars, a total of 16,882 men. In wartime, this force could be expanded to 25,000 or even more depending upon the defensive needs[46] (see table 3). This did not include the urban units in Mexico City and Puebla for duties related to internal security, nor the large number of untrained reserve companies (*compañías sueltas*) located in towns and provinces where there was too little population to merit a full battalion or regiment. On both coasts, armed companies of pardos or whatever residents were available would perform watchtower duty, guard against contraband, and serve as the first line of defense against enemy landings. In the interior, these companies were to serve as a pool of recruits for the regular regiments as well as manpower reserves to increase the provincial regiments to wartime strength. Finally, to bring regional control over the provincial units, urban militias, and reserve companies, Crespo recommended the introduction of twenty-three mixed infantry and cavalry legions. The first fourteen legions were to include all of the interior militias and the remaining nine would include the infantry and cavalry units stationed along the coasts. The army of New Spain would continue to total about forty thousand men, but Crespo was certain that his plan would end the history of wasted expenditures and empty units.[47]

Viceroy Matías de Gálvez submitted the Crespo Plan to the imperial government for ratification, but there were years of indecision ahead. Although many of the recommendations had been suggested before, time was needed before a ruling might be expected from Madrid. In the interim, confusion in the administration and attention to other reform programs further slowed any final resolution. When Viceroy Flórez inspected the army in 1787, he found all branches to be in a deplorable state. Referring to the numerous plans and proposals to improve the defensive system, he soon concluded that Crespo's ideas, while not the best in theory, at least recognized the Mexican reality. The plan by the Marqués de Torre, for example, presented the prospect of a

TABLE 3
The Provincial Army Proposed by Colonel Crespo.

Units	Peacetime Force	Wartime Force
INFANTRY		
Regiment of Mexico	833	1,361
Regiment of Tlaxcala	833	1,361
Regiment of Córdoba	833	1,361
Regiment of Toluca	833	1,361
Battalion of the Prince (Guanajuato)	417	681
Battalion of San Carlos (San Luis Potosí)	417	680
Battalion of Oaxaca	417	681
Battalion of Valladolid	417	680
Pardo Battalion of Mexico	417	681
Pardo Battalion of Puebla	417	680
Regiment of Provincial Grenadiers	1,139	1,139
Regiment of Provincial Light Infantry	1,139	1,139
CAVALRY, DRAGOONS, AND LANCERS		
Regiment of Querétaro	361	613
Regiment of the Príncipe (Guanajuato)	361	613
Regiment of San Carlos (San Luis Potosí)	361	613
Regiment of San Luis (San Luis Potosí)	361	613
Dragoon Regiment of Puebla	361	617
Dragoon Regiment of Michoacán	361	617
Dragoon Regiment of Volunteers	617	617
Lancers of Veracruz	180	306
Totals	11,075	16,414
Urban and Coastal Militia Units	6,693	
Reserve Companies (compañías sueltas) (134 infantry companies and 76 cavalry companies)	22,232	
Grand Total	40,000	

Source: Proyecto militar de 1784, AGI, México, leg. 2418. Resumen de fuerzas de los cuerpos provinciales que se proponen.

better army based upon regular troops, but did not take economic factors into account. Flórez accepted dependence upon provincial militias even though he expressed some reservations over whether or not they could be adequately disciplined.[48]

Flórez submitted his own impressions of the army to Sub-Inspector General Pedro Mendinueta,[49] a former governor of New Mexico, and ordered him to make a thorough study of militia weaknesses and Crespo's proposals. Mendinueta, while impressed by the sheer number of plans drafted since 1764 and the amount of money wasted without noticeable results, was no more positive about the militia regiments than had been his predecessors. Beginning a series of inspections in Mexico City, he compiled a list of negative factors similar to those listed since 1764. Any man in the capital who might have been useful to the provincial infantry regiment managed to gain deferment or joined the Urban Regiment of Commerce or the cavalry companies of the guilds to avoid service outside of the immediate precincts of the city. Men from the very poorest classes ended up filling the ranks. Some of the other provincial regiments enlisted men of better quality, but distance and other factors intervened. The Regiment of Jalapa and Córdoba, for example, was spread over such a wide territory that organization was extremely difficult. Besides, the small population limited the number of replacements available to fill vacancies. Most inhabitants of Córdoba and Orizaba worked in the tobacco industry and during harvest time every hand was needed in the fields—so much so in fact that the regime granted them a blanket exemption from militia duty.[50] Similar problems existed in Toluca, Oaxaca, Guadalajara, and throughout the province of Michoacán; the people were excellent and well suited to the military, but could not be spared from agriculture, commerce, and industry. In the mining districts of Guanajuato and San Luis Potosí, where Gálvez raised the mixed infantry and cavalry Legions of San Luis and San Carlos, distance prevented adequate training and discipline. Moreover, full exemptions extended to mineworkers kept these units understrength. Mendinueta was doubtful about solving these problems, but by no means as pessimistic as some previous observers.

It is noteworthy in the light of future events that both Flórez and Mendinueta rejected proposals to reduce the provincial militia regiments into untrained reserve companies. On the contrary, one of their criticisms of the Crespo proposals was that he recommended the reduction of the regular army cadre attached to each militia unit.[51] The reserve companies could not be depended upon to present adequate reinforcements. When they might be most needed, they could do little other than to add large numbers of green civilians to the units they were to strengthen. Rather than helping, these men might reduce regimental efficiency and possibly hinder the capacity of the army to withstand an enemy attack. The same was true of the provincial regiments. It would not do to have the regular army cadre training provincial soldiers only when danger threatened New Spain. Since the provincial officers were incapable of training their own men, the mission of the regulars was essential. More than anything else, Mexicans needed strong doses of discipline, subjection, punishment, and training.[52] To attain these ends, Flórez and Mendinueta accepted the main proposals of the Crespo Plan. The viceroy wanted to begin implementing some of the major recommendations as soon as possible, but he dared not initiate any expenditure until he received royal assent. The first priority would be to raise the three new regular infantry regiments before altering the militias. Besides, a full census was necessary in all provinces to give data on the availability of manpower. Bernardo de Gálvez's effort to enumerate the population had not been continued after he died in office.

For once, the approval of the crown was not long in coming. Royal orders of September 26, 1786, and April 13, 1787, adopted the first parts of the Crespo Plan and accepted Flórez's proposal to organize the new regular infantry regiments. The king sanctioned the formation of the Infantry Regiments of New Spain, Mexico, and Puebla, but made no mention of the Fixed Battalion of Veracruz, considered essential by all knowledgeable observers. The regiments of the interior had to be kept away from the disease-ridden coastal garrison if the army was to be made a success. At first, the imperial government was as enthusiastic about the proposed reforms as were the Mexican authorities. The first royal order proposed to dispatch a number of Spanish sergeants, corporals, and soldiers with weapons and uniforms for all of the new regiments. The second order, however, while continuing to approve the new regiments, withdrew the offer of peninsular troops. A reform in the Spanish army increasing infantry regiments from two to three battalions had absorbed all available manpower.[53] Although the significance of this change was not understood in New Spain, there were to be no more European troops for many years. If there was to be an army, it would have to be formed from available resources. To soften the blow somewhat, the sub-inspector general received permission to recruit soldiers and NCOs from the Spanish Regiment of Zamora before it departed from Mexico for Havana. If there were still shortages, additional troops might be obtained from the Regiments of the King and Hibernia stationed at Havana.

There was considerable interest in military circles to see how many soldiers of the Regiment of Zamora might be induced to volunteer for permanent service in the new regiments. Mendinueta cautioned against coercion and irregular recruiting procedures and was pleased when 565 soldiers asked to remain in Mexico. Many of these of course were Mexicans who had little desire to experience European duty. A lottery divided the total, placing 282 men in the Regiment of New Spain and 283 in the Regiment of Mexico. Four companies of the existing Infantry Regiment of the Crown were transferred intact to the new units. By these methods, a relatively strong corps of veterans gave some semblance of military discipline to the first stage of Crespo's program. Flórez published a viceregal pardon of any deserter who would return to service and issued orders to municipal authorities and local magistrates requesting their aid in locating men and promoting recruitment.[54] Despite shortages of muskets and disturbing desertion rates, which will be examined in subsequent chapters, Flórez had three of the new regiments at least half formed by the end of April 1788.[55] It now remained for the viceroy to continue applying pressure upon the crown to approve the rest of the regular units and then to begin the larger task of implementing the militia program.

Defense remained one of the major preoccupations of the viceregal regime. Worrisome Indian risings at Papantla and Acayucan near Veracruz bothered Flórez and he was concerned about the dangers of any further weakening of the external defenses during the period of army reorganization. The captain general of Cuba, José de Ezpeleta, wanted the Regiment of Zamora sent to Havana at the earliest possible moment because his garrison was short more than 2,000 soldiers.[56] The viceroy managed to delay the departure until his own forces took shape, but a major setback occurred when the crown suspended the formation of the fourth regular infantry unit, the Regiment of Puebla. Without the fourth regiment, the net increase in the number of regular troops was not worth the time and labor expended on reform. The three regiments of 979 soldiers each increased the total regular infantry complement by only 183 men over the two existing Regiments of the Crown and Zamora, which each had held a total of 1,377 men.[57] Obviously, the imperial government was not aware of or did not place great emphasis upon Mexican needs. There was no alternative to continued pressure for total adoption of the Crespo Plan—underscoring the essential role of regular troops to lead the provincial army. Such arguments elicited support in Spain and when Flórez turned over command to the Conde de Revillagigedo, the Regiment of Puebla was under formation.

In the meantime, royal orders of September 24, 1787, May 5, 1788, and October 20, 1788, introduced legislation dealing with Crespo's recommendations for the provincial militias.[58] A number of reductions were made in the size of the army, but the crown adopted all of the essential proposals. At long last there appeared to be a reasoned formula for the army of New Spain. When the Conde de Revillagigedo was appointed to replace the ailing Flórez, his instructions from the king dealt with the military even before the controversial subject of the intendancies. Revillagigedo was to complete the new regular regiments and proceed to establish the various classes of militia.[59]

There were few similarities between the regime of Flórez and that of the Conde de Revillagigedo. Flórez was cautious and conservative, delaying policy decisions until he could be certain of full consultation with Madrid and approval of the crown. Revillagigedo on the other hand devoted his administration to efficiency and reform; where his policies did not match those of the imperial government, he was willing to risk censure if he believed his approaches to be better. A close colleague and friend of the Conde de Floridablanca, the Conde de Aranda, Alejandro Malaspina, and others in governing circles, he was an active representative of the spirit of enlightened despotism which ruled metropolitan Spain. At the same time, however, while Revillagigedo was born in Havana, he doubted the loyalty of Spanish Americans and opposed any policy that might place them in positions of power. He had run into difficulties with provincial militias in 1768 when commissioned to reorganize the defenses of the Isthmus of Panama. The result of his efforts had been frictions with the militiamen, outright rebellion in his own regiment, and finally his own ignominious withdrawal and return to Spain. Had it not been for the friendship of Floridablanca, Revillagigedo might never have recovered his reputation.[60] As it was, he had to await the death of Charles III before he could expect to obtain any senior appointment.

Besides his own negative experiences with Spanish Americans, Revillagigedo reflected many of the attitudes of Spanish intellectuals in the wake of the traumatic events destroying Bourbon France. He worried about the ramifications of the "foolish new system of the French," fearful that "the contamination might spread its fatal plague to others."[61] Like so many other Spaniards, he looked on with a mixture of horror and fascination; as he wrote from Mexico City to Alejandro Malaspina, ". . . the French appear more and more insane, working toward their own ruin through the fanaticism of a badly understood liberty."[62] His constant study of foreign gazettes and reports on the events in the French West Indies tended to confirm his apprehensions and solidified his existing low opinion of the Indians, Negroes, and other castas.[63] These feelings translated into policy when Revillagigedo took command of New Spain. He did everything in his power to prevent Indians from carrying weapons and he disbanded the existing pardo and moreno militia battalions in Mexico City and Puebla. Although he disliked all militias, his treatment of the pardos demonstrated a special contempt he reserved for a people whom he held in low regard.[64]

Had anyone in the imperial government read through Revillagigedo's statements on the defense of the American empire, written in Madrid just prior to his embarkation for Mexico, there might well have been concern about how he would react to the Crespo Plan. The new viceroy made no attempt to withhold his own strong opinions. If ever there was a concerted general rebellion in New Spain, he doubted the capacity of Spain even with the assistance of her European allies to restore imperial rule. Yet, he could not see how any foreign power could conquer the country without the aid of the Mexicans. The secret of maintaining Spanish rule, he concluded, depended upon two factors—love and illusion: the first meant that Mexicans must be kept relatively happy through good treatment so they would not wish to sever the imperial tie, and the second that they should be impressed with the formidable power of the mother country so as to discourage any revolutionary effort even if they desired it. Experience demonstrated the complete failure of garrisoning peninsular regiments in New Spain. They rapidly lost all usefulness and in the end prejudiced rather than enforced Spanish rule. The only convenient solution would be to maintain competent garrisons in Andalusia and Galicia ready for rapid dispatch to trouble spots in the Americas. He supported the policy of recruiting regular regiments in the colonies so long as they contained a strong cadre of officers and troops drawn from Europe. At the same time, Revillagigedo understood that much of the American criollo discontent was inspired by their exclusion from high offices and positions of honor. To alleviate the problem somewhat, he proposed greater interchanges between the colonies and the mother country. He thought an American regiment of royal guards raised in Spain might attract the sons of important criollo families.[65]

Revillagigedo did not even consider the possibility of using provincial militia commissions to satisfy some of the criollo aspirations. He questioned the abilities of part-time soldiers and often referred to the Spanish failure to defend Havana against the British in 1762 as clear proof of militia incompetence.[66] When Pedro de Gorostiza became sub-inspector general of the army of New Spain, a meeting of two like minds took place. Both officers sailed from Spain on the same vessel and during their sixty-seven-day voyage, they discussed the composition of the Mexican army at great length. Having read it in Madrid, Gorostiza was familiar with the Crespo Plan and he formed an early impression that it was "impractical, chimerical, and costly." Since he had a great deal of experience in New Spain, he prepared a report which would serve as a discussion paper. Arriving in Mexico, the viceroy and sub-inspector spent four and a half months laboring over the future of the army. In their opinion, the population of the viceroyalty simply could not support the army envisaged by Crespo without relying upon classes they considered unacceptable for service. Racial composition and geographic factors were reason enough to give up any hope of enlisting provincial units based in Michoacán, Oaxaca, and some other provinces. In Guanajuato, for example, the Legion of San Carlos never enlisted more than half of its total strength and in 1785, Sub-Inspector General José de Ezpeleta had to retire 517 men between the ages of fifty and ninety years.[67] The result was the preparation of a new military plan, or, to be exact, a reintroduction of many proposals submitted by Gorostiza in 1776. In adopting this course, Revillagigedo challenged the criollos in one of the few areas in which they possessed any claim to position and power.

In Revillagigedo's military plan of February 6, 1790, the militias became "truly metaphysical creations of no real utility whatsoever." Instead of following explicit instructions from Madrid, the new viceroy set out to reconstruct the army from the ground up. Once again, the pendulum swung back to the position of those who for so long had emphasized the development of a strong regular army and reduced the militia forces to the least possible role. All of the old arguments were repeated—the economy could not stand the imposition of militia units, and "... the major part of the population showed a propensity toward laziness, vice, and the life of vagabondage."[68] Money invested in such units was squandered and even the regular cadre assigned to Mexican provinces soon became groups of idle men who had too much liberty and no hope of promotion. Since Mexicans who engaged in mining, agriculture, and commerce deserved exemption from duty, the militiamen were the vagabonds and outcasts of society. Instead of improving under the discipline of the regular cadre, these men debauched the Europeans, whose morale was already very low. Most of these soldiers viewed colonial service as a form of involuntary exile.[69]

The solution was to create an efficient regular army. High-quality officers, NCOs, and soldiers had to be transferred from Spain without prejudicing their army careers. These men would furnish the good example Mexicans might eventually emulate. As matters stood, even the regular regiments raised in Mexico—in theory the shining examples for the provincial militias—were of little value and without the training needed to shoulder the defensive burden. To correct existing faults, at least one-third of the regular army must be European and there should be as many peninsular sergeants and corporals as criollos in each company.[70] The criollos might be useful for service, but they lacked the vigor to command without the discipline and stimulus of Spanish leadership. To prevent Mexicanization and to retain morale, the Europeans were to be transferred regularly and prevented from making close connections with Mexican society. After years of residence in New Spain, Spanish officers developed business interests, friendships, and marriage ties; according to Revillagigedo, they became "true American patriots." He considered ten years to be the absolute maximum before officers rotated back to Spain.[71]

Under the new system, Revillagigedo increased dependence upon the four existing regular infantry regiments and the two dragoon regiments, proposing an additional infantry regiment called the Regiment of Tlaxcala and the much discussed Fixed Battalion of Veracruz. He planned to expand the number of engineers, the artillery companies, and the Companies of Catalonia. The Catalonian companies would be used to garrison Guanajuato and Guadalajara, replacing militia pickets that had failed to prevent outbreaks of violence among the "vicious plebeian classes." The plan projected a peacetime operational army of 10,386 troops which could be increased to 14,176 in wartime.[72] To replace the provincial regiments and battalions, the viceroy fell back on the idea of loosely organized reserve companies which would cost little, serve only in the event of emergencies, and possess no special privileges to cause jurisdictional disputes.[73] Along both coasts, a series of militia divisions would protect local populations and guard against contraband traffic.[74]

Long before he received any reaction from the crown, Revillagigedo implemented portions of his plan. Fully confident of gaining absolute support, he congregated the regular cadres assigned to provincial militia units at Mexico City for a thorough inspection. Of the 453 sergeants, corporals, and drummers who appeared, 196 were retired for completion of enlistment, irredeemable indolence, illegal marriages, and uselessness to the royal service. Another 127 men were retired, leaving only 130 fit for assignment to the regular infantry regiments.[75] Of the 117 regular army officers who had been stationed with the provincial units, 80 continued service, 33 were retired, and 4 transferred to Spain.[76] Less attempt was made to soften the shock to provincial officers who found their regiments and battalions crumbling and with them the prestige of holding the king's commission. Some criollo officers received vacant subdelegations, minor posts in treasury offices, and duties in the general census, but most were left without any compensation or reward. In the case of the pardo battalions—viewed by the viceroy as particularly despicable—militia officers were not considered fit for posts as common soldiers in the regular regiments.[77]

It was one thing to demolish the provincial militia system and quite another to replace the part-time soldiers with regulars. Revillagigedo lacked authorization from Spain and he dared not initiate the major expenditures necessary to raise regiments without some emergency to justify his actions. As time passed, the specter of having his plan rejected caused him to dispatch anxious reports defending his ideas.[78] The minister of war, Marqués del Campo de Alange, resisted any hasty rearrangement of the military structure and warned that there was little hope of the Spanish army being able to spare troops for Mexico. Naturally, he did not oppose saving funds which had been paid out to operate the provincial army, but he delayed any decision. Meanwhile, the recommendations passed from committee to committee for information before any final adoption or rejection.[79] After a series of rebuffs, Revillagigedo placed the matter before his old friend the Conde de Aranda. Once again, however, no reply came from the imperial government. Aranda was losing power in the struggle and intrigue surrounding the court of Charles IV. Manuel Godoy, now elevated to the nobility as the Duque de Alcudía, received the dispatch addressed to Aranda and passed it to the ministry of war without comment.[80]

The Mexican defense system was a low priority item in the imperial ministry of war. Repercussions of the French Revolution caused far more anxiety both in the peninsula and in Spanish colonies in close proximity to French possessions. At a time when war in Europe appeared to be a distinct likelihood, Revillagigedo's pleas for troops were ludicrous. Cuba, Santo Domingo, and Louisiana needed troops much more than did the viceroyalty. The French were said to have 18,000 troops in Saint Domingue and the Americans threatened to invade and occupy Louisiana. By July 1792, Louisiana had absorbed a full battalion of Cuban infantry, three companies of light infantry, and 300 soldiers of the Regiment of Havana. Two additional full battalions had been dispatched to Santo Domingo to meet the threat there, but local commanders begged for more men. As a result of these troop movements, the strategic island of Cuba was left with only 1,430 regular soldiers in three dismembered battalions. Anticipating just this eventuality, the minister of war had issued an order on April 23, 1792, authorizing the captain general of Cuba to requisition an infantry regiment from New Spain.[81] As might be expected, the precedent of transferring one regiment made all Spanish governors in the Caribbean area aware of a new source of manpower. By 1793, Spain was at the brink of war with France and in both Santo Domingo and Louisiana the dangers of invasion or revolutionary ideology threatened Spanish control. Under growing pressures, the crown transferred two more Mexican infantry regiments to Havana. By 1794, the Regiment of the Crown was the only regular infantry unit left in all of New Spain. Having disbanded most of the provincial regiments and battalions, Revillagigedo found that he did not have sufficient troops to guard the cities let alone to defend against the possibility of an enemy attack.[82]

With these events, the military situation in New Spain went from bad to worse. Regulars of the interior garrison went first to guard Veracruz and then were sent to Havana. General pardons issued to attract fugitive deserters had no result.[83] To protect the strategic port, Revillagigedo moved to raise the long-discussed Fixed Battalion of Veracruz. In theory, the recruits were to be drawn from the coastal region, where the population was almost immune to tropical diseases. Normal racial qualifications for regular infantry units were lowered to admit pardos and morenos because few whites resided there.[84] In the interior, the complete lack of regular troops forced the viceroy to rely upon what remained of the provincial militias. He mobilized the Provincial Infantry Regiment of Mexico, but was to find that his previous policies had alienated the officers and the city government of the capital. Elsewhere, the liquidation of the provincial units had been completed and there were few units to mobilize. Even worse, the plans for the reserve companies and for coastal militias had not been introduced; lengthy illnesses of Sub-Inspector General Gorostiza left the army without adequate leadership at a time when quick action was essential.[86]

The Marqués del Campo de Alange left little doubt that the military policies of Revillagigedo did not satisfy the imperial government. Even after the declaration of war against France, no increases of military expenditures were permitted in New Spain. France was not considered capable of mounting an attack against the viceroyalty, particularly with the combined fleets of Spain and Britain to ensure naval superiority. While no final decision had been reached on Revillagigedo's military plan at the end of 1793, it was made quite clear that no reinforcements were forthcoming from the Spanish army.[87] In 1794, a memorandum circulated within the ministry of war acknowledged some of the pleas coming from New Spain, but continued to place its defense in a very low priority. Rumors of planned French expeditions were dismissed as lacking any real substance.[88] In the event more troops were needed to police Mexican cities, the viceroy could activate the Urban Regiment of Commerce since it was funded by merchants and needed no public support from the treasury. When Alange was informed that the provincial regiment of the capital already was in service, he decided to leave the merchants alone.[89]

Clearly, the brilliant record of legislation and reform left by Revillagigedo did not extend to his efforts as captain general. His plans to create an army of highly motivated Spaniards and Mexicans reflected a kind of inflexibility which hindered many of the Spanish administrators most influenced by the spirit of enlightened despotism. In their desire to introduce a rational system of efficient, reformed institutions and to further the interests of imperial Spain, they found Mexican society, with its divisions and factions, difficult to comprehend. The tendency was to keep the criollos away from any levers of power and to dismiss the other castas as idle vagabonds. As Revillagigedo admitted, his political maxim was that the natives of the country should not if possible be permitted control over arms.[90] Mexico challenged the reformer much more than the conservative who was willing to work with the existing system and those who held power in the provinces. For Revillagigedo, his years of isolation away from the mainstream of events were not a happy time. As he explained to his friend the scientist and explorer Alejandro Malaspina, "Perhaps you think that I am of good humor in this position, but I assure you that it is not so. . . ."[91] Much overworked and weakened by frequent migraine headaches, which he treated each night in baths from 12:00 to 1:00 A.M.,[92] Revillagigedo was not unhappy when the Marqués de Branciforte entered Mexico City to relieve him on July 12, 1794.

Branciforte arrived in Mexico when the Spanish empire was at war with republican France and its revolutionary ideologies. To his amazement, he discovered the army in disarray and the defenses of the viceroyalty unprepared. Three of the four regular infantry regiments were overseas, the provincial militia had been disbanded, and the new orders for the enlistment of reserve companies had been published just six days before his arrival. Nothing had been done to begin the formation of these units.[93] Although there was comparatively little expectation of an enemy attack, Branciforte saw the potential for disaster if defensive measures were not improved. He transferred the Regiment of the Crown and the remaining Provincial Battalion of Puebla to garrison Veracruz. In Mexico City, he activated the Urban Regiment of Commerce to guard public buildings and to prevent civil unrest. A rapid survey of the army underscored the potential danger—the total force available, regular and militia, amounted to only 4,767 troops. Since at least 2,000 of these were needed to garrison Veracruz, only 2,767 were left over to form an army of operations.[94] Furthermore, the commanders of Caribbean jurisdictions clamored for new reinforcements from Mexico.[95]

Examination of the military plans—including those of his immediate predecessor—convinced Branciforte that the failure to maintain an army could be traced directly to overemphasis upon regular units. The rejection of the approved Crespo Plan was unpardonable and events had proved the need for large reserve forces. Revillagigedo's proposals established enlistment figures similar to those of Crespo, but with the inclusion of 9,120 untrained men of the reserve companies in a total wartime defense force of 20,000. Not only did this threaten to swamp the regular regiments with green recruits, but it left few replacements in case of battle or disease casualties. The Crespo Plan on the other hand made available 8,000 men from the reserve companies simply to reinforce the regular and provincial regiments, and another 5,000 to meet wartime shortages. Even more important, the imperial government had not approved the creation of the Regiment of Tlaxcala and had refused to send large numbers of Spanish regulars to bolster the Mexican army. This lack of official endorsement limited the possible effectiveness of Revillagigedo's plans even before the transfer of the three regular regiments overseas.[96]

To Branciforte, economy and efficiency were fine ends in themselves, but like all virtues they could be pressed to such lengths that the result might be defeat and possibly the loss of the Spanish dominions. If he was to continue the monotonous history of military planning his approach might have been to disband some of the regular units, augmenting the training cadres in the provincial regiments to improve the level of training. If annual militia assemblies were extended to a full month, the result would be perfection of standards and a general improvement in discipline. Not only would this approach save money that was being wasted on the regular army, but it would also slow the manpower loss caused by the exile to Cuba and the Philippine Islands of deserters, gamblers, petty criminals, and the profligates from the regular regiments. These crimes were much less frequent in the provincial militia regiments among men who maintained their love for family, home, and country.[97]

Although Branciforte has been condemned by historians for any number of evils—marriage to Godoy's sister, peculation in the sales of militia commissions, militarizing Mexican society, and numerous other "crimes"[98]—his main offense was to restore a more conservative and traditional style of government to New Spain and to the army. It has been suggested that his major mission was to separate the viceroyalty from the "ideologies and revolutionary tendencies of Aranda."[99] Whether or not this was the case, Branciforte was cut out of different cloth than his predecessor. Authoritarian, aristocratic, and somewhat old-womanish in temperament, and certainly reactionary when it came to the French Revolution, he recognized the best means of defending New Spain and was willing to strike a reasonable relationship with the criollo elites. Branciforte cast aside the fear in which Mexicans were held and sought to utilize the manpower available in a reasonable program to develop a provincial army. He admired the approaches used by Viceroy Flórez and decided to reestablish the provincial militia system on a similar plan. Because of the large sums collected from the sale of commissions, the regular infantry regiments had been formed without great cost to the exchequer. Using this lead, Branciforte saw no reason why militia regiments and battalions could not be raised within the guidelines of the Crespo Plan.[100]

The one barrier remaining to the full implementation of the Crespo Plan was Sub-Inspector General Gorostiza, who persisted in his own opinions about defense. A bitter dispute soon broke out between Branciforte and his military commander. When Gorostiza attempted to begin enlisting reserve companies,[101] the viceroy refused him permission and in the process attacked every aspect of the previous regime's military planning—refusal to obey royal orders, unlawful suppression of militia units, and failure in introducing the *compañías sueltas*. Troop reserves had been reduced to insignificance and the urban, coastal, and frontier militias could not serve outside of their immediate localities. In the event of need for an army of operations, Branciforte could anticipate little other than untrained recruits unaccustomed to discipline or the management of weapons. Since the men of the reserve companies were to serve as nothing more than a pool of untrained manpower, his first priority was the formation of an army of operations. To facilitate this goal, he suspended the formation of reserve companies and concentrated all efforts upon the reestablishment of provincial cavalry, dragoons, and infantry.[102]

Gorostiza, very ill and isolated at his estate in Jalapa, could not resist Branciforte's will. He argued that Revillagigedo had secret orders from the minister of the Indies to alter the military plan, but since he furnished no evidence the viceroy dismissed the claim as pure fabrication. Branciforte rejected the sub-inspector general as an old man blinded by ambition for his own projects. After all, the imperial cabinet accepted the Crespo Plan in October 1788, making highly unlikely a reversal of the decision when Revillagigedo received his instructions at the beginning of 1789. Moreover, a great deal of effort had gone into the original approval with the votes of numerous committees that hardly could be set aside.[103] The viceroy requested the immediate recall of Gorostiza to Spain, but the conflict ended when the sub-inspector died suddenly on November 8, 1794.[104] Liberated from the final obstacle impeding full introduction of the Crespo Plan, Branciforte requested the imperial government not to appoint a replacement. He preferred to have the duties of inspection attached to his own office rather than risk further conflict with a new sub-inspector general.[105]

The obstacles to the Crespo Plan with its dependence upon the provincial militia units did not disappear, but they were not insuperable. Wealthy criollos, many from families with traditions of militia service, who had been dismissed by Revillagigedo, needed little prompting. As will be seen, they were more than willing to donate large sums of money toward the reestablishment of the militia in exchange for the prestige of a royal commission. Branciforte's concern about the need for an army of operations was not ill-founded. Although the war against France concluded in September 1795, it was followed by a renewal of the old alliance with the French. Before the end of 1796, the Spanish empire was at war with Britain, and Mexico had need of its restored provincial army.[106] After this date, there was little time for debate over the constitution of the army. Even though regular officers continued to curse the Mexican soldiers, to condemn the ignorance of militia officers, and to damn the incorrigible NCOs assigned to train the provincials, the pressures of war left no alternative other than to make do with what was available.

2

STRATEGIC VERACRUZ

It would be almost inconceivable to discuss the army of New Spain without first understanding the problems presented by the defense of Veracruz. Until 1810, military planners were far more concerned with the possibility of an invasion by a foreign power than with domestic insurrection. In the event of invasion, Veracruz was the logical target. It was the only city of importance on the Mexican gulf coast and the single gateway to the interior. No wonder then that officers described the port as "the key to the kingdom," "the throat of New Spain," and other, similar terms.[1] In many respects defense and Veracruz meant the same thing: no matter what form the army assumed in the populous interior, its real test would come in the tropical lowlands. At the same time, however, Veracruz presented both defender and potential invader with some very nearly insuperable difficulties. While Mexicans might have taken heart from a comment of the Duke of Wellington that "the cheap defense of nations is an unimproved frontier,"[2] it was doubtful whether climate and geography served Spanish interests. True, there were no safe anchorages along the gulf coast suitable for disembarking and sustaining an invasion force. The violent *nortes* which blew during the months from September to April threatened the very existence of shipping. Humboldt described the sudden barometric change, land wind, suffocating humidity, and veil of haze over the summits of Orizaba and Cofre de Perote which heralded the storm. Shortly after these signs, the tempest struck and "... before the lapse of a quarter hour it would be too dangerous to remain on the mole in the port of Veracruz."[3] Even within the comparative shelter of the port, vessels were caught by the teeth of the gale and driven against the rocky shoreline. Helpless witnesses in the city were unable to save the struggling victims of these disasters without great peril to their own lives.[4] In the summer months when the *nortes* were no danger, a guardian more formidable than the brooding fortress of San Juan de Ulúa stood watch and commanded access to the city. This was the feared *vómito negro* (yellow fever) that lurked in wait for any newcomer and stood ready to decimate any invasion force of men unacclimatized to the tropics and weakened by the debilitating conditions and diet of troop transports. The problem with this excellent deterrent was that it did not discriminate between Spaniard and foreigner, European or Mexican highlander.

Control over Veracruz itself was not seen to be essential by all Spanish officers. The idea of an enemy force bottled up in the city cut off from transport, denied provisions that had to be imported from the small coastal communities and from the interior towns as far away as Jalapa and Puebla, seemed better than seeking an engagement on the beaches in which defeat was a distinct possibility. With yellow fever eroding the occupation army, the defenders could bide their time before driving the weakened enemy into the sea. The real obstacle in this approach was the undeveloped frontier which protected the capital city. The road inland to Jalapa and Mexico City received the dubious distinction from Humboldt of being " ... the most difficult perhaps in all America."[5] Not only did it run through rough, unsettled country, but it was also often little more than a narrow path broken by swamps and unbridged torrents. Even in the dry seasons, deep ruts and rock slides made travel hazardous and there was no possibility of using wheeled vehicles. Indeed, lengthy notice was necessary before a carriage might pass over some of the better developed roads of the interior. When Viceroy Branciforte decided to take his wife and baby with him to Orizaba in 1797, his demand for a comfortable carriage route caused the chief of army engineers, Miguel Costansó, to spend weeks surveying roads and arranging road repairs. The subdelegates had to get out crews of Indian laborers at least fifteen days prior to the arrival of the viceroy. Nine days were needed to move Branciforte from Mexico City to Orizaba.[6] Generally, travellers could expect to reach the capital from Veracruz in about four days—a time that had not changed since the 1740s and even before.[7] To move an army was of course an entirely different situation and much more time was required.

The positive factor in all of this was the knowledge that even without holding Veracruz, the terrain sided with the defense. Defiles and gorges could be held by a very few dedicated troops who might delay an enemy army from achieving a sudden *coup de main* directed against Mexico City. Should the natural defenses fail, the fortress of San Miguel de Perote served as a secondary bulwark. Although it was not constructed to withstand a lengthy siege, its walls were strong enough to make any enemy carry full siege equipment.

This would slow their advance inland long enough to allow for the mobilization of the Mexican army.[8] Almost as important for the defenders, the mules that furnished the only reliable transport into the interior were easily removed in case of invasion. Again, however, experience proved that the advantages were also detriments. If an enemy force could not penetrate the interior, the Mexican army might encounter similar problems reinforcing Veracruz. To move approximately six thousand soldiers from encampments at Jalapa, Córdoba, and Orizaba, at least 1,635 mules were necessary.[9] This number of animals was not immediately available to the army and whenever there was an invasion scare, merchants and civilians competed with the military for the same animals. Over the years, the army acquired a poor reputation for requisitioning pack mules from private merchants. On those occasions when muleteers heard that mules were being seized for military use, they stayed well away from Veracruz, hiding in the mountains even at risk of losing perishable cargoes.[10]

While no one doubted the primary importance of defending Veracruz, each new viceroy or military commander recommended his own particular approach. There were two basic plans and innumerable variations: the first was to hold Veracruz, making it the front line of defense and the second was to garrison a respectable force at the port, stationing the bulk of the army in the interior towns of Jalapa, Orizaba, Córdoba, and Perote. Since neither approach satisfied all of the interests concerned, new plans were churned out until there was a terrible confusion of paper in the military archives. Finally, in 1775, a junta of the most senior army officers available produced a defense plan for Veracruz that was not altered appreciably until the end of the colonial period. Notwithstanding the importance of the port, no officer considered it capable of sustaining a concerted siege for more than a few days. The city, separate from the island fortress of San Juan de Ulúa, was guarded by a low wall that was usually covered by drifting sand from nearby dunes. An enemy could anticipate having a ramp leading to the very heart of the defenses.[11] The totally indefensible nature of the town caused many military planners to devote more time to the best means of retreat to prevent the loss of the garrison. They centered all hope for coastal resistance on the strong fortress of San Juan de Ulúa, postulating that if an enemy failed to capture it, there could be no major invasion of the interior.[12]

By almost all accounts, Veracruz was not blessed with many positive attributes. Without the benefits of modern medicine and sanitation which have made it one of the most pleasant cities in Mexico, the port was a place loved only by its natural and adopted citizens. Men congregated at Veracruz to make their fortunes from commerce or were attracted by high salaries to other positions, but they paid a high price in terms of their own lives and those of their families. If they survived the period of acclimatization, they ceased to have major cause for fear of *vómito negro* and other tropical diseases. After long residency, such men became the staunch defenders of the port; their hard work and entrepreneurial talents made the city advance in wealth and population. They were a tough, dynamic breed who propelled their own business interests and who often worked outside the law to make their fortunes. Smugglers made their way out to British or other foreign vessels awaiting them offshore. There they paid Mexican silver for textiles and other manufactured goods unavailable or much more expensive in New Spain after paying duties and taxes.[13] Others with brazen self-confidence traded openly at Kingston, Jamaica, regardless of whether Spain was at peace or war with Great Britain.[14] Some of these traders made fortunes and began to compete with the entrenched merchant interests of the *consulado* of Mexico. Recognition of the prominence attained by these men came in 1795 with the creation of the consulado of Veracruz. Having gained status, the Veracruz merchants turned their energies to the advancement of agriculture, improvement of mercantile techniques, application of new machinery, and the upgrading of the road inland to Jalapa.[15]

At the same time, however, the port city repelled those from overseas or the highlands who were well aware of its reputation as a graveyard for outsiders. When the Conde de Revillagigedo arrived in Mexico in 1789, he undertook an extensive study of Veracruz before moving inland to take possession of his command. Everything he saw regarding defense, government, and public health gave Revillagigedo cause for shock. The city fortifications were "not deserving of the name," and the walls had deteriorated to such a state that contraband trade flourished within the confines of the town. Residents threw their garbage and wastes into the streets and open ditches, presenting a sight "... not only ugly and indecent, but prejudicial to health."[16] The fortress of San Juan de Ulúa was in slightly better condition, but the few naval vessels were almost eaten through by worms. Though it was well known that wooden hulls lasted as little as four months in tropical waters, no effort had been made to sheath them in copper. Because there was a shortage of barracks, troops of the garrison were billeted in private residences where military discipline soon weakened. The army hospitals of San Carlos and San Juan de Montesclaros were overcrowded and in such frightful condition that Revillagigedo viewed them as hazards to patients and to the entire population of the city. He described the climate as so depressing and dangerous to his own health that he began to fear for his life. Well aware of the fate so many others had suffered from the foul odors emanating from cemeteries located in small patios next to the hospitals, he cut short his stay and left the port with precipitous haste for the healthier highlands.

Other observers confirmed this general picture. Colonel Diego García Panes, a long-time resident of the port, believed that the city walls served only to block adequate ventilation of streets and houses. He found almost all wells and cisterns fouled by dead insects and animals or by the filthy privies situated too close to water supplies. The water consumed by the lower classes of the city was especially bad.[17] Humboldt confirmed this opinion and stated that the only reliable source of water was to be found in the cisterns of San Juan de Ulúa used for army consumption.[18] The hospitals were as evil or more so than Revillagigedo reported. One study by the physicians and surgeons of the navy described the hospital of Montesclaros as:[19]

> ... a deposit of putrefaction and malignity situated against all rules of medicine in the center of the city where the causes of illness abound; one must view it as a focus that gives off contagious beams in every direction.

Army officers feared stationing their troops in this atmosphere where conditions and the climate were certain to exact a heavy toll. But even more they shuddered at the prospect of encountering an epidemic of *vómito negro* that might sweep through their regiments leaving little standing except the banners. Yellow fever was one of the most important single enemies the army had to deal with and weapons were of little use against it. Long after independence, the Mexican government offered a prize of 100,000 pesos to anyone who discovered a cure.[20] The army attempted any number of experiments to reduce casualty rates and to strengthen soldiers sent from the interior to the coast. Men were given two to three months at Jalapa with very light duties so that they might rest and build up resistance to tropical conditions. Then they were marched down to the coast at night without full packs so as to prevent sweating and exhaustion which were believed to invite yellow fever.[21] Despite these measures, physicians were certain that the trip into the suffocating humidity of the coast irritated the nervous system and disposed " ... the organs more easily to receive the deleterious miasmata of the yellow fever."[22] The speed and devastation of the disease horrified all observers. In 1801, Captain Juan de Abercrombi of the Regiment of New Spain wrote to Viceroy Marquina informing him that of one hundred vagabonds sent from Puebla to serve in the Veracruz garrison, eighty-five died before the completion of one month.[23] Even those who survived disease to become acclimatized residents struck observers as being less healthy and robust than other Mexicans. Padre Francisco de Ajofrín noted a general pallor as though the Veracruzanos were convalescing from severe illness. In his opinion, "in their actions and even in their speech they show a feebleness and great decay."[24]

In the face of such a major threat to life, eighteenth-century medicine offered precious little in the way of remedy. The first signs of pain in the lumbar region, yellowing of the eyes, and congestion in the head must have thrown most victims into mortal terror. The symptoms were quite clear; some residents of Jalapa familiar with travellers coming up from the coastal lowlands were able to identify victims of yellow fever even before it struck. Humboldt mentioned a barber who shaved the incoming Spaniards and informed those infected of their probable death sentences.[25] Physicians were by no means agreed on what to do during the various stages of yellow fever. Humboldt, very interested in the impact of the disease and the methods of treatment, reported widespread use of baths, ice water, and sherbets during the first stages. As the illness progressed, patients were given sixty to seventy drops of tincture of opium per hour and more than one hundred drops of sulphuric ether. Bleeding, used extensively during earlier decades, had been discarded by the beginning of the nineteenth century.[26] Numerous experiments with quinine, mercurial compounds, pineapple juice, and other preparations were tried and then abandoned. For the lower classes as well as for the common soldiers, the treatment was more rudimentary but likely just as effective. Unable to afford ice, which was carried to Veracruz from the volcano of Orizaba, the poor gave fever victims lukewarm water and other liquids.[27] Other cures which prescribed tartar emetic to induce vomiting, enemas, and drugs to promote sweating probably hindered more than promoted recovery.[28] In 1800, the *Gazeta de México* published a cure for yellow fever that advised twelve ounces of the whey of milk mixed with a little sweet saltpeter; patients were to take this concoction as often as three times every two hours.[29]

Scientists and physicians did not connect yellow fever and the mosquito, but they did suspect that pools of stagnant water breathed "exhalations" harmful to men.[30] Numerous proposals were made at Veracruz to drain marshes and to move both hospitals and graveyards from the center of the city. Physicians were less certain about the communicability of the disease. When militiamen of the Provincial Regiment of Valladolid fell ill with fever in 1801 and began to die from symptoms similar to those of yellow fever, some physicians suggested that the source of contagion was the uniforms received by the militia unit from Veracruz. Although Valladolid (now Morelia) had never experienced yellow fever, investigations showed signs of sweat, blood, and dried vomit on the uniforms. Dr. Santiago Maureta de la Barrera proposed quarantining the men who had worn the uniforms and the immediate burning of all garments shipped from the port. In his opinion, it was quite obvious that these uniforms had been taken from the bodies of soldiers who perished from yellow fever. The Valladolid doctors believed that the disease passed like an electrical current from body to body and they resisted orders to perform autopsies on the bodies of victims for fear of releasing the disease and exposing the surgeon and all present. On the other side of the case, budget-conscious administrators wanted nothing to do with the suggestion of burning perfectly good uniforms. The Tribunal del Protomedicato settled the matter by arguing correctly that yellow fever could not be transmitted through the clothing of previous victims.[31]

Debates of this nature had an air of the unreal. For every proposed cure or prevention of yellow fever, there was some other case to be made for a radically different solution. When Veracruz fell into the grip of an extended epidemic of yellow fever in the 1790s, the authorities were hard pressed to suggest new approaches. The director of the royal botanical expedition, Martín de Sessé, went so far as to recommend either a reduction of the port population or the abandonment of the site of Veracruz.[32] As Miguel Lerdo de Tejada pointed out, this was an absurd idea by the early nineteenth century.[33] Despite the dangers of yellow fever, the port had attained a degree of prominence and power which made it capable of resisting much less radical solutions. Indeed, no viceroy could afford to risk alienating the port merchants, who were quite prepared to lay their complaints before the imperial cabinet if satisfaction was not forthcoming from Mexico City.

The real difficulty in defending Veracruz lay in balancing the conflicting interests of the port merchants and the poor soldiers who served in the garrison. The war against Britain, beginning in October 1796, coincided with the outbreak of a virulent epidemic of yellow fever. Before news of the hostilities reached New Spain, Branciforte decided to follow the basic approach of the 1775 defense plan.[34] He dispatched Lieutenant Colonel Miguel Costansó to survey the coastal defenses and to visit sites near the healthy inland towns which might be suitable for a small cantonment. A *junta de guerra* of senior officers convened at Veracruz to advise on defense and this body selected Orizaba as the best location for military headquarters. The region seemed to produce adequate surplus food, fuel, supplies, and fodder needed for an army of operations. The viceroy agreed to station twenty-two hundred men at Veracruz, but only if the city prepared adequate barracks and lowered the health hazards created by accumulations of garbage and other filth inside the walls.[35] The remainder of the army—about six thousand troops of the newly reestablished provincial militia regiments and battalions headed by the Infantry Regiment of New Spain now returned from duty in Havana—were to be stationed at Orizaba, Jalapa, and Córdoba. In the event of an invasion, this small army would be ready to engage the enemy. To make sure, Branciforte went to Orizaba himself to take command of the army and to conduct training exercises. He found his troops somewhat green, but they appeared diligent and willing to learn.[36]

The need for a strong defensive force was quite evident from dispatches arriving from Spain and Philadelphia. Britain was said to be planning a two-pronged attack—from Canada by way of the Mississippi River to invade the Provincias Internas and from Jamaica to land at Veracruz.[37] Ludicrous though these rumors were, other events tended to confirm the most bizarre apprehensions. News of the fall of Trinidad to the British threw the governors of Caribbean Spanish possessions into near panic and both Cuba and Puerto Rico prepared for assaults. The captain general of Cuba, Marqués de Santa Clara, undertook a feverish program to dig trenches to defend Havana and he requested immediate reinforcements from New Spain to fill the two Mexican infantry regiments still on duty in Cuba.[38] Branciforte said he would do what he could to send troops, but in reality he saw little hope of attracting volunteers. He could not spare men from the Regiment of the Crown stationed at Veracruz and the Regiment of New Spain had not made up its losses from its previous tour of duty at Havana. Fortunately, reports of the Spanish victory over the British at Puerto Rico relieved some of the tensions.[39]

While the fear of invasion decreased, enemy maritime activity and the weakness of the Spanish navy caused sufficient problems. The coasts of Veracruz, Tabasco, and Campeche were swept clear of merchant shipping by enemy corsairs protected by larger vessels of the British navy. The lancers of Veracruz and other coastal militia units had their hands full chasing off small parties of marauders who looted villages and ranches or landed with the intention of stealing provisions and water. Enemy blockades of Havana and persistent rumors that the Venezuelan revolutionary, Francisco Miranda, might attempt a landing near Veracruz gave reason enough for continued vigilance.[40] Coastal authorities watched constantly for any strangers and at Jalapa, where travellers were thoroughly inspected, the customs guards possessed a detailed description of the "unhappy brown eyes and suspicious, treacherous countenance of the traitor."[41] Knowing about Miranda's plans, army officers feared a sneak attack in which one or two vessels might surprise and capture the fortress of San Juan de Ulúa. Audacious officers, a few good troops, and use of Spanish flags and signals could convince the defenders momentarily that the vessels came to collect treasure. Once having gained entry to the port, as few as two hundred to three hundred men could overpower the fortress taking full advantage of confusion amongst the defenders.[42] As a precaution, valuable ornaments from the churches of Veracruz and

2,300,000 pesos in silver belonging to the crown were transferred inland to the fortress of Perote for safekeeping.[43]

Although the cantonment and the general defensive preparations appeared to be progressing, the epidemic at Veracruz soon jeopardized the entire military effort. Unacclimatized troops from the interior became the special victims of yellow fever. On March 1, 1797, the army hospital of San Carlos reported 365 yellow fever patients and in the following three days, 57 new cases were admitted and 17 men died of the disease. Of the 56 who recuperated sufficiently to leave the hospital, all had to be carried inland to regain their health and could not be returned to active duty for many months.[44] By September 1797, the Regiment of the Crown had lost nearly 500 men to disease, and desertion had become an alarming problem among the remaining troops. Reluctantly, Branciforte sanctioned the transfer of two militia battalions from the cantonment, but he delayed their departure when the epidemic continued into the normally healthy season.[45] As if yellow fever was not sufficient cause for concern, smallpox, which had been raging through the interior cities, swept down to the coast. The cabildo of Veracruz opened a provisional contagious disease hospital funded by the public revenues of the city, but there were strenuous objections from civilians when it was found that almost all the patients were soldiers. If the troops were the only ones contracting smallpox, the city wanted the army to pay for the full costs of their hospitalization.[46]

Since no reports of peace negotiations arrived from Europe by January 1798, Branciforte reconvened the *junta de guerra* at Orizaba to discuss strategy and the growing disease crisis at the port. According to rumors, the British were constructing forty launches at Jamaica—a matter for anxiety because such craft might be intended to support an invasion.[47] Of much more immediate worry, however, were the increasing death rates and desertion levels at Veracruz, which made all defense plans inoperable. The garrison, consisting of the Regiment of the Crown, the first battalion of the Provincial Regiment of Puebla, the Fixed Battalion of Veracruz, two Companies of Pardos and Morenos, and 360 militiamen of the Corps of Lancers, should have totaled 2,486 troops. In reality, less than 1,900 men were available although many replacements had arrived for the dead and sick. As Veracruz slowly eroded the army of operations, the total number of troops at the cantonment declined from 6,000 to fewer than 5,600. Branciforte was not at all pleased by any reduction of his provincial army even though he was certain he could increase the army of operations to 10,000 troops without hindering internal security.[48] He was less able to respond to the growing demands of the consulado and cabildo of Veracruz. Merchants began to fear that the weakness of the port garrison and the low morale of the panic-stricken troops might well encourage an enemy raid.

After considering the alternatives, the *junta de guerra* advised Branciforte not to bolster the Veracruz garrison without definite enemy provocation. The impact of yellow fever, desertion, and the question of naval use of soldiers to man the chronically shorthanded vessels were discussed at length, but no new solutions came to mind. Some officers proposed moving a part of the cantonment to a site closer to Veracruz where the climate was more benign and the health of soldiers could be protected. The junta also examined requests from the cabildo of Veracruz for fifteen hundred to two thousand muskets. If the army refused to guarantee adequate safeguards, the city government proposed to raise urban companies of armed civilians.[49]

In the meantime, the port garrison continued to decline. By the beginning of March 1798, only 114 men were available to stand watches in the fortress of San Juan de Ulúa. Branciforte, convinced that men from the interior would stand little chance of surviving at the coast, delayed sending any further reinforcements. He left the final decision on what he stressed was a life or death sentence for the soldiers up to the interim governor of Veracruz, Colonel Diego García Panes. By employing numerous postponements and forcing the governor to accept responsibility for any disaster, Branciforte fought for time, hoping to withhold the departure of troops until the epidemic abated. He chided the governor for requesting troops and asked him to follow the dictates of honor and conscience. After all, in the event of an enemy attack, immediate reinforcements would be sent from the interior cantonment.[50]

For García Panes, the explanation of troop shortages became impossible as the powerful merchants and business elements pressured for more adequate defenses. At first he agreed with Branciforte's delay of reinforcements until the epidemic subsided, but he was soon caught between the interests of the port and those of the interior. Branciforte's refusal to dispatch replacements left the governor in a real quandary; if he did nothing to obtain fresh troops he faced the wrath of merchants and if he challenged viceregal decisions in defense matters he faced a possible charge of insubordination. The continual offer of two provincial battalions followed by permanent postponements finally drove García Panes to a state of complete frustration. Delays blamed by Branciforte on the unavailability of housing were ridiculous since the Regiment of the Crown had been moved to San Juan de Ulúa with the specific purpose of opening their barracks for the battalions. If these quarters were not adequate, the governor offered to requisition the best private residences in the city for the defenders of the *patria*. Finally, García Panes spoke out in favor of the Veracruz interests, arguing that he had no alternative since he had sworn an oath to defend the port when he accepted the post as interim governor. The result was a stinging denunciation of the policy of interior cantonment and the security it appeared to allow for the defense of Veracruz. To the merchants as well as to knowledgeable officers, the basic premise that troops cantoned in the interior protected the port was completely false. At least five days would elapse from the first enemy landings and even then, the strenuous marches might weaken the ability of the soldiers to resist the climate. Yet, an enemy force of three thousand or more might land within twelve hours after being sighted by the defenders.[51] This fact alone made it essential for the Veracruz garrison to be at least strong enough to withstand the primary assault. Since the governor could field only six hundred to seven hundred troops, there was little likelihood of success: in the event of an attack, the garrison would have to retire to San Juan de Ulúa while the enemy sacked and burned the city.[52]

When Branciforte asked for a list of potential cantonment sites just outside the port, but close enough to give rapid aid to the city garrison, the governor replied in utter exasperation: "There are none, Your Excellency! There are none, except within the walls of Veracruz!" Previous searches for bases always returned the army to the port because no town in the vicinity even began to offer adequate facilities. Soldiers needed good housing to protect them from the climate, hospitals to treat those who succumbed to tropical diseases, and supplies, medicines, and many other essential items. At any other locations, barracks and hospitals would have to be constructed before a cantonment might be considered. Antigua was the only town near Veracruz, but it was a poor community of straw huts without any buildings suitable for military use. Besides, forced marches over the six leagues from Antigua to Veracruz would leave the troops in a state of exhaustion by the time they arrived to engage the enemy. As for other locations which had been recommended from time to time—Satanás was only three leagues from the port, but the name described the place better than words. Like other sites it was exposed to flooding during the rainy season, heat and oppressive humidity in the summer months which rotted tents and clothing, and the angry *nortes* of the cooler months would complete the destruction. To further deter those who promoted these plans, García Panes reported that even the climate-hardened lancers of Veracruz could not survive without adequate facilities. A small garrison sent to guard the coastal defense cannon launches at Vergara had to be withdrawn when it was found that the men fell ill even though they were relieved every eight days. The governor warned that if encampments were set up in these unhealthful areas, soldiers must not be stationed in them for more than a week at a time.

As might be expected, Branciforte developed an intense dislike for García

Panes. The *junta de guerra* reconvened to examine the validity of the charges and agreed with the viceroy that the governor had used his "capricious imagination" in misrepresenting the true facts about the availability of troops. He had not taken into account the coastal militias, which on paper listed 954 infantrymen and 476 cavalry. That these coastal units were not to be moved from their home districts was forgotten in this dispute. Disregarding the statistics from Veracruz, the officers found García Panes guilty of having become involved in the politics of the port and of adopting a biased view rather than serving the best interests of New Spain.[53] In fact, this conclusion was wishful thinking more than anything else. Although the defense plan of 1775 was still logical in strictly military terms, the situation in 1798 was quite different. No longer was Veracruz a transit point where vessels of the *flotas* dropped their cargoes of merchandise, quicksilver, and other European imports and picked up Mexican silver, cochineal, and other exports. In 1775, all of the negotiations and business had been transacted at the trade fairs of Jalapa. The port was very nearly a dead city once the muleteers transferred their wares to the outbound fleet. Only six thousand to eight thousand people inhabited the city permanently, about half the population of sixteen thousand who lived there in 1798.[54] There were fewer warehouses, businesses, or private residences and an enemy would have gained relatively little from sacking the city.

With freer trade, its own dynamic merchant consulado, and the right to trade with foreign neutrals between 1797 and 1799, Veracruz had become a very different kind of defensive problem. In 1798, Lieutenant Colonel Pedro de Laguna, artillery commander in New Spain, described the port as the "warehouse for the commerce of Spain and Mexico."[55] Not only had the population increased dramatically, but wealth in buildings and improvements made it a more attractive target for enemy attention. Because of the uninterrupted flow of commerce, there was a sizable amount of minted silver in the city. When one added the value of private residences and churches with their furnishings, ornaments, and jewelry, the potential value of booty was very large. While merchants dispatched much of their money and trade goods to Jalapa at the outbreak of every war, the value of permanent fixtures and unmovable property was much more than the planners of 1775 could have imagined.[56] Merchants who in 1798, for example, had eight thousand bags (*zurrones*) of cochineal, sugar, and a large inventory of indigo stored in warehouses refused to accept the idea that Veracruz might be surrendered to the enemy without a fight.[57] Like their colleagues in the consulado of Mexico, these men were largely immigrant Spaniards who were unwilling to play a passive role in events they considered crucial to their future (see table 4). Dominating the

TABLE 4
Origins of Some Prominent Veracruz Merchants, 1810.

José Ignacio de la Torre	Santander
Pedro Miguel de Echeverría	Navarra
Domingo Escandón	Santander
Pablo Frayle	La Rioja
Manuel Antonio del Valle	Vizcaya
Genero Garza	Galicia
José Givert	Isla de León
Bruno Barnolla	Genoa, Italy
Juan Antonio Fernández	Reynosa, Castilla
Antonio de Zúñiga	Cádiz
Juan Tómas de Miguelena	Navarra
Juan Felipe Laurnaga	Navarra
Jorge de la Serna	Santander
Juan Salcedo	Vizcaya
Tomás Murphi	Málaga

Source: AGN, Infidencias, vol. 30.

cabildo of Veracruz, the merchants had begun to demonstrate an aggressive determination to force defense policy to meet their needs. Branciforte encountered some rather stiff resistance to his deployment of the army, and his successors would find Veracruz even more difficult in the years down to 1810.[58]

At the time Branciforte transferred command of New Spain to José Miguel de Azanza, he stressed the fact that his personal success with army building depended upon his determined refusal to send large numbers of troops to Veracruz where morale and health would be destroyed. Despite repeated demands from Governor García Panes and the port merchants, he maintained a firm stand in a matter he considered to be absolutely crucial.[59] Azanza agreed, for he found the provincial army at Orizaba and the other towns of the cantonment to be in a remarkably good state of training and discipline. There were some signs of fatigue among militiamen who desired to return to their homes and occupations, but this was to be anticipated. Much of this restlessness resulted from pressures exerted by their families and employers who argued that the men were needed at home to support dependents or to labor in the various branches of industry and agriculture.[60]

Having recently completed a term as imperial minister of war, Azanza knew all about the Veracruz merchants' dissatisfaction and their tendency to bypass the viceroy. He had received numerous petitions asking for a larger garrison, more ordnance, and a defense plan that would commit major forces to defend the port. To head off further dissension, Azanza commissioned two lieutenant colonels, Miguel Costansó and Pedro de Laguna, to make a full study of defensive strategy. To begin with, both officers discovered numerous obstacles preventing the interior army from carrying out a rapid descent to the coast. Troops quartered in the cantonment towns paid for their own maintenance from their daily allowances, purchasing food and fuel out of the surrounding countryside at current prices. Although this system was much more economical than if the treasury supplied rations, it could not be used during marches to the coast. The sparsely settled routes lacked anything near the agricultural or animal production needed to provision an army. The government would have to construct warehouses and be prepared to underwrite the full costs of troop maintenance. Lodging posed similar difficulties since the small villages along the roads were not large enough to accommodate the existing flow of travellers. Tent encampments could be used, but the climate made dependence upon temporary shelter very risky. Tents might serve in the dry season, but during much of the year the rainfall was too heavy and grass or straw bedding would always be damp. Costansó recommended the construction of large barracks or sheds with thatched roofing situated at the end of each day's march. These would protect the soldiers from heavy rain, burning sun, and at night from "an atmosphere charged with noxious vapors dangerous to the health of men."[61] In theory, the barracks might evolve into travellers' inns and perhaps serve as focal points to attract much-needed settlers to the region. To further protect the soldiers, Costansó proposed issuing each infantryman a goatskin waterbottle and each cavalryman a wineskin large enough to carry water for himself and his horse. Canoes or bridging materials would have to be purchased in advance and made ready at river crossings where timber was not available. With all precautions, however, the reports warned that of the six thousand troops marching to the coast, as many as fifteen hundred would fall ill in normal times and perhaps as much as a third of the force if disease conditions were high.

These findings corroborated the conclusions of Colonel García Panes. It became quite obvious that if a large force was sent to the coast, the troops might be too weak to add much immediate assistance against an invading enemy. Certainly the costs of moving six thousand men from the interior cantonment and supporting them for a six-month campaign shocked all observers. The intendant of the army, Francisco Rendón, submitted a detailed estimate outlining all possible expenditures—his total came to 2,207,223 pesos[62] (see table 5). Aware of the imperial government's attitude on extraordinary defense costs, many officers were convinced that the only solution was to move the army of operations closer to Veracruz. Indeed, the crown acted to cool the activities of military planners in New Spain. Not only were

TABLE 5
Cost of Sending an Army of 6,000 from the Interior Cantonment to Veracruz and Maintaining It for Six Months

Provisions and Forage	436,680 pesos
Barracks, hospitals, canoes, and the Intendancy	356,000
Utensils	15,958
Utensils for hospitals, kitchens, and chapels	85,694
Special rations for hospital patients	135,000
Drugs	45,000
Washing and cleaning in hospitals	9,000
Hospital equipment	30,000
Mules	360,000
Officer's Utensils	2,945
Pay and Allowances	654,716
Pay for non-military employees	40,070
Pay for hospital employees	33,100
Pay for bakers	3,060
Total	2,207,223 pesos

Source: Propuesto general de los gastos para en caso de que las tropas acantonadas hubieron de trasladarse a los puntos de la costa de Veracruz, 1798, AGN, IG, vol. 328-A.

all capital expenditures on defense projects postponed, but a royal order of April 10, 1798, retired all provincial militia units stationed at the cantonment.[63]

Although invasion was still a major concern, the royal order reduced the available infantry force to the two regular regiments and the Battalion of Veracruz. French intelligence reported an impending alliance between Britain and the United States which would be sealed by a joint invasion of Florida and a new attempt against Havana.[64] Conquest of this port was supposed to anticipate a general assault directed against other Spanish and French possessions. While the imperial government accepted the gravity of this information, the defense of exposed Caribbean possessions took precedence over New Spain. Viceroy Azanza received orders to transfer another regiment or at least a battalion to Havana.[65]

The viceroy had no alternative other than to send a large percentage of his veteran soldiers to Havana. His position was made even more difficult since the Regiments of the Crown and New Spain along with the Battalion of Veracruz were occupied fully in the port garrison. Already weakened by yellow fever and desertion, they had no reserves available for overseas duty. The two regular dragoon regiments could not be considered because they were vital for the provincial army's support. If a regiment was to be sent to Havana, it had to be one of the two stationed at Veracruz. One of the provincial regiments would have to fill the void although these men had just returned to their homes after a year and a half in the cantonment.[66] Further limiting the options was the fact that the Regiment of New Spain had completed a tour of overseas duty only two years before. At that time it returned with less than 50 percent of its total and it was still basically a unit of green recruits. The Regiment of the Crown, the obvious candidate for Havana, was also the cream of the Mexican army and considered essential to lead the provincial forces. Examining the few options, Azanza decided to select the least damaging solution. Instead of losing a full regiment or even a battalion, he transferred 760 troops from the two regular infantry regiments to Havana. This number was sufficient to fill 400 vacancies in the Regiments of Puebla and Mexico and to add 180 men to each regiment.[67] The shortages in the Regiments of the Crown and New Spain were to be filled from the provincial units when the invasion season began at Veracruz. A total of 1,680 militiamen were drafted with each provincial regiment contributing 240 men and each battalion 120. The only units exempt were the Regiment of Mexico, assigned to garrison duty in the capital, and the Battalion of Guadalajara, which was located too far from the port.[68] By the end of February 1799, militia troops had begun to arrive at Jalapa. They would join the regular regiments at Veracruz as soon as a British blockade of Havana terminated and the reinforcements sailed for Cuba.

At the same time, merchant interests at Veracruz achieved their objective of making the port a primary focus of defense. Instead of a garrison of only 2,200 men and a plan to relinquish control over the city in the event of a concerted enemy attack, Azanza concentrated a significant part of his army at Veracruz. A garrison of 4,230 troops employed almost all of the regular infantry available in New Spain as well as a large number of militiamen.[69] Besides this force, the consulado and cabildo were given permission to enlist a civilian militia of 1,000 men capable of firing at any invader from the parapets. If an attack came, 500 infantrymen were to garrison San Juan de Ulúa and be prepared for a possible siege of up to six months, 300 men were to assist the armed civilian militia of the city, and the remainder of the garrison, over 3,000 men, would be divided into two mobile columns. Supported by field artillery, the enemy would be resisted at the points of attempted landings.[70]

To combat yellow fever and to place the defense force in a better position to intercept the enemy, the *junta de guerra* recommended stationing some of the troops in a cantonment near the city. After the completion of surveys and estimates, Azanza approved the creation of a cantonment of six hundred infantry and two hundred cavalry at Arroyo Moreno, only two leagues from

Veracruz.⁷¹ To add strength to the forces available, attempts were made to extend the enlistment of the Lancers of Veracruz. This was a popular move with army officers because the pardo and moreno inhabitants resisted the diseases which felled most soldiers and they were excellent horsemen with perfect knowledge of the coast. A census conducted by Colonel Nicolás de Monteagudo, commander of the Corps of Lancers, enumerated an eligible male population of three thousand in the coastal zone close to the port.⁷²

It was at this point that the carefully conceived coastal defense plan began to crumble. The imperial government balked at the prospect of doubling the annual budget for the lancers and sent Azanza's reports to the Marqués de Branciforte for evaluation. He responded that he too had considered expanding the Corps of Lancers, but did not because of overriding social and economic factors. Any further expansion of the coastal militia might well damage the economic system of the region, resulting in food and supply shortages in the port city.⁷³ The attempt to raise a civilian militia force at Veracruz also failed. Lieutenant Colonel Pedro de Alonso, commander of the Arroyo Moreno cantonment, described the five hundred muskets shipped to the port for this purpose as "... truly useless, not only for inexperienced militiamen, but even for regular troops fully trained in the use of firearms." They were of English manufacture, heavily reinforced along the full length of the barrel, which not only raised doubts about safety for those discharging them, but also made the muskets so heavy that no degree of accuracy was possible. The bayonet also was heavier than usual and when it was attached to the musket, few citizens of Veracruz were strong enough to aim the weapon. Since the muskets were of rather rough iron construction, they would soon rust away in the humidity of Veracruz.⁷⁴

In 1800, Spain's maritime defense posture at Veracruz caused growing alarm. Although fourteen cannon launches had been constructed and armed with a medium caliber cannon placed on a swivel, there were few experienced officers or seamen to man them. Often, infantry officers had to be employed to command the launches and the crews were made up of recuperating patients from the port hospitals.⁷⁵ At the same time, British naval blockades of Havana increased the number of ships in the harbor, adding to the potential for an epidemic. Three frigates, the *Esmeralda, Medea,* and *Clara,* had been in port since the previous autumn loaded with silver for Spain. In February 1799, two warships of the Havana squadron, the *Anfitrite* and the *Juno,* arrived from Havana to announce that all was well and the blockade had been lifted. They took on the large cash subsidies (*situados*), gunpowder, and supplies New Spain furnished for less wealthy Caribbean possessions. The fleet was prepared to sail when two more warships, the *San Ildefonso* and the *San Fulgen-*

cio, dropped anchor, thereby delaying the fleet until they could sail with the convoy. In the meantime, two frigates, the *Minerva* and the *Nuestra Señora de la O,* were sent from Havana to convey the *situados* and the reinforcements destined for duty with the Mexican regiments at Havana. The fleet was ready to sail once again when it was learned that the enemy had five warships of the line and six frigates lying in wait off Havana and in the Bahama Channel.[76] The captain of the *San Fulgencio,* Dionisio Alcalá Galiano, by seniority the commander of the growing fleet, conferred with Azanza and with the other captains at Veracruz to decide on a plan in the face of continuing enemy blockades. On one point they were in full agreement: the risks of navigation were much less than those of remaining idle at Veracruz. Disease and desertion had diminished the crews to such an extent that it would soon be impossible to sail at all.[77] The convoy sailed and arrived safely in Havana after an uneventful voyage.

The concentration of so many *arribeños* and *guachinangos,* as the highlanders and those from overseas were called, was bound to increase yellow fever casualties. Indeed for the past few years the number of cases amongst soldiers had been a source of growing concern to army and medical authorities. What occurred in 1799, however, was a catastrophe of totally unexpected proportions. More than half of the provincial militiamen cantoned at Arroyo Moreno perished in the sweltering heat and humidity of their encampment, and many of those who survived were maimed for life.[78] In the Regiments of New Spain and the Crown, the epidemic killed 875 officers and soldiers and caused 358 desertions. As the garrison declined, Azanza found no alternative other than to withdraw additional militiamen from the provincial regiments. Another 460 young bachelors were sent into active duty with the regulars, dangerously depleting some of the militia units.[79] As table 6 shows, 14,672 soldiers were admitted to the Hospital Real de San Carlos and 891 of these men died.[80] It is no exaggeration to say that Azanza lost half of his regular infantry troops in a single year.

This was the crisis which confronted Viceroy Marquina in March 1800, when he assumed command of New Spain. Horrified by the appalling statistics listing deaths and desertions, Marquina halted the drain of militiamen from the interior to Veracruz. Discovering a satisfactory alternative was another question. In the end, Marquina returned to Branciforte's position and the Defense Plan of 1775. One battalion of the Regiment of the Crown was withdrawn from the port and replaced with several militia companies of the Corps of Lancers.[81] As might be expected, the merchants of Veracruz interpreted the withdrawal of any troops as a reversion to Branciforte's policies. They viewed the mobilization of coastal militiamen as a particularly danger-

TABLE 6
Entries, Departures, and Deaths in the Military Hospital of San Carlos and the Poor Hospital of Montesclaros, Veracruz, 1787–1804.

	Hospital of San Carlos			Hospital of Montesclaros		
Year	Entries	Departures	Deaths	Entries	Departures	Deaths
1787	2087	2041	46	2304	1857	447
1788	2415	2331	84	1775	1450	325
1789	2625	2514	111	1443	1118	325
1790	1844	1805	39	1405	1201	204
1791	2070	2032	38	1568	1352	216
1792	2887	2816	71	1973	1669	304
1793	2907	2830	77	1507	1244	263
1794	4195	3742	453	1496	1105	391
1795	3596	3175	421	1890	1485	405
1796	3181	3005	176	1687	1245	442
1797	4727	4249	478	1354	980	374
1798	5186	4991	195	976	785	191
1799	14672	13781	891	1952	1514	438
1800	9294	8789	505	1818	1308	510
1801	7120	6894	226	2069	1649	420
1802*	5242	4700	441	1905	1182	654
1803*	2217	1962	162	1601	1236	295
1804*	3432	3599	267	1967	1325	525
TOTALS	79697	75256	4681	30690	23705	6729

*There are statistical discrepancies for the last three years.

Source: Unsigned report from Veracruz, 1804, AGN, Archivo Provisional, Hospitales Militares, Caja 1.

ous step that might further damage the delicate balance between agricultural labor and food production for the port city. Other than staples such as ham, butter, flour, and some grain, most of the food consumed in Veracruz was grown on the small farms along the coast. Militia mobilizations meant the removal of farmers and subsequent losses of agricultural output. Some of the small communities in which the lancers resided had been so hard hit by lengthy service that they had not been able to harvest food for their own use let alone for the markets of the port. Food prices had been driven upward until some items such as eggs and vegetables cost four times their normal value.[82]

Much of the price inflation resulted from the activity of enemy warships and privateers that drove most coastal commerce from the sea. Watchtowers from Coatzacoalcos to Alvarado reported continual sightings. Occasionally, the enemy approached the fortress of San Juan de Ulúa and on June 16, 1800, a frigate chased a Spanish schooner to within four leagues of the port. The captain of a fishing boat informed the governor of Veracruz that the British frigate confiscated his cargo of fish and he had been questioned as to whether or not the warship *Gloria* was in Veracruz. The schooner *Guadalupe,* sailing from Campeche for Veracruz, was captured by a forty-eight-gun frigate. The enemy removed the best of the cargo, food, and documents before permitting the vessel to proceed. Before releasing the schooner, they placed on board the captain and crew of another Spanish vessel, the *Fidela,* taken on the way to Veracruz with a cargo of pitch and tar for the government shipyards. The *Guadalupe* continued her voyage, but was stopped again by another enemy frigate, the *Amphion,* only to be freed when it was discovered that the best cargo had been picked clean.[83] Marquina convened a *junta de marina* to see what if anything could be done to forestall the disruption of commerce. There were four Spanish frigates at Veracruz, but they had deteriorated to such a degree that they could not sail without extensive repairs, let alone protect merchant shipping against corsairs. Since the only operational naval defense came from the small cannon launches, little help could be expected. These vessels were not permitted to leave port except at night and then under strict orders to avoid contact with superior forces and to keep an avenue of retreat open at all times.[84]

The merchants of Veracruz, much more aggressive than the naval officers, found nothing positive about the lackadaisical maritime effort. On one occasion a single enemy frigate, the *Cleopatra,* a warship of only thirty-two cannon and a crew of about two hundred men, was able to blockade the port of Veracruz. The merchants' criticism became even more harsh when this frigate captured the *San Sebastián,* a merchantman from Cádiz, the *Perro,* a brig from Havana, and two vessels of the coastal commerce. When the naval commander, Juan Ignacio Bustillo, excused the navy of any negligence, the consulado turned to the viceroy, urging him to force the navy to engage the enemy and to protect what remained of the commerce of New Spain. Marquina, a vice-admiral himself, agreed with the civilians and convened yet another *junta de marina,* this time with a member of the consulado in attendance. Bustillo attempted unsuccessfully to block civilian participation in defense proceedings: it was not that he opposed the idea in principle, but he did not want to risk the possibility of word leaking out about the disastrous state of the Spanish frigates.[85] In January 1801, another enemy frigate, the *Acasta,* blockaded Veracruz and terminated all commercial activity. When the British captain sent a small pinnace toward the port under a flag of truce to request a conference on prisoner exchange, the governor of Veracruz, García Dávila, the commander of the port artillery, and Bustillo of the navy rowed out to parley about a league off the coast. The incident angered Marquina, who saw the possible conclusion of this adventure being the loss of all senior commanders in Veracruz. He issued a strong reprimand, noting that the affair had become a matter for general amusement and conversation amongst the populace. The governor minimized any danger and in a response which was more arrogant than diplomatic he set the scene for a new series of clashes between the viceroy and Veracruz.[86]

The confrontation became more alarming when on January 26, 1801, Governor Dávila issued emergency orders preparing the port for an enemy assault. Currency, valuables, and articles of commerce were to be shipped inland away from the coast. Children and the aged were to be evacuated to locations considered less dangerous. Veracruz awaited the first sign of enemy sails. Yet instead of notifying Marquina about the intelligence reports causing these preparations, the governor said nothing and permitted word to reach the capital by way of travellers' rumors. The viceroy expected an invasion and on the basis of Dávila's actions he ordered the light infantry companies from the provincial regiments to Mexico City and placed all army units on alert. When no message arrived from the coast with details on the situation, Marquina sent his own courier to discover what had occurred. Apprehensions turned to irritation when it became evident that there had been no particular motivation for the emergency. Dávila, while genuinely concerned with the weakness of his garrison during what he termed a period of ominous military preparations in Jamaica, used the alert to illustrate his need for reinforcements. He requested a minimum of 26 officers, 50 sergeants, 105 corporals, and 864 soldiers. Without these troops, fully two-thirds of the essential guardposts could not be covered. While the existing garrison totalled 1,841 soldiers on paper, 1,553 of these men were not available for day-to-day service. A mere 288 troops remained on active duty.[87]

Concerned by the growing controversy, Marquina decided to visit Jalapa and Veracruz to examine the defenses and to convene *juntas de guerra* to look into the major issues. In his own opinion, the invasion threat was not as great as Dávila indicated. Even so, there were good reasons for the journey—the season most suitable for attacks was approaching, something had to be done about the Veracruz garrison, and a new interior cantonment needed to be discussed. Jamaica, the source of most rumors, did not frighten Marquina as much as it did his subordinates. He believed that the primary interest of the British was contraband trade, a source of profit far greater than any invasion might produce. There was one consolation to be had from illegal commerce; it was simple to hire spies who gave fairly accurate information if they were well paid. Miguel Costansó suggested that this channel of communications should be employed to maximize the propaganda value of defense preparations. Foreigners might be led to believe that there was an army of fourteen thousand to sixteen thousand prepared to repel any invasion. News of Branciforte's cantonment in 1796 had come to the attention of some American gazettes.[88]

On March 12, 1801, Marquina convened a new *junta de guerra* at Veracruz. He opened the meetings with a general statement on the army and outlined what he stated were disastrous errors in almost every aspect of defense policy.[89] Members of the junta were to examine the problems of defending Veracruz, the population available for military service, and methods to combat yellow fever epidemics, which increased in intensity whenever large numbers of soldiers concentrated at the port. Each officer was to tour the defenses and to draft a detailed report answering a series of questions relating to the objectives of port defense—how long the city might withstand a siege, whether the army was effective if garrisoned in the interior, and what steps might be taken to improve communications between the levels of command and other interested groups.[90]

Most officers were in basic agreement with Manuel de Flon, who wrote, "... the walls of Veracruz are not strong enough to withstand the assaults of a gang of boys against an orchard."[91] The basic approach of the 1775 defense plan continued to receive general support although the officers differed over the number of troops needed at Veracruz and in the interior cantonment. Governor Dávila wanted a garrison of at least four thousand men and he received some support from other officers stationed at the port. Most officers supported the theory that the best defense of Veracruz was to maintain a small but strong force at San Juan de Ulúa, to protect the harbor with the fleet of cannon launches, and to canton the bulk of the army in the immediate upland interior. Again there was considerable difference of opinion over how many troops should be placed in the cantonment. Estimates ranged between thirty-five hundred and eight thousand men.[92]

Although the Peace of Amiens relieved some of the pressure for troops in Veracruz, yellow fever continued to decimate the garrison. By the end of September 1802, the Regiment of New Spain was short 407 soldiers and of the 506 remaining on the roster, 230 were in hospital, convalescing at Jalapa, or serving outside of the port on the coast guard brigs.[93] Governor Dávila complained he did not have enough guards to prevent the simplest kinds of contraband traffic. He illustrated his point on one occasion by refusing to send two or three soldiers to guard an American merchant vessel which had arrived from Philadelphia.[94] Marquina condemned this sort of irresponsible behavior, noting that even if he wished to send troops, he had none available. All of the militia regiments had been retired from active service and the Regiment of the Crown was the only unit in the colony available to garrison Mexico City and protect it against violence from the lower classes.[95] He continued to pressure the imperial government and the captain general of Cuba, the Marqués de Someruelos, for the return of the two Mexican regiments stationed in Havana. Someruelos delayed, arguing that no matter how severe troop shortages were in New Spain, there were greater problems in Cuba. Regular exchange of correspondence on the question gave little cause for hope although the captain general did promise to return the second battalion of the Regiment of Mexico from New Orleans when the French commissioners arrived to take charge of the province of Louisiana. Marquina appealed to the minister of war for the full restoration of both regiments and was finally successful in obtaining a royal order to this effect. But even with the support of the imperial government, Someruelos simply suspended the order under the pretext that he could not afford to release any soldiers.[96] With a new war threatening, only three companies of the Regiment of Mexico were returned to New Spain.

3

THE PORT VERSUS THE VICEROYS

The situation in Veracruz remained unchanged at the beginning of 1803 when José de Iturrigaray became viceroy of New Spain. The Regiments of the Crown and New Spain had suffered 1,220 deaths and 1,558 desertions since 1799, making a mockery of the effort to develop strong regular forces. The figures compiled by the consulado of Veracruz listed 1,500 persons from the interior and abroad who succumbed to disease in the port during 1802.[1] Although the total number of deaths declined somewhat, to 959 in 1803 and 997 in 1804,[2] there was no prospect of a marked improvement. Like Marquina, Iturrigaray had no intention of sending more troops into what he described as the "horrible cemetery" of Veracruz. He transferred the Regiment of New Spain, now almost skeletal in condition, to the uplands, where it could be rebuilt.

As might be expected, this step provoked the immediate opposition of Governor García Dávila and the port merchants. The governor, also commander of the Third Militia Division, which included the lancers and the coastal militia units, wanted to expand the militia so that every male inhabitant, no matter what color or social status, could serve.[3] He refused to accept responsibility for any disaster resulting from shortages of troops. If Veracruz fell, he would place full blame upon viceregal policy and not upon any advantage the enemy held in numbers or astuteness. His officers were disgusted with their position and low in morale; by March, only fifteen officers were left in the Battalion of Veracruz and of this total all but four were not healthy enough for regular duty. The battalion maintained a paper enlistment of 502 troops, but there were fewer than 150 men actually available. Although manpower was to have come from the acclimatized mulatto population of the coastal region, few men wanted to ruin their opportunities for high wages by committing their future to the army. This failure to attract recruits meant that much of the battalion came from the interior and a significant percentage of the men were petty criminals and chronic deserters. They continued to desert whenever the occasion arose and fell victim to the whole range of tropical diseases.[4]

Unlike so many of his predecessors, Iturrigaray suffered no illusions about receiving military aid from Europe if renewed war centered on the Caribbean or even if there was an invasion of New Spain. A royal order of September 1803 stated quite bluntly that no reinforcements would be sent from Spain.[5] Since the concentration of the Mexican army at Veracruz served no logical military purpose, Iturrigaray followed the lead of Branciforte and Marquina rather than the demands of the port merchants. The fortress of San Juan de Ulúa would be defended, but if the enemy attacked the city of Veracruz with superior force, no real resistance would be attempted. All valuables were to be shipped inland, leaving little for the invader other than the harassment of Spanish artillery fire and the slow encroachment of diseases, which would consume more victims than the battlefield. If an attempt was made to march into the interior, a healthy Mexican army would deal with the situation.[6] In order to raise a force large enough to cover watchtowers and to man sentry posts, Iturrigaray increased the three recently returned companies of the Regiment of Mexico to almost six hundred troops and the Battalion of Veracruz to a total of one thousand.[7]

The crown approved this restatement of the 1775 defense plan just prior to the arrival of word that a new war had broken out against Britain on December 12, 1804.[8] This was fortunate because both the cabildo and consulado of Veracruz rejected what the merchants viewed to be a suicidal policy. In many respects, Iturrigaray failed to see the political ramifications of his viceregal office. Having obtained official confirmation of his plan and interviewed his own subordinate officers, who told him the walls of Veracruz would collapse in the first cannonade, he issued a decree to the consulado which dismayed and infuriated the port merchants. Even the niceties of diplomatic language were neglected. Iturrigaray stated, "I have resolved absolutely that in the event of an invasion, the city with the exception of San Juan de Ulúa shall not be defended." All treasure, valuables, and articles of commerce were to be shipped inland to Jalapa under the system employed during the time of the *flotas*. Moreover, until further notice there was to be an absolute ban on all commercial transactions at the port and on maritime traffic along the gulf coast.[9]

When these orders arrived at Veracruz, the cabildo was in special session to thank Iturrigaray for his aid in funding the hospital of San Sebastián. Word that the city might be abandoned to the enemy and denied even the right to engage in its primary business functions dissolved the meeting into bedlam. Many refused to believe what they heard and to end the confusion asked for further clarification of the order. To the rulers of Veracruz, if the viceregal orders conveyed the correct meaning of Iturrigaray's intentions, the labor of three centuries could be destroyed in a moment. This would precipitate a disaster for the whole empire, especially after the remarkable expansion in the volume of commerce over the twenty-five years since the beginning of free trade. To the merchants, the unfortunate climate of their city—certainly hard on highland Mexicans and foreigners—was not their fault and should not cause economic ruin more devastating than if the port was invaded by the enemy. Even if they did send movable valuables into the interior, there remained between 18 and 20 million pesos in fixed assets—more than sufficient to stimulate the greed of the British once word spread that there would be no defense of Veracruz.[10]

Lack of diplomacy in applying a most unpalatable defensive arrangement was a terrible blunder. On the question of defending the port city, it was not so much that Iturrigaray introduced any new system but rather that he overstated a policy long accepted by the majority of army officers. In the view of the port merchants, however, Veracruz had been the essential cornerstone of the Mexican defensive preparations during the four wars since 1760. The climate, which always decimated the troops in their first weeks and months of tropical service, had to be viewed as one risk of the military profession. The maintenance of Veracruz was of such primary importance that it could mean the difference between continuance of Spanish rule or the loss of New Spain. Although the cantonment of troops in the interior was a humane solution to high levels of disease and death, it was unrealistic in a situation demanding immediate response to surprise attacks. As Spaniards and nobles, the port merchants asked permission to undertake their own defense the way their ancestors had for the past eight centuries. They asked for two thousand to three thousand muskets for distribution among a civilian militia determined to fight for Veracruz and its nearly twenty thousand inhabitants.[11]

Iturrigaray saw the intervention of civilians into military affairs as an unpardonable intrusion by persons who had no competence in such matters. Although his policies had received royal approval, he was at a loss to suggest any other reasonable approach to coastal defense. Mexicans feared the death-dealing climate and remembered the events of past wars. Officers and soldiers who survived Arroyo Moreno or the epidemic of Veracruz spread the word about the extent of the disasters. As the situation stood, the only persons sent from the interior who arrived at the coast were the *presidarios* and this was because they were chained together and marched under military escort.¹² The viceroy pointed out that his responsibility as army chief required consideration of the total defensive picture and not just the needs of one city. Since the fortifications of Veracruz would not stand up to three days of siege, an attack might well cause the loss of the garrison, the civilian population, and considerable treasure. The only safe means to avoid this potential danger was to move valuables and nonessential population inland. If a defeat did occur, no town was close enough to shelter the refugees and the roads were so poor that only those able to travel on horseback or in litters could escape. Iturrigaray's experience in European wars gave him sufficient proof that the result would be heavy loss of life and disorders from looting and robbery. The same was true in the case of civilian militias. The offer to raise an untrained force was ridiculous because the port residents lacked experience in handling weapons and were not trained to repel enemy landings. During the recent war against France in Catalonia, Iturrigaray had seen forty thousand civilians placed under arms. At the first hint of danger, most of the men deserted and were not seen again. The only result was the loss of up to fifteen thousand muskets, which the regular troops soon needed.¹³

The opposition from Veracruz did force the viceroy to explain his defensive reasoning more fully and to point out the legal basis for the closure of commerce. On November 8, 1804, the Prince of the Peace had ordered the closure of the ports of the Spanish empire to protect government and private interests against British naval assaults. Only mail packets without specie, cargo, or anything of value except official correspondence were permitted to sail. Extension of this order to cover local coastal traffic had been Iturrigaray's own innovation designed to cut contraband trade and other contacts with the enemy. He was convinced that enemy captains received almost daily reports which allowed them to capture a large percentage of the vessels departing from Veracruz. By his plan, Iturrigaray hoped to make contraband and privateering unprofitable, forcing the enemy to depart from the Mexican coasts.¹⁴

This policy admitted the continuing weakness of the Spanish naval defenses. Maritime authorities at Havana refused to release warships to patrol the coast of New Spain and three frigates sent from Spain with naval supplies for Veracruz, the *Matilda, Anfitrite,* and *Pamona,* did not reach their intended destination. The first two were captured and the *Pamona* was blockaded at Havana. The commander of the Veracruz naval station, Ciriaco Cevallos, had only three warships and even these were not efficient fighting units. The one frigate, the *Nuestra Señora de la O,* had no crew and needed extensive repairs. The coast guard brigs *Alerta* and *Saeta* were underarmed because cannon and mortars ordered from Havana had not arrived. Most unfortunate of all, the fleet of cannon launches constructed by Branciforte during the past war had deteriorated to such a degree that they were useless. All of these vessels were sold to private interests.[15] In spite of the situation, Cevallos did what he could to keep his crews ready for action. As the officer responsible for implementing Godoy's policy of port closures and suspension of commerce, Cevallos soon drew the wrath of the merchants and many others who held him responsible for their misfortunes. Cevallos did ask for twenty new cannon launches to help protect some coastal commerce and he warned that the British frigate *Acasta* had been surveying the coast and taking soundings.[16]

Apprehensions about the danger to merchant shipping proved to be quite justified. A former French frigate of forty-four cannon, the *Sourvailante,* commanded by John Bligh, captured a frigate, three brigs, and numerous smaller vessels of the Veracruz coastal trade. Another British warship, the *Diana,* arrived off Veracruz on July 17, 1805, showing a flag of truce. A boat was sent ashore with a letter from Captain John Maling, who said that he had a number of Spanish prisoners on board and wished to exchange them. The governor replied that he was under specific orders neither to communicate with the enemy nor to conduct prisoner exchanges. While this negotiation continued, a Spanish brig appeared on the horizon and the British hauled down the truce flag and raised the Spanish ensign in hope of tricking the newcomer. After a lengthy chase in which the brig escaped safely into the port, the enemy raised the truce flag once again. After such perfidious behavior, however, the governor refused to respond.[17]

By the beginning of September 1805, the most dire predictions of the Veracruz merchants appeared to be coming true. Although enemy raids on commerce gave cause for concern, the prohibition against trade proved much more damaging. When coastal traffic halted, crops rotted in the fields, lime and brick factories ceased to operate, and workers suspended the harvest of valuable dye-wood. Because salt meat, poultry, fruit, and vegetables were not introduced into Veracruz, prices rose at an alarming rate. Export commodities such as cotton, vanilla, pepper, and dye-wood which normally went to the peninsula remained in warehouses. Producers of indigo and cochineal from Oaxaca begged the viceroy to permit these commodities to be shipped from Veracruz.[18] Unemployment at the port caused growing unrest amongst the laboring classes and the crime rate increased. Merchants demanded an immediate reopening of coastal commerce, arguing that these vessels were never involved in contraband. Furthermore, they asked for permission to take their own chances in shipping cargoes to Spain.[19] Similar reports came from Campeche where corsairs caused even more havoc than at Veracruz. Merchants learned of the declaration of war when an enemy frigate attacked and captured six vessels laden with local exports. This blow, severe enough to the local economy, was nothing compared with the viceregal prohibition of all commerce. Merchants reported that agriculture, industry, and shipping had entered a most profound depression.[20]

The pressure of merchants and producers caused Iturrigaray some concern. He commissioned Ciriaco Cevallos to investigate the charges and agreed to permit occasional convoys of merchant vessels if they were guarded by naval units. Certainly during wartime he had to guarantee supplies of lime, brick, and building materials needed to repair fortifications.[21] Cevallos confirmed the economic dislocations—the order prohibiting trade had resulted in complete stagnation of commerce. Small coastal communities which made their living from fishing and agriculture had no markets. The port lacked adequate supplies of food as well as materials for military construction and the repair of naval vessels. At the same time, naval escort for coastal convoys would be difficult because only two brigantines remained in service and they already had far more work than they could handle. Besides, the brigs drew too much water and would not be able to accompany the smaller merchant vessels through the bars into small ports. If contraband was to be avoided, the escort vessels would have to be the same type of craft used by the merchants.[22]

As might be expected, the Veracruz merchants lost little time in carrying their grievances to the imperial government. Their importance and political astuteness enabled them to gain access to the most powerful figure in Madrid. The Prince of the Peace, Manuel Godoy, listened to their complaints and issued a royal order designed to pacify the merchants. Godoy lectured Iturrigaray on the strategic importance of Veracruz: not only was it the single port for imports and exports from Cape Catoche to the Mississippi River, but it was also the "gateway and principal key to the roads and communications of all New Spain." To deter an enemy attack, Veracruz must be maintained in the best possible state of preparedness. The fortifications were to be repaired and heavy artillery mounted in the bastions of the city. Clearly, Godoy knew very little other than what the agents of the Veracruz merchants told him because his order contravened existing legislation and made impossible demands upon the viceroy. Iturrigaray was to send four thousand to five thousand muskets from the Perote magazine to arm a civilian militia. In fact, there were not that many spare muskets in Perote or anywhere else in Mexico. Finally, the naval defenses of Veracruz were to be upgraded by the construction of twenty cannon launches.[23] Complicating matters further, Iturrigaray did not receive Godoy's instructions until 1807, or two years after they had been issued. He insisted—probably with justification—that no disobedience had been intended and that the official dispatches had probably been lost. While Iturrigaray continued to pursue his policies, the cabildo of Veracruz engaged in regular correspondence with Godoy through agents in Madrid. As a result, the merchants knew more than Iturrigaray did about changes in defense policy. Misunderstandings and disputes could not be avoided: for example, the cabildo of Veracruz charged that he removed cannon from the shore batteries and further exposed the city to attack. In reality, the withdrawal of most heavy caliber cannon was in line with good military strategy. Eight cannon had been left in the batteries of Santiago and Concepción, quite enough to keep small vessels from entering the bay. Because larger warships had to pass under the guns of San Juan de Ulúa, there was no reason to duplicate the defenses. A formal *junta de guerra* had investigated the situation fully and proposed these changes.[24]

In the meantime, dispatches arriving in Mexico brought ominous news from Europe and the United States. The Spanish minister in Philadelphia, the Marqués de Casa Irujo, reported the departure of a British expeditionary force of twelve thousand troops from Madeira on October 3, 1805, under the command of Sir Home Popham. Although the army's destination was unclear, it was known to be headed for either South Africa or South America. Francisco Miranda had sailed from New York with a small number of revolutionaries, but there were rumors that a large force of mulatto troops from Haiti would join him. Since no one could anticipate how many men Miranda might recruit, there were new fears of an attack upon Veracruz.[25] More ominously, however, Spanish intelligence gave notice of increased British interest in New Spain. Casa Irujo warned of this danger, convinced, as Napoleon strengthened his grip on Europe, that the British would attempt to conquer Spanish American colonies to open new markets. Victories in the Americas would furnish the British nation with the will to continue the war and possibly improve their bargaining position when peace returned. The attacks on Buenos Aires and news from Britain of two or three new expeditions reinforced these fears.[26] Indeed, the Spanish intelligence regarding British interest in Mexico proved to be correct. A number of individuals and semiofficial sources in London had begun to collect information on the best means of achieving a successful landing on the coast near Veracruz. One report submitted by a William Jacob to Viscount Castlereagh gave an accurate description of the climate, the dangerous *nortes,* and the disease factor. Jacob pictured the port city as a place that would surrender without a battle.[27]

Sir Arthur Wellesley, designated to lead any invasion of Mexico, gathered information and interviewed merchant contrabandists who were familiar with the gulf coast. At one point he projected a coordinated attack on New Spain from both coasts, with troops from India crossing the Pacific to assault Acapulco. Although this part of the plan was dropped, by the end of November 1806, Wellesley had a detailed proposal for an attack on Veracruz. He planned to use a force of six thousand European infantry, three thousand Negro infantry, fourteen hundred cavalry, and two hundred pioneers.* Following a rapid takeover of San Juan de Ulúa to open the harbor, the unseasoned troops were to march into the interior. In case the fortress of Perote proved to be much stronger than anticipated, full siege equipment was to be carried by the invaders.[28]

Concerned by persistent rumors of attacks against New Spain, Iturrigaray mobilized the largest army of operations yet seen in the viceroyalty. By the end of August 1806, more than 11,000 troops garrisoned the small upland towns close to Veracruz.[29] The arrival of the mailship *El Dulce* at Veracruz on February 26, 1807, appeared to confirm the danger and to more than justify the preparations. Godoy warned that a British expeditionary army of 10,000 to 12,000 troops had sailed from Falmouth; the probable destination was Veracruz. Due to the extreme urgency of this threat, the dispatch was sent by three different routes. Alarmed by what appeared to be a certain invasion, Iturrigaray mobilized additional provincial units and began to scour the interior for new sources of manpower. The day after he received the warning, he departed from the capital to assume personal command of the army. He increased the Veracruz garrison to 2,742 men and by the end of October 1807, the cantonment had been raised to a total of 15,516 troops.[30]

In an effort to convince foreigners and the Veracruz merchants that the army was real, the *Gazeta de México* published a rather exaggerated and idealized version of what went on at the cantonment. The troops were said to have developed "a warlike spirit similar to that of the soldiers of old Spain." Reports on maneuvers written by Captain Cristóbal Domínguez of the Regiment of Valladolid stressed the tactical mobility of the army and the fact that it would be able to move quickly to intercept an enemy landing on the coast.[31]

The merchants and other sectors of the port population remained unimpressed by the interior cantonments or the propaganda of the *Gazeta de México*. During the first months of 1806 they observed the beginnings of repairs to the fortress of San Juan de Ulúa, but saw nothing being done to improve the city defenses. This inaction coupled with their deep distrust of viceregal defense policy raised new fears of abandonment. Despite their continual offers to defend themselves, Iturrigaray made the idea unpalatable by

---

*Foot soldiers who do advance work, such as opening roads, for the main force.

asking civilians who wanted to take up arms to report to the Battalion of Veracruz for instruction. This was a logical but thoroughly unacceptable solution.[32] The Veracruzanos balked at the thought of association with the regular battalion. Their nobility, professions, and occupations could not be degraded by association with the lowest plebeian elements, many of whom were criminals serving out prison terms. They placed little or no trust in such troops and wanted no part of Iturrigaray's proposal.[33]

The viceroy visited Veracruz in March 1807, meeting with army and navy commanders as well as with the city government. The report in the *Gazeta de México* described a banquet at San Juan de Ulúa during which Iturrigaray attempted to pacify some of the opposition from the consulado and cabildo. He promised that the army would make a determined stand before any enemy gained entry to the port.[34] Unfortunately, however, this reconciliation attempt came after years of dispute over defense strategy had accumulated considerable animosity. The cabildo continued to correspond with its Madrid agent, Manuel de Quevedo y Bustamante, who carrried grievances to the imperial cabinet. Already, viceregal defense policies had been overturned by royal orders of September 27, 1805, and August 29, 1806, but a new royal order of April 20, 1807, left no doubt about where the crown stood regarding Veracruz. The minister of war, José Antonio Caballero, brushed aside the defensive measures implemented by Iturrigaray and agreed with the Veracruz merchants that interior cantonments had to be accompanied by equally strong port defenses. To hasten this end, the walls and esplanades of the city were to be repaired and the cannon returned to the seafront bastions. Caballero applauded the offer of Veracruz to raise civilian forces and renewed the order for the immediate distribution of four thousand to five thousand muskets.[35] In summarizing the lengthy conflict between the viceroys and the population of Veracruz, the minister declared that the people had struggled to defend themselves despite arguments belittling their efforts. When they attempted to organize civilian militia forces for their own protection, Iturrigaray had debased their honest petitions and tried to join them to the low mulattoes, presidarios, and delinquents who served in the Battalion of Veracruz. Such moves dampened the ardor of noble citizens who asked for nothing more than the opportunity to aid the *patria*. Finally, Caballero accepted the opinion that the cantonments were too far away to relieve the port should the enemy attempt a hit and run attack.

Remarkably, Caballero's decree failed to mention any of the arguments in favor of Iturrigaray's defense strategy. The disasters of the cantonment of Arroyo Moreno were forgotten. No mention was made of the fact that the viceroy had obtained the support of *juntas de guerra* before making policy and that his decisions were approved by the crown. All of the experience gained since the 1775 defense plan, and, more specifically, since the cantonment of Viceroy Branciforte, was lost upon the minister of war, who, like Godoy, appeared to obtain his information directly from the Veracruz merchants. The apparent refusal to send arms to the port was another matter. Iturrigaray avoided public explanation of his refusal because he did not want the arms shortage to become generally known. Even the provincial regiments used weapons that had been repaired so many times they were nearly useless. Even so, he managed to locate 500 muskets of the type used by the militias, 139 carbines, 435 sabers, and 500 lance points.[36]

Confident of the imperial government's support, the merchants rode roughshod over the viceroy. They expressed irritation when only an eighth of the weapons they demanded actually appeared. This was only the beginning, however, for they raised an even louder howl of protest after learning that their militia was to be subject to a certain degree of regimentation. Any civilian militiaman wishing to depart from the city was to require a pass with a statement indicating how long the individual planned to be absent. Most merchants preferred the idea of an informal structure—perhaps a list at the cabildo or merchant headquarters to be signed by those present for duty.[37] Iturrigaray's patience, long since dissipated after the intervention of merchants in military matters, was now at an end. Civilian militia or not, he demanded a degree of formality in line with army practice. He vented his anger in the rough draft of a dispatch to the minister of war, accusing the cabildo of "great inexactness," but crossing out a section in which he described their arguments as "capricious falsehoods." The cabildo had attempted to convince Governor García Dávila to abandon his command of the interior cantonment and to return to Veracruz. Pedro de Laguna, the artillery commander, refused to obey the approved defense plans and had drafted new "subversive plans" to satisfy the port merchants. Members of the cabildo were described as having been motivated by greed and self-interest when they refused to implement orders to ship valuables and commercial inventories inland. Port merchants seemed willing to take any risks in order to maintain their monopoly over the deposit of goods. Governor García Dávila opposed any orders which threatened to deprive him of his share of seizures, and the entire community forgot all about the war and the Spanish cause if they saw any danger to their personal fortunes. As for the *regidores* of the cabildo, Iturrigaray declared them guilty of near-insurrectionary behavior against the government—conduct that should be contained everywhere, but especially in a province so far removed from the crown. Having vented his spleen and said exactly what he thought, Iturrigaray reconsidered and struck all of these allegations from the finished dispatch. Instead, he asked the king and Prince of the Peace to examine his record: they would find it clear of any wrongdoing.[38]

The 500 muskets became another source for contention when they were found to be the same weapons declared useless for the civilian militia in 1800. The carbines had been lying around the Mexico City armory for almost fourteen years, totally unserviceable, and the sabers were discards from the provincial militias. No one in the port saw much point in resisting an enemy with these weapons since the effort would accomplish nothing. If the British captured Veracruz, there could be no hope of repeating the noble defense of Buenos Aires.[39] Iturrigaray did not attempt to make a case for the muskets, but he did point out that the militiamen would fire them from the city walls where weight was no consideration and bayonets were not necessary. To mollify somewhat the port merchants, however, he dispatched 1,244 new carbines and 282 shotguns to bolster the militia. With the previous arms shipment and the addition of 1,000 shotguns promised by the cabildo, there would be sufficient weapons to arm four thousand volunteers. Even so, Iturrigaray expressed grave suspicions about the motives of certain people in Veracruz who seemed intent on frustrating his policies. He wondered if reports of unrest in Mexico appearing in American journals originated at Veracruz.[40]

After threats to place the Veracruz civilian militia under the direction of regular army officers, the cabildo compiled a list of 2,634 volunteers. This figure was hardly the 4,000 men mentioned in the demands for weaponry, but the city governors excused their inaccuracy, arguing that there were numerous persons from the interior, seamen, and government employees who would take up arms if an invasion took place.[41] The assemblies began in March 1808, and the cabildo received the first of many reminders of its offer to donate one thousand shotguns.[42] Only 1,379 men appeared to receive weapons for firing practice and of this total, only 738 completed the full training program. When the time came for the return of the muskets, officers discovered that many had been damaged and some could not be located. In the end, about thirty muskets were lost to men who sold or stole their weapons and then left the port. Coupled with the poor behavior of the volunteers, Iturrigaray felt his own opinions had been confirmed. Moreover, only fifty-eight of the one thousand shotguns promised were ever delivered.[43] Reviewing the discord, the *fiscal de lo civil,* Ambrosio de Sagazurieta, urged the viceroy to take stronger action against the "... excess, disorder, illegality, and the abuse of power" demonstrated by the cabildo. If certain individuals dared to foster additional suspicions amongst the populace, the guilty parties must be arrested.[44]

While Iturrigaray struggled with Veracruz, the British continued to rank the city as a target of primary interest. Detailed intelligence data obtained from merchants who knew the Mexican gulf coast gave an accurate picture of the port and its weaknesses. A Mr. J. D. R. Gordon, a businessman who had resided in Mexico for six years, dismissed the fortifications of San Juan de Ulúa as no substantial barrier to conquest; the walls were decayed and the gun carriages rotten with age. The city, surrounded by "a slight stone wall," posed no difficulties. Since the lower classes of the country had no trace of patriotism, Gordon was certain an army of fifteen thousand could conquer all of New Spain and reap a fabulous treasure in precious metals for its efforts.[45] With Mexico still a priority, Sir Arthur Wellesley began to mobilize an expeditionary army at Cork. News of the British defeats at Buenos Aires diminished some hope of easy victories in Spanish America, but Francisco Miranda and others continued to press for new adventures. By June 1808, plans against Mexico had been downgraded by proposals to land an army near Cádiz or to attack Caracas.[46] Events in Europe overtook the schemes to destroy Spanish power in the Americas. With the French occupation of Spain and the tenacious resistance of the Spanish populace, the British seized the opportunity to attack Napoleon in Europe. Wellesley's expeditionary army went to the Iberian Peninsula rather than to Spanish America. In the process, it is likely that the future Duke of Wellington was saved from the very real possibility of a disaster which would have changed his career.

Following the Mutiny of Aranjuez and the abdication of Charles IV in favor of Ferdinand VII, the situation in Mexico became more and more complex. The *Gazeta de México* reported the events in some detail, and by the end of May 1808, Mexicans learned about the French intervention in Spain. The vessel *Ventura,* which departed from Cádiz on May 26, 1808, brought news of the events of Bayonne; the Spanish Bourbon kings had abdicated the throne in favor of Napoleon's brother Joseph Bonaparte. The Mexican political situation clouded, but the great majority of the population was momentarily dumbfounded by the events. While in theory the Spanish Empire remained at war with Britain, it was obvious France was now the enemy.[47]

Iturrigaray ordered the military and political officials at Veracruz to exercise every precaution with vessels arriving from Spain. All passengers were to receive thorough investigation and their correspondence, books, and other papers had to pass through a process of rigorous censorship. Vessels deemed suspicious were to be held under strict guard until investigation by the military governor, Pedro de Alonso. Foreign and even national warships were to be treated with the same suspicion as merchant vessels and a close watch was to be kept for the agents of Napoleon.[48] At first, the response from Veracruz was encouraging. Like other cabildos throughout New Spain, the port authorities pledged their most profuse loyalty to King Ferdinand VII and to Viceroy Iturrigaray. Released at once from the dread of a British invasion, the populace of Veracruz whipped itself into a state of angry indignation against the machinations of the evil Bonaparte. The atmosphere was tense when on August 10, 1808, a French schooner, the *Vaillant,* appeared off San Juan de Ulúa. The fortress opened fire, but ceased hostilities when the French captain showed a flag of truce and requested a conference. The naval commander, Ciriaco Cevallos, negotiated the surrender of the enemy vessel, which was found to be carrying documents from France addressed to the viceroy and other authorities of New Spain.[49]

With the populace aroused against the French yet at the same time curious about the arrival of an enemy vessel, the situation was extremely delicate. Cevallos feared an effort by enemy agents to circulate seditious documents or possibly even to form a party dedicated to furthering the cause of Napoleon. To prevent any communications, he stationed guards on the wharf to expel curiosity seekers and issued a decree threatening death as traitors to persons who attempted to approach or exchange messages with the vessel.[50] The people misinterpreted the meaning of Cevallos's actions; word spread condemning the naval commander for attempting to protect the French and certain important passengers who were said to be on board. A mob formed and almost immediately cries for Cevallos's head were heard throughout the city. Before long, everyone accepted a rumor that he was protecting a French general and former viceroy, Miguel José de Azanza, a known *afrancesado* who was supposed to have come to take over New Spain for Napoleon. The hatred for France focused on Cevallos. When gossip spread that Cevallos had sent the French agents to Antigua in small boats, the rioters went to Governor Alonso to demand action. Although he considered the request to be ridiculous, the pressure upon him became so great that he agreed to send thirty lancers and ten or twelve representatives of the populace to Antigua. Accompanied by a multitude of spectators, they went to search for the nonexistent French agents and returned satisfied that their suspicions were unfounded.[51]

Colonel Alonso, accompanied by two regidores, removed all correspondence from the French vessel and carried it to the city hall for evaluation and safekeeping. There the mob became so dangerous that it was necessary to distribute some of the documents which were read, found seditious, and burned on the spot. The crowd then demanded additional documents, some of which were read before being destroyed. It was no longer possible to maintain control and increasing numbers made the situation extremely volatile. Efforts to turn the riot into a popular demonstration in favor of Ferdinand VII were partially successful. Cries of *"Viva Fernando y muera Cevallos"* rang through the city. According to an anecdote which later spread through the city, a muleteer asked his companion, "Who is this Cevallos? What has he done?" His companion replied, "I don't know, but I am doing what everyone else is and you do the same."[52] Many of the less politically motivated elements used the temporary breakdown in law and order to pillage, drink, and sack commercial establishments. During the afternoon, a liquor warehouse was broken open—brandy, wine, and other alcoholic beverages flowed like water, further arousing the mob's misguided patriotism. Cevallos was sent to San Juan de Ulúa for his own protection while the rabble vented their passion against his two houses. His furniture and possessions were hurled into the streets, where everything was burned. Besides the loss of Cevallos's personal property, the mob destroyed most of the instruments of the hydrographic commission, charts of the port, and detailed observations on the gulf coast. Only the timely intervention of Colonel Alonso and *Regidor* Juan Manuel Muñoz prevented the burning of the houses.[53]

Excited by the taste of success, the rioters threatened to expand their attacks to the property of other prominent residents who were known friends of Cevallos. The wealthy merchant Thomas Murphy had to admit representatives of the populace to his home as the search for the naval commander continued. Finally, Alonso and members of the city government were able to divert attention elsewhere.[54] At midnight, what remained of the French documents were moved in preparation for shipment to Mexico City under armed guard, but at 4:00 A.M. almost three hundred men were on hand to impede the departure. Once again, documents were opened, read to the crowd, and then destroyed before the remnant could be slipped out of the city. The next morning, representatives of the populace went to Colonel Alonso to request an increase in the military preparations to defend Veracruz. He promised to bring the matter before the attention of the viceroy and agreed to prevent Cevallos from returning to his duties. Since no blood had been spilled during the events of the previous day, he petitioned the viceroy for a general pardon for all those who had participated in the riots. Although Iturrigaray believed that the affair could have been avoided in the first place if Alonso had taken the proper steps to isolate the French vessel when it entered the harbor, he did issue the pardon.[55]

It is impossible to determine how much the opponents of Iturrigaray had to do with the *Vaillant* affair. Cevallos fled to New Orleans, where he found himself overtaken by the destruction of the regime that might have declared his innocence. He remained in a state of political limbo, under suspicion of treason and other capital crimes, until December 1810, when the Junta de

Seguridad y Buen Orden in Mexico City heard his case and exonerated him. In his opinion, certain elements in the port encouraged and incited the masses to their criminal fury. Since he had confiscated over half a million pesos in contraband and jailed many offenders, there was no shortage of men who had scores to settle. In the testimony leading to Cevallos's acquittal in 1810, several merchants mentioned the impact of Iturrigaray's orders suspending coastal commerce. According to one witness, Manuel Antonio de Ysassi, the rapid rise of food prices resulting from the prohibition against commerce caused the ill will against Cevallos. As the officer responsible for the implementation of this policy, he became the most accessible target for attack. Other merchants charged Cevallos with having engaged in contraband trade himself.[56] In reviewing some aspects of the case, Lucas Alamán suggested that Cevallos permitted British vessels belonging to the House of Murphy to enter Veracruz. Even though there was no hard evidence of wrongdoing and much reason to exonerate the naval commander, the increase in neutral vessel trade during 1806 and 1807 made suspicions unavoidable.[57] (See table 7.)

Without any doubt, the controversy over the defense of Veracruz had something to do with the riots and the lack of effective action to contain the violence. The port merchants who felt most strongly about the weakness of the garrison lost no time in pointing out the incapacity of the available troops to curb the mob. The cabildo continued to oppose Iturrigaray, threatening to precipitate a new crisis at the beginning of September 1808, with a general resignation of all members of the city government to protest against the lack

TABLE 7
Neutral Vessel Commerce at the Port of Veracruz, September 26, 1805, to March 31, 1807.

Imports:		
Date	Number of Vessels	Value of Cargo
September, 1805 to December, 1805	3	245,252 pesos
All of 1806	37	3,641,263
January 1, 1807 to March 31, 1807	24	976,041
TOTAL	64	4,862,556
Exports: September, 1805 to March 31, 1807.		
Silver		10,857,914
Cochineal		927,746
Other products		670,794
TOTAL		12,456,454

Source: Noticia del comercio que han hecho los buques neutrales desde 26 de Septiembre de 1805 hasta fin de Abril de 1807, MN, vol. 317.

of troops. The interim intendant, Pedro Telmo Landero, described the regidores as "subjects of known honesty, wealth and patriotism"; they, more than anyone else, deserved primary responsibility for having calmed the angry populace during the *Vaillant* crisis. The merchants now feared a French invasion even though British naval squadrons patrolled the Caribbean. After all, Napoleon had managed to send expeditions against Egypt and Newfoundland in the past war.[58]

Not at all deterred by the collapse of the Spanish monarchy, the merchants of Veracruz carried their cause to the Junta Suprema, the provisional government of Spain. Although they had won powerful support from the imperial cabinet before disaster struck the mother country, their most damning charges had not reached the peninsula until Ferdinand was on the road to captivity. They feared a French expeditionary force might attempt to seek revenge for their treatment of the *Vaillant* and used the riots as positive proof that the port garrison should be enlarged to six thousand troops from the less than two thousand available. To guarantee effective defense, these troops would have to be backed by a cantonment of twenty-thousand infantry, three thousand cavalry, and two thousand artillery armed with one hundred mobile field cannon and twenty-four mortars. Furthermore, at least one hundred cannon launches were necessary to protect Veracruz and the adjacent coastal waters. The epidemic of yellow fever which had prevented viceroys from stationing a large force at the port ended in 1806 and, according to experience, it would not return for at least sixteen to eighteen years. Finally, because of the extreme risk of invasion and the fact that Iturrigaray could not comprehend the strategic importance of the port, they asked for his removal from office and replacement by a person more worthy of confidence.[59]

In more peaceful times, the Veracruz merchants' delusions of grandeur and self-importance might have been dismissed without much difficulty. But during the late summer of 1808, Iturrigaray came to view the port merchants and their allies as a real danger to the regime. He ordered Colonel Félix Calleja, the active commander of the Tenth Militia Brigade, to report to Mexico City for instructions and then to take command at Veracruz. Besides the near insurrection caused by the activities of the cabildo, some of the more volatile elements were said to have planned a march to the town of Antigua with the purpose of removing the heavy artillery and taking it back to Veracruz. Iturrigaray commanded Brigadier García Dávila at the cantonment to make ready the Dragoon Regiments of Spain and the Prince to intercept and crush any such attempt should it occur. He found the rumors difficult to believe, but in the event of trouble the instigators were to be apprehended and treated with the full rigor of the law. Like so much of the hearsay and gossip circulating through the colony, this rumor appeared to be groundless. The merchants of the Veracruz cabildo did not carry out their mass resignation and Calleja was sent back to his command at San Luis Potosí.[60]

Distracted by turbulence at the port and elsewhere, Iturrigaray neglected the opposition closer to his palace. On the night of September 15, 1808, a conspiracy of Spaniards in Mexico City overthrew the viceroy and set up a provisional regime. Although the Veracruz merchants do not appear to have been directly involved in these events, they welcomed the outcome and threw their full support behind the interim viceroy, Field Marshal Pedro Garibay.[61] The cabildo of Veracruz was quick to join in the general condemnations of the deposed viceroy; after all, Iturrigaray had described them as traitors or at least as suspect of grave crimes. To prevent such injurious documents from remaining in the archives of New Spain, they requested permission to have an executioner burn any papers which damned their good character and patriotism.[62] Indeed, one of Garibay's first acts as viceroy was to deal with the causes of discontent alienating the Veracruzanos. In his opinion, a more dangerous popular uprising would take place if steps were not quickly taken. The artillery commander, Colonel Pedro de Laguna, one of Iturrigaray's most vigorous detractors, received orders to march from the cantonment to Veracruz with all of his troops and ordinance. Cannon removed from Veracruz for use by the army of operations were to be restored to their original bastions.[63] Brigadier García Dávila was to return from the cantonment to his office at Veracruz, where his first tasks were to solve disputes over the artillery removed to Antigua and to calm the populace. Quite generally, the fortunes of the coastal interests appeared to have changed for the better.[64]

Back at the port after his term in command of the army of operations, García Dávila encountered the same problems he had left. Lengthy mobilization of the provincial lancers and coastal militiamen continued to hinder agricultural production—particularly grain, fresh vegetables and fruit needed in the city. Militiamen of the pardo and moreno companies and of the coastal divisions did not have sufficient pay to support their families and there was chronic trouble with begging and thievery.[65] Even the merchants who had been loudest in welcoming the overthrow of Iturrigaray began to wonder about the advantages of the change. The cabildo raised and paid for a volunteer unit of twenty men to guard the ex-viceroy until he embarked for Spain, but the enthusiasm of these militiamen declined when they were kept in service long after the departure of their prisoner. Most were merchants or employees of commercial houses and they wanted to get back to their primary occupations. Since the alliance with Britain, the port had experienced greatly renewed activity and both warships and merchant vessels awaited the merchants' attention.[66]

Much worse than these annoyances, Garibay did nothing to strengthen the port garrison. Like his predecessors, he wanted the regular units stationed at Jalapa, where the climate was benign. When unrest in the capital diverted his attention, he stunned the port by transferring the three regular regiments at Jalapa to Mexico City.

After a short interregnum of cooperation, Garibay experienced the same troubles with the port as his predecessors. Governor García Dávila and private interests in the cabildo and consulado continued to correspond directly with the Junta Suprema in Spain about their inability to defend against a viceregal policy of isolating their city without proper protection against the enemy. More accustomed to the army than political office, Garibay attacked the governor and cabildo for breaking the chain of command. Like Marquina and Iturrigaray, he explained that there were troops at the cantonment ready to give aid in case of an invasion. When García Dávila replied with some elementary lessons on the defense of fortifications, the viceroy interpreted the approach as a direct insult to his office and his long military career. Although he had no intention of justifying his decisions to subordinates, he did inform the governor that he had orders to retire the cantonment. The immediate task was to prevent frictions between the levels of government, to maintain public tranquility, and to economize wherever possible in order to raise funds for the support of the struggle against Napoleon.[67] In Garibay's opinion, there were sufficient troops at the port to garrison San Juan de Ulúa, protect the city, and guard French prisoners, including the Napoleonic agent, General Gaëten D'Alvimart, who was locked up in the fortress dungeon.

There were more blows to come. The heavy artillery returned to Veracruz from Antigua had to be removed from the port bastions when the parapets were declared unsafe. Even worse, Garibay issued an order on July 1, 1809, transferring the companies of the Regiment of Mexico from duty at San Juan de Ulúa to Jalapa. Replacements were to be drawn from the coastal militia companies. García Dávila expressed outrage at seeing his best climate-hardened infantrymen being marched away and replaced by militiamen who knew nothing about army life and who resented mobilization.[68] He wrote to the Junta Central in Seville denouncing Garibay's policies and requesting the return of these troops. The men of the Regiment of Mexico had been in the port since April 1805, and they were indispensable. No regulars or militiamen could replace disease-resistant veterans—particularly with a new epidemic of yellow fever introduced by the warship *San Francisco de Paula*. Even though a *junta de guerra* had begun to discuss ways to expand the Battalion of Veracruz to regimental size, this force could not be of much use for at least another year.[69]

By 1810, growing internal dissension combined with continuing fears of invasion by the victorious French. Viceroys Garibay and Francisco Javier de Lizana concentrated most of the regular troops in Mexico City and left coastal defense to the British navy. Even before the audiencia replaced Lizana, however, the fear of France focused attention on the Napoleonic menace. Over eight thousand troops of the provincial militia regiments congregated at Jalapa and the other interior towns to guard against a surprise attack. Lizana ordered Félix Calleja to go to Mexico City to advise on matters pertaining to defense.[70] With two new battalions being added to the existing Battalion of Veracruz and another new battalion of freed criminals, Veracruz prepared once again to meet an enemy.[71] When José Luyando, a delegate from the Council of Regency in what remained of independent Spain, arrived at Veracruz in May 1810, he expressed surprise at the intensity of military preparations. His reaction was natural; there was an alliance with Britain, and he was not aware of any danger from the United States. In talking to the inhabitants of the port and along the roads into the interior, Luyando found no one who could explain the need for military preparedness. The only clear sentiment expressed was the panic felt by militiamen who were certain they would perish if sent to the coast. The epidemic of yellow fever, reported at an end by the cabildo, reappeared to devour the latest crop of tender *arribeños*.[72] In the interior, Luyando found militia units under arms and new battalions being formed. At a time when New Spain was supposed to be sending all surplus funds to aid the mother country, he could not understand what fear gripped the administration.[73]

4

THE PERCEPTION OF DANGER

As much as Spanish officers in Mexico dreaded the prospect of an enemy attack, it was a possibility they were trained to anticipate and a strategic problem to be dealt with according to the available resources. But defense was by no means this simple in a world disrupted by continuing shock waves emitted from the independent United States and after 1789 from revolutionary France. Great Britain, the traditional enemy and the power most capable of landing an invasion force, presented the Spanish regime with little ideological danger, but there was always the possibility that the British might attempt to cooperate with separatist sectors in the Mexican population. The motivations of the United States and France caused greater anxieties since both nations furnished models for an independent republic. In Mexico, any mention of revolutionary change or even minor criticisms against existing policies came to be seen as attacks against the system. By the turn of the century, officials readily believed rumors of the most nefarious plots to subvert and overthrow the regime, and were quick to blame foreign agents or American and French examples for encouraging whatever noxious elements might exist within the viceroyalty. Very often, metropolitan army officers and administrators lacked adequate understanding of Mexican society and feared the worst if Mexicans received offers of military aid or ideological support from abroad. The criollos' aspirations for position and power, and the lower classes' chronic violence and deep hostility, were interpreted as signs of insurrectionary behavior. Traditional fears of Indian uprisings became more ominous when officers considered the prospect of British aid or a leadership inspired by revolutionary programs.

The relative peace following the War of the American Revolution appeared to end in 1789 when Spain and Britain clashed over the rather unlikely issue of possession of the isolated northwest coast of North America. For Spain, it was simply a matter of strategic considerations and traditional claims to sovereignty over the Pacific rim of the American continents. Until the advent of foreign interest, little had been done to survey the potential wealth of the region let alone to establish permanent settlements. Proximity to California and the continuing myth of a Northwest Passage through the continent were sufficient causes for Spain to invoke the Family Pact with France and to prepare for hostilities. The arrest of British mariners at Nootka Sound on Vancouver Island edged both sides to the brink of war in 1790,[1] but the Spanish government soon realized that the French could not be depended upon to support the alliance. Indeed, as the Marqués del Campo wrote a little later from London to the Conde de Floridablanca, "Who knows if upon incorporating our troops and sailors with theirs, there could have been consequences fatal for the present epoch and for the future?"[2] These anxieties appeared to be confirmed by subsequent events: pocket watches, snuff boxes, and coins engraved with a woman dressed in white with a flag in her hands surrounded by the inscription "Libertad Americana" appeared in Spanish colonies, as did literature lauding the revolution in France.[3] Viceroy Revillagigedo stepped up customs surveillance over crates of books and other goods imported through Veracruz, but despaired of ever closing off the flow because of the sheer volume of commercial traffic and private correspondence. Much of the material appeared to originate in Havana, where there was ample opportunity for contacts between Spaniards and foreigners.[4] It was impossible to deny Mexicans access to modern ideas and their knowledge of exciting changes taking place in the world spurred interest in forbidden publications.[5]

Besides the flow of revolutionary propaganda from Europe and Havana by way of official commerce, Revillagigedo suspected the loyalty of Louisiana, whose population was still largely French and ideologically untrustworthy because of proximity to the United States.[6] Of even greater concern, however, was the revolution in the French sector of Hispaniola, where the rebellious Negroes offered a clear example to subject peoples. Despite these concerns, Revillagigedo was not convinced New Spain would be drawn into revolution. While he investigated rumors of French agents said to be active in Mexico,[7] most Mexicans did not appear to show much interest in what occurred overseas. Since most of the population failed even to keep stride with the fashions, usages, and customs of the mother country, he doubted their ability to be more successful in absorbing foreign ideas. Those interested in European affairs and the modern ideologies formed small, secret associations to discuss the events. Revillagigedo believed that the spread of revolutionary ideas would take years to reach a dangerous level because there was no united effort to propagate dangerous philosophies.⁸ In the meantime, the minority in New Spain that might support revolution could be redirected in their thoughts if the regime undertook an active program of public works—urban sanitation, street lighting, and the construction of impressive buildings.⁹

The outbreak of war against France after "the horrible detestable act of regicide" caused increased efforts to reduce French influences in Mexico.¹⁰ This was not an easy task since for many years the French had been able to settle in New Spain and even to serve in the regular army.¹¹ While Revillagigedo was fairly moderate in his approaches to French residents, the Marqués de Branciforte shared none of his toleration. Fresh from a Spain gripped by a bloody war against France and its revolutionary ideology, Branciforte found the policies of his predecessor to be lax beyond belief. In his opinion, the French were a creeping menace who could be found in every quarter seeking to infiltrate and seduce the population. While many Mexicans shared Revillagigedo's belief that the French residents were neither dangerous nor committed to revolution, the new viceroy was certain they engaged in meetings and other activities designed to gain converts to their ideology. His views appeared to be confirmed when on August 24, 1794, a broadside was nailed to the wall of the viceregal palace:

> Los más sabios
> son los Franceses
> El seguirlos en sus
> Dictámenes, no es absurdo.
> Por muchos que hagan las leyes,
> Nunca podrán sofocar los gritos
> Que inspira Naturaleza.¹²

The investigation which followed the appearance of this statement unearthed a number of Frenchmen and at least some evidence that they had discussed liberty and independence, eulogized the French Revolution, and circulated propaganda material. Among the persons arrested was one Jean Lausel, a French baker, formerly in the employ of Viceroy Revillagigedo.¹³ Rumors flew all over the country concerning plots; a merchant at Veracruz, José María Bejarno y Frías, wrote to his brother in Granada describing a conspiracy which included among its aims the murders of the viceroy, archbishop, and corregidor of Mexico, the destruction of public buildings and the bullring, and finally an attempt to seek the independence of Mexico. More than one thousand French and Spanish advocates of revolution were supposedly arrested on the night the plot was exposed.¹⁴

Alarmed by the rumors and fearful that some might contain a grain of truth, Branciforte ordered the provincial intendants to investigate all foreigners and any Spaniards who showed signs of having fallen under the influence of French "fanaticism." In his opinion, the safest and best solution to the depravity caused by French residents might be to expel them from New Spain. If so, the best way to accomplish the task would be to follow the method used to eradicate the Jesuits. All Frenchmen and any other dangerous foreigners would be rounded up on a given night and their properties forfeited to the government. This seemed to be a sensible way of purging an element that had long been attacked for perverting the life of Mexico.[15] As far as Branciforte was concerned, the French had never contributed anything to the development of New Spain. Most were barbers, cooks, and dressmakers "who introduce little but corruption, madness, and effeminacy."[16] Reports from the Real Sala del Crimen and the audiencia reinforced this conviction. The French were described as "the lepers of the world who infect the healthy" and their mere presence in Mexico would introduce some kind of horrible plague. The French residents, many of whom were illegal immigrants, would spread maxims destructive to good government—that all men were naturally free, that all men were equal, and that monarchy was tyranny.[17] The majority of the judges in the Sala del Crimen supported extreme measures. Frenchmen who had entered New Spain since the beginning of the French Revolution were probably the worst offenders: they must be arrested, their properties sold, and the proceeds used to pay their expenses and transportation to Europe. Those who had taken up residency prior to 1789, but had not completed ten full years in Mexico, were to receive the same treatment. Those of even longer residence deserved some penalty, but their properties and possessions could be transferred to their families. Finally, the few French immigrants who came to New Spain with proper licenses would be left alone unless they exhibited signs of suspicious behavior. It should be noted that two judges opposed the severity of the majority view. Since the imperial government had done everything possible during the war to act as a model of humanity—even encouraging French deserters to join the Spanish side—punishments based simply upon place of birth appeared extreme.[18]

Branciforte rejected toleration as a way of dealing with what he thought was a truly dangerous minority. The roundup of French residents took place on January 15, 1795, employing surprise to prevent resistance or flight. A number of individuals had no legal grounds for residence in New Spain and they were detained for deportation. Generally, the public accepted the action, which had little real impact upon society. The audiencia commended the viceroy for having removed a dangerous element with the greatest possible efficiency while at the same time protecting the criminal Frenchmen from violence by Mexicans who clamored for their blood. A royal order of March 22, 1795, approved the operation, but by the time the deportations began, relations with the French republic had changed. While no orders arrived pertaining to the final disposition of the prisoners, it was quite evident that the traditional alliance against Britain had been renewed. Branciforte found himself in an embarrassing position and, after some delay, only those Frenchmen of known seditious intentions were transported to Cádiz. The others were awarded provisional pardons and permitted to return to their families.[19]

Although the new alliance with France halted overt action against the French, Branciforte did not have to look far to find new dangers. The Americans appeared to pose yet another ideological menace. A book titled *El Desengaño del hombre,* published in Philadelphia, turned up in Mexico and was declared to promote sedition and placed on the index of the Inquisition.[20] Quick to see the worst, Branciforte condemned the book as part of an American plan to cooperate with the untrustworthy French inhabitants of Louisiana in order to gain free navigation of the Mississippi River. The viceroy expressed alarm about the possibility of losing Louisiana and having to face the unpalatable prospect of sharing a common frontier with the Americans. Texas with its population of less than three thousand was a natural target in any new stage of American expansionism.[21] From a base in New Orleans, countless new American enterprises became conceivable. Branciforte wrote, "I do not consider these risks to be immediate, but they are not very remote." Despite the successful negotiation of the Treaty of Friendship, Limits, and Navigation (Pinckney's Treaty) with the United States, American disputes with France and negotiations with Britain kept New Spain's defenders on constant alert. In 1798, when the American Congress broke off diplomatic relations with France, declared hostilities against French ships, and approved the formation of an army of ten thousand men at President John Adams's initiative, Viceroy Azanza worried that Spanish ties with France might well provoke an American attack against Spanish possessions.[22] After all, the imperial government was certain that the Congress had been bought by the gold and intrigues of British prime minister William Pitt. Dispatches from the Spanish minister in Philadelphia, Carlos Martínez de Irujo, revealed that the mass of the American population had been deceived into wanting war. In Irujo's view, President Adams accepted the propaganda of British agents because he wanted to promote Federalist Party interests, which would be served by a war against France.[23] This information corroborated other reports from French sources that the British had attained significant influence over the American administration. The French were certain an alliance was near and warned Spain to anticipate possible Anglo-American attacks against Havana or other important Spanish possessions in the Caribbean.[24]

While nothing came of these rumors, Spanish army commanders in Mexico continued to watch American intentions. The prospect of an army of wild frontiersmen falling upon the Provincias Internas threw the calmest officers into a cold sweat. When news reached Mexico City in 1800 that the American adventurer Philip Nolan planned to enter Texas with a band of men to capture horses, Viceroy Marquina demanded vigorous action to make an example of the intruders.[25] This particular incident gained importance because the reports suggested that Nolan intended to smuggle goods into the province of Nuevo Santander, which came under the military jurisdiction of Mexico City rather than the commandancy of the Provincias Internas. Colonel Félix Calleja mobilized elements of the Tenth Militia Brigade at San Luis Potosí and notified the commanders of frontier detachments to prevent any southward movement of the Americans.[26] What worried the viceroy besides the American presence was the apprehension that Nolan might attract support from Indians who opposed Spain. Even a temporary alliance could draw attention to the military weakness of the northern frontier and inspire other Americans to undertake similar intrusions. Doubts about Nolan's motives were increased when Mordecai Richards and two companions deserted from the expedition and fell into Spanish hands. According to Richards, Nolan planned to construct a fort in Spanish territory and to search for mines and other sources of potential wealth. In relating what they remembered of Nolan's conversations, the Americans mentioned the formation of a large mounted force in Kentucky to be used against New Spain.[27]

Troops from the Provincias Internas and the Tenth Militia Brigade combed their territories for weeks without finding a trace of the Americans. Finally, on March 21, 1801, Lieutenant Miguel Músquiz with some hastily organized militia forces from Nacogdoches encountered Nolan in the territory of the Tahuacana Indians. The Americans had constructed three temporary forts and were ready to fight rather than lay down their arms. Músquiz ordered his men to open fire and in the ensuing exchange, Nolan received a mortal wound from the ball of a small campaign cannon. Once the excitement died down, the Spaniards were better able to assess the situation. They had spent a great deal of money and mobilized large forces to crush what turned out to be only twenty-eight intruders. The Indians, who might have supported the Americans, paid no heed to either side. Despite the overreactions of military and political officers, the Spaniards viewed American encroachments as a threat that had to be countered before it became worse. Well aware of the power of the American frontiersmen once they heard of good land, they tended to see grand expansionist designs in any exploratory expedition into Spanish territories.[28]

If Madrid failed to respond to the warnings of colonial administrators, it was not because of a shortage of information. About the same time that news reports mentioned Spanish Florida as a possible target of Burr's ambitions, but in November 1806, Casa Irujo added a postscript to a dispatch, cautioning that Burr might attempt an invasion of Mexico to attract additional support from the western states. Although these projects seemed preposterous, Burr was known to possess charts of the coasts of Veracruz and Tampico. One of his plans was said to contain reports on Veracruz indicating that the Spanish defenders would evacuate the port in the event of an attack. While Burr did not appear to possess any naval force, merchant ships were always available at New Orleans together with adventurers willing to gamble their lives if there was any likelihood of obtaining riches.[31] In some respects, the Burr revolt was received in New Spain as a real godsend: Iturrigaray had been expecting a clash along the Texas border between Spanish forces and troops under the command of General James Wilkinson. Instead, the Americans retired to New Orleans when word spread of Burr's plan to fall on the city with an army of between fifteen thousand and twenty thousand men.[32]

Never at a loss when it came to intrigue, the ubiquitous Wilkinson changed his tactics and adopted the mantle of protector of New Spain. He sent his aide-de-camp, Mr. Burling, to Mexico City with what he termed full information on Burr's plans. Wilkinson claimed to have spent 121,000 pesos stopping Burr and, quite typically, he asked Iturrigaray to reimburse the full amount and any other expenditures needed "... to sustain the common cause of good government, order, and humanity."[33] Iturrigaray went along with some of the cloak and dagger procedures requested by Wilkinson; he burned the originals of letters sent with Burling, but he had to admit that the documents contained no more about Burr's projects than what he had seen in public papers. He replied that the army of New Spain would deal with Burr even if an army of twelve thousand mentioned by Wilkinson appeared on Mexican territory. As for the request for money, Iturrigaray dismissed the matter and sent Burling back to New Orleans.[34]

The real intentions of the United States toward New Spain were to remain a most perplexing enigma for Spanish observers. A number of groups in New Orleans and elsewhere promoted some farfetched schemes designed to conquer new lands or, more often, to grab the "golden candlesticks and silver platters" believed to be so common in Mexico.[35] Since many of these projects were enveloped in the righteous propaganda of a new American Revolution to free Mexico from Spain, it was not surprising that the Spanish regime mistrusted the northern neighbor. After the French invasion of Spain and the disruption of the imperial government, it became almost impossible to evaluate the true situation. New rumors in 1809 about American troop concentrations at New Orleans caused officials in the Provincias Internas to request immediate reinforcements and a cantonment of at least five thousand troops stationed in Nuevo Santander. The letters of General Wilkinson were more mysterious than usual and correspondence from Spanish residents of New Orleans confirmed the presence of troops and naval units. According to hearsay, attacks were planned against Tampico and Campeche. President James Madison was supposed to be dominated by French interests in the United States and gossip indicated that Ciriaco Cevallos, the exiled commander of the Veracruz naval station, had joined the conspiracy to bring independence to New Spain.[36] Viceroy Garibay convened a *junta de guerra* to consider the possibility of deploying troops to meet these dangers and he dispatched an officer to Jamaica with a commission to purchase twenty thousand muskets, six thousand pistols, field artillery, and any other arms the British could spare.[37] His anxieties increased when American merchant vessels were detained at Isla del Carmen and Campeche for carrying cargoes of seditious documents, information on the government of the United States, and material promoting revolution in New Spain. It could not be determined whether these ships carried the official sanction of the American government.[38]

While there were those Spaniards and Mexicans who believed in the unremitting evil of American plots to promote independence in Spanish America and insurrection along the frontiers of New Spain,[39] other observers were certain such activities were the work of very small minorities. According to José Vidal, the Spanish vice-consul at New Orleans, the majority of the American population supported the Spanish people in their struggle against Napoleon. Only the government wanted to see the French subjugate Spain so that the colonies could declare independence. If this occurred, Vidal postulated that the United States would obtain great advantages and could use the Latin American states to help form a united barrier against the powers of Europe.[40] Ciriaco Cevallos, now an involuntary resident of the New Orleans listening post, adopted an even more positive view of American intentions. Although he submitted full intelligence reports on the size of the United States army and navy, he stated that the government desired a Spanish triumph against France. In the event Spain failed in Europe, one American had told him, "Aragon and Castile must revive in the New World." If such support was not motivated by friendship for Spain, he was convinced the Americans opposed the idea of France gaining control over Spanish territories. Voicing what was an idealistic but not uncommon Spanish view of the United States, Cevallos wrote, "the fundamental laws of the Anglo-American Union do not favor the spirit of conquest." Armies and wars would elevate ambitious men who would kill republican institutions. To prove the antimartial qualities of the Americans, Cevallos pointed out that such a wealthy nation of almost eight million did not have a navy or regular army worth mentioning. Fearing mercenary soldiers, Americans placed their trust in a national militia which could not be used in foreign wars. Cevallos did see the possibility of the fundamental principles underlying the American union being changed, but not until the distant future.[41]

Other prominent Spaniards supported this opinion; Luis de Onís, the minister plenipotentiary to the United States, grumbled about the failure of the Americans to recognize the interim regime in Spain and complained that this was poor behavior from a people who in large measure owed their own independence to Spain, but he did not see the prospect of hostilities.[42] Another Spanish diplomat in the United States, Ignacio Pérez de Lema, supported the view of Cevallos. During May 1809, he detected a definite spirit of reconciliation developing between Britain and the United States which would end the possibility of an alliance with France. But even if this trend proved illusory, he did not think the president could obtain the required two-thirds vote in Congress to support a war against Spain. Even though former President Jefferson and the Republican Party were the enemies of Spain, the Federalists possessed sufficient power to destroy any warlike projects. At the same time, however, a small, vociferous minority in the United States had made the idea of conquering New Spain into a favorite subject for discussion. In reality, Pérez de Lema considered such a project well beyond the capacity of the Americans under their existing constitution. Very few men wanted to be soldiers and an insignificant percentage of the national budget went for military expenditures. Congress refused to vote sufficient funds for regular troops, placing great dependence upon militiamen, who disliked discipline and generally had large families to support. Such troops rejected the prospect of service beyond the boundaries of their home states. They were not at all warlike and showed no proper respect for their officers. Pérez de Lema pictured the lowly common soldiers drinking and carousing with their superiors in the taverns—a truly scandalous situation for the maintenance of any proper military discipline. In his opinion, the Americans could deploy a maximum of six thousand troops along the Texas frontier. It would not be difficult for Garibay to put on a show of Spanish force which would impress the United States and end the notion that Mexico would be an easy conquest.[43]

The question was whether the Americans were the raving expansionist Kentuckians capable of any violence or the tavern-loving homebodies described by Pérez de Lema and Cevallos. Certainly Viceroy Garibay accepted the former interpretation since he felt that the United States wanted either to expand its national territory or to aid the projects of Napoleon. As has been seen, Garibay activated militia units and proposed to dispatch seven thousand troops to Jalapa, but his *junta de guerra* advised against further expenditures unless an invasion appeared inevitable.[44] Although the conclusion of the new alliance against Napoleon ended the possibility of a British invasion, the defenders of New Spain could not relax their vigil. Already, some officers had begun to warn about the even more frightening prospect of internal unrest and insurrection.

Generally speaking, the army officers who planned the defense of New Spain had attached remarkably little importance to the possibility of a major outbreak of violence from within the country. Some mentioned revolution in vague terms, but unlike the concentrated study that went into defense against invaders, there were no specific schemes on how to react to an uprising. Yet there was evidence enough of violence and a procession of minor episodes indicated a dangerous state of incomprehension between the way viceroys and army officers viewed unrest and the true situation as demonstrated by later investigations. The heavy-handed reaction of the regime to these minor events illustrated its concern about potential trouble from the population. At the same time, however, the officers found that to even discuss internal frictions or the possibility of insurrection was considered in itself a disloyal act. As a result, the incidents continued and both the army and the administration delayed meaningful investigation of problems. Even worse, lack of clear information on the attitudes of Indians or any other groups caused overreaction to non-events and underreaction to real dangers. By the time the regime suffered massive dislocation in 1808, the army and other agencies of law enforcement lacked the flexibility to identify symptoms of trouble and to act before minor revolts became major convulsions.

The military did maintain relatively close touch with some of the more turbulent sectors of the population. In most urban centers where crime and violence had grown beyond the enforcement capacity of the Acordada officers, local *alcaldes,* and *alguaciles,* the regulars and provincial militiamen had been used in many police functions. No viceroy wanted to permit a repetition of the urban riots of 1767, which had been directed against taxation, militia recruitment, and the expulsion of the Jesuits. José de Gálvez showed no sympathy with those who expressed grievances through disorder; he used exemplary punishments to crush any vestige of revolt. Once peace was restored, 85 persons were executed, 73 sentenced to the lash, 674 to prison terms, and 117 to banishment from their home provinces.[45] In Guanajuato and San Luis Potosí, two of the cities most affected by the disturbances, permanent army pickets from the local militias were established to help the *alcaldes de barrio* enforce order. Viceroy Bucareli introduced a similar picket at Oaxaca in 1776 when the city authorities failed to prevent innumerable robberies and homicides.[46]

In Guadalajara, a city well known for its underworld of vagabonds and criminals, rioting and unrest were common. During 1789, the audiencia of Guadalajara begged Viceroy Revillagigedo to send regular troops to suppress what was becoming an epidemic of major crimes. Rapid growth in the population had increased the numbers of robberies, muggings, and murders. The criminal element no longer confined its activities to the lower levels of society. Robberies and violent assaults were reported by the officer of the tobacco monopoly, the Colegio de San Diego, some *oidores* of the audiencia, and many individuals of leading families. The city lacked funds to hire extra police constables let alone to pay the costs of an army garrison. There were not sufficient men to fill city patrols or to furnish adequate security in the prisons. When a similar crime wave had threatened the city some years before, Viceroy Bucareli sent two regular companies to strengthen the forces of law and order. Now the cabildo requested a full battalion. Unfortunately, however, Revillagigedo had no troops to spare for ordinary police duty.[47]

By 1795, not only was the city of Guadalajara unsafe at any hour, but gangs of thieves made travel difficult throughout the intendancies of Guadalajara and Valladolid. Subdelegates lacked sufficient force to contain banditry and the local residents were so intimidated that they dared not leave their homes. On several occasions gangs raided the offices of royal administrators or robbed treasury funds during transit. Angered by growing losses and official inaction, merchants of the consulado petitioned the viceroy for aid, stating that the dangerous situation had them terrified and that they were unwilling to continue risking their property. Viceroy Branciforte condemned Revillagigedo for having disbanded the provincial militia, thereby endangering the safety of magistrates and the general population. The one source of relief in this situation was the knowledge that the French residents who might have been behind the activities of the criminal bands were no longer free to give leadership. Branciforte appointed the Acordada judge, Manuel de Santa María, to take charge of the crisis and to use measures harsh enough to deter potential criminals. To add muscle, he sent a detachment of the Dragoon Regiment of Spain composed of men selected for their valor, strength, and good conduct.[48] This force was successful in driving the major bands into cover. However, no evidence of any links between bandits and French or other revolutionary elements could be established. As a matter of fact, many of the two hundred criminals captured turned out to be army deserters.[49]

Elsewhere, however, gangs of criminals continued to test the efficiency of the acordada and to demonstrate Branciforte's arguments for increased militia forces. The administrator of the post office at Huautla in the intendancy of Puebla was robbed in his own home; 1,697 pesos belonging to the Renta de Tabaco, other government monopolies, and his own savings were stolen. A second major robbery took place twenty-five leagues from the capital on the road to Zimapán, where highwaymen attacked a merchant mule train, making off with more than 11,000 pesos in goods and coin. Several of the perpetrators were captured and their cases placed in the hands of the tribunal of the Acordada. Once again, Branciforte expressed fears that the constant bandit activity might presage a general insurrection.[50]

Despite bursts of activity to contain crime in cities and on public highways, violence increased as soon as the authorities showed any sign of relaxing their vigilance. A new wave of assaults and robberies plagued Guadalajara throughout 1799, compelling the audiencia to take measures to tighten up urban security. As usual, nothing was done until a spectacular and horrifying crime caused popular pressure for action. In this case, three robbers with painted faces forced their way into the residence of the prominent widow Doña Rosalia María del Valle. The criminals stabbed the gatekeeper to death, tied up two servants, and escaped with some valuable clothing and all of the family silver. The audiencia ordered that the local provincial infantry battalion conduct a night patrol, but the commander, Francisco de Escovedo, opposed this as inadequate. "What would be accomplished by this?" he asked. And answering his own question, he stated, ". . . dispatching a patrol to keep order amongst the population of this city and to guard the full expanse of its jurisdiction is the same as damming a turbulent river with a little stone." To make any impact upon criminal activity, two patrols would have to be on duty serving four shifts during the day and night. This would mean the mobilization of at least sixty militiamen with a number of sergeants and corporals.[51] In Viceroy Azanza's view, the *alcaldes de barrio* and the *alguacil mayor* had primary responsibility for rounding up robbers, but if they could not handle the volume of criminal activity, it was high time Guadalajara adopted the system used in Guanajuato, San Luis Potosí, and Oaxaca. In all of these cities, the cabildos paid for militia pickets from local taxes levied for the purpose.[52]

The viceregal orders to crush criminal elements and to inflict severe punishments upon perpetrators seldom took into account the basic social ills of New Spain. In Oaxaca, one of the Mexican cities requiring very strong militia patrols to enforce the law, alcohol consumption was a major cause of the high incidence of homicides and violent crimes. Bernardino Bonavía, commander of the Seventh Militia Brigade, expressed incredulity at the way plebeian classes abused alcohol. No measures seemed effective in preventing excessive consumption and an exasperated Bonavía stated, "... in Oaxaca drunkenness has taken his throne." At the same time, however, the very alcohol which contributed to turbulence paid a tax supporting the operating costs of the militia picket charged with maintaining the peace. Each barrel of brandy carried into the city was taxed three reales, which each year resulted in a tax income of about 10,500 pesos.[53]

Very often the army was used to control the lower classes. In Mexico City, where soldiers performed many of the guard and police functions, they were even responsible for traffic control and for regulating access to the Alameda park. On fiesta days, an officer, a sergeant, two corporals, and eighteen grenadiers watched the entrances to the park and turned away anyone of the "*clase de mantas*"—the beggar, barefoot, naked, or otherwise "indecent" classes of the capital. Patrols within the park removed any of these individuals who had gained entry; even the hawkers of sweets and food were denied access if they were barefoot or improperly attired.[54] It took little to turn the floating population of vagabonds and beggars into a dangerous mob or a panic-stricken multitude. When for example, on October 14, 1789, Mexico City viewed a brilliant exhibition of the Aurora Borealis, the plebeian classes were thrown into panic. Rumors spread that flames dropped from the skies would consume the city. The clergy, rather than calming the ignorant, whipped up the frenzy by demanding prayer, confession of sins, and processions of sacred images through the streets. Many people congregated at the shrine of Guadalupe, where they commended themselves to the Virgin. Army officers went into the streets to explain the true meaning of the natural phenomenon and patrols were sent out to prevent the looting of abandoned property.[55]

The unpredictability of the plebeians caused officials to fear riots which might conceivably turn into popular insurrections. All of the late eighteenth and early nineteenth-century viceroys were apprehensive about unemployment in the mining industry and tobacco factories resulting from shortages of European quicksilver and paper. During any war with Britain, naval blockades, capture of merchant vessels, and interruption of trans-Atlantic commerce endangered the flow of these vital commodities and forced a number of viceroys to agree to sending illegal commercial expeditions to Jamaica to ransom captured cargoes. With eleven thousand families dependent upon employment in the tobacco factories, paper shortages could result in widespread unemployment and the possibility of violence.[56] The warnings were stronger regarding supplies of mercury, so necessary in refining silver ore. Many mines could neither maintain costly drainage operations nor refine their ores by fire and other methods. An extended interruption of the mercury supply would shut down the mines and cause a ripple effect through the entire economy. Depression and unemployment could have dire results once a large sector of the population began to suffer hunger and other hardships. Fortunately, during most of the period, the imperial government was the first to recognize the full ramifications of disruptions in mining. Naval ships carried cargoes of mercury and paper when merchant traffic was interrupted.[57] However, once Britain deployed overwhelming naval forces and blockaded Cádiz and Havana, supplies of these key ingredients declined to a trickle. By 1806, Viceroy Iturrigaray asked the imperial government to use any means at its disposal to transport mercury; if Spanish warships and merchantmen could not do the job, vessels of neutral nations must be hired.[58]

The concern about unrest and violence in cities or mining districts rested upon a series of unknown variables. Viceroys and army officers understood economic problems and unemployment, but they were not certain how the diverse Mexican population might react to a given set of circumstances. Many recalled the Indian commotions of 1608, 1624, and 1692 in Mexico City or the frightening events of 1767 in San Luis Potosí, when Indians had stoned an agent of the alcalde mayor and then threatened a general massacre of all Spaniards.[59] In 1781 when the Indians of Izúcar rebelled against their alcalde mayor over repartimiento conflicts, Viceroy Mayorga drew parallels with the revolt of Tupac Amaru in Peru.[60] In the cities, it was possible to dismiss the Indians as little more than a noxious influence and a social problem. Humboldt described how the police in Mexico City sent tumbrils through the streets each morning to collect Indian drunkards, who were carried to jail and then sentenced to three days' labor cleaning the streets.[61] But in more isolated regions, where Indians were often the majority, the regime was less certain about their basic motives. Indeed, there were sufficient incidents to give the Spanish governors cause for cold shudders: from time to time they suspected some unknown conspiracy working to weld the disunited opposition into a massive force dedicated to the destruction of New Spain.

Two of these Indian uprisings occurred in 1787 at Papantla and Acayucan. While both centers were isolated from each other, proximity to the strategic Gulf Coast made Viceroy Flórez very much aware of the potential ramifications. The insurrection at Papantla broke out on August 23, 1787, when a mob of angry Indians rose up against the district alcalde mayor. The militia commander, José María Morcillo, attempted to mediate, but he was gravely wounded for his efforts. The mob turned on three officers of the tobaccc monopoly guard and began to stone any Spanish residents who had not escaped from the town. Several deaths and injuries resulted from skirmishes, but the Indians were left in clear possession of Papantla. Word about the uprising did not reach Veracruz for nearly a week, allowing the Indians time to celebrate their victory and to consolidate their positions. Not at all certain about the magnitude of the revolt, Governor Bernardo de Troncoso decided to act even before seeking the approval of the viceroy. He sent a force of 171 troops of the Regiment of Zamora by sea and they marched inland to quell the unrest. They encountered little coordinated resistance; one lieutenant received serious injuries which were considered fatal, but he recovered.[62]

Although the Indians showed no taste for combat against regular troops, the Papantla rising raised a number of important questions. First, the Indians managed to win possession of the town despite the presence of two infantry companies and one lancer company. Clearly, the militia failed to perform when faced with the slightest resistance. Instead, the burden of restoring order fell upon the limited regular troops available at Veracruz. The expedition to Papantla temporarily weakened the coastal defenses and at the same time cost the treasury over 8,600 pesos. Flórez pointed out that if an enemy squadron had appeared off the coast at the same time, the Indians could have contributed to the loss of the kingdom.[63] An investigation of the Papantla militia revealed numerous weaknesses and caused some officers to renew their old suspicions about the basic worth of militias. Few of the officers were able to perform their training functions or to enforce discipline. Five were itinerant merchants who were home for only a few days during the year and another six or eight held similar positions which required extensive travel. This left only the administrator of the tobacco monopoly, the local school teacher, and a few old men whose health prevented much activity. Some militiamen described in the military census as belonging to the *castas de razón* were mulattoes; even they were employed permanently outside Papantla on haciendas, ranches, or in the river fisheries. In order to visit the town, they had to travel anywhere from four to fourteen leagues, so they made the trip only on the most important holidays.[64]

Many of the causes of the Papantla uprising could be traced to deep social problems. Colonel Esteban Tizón, subdelegate of the district, described the Indians from their governor on down as vicious and quite generally addicted to alcohol. Tizón claimed to have labored to correct their behavior through love and charity, but with more than three hundred stills turning out the powerful sugar-based *chichique,* his efforts had no impact. Indeed, the Indians produced enough liquor to keep men, women, and children in a continuous state of intoxication. When gentle means failed, Tizón tried other means to chastise offenders, from fines to whippings, but he could not combat alcohol. Moreover, despite his attempts to settle the Indians and to find them permanent employment, many continued to wander through the mountains. In his opinion, the uprising resulted from local causes; the Indians resisted taxation and felt that they had been cheated by local officials. No resentments had apparently been expressed against the king, viceroy, or government, and even if there had been, Tizón would not have believed them. He reported that Indians said many nonsensical things when drunk which they could not remember once they sobered up.[65]

The Papantla incident would have been forgotten had there not been a similar rising at the town of Acayucan—this time south of Veracruz. Since Acayucan was sixty leagues down the coast and then inland in the Sierra de San Martín, the prospect of Indian insurrection caused even more anxiety. The Indians revolted on Sunday morning, October 20, 1787, catching the Spaniards and mulattoes off guard. Some attempted to resist, but they were overwhelmed in a clash which left several dead including the lieutenant of the alcalde mayor, Andrés Antonio García. The administrator of the *alcabalas*, Juan García Amoroso, disguised himself and rode out of town; he took a canoe down the San Juan River to Tlacotalpan, where he was able to report the events to Governor Troncoso. García Amoroso left little to the imagination. If God had not moved the Indians to compassion, he was certain that Acayucan would have been burned and the people slaughtered "at their tyrannical and impious hands."[66] According to a report from Manuel Sabón de Oliveros, the administrator of the post office and customs at Acayucan, the violence originated from a struggle among the Indians over the governorship. Apparently, a local Indian leader, Gaspar de los Ríos, and his wife, Ana Pasquala, alias "La Filota," led a faction which was intent upon ousting the existing Indian governor. Ríos went to Mexico City to petition the viceroy for recognition and apparently received a commission. Returning from the capital and by now supported by his followers, he went to the alcalde mayor, who rejected his claims and sided with the existing Indian governor. On the following Sunday after Mass, La Filota with a group of women attacked the Indian governor, whipped him, beat him, and were about to castrate him when his wife managed to obtain the aid of some local militiamen. Between thirty and forty soldiers armed with muskets—most of which lacked flint, powder, or ball—joined the fray. The Spanish and mulatto residents rushed to support the alcalde mayor, who was with the militiamen, in what developed into a confrontation of two angry mobs. Someone opened fire, and in the first volley not more than five muskets discharged: three Indian men and one woman fell dead and the Indians, "like bloodthirsty wolves," fell upon the troops, killing two officers and capturing Andrés Antonio García, who was executed and mutilated.[67]

The Indians captured the alcalde mayor, tying him up and beating him.

They were carrying him to the jail when he broke free and bolted into the church. There, the curate and vicars gave him protection and the mob turned its attention to looting the houses and property of government administrators. According to Oliveros, the curate attempted to parade the consecrated image of the Lord to calm passions, but the Indians ordered him to take it back or they would break its arms, legs, and head.

Upon receiving this disquieting news, Governor Troncoso convened a *junta de guerra* and appointed Colonel Miguel del Corral to prepare a detachment of 100 troops from the Regiment of Zamora. These regulars were to incorporate with 150 militiamen from Alvarado, Tlacotalpan, and Cosamaloapan. The militia commander of San Andrés Tuxtla was to send another 150 men to join this force. Since none of the militia units possessed any usable munitions, the governor ordered thirty thousand cartridges loaded on coastal vessels used to transport the regular troops and supplies to Tlacotalpan. Corral received a fund of three thousand pesos to pay militiamen and the authority to draw money from regional administrators of the alcabalas against the Veracruz treasury.[68] The problem at Veracruz was that, with some regular troops still stationed at Papantla, few soldiers remained to guard the port. The governor mobilized two militia companies, but worried about fragmenting his small regular garrison.

By the time Corral and his forces arrived at Acayucan, the Indians had lost their taste for insurrection. In fact, while they had been in full possession of the town from October 21 to November 3, after the first outbursts of looting, relatively little damage had been done to the property of those who fled. Some brandy disappeared from the houses of the deceased Spaniards, but other valuables and clothing were not touched. From one house, only five pesos were taken, to buy a shroud for one of the slain Indians, and some soap to wash bloodstains out of clothing. Corral set about to discover the origins of the violence. He blamed the Indian, Gaspar de los Ríos, and his wife, La Filota, for creating a faction and promising their supporters that they would end taxation and forced labor.[69] At the same time, however, the alcalde mayor was negligent in permitting matters to have gotten out of hand before he took steps to restore order. As in the case of Papantla, the militia failed to give any protection. While the two local companies were supposed to be armed, uniformed, and fairly well trained, not even twenty-five muskets remained in serviceable condition. The rest were either rusted or lacking vital parts—despite the fact that the weapons had been new or in good shape less than four years before. Much of the trouble as usual was traced to Indian grievances over tithes, taxes, land claims, and involuntary labor. They rejected a tithe of one peso on each cow killed for their own consumption and they were angry of Nolan's failure became known, the intendant of Louisiana, Ramón López de Angulo, presented an exposition to the imperial government detailing why the United States must be feared. First, proximity to the wealth of New Spain generated jealousy: Americans who had little more than grain, tobacco, and maritime supplies could not repress their greed when they thought about the precious metals, cochineal, indigo, sugar, cotton, coffee, dye-woods, and other products of the Spanish colonies. Second, the Americans had become the most infamous of contraband traders. Spain and France committed a cardinal error in supporting the American Revolution because instead of destroying trade between Britain and her colonies, they had achieved exactly the the opposite. During wartime, the British merely adopted the American flag; since they spoke the same language as the Americans, few Spanish officials were able to distinguish one from the other. López mentioned a conversation reported to him in which an American questioned a New Orleans resident who had just returned from Veracruz about the state of discontent or satisfaction expressed by Mexicans toward the Spanish regime. The American had indicated that the colony would not be around much longer. As if to underline the danger, López mentioned that among a certain class of Americans, when their children did something pleasing, they said, "You will go to Mexico." Basically, American children grew up inculcated with expansionist ideas. In López's view, they could raise an army of 100,000 to 150,000 for an expedition to conquer Mexico. This prospect was all the more fearful if one looked at the Kentuckians who came to New Orleans to sell flour; all of the men looked like the powerful grenadiers or pioneers of Spanish regiments. They were accustomed to hardships and exceptionally ferocious from their constant struggles against the Indians. Only a concerted effort by all of the major European powers could prevent the United States from carrying forward its designs.[29]

For the rulers of New Spain, Louisiana was an essential buffer province. Small wonder, then, that the news of the cession of Louisiana to France and then the secret negotiations in which Napoleon sold the province to the United States in 1803 came as a terrible shock. To make matters even worse, since the frontier between Louisiana and the province of Texas was unclear, Spanish and American troops were soon glaring at each other across the border at Natchitoches. From Philadelphia, the Marqués de Casa Irujo declared that the United States did not oppose the idea of war with Spain in order to obtain a favorable solution to the Texas boundary question and to gain control over Florida.[30] The situation clouded even further in 1806 when rumors began to circulate that former vice-president Aaron Burr planned a revolution to separate the western states from the American union. The first about attempts to collect the alcabala on sugar cane. Little wonder the reforms proposed by Gaspar de los Ríos attracted support. Corral concluded that the uprising could have been much worse. At least half of the town seemed to have joined the original mob, but only twenty men and eight women were considered to be principal offenders. Many more could have died, and the rebellion did not attract support from Indians of other towns or from any of the pardos of the region.[70]

Despite the fear of more general insurrections, the prompt but measured response concluded the incidents. This would be in marked contrast to the way the regime responded to a new threat of Indian uprising in 1801. Of course, the world view of Spanish administrators had changed rather dramatically in the intervening years; with the specter of revolutionary ideologies, war against Britain, and fear of the United States, the authorities were prepared to read almost anything into the most obscure rumors. This tendency, along with continued incomprehension of Indian motivations and the view that they might be able to organize a general secret conspiracy embracing all of New Spain, led to the brutal suppression of a nonevent. The so-called rising of Mariano of Tepic coincided with a British invasion scare which had drawn Viceroy Marquina's full attention. The first information came from the naval authorities at San Blas and the subdelegates of Compostela and Aguacatlan in Nueva Galicia, who obtained copies of some incendiary letters reported to have originated in the town of Tepic. From the beginning, the conspiracy sounded dangerous and it became more and more fantastic as new information became available. Mariano, believed to be the son of the Indian governor of a town called Tlaxcala in Nueva Galicia, had issued a summons to an unknown number of Indian communities convoking a general meeting at Tepic.[71] There was mention of an Indian king or the election of a leader and of an army of thirty thousand ready to march under his command. Indians throughout the viceroyalty were reported to have established communications with each other and with the Tlaxcalan nation.[72] An unnamed gentleman from Mexico City was supposed to be implicated and armed horsemen were alleged to have been sighted with groups of Indians. The plan was to become operative on the feast day of the Virgin of Guadalupe at the moment the tapers were lit in her shrine. These were to contain explosives which would blow up the temple. In the confusion, the insurgents would attack the viceregal palace, which was to have been mined at the corners.[73]

As these revelations and others circulated in Nueva Galicia, Commandant General José Abascal, the audiencia of Guadalajara, and Captain Francisco de Eliza, commandant of the Naval Department of San Blas, moved to suppress the revolutionary uprising before it took hold. Abascal ordered the colonel of the provincial Dragoon Regiment of Nueva Galicia to march into the danger zone with two squadrons and to leave the remainder of his regiment mobilized for action. The provincial Infantry Battalion of Guadalajara was placed under arms and coastal militia units alerted.[74] In the meantime, Eliza dispatched Captain Salvador Fidalgo to Tepic with a force of troops and sailors under orders to surprise the Indians in the midst of their illegal gathering. Apparently, most residents of Tepic either had not heard of Mariano or paid no heed to the letters. Others, believing that they were assembling to meet some important personage, perhaps even the king of Spain, went to the town to see what the affair was all about. Fidalgo encountered a gathering of Indians as planned and they surrendered, throwing down their machetes and calling out that they had come in peace. Some, however, fearing arrest, made a run for freedom. In what became a panic-stricken melee, the troops opened fire killing two Indians, wounding a number, and taking seventy-two prisoners. Over two hundred were rounded up and eventually marched to Guadalajara, where many perished in prison before their cases came to trial.[75]

Upon receiving the first confused reports from the north, Marquina could scarcely avoid interpreting the events as a major threat to internal security. He ordered Captain Eliza to prepare for a possible evacuation of the San Blas naval base to Acapulco if an assault materialized. The evil intentions of the Indians seemed to be confirmed by their precipitous flight into the mountains whenever troops approached their villages. No one considered the possibility that they might be terrified of the Spaniards and seek safety through flight. New reports of horsemen and Indians accompanied by Europeans of strange speech and dress added to the atmosphere of fear. After all, Spain was at war with Britain and there had been skirmishes with either American or British corsairs along the Pacific coast. The viceroy did not discount the possibility of some foreign-inspired plot.[76]

Perhaps the most alarming aspect of the Tepic affair was the supposition that the Indians had the capacity to create a chain of communications tied together by one means or another through the mountains into Tlaxcala. Great efforts were made to confirm the existence of this network, particularly since in the early nineteenth century no one was certain what the Tlaxcalan nation was. Marquina was still nervous about these rumors when he received news from Veracruz which appeared to confirm his worst fears. The governor reported that two Indians from suspicious Acayucan had not only discussed the election of an Indian king, but departed from their homes to visit him. Marquina alerted the militia of Veracruz and issued orders to arrest and remit to the port any person who behaved suspiciously. Probably because of the memory of the poor performance of the Acayucan militia in 1787, a coast guard brig and two small corvettes were made ready to transport reinforcements. These precautions having been taken and complete secrecy maintained to prevent rumors from reaching the populace, everyone waited in vain for any sign of unusual activities.[77]

By as early as February 1801, the Indian plot began to appear a reflection more of Spanish insecurity than of Indian belligerency. The census for the region most infected by the revolt was found to list only about two thousand inhabitants—hardly sufficient population for a massive insurrection. Even though the evil Mariano evaded arrest, no Europeans or foreigners turned up. As for the more outlandish aspects of the plot, José Verdía, a royal navy pilot, reported that the plan utilizing incendiary candles was not new and for many years had spread as gossip among the common people.[78] Then came word from Veracruz of the arrest of the two Indians who had gone to interview the Indian king. Their testimony reflected total innocence and naïveté. They had gone to Tlaxcala with the purpose of requesting a little money from the Indian governor there, who could give them sufficient funds to alleviate their misery. In reality, however, the Indian governor of Tlaxcala, while he was sympathetic with their plight, had not been able to help since he needed all of his money to build a church. He gave each of them two reales and sent them back to their homes.[79]

The plot received one last flutter with the arrest of a suspicious character near Potrero Grande, Nuevo León, during an attempted mule robbery. Sent to prison at San Luis Potosí, the man, whose name was Juan José García, refused to eat and after several days called himself Alejandro I; he assured his jailers that the king had granted the title and he had confirmation from the pope in Rome. At first, the jailers believed that García was demented, but under recommendation from the *fiscal de lo civil* in Mexico City, he was placed in irons under harsh, isolated conditions.[80] Following several days of this treatment, he was questioned once again and ordered to tell the truth. If anything, isolation accentuated the madness, for García described a trip to Mexico City, where he had been supposed to see the viceroy and to receive a commission as commandant general of the Provincias Internas. Not finding the viceroy, he had gone to Tlaxcala and finally to Veracruz, where he was named Mariano I. Interrogated in detail about this last statement, García responded that he had received a royal order granting him the name. He was returned to his cell in irons and with his head placed in a stock. After five interviews during which nothing more was learned, the physicians of San Luis Potosí declared García to be insane—the victim of *"verdadera demencia melancólica."* No one was quite sure what to do with the prisoner. Since there was no insane asylum in San Luis Potosí, Calleja wanted him shipped to the capital—or anywhere, for that matter, to get him out of the barracks, where his upkeep cost a large amount. No one wanted to take responsibility for a final decision on García, and there were still some who believed that he might be the real Mariano. Finally, however, a very weak García was committed to the hospital of San Hipólito in Mexico City.[81]

In retrospect, observers from the viceroy on down realized the true insignificance of the Mariano revolt. By June 1801, Marquina complained that recent dispatches from subordinates had "notably diminished the history of the intended rising" and, to reveal the true situation, he ordered priests, who knew the Indians better than anyone else, to interview their parishioners.[82] As the facts were pieced together, it became clear that the regime had reacted to a hoax engineered by possibly only one man, an Indian named Juan Hilano, who either died in prison or on the way to prison at Guadalajara.[83] Hilano seemed to have written the letters himself and the existence of Mariano was doubtful to say the least. No evidence turned up to implicate any Spaniard or foreigner, and the region around Tepic was quiet following these events. Although Hilano received traitor's treatment—his goods and property were confiscated, his house destroyed, and the site spread with salt—there are many questions to be answered about the behavior of officers connected with the affair. There was no evidence whatsoever to justify the heavy-handed repression. By mid-1801, the troop mobilizations, supplies, prisoner maintenance, and other expenditures amounted to almost 56,000 pesos. All concerned wished that they had never heard of Mariano or Tepic.[84] In reviewing the uprising in 1805, the Council of the Indies condemned several officials for having acted without due caution; Captain Fidalgo, who was in command during the assault on the peaceful Indians, was issued a harsh reprimand, although it never reached him.[85]

The inability to bridge the cultural gap between Spaniards and Indians was dangerous, but understandable. Yet Indians were by no means the only victims of policies based upon ignorance of conditions and true motivations. At the highest level, viceroys such as Miguel José de Azanza and Félix Berenguer de Marquina could not in a two- or three-year term of office gain the kind of expertise needed to govern New Spain. Worse than this, a viceroy could find himself almost completely isolated except from the members of his immediate official family who accompanied him from Spain. Not knowing whom to trust or where to turn for correct information, viceroys found that minor difficulties sometimes became major concerns. Viceroy Marquina was plagued by one of these situations; for some time he was almost powerless in the hands of a bogus informant. Scarcely having recovered from the shock of capture by the British as his ship approached New Spain and then from slanderous rumors that he had imported contraband from Jamaica, Marquina received a secret letter informing him of a well-planned criollo conspiracy to separate Mexico from Spain. Apparently a large faction with British support had plotted for two years to establish an independent republic. The viceroy accepted the fact that there must be some group in New Spain espousing the ideas of liberty and independence; obviously, "... some sparks of revolution must have jumped to these almost indefensible dominions, so far distant from the throne."[86] But to make matters difficult the denunciant, who signed his name Francisco Benítez Gálvez, warned of a powerful alliance of prominent Mexican families who supported the plan. Their agents were said to be in positions close to the centers of power in Mexico City. Marquina had no idea which among his subordinates might be implicated and he dared not trust anyone with the information.

The viceroy considered the danger grave enough to merit moving regular army units to positions where they might be able to prevent a domestic upheaval. The two regular dragoon regiments were stationed in Mexico City and Puebla, and the first battalion of the Regiment of the Crown, recently withdrawn from Veracruz, was to be reinforced as rapidly as possible from the reserve companies. At the same time, a dark suspicion bothered Marquina: since both regular and militia units were predominantly Mexican in composition, he wondered if they would join their relatives at the first hint of a separatist movement. Not able to trust the army, he demanded the return of the two infantry regiments from Havana and asked for two Spanish field marshals to give better leadership while he directed operations from the capital.[87]

The mysterious Benítez Gálvez continued to write letters from various points in northern Mexico. He promised to send documents from a British general, James Smith, outlining the extent of Jamaican aid for the republican conspiracy. He implicated Colonel Antonio Pérez Gálvez, commander of the provincial Dragoon Regiment of the Prince, and named a number of militia officers on the Tampico coast who were supposed to have many Indian auxiliaries ready to support the rising. Furthermore, he warned Marquina that one of the first acts of the revolutionaries would be to murder the viceroy and other senior officials in order to disrupt the government at the moment of the attack. Despite the persuasiveness of these charges, Marquina began to suspect the veracity of his informant. Detail after detail lacked any corroborating evidence. Yet, he wanted to humor Benítez Gálvez, whose ideas were extremely dangerous even if unsupported by fact. Gaining confidence, Marquina selected the *alcalde del crimen*, Joaquín Mosquera, a man he had known and trusted since they worked together in the Philippines, to investigate the continuing flow of information from the north. Suspicions of a complete fraud grew deeper when Benítez Gálvez forwarded some original letters which were supposed to have come from Jamaica; obviously, his coconspirators would not have permitted such important documents to remain in the hands of a minor participant.[88] Continuing to humor Benítez Gálvez, Marquina finally lured him to the capital, where he was arrested and jailed without any word escaping to the general public. After seven days of intensive interrogation in the acordada prison, Benítez Gálvez confessed to having perpetrated a great fabric of lies conceived primarily as a means of obtaining revenge against his former employer, Colonel Pérez Gálvez. Apparently, he bore a grudge over a matter having to do with recommendations for service and loyalty. His real name was Francisco Antonio Vázquez Fernández, a native of Cádiz with a lengthy criminal record for offenses ranging from bigamy to impersonation. This time he had bitten off a little more than he could chew: as a start, he was charged with writing false and inflammatory statements, impersonating a Spanish naval officer, and obtaining money under the forged signature of the viceroy. Although Vázquez Fernández was locked in a secure cell, Marquina viewed him as a potential danger because his mind was full of schemes to destroy the government. Rather than risk having such a prisoner, and worried about the possibility of a public stir when information about the bizarre letters came out at the trial, Marquina deported Vázquez Fernández to Spain.[89]

Some of Marquina's apprehensions about criollo motivations can be explained in part by an antigachupín plot he inherited from Azanza. The affair, called the Conspiracy of the Machetes, had been accepted by Azanza as a legitimate danger which if nothing else publicized the "... ancient division and rooted hatred between Europeans and criollos."[90] The first word of trouble came in October 1799, when a man named Teodoro Francisco de Aguirre denounced his nephew and a small group of criollos for plotting to achieve the independence of Mexico and the expulsion of the gachupines. From the beginning, no one placed much faith in the abilities of the conspirators; the leader, Pedro Portilla, aged twenty-four, was a minor civil servant from Toluca and the others were young criollos from the lower classes. None had the connections, abilities, ideas, or capacity for leadership needed to inspire revolution. But the mere mention of the criollo-gachupín split was cause enough for Azanza to treat the plot as if it endangered the regime. All efforts were made prior to the arrest of suspects to determine the full scope of the conspiracy. Joaquín Mosquera took charge of the investigation and presided over a junta formed to discuss procedures. When sufficient evidence had been collected, thirteen suspects were arrested—the majority during one of their meetings.[91] The case was handled with full security to prevent public discussion of the matter, but these precautions did not prevent widespread comment and interest.

All of the most incriminating evidence hinged upon the testimony of Aguirre, whom the viceroy described as having proved his loyalty and honor in twenty-seven years' service in the army, Acordada, and royal treasury. For denouncing the plot, Azanza rewarded Aguirre with a government post outside Mexico City to protect him from possible harassment or physical harm. When Marquina checked into Aguirre's past record, however, he found the principal denunciant in the case to be a distinctly unsavory and untrustworthy character. The director general of the Tobacco Monopoly, for whom Aguirre now worked, reported that he was useless and often absent without permission. Even worse, the chief judge of the Acordada testified that while Aguirre was employed as a lieutenant of the tribunal, not only had his behavior been questionable, but he had been dismissed for negligence in the deaths of two prisoners.[92] Marquina suspected that Aguirre had supported and even nourished the plot with the full intention of exposing it and gaining recognition for his loyalty.

Marquina, like the Council of the Indies which reviewed the evidence, doubted the gravity of the conspiracy. After reexamination, it was obvious that the whole project lacked planning; it was the work of young, uneducated, socially inoffensive and even humble men who possessed none of the talents needed to act upon the ideas attributed to them. Correction rather than punishment seemed to be the best way to proceed.[93] For these reasons, Marquina saw no reason to submit the case for trial in the Real Sala del Crimen where the affair would gain a prominence or notoriety it did not deserve. Once the evidence got into the hands of lawyers, scribes, and the families of the accused, the charges would draw considerable attention. When the criollos considered the fact that the audiencia judges who had to decide on guilt or innocence in such cases were gachupines, the general ramifications might be disastrous. Certainly, the discussions about the conspiracy could not help but spawn rumors and exacerbate the relationship between Europeans and criollos. In Marquina's opinion, the old disaffection between the two groups was an antiquated fantasy that had no place in the nineteenth century. Everything possible should be done to end disputes between Spaniards of the two origins.[94]

In this case, Marquina made a wise decision although his knowledge of the bad blood between criollos and gachupines was superficial. Within a few years, the pressures of nearly two decades of war, which had weakened the Spanish Empire and caused constant internal and external disruptions, culminated with the Napoleonic invasion of mother Spain. In the confusion, what had been mere suspicions or minor disagreements became deep rifts. The

European Spaniards came to see more and more signs of separatist tendencies amongst the criollos. Both sides believed rumors of expulsion, death threats, and other gossip that in normal times would have been dismissed out of hand. Both ruling groups were paralyzed by mistrust which led them to make the worst possible decisions. The enemy was no longer a mass of plebeians or a foreign nation intent upon acquiring the wealth of New Spain; now it was a fearful revolutionary tide undermining the very pillars of society. This feeling was what had motivated Ciriaco Cevallos to issue his decree isolating the French schooner *Vaillant*. In his opinion, the slightest brush with the infection of French ideas was enough to pollute the entire society.[95] Fears which fueled the riots at Veracruz strained relationships between groups that had to work together if the regime was to be maintained. In Mexico City, the overthrow of Iturrigaray appeared to confirm the darkest charges. For the army and its commanders, the situation assumed nightmare proportions.

5

THE ARMY BUREAUCRACY AND THE BOURBON ADMINISTRATION

It was one thing to introduce an army into a predominantly unmilitary society and quite another to do so during a period of far-reaching administrative reform. Beginning with the expulsion of the Jesuits and the Gálvez visitation (1765–71), Mexicans were to be challenged by constant change inspired by the reform-oriented regime of Charles III. The criollo elite, far more powerful than historians have traditionally believed, discovered that enlightened despotism meant an effort to stimulate the economy, to regain imperial control over lost or diverted revenues, and, most important of all, to replace criollos who held senior posts in the colonial administration. Throughout the Americas, the audiencias, long dominated by the criollos, became the targets of José de Gálvez when he became minister of the Indies. By the end of the 1780s, peninsular oidores replaced most criollos, and in New Spain only three of eleven judges were American-born.[1] With the introduction of the system of intendancies in 1786, Mexico received a new group of powerful peninsular administrators who had to establish their own personal authority and to implement a governmental structure untested in the Mexican situation. Since many of these officials came directly from the Spanish military, they were to bring a particularly disciplined view to their new tasks.[2]

Well before the implementation of the administrative reforms, it was evident that the army with its own bureaucracy and privileged fueros did not fit easily into the existing political system. Each jurisdiction, jealous of its own rights and prerogatives, struggled to prevent encroachments into its own special preserves. Even within the high command of the army, viceroys and inspectors general were often at complete loggerheads. Reduction of the second-in-command to sub-inspector general after 1783 did nothing to end conflicts whenever personalities did not mesh. Yet despite their reluctance to delegate control over the army, few viceroys could hope to release themselves from the enormous executive pressures of their office to find time for military affairs. Defense planning, monthly status reports for the imperial government,[3] recruitment, finance, promotions, service records, and regular inspections required the introduction of a substantial bureaucracy headed by an officer who had sufficient power to make routine decisions on his own. In theory, the office demanded constant travel to conduct inspections, training missions, and audits. Wherever the sub-inspector went he was accompanied by his secretarial staff to record his findings and to maintain the extensive military archives. If, on the other hand, the sub-inspector decided to settle in Mexico City or Veracruz where he could do justice to his other duties, inspections became more infrequent and haphazard, officer and soldier debts accumulated, and the general level of military efficiency and discipline declined.

During the 1780s, there were efforts to define the duties of the sub-inspector general and to have him take interim military command of the viceroyalty in cases of indisposition or the viceroy's death.[4] Probably this was done to end some of the problems stemming from the lack of continuity in the chief executive's office, but the idea caused more difficulties than it solved. The sub-inspector interpreted the situation to mean that he had the right to succeed the viceroy. The audiencia, which normally assumed the executive power when there was no *pliego de providencia*,* challenged the right of a military officer to hold command independent of the other senior branches of government. After much debate, a royal order of January 26, 1786, placed succession to the captaincy general under the control of the *real acuerdo* of the audiencia. Command of the army succeeded directly to the audiencia with the sub-inspector general serving under the orders of the *real acuerdo*. In the event of a defensive emergency, the regent of the audiencia was to act in accord with the sub-inspector—with a full account, at the earliest opportunity, of any decisions being submitted to the full body.[5] When this order was repeated in 1789, Viceroy Revillagigedo opposed it arguing that civilian magistrates were ill-equipped to command the army. He recommended passing military command to the governor of Veracruz or to the sub-inspector general and political command to a civilian judge.[6]

Although nothing was done to implement this proposal, Revillagigedo was

---

*A sealed document indicating the king's orders on who should assume power in case of the viceroy's death or incapacity.

successful in uniting the sub-inspectorship to the office of governor-intendant of Veracruz in the person of his colleague, Pedro de Gorostiza.[7] The amalgamation of these important offices was considered to be a cheap and efficient means of terminating chronic disputes between the intendant of Veracruz and the commander of the garrison. In fact, the new arrangement did not work out as anticipated. Gorostiza was torn between his responsibilities as sub-inspector and executive officer needed in the capital to advise the viceroy on promotions and military policy, and his equally important duties as governor-intendant at the port. By isolating his sub-inspector general, Revillagigedo's reform reduced army efficiency and weakened his ability to introduce new military policies. To make matters even worse, Gorostiza fell ill and passed the last few years of his office at Jalapa away from the unhealthful climate of Veracruz. While Revillagigedo was willing to tolerate this situation during Gorostiza's lifetime, he suggested that, in the future, inspection and record keeping could be transferred to the provincial intendants. In this case, a central office within the viceregal secretariat would be sufficient to maintain the military archives and to perform the essential task of keeping the service records.[8]

If Revillagigedo was willing to delay these changes to protect Gorostiza, the Marqués de Branciforte felt no similar restraints. As has been seen, the two officers disagreed over the form of the army and they soon developed a hearty dislike for each other. By the time of Gorostiza's death in November 1794, Branciforte had by-passed the sub-inspector and taken full control over the army.[9] Now liberated from interference, he lost no time in absorbing the office into the viceregency. Branciforte justified this action on a number of grounds. First, the sub-inspector general had not been able to devote adequate attention to Veracruz; this led to increased contraband and other problems prejudicial to the port city. Second, his studies of the military archives showed a recurrence of disputes between viceroys and sub-inspectors dating back to the formation of the army. Third, Branciforte wanted a free hand to implement his own program of militia reorganization.[10] Once the new army took shape, he planned to adopt Crespo's proposal for a series of militia brigades. Each commander could handle the inspection of units within the jurisdiction of his own brigade. The commander of the brigade encompassing Mexico City would also be responsible for the regular army units stationed in the capital, Puebla, Perote, and Veracruz.[11]

In reality, however, the administration of the army fell to a few overworked officers in the viceregal secretariat. The brigades were not formed until 1800 which meant that there was no one specifically encharged with this vital function. Colonel Antonio Bonilla held the office of secretary of New Spain from 1788 to 1800,[12] but since he was occupied with other responsibilities for much of the period, he did not play a major role in army government. This task fell to Major Manuel Pastor, a Spanish officer who had come to Mexico with Sub-Inspector General José Ezpeleta. Pastor's administrative career began in Spain and North Africa and he served for two years as secretary of the captaincy general of Louisiana. Transferred to New Spain in 1786, Viceroy Conde de Gálvez appointed him *secretaría de cámara* or third officer of what was supposed to become a department of war. Viceroy Flórez had not permitted the department of war to separate from the secretariat, but Pastor remained in his post where he developed outstanding expertise on the confusing military constitution of New Spain. Sub-Inspector General Mendinueta appointed him to take charge of the service records and military archives and Pastor moved to Veracruz, Jalapa, or wherever necessary to act in the same capacity under Gorostiza. When Branciforte took over the duties of sub-inspector general, Pastor continued to serve as senior officer in the department of war of the secretariat.[13]

Unfortunately, the viceroys who depended upon Pastor to perform the duties of *de facto* sub-inspector general failed to recognize him as anything other than a quiet, efficient, and economical officer. By 1800 he had made four long journeys with the military archives to follow his superiors and to serve in the cantonments. Not only had these trips cost him a great deal of his own money, but he found that other officers of his rank and seniority who had much less responsibility were being promoted before him. Indeed, Pastor, who was nominally the major of the provincial Cavalry Regiment of Querétaro, had become so valuable in the secretariat that Viceroy Marquina blocked his resignation. The viceroy was new to Mexico and with the complications of wartime defense, he needed an experienced officer to look after army administration. Finally, Pastor complained to the crown about his condition. Marquina denied having exerted pressure to keep him in the secretariat, but he agreed that no officer possessed a similar knowledge of the military constitution and the operations of the inspectorship.[14]

Quite clearly, the militia brigades were needed to alleviate some of the pressures upon the viceroys and the secretariat. Branciforte attempted to find a solution to the confusing military structure and in 1797, he began to collect data and to consider the formation of an *ordenanza general* for the army of New Spain. The different types of troops and the varying privileges made the task exceptionally difficult and he fell back upon the brigade system to bring better organization. Branciforte started to establish some of the brigades, suspending his efforts when he received word that he was to be replaced. Since no successor appeared, he returned to the task which he considered crucial to proper administration of the army.[15] There were to be ten brigades, some led by existing military commanders and others newly created. The viceroy saw the possibility of saving salaries by posting military intendants to some provinces and investing them with the command of a brigade. In the end, however, only the Tenth Brigade of San Luis Potosí came into active existence under the command of Félix Calleja. Viceroy Azanza received the royal order confirming Calleja's appointment and he introduced the remainder of the brigades, making use of the intendants as commanders wherever possible.[16] (See table 8.)

TABLE 8
Militia Brigades of the Army of New Spain, 1800–1810.

First Brigade of Mexico: Commander, Carlos de Urrutía.	
Provincial Infantry Regiment of Mexico	845
Provincial Infantry Regiment of Toluca	845
Urban Regiment of Commerce of Mexico	702
Urban Squadron of Mexico	129
3rd Division, Costa del Sur	250
Reserve Companies of the Intendancy of Mexico	—
TOTAL	2,771
Second Brigade of Puebla: Commander, Intendant Manuel de Flon.	
Provincial Infantry Regiment of Tlaxcala	845
Provincial Infantry Regiment of Puebla	845
Provincial Infantry Regiment of Tres Villas	845
Provincial Dragoon Regiment of Puebla	367
Urban Battalion of Commerce of Puebla	228
Reserve Companies of the Intendancy of Puebla	—
TOTAL	3,130
Third Brigade of Veracruz: Commander, Governor-Intendant of Veracruz.	
Provincial Lancer Corps of Veracruz	1,000
Companies of Pardos and Morenos	210
1st Division, Costa del Norte	400
2nd Division, Costa del Norte	670
3rd Division, Costa del Norte	789
4th Division, Costa del Norte	600
TOTAL	3,669
Fourth Brigade of Tabasco: Commander, Governor of Tabasco.	
Militias of Tabasco	910
Fifth Brigade of Presidio del Carmen: Commander, Governor of the Presidio	
Regular Infantry Company of Presidio del Carmen	143
Militias of Presidio del Carmen	300
TOTAL	443

continued

TABLE 8, continued

Sixth Brigade, Costa del Sur: Commander, Castellano of Acapulco	
Regular Infantry Company of Acapulco	77
4th Division, Costa del Sur	300
Reserve Companies of Tuxtla and Chilapa	—
TOTAL	377
Seventh Brigade of Oaxaca: Commander, Lieutenant Colonel Bernardino Bonavía	
Provincial Infantry Battalion of Oaxaca	423
5th Division, Costa del Sur	450
6th Division, Costa del Sur	580
7th Division, Costa del Sur	400
Reserve Companies of the Intendancy of Oaxaca	—
TOTAL	1,853
Eighth Brigade of Querétaro: Commander, Colonel Ignacio García Revollo	
Provincial Infantry Regiment of Valladolid	845
Provincial Infantry Regiment of Celaya	845
Provincial Infantry Battalion of Guanajuato	423
Provincial Cavalry Regiment of Querétaro	367
Provincial Cavalry Regiment of the Príncipe	367
Provincial Dragoon Regiment of the Queen	367
Provincial Dragoon Regiment of Michoacán	367
Frontier Militia of Sierragorda	240
TOTAL	3,821
Ninth Brigade of Nueva Galicia: Commander, Comandante General of Nueva Galicia.	
Provincial Infantry Battalion of Guadalajara	423
Provincial Dragoon Regiment of Nueva Galicia	367
Frontier Militia of Colotlán	720
1st Division, Costa del Sur	680
2nd Division, Costa del Sur	774
Regular Infantry Company of San Blas	105
Reserve Companies of the Intendancy of Guadalajara	—
TOTAL	3,069
Tenth Brigade of San Luis Potosí: Commander, Colonel Félix Calleja.	
Provincial Dragoon Regiment of San Luis	367
Provincial Dragoon Regiment of San Carlos	367
Frontier Militia of Nueva Santander	360
Flying Companies of Nueva Santander	225
Militia Companies of Nueva Santander	2,000
Flying Company of Nuevo León	100
Militia Companies of Nuevo León	1,000
TOTAL	4,419
TOTAL ENLISTED IN ALL BRIGADES	24,462

Source: Noticia que manifiesta el número de tropas de que constan los Cuerpos provinciales, urbanos, y demas milicias del reino de Nueva España con algunas veteranas fixas, su reparto en divisiones ó brigadas... , March, 1800, AGN, IG, vol. 386-A.

Azanza agreed with Branciforte that the brigade system would end any need for a sub-inspector general. Such an officer could not be expected to inspect all of the militia units; the new brigade commanders would have the advantage of knowing their units, the best time for inspections, and the troops' social composition.[17] The commander of the First Brigade of Mexico could look after the inspection of the regular army, relieving the viceroy of this responsibility. In order to make the new system even more effective, Azanza proposed that all brigade commanders be promoted to the rank of brigadier so they would not be outranked by the colonels of regular regiments. He strongly recommended the merits of Colonel Calleja, who had his brigade formed and in an excellent state of training.[18]

Although the crown was not prepared to create ten new brigadiers, the system itself received royal sanction.[19] Azanza prepared a set of regulations to govern the brigades until such time as an *ordenanza general* for the army might be adopted. Commanders received full and exclusive control over all legal cases of individuals who held the *fuero de guerra*. Appeals from the brigade commander in criminal or civil cases and in jurisdictional disputes went to the captaincy general. Brigade commanders were to watch over the militia units and to make sure that local officers enforced army regulations, avoided delays in bringing cases to trial, and maintained proper relations with other legal jurisdictions. In cases against militia colonels and commandants, the brigade commander served as the judge of the first instance. Finally, these officers exercised all inspection functions and were responsible for keeping the units under their command up to full strength.[20]

Despite some relief from routine administrative duties for the viceroys and the secretariat, the brigade system was by no means a panacea. By the beginning of the nineteenth century, far too much power had been concentrated in the viceroy's hands. Like his predecessors, Viceroy Marquina had difficulty finding time for even five hours' sleep per night. The pressure of mechanical tasks—principally signing documents—was enough to exhaust any man. There was no time left over for mature reflection upon important decisions. The viceroy still had to pass judgment upon the merits of officers recommended for promotion although in most cases he had no acquaintance with the men or the places where they served. Marquina asked to have some of the more routine military duties of his office assigned to subordinates, who might also be given some authority to sign service records and promotion proposals being forwarded to the imperial government. The crown rejected this request, recalling Branciforte's argument that the brigade system would distribute the duties of inspection among the various commanders.[21] In Marquina's opinion, however, the brigades had increased rather than diminished the administrative load upon the viceroy. It was now necessary to examine many more reports and proposals of the brigade commanders as well as to investigate some of the complaints made against them.[22] Moreover, full responsibility for the regular infantry and dragoon units, including those serving overseas, remained directly attached to the viceroy. Marquina and then his successor, José de Iturrigaray, did not have any time to devote to these units. As a consequence, the regular army ceased to function with any degree of efficiency; instead of posing an example of martial virtues, the regulars became a real detriment to the army. Both viceroys saw no possibility of improving this situation without the restoration of the sub-inspector general.[23]

The regular regiments went for years without inspections or any controls other than those of the internal command structure. Errors were permitted to become chronic abuses—training and discipline deteriorated, debts to the regiment were not paid off, and records were not maintained. Much of the trouble could be traced to the transfer of the regiments to overseas duty, the high death and desertion levels at Veracruz, and the green militiamen who were pressed into regular service. On the other hand, the lack of direction from a sub-inspector general or some other senior commander contributed to the general decline. Once the damage had been done, it was very difficult to restore an acceptable level of efficiency. In 1798, for example, Azanza discovered that the Regiments of Puebla and Mexico had not been inspected since 1790.[24] Although both units were stationed overseas, the Mexican authorities had blocked efforts by the sub-inspector general of Havana to investigate recruitment and internal administration. The argument was that once Havana officers took over this function, there would be no possibility of obtaining the return of the regiments.[25] Azanza commissioned Brigadier José Fernández Abascal, lieutenant of the king at Havana, to conduct full inspections. He reported that the Regiment of Puebla was in disastrous condition and that he could not conduct a meaningful inspection of the Regiment of Mexico since it was split between Havana and New Orleans.[26]

The Regiment of New Spain was not inspected from the time of its formation in 1788 until 1804, when Viceroy Iturrigaray had no alternative other than to take action or watch the unit disintegrate entirely. He commissioned Brigadier Conde de Alcaraz to inspect the regiment and to curb absolutely enormous debts. The accounts were in such chaos that verification of what had taken place over the years was impossible.[27] Between 1798 and 1803, a total of 2,418 soldiers had passed through the unit—698 deserted without recapture, leaving debts of 8,272 pesos, and 866 died, leaving debts totalling 8,904 pesos. Officers had run up debts of 39,747 pesos, including one sum of 8,912 pesos left by Field Marshal Pedro Garibay, who was then in Madrid.[28]

Needless to say, Iturrigaray used this evidence to request the immediate appointment of a sub-inspector general.

Despite this evidence, nothing was done until 1809 when Archbishop Lizana became viceroy. The appointment of a nonmilitary viceroy made further delay impossible. Brigadier Carlos de Urrutía, commander of the Brigade of Mexico, was made governor-intendant of Veracruz and sub-inspector general of the army of New Spain.[29] The inexcusable neglect of the regular army is difficult to explain except in terms of the over-concentration of authority and the refusal to delegate administrative functions to subordinates. As will be seen in subsequent chapters, fiscal chaos was not the only weakness to be found in the regular army. Officers who permitted these abuses to accumulate over the years were no more dedicated to training, discipline, or any other aspect of regimental government.

Besides this inability to carry out inspections, the viceroys could not possibly manage the volume of legal cases and appeals directed to the captaincy general. To obtain the best legal assistance, they turned to one of the oidores of the audiencia, who, in addition to his regular duties, assumed the office of *auditor de guerra*. The system operated smoothly enough when there were few military units in New Spain, but after 1764 the expansion of the army multiplied the numbers of appeals and conflicts. By 1789, there was a heavy backlog of cases awaiting the attention of the *auditor de guerra,* Miguel Bataller y Vasco. These included important criminal cases, appeals where severe penalties had been assessed by courts-martial, jurisdictional disputes (*competencias*) between the army and other tribunals, and a wide range of legal matters relating to the regular and militia forces.[30] In fact, the *auditor* had to examine the transcript of every case involving most common crimes such as desertion. His obligation was to watch over proper form and judicial procedures and he often altered sentences before passing the cases to the viceroy for final decision. As might be expected, this last step was almost always a perfunctory signature accompanied by the statement, *"como parece al Señor Auditor."* Not only did this magistrate exercise considerable discretionary power over the army, but he could also either speed or retard the legal process according to his need. To prevent delays and disruptions of justice, Viceroy Flórez recommended the removal of the *auditor* from his regular duties in the audiencia so that he would devote full time to the army.

The proposal was not adopted and by 1791, Bataller had to review a total of 1,236 cases. While he left only 11 cases pending at the end of the year, the pressures of his other obligations as a *juez de colegios* and on the appeals court for the mining tribunal left him almost no free time. Though Viceroy Revillagigedo showed no sign of questioning Bataller's ability at seventy years of age to manage this administrative load, the *auditor de guerra*'s health suffered. Noticing this, one of the most junior oidores, Hemeterio Cacho Calderón, took matters into his own hands and wrote to the imperial government requesting the position. Revillagigedo reacted angrily; he saw no reason why Bataller should not continue in office and he opposed the idea of any subordinate going over his head to petition the crown. Furthermore, since Cacho lacked seniority his promotion would cause great scandal among his colleagues. It was the custom for the viceroy to select the oidor he considered best suited for the office.[31] Bataller, a strong supporter of Revillagigedo's policies, could be trusted to support him on crucial political issues.[32]

At the end of October 1794, Bataller requested a three-month vacation to regain his strength. Viceroy Branciforte, looking for an excuse to appoint an *auditor* more attuned to his policies, agreed to the leave of absence, noting "this worthy minister suffers the incurable attacks of old age." He selected the ambitious Cacho Calderón to take the interim post pending royal appointment, oblivious to his predecessor's arguments about audiencia seniority.[33] A most adept politician, Cacho had become an early supporter of Branciforte's military policies. While he was a comparative newcomer to New Spain, he had made a good reputation for hard work in the audiencia of the Philippines (he had also survived a shipwreck in the Marianas Islands and attacks by Philippine Moro pirates). In 1787, he was promoted to *alcalde del crimen* in the audiencia of Mexico. As *auditor de guerra,* Cacho dealt with an increasing volume of military litigation and he gave Branciforte the legal help necessary to overcome obstacles to rapid army expansion. During the cantonment of 1797 and 1798, Cacho moved his office to Orizaba where he could dispense military justice without lengthy delays. Viceroy Azanza ordered him back to Mexico City to look after accumulating cases, but in 1800 he returned to Orizaba when Viceroy Marquina raised a new cantonment. By this time, however, the pressures of office had weakened his health, and the recurrence of an old illness dating back to his days in the Philippines forced his resignation. He died in December 1803, leaving a wife and a young family.[34]

Iturrigaray selected *Oidor* Guillermo de Aguirre to take charge of the auditorship, but he refused because of delicate health and his fear that the challenge of the position was simply too much for him.[35] The weight of criminal cases, appeals, and other litigation entering the auditor's office and the noticeable increase in the volume of work convinced the viceroy to divide the position into two parts—one including the regular army units and the war department of the secretariat, and the other, the provincial and urban militias. *Alcalde del Crimen* Joaquín de Mosquera received the appointment to take charge of the regular army and Miguel Bataller, son of the former *auditor,* the militia units.³⁶ The division ended the backlog problem, but in 1806 Mosquera was commissioned to investigate unrest in Caracas and Bataller was given control over both sections.

This was a temporary expedient because Iturrigaray needed an *auditor de guerra* to prevent legal disputes at the cantonment towns of Jalapa, Orizaba, and Córdoba. Rather than appointing another *oidor* whose absence from the audiencia—particularly if he was an *alcalde del crimen*—damaged the administration of justice, the viceroy named a civilian lawyer, José Antonio del Cristo y Conde, to serve as *auditor* of the regular and provincial units stationed at the cantonments.³⁷ After the dissolution of the cantonments, Bataller assumed control over both branches of the army, but he could not handle the number of cases which came before him. When Mosquera was elected to the Junta Suprema government in Spain by the province of Caracas, *Oidor* Melchor Foncerrada became *auditor* for the regular army.³⁸

Despite Bourbon reliance upon army officers to fill a large number of the administrative positions in New Spain, the *auditor de guerra* was always a civilian. Through this important position, the audiencia was able to keep the army within certain limits and to monitor martial justice at a time when military privileges were extended to a fairly wide sector of the population. Although the position was not used to resist viceregal decisions concerning the army, the fact that the *auditor* did all of the work and wrote the decisions in cases that had been appealed to the captain general meant that he could modify anomalies emerging from the courts-martial or more specifically from military magistrates intent upon expanding their powers at the civilian tribunals' expense. Using the mechanism of the *auditor de guerra*, military justice was brought under the same appeals framework as ordinary criminal and civil cases.

Before proceeding any further, we must examine the relationship between the army and the intendancy system. As might be expected, the intendants exerted significant influence over the military. The first intendants in Spain had been *intendentes de ejército* and the provincial intendants retained many of their fiscal and administrative powers over the army.³ In New Spain, José de Gálvez and the intendant system's supporters encountered stiff resistance from entrenched interests and from some of the more intelligent conservatives who saw little advantage to be gained through a wholesale administrative upheaval. Viceroy Bucareli, supported by the Conde de Tepa and others, recommended continuation of district administration in the hands of the alcaldes mayores; they denied the need for a new level of officials who would become powerful provincial governors.⁴⁰ In Tepa's opinion, the military duties of the Spanish intendants could not be adapted to Mexico, where the army was almost nonexistent and there were no *quintas* or levies.[41] Even with temporary delays, Gálvez was not to be denied in his effort to modernize the bureaucracy, end the abuses of the alcaldes mayores, and increase imperial revenues. The *Ordenanzas de Intendentes* of 1786 created twelve new intendancies—México, Puebla, Veracruz, Guanajuato, Valladolid, Oaxaca, Guadalajara, Zacatecas, San Luis Potosí, Sonora, Durango, and Yucatán. The powers of the intendants were divided into four general areas—justice, war, exchequer, and *policía* (general administration).

Under the heading of war, the intendants received broad powers to govern the relationship between the army and the royal treasury—pay, supply, provisions, and responsibility for military hospitals. Each month they were to inspect all units within their jurisdiction to verify that no attempts were being made to collect salaries for soldiers who were not present. In view of these duties, they were always to be included in the discussions and decisions of the *juntas de guerra*.[42] Finally, article 302 of the *Ordenanzas* left no doubt about the importance the regime attached to the new administrators; all intendants were to receive the military honors and guard of a general field marshal. To direct the provincial intendants and to reduce the viceroy's powers, Gálvez created the office of superintendent or *intendente de ejército y real hacienda*. This post went to Fernando José Mangino, a Gálvez loyalist and superintendent of the Mexico City mint. As might be expected, Mangino encountered heavy opposition even before he assumed control over military finance. He managed to assume some of the routine treasury functions connected with the regular army in 1787, but he was severely hindered by lack of knowledge about the military ordinances. His office requested copies of various regulations, *ordenanzas*, and royal declarations on the army needed in the library of the new secretariat of the *intendencia general de ejército*.[43] Before these documents arrived from Spain, viceregal hostility to the superintendent halted any degree of cooperation. Flórez, like the viceroys of other provinces confronted by a competitor for control over the purse strings, did his best to exclude Mangino from any of the prerogatives he defined as the exclusive possession of the captain general.[44] The death of Gálvez and the opposition to every initiative of the superintendent induced the imperial government to change its policy; Mangino was promoted to the Council of Indies and his office was reincorporated into the viceregency.[45]

The controversy for and against the intendancies became so intense by 1789 that officials in Spain could not determine whether or not the reforms served any purpose. Revillagigedo was given specific instructions to investigate the welter of charges and to make definite proposals.[46] His reply, "Everything here is a chaos of confusion," described the situation very well. In the last seven years, Mexico had been governed by four viceroys, the audiencia, and the archbishop. To compound the lack of continuity, bureaucratic reforms had disrupted the lower levels of the government and created an entirely new set of provincial governors. The result was fiscal turmoil and a general breakdown of proper administrative practice. To Revillagigedo, the intendancies, considered by many as a remedy for all ailments, were no such thing in a country which lacked sufficient police and a solid laboring population.[47]

At the same time, however, Revillagigedo viewed the new system as an essential precondition to reform and as a significant improvement over the previous administration. Like Flórez, he blamed some of the early problems upon the appointment of a superintendent who controlled the provincial intendants and the royal exchequer. This official interfered with viceregal power and created "a two-headed monster" that could not govern New Spain. As for those who opposed the provincial intendancies, Revillagigedo dismissed their reactionary caviling: they were the same prophets of gloom who predicted disaster from the creation of the royal mint, the administration of the *alcabalas* by government officials, the policies of Visitador Gálvez, and the military expedition of Juan de Villalba to raise defensive forces.[48] Rather than supporting those who wanted to suppress the intendancies, Revillagigedo wanted to create new ones—particularly in the Provincias Internas where the economy needed stimulation and hostile Indians paralyzed settlement, commerce, and mining. In these provinces, the new administrators would have to be the senior military commanders as well as the political leaders. Elsewhere, the intendants would serve to overcome distance, a dispersed population, and the "natural laziness" of the Mexican people.[49]

Even in the more settled regions of New Spain, Revillagigedo wanted some of the intendancies governed by army officers. Although the army might be increased as needs dictated, he was concerned about the shortage of generals or senior officers to command the garrisons of ports, cities, and frontiers. The contrary was true in the fields of justice, administration, and royal exchequer where there were civilian magistrates "in their multitudes"—albeit at high salaries that strained the treasury. There seemed to be little sense in appointing new civilian intendants if army commanders were also needed. The result would be too many heads and difficulty in reaching any decision that required a combination of separate civilian and army governors. One intendant invested with a broad range of powers would be able to avoid jurisdictional clashes, economize on salaries, and simplify the administrative structure. Veracruz was the most obvious choice for rule by a governor-intendant. The same arguments were made for Puebla where there was a large regular garrison, a number of provincial units, problems with troops in transit, and obligations to produce adequate provisions during cantonments. Without conferring military command upon the intendant, he would be subordinate to the ranking officer of the garrison who might be in Mexico City or elsewhere. As his ideas formed, Revillagigedo proposed to rank the intendancies in three classes according to their military status. Veracruz, México, Guadalajara, and Yucatán would be the senior posts, commanded by field marshals or brigadiers, while Puebla and Sonora, in the second category, might be governed by officers of the rank of colonel. Other intendancies, such as Guanajuato, Valladolid, and Oaxaca, did not necessarily require a military officer.[50]

It was one thing to plan the intendancies and quite another to make the system live up to expectations. From the beginning, conflicts of authority and jurisdictional disputes marred the relationship between the army and the intendants. In 1788, Viceroy Flórez dispatched the Dragoon Regiment of Spain to help defend the population of Sonora against Indian incursions.[51] The unit arrived in Durango to encounter food shortages and a complete lack of adequate housing—matters which fell under the responsibility of Intendant Felipe Díaz de Ortega. Harvest failures and frontier conditions caused some of the difficulties, but the dragoon commander, Colonel Vicente Moreno, lost patience when his men did not have sufficient food. The result was an acrimonious dispute between the colonel and the intendant. The regiment failed to perform any of the duties assigned to it and many soldiers deserted. Rather than fighting Indians, the remainder of the troops requisitioned and ate the limited supplies of seed grain possessed by the inhabitants. Before the unit could be withdrawn to Querétaro, both soldiers and civilians had begun to suffer from hunger.[52]

Although the frontier aggravated relationships, the intendants of most provinces experienced difficulties with local army commanders. In Puebla there was so much confusion over seniority that some officers questioned orders originating from the intendancy. When militia Lieutenant Antonio Junco denied the right of Intendant Manuel de Flon to give him any commands, the issue came to a head.[53] Flon lost his temper and ordered some regular dragoons to throw Junco into jail. The outraged lieutenant emerged from this experience to petition the imperial government for redress and to demand the removal of the intendant from office. Revillagigedo did not condone Flon's actions, but used the incident to press for unification of military command with the intendancy. Because of its importance, Puebla had been designated as a military governorship in 1754.[54] With the new administrative system, however, military command had been awarded to the most senior officer stationed in the city. In the short time Flon had been intendant, the military governorship was held by the colonel of the Dragoon Regiment of Mexico, the colonel of the provincial Dragoon Regiment of Puebla, and the colonel of the Dragoon Regiment of Spain. Each time the office changed hands, the level of law and order deteriorated. By 1790, a criminal gang led by José Madera attempted a daring assault on the prison of the acordada to liberate some of the prisoners. Fortunately, the gang had been intercepted by an army patrol which drove them off after an exchange of fire. Revillagigedo sent the Dragoon Regiment of Spain and six companies of the Regiment of the Crown to help the local law-enforcement officials end the rising crime wave. With this sort of evidence to back his arguments for a unified political and military intendancy, Revillagigedo obtained a royal order granting his request.[55]

There were similar frictions in Guanajuato where Colonel Antonio Pérez Gálvez disputed the right of Intendant Antonio Riaño to exercise military command. Riaño held the naval rank of frigate lieutenant, much inferior to the colonelcy that Pérez Gálvez had purchased. Since the intendant based his claim upon the royal order dealing with Puebla in 1790, Pérez Gálvez argued that his regiment had been raised subsequent to the ruling and that military command of Guanajuato belonged to him.[56] Azanza ruled for the intendant, but Pérez Gálvez raised the issue again in 1802 and 1809. On both occasions, the *auditor de guerra* and the viceroys rejected his pretensions.[57]

Much of the trouble in Guanajuato resulted from the fact that Riaño took his duties seriously and intervened actively in military matters which also came under his jurisdiction. Concentrating upon his first mission, which was to increase royal revenues, Riaño suspected that many militiamen enlisted in the provincial Cavalry Regiment of the Príncipe were *tributarios* who joined the militia to escape annual payment of the head tax. Instead of requesting information from the colonel, Riaño sent his agent, Antonio Ojanguren, to investigate enlistment in Silao. The local militia commandant was ordered to produce the regimental registers. Ojanguren declared at least ten militiamen to be *tributarios* and Viceroy Branciforte demanded a full examination of the regiment and enlistment procedures.[58] In fact, the baptismal records of the ten men had not been located. When the regiment conducted its own inquiry into individual cases, it was determined that two of the men were mulattoes and the rest were from castes eligible for enlistment. Pérez Gálvez blamed the dispute upon the confusing racial picture and the incapacity of bureaucrats who had to determine who paid tribute and who was exempt. Since even the oldest inhabitants of his regimental jurisdiction were perplexed when asked to identify the racial origins of their neighbors, the intervention of the intendant was pointless. The parish records shed no light upon classifications because those who registered the infant claimed to be white (Spaniards); if they were not well known, very few questions were asked. Besides, infants were difficult to place in a specific racial category and many mistakes occurred. Pérez Gálvez resented what he termed to be an unjustifiable encroachment upon his own personal authority.[59]

In Oaxaca, relations between Intendant Antonio de Mora y Peysal and the military were aggravated by economic issues and personal animosities. Lieutenant Colonel Juan Francisco de Echarrí, commander of the provincial Battalion of Oaxaca, blamed the intendant for numerous disputes between the military and the ordinary jurisdictions. According to Echarrí, Mora had attempted to convert the militia picket used to supplement police forces into a personal guard designed to flatter his own vanity. While Echarrí was aware that article 302 of the *Ordenanzas de intendentes* granted certain military honors to intendants, he refused to accept these in Oaxaca, where there were no troops on duty except the twelve men of the police picket. All of these men were needed to assist the city magistrates and to guard the jail which housed over two hundred criminals. Ever since the intendant had drawn off a corporal and four soldiers for his own residence, escapes from jail had become a significant concern. Besides, if the intendant deserved a special guard, then Echarrí wanted the same recognition as the battalion commander. Mora did not even have military rank to entitle him to this honor.[60]

Responding to the charges, Mora prepared a rebuttal with 191 articles which discredited much of Echarrí's case. The guard was sanctioned by viceregal decree and he denied any allegation that militiamen of the picket were being turned into his personal servants. More important, however, Mora described the atmosphere of intrigue and resentment common in Mexican provincial society. Echarrí, one of the most successful miners in the region, had attempted to befriend the intendant, offering him money, protection, and other favors. At one point, he proposed to smooth Mora's entry into the mining business, offering him investment capital and advice so that he might avoid the pitfalls of speculation. All had gone well until Echarrí became entangled in a legal battle over the Aurora mine—one of the richest in Oaxaca. When the intendant decided the case against the pretensions of Echarrí and in favor of the mine's legitimate owners, their friendship began to sour. Although the colonel made no effort to hide his disgust, he continued to look for favors and asked Mora to support his claim for deferment of the royal *quintos* and other taxes on silver produced from some of his mines. Since these mines were in full production, Mora saw no reason at all to support any subsidies. The final blow came in 1796 when the mining tribunal granted Oaxaca the privilege of electing a local deputation. Echarrí suffered a narrow loss in the race for the post as first deputy and then he attempted to invalidate the credentials of his opposition. Once again, Mora stepped in to demonstrate that the election had been legal. From this point forward, Echarrí stopped visiting the intendant and began to block his policies wherever possible.[61]

With the introduction of the militia brigades, the quarrels between Mora and the military became even more disruptive. The commander of the Seventh Militia Brigade of Oaxaca, Bernardo Bonavía, condemned the intendant for taking five soldiers away from essential police and guard duties; he added that the militiamen were locked in the entry hall of Mora's house from 10:30 P.M. to 6:30 A.M. Crime and chronic drunkenness were common in the city and the militia picket had to be available for patrol duty and to protect public buildings. Bonavía proposed an immediate increase in the size of the militia picket, but was not sure how to attract men to an obligation that was exceptionally unpopular.[62] They abandoned guardposts, slept during the night rounds, sold their badges and uniforms, and committed numerous other misdemeanors. Since there were so few men willing to serve at all, the officers were loath to impose even minor penalties.[63] Of course the results were disastrous. Law-enforcement officers such as Antonio María Izquierdo, *teniente letrado* of Oaxaca, lacked sufficient backing to enforce public order.

Mora blamed much of the trouble in Oaxaca upon the rivalries between the military authorities and the civilian magistrates. His own approach of using peace and harmony to settle petty disputes had been frustrated. By the end of 1807, the city was a hotbed of unrest and discord. The campaign to take away his small honor guard was, in Mora's view, the work of men who had old grudges to settle. When Bonavía had been subdelegate of the wealthy district of Villalta in Oaxaca, Mora encountered constant grievances and had to act on numerous occasions to halt illegal repartimientos and other despotic acts against the lower classes of the population.[64] Entrenched merchant and mining interests resisted the reforms introduced by the intendant system and used the provincial militia as one platform for this resistance. Bonavía, Echarrí, and other militia officers had complete control over the provincial battalion and also of the vitally important subdelegations. Mora, like other intendants, could not introduce a reform program on his own and he needed full cooperation to administer his province. Confronted with tenacious opposition at every step, he despaired of ever achieving sufficient control to introduce the *Ordenanza* of 1786.

In many of the new provinces, the intendants failed to attain sufficient mastery to make them effective agents of the army. With the suppression of the superintendent who was also to have been *intendente del ejército,* the viceroys discovered that it was often better to use special commissioners or to deal directly with authorities at the local level. Beginning with the cantonment of troops at Orizaba in 1797, however, Branciforte required much better organization and a fairly large staff to administer a force of seven thousand men. Indeed, the regiments and battalions were on the march to Orizaba before barracks, utensils, hospitals, and supplies were ready; no one understood the economic and social pressures created by the concentration of troops or by large-scale purchases of food and fuel.[65] To supervise these matters, the viceroy appointed the intendant of Zacatecas, Francisco Rendón,[66] to act as *intendente general provisional del ejército*. Rendón went to work immediately to transfer staff from other administrative offices to the new army intendancy. He selected a secretary, a treasurer, several good accountants, and some arithmeticians to manage accounts and to enforce treasury regulations. Since matters pertaining to pay and regimental expenditures were determined from the monthly inspections, Rendón named three *comisarios de guerra* and three subaltern treasurers who would reside in the towns of the cantonment. Their main function was to serve as guardians of the treasury and paymasters for the troops.[67]

Rather than organizing extensive warehouses and distribution centers to supply the army, Rendón chose to regulate the market place and to freeze commodity prices. Soldiers were given a maintenance allowance sufficient to pay for their own food and fuel needs.[68] The intendant would then regulate the activities of the cabildos and other provincial authorities so as to control prices and to ensure adequate supplies. Generally speaking, the system worked well; Rendón experienced some conflicts with the quartermaster general of the cantonment, Miguel Costansó, but these ended when Branciforte stationed both officers in Orizaba, where they could coordinate their operations.

When the crown disbanded the cantonment in 1798, Rendón returned to what he termed the "obscurity of Zacatecas." Although he pressed for the creation of a permanent army intendancy, the logic of his arguments escaped other observers. Viceroy Marquina attempted to do without a special intendant and fell back upon the services of the provincial intendants. When he raised a small cantonment at Jalapa in 1801, he ordered the intendant of Puebla, Manuel de Flon, to fix prices on essential food products and to regulate agricultural production so that there would be plentiful supplies of grain, meat, and vegetables.[69] Flon's inability to control prices let alone to enforce an agricultural plan led to the reestablishment of the *intendencia de guerra* in 1804. Viceroy Iturrigaray recalled Rendón, this time to Jalapa. As we have seen, the cantonment grew to eleven thousand in 1806 and, including the garrison of Veracruz, to seventeen thousand by 1808.[70]

The rapid expansion of the cantonment strained the supply system and alienated citizens who were thrown out of their homes to make way for the soldiers. At the same time, with economy the watchword of the army of operations, Rendón experienced difficulties maintaining the army in place let alone preparing for a possible rush to the coast to intercept an enemy invader. Since there were no towns between Jalapa and Veracruz which could furnish barracks, food, or forage for animals, the intendant could not rely upon the system of paying daily food allowances. Rendón labored to prepare supply bases and to accumulate provisions, but encountered spiraling prices, inferior goods, and untrustworthy civilian contractors. Even in the cantonment towns, facilities were not available to serve the expanded population. Hospitals at Jalapa, Córdoba, and Orizaba founded by religious orders to help the indigent were hopelessly overtaxed. Rendón pressed the government to establish a permanent *intendencia de guerra* similar to those of Spain, Havana, or Caracas, but his recommendations were not accepted. Instead, in June 1810, he returned once more to his civilian post at Zacatecas.[71]

By virtue of their position, high salary, and the rigorous selection process, the intendants retained a good reputation even if they could not perform any miracles once they took office. One of the real weaknesses of the new system lay in the failure of the intendants to extirpate the abuses and illegal practices of the old alcaldes mayores and corregidores. Changing the name of the local governor or district administrator to subdelegate and applying the *Ordenanzas de intendentes* did not alter the social system, the economic conditions, or the attitudes and relationships developed since the sixteenth and seventeenth centuries. It was at this level that the reformed institutions would receive their greatest test. The subdelegate, much more than the intendant, was the man at the focal point between the regime and much of the population. Unlike the viceroys, intendants, and others who engaged in rather speculative discussion about the ills of Mexican society, how to reform the economy, and so forth, the subdelegate actually had to implement policy and to find some means of balancing the often irreconcilable racial, social, and economic interests. At the same time he was to fulfill these missions, he found that the reforms curtailed his old freedom to make profits from his office. Throughout the viceroyalty, the alcaldes mayores had developed methods of generating income—particularly through the manipulation of judicial powers within their provinces.[72] Corruption, bribery, and extortion were endemic. Where possible, they monopolized commerce and, using the repartimiento, they issued goods or money to the Indians and castas in exchange for commodities or crops which they sold at much higher prices through merchants in the cities.

José de Gálvez and the reformers wanted to regain control over lost revenues and to place more trustworthy administrators into all levels of the bureaucracy. Although committed to these kinds of reforms, they had little interest in striking at the real inequities and inequalities of Mexican society.

Indeed, as we have seen before, some of the most enlightened reformers were at the same time the least sympathetic with Indians and castas. To compound the problems, the subdelegates received very poor salaries—often their income was not sufficient to permit a decent level of survival. It was difficult to find good men to take the subdelegations and quite naturally those who were willing reinforced the old illegal practices of supplementing income.[73] As historians of the eighteenth-century administrative reforms have pointed out, the subdelegates were the basic weakness in the new system.[74] The reformed administration served to expose the weak foundations, but did not strike at the real problems, which were shored up only temporarily by efforts at reform.

From the beginning of the defense program in the 1760s, the army posed as much a threat to the alcaldes mayores and later to the subdelegates as to any other legal jurisdiction. In order to maintain dominance over trade and repartimiento, as well as to control the population, these officials needed to monopolize the judicial system within their provinces. The moment they lost this control, their activities became easier to scrutinize and the possibilities of judicial conflicts and appeals to higher authorities increased. The army presented the most significant challenge because it granted some privileges through the *fuero militar* and exerted a presence which could serve as a focus for opposition. Since it extended some protection to nonelite sectors rather than exclusively to wealthy residents, it was considered more dangerous than other privileged jurisdictions. As a result, the subdelegates attempted to retard the militia and to enlist the most useless men in their districts.[75] It did not take long for militiamen or, more often, elements in local elites opposed to the subdelegate to see the possibilities in manipulating the military jurisdiction to escape the controls of the ordinary magistrates. Since most militia officers possessed only the vaguest notion of what privileges they enjoyed, the potential for disputes increased.

It is often exceptionally difficult to sort out the guilty and innocent in the large numbers of *competencias* (jurisdictional disputes) filed in the Mexican archives and to do so would not really advance our purpose. In most cases involving the alcaldes mayores or the subdelegates, however, the root of the quarrel was the basic divergence of interest and the realization that the army threatened their grip upon the population. When, for example, Colonel Pedro de Laguna visited Pacific coast communities in 1796, he found the conflicts between the civil and military authorities to be so detrimental to good government that he recommended the amalgamation of the two commands under one person. In his opinion, much of the trouble could be traced directly to a lack of intelligence on both sides and by officials each determined to extend their powers at the expense of the other. Frivolous quarrels soon became grave conflicts because each *teniente de justicia* believed that his powers were being trampled and each militia officer felt his poorly understood *fueros* were under attack. Both sides hastened to their respective superiors, painting the incident in their own favor so that the local commander and subdelegate were drawn into the fray. They interpreted the evidence from the reports of their subordinates and took up their arguments. Laguna saw these cases developing daily and described the situation as "a cancer which is propagating rapidly and must be remedied quickly."[76]

Once militiamen learned they could sometimes escape punishment from the ordinary royal jurisdiction, they exploited their new freedom. In Tehuacán, for example, workmen wearing the militia cockade formed gangs and went about at night drinking, playing guitars, and insulting the better residents of the town. They molested the guards at the customs house and tobacco monopoly, teasing the *comisarios* (police), who could not arrest them. On one occasion, the subdelegate and the administrator of the alcabalas were dining when they heard an enormous racket in the streets. Suspecting that some contrabandists had been apprehended, they rushed to give assistance. Instead, they discovered ten of the disruptive militiamen brawling with the customs guards. One of the troublemakers was caught and turned over to the comisario, but his accomplices freed the prisoner, beat the police officer, and then sought sanctuary in the parochial church. Later they thought better of their activities and returned a stolen musket. Their captain looked into this incident and then refused to take any disciplinary action.[77]

At Xalacingo in the intendancy of Veracruz, Subdelegate Baltasar Ruiz encountered similar abuse from militiamen of the local reserve company even though the unit did not possess a single musket. Neither the subdelegate nor the militia officers were certain how to interpret viceregal orders on the fuero militar. The subdelegate was willing to enforce Viceroy Branciforte's *bandos* requiring all authorities to send militiamen charged with crimes to the nearest military judge, but he was not sure whether this meant the colonel, some specially designated officer, or the local subalterns who happened to reside in the place where the offense had been committed.[78] The acting intendant, Colonel Diego García Panes, replied that according to the 1793 regulations on these militias, soldiers did not enjoy the civil fuero and came under the ordinary royal jurisdiction of the subdelegate.[79] This information did nothing to end conflicts in the small towns around Xalacingo between subaltern officers and the *tenientes de justicia* appointed by the subdelegate. Ruiz was not certain how many men in his province were enlisted, and had to write to Jalapa for the information. There were supposed to be eighty-four militiamen, but the justice of nearby Altotonga reported that the resident sublieutenant was enlisting men as fast as he could. All prospective recruits were told that they were free of the ordinary royal jurisdiction.[80] The militia commander, Captain Juan Baptista de la Torre, answered this accusation, stating that the royal magistrates under the subdelegate were going out of their way to harass militiamen. Finally, the competencias from Xalacingo had to be decided by the *auditor de guerra,* who explained the laws once again and ordered both sides to prevent minor disputes from degenerating into personality conflicts which obstructed the proper course of justice.[81]

Quite generally, the subdelegates resented the reduction in authority, the administrative confusion, and the obstructionism presented by the military. Militiamen arrested for minor offenses often had to be sent many leagues to their commanding officer for trial. In isolated Real de Catorce, Subdelegate Tómas Anteparaluzeta was accustomed to running the town according to his own interpretation of the laws. On one occasion, when Sergeant José Basilio Medellín of the provincial Cavalry Regiment of San Carlos arrived from Matehuala to sell charcoal to his regular customers, he was arrested by the comisario for not having obtained a written license. During the incident, Medellín resisted the authorities, received a severe beating, and lost his militia identification and fifty pesos. While he did not deny having behaved in a loud and rude manner, he claimed to be well known and respected in the valley. Since he was accustomed to selling charcoal at Catorce, the actions of the local authorities had angered him and caused his poor behavior. Medellín now petitioned his commander for restoration of his property.[82] In another dispute at Catorce, a soldier of the Cavalry Regiment of San Carlos, José Luz Mazatán, was arrested for gambling and jailed by the comisarios. When his militia commander, Captain Antonio Ynquanzo, sent a sergeant to transfer Mazatán into army custody, the subdelegate denied military jurisdiction over the case. Ynquanzo appealed to the regimental commander at San Luis Potosí; he demanded an end to opposition from Anteparaluzeta and to legal conflicts that left accused militiamen in jail for long periods while their superiors debated over jurisdiction.[83]

As might be expected, the subdelegate defended his policies against the military. On the Medellín complaint, he stated that a local ordinance required charcoal dealers to sell their product in the main plaza to prevent hucksters from cornering the market and inflating prices. Medellín insulted the *ministro de vara* and continued his business despite warnings of the infraction. After the arrest, a thorough search had failed to turn up any documents or money.[84] In the Mazatán case, Anteparaluzeta insisted that the prosecution of gamblers fell under his authority, although he had not bothered to draw up formal charges or to inform the military jurisdiction.[85] At this point, Major Manuel de Santa María of the cavalry regiment appealed the cases to the viceroy. He was exhausted by constant conflicts in which the subdelegates and their subordinates walked over the fuero militar. The legal machinery to solve competencias was no longer sufficient to handle the volume of complaints and he dared not send troops to transfer the prisoners for fear of scandal or even of bloodshed—particularly in a violence-prone community like Catorce.[86]

Félix Calleja, commander of the Tenth Militia Brigade, blamed the disputes upon the way the subdelegates and the ordinary royal judges interpreted the fuero militar. They treated soldiers as if they enjoyed only the *fuero criminal*. Since the distinction between civil and criminal cases was seldom clear cut, they took advantage of obscurities to molest the militiamen. In his opinion, official harassment lowered the will of many men to serve the king. The *auditor de guerra* agreed; he condemned Anteparaluzeta for his high-handed and despotic acts. Both militiamen should have been sent to their commander for punishment and not jailed by the ordinary jurisdiction. Moreover, he dismissed the law on charcoal sales as illegal and certainly not a matter a dealer from Matehuala would know about. Both accused militiamen were released and the subdelegate was fined fifty pesos besides having to pay restitution for any losses suffered.[87]

The crimes against the populace committed by some subdelegates equaled the worst abuses of the old alcaldes mayores. In isolated districts far away from the controlling influence of Mexico City, the reformed administration exercised only limited control. Where a heavy Indian population coincided with the production of valuable commodities such as cochineal, the subdelegates attempted to maintain repartimiento.[88] Even in the intendancy of Mexico where one might expect to find the best controls over the forty-three subdelegations, the intendant was little more than a powerless functionary. Although he achieved some control over aspects of government in the capital, his presence outside the city was limited. Indeed, the abuses which were to have been corrected in 1786 were still evident in 1810. The subdelegates used their control over police and judicial powers to erect thoroughly despotic regimes independent of Mexico City. The only real hope for the populace in these situations was to depend upon another privileged group that might espouse popular causes in order to advance their own special interests. Merchants, miners, the clergy, or members of a strong cabildo were able to place grievances before the viceroy. With the recruitment of militia units, the army functioned in a similar manner; officers resisted subdelegates who abused their men and, in some cases, militiamen utilized the organization of their companies to petition the viceroy for relief against illegal acts and other forms of mistreatment.

The subdelegation of Mextitlán, today in Hidalgo state, furnishes excellent examples of subdelegate exploitation and how the militia served to organize effective resistance. The town of Mextitlán was the home of two *compañias sueltas* (reserve companies) raised in 1797 when Branciforte expanded the provincial army. Like other reserve forces within easy reach of the capital, these companies often served in the Mexico City garrison, the cantonments, or as reinforcements for the regular regiments. By 1807 active duty caused severe hardships for the men and their families. When Iturrigaray agreed to receive petitions for release, he was deluged by the requests of men who had large families to support, fields to cultivate, mules to employ in the carrying trade to the north, and other legitimate reasons for deferment. According to the evidence of many militiamen, they had been drafted while many unattached bachelors in their towns escaped duty.[89]

One man, José Antonio Fernández of Tlanchinol in the *partido* of Mextitlán, stated that his wife and two children were in danger of starvation because he was not at home to cultivate his fields. He named thirteen bachelors of his town who were eligible for service.[90] Antonio Castillo of the village of Molango was posted to guard duty in Mexico City for four months before he realized that the pay of a common soldier was not sufficient to send any money to support his wife, two small children, and his old parents. His wife, a tributary Indian, fell ill from malnutrition and had to be hospitalized. Normally, Castillo earned four pesos monthly as an employee of muleteers—quite enough when supplemented by food grown on his *milpas*.[91] The curates of Zacualtipán, Lolotla, and Molango supported these petitions; many of the militiamen had served for ten years since the companies' original formation. Even if they had been young bachelors in 1796, they now had dependent wives and three or four children to support. Fathers dreaded abandoning their families and the priests warned that young girls might become the victims of necessity if the breadwinner was not at home. If this was not compelling enough reason for releases, most of the men were muleteers, merchants, and traders needed to keep commerce moving.[92]

When thorough investigations confirmed all of these petitions, Iturrigaray released 147 militiamen from Mextitlán.[93] While the dismissal of so many men from two companies cast doubts upon the recruiting policies of the subdelegate of Mextitlán, Ignacio Muñoz, who was the nominal commander of the local militia, the viceroy furnished no explanation. He agreed with the curates that mobilization hurt the families of militiamen, reduced tax income because the traders and muleteers were not working, and lowered crop yields. Although none of the militiamen were *hacendados,* most of them owned small fields where they grew maize and grain for their families.[94] At the same time, however, Muñoz claimed to be short of replacements, and he asked the viceroy whether he might begin to recruit men who were registered as Indian tributaries. His argument for proposing this radical departure in recruitment was that many who paid tribute were mestizos who declared themselves to be Indians in order to gain access to communal lands or to free themselves from payment of the alcabala.[95]

There was no outright charge of corruption in Mextitlán until October 1807, when eighteen married militiamen stationed in the capital sent a joint petition to Iturrigaray. According to their testimony, Subdelegate Muñoz and other officials had engaged in a well-planned conspiracy to sell militia exemptions. To bolster their case, they listed 169 men who had paid sums as high as two hundred pesos for deferment and this included only two-thirds of the partido of Mextitlán.[96] Other petitions soon added corroborating evidence. Rafaela Manuela Hernández, an old widow from Mextitlán, complained that her only son, Pedro, had been arrested, jailed, and then marched off to the capital to join the companies. She wrote to the subdelegate who was at the town of Zacualtipán, explaining that she was a poor widow with no other means of support than her son. He replied demanding thirty-five pesos to consider the case. Unable to raise the money, she decided to write a letter to the viceroy explaining her situation and begging for her son's release. This time the subdelegate and his lieutenant, Francisco Lezama, attempted to charge her fourteen reales postage to send the letter to Mexico City. Probably doubting their motives, the widow herself carried the letter over the fifty leagues to the capital and delivered it in person to the viceroy.[97]

Iturrigaray passed the matter to the *auditor de guerra*, José de Cristo, who sent it to the intendancy of Mexico. The *fiscal* of the intendancy proposed a secret inquiry into the charges against the subdelegate. A lawyer, Joaquín Miramón, received the commission. From December 1807 to February 1808, he conducted what he termed secret interviews of officials and residents of the subdelegation. No evidence of wrongdoing turned up, but there were unsubstantiated rumors spread by women in the markets about bribery concerning enlistment. Miramón did confirm the difficulties in enlisting bachelors, many of whom escaped into the mountains, joined muleteers heading for the Provincias Internas, or sought other means of avoiding their duty. These were chronic problems and certainly not the result of negligence on the part of the subdelegate or his subordinates. Witnesses mentioned that as soon as the militia mobilization became public knowledge, the number of young men to be seen in the region declined, leaving only young boys and old men. There was now a real shortage of muleteers, tanners, servants, and laborers. The only sum paid to the subdelegate was a six-to-eight-peso fee to pay for the *expediente* declaring the reasons for military deferment. All of the evidence given by government functionaries, curates, merchants and tradesmen exonerated Muñoz and his officials.[98]

According to Miramón's report to the intendant of Mexico, Manuel Francisco de Arce, Muñoz had behaved with complete honesty and prudence. Those men excused from service had good reasons for being awarded deferment. The only sums paid were the minor fees for the judicial inquiry and process.[99] Even at this, however, Miramón neglected to mention that the subdelegate had committed a breach of regulations punishable by a fine of one hundred pesos. No justice or scribe was permitted to charge any fee for the investigation of exemption petitions.[100] Before Iturrigaray received this information, the angry militiamen rebutted Miramón's findings and expanded the scope of their charges. They condemned Muñoz and his lieutenant, Lezama, for gambling, engaging in illegal repartimiento, and for dominating trade in the valuable export commodity *purga de jalapa,* a well-known purgative drug.[101] Two militiamen, Mariano Morales and Felipe Razo (alias Felipe Calva), compounded the charges when they informed the intendant of Mexico that Miramón's investigation was a complete farce. To conceal the truth, Miramón cooperated with the subdelegate and permitted the use of intimidation and bribery. Threats terrified witnesses and they falsified testimony about having made payments to local officials. The curate of Zacualtipán was involved with the subdelegate in what was an extortion racket that permitted the wealthy to buy exemptions for themselves and their employees. While this priest had not spent a single day in the past three years teaching Christian principles to his flock, he labored for eight days instructing those who were to testify in the investigation.[102]

Confronted by this new evidence, the intendant of Mexico, in agreement with the *auditor de guerra* and Viceroy Iturrigaray, named a new investigator, Antonio Lavin, to conduct a secret inquiry. Beginning in June 1808, Lavin toured the subdelegation of Mextitlán questioning witnesses and interviewing those purported to have paid for deferments. One of the major denunciants, Mariano Morales, now released from the militia, admitted he was illiterate but he renewed all of his charges and refused to disclose the name of the person who had written the original petitions.[103] When Muñoz attempted to interfere with the witnesses, Lavin reported the matter to Arce. The intendant authorized Lavin to levy fines of five hundred pesos and gave him full power to remove the subdelegate or any other official who interfered with the investigation. When the people continued to be reticent to discuss militia recruitment, and some who had agreed to make depositions later refused, Lavin exiled Muñoz, his lieutenant, and his associates, Manuel Machín, Agustín Dorantes, Manuel Parodi, and Sergeant José María Acosta. There was already enough evidence for Acosta to be jailed for two months and Parodi was removed from his post as administrator of the town of Mextitlán. All of the accused were to stay at least twenty leagues away from the subdelegation.[104]

Having taken these steps, Lavin soon turned up evidence corroborating the charges against the subdelegate and the commission of Miramón. Tomás Contreras, a merchant who travelled in the Huasteca, admitted having paid 20 pesos to obtain an exemption for his son. Later when he was away on business, the curate returned 10 pesos to his wife and informed her that the remaining sum had gone to pay for the judicial process. Nicolás Hernández, a muleteer, testified that he paid 60 pesos for his son's deferment. All except 10 pesos had been returned when Miramón visited Mextitlán. Others told of having to borrow sums up to 150 pesos or paying with horses, mules, and other property. Some of the best evidence came from the wives of those who purchased deferments. Once the lid was off many of the witnesses furnished the names of others they knew who had followed the same course. As might be expected, there was new fear among those who had escaped military duty. Guadalupe Gómez stated that her brother-in-law berated her for babbling before the commission. It was now said in street gossip that those who had bought their freedom from Muñoz and his men would be dragged to the capital, where they might replace their less fortunate neighbors.[105] Guadalupe Gómez expanded the scope of the investigation beyond Muñoz and his men to other prominent residents; she paid 80 pesos to the subdelegate at the curate's house and 19 pesos to the local physician who was the curate's nephew. He gave her a document certifying that her husband was crippled. At first the physician demanded 50 pesos for this document, but after much haggling the figure was lowered to 20 pesos. She still owed one peso and had later been required to pay an additional 6 pesos to Sergeant Acosta. As in the other cases, the subdelegate returned 70 pesos when Miramón arrived on the scene.[106] Josefa Hernández, the wife of a merchant named Patricio Hernández, stated that her husband had gone to Mextitlán when ordered to join the militia, but he returned the following day with a deferment. He had been troubled at the prospect of leaving his family, home, and business, which would be destroyed in his absence, so he went to Manuel Machín and, after three negotiating sessions, he pledged 250 pesos, which were delivered to Lezama at the courthouse. Josefa Hernández later received most of the money back from the curate.[107]

The involvement of Miramón in the cover-up was not made fully clear although the circumstantial evidence was strong. Several witnesses testified that he had become implicated with the subdelegate and his clique—

particularly after he formed a close friendship with Machín. Paula Gertrudis Olivares, in whose home Miramón resided during his visit to Zacualtipán, stated that she heard people tell him about the payment for deferments; on one occasion a woman from Tianguistengo asked for the return of her money. Miramón replied that he did not disperse funds and advised her to see Muñoz. Paula Olivares felt that at first there had not been close contacts between Miramón and the subdelegate's men; however, after he destroyed some papers, Machín and the others had come to dine and visit on many occasions.[108]

Lavin was equally successful in turning up evidence relating to repartimiento. As in the case of deferments, the original charges came from the petitions of the militiamen. According to their information, Subdelegate Muñoz used his *teniente* or *director* Lezama, who with a number of servants managed the production of *purga de Jalapa*. In August and September of each year, they advanced six pesos per *quintal* to the Indian farmers and by harvest time three or four months later, they could market the purgative for about four times the sums paid to the Indians. To prevent sales to independent merchants or failure to deliver the amount contracted, Lezama's men used their legal powers or outright force. Indians who for any reason could not produce their quota had their possessions and draft animals confiscated and sold at the harvest rates of twenty-four pesos per quintal and not at the six-peso rate they had been paid. Others, lacking sufficient property, were obliged to present two *quintales* the following year for every one they failed to deliver. This gave the subdelegate a potential profit of forty-two pesos for a six-peso investment. Anyone who attempted to buy purgative from the Indians was jailed, whipped, or expelled from the region.[109]

Confirmation of these charges was swift. The administrator of the post office in Zacualtipán, Manuel Mateos, testified that Muñoz paid a sum of six pesos, two reales to the Indians for purgative which at harvest time was worth between twenty-four and twenty-eight pesos. He supported the militiamen in their claims against the moral standards of the local regime; illegal card games and other forms of gambling run by the subdelegate brought together both people from the lowest plebeian elements and those of the distinguished classes. On one occasion at the subdelegate's residence, Muñoz drank to such excess that he lost his senses and vomited all over his bed.[110] The village curate of Tianguistengo, Juan de Bustamante, cited the case of an Indian named Francisco Méndez who had not delivered his quota of purgative. Fearing punishment, he took his wife and fled into the mountains. When the subdelegate's enforcers arrived, Méndez's mother was the only member of the family to be found; they arrested her and marched her off to jail in irons.[111] A merchant of

Zacualtipán, Mariano Cuello, stated that the only way for Indians to sell purgative to merchants was to arrange secret meetings at night in isolated locations—and even then they were very frightened.[112]

Lavin did not restrict his investigation to the upper classes of the subdelegation. Some of the most devastating testimony came from the Indian producers who had felt the oppression of the subdelegate at first hand. José Martín, an Indian tributary and former alcalde of his village of Santiago Acapa, said that those who did not deliver their full quota of purgative at harvest received a visit from Ildefonso Castaneira who confiscated their mules and supplies of maize. Martín experienced this first hand; during a previous crop failure, his family was left exposed to hunger when he lost two mules, a quantity of purgative, and other property. Notwithstanding his offer to repay 12 to 15 pesos per quintal, although he had received only 6 pesos, 2 reales, Castaneira would accept nothing less than the inflated harvest price. The year he became alcalde, Martín avoided involvement with repartimiento for fear his people could not complete their quotas and would suffer confiscation of their animals and food. However, Castaneira pressured him to distribute money promising that there would be no seizures because of crop failures. In spite of this, Martín was able to recount numerous cases of families losing mules, maize, furniture, and other property. While alcalde, he had standing orders to jail anyone who came to purchase purgative directly from the Indians.[113] Another witness, Antonio Mercado, who described himself as a Spaniard (white), had been teniente of the village of San Lorenzo. Two years previously, Muñoz gave him 600 pesos for distribution to the Indians, who were to deliver one hundred quintales of purgative at harvest time. When he explained that it would be difficult to hand out such a large sum in his area, he was ordered in no uncertain terms to allot the money and then to gather the harvested crop. As Mercado suspected, he was able to distribute only 475 pesos and could not even give away the remaining 125 pesos. That December, the authorities confiscated his household possessions: five mules, four mares, and 207 pesos; they even went so far as to take three mules from his married son.[114] The final proof came from the local schoolmaster, Rafael Bermudo, who confirmed these events; he had seen many cases of Indians and poor Spaniards being jailed, flogged, and dispossessed of their possessions if they did not deliver their purgative on time.

By the end of July 1808, Lavin completed his report and returned to Mexico City. The Mextitlán militiamen's persistence had broken the corrupt and despotic rule of one subdelegate. The case of Mextitlán demonstrates why some subdelegates raised such vigorous opposition to the introduction of militia units. Army officers might protect their men or, as in this case, the experience of contact with other regions and the means by which justice might be obtained made otherwise docile *campesinos* capable of resisting exploitation. In some respects, the army brought positive benefits to society. On the other hand, the confused tangle of overlapping jurisdictions made competencias inevitable. As will be seen in subsequent chapters, the crown sometimes passed legislation without fully understanding the legal ramifications in New Spain. It took years for the *auditor de guerra,* sub-inspector general, and viceroy to untangle some complex disputes and to ask for a definitive ruling. In partial defense of the subdelegates, however, their police and legal functions were complicated by the introduction of militia units. Unlike most other privileged jurisdictions that enjoyed special legal status and their own tribunals—merchants, miners, and the clergy, for example—the army drew its manpower from a broader spectrum. This was the first fuero open to almost anyone who could shoulder a musket, and it was only natural that elements to be found on the borderline of legality in any society would flaunt their privileges and use legal loopholes to escape punishment.

6

THE ARMY AND THE CABILDOS

The *ayuntamientos* or cabildos, the municipal governments of cities and major towns, played a significant role in the implementation of the provincial militia system.[1] While the responses to challenges posed by the military reflected regional, demographic, and economic factors among others, a number of general themes stand out. First, the local elites, through control of the cabildos, placed their own stamp on the provincial regiments and battalions. The viceroys had to come to grips with this reality or face severe difficulties with the militia. Although cooperation between the regime and the elites was quite possible, efforts to diminish the participation of the cabildos endangered militia formation. Second, through their domination of the municipal governments, the criollos acted as a check on the bureaucracy and as spokesmen for regional interests. A good working relationship between the captain general and an urban administration usually was sufficient to avert problems with the militia. On the other hand, attempts to remove powers from the cabildos or other frictions between the Bourbon centralizers and the local governments produced shortages of recruits, disappearance of tax support, and a constant stream of complaints, jurisdictional battles, and irritation of the old criollo-gachupín mistrust. Third, the cabildos were so important in the provincial militia system that the provincial intendants were often left out in a direct city-to-viceroy connection. Clearly, some cabildos were more favorable toward the army than others. In cities and towns where a militia picket performed police functions or where there were traditions of plebeian violence, there was greater support for the militia or even for a regular army detachment.[2] Elsewhere, the advantages to be gained from a military presence could be outweighed by other factors. High support costs or feared loss of jurisdiction to the army sometimes provoked sustained opposition which frustrated attempts to create an effective militia.[3] What the cabildos lacked in actual power, they made up in their expert use of manipulation, petitioning, and delay. Furthermore, the privilege of nominating officer candidates translated into real power in struggles against gachupín governors.

According to accepted practice, when a regular army officer received a viceregal commission to raise a new militia regiment or battalion, his first obligation was to visit the headquarters town. Addressing the cabildo, he explained his mission, pointing out the benefits accruing to the community— more adequate security, troops to aid in law enforcement, and the honor of having been selected in the first place. On an appointed day, recruitment to fill the ranks took place in the town and in surrounding communities. Two deputies from the cabildo known to possess the best knowledge of the population joined the army officer and other officials during the selection process. On a subsequent occasion, the owners of haciendas, ranches, shops, and other businesses were convoked. Each individual was asked to furnish a donation toward the new unit or, in the case of a mounted regiment, to present a number of horses. Ranchers and landowners were to sign contractual agreements to maintain the animals when they were not in use. Finally, the viceregal representative went to the cabildo to request that it propose candidates for militia commissions. These were to be drawn from the cream of the community—the most respected patricians of greatest wealth and highest social position.[4] As might be expected, the most senior ranks, the colonelcy and lieutenant colonelcy, usually went to the men who donated the largest sums toward regimental or battalion formation.

All of this was theoretical since militia units could not be raised without long-term commitments, and even then success might be ephemeral. The provincial Cavalry Regiment of Querétaro, one of the senior militia units and considered among the best in Mexico, illustrates the difficulties. This regiment was formed in 1765 when Field Marshal Marqués de Rubí was sent to Querétaro by Juan de Villalba to look into the possibility of forming a militia. After lengthy discussions with the cabildo, it was decided to enlist a regiment of 493 horsemen divided into twelve companies of forty men, twelve trumpeters, and one drummer. Two regidores were appointed from the cabildo to hold an enlistment lottery and collect donations. They encountered few immediate problems recruiting six companies in the city of Querétaro or the six companies assigned to Celaya, Salvatierra, and Valle de Santiago. Besides donating five thousand pesos in currency, residents presented the militia with many horses and a large amount of cloth for uniforms.[5] To maintain the regiment, the cabildo of Querétaro voted to impose taxes or *arbitrios* of one real per *carga* of flour entering the city, two reales on each carga of wool, and four reales per barrel of Spanish wine or brandy.[6] The annual income from these taxes varied between two thousand and four thousand pesos between 1765 and 1800—sufficient to pay many of the minor operating expenditures and part of the salaries of the regular training cadre.[7] In Querétaro, this payroll was higher than in other militia regiments because the colonel, lieutenant colonel, major, two adjutants, twelve lieutenants, twelve sergeants, and twenty-four corporals were all regular army men.[8]

Following the first flush of enthusiasm over the regiment, the hacendados and artisans of Querétaro lost interest in their militia connection. Training and duty took up time and a cavalry regiment cost much more than anyone had been led to believe. The hacendados were not at all impressed with their obligations to look after the regimental horses and to present them in good condition whenever necessary. After all, horses aged, became ill, got lost, or died on the range and the landowners refused to accept responsibility for replacements. Although the army paid twelve pesos for each animal in the first place, this was a small sum compared with the long-term obligation and commitment. Many ranchers simply did not have year round pastures to graze the cavalry horses. Even worse, the encumbrance of having to care for these animals reduced land values since prospective purchasers did not wish to buy perpetual agreements signed by previous owners.[9] One *alcalde ordinario* of the cabildo, José González Roxo, sold sixteen horses to the regiment and then denied any further liability. His hacienda was twenty-five leagues from the city in rugged mountainous terrain which simply did not offer adequate summer pasture. Even if he received 100 pesos per animal, the high mortality rate and replacement costs caused him to lose money. Roxo wanted to return the 192 pesos he received from the original sale of horses to the regiment if he could escape the heavy obligation of caring for them.[10]

Of course, horses purchased off the range were by no means good cavalry mounts. They were untrained and lacked the docility needed for military maneuvers. When these animals were brought into the city away from the freedom of their pastures, they needed months of work with expert horsebreakers who knew how to subdue the most rebellious mounts. Instead, they were assigned immediately to a militia regiment made up in large part of tailors, shoemakers, barbers, and other tradesmen who possessed only a vague notion about equestrian skills. Besides having to manage these horses, the militiamen were supposed to be ready for offensive and defensive maneuvers using weapons and following the orders of their commander.

During the risings of 1767 in San Luis Potosí, Guanajuato, and Pátzcuaro, the regiment had managed to send 230 mounted militiamen to serve under José de Gálvez. From then on, however, the unit's major obligation was to escort silver shipments and the *cuerdas de presidarios* (convoys of criminals) on their way through Querétaro to Mexico City and Veracruz. They escorted prisoners as far as San Juan del Río and bragged that the regiment had never permitted an escape.[11] The real test of preparedness came during the war against Britain in 1780 when Viceroy Mayorga ordered one squadron of the Querétaro cavalry to garrison Mexico City. To his shock and embarrassment, Colonel Pedro Ruiz Dávalos discovered that forty of his horses were dead and the remainder were so feeble they could not be ridden. He dispatched two officers to select sixty of the best horses for fattening prior to the march to the capital. There would be considerable delay, but, the colonel warned, "the roads will be left sown with horses if they are used in their present condition."[12] The colonel blamed the cabildo and hacendados for refusing to abide by the regulations for those who furnished and cared for horses. After waiting several months for the Querétaro cavalry, Mayorga gave up and ordered a squadron of provincial dragoons from Puebla to the capital.

An opportunity for redemption came in 1782 with new orders to send a cavalry squadron to Mexico City. This time, 137 horses were selected from the 500 belonging to the regiment and Ruiz Dávalos chose his best officers and men. In fact, all of the regular officers accompanied the squadron, which took eleven days to cover a distance that took ordinary travellers less than five days. To keep up morale, the officers assured the troops that once they arrived in the capital their only duties would be to present a brilliant martial display and to promenade through the streets.[13] Although the squadron carried adequate supplies of hay and grain for the march, the colonel found the animals were in bad shape shortly after they arrived. Before two months had passed, he requested new horses and militiamen to replace those on duty. By the end of the first year, he had rotated almost all his men and horses.

Reviewing the spectacle of ineptitude and other deficiencies, Inspector General Pascual de Cisneros condemned the deceit and bad faith of the Querétaro cabildo. Factions within the city government had frustrated efforts to introduce an adequate system for monitoring the militia. As a direct result, for the past two years the regimental horses had been pastured in an area where there was little grass or water. Ruiz Dávalos attacked *Regidor* Pedro Antonio de Septién as a troublemaker and *"espíritu lusiferino,"* accusing him of leading a faction which had misled the cabildo and the populace.[14] According to Ruiz, Septién, who was also an ensign in the cavalry, spread all sorts of rumors and smears directed against his senior officers.[15] To end dominance of the cabildo by provincial or, one might say, criollo elements opposed to the militia, the colonel proposed that a number of new *regidores honorarios* should be named to the city government. José de Gálvez had employed this method of crushing opposition in Mexico City, Puebla, Guanajuato, and Valladolid. The essential step was to keep the existing cabildo out of the selection of new appointees or they would nominate individuals from their own factions. If this happened, the situation would be even worse.[16]

Through effective use of petitions and procrastination, the Querétaro cabildo avoided any reform which would regularize regimental finance and the maintenance of horses. In 1785, the climate dealt a blow, adding support to arguments opposing the regiment. Droughts in 1784 destroyed much of the maize crop in the province, pastures burned off, and wells dried up.[17] The result was disastrous livestock mortality; some hacendados lost at least two-thirds of their herds and some had only ten out of every hundred oxen by the end of the year. Rain did not fall until July 6 and then it came in a deluge causing severe flooding. After July 30, when the rains finally relented, there were few crops left in the ground. In August and September, killing frosts compounded the calamity. By this time much of the range was totally barren or covered with coarse, inedible grasses and weeds. Many hacendados dismounted their servants and not even the hardy mules and oxen which normally withstood drought were in any condition to be worked. Now there could be no question of asking landowners to accept responsibility for cavalry horses.[18]

The disaster of 1785 was insufficient reprieve. The very next year, Viceroy Conde de Gálvez and Sub-Inspector General Mendinueta imposed the long-dreaded plan for the selection and maintenance of horses.[19] Each hacendado had to accept regimental mounts according to the size of his landholdings; he was to sign a perpetual contract obliging himself to present horses of at least seven *cuartos* (about five feet in height) and without any physical imperfections. If an estate was sold or inherited, the new owner was bound to continue the contract. To prevent further delays, the viceroy denied the cabildo the right to file any representations or objections. Under the new militia plan of Francisco Crespo, the Regiment of Querétaro was reduced to twelve companies or a total of 361 men. The city of Celaya accepted the new arrangement without argument, but opposition remained in Querétaro. Although the viceroy prohibited members of the cabildo from direct or indirect meddling in the affairs of the regiment, *Regidor* Tomás Ecala led a movement resisting the militia.[20]

The issue of horses was only one of the sources of irritation between the cavalry regiment and the cabildo. Another was the administration of the taxes established to operate the regiment. At first, the cabildo received permission to control these funds, but charges were soon made that the administrators manipulated the income and obscured the true financial picture. Ruiz Dávalos recommended the use of a strongbox with three keys and the appointment of wealthy citizens to the positions of treasurer—men who "would not have to stoop to petty thievery in order to live."[21] He was disturbed that his militiamen still wore uniforms issued eighteen years before; although the garments had ceased to be of any use, there was never enough money in the tax fund to replace them. The final impetus to reform came when *Regidor* Antonio del Solar Iglesias declared bankruptcy; besides losing his own money he lost eleven thousand pesos belonging to the militia tax revenues.[22] As in the case of the horses, the cabildo lost its right to intervene in any matter having to do with the militia taxes. The viceroy formed a new *junta de guerra y de arbitrios* including the corregidor as presiding officer, the colonel, the administrator of alcabalas, and the *procurador síndico del común*. The last three members held the keys to the strongbox and they were to keep exact account of all transactions. Any expenditure of more than twenty-five pesos had to be approved by the captaincy general.[23]

Another of the Querétaro regiment's chronic weaknesses resulted from the refusal of the Querétaro and Celaya cabildos to conduct a proper population census. Quite clearly, Celaya was declining in population and the squadrons assigned to that city were often short of manpower. Celaya had little other than agriculture to drive its economy and many workers migrated to Querétaro where there were greater job opportunities. The city had grown from medium status to a position of importance as the main entry and distribution center for the interior.[24] By 1810, the population totaled more than sixty thousand inhabitants; three thousand workers labored in the new tobacco factory and the textile industry was booming.[25] Lacking adequate census data on the number of eligible bachelors available for the cavalry, the urban magistrates had to collect men from the streets when the colonel asked for replacements. For several years, the corregidor of Querétaro pressured the cabildo to name streets and number houses to facilitate the census as had been done before in Puebla and Mexico City.[26] Even so, no accurate statistics were collected until 1786.

Although the passage of time reduced the frictions between the cabildo and the cavalry regiment, Viceroy Revillagigedo included the unit in his general disbandment of provincial militias. Regimental equipment, arms, and the tax fund were sent to the capital for use by the regular army.[27] It is likely this development pleased the hacendados who controlled the cabildo of Querétaro, but they did not have long to enjoy their freedom. Viceroy Branciforte ordered the cavalry regiment to be reestablished. The cabildo made a show of pleasure at this development, but did nothing to implement major aspects of the commands. In 1797, three years after the regiment was to have taken shape, there were no horses. Branciforte became exasperated by the dissidence and slowness of the cabildo; this regiment was in much worse condition than new cavalry units being raised in San Miguel el Grande and San Luis Potosí.[28] At first, the cabildo claimed there were no funds available for the purchase of horses; the regidores asked for permission to draw money from the public land and tax funds. When Branciforte dismissed this proposal, they agreed to buy horses but did not implement the *plan de caballos* to maintain the mounts when they were not in use. From the point of view of Querétaro interests, the financial crisis brought on by the militia's reestablishment was artificial: Revillagigedo transferred twenty-four thousand pesos of the local tax fund to Mexico City, the bankruptcy of Antonio del Solar Iglesias cost eleven thousand pesos, and there were six thousand pesos remaining in the treasury. Once these sums were recovered for use by the cavalry, the Regiment of Querétaro would be wealthier than any other.[29]

A very angry viceroy terminated the delays caused by the cabildo. There were 348 horses to place on haciendas and if the *plan de caballos* was not accepted quickly, the "notorious disobedience" of the city would be punished.[30] A *cabildo extraordinario* convened immediately upon receipt of this information and with prudent haste agreed to the plan. There was still some mumbling about the difficulty of locating horses, but this was a weak argument in a province renowned for excellent mounts. According to the cabildo, most haciendas produced cattle or sheep and the few horses were not of acceptable size or quality. In any event, the regidores decided to distribute the cavalry animals among eighty-seven haciendas of the province; smaller estates would be responsible for one horse and the largest for as many as fifteen or sixteen. A general junta of hacendados met on August 4, 1797, at the treasury offices because the cabildo building was not made available.[31] The purpose was to inform landowners of how many horses they were to support and of the terms of the agreement. As in the previous contract, they were obliged in perpetuity to present horses upon demand; in return, they were to be paid twelve pesos from the tax fund over a ten-year contract. Upon notification from the regiment, the hacendado or his employee was to deliver the horses in Querétaro with a paper indicating the name of the hacienda and a description of each animal by color, marks, and brand. This was done because if the horse was injured or killed in service, it would be replaced without charge to the hacendado.[32]

The instructions to hacendados were made very clear. Landowners were not to ignore the contract and the slightest sign of disobedience would be severely punished. In fact, however, the responsibility to furnish horses was divided as evenly as possible with two or three horses going to most estates. There were few hacendados obliged to care for as many as 16 horses. One of these, José Rengel, Conde de Alcaraz and colonel of the regular Dragoon Regiment of

Spain, was married to a daughter of the millionaire Fagoaga family.[33] He owned seven haciendas in Querétaro—Atongo, Zamgrano, Aljajayucán, Rayas, Carbonera, Monte de Lobo, and San Rafael. In 1799, he had 238 brood-mares on his estates and 339 horses in general use. He was by far the largest landowner and horse raiser in the province—outdoing even the fabulously wealthy Conde de Regla. Regla also supported 16 militia horses on four haciendas—Tuchitlán el Grande, Santa Rosalia, Las Animas, and Rancho de la Vega.[34]

Wealthy or not, a good many of the Querétaro hacendados refused to accept the imposition of a contract to furnish horses. Claiming that the system would doubtless bring "total ruin to all inhabitants and complete desolation to towns and districts," a junta of forty-six landowners elected three representatives to lay their case before the king.[35] Through their agent in Madrid, Nicolás Rivera, they placed their grievances before the imperial government. Their argument was quite simple: if the plan went into effect, agriculture and stock-raising essential to the provincial economy would be hampered. The total annual output of horses was about one thousand head of which only about a third would be stallions needed by the cavalry. Even supposing 500 stallions were produced annually, one had to remember that many died on the range or were killed, injured, or crippled while still suckling. Even then, numerous accidents reduced the eventual output to a total of not more than 182 stallions. This small number had to meet the needs of 112 haciendas and their mayordomos, adjutants, keepers, *vaqueros,* and other employees. Each hacienda required about six horses per mayordomo and as many as sixteen to twenty animals per *vaquero*. One of the Querétaro representatives, Mariano Pérez de Tagle, explained that harsh treatment by the vaqueros ruined many horses during the course of a year. To complicate matters further, horses produced in Querétaro were not selectively bred, which meant many were too small to meet cavalry needs. If this was not proof enough, Rivera added an argument which might not have been well received by the criollos: it was well known from the reports of travellers and scientists that "all races of animals from Europe are much smaller, weaker, and more emaciated in America."[36] The petitioners stated that for the twelve pesos they received for their horses, they would have to anticipate spending fifty pesos or more to keep a good cavalry animal. Since many were weighed down by mortgages, leases, and taxes—some for two-thirds of their income and others for nearly the full value of their assets—they could not afford this duty. In the opinion of Pérez de Tagle, the regimental officers contributed to the low efficiency of the unit because they could enjoy their homes and business interests without fear of active service.[37] The hacendados denied any antimilitary sentiments from their opposition to the cavalry; to show their good intentions, they requested that the existing regiment be converted to infantry.

Minister of War Alvarez received the petitions from Querétaro and asked for recommendations to improve relationships between Querétaro and the militia.[38] As might be expected, the proposal to convert the cavalry into infantry was not well received within the regiment. Colonel Ruiz Dávalos considered the idea an attempt by the hacendados to escape responsibility. In his opinion, they could not have considered the impact of enlisting a foot regiment of eight hundred to one thousand men from a region where "horses are abundant and men scarce."[39] Instead of just 348 men, the infantry would have to draft agricultural laborers, whose absence might endanger planting and harvests. If there were not enough Spaniards and mestizos, the hacendados themselves would be enlisted—then there would be a cry for a return to cavalry. Ruiz Dávalos concluded, "the hacendados love 348 horses more than the 1,000 men needed for an infantry regiment and they do not care about the damage to workmen."[40] Lieutenant Colonel Ignacio García Revollo and twenty-two officers submitted their own petition, expressing pride in their regiment and attacking the idea that it could be converted into infantry. In a country where three out of four regular infantry regiments were stationed overseas and where desertion was epidemic, a solid provincial unit like that of Querétaro was essential.[41]

Viceroy Azanza considered the idea of converting the regiment from cavalry to infantry to be an impractical solution to disputes at Querétaro. Had the idea been serious, the time to have made the change was in 1794 when the unit was disbanded and Branciforte began to rebuild it. All of the equipment, uniforms, and arms would have to be changed and there would be major expenditures as well as opposition from those who served in the existing regiment. Since the method of supplying and maintaining horses was similar elsewhere in Mexico, and without the grumbling of a "junta of malcontents," Azanza rejected alterations except perhaps from cavalry to dragoons.[42] However, he did order a thorough census of the province's horse population to verify the validity of the hacendados' charges. As a result, the corregidor of Querétaro, José Ignacio Ruiz Calado, prepared a detailed report on each hacienda. In total there were 550 brood-mares, 1,000 unbroken colts, and 3,327 horses in daily use for a total of 4,877.[43] Although these statistics were used by both sides to give weight to arguments for or against the regiment, the only change adopted by the imperial government was the technical alteration from cavalry to dragoons.[44]

Difficulties between the army and cabildos dominated by powerful landowners or business interests were by no means confined to Querétaro. The case

Provincial Mexican militiaman, 1795. *From AGI, Estado, leg. 23, in Mapas y Planos, Uniformes, 73.*

Provincial Mexican dragoon, mounted, 1795. *From AGI, Estado, leg. 23, in Mapas y Planos, Uniformes, 77.*

Provincial Mexican cavalryman, mounted, 1795. *From AGI, Estado, leg. 23, in Mapas y Planos, Uniformes, 80.*

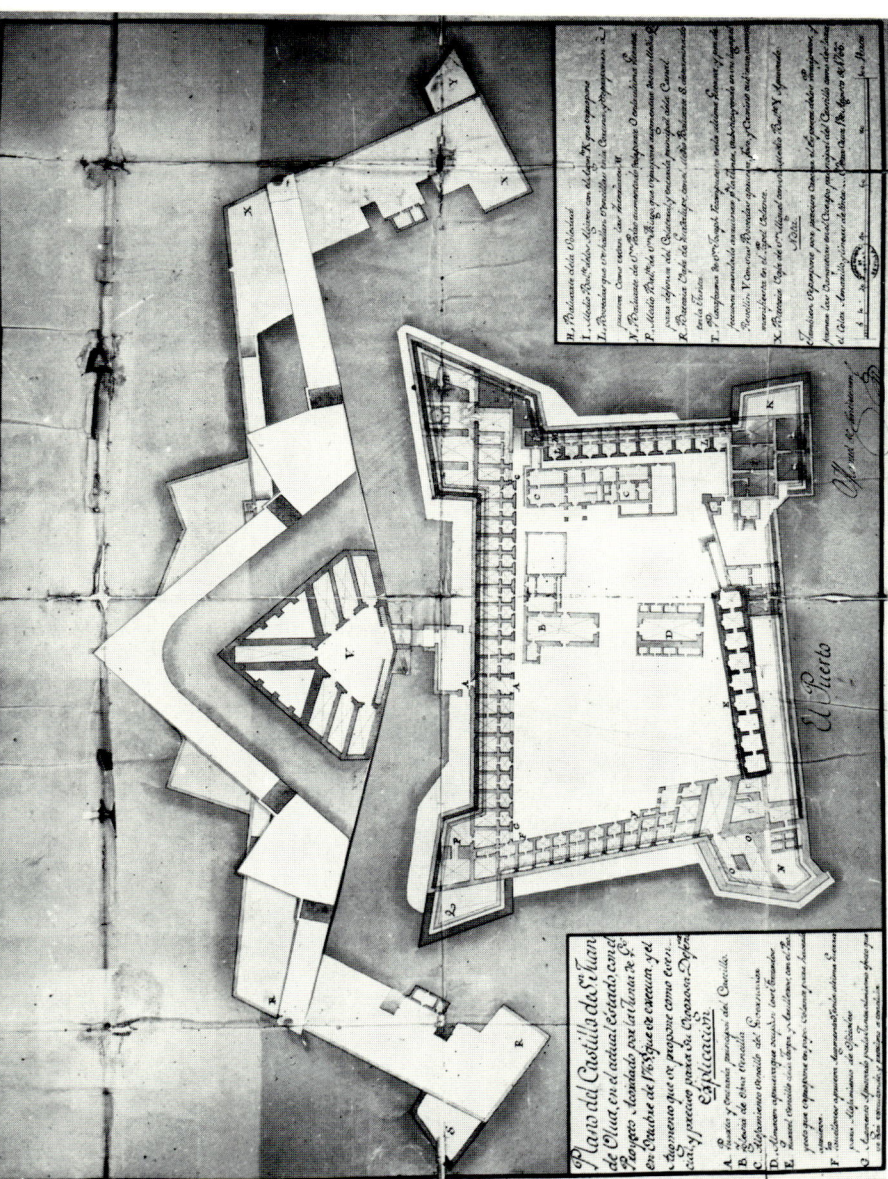

Plan of the fort of San Juan de Ulúa, 1765. *From AGI, Mapas y Planos, 233.*

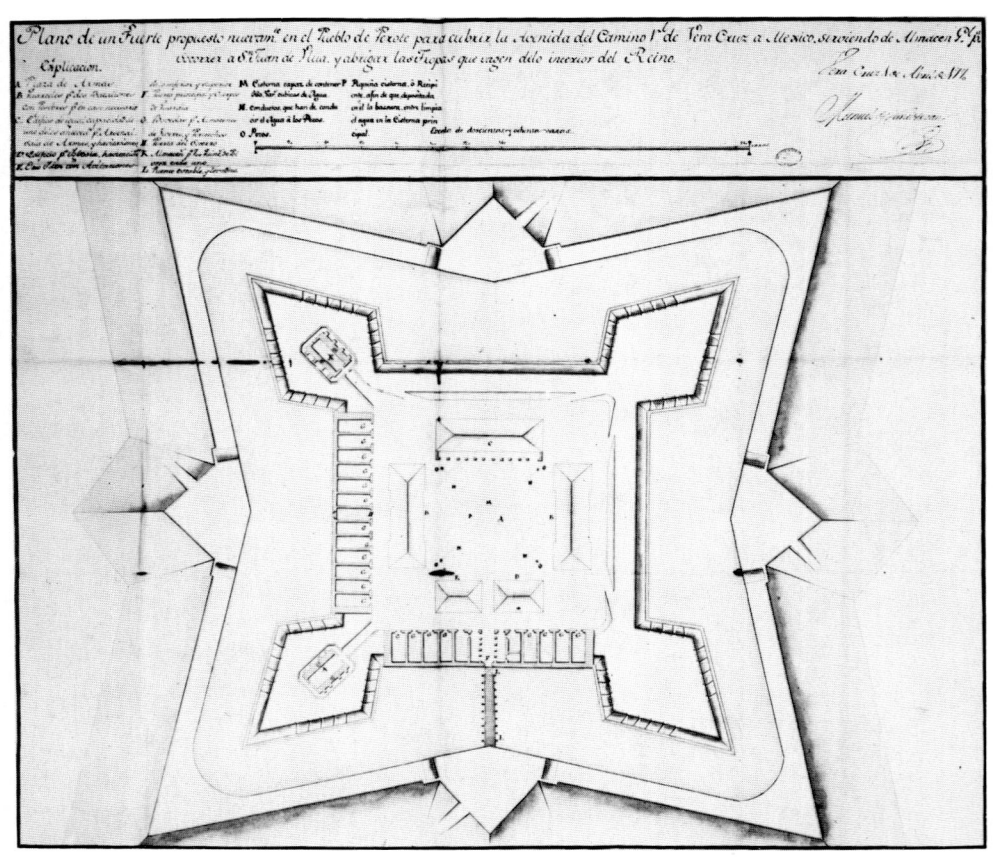

Plan of a proposed fort for the town of Perote, 1770. *From AGI, Mapas y Uniformes, México, 254.*

of Veracruz, which has been examined separately, was the most outstanding, but other cities experienced conflicts over their provincial units. In Oaxaca, resistance to the militia from the cabildo and rural magistrates reflected legal and jurisdictional struggles. As in the case of the Querétaro regiment, the Infantry Battalion of Oaxaca was reestablished by Branciforte after Revillagigedo's general militia demobilization. Branciforte dispatched Lieutenant Colonel Pedro de Laguna to carry out the commission. He arrived in the city during February 1796, took precautions to prevent an exodus of potential recruits, and then published the viceregal order informing the populace of his mission. Since Laguna could not enlist tributary Indians or unacceptable castes, he asked for the full cooperation of the provincial intendant and the cabildo.

The battalion was formed in the main plaza before the regidores, the tribute collector, and guild officers, who brought their membership lists to verify family and racial status. During the process Laguna appeared perplexed and asked repeated questions. Obviously, he was not completely happy with either the procedures or the recruits. Afterwards, he ordered the battalion commander, Lieutenant Colonel Juan Francisco Echarrí, and his captains to use their knowledge of the population to refine and improve their companies. Although Laguna was able to generate some enthusiasm for the militia among officer candidates, he ran headlong into the factious politics of a provincial town. After several weeks in Oaxaca, he wrote, "slander and backbiting abound in this city and there are not two people who are united." He identified five individuals in the cabildo who, with the intendant, governed the city. These men drew Laguna's special ire, for they opposed his every move and seemed to be the source of his difficulties. Worst of all, the opposition came from men who did not possess great fortunes and according to Laguna they lacked the circumstances needed to hold their offices. Not only did these men abuse their positions, but they also selected the *alcaldes ordinarios* who made a mockery of their police and judicial powers. In Laguna's opinion, the first object of the alcaldes upon assuming office was to provoke militiamen and to stir up legal disputes and jurisdictional conflicts with the *jefe militar;* minor misdemeanors quickly were transformed into execrable crimes. Most of the alcaldes lacked legal training and "none have ever seen any other city except Oaxaca."[45] Laguna predicted serious trouble in the future between the magistrates and the militia because of the "immortal hatred they have for militiamen."

To terminate some of the worst conflicts, Laguna proposed alterations in the cabildo's membership. Using the precedents set by José de Gálvez and the method used to reduce the dominant faction in the Querétaro cabildo, he recommended an increase in the number of regidores to twelve with the addition of two honorary regidores for a total of fourteen. Consulting with trustworthy residents, Laguna listed nine prominent citizens whom he considered of the quality needed to upgrade the urban administration and to end resistance to the provincial militia. At least five of these men were merchants connected with the consulado of Mexico.[46] Quite clearly, the purpose of the move was to replace or dominate the men who were identified most closely with Oaxaca; once again, the narrow criollo interests had to be brushed aside by those who espoused a wider view and accepted the imperial prerogatives. At the same time, Laguna asked the militia officers to do everything in their power to eliminate the abuse of fueros and other military privileges. Uniformed militiamen were to be kept away from *fandangos* and other public occasions, where they invariably ended up in trouble with the ordinary magistrates. When crimes were committed, punishments under army justice were to be so severe as to act as a deterrent to would-be offenders. To aid in this process, Laguna ordered that stocks be erected in the militia barracks.[47]

Reservations about the Battalion of Oaxaca were soon made plain to all observers. When, in late 1796, Branciforte mobilized the unit for duty in the Orizaba cantonment, Major Luis de Zárate reported a shortage of sixty-one soldiers. Despite his requests for new recruits, neither the cabildo nor the intendant produced any bachelors. All of the prospective recruits were married men with large families. Zárate saw little purpose in enlisting them because they would desert as soon as their dependents began to suffer. After an inspection he found men in the battalion who in his opinion did not belong to castes eligible for duty or who deserved exemption for other legitimate reasons. Obviously, there had not been sufficient controls over enlistment at the time of the battalion's formation.[48] The cabildo managed to scrape together a few men, but the municipal governors doubted their ability to find more. Once news spread that the battalion was to be sent out of its home province, the populace's restlessness and insurrectionary behavior ended recruitment. Pressures for replacements increased after the battalion reached the cantonment and Branciforte found himself beset by the hardship petitions of married men asking for releases. The cabildo dredged the city for victims— eventually rounding up thirty-eight men from the jail. Examination for disease, racial characteristics, height, and other possible exemptions reduced this number to eleven soldiers. Young men who might have been eligible for duty were by this time in hiding; this left only the tributary castes, married men with large families, and the chronically ill.[49]

Shocked by the numerous complaints from the Oaxaca militiamen, Branciforte asked Colonel Laguna to explain just where recruitment had gone wrong and which authorities were to blame. Laguna answered, stating that he would speak with candor. From the moment of his arrival in Oaxaca, he encountered the declared opposition from judges and magistrates who feared any diminution of their powers. The cabildo "feigned zeal" in its relationship with the militia, but the regidores either failed to fulfill their promises or acted "with the greatest indolence."[50] Most of the eligible young bachelors escaped service and even the lists of guildsmen were incomplete. Despite these obstacles, Laguna managed to fill the battalion and he failed to see why the city could not locate replacements. In his opinion, the culpability lay with the cabildo and with Intendant Mora y Peysal, who went to any lengths to escape responsibility; on one occasion he feigned illness to avoid association with the battalion.[51]

Besides these issues, some elements in Oaxaca opposed the militia arbitrios levied to support the thirteen-man militia picket used to bolster the police officials. In the 1770s, disorders caused by vagabonds and the plebeian classes grew beyond the capacity of the three city magistrates to control. To restore order, the crown permitted the use of militiamen; four soldiers were assigned to accompany each police official on his nocturnal rounds. A tax of four reales per carga of sugar and four reales per *tercio* of cacao introduced into the city would pay the costs of this protection.[52] While the tax was very successful in raising funds,[53] many considered levies upon food to discriminate against the poor. In 1794, for example, Antonio de San José Muro, a well-known Bethlehemite friar, condemned the concept of taxing what he described as basic food staples. Poor peons who subsisted on a diet of corn could not afford their morning cup of *champurrado* (a mixture of corn, sugar, and chocolate) before they went out to toil in the fields. Although Muro wanted the militia picket on duty to catch thieves, pickpockets, and gamblers, he believed that the wealthy classes should pay all of the costs through taxes on imported luxury goods.[54]

The cabildo of Mexico City encountered similar difficulties with its provincial infantry regiment and with the army in general. Considering the size of the population—in 1788 the guilds enumerated 18,642 artisans and tradesmen[55]—the task of recruiting 810 militiamen would not appear particularly difficult. Puebla after all raised two militia regiments and smaller towns encountered few major obstacles during peacetime. One of the problems in the capital seems to have been over-scrutiny of viceroys and senior staff officers, but the provincial Regiment of Mexico simply was not popular with the classes who had to fill its ranks. Despite the enormous pool of manpower in comparison with any other city, the statistics did not reflect the citizens' attitudes and aspirations. Many of the capital's inhabitants were there to make their fortunes, to gamble, or to live as free vagabonds; their contribution to the military was negative to say the least.

When Viceroy Revillagigedo disbanded most of the militia units, he decided to keep the provincial Regiment of Mexico. The capital was too large for the existing police forces and in the event the regular regiments had to meet an invasion threat at the coast, there would be troops to guard public buildings and to maintain internal peace. Revillagigedo did not take into account the possibility of losing his regular regiments to Caribbean stations. He watched with increasing distress as the regular Infantry Regiments of New Spain, Mexico, and finally Puebla were shipped off to Cuba, Santo Domingo, Louisiana, and elsewhere. By May 1793, the Regiment of Mexico was on its way to Havana and the Regiment of Puebla had to be transferred from garrison duty in the capital to guard Veracruz. The viceroy informed the city government that he intended to mobilize the provincial regiment. In an outburst of apparent generosity during a *cabildo extraordinario* convened to discuss the militia, the regidores agreed to underwrite the full cost of supporting the regiment while it was activated. The cabildo proposed a voluntary subscription: one thousand honorable residents were to donate 100 pesos, seven hundred to offer 50 pesos, and fourteen hundred to offer 25 pesos. The plan was to raise 170,000 pesos annually to cover estimated regimental expenditures of 126,235 pesos.[56] In reality, Revillagigedo was behind the whole idea and he made support of the regiment into an act of loyalty. Under these circumstances, the *cabildo extraordinario* felt it had little choice other than to capitulate to the viceregal desire. While members of the cabildo took out subscriptions for 100 pesos, this did not mean that other residents felt the same compulsion.[57] Despite strenuous efforts, the cabildo collected only 11,496 pesos to cover costs which by the end of October 1794 rose to 159,441 pesos. The royal treasury had to make up the difference of 143,152 pesos since the local militia arbitrios contributed only 16,289 pesos.[58]

This fiasco was yet another example of Revillagigedo's failure to understand the Mexican reality. He had reduced the size of the regiment and angered officers who could have been instrumental in furnishing donations and making sure that the subscription was taken up. Not long before, Sub-Inspector Gorostiza informed two Mexico City militia officers that provincial service was not worth "reward, attention, or prize."[59] It came as little surprise when Revillagigedo refused to pay the mobilized officers and soldiers the full salaries accorded to their ranks. Although there were many precedents for paying militiamen full regular army remuneration, the viceroy had no intention of granting this kind of recognition. Men of the lower ranks who normally earned good incomes in the guilds discovered that they could not support their families on reduced army wages.⁶⁰ While Revillagigedo permitted militiamen to continue working at their regular trades in their off-duty hours, there was little time or opportunity for this. A junta of regimental captains did not see how any man could hold down two jobs without broken health, overwork, and poor concentration at either task.⁶¹ When the viceroy did not respond to their letters, they dispatched a petition to the king; in the opinion of most officers, not only had the regiment been made inferior to a regular army unit, but its degraded state also deterred any voluntary recruits. Revillagigedo threatened to charge the captains with sedition and went as far as ordering the regimental major to read the army ordinances concerning seditious behavior to the captains. In the end, however, he could do little other than to condemn them for their ignorance of military service and of the regulations governing the army.⁶²

The embarrassment to the viceroy was quite evident and it was not helped when the king thanked the city for its generosity in supporting the regiment. No one was quite sure how to force the cabildo to make good its offer, and the idea of compulsion was ruled out when Gorostiza stated that the city could not be held responsible. Later the imperial cabinet discussed the question, concluding that the few who had contributed had done so out of consideration for the viceroy and not because they wanted to do something for the good of the state. Once Branciforte replaced Revillagigedo, the promised subscriptions were forgotten.⁶³ No one wanted to adopt the Mexico City cabildo's suggestion to raise taxes on imported wine and brandy entering Veracruz. In the end, the treasury paid the deficit between the amount collected and the real expenditures. Always pleased to show his predecessor's policies in the worst possible light, Branciforte made no effort to press the cabildo.⁶⁴

Branciforte should not have been so hasty in this criticism of Revillagigedo because his own experience with the cabildo and the provincial Regiment of Mexico was little better. The declaration of war against Britain in October 1795 increased pressures to locate manpower reserves for both regular and militia units. Mexico City, the largest population center and the home of a significant floating or transient population, became the happy hunting ground for recruiters. All cabildos were ordered to make careful scrutiny of urban areas to locate vagabonds, the unemployed, and other useless males who had no fixed domicile or occupation.⁶⁵ Warnings to exercise caution and to avoid detaining innocent citizens were often neglected. Corruption crept into the process as petty officials recognized the potential for extracting money. In the capital, a number of the *alcaldes de cuartel, alguaciles, cuadrilleros,* scribes, and others began to apprehend civilians and to extort ransoms from their families. In 1797, the famous scientist José Antonio Alzate wrote a series of letters to Viceroy Branciforte pointing out the growing level of abuse. When the viceroy left Mexico City to command the army of operations, the mistreatment of the populace became intolerable. Agents commissioned by the cabildo to fill the provincial regiment began to arrest any man who dared to show himself upon the streets, and to enter private homes. Masters were afraid to send their servants out on errands for fear that they would be swept up by the police or militia patrols. The goal was simply to gather as many men as possible and then either to draft them or to allow them to purchase their freedom. Whether or not they deserved exemptions was irrelevant. The true vagabonds hid themselves in churches, monasteries, and schools or departed the city altogether, leaving the peaceful workers to suffer the full brunt of the attack. Alzate gave numerous examples to back his charges: the scribe Espinosa conspired with the *alcalde de corte* Alosqueira to extort nine pesos from a poor tailor who went out to buy bread for his uncle.[66] The *alcalde de cuartel*, José Conejo, a man who already had dissipated his own fortune through gambling, stooped to anything if he could make money; he detained little boys as young as eight years of age, confident that he could extort money from their parents.[67] Sergeant José Salazar and Corporal Manuel Cristalinas of the provincial Regiment of Mexico, commissioned to apprehend beggars and vagabonds, used their positions to build up a considerable fortune. The poor artisans, tradesmen, and laborers suffered while any man with connections could escape. In the meantime, professional gamblers and vagabonds who had bought immunity from arrest or the army gathered as usual at the cockfights.[68]

Although the investigations into Alzate's charges appear to have curbed some of the worst abuses, the cabildo experienced even more difficulty finding men for the provincial regiment. By this time the unit was on duty at the cantonment where the men encountered food shortages, colds, and fever.[69] At the beginning of November 1797, the regimental commander, Colonel Joaquín Benito de Medina y Torres, reported shortages of about 100 men; repeated petitions to the cabildo for replacements produced excuses but no recruits. In fact, the only action was a study of 478 men who retired from the regiment between 1793 and 1797 to see whether 100 or more might be recalled.[70] Finally, after smallpox reduced the regiment even further, 82 replacements arrived. The colonel and regimental physician examined them and dismissed 11 men as useless for service.

A state of relative equilibrium appeared to have been restored until February 1798, when the regimental surgeons submitted a list of 72 men they considered unfit to continue active duty.[71] An uproar resulted. Major Tomás Rodríguez de Biedma, the senior regular army officer in the regiment, said the release of so many men resulted from poor judgment rather than good medical acumen. In one year, the regiment had retired 69 men, sentenced 4 to presidios, and lost 106 to desertion and 17 to disease, for a total of 196. These had been replaced by 92 recovered deserters and 106 replacements for an increase of 2 men over the year. Now, however, regimental stability was in jeopardy and Biedma wanted the 72 useless soldiers sent to Orizaba from Jalapa where full medical examinations could be made into their alleged disabilities.[72] When the colonel submitted a new list of 52 soldiers he described as fully or partially incapacitated, the officers looked for a scapegoat. They blamed the cabildo of Mexico for the poor quality of replacements. According to their information, the regimental reserves had been squandered, leaving no men who were fit for military duty. During 1796, for example, 150 supernumeraries were sent to reinforce the Regiment of the Crown and 25 to the Dragoon Regiment of Mexico. None were left for the provincial regiment except vagabonds, the vice-ridden, and the aged. Once in uniform they deserted or claimed legitimate exemptions from service because they supported families. Others suffered diseases and defects which made them liabilities rather than assets to the regiment.[73]

As table 9 demonstrates, the catalogue of disabilities covered everything from birth defects to the infirmities of old age. Besides this list of 124 men, 12

TABLE 9
Disabilities of Militiamen in the Provincial Infantry of Mexico Stationed at Córdoba, 1798.

Disability	Number	Disability	Number
Old and Exhausted	25	Dropsy	3
Old and Toothless	2	Hematosis	2
Old and Deaf	2	Fits	2
Skin Diseases	3	Demented	1
Crippled, Missing Fingers and Bone Diseases	16	Emaciation	1
		Hernia	1
Lung Disease	6	Epilepsy	3
Ruptures and Tumors	5	Perforated Palate	2
Nerve Problems	5	Humpbacked	1
Spasms	1	Asthma	1
Broken Ribs	1	Mentally Retarded	3
Deaf	2	Gout	2
Habitual Illness	2	Rheumatic	2
Kidney and Liver Disease	5	Dissipated	2
Poor Eyesight, Glaucoma, and Cataracts	6	Unidentified Conditions	12
		TOTAL	124
Urinary and Venereal Disease	5		

Source: Estados que manifiesta los soldados que se hallan inútiles, Regimiento Provincial de México, February 9, 1798, and August 11, 1798, AGN, IG, vol. 49.

of the replacements sent by the cabildo were found to suffer from venereal disease; they were dispatched to the hospital of San Pedro in Puebla for treatment with mercury. It is interesting to note the advanced ages of these militiamen. Of the 124 men listed, 43 had been in the militia for more than eighteen years and several had over thirty years' army service.[74]

Following these revelations, the cabildo experienced even more difficulties locating recruits. By 1800, there was so much resistance to the regiment that Viceroy Marquina threatened to reduce the number of officers in proportion to the number of soldiers.[75] Many companies consisted of little more than officers, sergeants, and corporals. The cabildo responded by suggesting a general levy of the capital to include childless only sons of widows and married men. Existing deferments should not be recognized because most lacked any veracity. The men of Mexico City were expert at utilizing legalities and dodging the census takers. The cabildo spent between six thousand and seven thousand pesos to collect accurate data, but discovered that the census consisted of a list of those who held military deferments of one kind or another. The eligible young men went into hiding, and no one knew the true size or composition of the population in the crowded barrios. The municipal governors claimed to have done everything within their power to promote recruitment; since the beginning of the cantonments, however, opposition to military service made the task impossible. The smallpox epidemic of 1797 added further complications because many young men of military age died or were permanently disabled. When Viceroy Azanza transferred provincial militiamen into the regular regiments at Veracruz in 1799, the cabildo of Mexico found no alternative to drafting 120 young apprentices from the guilds. Militiamen who believed themselves protected from the frightening idea of regular army duty were forced to abandon their families and to endure the evil conditions of Veracruz. Terror of this prospect caused a precipitous flight of men out of the capital whenever rumors spread about draft lotteries or new efforts to recruit militiamen. Not only had family men been torn from their homes and employment, but the experience in the regular regiments was harmful. Many of the hardworking young apprentices who were sent to Veracruz returned as useless wastrels who abandoned their families and took up vagabond lives.[76]

The role of the cabildos in military affairs did not end with the exasperating task of enlisting and mobilizing unwilling manpower. Whenever there were congregations of soldiers in urban centers, the cabildos were expected to fill important regulatory and supply functions. Here again, the municipal governors were torn between their duty to obey the regime and their desire to defend their constituents' interests. Great strains occurred in the cantonment towns of Orizaba, Córdoba, Perote, and Jalapa, where large numbers of troops were crammed into compact urban centers where there were limited rental accommodations. In such cases, the pressure upon housing and supplies became intense and the resultant profiteering provoked angry reactions from both army officers and civilians. When Branciforte designated Orizaba as the headquarters for his army of operations, he named Colonel Miguel Costansó to the post of quartermaster general; he was sent to survey the town and to select a dwelling adequate for the viceregal residence. At Orizaba, Costansó informed a surprised cabildo about the honor that was about to descend upon the town; he expropriated three of the best houses and asked for more. The cabildo named the alcaldes, Pedro Andrés Marín and José Antonio Suárez, to act as agents of the town in subsequent negotiations with the army.[77] Despite the wide powers granted to Costansó, Orizaba was not easy to convert into a headquarters town and seat of viceregal government. The quartermaster general had to suspend all private construction just to put glass in windows, doors in frames, and to clean out the lower floor of the house to be occupied by the viceroy. The acute shortage of artisans and laborers forced him to ask the cabildo of Córdoba for additional masons, carpenters, tinsmiths, and ironsmiths. When this failed, he asked the commander of the provincial Regiment of Tres Villas to see whether he could release workers for construction and repair duty. Since the viceregal court and the provincial regiments were about to converge upon Orizaba, not an hour was to be wasted. The local *juez eclesiástico* extended permission for tradesmen to work on holidays and Costansó attempted to put on a night shift although he found that the workers were not particularly enthusiastic about this.[78]

When *Intendente de Ejército* Francisco Rendón arrived at Orizaba, he ordered the cabildo to guarantee the availability of provisions and forage and to maintain prices according to the season. Although the municipal government agreed, it was powerless to prevent rapid inflation of prices on anything needed by the army. Disorders resulted as *revendadores* (middlemen) and *regatones* (speculators) intercepted incoming goods before they reached the urban markets. The cabildo posted spies beyond the town sentry-boxes to catch offenders, but this had limited results.[79] Despite efforts to prevent speculation, it went on in public view right in the main marketplace. The residents of Orizaba soon protested against the rise in prices and the disturbance of their normally calm city.

To control price increases and rampant speculation, prices of primary food items were fixed by regulations to be enforced by the cabildo. All speculation was forbidden and there was to be no sale of goods outside of the markets. Suppliers were ordered to bring their products to the plaza for sale before the noon prayers: failure to do so would be punished by confiscation of goods plus a fine of four pesos for Spaniards and two pesos for other castes. In order to gain public support for these measures, half the value of condemned articles went to the denunciant and the other half to the public jail or the hospital.[80] Even with tightened controls, many merchants, shopkeepers, and producers attempted to monopolize the sale of certain items and to limit the availability of provisions in the markets. In one typical case, an Indian, Francisco Antonio, sought to buy up all eggs before they reached Orizaba. He was caught with eleven dozen in his possession and argued that he had been ordered to purchase eggs by a regidor of the *cabildo de naturales,** Ignacio Bonifacio; furthermore, he claimed to be supplying eggs and chickens to the viceregal palace.[81]

Although prices leveled off after the Lenten season, the cabildo was kept busy with complaints about food costs, quality of goods, and the rental of houses. To dramatize the price controls on food and forage, the cabildo increased the fines and penalties for speculation. Table 10 illustrates the price per unit established in March 1797.[82] Speculation was to be penalized by a ten-peso fine, and monopolistic practices by shopkeepers or hawkers was forbidden under penalty of two years' exile for Spaniards and two hundred lashes and two years in the galleys for the castes.[83] The cabildo appointed Francisco del Puy y Ochea to serve as commissioner for public cleanliness and control. Besides watching over supply, his duties included street maintenance, lighting, repair to house exteriors, removal of offal and filth from slaughterhouses, and the power to destroy spoiled or inferior food offered for sale in the markets. The housing shortage continued to give the cabildo cause for concern: many residents attempted to take advantage of the army's needs by raising rents to exorbitant levels. Pedro Andrés Marín, the *alcalde ordinario* responsible for housing, acted to establish rent controls. There were to be no increases unless the army insisted upon major repairs and even then all charges had to be approved by Marín.[84] The concentration of troops brought severe hardships to many permanent inhabitants. Officers tended to be arbitrary in their demands for good housing near their regimental barracks and some citizens were evicted from their own homes.[85]

The rental situation was even tighter in Jalapa, where the viceregal court did not exert a controlling influence. The army appointed Captain Juan Antonio Carraras of the provincial Regiment of Tres Villas as *comisario de guerra* to deal with the cabildo's representative, *Alcalde* Mateo Badillo. Carraras soon charged that Badillo recommended poor quality housing—even abandoned Indian huts—at very high monthly rates. One place which had never rented

---

*The Indian governing council.

TABLE 10
Food and Commodity Prices Fixed by the Cabildo of Orizaba, 1797.

Product	Amount	Cost	Product	Amount	Cost
Bread	28 onzas	1 real	Maize	1 cuartilla	3 reales
Maracaibo			Cinnamon	1 onza	10 reales
Cacao	1 libra	4 reales	Cloves	1 onza	5 reales
Tabasco			Pepper	1 onza	1 real
Cacao	1 libra	4 reales	Saffron	1 onza	1 peso
Guayaquil			Cooking		
Cacao	1 libra	2¾ reales	Oil	1 cuartillo	5 reales
White Sugar	1 libra	1 real	Vinegar	1 cuartillo	2 reales
Rice	1 libra	⅝ real	Tallow	8 onzas	1 real
Sea Salt	1 libra	½ real	Beef	4 libras 12 onzas	1 real
Chile	1 libra	2 reales	Lamb	26 onzas	1 real
Ham	1 libra	2 reales	Barley	1 carga	20 reales
Butter	1 libra	2½ reales	Straw	1 arroba	1½ reales
Cheese	1 libra	2 reales			
Shrimp	1 libra	2 reales			
Eggs	1 libra	2 reales			
Chick peas	1 cuartilla	3 pesos			
Beans	1 cuartilla	1 peso			
Lima Beans	1 cuartilla	5 reales			
Lentils	1 cuartilla	10 reales			

Source: El cabildo... manda que por ahora y hasta nueva orden los dueños de tienda y demas personas que les comprehende, observen y guarden la postura siguiente, March 16, 1797, AGN, IG, vol. 134-B.

for more than six to eight pesos per month was offered to the military at twenty pesos. Jalapeños were familiar with periodic pressures upon local housing because of their intimate connection with the merchants and commerce of Veracruz. Accustomed to raising rents in any shortage, they now either refused to rent to army officers and soldiers or demanded highly inflated prices. Carraras found his own job was almost impossible because the alcalde always sided with the renters against the army.[86]

Poor relations between the army and the cantonment towns continued in subsequent years. After some preliminary sparring over accommodations, Viceroy Marquina demanded that the cabildo of Jalapa furnish him with a suitable house and, in addition, supply food and drink at local expense.[87] In the opinion of most property owners, soldiers were exceptionally rough tenants. Commanders believed that it was bad for discipline to have their units billeted in various locations; if houses were not large enough, they attempted to rent contiguous buildings and then proceeded to knock down walls and to block doors and windows.[88] Even if the effort to make barracks out of private residences did not cause major damage, the presence of soldiers on the premises meant rough usage, wear, and a certain amount of vandalism. Even in the most rigorously controlled army barracks, unknown culprits smashed doors, windows, and any movable articles.[89] When, for example, Ana María de Leyra returned to her home in Orizaba in 1809 after it had been occupied by the Dragoon Regiment of Mexico and the provincial Regiment of Tlaxcala, she found it totally uninhabitable. Major repairs were needed before she could even contemplate moving in; she demanded compensation from the government and was successful in recovering some damages.[90]

On other occasions, disputes raged between homeowners and army officers or between merchants and the military over the expropriation of buildings. In 1805 when Colonel Miguel de Emparán and his wife arrived at the house designated as their residence by the cabildo of Jalapa, they discovered to their shock that most rooms were filled with bales of merchandise. The house had been rented to the Veracruz merchant house of Gibert, Tutzó, and Grau. Following Viceroy Iturrigaray's order to move all valuable commodities inland to Jalapa, they had begun the laborious process of shipping 400 mule loads of goods—part of a total inventory worth more than 600,000 pesos. This included 1,200 barrels of brandy, 500 barrels of wine, a large quantity of iron, 140 cases of steel, 42 cases of books, 80 bales of paper, and 17 bales of silk goods.[91] Already, Jaime Tutzó had moved 170 mule loads to the Jalapa warehouse and he did not have any intention of bowing to the army. He possessed a lease on the house in question and argued that the costly transfer of his business to Jalapa resulted from viceregal orders. In his view, merchants as well as soldiers had to have some rights. Colonel Costansó attempted to make the cabildo evict the merchants, but no action was taken. When both sides appealed to Iturrigaray, he left the merchants in possession of their property; since he was in more than enough trouble with the port merchants, it was likely he did not wish to create new grievances.[92]

As we have seen earlier, many of the disputes between the cabildos and the army reflected aspects of the criollo-gachupín rivalry as well as the normal conflicts between soldiers and civilians. Since the army represented centralized power and appeared to threaten local privileges and interests, the cabildos developed a protective attitude. Yet, it was possible to turn most cabildos into ardent supporters of army expansion. Branciforte achieved some remarkable successes in contrast to Revillagigedo's negative relationships with urban administrations. There was one thing the criollos wanted desperately—access to prestige, position, and power. Branciforte was successful because he found one way to satisfy some of these aspirations.[93]

Revillagigedo neither understood nor cared to understand the aspirations of the criollos. His mission and the reforming zeal which propelled him was to further the cause of Bourbon Spain. A true believer in the ideals of enlightened despotism,[94] close in spirit to the Conde de Aranda and José de Gálvez, he desired to strengthen metropolitan controls and to bring efficiency to the near impossible bureaucracy of the American possessions. As he explained to Alejandro Malaspina, "the only way to bring order and to advance affairs in these kingdoms is to send to them governors of satisfaction and performance."[95] He complained to Aranda about the "rivalries and antagonisms" he had to counter and the general level of inefficiency in the administration.[96] No wonder he had little sympathy for the cabildos over which he exercised the least control, or over the militias which seemed inefficient and a source of constant friction. His goal was to disband the provincial army and to replace it with a heavily European regular force.

Branciforte's approach was quite different. From the beginning of his tenure in New Spain, he sought to utilize and to channel the criollo aspirations. To do so, he employed the cabildos. He could see that if there was to be a significant army of operations, the criollos had to be involved. Revillagigedo's military planning was in ruins and the cabildos of Guanajuato and other cities which no longer had militia pickets on police duty were hard pressed to protect their communities against rising levels of crime. In these cities, the elites clamored for restoration of some militia units. Taking advantage of this need and the insatiable criollo thirst for office, Branciforte realized he could raise a large army with little immediate cost to the exchequer.[97] He ordered senior regular army officers to visit cities and towns which had been or were to be the headquarters of the new provincial regiments and battalions. Each officer received thorough instructions on how to approach the cabildos and other officials. First, they were to inform the cabildo of the limited funds available in the treasury and of the shortage of tax support for provincial militias. Without the full cooperation of the loyal subjects of New Spain, the formation of an adequate defense force would be impossible.

The second step was to stimulate the competitive spirit of municipal leaders by telling them about the zeal of the Puebla cabildo, which had collected enough voluntary donations to reestablish the local cavalry and infantry regiments. Finally, each cabildo was granted full control over the recommendation of candidates suitable to hold commissions. Of course, it was made crystal clear that those who desired commissions—the colonels, lieutenants colonel, captains, lieutenants, and sublieutenants—should underwrite all costs of uniforms and weapons, and, in the case of cavalry or dragoons, provide mounts and equipment for their prospective units.[98] As a guideline, they were to keep in mind that each infantryman cost thirty-five to forty pesos and each dragoon sixty to seventy pesos.

Branciforte set down very strict rules about how donations should be made. As might be expected, he received numerous personal petitions for commissions which mentioned sums of money to be offered for a specific rank or command. He rejected all of these out of hand because he wanted to avoid any suggestion of bribery or contractual arrangements. His purpose was to present a public display in which the only motive was the generosity of loyal vassals. Offers were to be made through the cabildos in terms of men uniformed, equipped, and armed—cavalry or infantry. Monetary values would be attached at a later date. The recommendations of the cabildo and finally of the viceroy and the king would decide what reward or rank to grant the honorable donors. Of course, the cabildo would inform wealthy aspirants of the amount of money needed to raise forces in their districts. The amount of donations almost always determined the rank to be awarded.[99]

In Guanajuato, the viceregal commissioner, Colonel José Antonio Rengel, carried instructions based upon the Crespo Plan to convert the extinguished Legion of the Prince into a cavalry regiment and an infantry battalion. The infantry was to be raised in Guanajuato and Silao and the cavalry in Guanajuato, León, Irapuato, and Pénjamo. The cabildo of Guanajuato was granted the right to propose candidates for commissions in the fusileer companies of the battalion and in cavalry companies based in the city.[100] Rengel carried copies of previous census reports and had a good idea of just how the units might be formed before he arrived in Guanajuato[101] (see table 11). Basically, however, there was no selling job needed in any of the towns assigned to these units. Guanajuato had used a militia picket for police protection until 1793, when Revillagigedo disbanded the legion. To fill the void, he garrisoned the Second Volunteer Company of Catalonia to police the city, but

TABLE 11
Ratio of Militiamen to Eligible Population in the Cavalry Regiment of the Prince and the Infantry Battalion of Guanajuato, 1796.

Jurisdiction	Militiamen	Eligible Males	Number of Eligible Families
Guanajuato	463	1,792	8,128
Silao	58	660	1,269
Irapuato	87	686	1,406
León	87	1,447	2,335
Pénjamo	58	646	1,012
Total	753	5,231	14,150

Source: Estado que manifiesta el número de milicianos establecidos en las jurisdicciones de Guanajuato, Silao, Irapuato, León, and Pénjamo, January 29, 1795, AGN, IG, vol. 156-B.

a few months later the war against France forced him to transfer the unit to Perote. Besides, the cabildo opposed the imposition of regular troops, who cost the city eight thousand pesos a year more than the militia. After this experience, the cabildo asked for the restoration of a system which permitted local troops to furnish police protection. In a city spread out over hills and ravines, residents were the only ones who knew the possible hiding places of criminals.[102]

The generosity of the cabildo and the elite of Guanajuato reflected the city's wealth and prosperity. The municipal government offered to use its own funds to uniform and arm the full infantry battalion and the two cavalry companies assigned to the city. This resulted in an outright donation of 20,260 pesos.[103] Not yet satisfied with their loyalty and patriotism, the regidores examined the city budget to see whether funds could be diverted from current fiscal programs to meet the greater needs of the state. They had to repair the Camacho bridge, construct a new bridge named San Pedro y Punta de Diamante, and undertake urgent repairs to the jail. These projects would deduct a total of 35,230 pesos from the total balance in the treasury of 72,087 pesos, 4 reales, 7 *granos*. The remaining 36,857 pesos, 3 reales, 1 grano had been earmarked for new construction on the *alhóndiga* de Granaditas* and the cobbling of streets. After consideration, the cabildo agreed to postpone these projects in order to make the full surplus available to the crown as an interest-free loan for the duration of the war.[104] Private donations from officer aspirants and other loyal citizens were equally generous. Wealthy miners and merchants offered to arm and uniform forces far larger than those to be raised. The figures in table 12 illustrate the sources of funds and the expenditures during militia formation.[105]

Despite the popularity of the Guanajuato militias, the units were not examples of overwhelming martial enthusiasm. Some members of the most outstanding families were not inclined to the militia and others simply lacked spare time away from mines, smelters, or other business interests. Some, such as Francisco de Septién, a wealthy smelter operator and financier, refused to accept a mere captaincy but jumped at the opportunity to become a lieutenant colonel. Quite often, the proposals made by the cabildo were submitted to Branciforte prior to adequate consultation with the individuals recommended for commissions. One candidate, Pedro Lozano, requested release from a lieutenancy and four others attempted to resign commissions on grounds of insufficient wealth, large families, poor health, or business pressures.[106] Others resided outside of Guanajuato and felt they could not attend assemblies or other

---

*Storehouse for grain and corn.

TABLE 12
Donations and Expenditures for the Formation of the Cavalry Regiment of the Prince and the Battalion of Guanajuato, 1795.

DONORS		CASH VALUE
Colonel Antonio Pérez Gálvez (300 cavalrymen uniformed and armed)		24,000 pesos
Colonel Ignacio Obregón (90 cavalrymen)		7,200
Cabildo of Guanajuato (2 cavalry companies)		4,800
Cabildo of Guanajuato (entire infantry battalion)		14,692.4
Private Donations—including offers by Lieutenant Colonel Manual García Quintana (100 infantrymen), Lieutenant Colonel Francisco Septién (150 infantrymen, and Colonel Diego Rul (100 infantrymen)		21,972
TOTAL		72,664.4
EXPENDITURES		
Cavalry uniforms for the regiment	30,159.3	
Infantry uniforms for the battalion	14,692.4	
Horses	4,176.	
Swords	1,568.7	
Barracks for the cavalry regiment	9,725.3	
TOTAL		60,322.1
SURPLUS FUNDS REMAINING IN THE TREASURY		12,342.3

Source: Noticia de las ofertas y gastos en el Batallón de Guanajuato y Regimiento de Caballería del Príncipe, August 1795, AGN, IG, vol. 157-B.

militia functions. Many of the cabildo appointments made in the surrounding towns demonstrate a rather haphazard approach to the junior commissions. Julián Pablo de la Peña of Irapuato renounced his commission as a cavalry standard-bearer because his business was just becoming established; he owed several large sums to Veracruz merchants and his finances were so precarious that he dared not abandon his shop for an instant.[107] José María de Lanuza, proposed as an ensign, stated that he had been a resident of Irapuato for only a few weeks and had decided not to open a permanent business there.[108] Ignacio Navarro Caziño rejected a lieutenancy in an Irapuato company because he was a resident of Valladolid and was in the town merely to visit a rented hacienda.[109]

As might be expected, some men who wanted commissions were passed over or received a rank below what they felt they deserved. Others were not at all satisfied with the degree of rigor practiced by the various cabildos. Pedro Salinas Medilla, subdelegate of Pénjamo, complained to Branciforte about the poor quality of officer candidates being proposed by the León cabildo. He described a number of the new officers in the cavalry regiment as being unworthy of commissions. Some possessed a total wealth of only a few hundred pesos in country property and others came from families that had never had noble status. One man, Juan del Río, owned a small shop valued at less than two hundred pesos. Moreover, he was fifty years of age and had six dependent children to support. The subdelegate warned against malcontent elements in the León cabildo who stirred up hostilities and created factions.[110] Another anonymous letter cautioned the viceroy about unworthy subjects from Pénjamo who were being appointed by the León cabildo. The worst was Manuel García Parra, also mentioned by the subdelegate, who made his living selling mezcal liquor and was married to a mulatta well known for her scandalous ways.[111]

While the cabildos of the Guanajuato jurisdiction were quite successful in raising militia forces, they did not neglect their role as guardians of the local interest. It was one thing to distribute officer commissions among the local notables, but quite another if any military enthusiast suggested the enlistment of laborers connected with mining. On this question, the cabildo was adamant; "mine work required ... constant presence, an indefatigable tenacity, extreme humiliation, and an attitude of servitude toward the administrators and managers of the mine." Not only would these qualities deteriorate when workers were absent for militia assemblies and garrison duty, but the respect shown the men as militiamen would ruin them as miners. Once they became accustomed to appreciation, distinction, and leisure, they would never want to return to the hard existence of the silver miner.[112] Since militia interference threatened to cause labor shortages, the cabildo protested in advance against any policy that might result in decreased production.

Elsewhere, the cabildos exhibited similar reactions to the restoration of the provincial militias. In the province of Michoacán, the criollo elite responded to the opportunity to obtain commissions, but there were other forces which raised obstacles to the viceregal plans. Branciforte's commissioner was Colonel Juan Velázquez,[113] commander of the Dragoon Regiment of Spain. His instructions were similar to those of Rengel for Guanajuato; he was to stimulate the provincial population's loyalty and patriotism, and leave to the cabildos the right to propose candidates. Once again, the cities and towns received control over much more territory than their immediate urban centers. Much of the enlistment for the provincial Infantry Regiment of Valladolid and the Dragoon Regiment of Michoacán came from rural districts rather than the towns. Indeed, although the Valladolid census listed 2,779 men of military age and status, only 976 actually resided in the city. The rest came from small villages, haciendas, and ranches in the surrounding countryside[114] (see table 13). Velázquez commenced his work in Valladolid, where the cabildo was to pre-

TABLE 13
Numbers of Whites, Castizos, and Mestizos Eligible for Militia Service
in the Ten Jurisdictions of Michoacán, 1794.

Valladolid	2,779
Pátzcuaro	1,117
Tlazazalca	1,990
Zamora	1,630
Xiquilpa	987
Maravatío	1,173
Ario	284
Sirándaro	712
Tlalpuxagua	806
Cuiseo	220
TOTAL	11,698

Source: Relación de los hombres útiles de las tres classes..., December 10, 1794, AGN, IG, vol. 211-B.

pare a list of aspirants for commissions in the infantry regiment. The only discordant note was the appearance of an anonymous letter nailed to the cathedral door which attacked the militia as a "destroyer of families and the ruin of people and souls."[115] Shocked by the vehemence of the attack, Velázquez reported the event to Mexico City. The secretary of the viceroyalty, Colonel Antonio Bonilla, dismissed the matter as a mere incident; although he felt it best to identify the author, he thought the letter was likely the work of "some crazy friar or some windy cleric who dislikes the gachupines."[116]

Outside of Valladolid, Velázquez encountered stiff opposition to any military formations. According to his plans, the Dragoon Regiment of Michoacán was to be centered in Pátzcuaro or Zamora with the cabildos sharing the privilege of officer selection and the obligation of recruiting 348 soldiers. At first, Velázquez sent one of his subordinates, Major José Gómez, to Zamora with instructions to begin recruitment. He even considered naming the unit the Regiment of Zamora until he arrived in the town to inspect Gómez's progress. Despite the mildest approach to the inhabitants, they fled to the Cerro de la Beata rather than permit their names to be enrolled in the militia. Velázquez found little more than apprentice merchants and married artisans in otherwise empty companies. He examined what men there were and then went to the cabildo to submit a list of the officer candidates he considered most deserving for the senior commissions. In all cases, he respected the seniority of officers left over from the extinguished militia; Lieutenant Colonel Francisco Menocal would be promoted to colonel and officers such as Captain José Bernardo Fonserrada who had held commissions since the 1770s and 1780s would fill the other senior posts.

The real trouble in Zamora began when the cabildo declined to accept any of Velázquez's recommendations. Asserting their rights, the municipal governors submitted three new names for the colonelcy—Alexo de la Mora, José Mariano Lasso, and Manuel Martínez de la Lastra. The first choice in the *terna,* Mora, had been a very junior captain in the disbanded militias; besides being the subordinate of Menocal and the senior captains, Velázquez described him as a man of such obesity that he could scarcely move from his house unless carried in a coach.[117] Although the cabildo declined to recommend Menocal because he resided in Pátzcuaro, Mora, temporarily a guest in the home of the local subdelegate, normally resided on his hacienda twelve leagues from Zamora inside the jurisdiction of Nueva Galicia. According to Velázquez's opinion, this candidate should have come under the control of the Guadalajara authorities. As for the others, Lasso lacked both the experience and the capacity to command, and Lastra was an altogether unknown quantity. For lieutenant colonel, the cabildo proposed José Torres, who had been a mere ensign, and two men who had no military experience at all. Finally, to confuse matters even further, some of the men suggested for commissions lived in Xacona and Tangancícuaro well outside of the control of Zamora.

Velázquez threw up his hands in disgust when he considered a regiment commanded by a junior captain and a mere countryman, filled with senior officers who must be gravely insulted by the affront. None of the candidates proposed by the cabildo offered as much in donations as Menocal and Fonserrada and they all withdrew their offers when told that they could not make donations in exchange for ranks, but had to leave the final appointments up to the viceroy. Velázquez stated that there were some reasonable men in the cabildo—the alguacil mayor, Alonso de León, for example—but they failed to sway the majority. In such a case, the commissioner requested viceregal intervention to force the city government back into line. Branciforte was willing to accept considerable local control over appointments to militia regiments, but not to the degree that experienced officers and the largest donors were not recognized. Threats were sufficient to restore full cooperation: Menocal became colonel, Fonserrada lieutenant colonel, and the cabildo offered to uniform and arm four companies as well as to donate one thousand pesos in currency.[118] Despite the apparent repentance, however, Velázquez continued to encounter resistance from the lower classes who were to fill the ranks; finally he did most of the recruiting in the small towns of Tarímbaro, Guango, Puruándiro, Angamacutiro, Maravatío, Tlazazalca, and Chocándiro.[119]

Where there was no truly wealthy elite of miners or landowners ready to underwrite the costs of militia formation, the cabildos had to collect money from a much larger segment of the population. In the Infantry Regiment of Tres Villas (Jalapa, Córdoba, and Orizaba), the cabildos and provincial subdelegates organized an efficient system of distributing regimental commissions and locating sources of funds to support the unit. Córdoba levied a tax of four reales per *carga* of tobacco harvested which in only three years yielded 7,160 pesos. Of course, where there was no single benefactor, the cabildos found that fund raising required a great deal of time and effort. In Córdoba, donations of 2,878 pesos to help finance the two local companies came from 107 citizens. The sums offered ranged from 1 peso to 200 pesos, but most contributors gave something less than 50 pesos. As table 14 illustrates, even the commanding officers could not afford to pay very large amounts for their commissions.[120]

Considering the complexity of Branciforte's militia program, the level of success was remarkable. Despite stiff opposition from the ordinary royal jurisdiction and from other privileged sectors, the prospect of royal commis-

TABLE 14
Donations toward the Formation of the Infantry of Tres Villas, 1795.

Source	Amount (pesos)
Cabildo of Córdoba	2,878
Cabildo of Orizaba	5,880
Cabildo of Jalapa	2,270
Cabildo of Tehuacán	2,555
Subdelegate of Jalapa	1,365
Subdelegate of Perote	420
Subdelegate of Teciutlán	102
Subdelegate of Xalacingo	105
Subdelegate of San Juan de los Llanos	2,555
Captain José de Cárdenas	875
Sublieutenant Juan de Barcena	980
Captain Gaspar de Yriarte	750
Lieutenant Colonel Marcos González	2,000
Captain José de la Fuente	100
Lieutenant José Simón de la Portilla	200
Sublieutenant Manuel Toledano	25
Anonymous Donation	400
Domingo Antonio de la Torre	1,050
Sargento Mayor of Perote Jaime Alzuvide	105
Colonel José Manuel Cevallos	1,000
TOTAL	25,615 pesos

Source: Listas de los sujetos de este vecindario que contribuyeron graciosamente para el vestuario de las dos compañías de milicias de esta villa... , 1795, AGN, vol. 374-A.

sions dazzled the provincial elite. Realizing exactly what motivated the outpouring of support, Branciforte was willing to suspend royal orders limiting the *fuero militar* or to do whatever he could to nurture the ceremonial role of the officer. Of course, this alliance with the cabildos and the community leaders did foster the "rage for titles" reported by Humboldt.[121] Branciforte felt that he had to take some risks since the formation of the provincial army was essential if New Spain was to be retained. Almost certainly, the charge laid by historians that he enriched himself through the sale of militia commissions lacks real substance.[122] Both the regular army commissioners and the cabildos kept careful records of all sums donated: had there been peculation, those who opposed the army would have seized upon the slightest trace of corruption. In fact, the authors of anonymous tracts attacking Branciforte's militia plan sought to unearth evidence to discredit the provincial army. Clergymen feared the impact of martial institutions and regular army officers continued to support Revillagigedo's idea of defense based upon a regular army. Since gossip, scandal, and rumor formed the staff of life in provincial society, secret bribes to the viceroy could not have been kept quiet.[123] The donations were large, but they were made through the cabildos and official channels. As early as February 1795, Branciforte boasted about voluntary offers worth 201,600 pesos.[124] By the time he left Mexico, contributions of over 550,000 pesos had paid for all uniforms, arms, and mounts; surplus funds remaining in the treasury were transferred to the general operating budget for the militias.[125]

The policy of sharing militia responsibility between the cabildos and the army remained after Branciforte departed from New Spain. From time to time, however, regular army officers and some of the brigade commanders attempted to restore Revillagigedo's view that cabildos had no right to interfere in military affairs. In 1805, for example, the colonelcy of the Dragoons of San Luis at San Luis Potosí became vacant with the death of the Conde del Peñasco. As was customary, the cabildo prepared a *terna* of three likely candidates; to help in this process they requested the service records from Brigadier Félix Calleja. Instead of cooperating, Calleja challenged the cabildo's rights. In his interpretation of the royal orders, he thought that the crown had declared its intention to create military ordinances for New Spain or for the Americas in general, but the project was not completed. Until such time as new orders superseded old *reglamentos,* the laws issued since 1766 remained in full force. Yet Calleja was not sure which of the conflicting sets of regulations applied to Mexico—the *reglamento* of 1766 and the *real declaración* of 1767 dealing with the European army, the militia *reglamento* of 1769 for Cuba,[126] or the militia *reglamento* of 1794 for Nueva Granada.[127] Long

Revillagigedo's protégé, Calleja could not help being appalled by the grant of militia appointment privileges to the cabildos and the consequent erosion of army authority.

In a survey of municipal-army relationships, Calleja agreed that the cabildo of Mexico City had been awarded permission to propose candidates for militia commissions. Then, beginning in 1795, Branciforte used this precedent to extend the same privileges to all cities and towns. This was pure political expediency motivated by short-term necessity; he wanted to stimulate contributions of arms, uniforms, and mounts. The plan had been successful, for officers such as the Conde del Peñasco gave so much money that the royal treasury did not have to spend a single "*maravedí.*"[128] At the same time, however, the power to propose officers was new to the cabildo of San Luis Potosí, where the commander of the disbanded legion had selected all candidates from the intendancy. As far as Calleja could see, the crown did not approve Branciforte's innovations. The *reglamento* of Nueva Granada—the latest militia ordinance for an American province—made no mention of a role for the cabildos. With the introduction of the militia brigades and the inclusion of powers over subinspection in the office of brigade commander, Calleja convinced himself that the king and his ministers wanted these officers to handle officer selection.

As far as Calleja was concerned, the cabildos did not have the legal right to intervene in militia matters. Only army officers could recognize and judge the capacity of a man to be an officer and whether he should be promoted. The city governments lacked the necessary service records and the civilian politicians could not possibly have the *ojo militar* needed for the selection process. At the same time, though, this challenge contained some highly important implications. This was one of the few areas in which the local elites—criollo or gachupín—controlled patronage and appointments. Of even more potential danger was the attitude Calleja represented; his frustrations with the cabildo of San Luis Potosí reflected the isolation of a highly intelligent professional soldier mired down in a boring militia command. What he advocated was greater military autonomy and freedom from meddling civilians. Fortunately, *Auditor* Bataller rejected Calleja's arguments out of hand. None of the ordinances Calleja cited took precedence over the royal order of September 24, 1794, concerning the cabildo of Mexico. Even more important, article 4 of the *Instrucción de Comandantes de Brigada*[129] declared that where there were cabildos, the right to propose militia officers belonged to them and not to the brigade commanders.[130]

Although there was not sufficient power in the cabildos to directly resist the viceroys or diverge radically from the regime's policy, the urban governments did protect and further local interests. In outright confrontations, the cabildos often had their way. When, for example, the colonelcy of the Infantry of Tlaxcala became vacant with the death of Colonel Conde de Contramina, the cabildo of Tlaxcala endorsed the candidacy of a prominent resident, Lorenzo Angulo Guardamino. He had given generously toward the formation of the regiment and while he had only eight years' service, the twenty signatories of the cabildo felt he demonstrated the military capacity of a regular commander. Viceroy Azanza disagreed with this choice, preferring to appoint Francisco de Luna, Marqués de Ciría, who was a senior captain in the provincial Infantry of Mexico. When the viceroy could not sway the cabildo to his opinion, he capitulated and named Angulo Guardamino.[131]

7

THE MERCHANTS AND THE MILITARY

If any Mexican army unit other than the small company of viceregal halberdiers could claim hoary traditions reaching back into the seventeenth century, it was the Urban Regiment of Commerce of Mexico City. In 1692, when food shortages and hunger drove much of the capital proletariat to violent insurrection, there was no army capable of restoring order. With the rabble in control of the central plaza and crying, "Death to the Spaniards and gachupines who eat our maize,"[1] the authorities assembled a force of merchants and guildsmen. Armed with fowling pieces (*escopetas*), pistols, and a few old muskets, the aroused merchants were the first to enter the plaza and to rout the disorganized mob.[2] Although such behavior was expected of the Spanish class during times of social turmoil, the king wrote to Viceroy Conde de Galve informing him that it was a good idea to regularize the involvement of those citizens who had the most to lose. The merchant militia was particularly attractive since the consulado of Mexico would be responsible for financing the new unit.[3]

While the Urban Regiment of Commerce received official sanction in a *real cédula* dated February 18, 1693, no new violence broke out. Without some impetus, the merchants forgot all about their newly acquired military status. The regiment had almost withered away entirely when on December 1, 1710, the Viceroy Duque de Linares asked the consulado to examine whether it was convenient for the security of commercial property to continue the militia; if not, it could be disbanded and the men united with the guild companies. To decide the issue, the consulado convoked a *junta de comercio* which voted twenty-one to four in favor of maintaining the regiment.[4] Because there were few troops in Mexico City and a repetition of the 1692 violence was possible, most merchants were willing to support a limited defensive force. Despite their unanimity, however, few wanted to lend their own services to the regiment; there was no colonel and captains had to be selected from the consulado's membership. To make militia service at least acceptable, the merchants agreed to allocate an annual subsidy of five thousand pesos from revenues on imported merchandise granted to the consulado by the crown.[5] There were to be eight companies and each captain would receive an annual allowance of five hundred pesos which was supposed to be used to cover expenses and to help out the sergeants, corporals, drummers, and fifers. The remaining one thousand pesos went to the regular army major who served as administrative officer; he was to use the money to pay for powder consumed in public ceremonies and to meet sundry other financial obligations. The most junior captains did not receive any allowance from the consulado. Subsequently, the regiment was expanded to ten companies, but there was no increase made in the annual subsidy.

The regiment was not mobilized during the War of the Spanish Succession and militia duty was not considered onerous by most merchants. They sent their apprentices and cashiers to serve in their places, and the keepers of small shops experienced little inconvenience even if they had to perform occasional guard duty. In fact, the regiment was seldom seen in public except at Corpus Christi or on important occasions such as the welcoming of a new viceroy. Even then, the militiamen appeared in their own personal, varied uniforms and armed themselves with diverse muskets and shotguns depending upon what they happened to have available for the protection of their businesses. There was little effort made to obtain regimental uniformity and the officers did not bother to hold assemblies for training or exercises.[6] Prior to 1764, the major service undertaken by the unit was the presentation of a few men for guard duty at the viceregal palace and royal jail. The labor was divided equitably allowing all merchants at least nine days for their businesses for every day they had to have a militiaman under arms.[7]

With army reform and the rise of better-organized regular and militia units, the merchant regiment became something of an anachronism. Privately funded and controlled by the unmilitary merchant barons, it did not fit into the new structure. Men of the regiment soon found themselves the objects of public condescension and derision whenever they appeared in public.[8] On the other hand, as the costs of maintaining an army became apparent, the viceregal administrations and even the imperial government saw the benefit of a regiment which cost nothing and was available at all times for garrison duty in Mexico City. Merchants who had been willing to donate some of their time on an occasional basis found themselves under growing pressures to present militiamen. They had to furnish daily guards for the mint, treasury, acordada, and archbishop's residence as well as to dispatch police patrols and to maintain various guardposts. By 1800, at least 175 men were needed each day to fill specific guard and police functions.[9] This did not take into account full regimental mobilizations when the regular and provincial units were needed elsewhere. Long before they suffered any harm to their businesses, the substantial merchants hired replacements called *alquilones* to serve in their places and those of their valuable employees. Merchants and shopkeepers who were less well off and could least afford the time were drawn more and more into guard duty. Since their regiment was almost as active as many provincial units, it did not take long before some merchant officers demanded parity of fueros with other militias. When this happened, conflicts of jurisdiction between the consulado and the military became inevitable. Any privileges extended to the semiprofessional merchant officers of the Urban Regiment detracted from the consulado's jealously guarded sovereignty over all merchants. Indeed, as the crown granted military fueros to make the provincial militias attractive to Mexicans, the consulado resisted any diminution of its own legal jurisdiction. Even within the merchant guild, the regimental officers and the merchant elite became embroiled in antagonistic debate. Many of the disputes were insoluble—the result of diametrically opposed commercial and military interests. But the struggle followed the course of the new army and tried the legal talents of each succeeding administration. In fact, much of the smoke generated by lengthy fuero conflicts developed from the complex problems of the merchant militia.

To begin with, the relaxed traditions of the merchant regiment were unacceptable when there were better-disciplined troops available for comparison. Viceroy Bucareli attempted to fill the chronically depleted ranks of the unit by imposing a one-month jail term and fifty-peso fine upon any merchant who did not present himself for service. Since many escaped connection with the regiment because they did not define themselves as merchants, the viceroy specifically included the owners of clothing stores, food sellers, wine, oil, and liquor merchants, and persons who sold sugar, chile, books, scrap iron, and all those who offered goods at market stalls.[10] In the month following enlistment, each man was responsible for purchasing a uniform, musket, bayonet, and other equipment at his own cost; when called, he was to present himself with sufficient ammunition to discharge his musket ten times. Without realizing the full ramifications of his decree, Bucareli struck directly at the welfare of the smaller businessmen who lacked apprentices or servants to serve in their place and who could not really afford to hire a replacement. Many were simply too old or physically disabled. The poor vegetable shop owners were the hardest hit because they seldom had servants; they faced the choice of employing alquilones or of closing up their shops to attend to their militia obligations. Most of these small shopkeepers went into business with capital of only one hundred to two hundred pesos and they needed to remain open on holidays if they were to make ends meet. Not only did they have to pay for their shops or stalls, but they were also obliged to purchase their inventories from the more substantial merchants who monopolized distribution and issued credit. There was limited profit to be made at the lowest retail level anyway; the small shopkeepers dealt with such poor customers that they had to accept pledged or pawned items in lieu of currency. Many soon fell into debt and then either fled or turned themselves over to the consulado. Few shopkeepers of this sort managed to remain in business for long. Upon declaring their insolvency, they sold their shops and tools to persons in the same basic position who inevitably followed them into debt and business failure.[11] As a result, the poorest merchants were the only ones who actually served in the Regiment of Commerce. The remainder of the unit was composed of affluent merchants' employees and mercenary alquilones hired as replacements. This meant that there was a constant personnel turnover in the regiment and by the beginning of the 1780s even more difficult problems had begun to emerge.

With the extension of the *fuero militar* to the provincial militia units, it was natural that the Urban Regiment's supporters would seek similar privileges. From 1781 to 1783, the regiment was mobilized and on active duty in the Mexico City garrison while the regular troops served in wartime defensive positions. This mobilization was to bring all of the unsolved problems connected with the unit into the open and to begin interminable struggles within the consulado between the powerful elite which governed the merchant guild and the merchant militiamen who wanted the same privileges as the provincial soldiers. It began with the petition of a merchant, Francisco Velasco, directed to the *auditor de guerra* in which he complained that his *fuero militar* as a member of the Urban Regiment had been abused when he was "scandalously" arrested and jailed in the public prison. As an hidalgo and a militiaman, he demanded to be transferred to his regimental barracks until such time as the case might be heard by the merchant court.[12] In his opinion, his brush with the law resulted from excessive creditor demands and poor economic conditions, but he neglected to state that he had been apprehended while attempting to flee the capital. In any event, the merits of the case were lost in what became a precedent-setting legal conflict.

When the captain of Velasco's company, Juan Manuel Pérezcano, suggested that the consulado had no right to throw merchant militiamen into the public prison, he began a jurisdictional battle which would continue until 1810. The consulado counterattacked on two fronts: first, it lashed out against a faction of officers who had become more interested in the regiment than in conducting their businesses; second, it interpreted the pretensions of Velasco and his supporters as a dangerous challenge to the merchant tribunal's jurisdiction. At first, the guild pointed out to the officers that they were, after all, merchants first and soldiers second, and they should recall that the consulado paid the regiment's costs and nominated candidates for commissions.[13] The officers reacted by forming a junta of twenty-two men which elected Manuel Pérez Fernández as their *apoderado general* to defend the unit's rights, fueros, and privileges. One of his first tasks was to petition Inspector General Cisneros for a permanent barracks and guardhouse. Pérez pointed out that all of the provincial regiments had barracks and that in Puebla, the urban battalion, the provincial regiment, and even the pardo battalion, composed of the most ordinary elements, all had barracks.[14] The sergeants of the Urban Regiment also organized themselves and elected Lorenzo José Cabrera as their spokesman. He supported the officers and went so far as to claim that since the Regiment of Commerce was mostly European Spanish in composition, it had to be more trustworthy than the provincial units. They and even the regular regiments enlisted a variety of castes and classes. Therefore, the merchant regiment was the only one to be counted upon to defend the king and *patria*.[15]

The rich almaceneros who dominated the consulado reacted to these petitions with anger and scorn against the merchant militiamen. Any major wholesaler or retailer simply did not have time to waste in the regiment and it was well known that merchants who were enlisted lacked financial substance. Besides, there were those in commerce, particularly some of the minor shopkeepers, who sold prohibited alcoholic drinks, used false weights and measures, or sold clothing pawned by the poor before the statutory time limit elapsed. These were the men who hoped to take advantage of the military jurisdiction to escape the consulado's honest regulating power. Some of the sergeants were not even merchants and had joined the regiment simply to escape the ordinary courts, to run illegal gaming houses, and to commit other crimes.[16] The officers' representative, Captain Pérez Fernández, was dismissed as a man without wealth or standing in the merchant community. What he did have, however, was a close friendship with Inspector General Cisneros, who sided with the officers against the consulado. The merchants blamed some of the trouble upon the obsolete system of paying five hundred pesos annually to eight captains, arguing that the money was seldom used for its intended purpose. With the passage of time, officers began to depend upon the subsidy as a salary rather than a fund to support their companies.[17] A short time before, the lieutenants, ensigns, and even the chaplains had asked for salaries. The consulado requested permission to terminate the payments made to captains; instead, the tribunal would accept responsibility for outfitting and equipment. Even as matters stood, the five-thousand-peso subsidy was nowhere near enough to cover expenses. During the past war, the consulado had been obliged to rent a house for a barracks and purchase furniture and three hundred additional muskets.

The challenge to the consulado looked innocent enough on the surface. The soldiers claimed the right to be arrested in their regimental barracks rather than to be exposed to the insult of being thrown into the public jail. The consulado, however, viewed this matter as a direct assault against its jurisdiction. Although Colonel Juan José Pérezcano, now the regimental commander, agreed that the militiamen must always be detained at the consulado's full disposition, the mere threat of diminished jurisdiction made the merchants reject any concessions.[18] The tribunal considered its power to detain merchants as an imperative regulatory and deterrent force to police commerce: in its opinion, "Jail is not only required to keep custody, but to afflict, shame, and to compel offenders to conduct themselves with good faith." To the judges of the merchant tribunal, the act of custody over a criminal was in itself a sign of jurisdiction. They suggested a parallel, hypothetical case of a civilian who aided a soldier to desert: the civilian would be arrested and incarcerated in a military prison and not in a public jail. The prisoner then must be jailed by the tribunal which held jurisdiction over the case.[19]

Prior to this time, there had not been any disputes over jails between the consulado and the officers of the Urban Regiment. In fact, the records showed only two cases of militiamen being held under arrest in their barracks for the merchant court. One worked out well and the other, the case of Lieutenant Joaquín Casades, was a total failure in the merchants' view. Casades was to have been held incommunicado, but in reality he had been permitted to speak freely with his friends and with one individual who was with him until after midnight. Even worse, Casades was permitted to spend at least two nights away from the barracks. In the consulado's opinion, since the militiamen were not accustomed to army subordination, "they look with scorn at the bond of military discipline."[20]

Much of the conflict stemmed from the Urban Regiment's unique status. Although neither side seriously contested the competence of the merchant tribunal to try cases of all connected with commerce, general ordinances and royal orders concerning the army confused the situation. For example, a royal order of January 10, 1773, conceded the same fueros and privileges enjoyed by the provincial militias to the merchant regiment. Inspector General Cisneros believed that the consulado was overzealous in defending its special jurisdiction—to such a degree in fact that it punished its own membership. At the same time, however, Cisneros tended to confirm the merchants' fears. In his opinion, those almaceneros and merchants who dedicated themselves to the king's service must not be exposed to the shame of public jail. Neither did he see any reason why a bankrupt merchant should be expelled from the regiment. As Colonel Pérezcano pointed out, bankruptcy meant a variety of things; if a merchant went broke because of shipwreck or enemy attack upon his cargoes, it would be unfair "to load more affliction upon the afflicted."[21] Both the colonel and the inspector general were enthusiastic in their support of the plan to establish a permanent barracks and guardhouse—a proposal which would cost the consulado an additional forty-five hundred pesos per year.[22]

Cisneros paid little heed to the apprehensions of the merchants. He doubted the consulado's capacity to make officer selections and challenged this power when the opportunity arose. After the sudden death of Lieutenant Colonel Juan Bautista Aldasoro, the consulado submitted its list of three candidates for the vacant commission. Instead of selecting one of these, Cisneros cast aside tradition and proposed his own man for the post. The result was an angry confrontation which was not settled until the imperial government issued a ruling. In a royal order of June 21, 1782, the crown equated the Urban Regiment's position with that of a provincial militia regiment. If the cabildos held the privilege of proposing officers to units within their districts, the consulado held the same powers over its regiment. To avoid further squabbles with the inspector general, proposals to fill vacancies in the Urban Regiment were to be submitted directly to the viceroy. Finally, the crown insisted that regimental officers had to be registered merchants. Whenever an officer ceased to be a merchant or declared bankruptcy, he would lose his commission and be deprived of his regimental rank.[23]

As far as the viceroys were concerned, the bickering and backbiting within the consulado and between merchants and the inspector general had to stop. Besides, all the rhetoric and debate did not make the merchant officers capable of opposing the consulado. Viceroy Matías de Gálvez had no wish to alienate one of the wealthiest tribunals in the capital—particularly since the merchants were generous in their support of worthy projects outside of their militia commitment. Over the past few years they had donated two warships to the crown, paid for the hospital of San Hipólito, built a new jail for the Acordada, and helped to underwrite the costs of the poorhouse.[24] Unwilling to permit further dissension, Gálvez took the unusual step of intervening personally to write a decree designed to end so many ". . . complaints, petitions, and haughty acts which are a bad example and produce worse results." He ruled for the merchants and against the officers. The consulado was to have full jurisdiction in mercantile matters over the colonel, officers, and soldiers of the Urban Regiment in time of peace or war. Furthermore, the tribunal could arrest and jail its subjects in the public jail. There was to be no further discussion of a regimental guardhouse.[25]

Left without recourse to appeal, the merchant officers found themselves without many friends. Indeed, the interim inspector general who replaced Cisneros, Francisco Crespo, had nothing good to say about the regiment. In his view, "there is no Regiment of Commerce; it is a truly imaginary body." Each time it was mobilized, it had to be formed from scratch beginning with proclamations ordering merchants to fulfill conveniently forgotten obligations. There were three classes of men available. First, the apprentices and servants of warehouses, stores, and shops belonging to wealthy merchants were enlisted in their masters' names. Second, there were the shopkeepers and traders of moderate, limited, and almost no income; some of these individuals possessed nothing more than a stall in a square or in the flea market where they sold a little chile, a few bits of old iron, some rebound books, or similar items.[26] Third, there were the vagabond alquilones who sold their services to merchants in return for a daily wage of four reales to one peso.

Crespo identified the alquilones as the most pernicious effect of the Urban Regiment. After six years as corregidor of Mexico City, he had sufficient firsthand experience to condemn their behavior.[27] Such men were "here today and gone tomorrow"; they could not be subjected to any law and he could not think of a less trustworthy group to place on guard duty at jails and in important posts such as at the viceregal palace where they were responsible for the treasury, the archives, and the viceroy. There was no case to be made for hiring mercenaries when the merchant guild's membership—without even including the poorest traffickers—totaled 1,122 men.[28] Surveying the impact of the Urban Regiment, Crespo exclaimed, "¡Qué anarquía! ¡Qué confusión!" Not only had the unit failed to serve the ends for which it had been created in 1692, but it drained available manpower from the provincial Regiment of Mexico. Insignificant dealers who in the sub-inspector's opinion did not deserve the name merchant managed to evade military duty by claiming membership in the Regiment of Commerce. In addition, the numerous idlers and vagabonds who sold their services as alquilones should have been available for the provincial militia. To end some of the most glaring inadequacies, Crespo offered a series of propositions: merchants or their employees must take up the full burden of manning the unit. Although all those enlisted would be fully entitled to the same fueros as were provincial militiamen, the consulado was to have no cause for alarm. The merchant tribunal retained full judicial sovereignty over its membership and the right to propose candidates for regimental vacancies. Finally, Crespo suggested the discontinuation of the five-hundred-peso annual subsidy to all officers except the colonel, the lieutenant colonel, and the major.[29]

While previous royal orders left very little room for the pretensions of merchant officers, José de Gálvez ended them once and for all. In a royal order of November 8, 1784, he expanded existing limitations: all officers had to be registered members of the merchant community, financial failure was to result in immediate suspension, and the consulado was confirmed in its right to propose officers from the lowest ensign to the colonel without any intervention of the sub-inspector general. To top this off, the payment of annual subsidies was to be terminated immediately and the consulado was to be given full control over regimental finance.[30] In the case of the Urban Regiment, there was to be no further challenge to civilian control.

Colonel Pérezcano made some rather perceptive observations about these defeats. To begin with, he connected the regimental fortunes to party politics within the consulado. In the elections for *prior* and *consules* which took place every two years, some factions supported the regiment and others expressed violent hostility to it.[31] As far as the colonel was concerned, those merchants who were the militia's most violent critics were the ones who had failed to achieve the rank of captain. Moreover, some elected officials wanted to use their offices to bypass those in the regiment who had worked their way up from the subaltern ranks. He also pointed out that the *priores, consules, diputados, consejeros, electores,* and *jueces de alzadas* were all selected from the wealthy almacenero class, which numbered only about 110 members. The other 900 or more merchants in the consulado had nothing to do with the operation of the guild.[32] On the question of the five-hundred-peso subsidies formerly paid to some captains, Pérezcano insisted that, contrary to popular opinion, the officers spent far more than they earned. Men who joined the regiment did so as common soldiers or standard-bearers and they served for at least twenty years before they could expect to achieve the rank of captain. Even then they did not advance to a position in which they received the five-hundred-peso payment until two of the existing captains died or retired. Many served until their deaths without ever attaining this goal. These officers paid out a large amount of their own money merely to purchase their scarlet uniform with its exquisite gold braid. All officers were elderly before they received any money from the regiment and most died before they recovered a tenth of the amount they had spent.[33]

Although the consulado had won a battle to maintain control over the merchant militiamen and the regiment, it was a Pyrrhic victory. The new challenge came not from the regiment, but rather from Viceroy Revillagigedo and Sub-Inspector General Pedro Gorostiza. Knowing the repugnance they felt toward all militia units, it is not difficult to imagine their attitude toward the Urban Regiment. They could not fault the merchants' racial origins as they might pardos and morenos, but the organization of the unit and the use of alquilones, "useless by their color and build," was more than sufficient to elicit biting sarcasm.[34] Gorostiza described the regiment as *"una farsa militar ridícula,"* a comment Revillagigedo included in his famous *Instrucción* and one which has been repeated by the historians of the Mexican army.[35]

When Gorostiza inspected the regiment, he discovered 608 men unequally distributed among the ten companies. The two grenadier companies were made up of merchants or apprentices, but the eight fusileer companies were found almost entirely to consist of alquilones. Not a third of the enlistment had any connection with the consulado. In many respects it was as if nothing had transpired since the 1690s. The men attired themselves in a profusion of different summer and winter uniforms; some carried muskets, others carbines, and a few had shotguns which did not have bayonets.[36] To remedy these abuses once and for all, Gorostiza set himself the task of drafting a full set of regulations to bring order and to end the practice of employing the plebeian alquilones. He was certain that this would curb many of the disputes over fueros, end jurisdictional conflicts resulting from poor understanding of the laws, and halt infractions of the mercantile and municipal codes.[37] Furthermore, the sub-inspector recommended a departure from the system of financing the regiment from funds collected on imports. This money, he argued, was a public tax which must be transferred into the general revenues designated for militia support. As matters stood, it was not the generous merchants of Mexico City who sustained the regiment, but the consumer public of the entire kingdom. He suggested that the operators of wineshops, vegetable stands, book shops, and other weak business concerns should be excluded from service. Once these changes had taken place, a full study would be made of how the merchants should pay for arms, equipment, and uniforms. Gorostiza estimated that the total sum per merchant would not exceed fifteen pesos annually. The final object would be to enlist the masters of businesses who up to this time had evaded service.[38]

All of these reforms became a part of Revillagigedo's military plan of February 1790, with its dependence upon greater numbers of regular troops. In fact, the viceroy considered the possibility of entirely disbanding the Urban Regiment until he considered the need for police forces in the capital.[39] Besides, once the crown adopted the concept of increasing the regular army, the merchants would not see much active service. Here of course he made a major miscalculation which would cause much trouble in the future.

In October 1791, Revillagigedo informed the merchants of Gorostiza's proposals and asked them to comment. The consulado responded by convoking all merchants in a *junta de comercio*. The first meeting took place in late October before all of the details of Gorostiza's plans were known. At first, the wealthy almaceneros presented their position to the commercial community and strengthened opposition to any new legislation which might harm business interests. On one point they agreed with the viceroy; a new constitution was needed to define the exact mission of the merchant militia and to curb abuses which had crept into the relationship between the unit and the government. In the merchants' view, the regiment existed to deal with sudden extraordinary events such as the 1692 insurrections and not to perform ordinary garrison duty when the regular regiments were absent from the capital. The 1767 *Real Ordenanza de Milicias Provinciales* specifically exempted merchants from any military obligations. It always had been royal policy to view commerce and public supply as indispensable services which could not be interrupted. This was the case in Mexico, where commerce was a full-time occupation. Merchants had to be on hand at all hours to deal with customs appraisers, pay taxes, prepare multiple invoices, examine shipments delivered by muleteers, and get the mules moving as soon as possible to avoid high maintenance costs. They had to honor and pay bills of exchange and to maintain detailed accounts with their correspondents throughout the kingdom. Finally, even the less important merchant had to keep his warehouse or store open for long hours for his customers' convenience.[40]

Since no merchant could run a major business enterprise on his own, he needed the service of a number of young men, depending upon the size of his operation. These were the *cajeros* (apprentices, cashiers, clerks, and accountants) who had to double as militiamen in the Regiment of Commerce. Most merchants felt as negative about sending their employees to serve as they did about fulfilling this obligation themselves. Few wanted their employees to have any opportunity for contacts with the low alquilones, or for that matter with any group which would weaken what Brading has described as the "spartan, novitiate, and semi-monastic"[41] life style taught to apprentices by the dominant almaceneros. When the young cajeros went to serve with the regiment, they invariably met less-disciplined young men and many were led astray. Without the restraint and subordination of their masters, they stayed out all night, began to drink, gambled, chased women, and fell into other vices.[42] By the time they returned after a few tours of guard duty, some of the most promising apprentices were corrupted. They lost their inclination for hard work, refused to accept the stern rule of their masters, and eventually had to be dismissed. Since these young men had to be kept on the job if they were to learn the business and to maintain the necessary spirit of subordination, many of the almaceneros hired alquilones who did not have careers to interrupt.[43] While many of the merchants' complaints might be termed special pleading to avoid interference in their profit-making enterprises, there were incidents enough to justify their fears. In one case, an entire patrol of the Urban Regiment—cajeros, alquilones, and some guildsmen who were replacing merchants—spent a riotous night tearing up a brothel in the Callejón de las Ratas.[44]

The wealthy merchants objected most strenuously to any proposal to exclude small shopkeepers and traders from the militia. Of the 818 soldiers enumerated in the 1790 regimental census, only 360 came from the *almacenes* and large businesses: the rest were drawn from the ranks of the small grocers, wine merchants, booksellers, and other minor traffickers. If the 360 major commercial establishments had to furnish 130 militiamen to cover the guardposts and royal palace, not only would the fatigue of service be intolerable but commerce itself would also inevitably suffer harm.[45] On the other hand, most merchants shared Revillagigedo's distaste for the practice of hiring alquilones; they were very expensive over long periods of duty and detracted from the luster of the militia.

On November 8, 1791, Gorostiza published his final report on the Urban Regiment. As the merchants feared, he recommended drastic reforms. The regiment was to be reduced to battalion size—340 soldiers and 15 officers. This might have been acceptable, but the sub-inspector attempted to make the regiment conform to the organization of the provincial militias, which meant the addition of a regular army training contingent. The unit would need barracks for the regulars, storage for equipment, and the long-dreaded guardhouse. Annual costs of five thousand pesos were to be paid by the merchants according to some system devised by the consulado. As if this were not bad enough, the regimental officers were to enjoy the criminal and civil fueros of the provincial army. The merchant tribunal could decide whether the *fuero criminal* of the enlisted men would go to those who actually served or to the merchants who sent their employees.[46]

Subjected to what they termed ridicule and harassment, the merchants convened on November 25 another *junta de comercio*. Though they were embarrassed by the sub-inspector's derogatory remarks, they tolerated his insults, knowing that military service was not their first occupation. Their errors would be the same "as those of the farmer who attempts to contend with navigation and the ship's pilot with driving oxen."[47] Besides, Mexico was a far different place than it had been in 1692 when civilian merchants resisted the angry mobs. The consulado opposed the size and cost of the unit proposed by Gorostiza. As for the statement on fueros, the merchants pointed to the rulings of Viceroy Matías de Gálvez and the royal orders of the 1780s. Most businessmen saw no advantages to be gained from the *fuero militar.* They lived quiet and honorable lives within the laws. For the few who did not, arrest and jail were incentive enough to force offenders to reveal hidden property and to pay their debts. The *fuero militar* caused nothing but trouble—competencias between the regimental commander and the consulado, frustrating delays over litigation, and bad blood between colleagues. In the opinion of the merchant tribunal, much of the fuss over fueros was inflamed by the regimental officers who built up the hopes of litigants.[48]

Gorostiza's temper, never far from the surface at the best of times, was aroused by the consulado's delays and lengthy memorials. Busy with other aspects of government and military reform, he was not at all pleased by the prospect of an interminable exchange of charges and countercharges. He could not understand why Colonel Antonio Ravago, Lieutenant Colonel Conde de la Cortina, and Major Tomás Urizar of the Urban Regiment had not been invited to the *junta de comercio* of November 25 if it indeed had been so important. If the merchants were so upset by his remarks about the regiment, they should adopt the reforms. He wondered aloud whether the merchants would be willing to accept full responsibility for the alquilones' acts. There were only two possible solutions—either to disband the regiment or to improve it.[49]

In the long run, delay proved to be the consulado's most effective tool. The provisional regulations, amended to meet some of the opposition, were not completed until May 1793.[50] This was not to say, however, that the merchants were any more willing to accept the reforms. The consulado still stood to lose some control over the regiment and the fuero question remained in doubt. Gorostiza managed to retain most of the proposals he considered essential—merchants who hired replacements, for example, were liable to a fifteen-day jail sentence. To prevent implementation of the new regulations, the consulado engaged in a voluminous correspondence which gradually exhausted Gorostiza. By the beginning of 1794, both the viceroy and the sub-inspector would have gladly disbanded the regiment and removed the import taxes collected by the consulado. Now their hands were tied because they needed the Urban Regiment to garrison the city.[51] The transfer of regular troops overseas and the dismemberment of the provincial units left no alternative.

Successful in outwaiting Revillagigedo's reforms, the merchants welcomed the Marqués de Branciforte as a savior.[52] At first, the campaign appeared to have paid off; the new viceroy expressed little real interest in the new regulations. But a much more ominous challenge soon appeared to erode the jealously guarded prerogatives of the consulado. It stemmed from a royal order of February 9, 1793, which had thrown many privileged jurisdictions, judges, and even the viceregal court into a quandary.[53] The decree stated baldly that henceforth the military jurisdiction would have full cognizance over all civil and criminal cases of soldiers and there should be no competencias with other tribunals. This was a general statement rather than a reply to specific issues raised in the context of New Spain. At first, Revillagigedo merely published the order, but with a growing storm of protest from all sides he realized that greater clarification would be necessary. If the decree were taken at face value, the military jurisdiction would receive enormous new powers over the provincial militiamen. Specifically, the legal cases of merchants or miners who happened to be enlisted in a militia unit would be tried in courts-martial by their commanding officers.

While the February 9 decree was anathema to the consulado, it was received by the Urban Regiment's officers as a most welcome if unexpected godsend. Here was legislation which appeared to overturn or supplant the restrictive Matías de Gálvez rulings and royal orders maintaining the consulado's dominance. Judge Manuel Antonio de Santa María of the acordada complained that within only ten days after publication of the new order, the forbidden alcoholic drink *chinguirito* had appeared in at least three wineshops belonging to members of the Urban Regiment. These individuals claimed total exemption from any jurisdiction except the army. Indeed, Colonel Ravago supported this position and denied that the Tribunal de Bebidas Prohibidas had any control over cases pending against his merchant militiamen. In his view, the February 9 decree granted the full *fuero militar* to militiamen and his jurisdiction must process all cases against men of the Urban Regiment. In rebuttal, Santa María pointed out that the Urban Regiment was not under arms and it simply did not deserve the privileges granted to the regular army.[54]

Despite Revillagigedo's personal aversion to militia privileges, he had some difficulty discovering grounds which could be used to modify the royal order. With the opposition coalescing, however, he issued his own order limiting the February 9 decree to the regular army and to regular soldiers who served in training cadres of militia units. This meant that there was to be no change from existing practice. When this seemed overcautious, he permitted the colonels and commanders of militia units to hear the criminal cases of their soldiers; there was to be no intervention from judges and magistrates of the ordinary royal jurisdiction. Very much concerned by the turmoil caused by the original royal order, Revillagigedo dispatched urgent letters to the crown requesting clarification of just who was to be granted the *fuero militar* and explaining the nature of the conflicts that had resulted.[55]

Specifically regarding the Urban Regiment, Revillagigedo met with *Auditor de Guerra* Bataller to deal with the representations of Colonel Ravago. Bataller identified the dispute as the same one which had taken place in 1782 resulting from the imprisonment of Francisco Velasco. He saw no reason whatsoever for altering the existing relationship between the consulado and the regiment. As far as he was concerned, Viceroy Gálvez's decision of 1784 still stood. Revillagigedo agreed and once again the consulado's jurisdiction in mercantile matters was upheld.[56]

An inevitable result of the confusion was a sharpening of partisan attitudes. Both the merchant tribunal and the militia officers were aroused by the continuing debate over Revillagigedo's regulations for the Urban Regiment. When the unit was mobilized for garrison duty in 1794, Colonel Ravago renewed his demands for permanent barracks and the right of arrest for militiamen under military jurisdiction rather than having them detained in the public jail. The consulado, more than ever fearful of a loss in power, reiterated its old position and added new information to bolster the mercantile case. In 1793, a merchant named Pablo del Villar had been arrested and held in the regimental barracks until his case came before the court. When the scribe of the tribunal was sent to notify him of some matters relating to his case, he could not locate the prisoner; eventually Villar was found at liberty in the streets. The same thing happened in the case of José María Velázquez, whom an officer of the tribunal encountered in public when he was supposed to be under arrest in his quarters. Such persons were able to hide their property from their creditors, and a few escaped from the city to avoid prosecution.[57]

During May 1794, the consulado sanctioned the forcible removal of a merchant corporal named Yriarte from the barracks to the public jail. Yriarte had ordered some supplies of meat from a pork butcher to stock his grocery store located on the Puente de Zavala. When he did not pay, the butcher registered a charge with the *alcalde de barrio* who already had another complaint against Yriarte from a merchant who furnished him with sugar and grain. The alcalde visited the shop, where he encountered a group of twenty-eight poor people who had pawned items. They clamored for their possessions, but none were found; it later turned out that Yriarte had sold them. When asked by what license he had taken such a step, he replied in a haughty manner that he needed none. To the judges of the consulado, Yriarte's behavior and attitude meant that he intended to fall back upon his *fuero militar*. They went on to defend their methods and the use of the public jail to contain such malefactors, concluding ". . . those who will not abstain from crime for love of virtue will do so from fear of punishment."[58]

It was at this point the Marqués de Branciforte assumed command in New

Spain. Finding himself almost without an army and in a war against France, he decided to use the privileges of the *fuero militar* as an incentive during the rebuilding of the provincial militias. On November 28, 1794, he published a decree enforcing the broadest interpretation of the royal order of February 9, 1793. All cases against subjects who happened to be militiamen were to be transferred immediately to the army jurisdiction.[59] To Branciforte and *Auditor de Guerra* Cacho Calderón, the crown meant to restore old privileges to the militia. Besides, the *fuero militar* was strictly honorific, "a prize to animate the subjects upon whom the regime depended for the defense of religion and the state, the peace of the country, observance of the laws, the development of commerce, the prosperity of mining, and the well-being of all."[60] Without offering the incentive of the fuero, Branciforte doubted he would be able to attract many wealthy men to offer donations and accept militia commissions.[61] In his opinion, the fuero was "a small but showy laurel" needed to animate the Mexican population.[62]

The viceroy rejected complaints from the consulado and other tribunals opposing military privilege. He found no evidence to back exaggerated fears of other privileged sectors; tax revenues did not decline, and there was no apparent harm to the public good. After all, the officers of the provincial and urban militias were wealthy merchants, miners, and hacendados drawn from the richest classes in New Spain. Many held the fueros of their own tribunals and none needed the protection of the army. To these men the *fuero militar* would never be anything more than an honorific title.[63]

As might be expected, the consulado of Mexico rejected these arguments. Once again, the merchants predicted an erosion of the mercantile jurisdiction.[64] They were not without support from other sectors. The corregidor of Mexico City, Bernardino Bonavía, reported difficulties maintaining order because men who claimed the *fuero militar* refused to answer questions. Other officials were frustrated by the problem of identifying militiamen—particularly those of the Urban Regiment, where the master, an employee, or a hired replacement might be serving.[65] Provincial subdelegates outside of Mexico City were critical of the dangers they saw to their own powers, and the Mining Tribunal submitted a strongly argued petition which mirrored the merchants' fears.[66]

With questions mounting about the crown's purpose in promulgating the 1793 decree, the audiencia took up the issue. The judges considered the evidence and arrived at three conclusions: first, the king meant his statement on the *fuero militar* to refer to the regular army; second, provincial and urban militias were included only during active service; and third, the controversial decree had not been designed to extend military jurisdiction into new areas.[67]

In other words, the audiencia adopted the position expressed by Revillagigedo and rejected that of Branciforte.

Unhappy with this interpretation, Branciforte submitted the question to *Auditor de Guerra* Cacho Calderón.[68] Unlike his colleagues in the audiencia, Cacho adopted the viceregal view of the crown's intentions on the *fuero militar*. In his opinion, the king left no room for argument. The consulado's protests based upon earlier rulings were out of order because the new decree superseded previous legislation. Viewing the general picture rather than the merchants' special interests, he stressed that the army judges would not release militiamen from the full vigor of the law or pardon their criminal acts. On the contrary, the only difference would be that cases involving soldiers moved to military courts. The penalties were the same and no one could use the new situation to escape the law.[69] Cacho was unimpressed by the merchant position that judges needed special training in order to hear mercantile cases. After all, appeals from the merchant tribunal to the audiencia were not tried by merchants. If such claims were pursued to the extreme, "only land surveyors would be able to judge cases dealing with real estate, and physicians those of deaths caused by wounds."[70] Since most merchants were not connected with the militia, he could not see why the issue had become so controversial in the consulado.

While the various litigants lost little time in carrying their pleas to the imperial government, the dispute was to last for several years. Once Viceroy Branciforte became adamant in his opinion about the fuero, there was little anyone could do to resist his policy. The petitions from the consulado and other tribunals convinced Secretary of State Pedro de Varela to overturn Branciforte's interpretation. He found that the actions of the viceroy ran counter to the spirit of the 1793 decree. The crown had not intended to alter existing jurisdictions and there was to be no doubt about the ascendancy of the consulado in mercantile matters. Far from being useful to merchants, the *fuero militar* could be exceptionally damaging. Having discussed the matter with the king, Varela restored the balance existing when Branciforte arrived in Mexico.[71] Rather than accepting defeat, the viceroy suspended the order. His reason for doing so was that the formation of the army simply could not be thwarted by legal niceties. Since the termination of the Ministry of the Indies and the transfer of its powers to the other ministries of the imperial government, Branciforte saw increasing problems with colonial government. Much less attention was paid to the affairs of the Indies despite the great increase in red tape and bureaucracy.[72]

If in Madrid heretofore there had been little interest in the dispute over militia privileges, Branciforte's suspension of Varela's order changed the situation. Because of confusion between departments over the fuero issue, the king formed a junta of four ministers—two from the Tribunal de Guerra and two from the Council of Indies. The junta was given the task of examining the petitions from the consulado and other tribunals in New Spain as well as ruling on viceregal policies.[73] It restated Varela's opinion and the Council of the Indies confirmed that the consulado's jurisdiction must not be limited by expansion of the *fuero militar.* On May 16, 1798, the crown issued a new royal order, but by this time Branciforte had formed his army.[74]

Although this decision guaranteed the predominance of the consulado, the relationships between the merchants and the Urban Regiment did not improve. After May 1794, the unit formed an almost permanent part of the Mexico City garrison. Constant friction occurred as businessmen struggled to provide soldiers without damaging their primary interest in commerce. Regimental enlistment varied according to daily needs in the business community. Some merchants employed five or more cajeros in each of several retail outlets scattered throughout the city.[75] Others could not afford any help; they either served themselves or contributed the costs of a half or even a third portion of a soldier's duty to the regiment. The difficulty for the consulado and for other legal jurisdictions resulted from the confusion over just who belonged to the unit. One day an employer would send an apprentice, servant, or hired replacement, and the next day it could be someone else. Unlike the better-regulated provincial militia units, the Urban Regiment was unable to send an accurate list of personnel to the city's magistrates and police officials. Since the mobilized merchant militiamen or their replacements continued to hold the *fuero criminal,* conflicts over jurisdiction continued in cases of public drunkenness, disorderly behavior, and in other minor offenses. Efforts to keep an up-to-date regimental roll in the office of the major proved to be unsatisfactory.[76]

The lengthy mobilizations and constant financial drain upon the merchants exacerbated these chronic weaknesses. By 1798, the tendency of many merchants to shirk their obligations to the regiment left some patrols and guardposts undermanned. Some officers sought to enlist soldiers from outside the merchants' ranks while others attempted to enforce existing regulations. This led to new friction with the consulado about the definition of the term "merchant." In one such case, Captain Juan Gallo of the Urban Regiment arrested a chocolate dealer named Felipe Mendoza. Mendoza was taken before the merchant tribunal where he argued that as a *chocolatero* he did not sell his product in the form he purchased it and therefore he was not a merchant. He mixed the chocolate with sugar and cinnamon, which made him into an artisan like a carpenter or candlemaker who purchased raw materials and sold them after making a new product.[77] Colonel Tomás de Urizar of the Regiment of Commerce refused to compare Mendoza to most chocolate sellers, who were humble and who barely made a living. This man shipped large supplies of chocolate into the interior and made a comfortable living compared to the poor shopkeepers and winesellers who served the regiment. Urizar viewed Mendoza not as a chocolate seller, but as a wealthy merchant who managed a major business enterprise. The consulado rejected this new intervention of the regiment into purely mercantile affairs—it and it alone established who belonged to the merchant guild. The militia could have no claim to Mendoza because he was not engaged in a business subject to the consulado. The fact that he happened to make more money than some merchants was irrelevant: even if he was a millionaire, his income was derived from a source beyond the consulado's jurisdiction.[78] Clearly, many merchants had come to view their regiment as a most noxious liability. Their long claim that business and soldiering could not be combined had been borne out by torturous experience. Incensed by the Mendoza case, the prior of the consulado, Antonio de Bassoco, asked Branciforte to review a confidential report he had given Revillagigedo in 1794. Bassoco and many other principal merchants had argued in favor of disbanding the Urban Regiment. Since there were other regular and militia units capable of guarding the capital, they saw no purpose to continuing a unit which did little other than to create discord.[79]

By 1800, the merchants were openly hostile to the regiment. After nearly six years of garrison duty at their own expense, few businessmen wanted to continue the burden. The practice of hiring alquilones had become the rule rather than the exception. Since the merchants paid up to one peso daily, which was triple the wage of a regular soldier, there was no real difficulty locating replacements. The regimental sergeants and corporals looked after hiring and took a percentage of the sum provided by the merchant as a finder's fee. This was permitted despite the potential for corruption because the merchants did not have the time to establish contacts with the elements who filled the positions. Occasionally, the officers rejected the unwholesome individuals who appeared.[80] Almost everyone agreed that most alquilones were "*gente abandonada*" who spent most of their time in taverns and who were impossible to subject to military discipline. Many deserted whenever they felt the impulse and thereby cheated the merchant contributor who lost his uniform and equipment as well as the salary he paid.[81] But even with these problems, the system was cheaper than either sending skilled employees or accepting personal service.

Even if the merchants had been willing to continue paying the alquilones, pressures increased for improvements. On surprise visits to guardposts during the night, Viceroy Azanza found the members of the Urban Regiment to be lax and disrespectful toward their officers. In his opinion, the consulado was wasting its money to sustain "... the illusion of a regiment which could not be counted upon in case of need."[82] The normal strength was about 100 alquilones who were on duty continuously to replace the merchants. Although Azanza saw little possibility of undertaking reforms until the war ended, he began to study methods of forcing the merchants back into the unit. There were 434 merchants and 484 cajeros listed on the regimental rolls—a potential total of 918 men—quite sufficient to form patrols without a single mercenary.[83]

An even stronger advocate of reform was Colonel Joaquín Colla, who had recently assumed command of the regiment.[84] Supported in principle by the viceroy and by a junta of regimental captains, he issued an order on February 1, 1800, requiring all contributors to send a properly uniformed militiaman and not a sum of money to hire a replacement. The high pay for guard duty had begun to attract some artisans and guildsmen away from other militia units. As a result, the *juez de gremios* responsible for recruitment into the provincial Infantry of Mexico experienced more trouble than ever finding men.[85] Even if the pay was no incentive, guarding public buildings for the Urban Regiment was inestimably better than the possibility of transfer to the cantonments or, even worse, a tour of duty with one of the regular infantry regiments.[86] Colla was angry about the continual misdemeanors of the alquilones, whom he could neither command nor trust. When they were short of money they appeared at the barracks for duty, but if not they disappeared into the *pulquerías,* taverns, and gambling dens.[87]

Like previous exponents of regimental reform, Colla found himself in trouble with the consulado. The merchants obtained a viceregal suspension of the order requiring an end to the use of alquilones, but this was only the beginning.[88] In 1801, Colla attempted to conduct a full regimental inspection in order to force the merchants onto the parade square. They caused acts of insubordination and near mutiny before the viceroy again intervened to overrule the colonel.[89] Not visibly disheartened by these setbacks, Colla prepared a new regimental register designed to rationalize service and to exclude mercenaries. According to his estimate, if wealthy almaceneros contributed one soldier and modest shopkeepers sent a man one day out of four, a total of 634 men would be available at all times. This number was quite sufficient to cover all of the duties assigned to the regiment.[90] Finally, Colla attempted to intervene in the selection of officers—one of the consulado's most jealously guarded prerogatives.[91]

With the harassment of Colla, the merchants accelerated their campaign to disband the regiment. To make this more palatable to the regime, they proposed to contribute an annual payment of twenty thousand to fifty thousand pesos toward the provincial militia.[92] Many merchants believed that the regiment was bringing about the ruin of commerce. Even the wealthy almaceneros supported this opinion. The long war had forced prices upward and driven away potential customers. Those who normally would have bought new garments, for example, were repairing their old ones, and the poor who received the castoffs were in a shameful state of nakedness. Businessmen were left with large inventories of unsold goods and merchandise.[93] In this situation, the expenditure of one peso per day to hire a replacement three or four times per week for guard duty was sufficient to drive some insolvent merchants into bankruptcy. Since May 1794, when the regiment was mobilized, more than 150 shops had closed. The consulado traced many of these failures to the burden of serving and contributing to the Urban Regiment. As the weaker businesses succumbed, those which remained had to increase the amount of time and money given to the militia. Oppressed by these matters, the merchants had to deal with what they described as "the ungovernable temperament of Colonel Colla." His intervention into the affairs of the consulado was the last intolerable straw.[94] Though the regiment was released from active garrison duty in February 1802, Viceroy Marquina's vote of thanks for eight years' misery and expenditure did nothing to remedy the real issues.[95]

Over the years, the poor relationship between Colonel Colla and the consulado became one of undisguised contempt. Despite continuing discussions about the regiment, the consulado could not obtain viceregal permission to convene a *junta de comercio* to discuss the future until the end of October 1807. The first problem was who should have a vote in deciding whether or not to disband the merchant militia; a junta of all contributors would mean convoking 929 individuals from all walks of merchant life. Many were poor men who contributed a half, third, or even a quarter cost of a soldier. The consulado asked permission to form the junta from the inner circle of wealthy merchants, the 177 *matriculados* who ruled the business community and could represent the others.[96] The regimental officers were invited to take part in the discussions.

Colonel Colla and Major Angel Michaus rejected the right of any junta of merchants to reform or disband their regiment. After 115 years' loyal service, they insisted that the king was the only one competent to decide such an important issue. They claimed that the consulado had acted without adequate consultation with the officers; no merchant militiaman, officer or soldier, would vote on any of the questions being raised. While opposed to any junta, Colla was even more vehement in his objections to the suggestion that only the merchant elite should decide upon important policies. Every contributor must be heard or at least represented. In his view, the matriculados would reach quite different decisions than would a junta of all merchants.[97]

Despite opposition, a junta of fifty-six merchants convened amidst a most confusing and even rancorous atmosphere. Many of the contributors demanded the immediate suppression of the regiment and some of the younger merchants shouted insults at their militia officers. Various documents were read to the junta—letters from the viceroys, the reform plan proposed by Revillagigedo, and various petitions for disbanding the regiment submitted by the consulado. After all of the material had been read twice, the junta was asked whether the purpose behind the voting was fully understood. Colla stated that he did not understand and all of the documents were read again. After this delay and discussions which permitted every opinion to be heard in great detail, it was agreed to hold a secret ballot. Members could vote either to disband or to adopt the Revillagigedo-Gorostiza regulations for the regiment. The colonel caused a most terrible scene during this portion of the meeting, threatening and insulting all who seemed ready to extinguish his command. Even with this confrontation and the abstention of all officers, the junta was close to unanimous in its decision to disband the regiment. Because some merchants were absent, another junta was held on December 24, 1807, in which fifty-three men voted: forty-three were in favor of dissolving the militia, two for adoption of the Revillagigedo reforms, and eight officers abstained. The matter was decided although some merchants feared physical harm from Colonel Colla. Several asked the consulado to petition Viceroy Iturrigaray for help in preventing violence from the officers.[98]

It was not long before the merchants had their opportunity for revenge. The day after the overthrow of Iturrigaray, Pedro Garibay received a petition from sixty merchants demanding the removal of Colla from his command. According to their information, the colonel had mocked the entire garrison of the city.[99] Opposed to the circumstances of the coup d'etat, he had remarked that with only his two companies of grenadiers, he could disperse all of the Volunteers of Fernando VII.[100] Major Michaus became another focal point for the merchants' enmity. He was denounced by more than 180 members of the consulado for "seditious expressions" about the imprisonment of Iturrigaray. Garibay sentenced him to six months' arrest in the fortress of Perote and suspended his rank until a royal decision on his case.[101] Remarkably, Colonel Colla did not undergo this fate; after a few weeks he was restored to his command, where he continued the old debates during the early years of the revolutions for independence.[102] As he wrote in his own defense, commanders made enemies and during the years of his colonelcy, the merchant militia had suffered greater strains than ever before in its history. For eleven years, the unit had been mobilized almost full time, making it more like a regular regiment than an occasional force designed to bolster the city garrison.[103]

For the merchants and particularly the rich gachupín almaceneros who ruled the consulado, the struggle against intruding militia officers, new regulations, and outside control over what was defined as merchant jurisdiction entered a new stage in 1808. In the near anarchy following the collapse of the Bourbon monarchy, the very men who had argued most consistently against any participation in martial endeavors were now the most enthusiastic about organizing the Volunteers of Fernando VII. Now, however, the shoe was on a different foot. Instead of the officers of the Urban Regiment complaining about alquilones, laxity, and lack of support from the consulado, it was the merchant elite which had demonstrated the greatest militancy during the overthrow of Iturrigaray.[104] They had to find the key to restoring the *esprit de corps* and patriotism of 1692. In taking on this mission, they were no more successful than the regimental officers. By as early as the first week in October 1808, only two weeks after the removal of Iturrigaray, many of the lesser merchants who had rallied to the cause began to excuse themselves from further participation in the militia. Gabriel de Yermo, the leader of the reactionary movement, complained to the consulado that none of the thirty-three enlisted men of the Gran Guardia de Fernando VII had shown up for duty.[105]

8

THE OFFICER CORPS

Perhaps the best-known impression of the Mexican army officer comes down to us from the pen of Alexander von Humboldt, who described his amusement and astonishment at the transformation of civilians. "Sometimes these militia officers are to be seen in full uniform, and decorated with the royal order of Charles III, gravely sitting in their shops, and entering into the most trifling detail in the sale of their goods."[1] The Intendant of Oaxaca, Antonio de Mora y Peysal, corroborated this picture: few officers of the provincial militia battalion possessed much in the way of wealth or property to support their pretensions to a genteel way of life. These merchants and shopkeepers conducted business " . . . in their uniforms and badges, the same way they had done before joining the battalion."[2] Elsewhere, however, some of the militia units drew upon the wealthiest members of the colonial elite. Diego Rul, Ignacio Obregón, Antonio Pérez Gálvez, Narciso de la Canal, and others were able to contribute enormous amounts of money in exchange for the honor and prestige of command.

The officers of the army of New Spain were a diverse group who reflected the regional, economic, and even the racial diversities of the country. Naturally, there were great differences between the career officers—most of whom were *peninsulares*—with their concern about promotions, salaries, and conditions of service, and the provincial officers—criollo or peninsular—who used the army to obtain power and prestige. Mining regions such as Guanajuato produced a surplus of truly wealthy men who could afford to purchase a full colonelcy, while in less opulent provinces, men had to pool their resources in order to cover the costs of outfitting regiments or battalions. As might be expected, the criollo-gachupín rivalry was very much in evidence. Spanish officers were critical of Mexicans and often racist in their attitudes. Félix

Calleja, for example, grumbled about the "bad" population of the Americas and about the shortage of candidates suitable for militia commissions. Where there were such men, they seemed to be fully occupied in mining, commerce, agriculture, or in some other profession which kept them away from their homes for much of the year. The obstacles increased with the remoteness of the place where militias were to be raised.[3] If the criollos detected a certain haughtiness from their peninsular comrades, the pardos had even more cause for animosity. In 1793, Revillagigedo did not even bother to engage in consultation when he disbanded the Pardo Battalions of Mexico and Puebla. The officers looked to the king for justice and begged him to "... free us from the yoke of European officers who always have been our capital enemies and have attained our ruin."[4]

As we have seen throughout this study, pardo officers were wasting their time if they expected the imperial government to relax the dominance of European army officers. Lingering doubts about the trustworthiness of Mexicans were cause enough for caution and it was the rule to appoint Spaniards to important posts in all sectors. Even in the provincial militias, where the colonels, lieutenant colonels, and many of the officers were criollos, there

TABLE 15
Regular Army Majors Assigned to the Provincial Militia Units in the 1790s.*

Name	Unit	Town or Province of Origin
Manuel Pastor	Cavalry of Querétaro	Castilla la Vieja
José Gómez	Dragoons of Michoacán	Andalusia
Melchor de Sequera	Dragoons of Michoacán	Catalonia
Vicente Barros de Alemparte	Dragoons of the Queen	Galicia
Miguel del Pino	Dragoons of Nueva Galicia	Málaga
Vicente Mediamarca	Cavalry of the Príncipe	Barcelona
Antonio Mendivil	Dragoons of San Luis	Navarre
Manuel de Santa María	Dragoons of San Carlos	Seville
Pedro Antonio de Queredo	Infantry of Tlaxcala	Santander
José Porras	Dragoons of Puebla	Burgos
Juan Antonio López	Infantry of Puebla	Castilla la Vieja
Francisco de la Cuesta	Infantry of Valladolid	Seville
Juan de Noriega	Infantry of Mexico	Asturias
Manuel Rengel	Lancers of Veracruz	Málaga
Tomás Rodríguez de Biedma	Infantry of Mexico	Andalusia
Manuel de Iturbe	Battalion of Guanajuato	Galicia
Francisco Ulloa	*Infantry of Toluca*	*New Spain*

*Officers of criollo origin are in italics.
Source: Patentes, nombramientos militares, AGI, México, leg. 2427; and hojas de servicio, AGS, GM, legs. 7270–7278.

were always a regular army major (*sargento mayor*), several adjutants, lieutenants, and NCOs to keep close watch over all developments. It was no coincidence that almost all of the majors and the great majority of subaltern officers assigned to the training cadres were of direct European origin (see table 15).[5] The major, third in command as well as chief training and administrative officer, was usually the effective commanding officer since the militia colonel and lieutenant colonel devoted most of their attention to their civilian professions.

European dominance over the regular regiments was almost total. In 1788, of sixty-two officers and first sergeants in the Regiment of the Crown, thirty-eight were of Spanish origin, three foreigners, and twenty-one from New Spain. Peninsular control over the regiment was more complete than these figures indicate because Europeans held all of the senior posts. In the rank of captain and above, there were eleven Spaniards, two foreigners, and only four junior captains of Mexican or American origin. And these four criollos were the sons of Spanish officers or had served either in Europe or overseas (see table 16).[6] A study of the top-echelon regular officers during the 1790s dem-

TABLE 16
Age and Origins of Senior Officers in the Regiment of the Crown, 1788.*

Name	Age	Province, Country, or Town of Origin
Brigadier Juan Cambiazo	56	Catalonia
Lieutenant Colonel Santiago Espalunge	47	France
Major Luis Duprat	59	France
Captain Diego Lazaga	63	Navarre
Captain José Obispo	61	Murcia
Captain Gaspar de Burgos	62	*Veracruz*
Captain José Alcaraz	62	Andalusia
Captain Ignacio Ruanova	62	*Veracruz*
Captain Juan Manuel Bonilla	38	Cádiz
Captain Juan de Soto	47	*Veracruz*
Captain Bernardo Gallegos	49	Canary Islands
Captain Manuel Páez	42	Seville
Captain Francisco Ulloa	44	*New Spain*
Captain Dionisio Armona	32	Madrid
Captain Antonio del Toro	38	Ceuta
Captain Ramón de Oromi	41	Catalonia
Captain Manuel de Santiesteban	32	Barcelona

*Officers of criollo origin are in italics.
Source: Documentos de revista de inspección del Regimiento Fixo de Infantería de la Corona, July 26, 1788, AGI, México, leg. 1518.

onstrates why the imperial government had little to fear from the colonial army. As table 17 illustrates, there was almost no criollo participation at the command level.[7]

When the imperial government approved the formation of the Infantry Regiments of New Spain, Mexico, and Puebla (1787–89), peninsulares received all of the important commands. Lieutenant Colonel José Manuel Alava of the Infantry of Seville became colonel of the new Regiment of Puebla. Pedro Gorostiza, commander of the Regiment of the Prince, used his promotion to the sub-inspectorship general to carry with him a number of his relatives and fellow officers. Viceroy Revillagigedo selected some young officers who had impressed him in the campaigns of the past war against Britain including a young captain of the Regiment of Savoy, Félix Calleja.[8] Yet there was no policy to deny army commissions to those criollos who had sufficient family status to merit access to the profession. In each of the new regiments, consisting of two grenadier companies and twelve fusileer companies, a total of eight captaincies, eight lieutenancies, and eight sublieutenancies were offered for sale.[9] The remaining companies and staff positions were filled by merit appointments to regular officers from the European army and to those already serving in Mexico.

Minister of the Indies Antonio Valdés proposed the sale of company captaincies for 6,500 pesos, lieutenancies for 3,000 pesos, and sublieutenancies for 2,000 pesos. Although the captaincies paid the moderate salary of 912 pesos annually, Valdés depended upon "the immense wealth of Mexicans" to make the offer attractive.[10] Indeed, by the beginning of 1788, there had been twelve requests for captaincies. Only four candidates had expressed interest in a lieutenancy and no one wanted to be a lowly sublieutenant. To meet the imbalance, Viceroy Flórez increased the price of a captaincy to 9,000 pesos and added the sublieutenancy to the package. Within the regulations governing army appointments, the purchaser of a company could fill or sell the junior post at his discretion.[11] Despite the availability of regular army commissions, few Mexicans took advantage of the offer. Most of the candidates were either peninsulares or first-generation sons of European army officers and civilian administrators. Heading the list for captaincies were Juan Flórez, son of the viceroy, and José Núñez de Haro, a nephew of the archbishop. Some regular army officers and cadets used the opportunity to speed promotion or to escape from a dead-end post in one of the provincial training cadres.[12] Lieutenant Nicolás Monteagudo of the Infantry Regiment of Zamora, for example, was able to purchase a captaincy and thereby to bypass his fellow lieutenants. Although he had seventeen years' service and had seen action against the Moroccans, many officers enjoyed

TABLE 17
Senior Regular Army Officers of the Army of New Spain, 1799.*

Name, Quality, Rank, and Assignment	Age in 1799	Date of Death or Transfer	Country or Province of Origin
Brigadiers			
Pedro Ruiz Dávalos (noble)	79	(1810 +?)	Valencia
Colonel, Provincial Cavalry of Querétaro			
Agustín Beven (noble)	76	(1797 +)	Bayonne, France
Colonel, Dragoon Regiment of Mexico			
Pedro Garibay (noble)	69	(1811 +?)	Navarre
Colonel, Infantry Regiment of New Spain			
Marqués de Moncada (noble)	59	Unknown	Palermo, Italy
Colonel, Provincial Dragoons of Puebla			
José Manuel de Alava (noble)	49	(1796–99 Tr)	Vitoria, Alava
Colonel, Infantry Regiment of Puebla			
Pablo Sánchez	62	(1797 +)	Spain
Commander of Artillery			
Antonio Bonilla (noble)	60	(1807 +)	Spain
Colonel, Dragoon Regiment of Mexico			
Conde de Alcaraz (José Rengel) (distinguished)	48	(1813 +)	Málaga
Colonel, Dragoon Regiment of Spain			
Nemesio Salcedo (noble)	45	(1809 Sp)	Bilbao
Colonel, Infantry Regiment of the Crown			
Francisco Villalba (noble)	60	(1802 + Havana)	San Sebastián
Colonel, Infantry Regiment of Mexico			
Vicente Nieto (noble)	53	(1809 Tr Montevideo)	Castilla la Vieja
Colonel, Infantry Regiment of Puebla			
García Dávila (noble)	51		Spain
Governor-Intendant of Veracruz			
Colonels			
Juan Velázquez (noble)	65	(1795 +)	Zamora
Colonel, Dragoon Regiment of Spain			
Pedro Ponce (son of a lieutenant colonel)	49	(1797 +)	Catalonia
Commander of Engineers			
Diego García Panes (noble)	68		Granada
Lieutenant of the King, Veracruz			
Joaquín Posada (noble)	58	(1802 +)	Asturias
Governor, Fortress of Perote			
Carlos Urrutía (noble)	47		*Havana, Cuba*
Lieutenant Colonel, Infantry Regiment of Puebla			
Diego Borica (noble)	56		Vizcaya
Governor of California			

continued

TABLE 17, *continued*

Name, Quality, Rank, and Assignment	Age in 1799	Date of Death or transfer	Country or Province of Origin
Ignacio Maneiro (career soldier) Lieutenant Colonel, Provincial Infantry of Puebla	59		*Veracruz*
Francisco Lisa (noble) Governor of Tlaxcala	73		Cartagena, Spain
Manuel Flon (noble) Intendant of Puebla	53	(1810 +)	Spain
Miguel Costansó (noble) Commander of Engineers	59		Barcelona
Jaime Alzuvide (noble) Sargento Mayor, Fortress of Perote	68		Catalonia
Ignacio García Revollo (noble) Lieutenant Colonel, Provincial Cavalry of Querétaro	57		Rioja, Spain
José Muñoz (noble) Lieutenant Colonel, Dragoon Regiment of Mexico	61		Zaragosa, Spain
José Barreiro (noble) Governor of the Castle of San Diego, Acapulco	52	(1809 +)	Spain
Félix Calleja (noble) Commander, Tenth Militia Brigade of San Luis Potosí	42		Castilla la Vieja
Lieutenant Colonels			
Miguel Emparán (noble) Lieutenant Colonel, Dragoon Regiment of Spain	41		Azpeitia, Spain
Casimiro Montero (noble) Lieutenant Colonel, Dragoon Regiment of Mexico	54		Cádiz
Manuel Bonilla (noble) Commander, Battalion of Veracruz	50	(1809 +)	Cádiz
Pedro de Alonso (son of a brigadier) Lieutenant Colonel, Infantry Regiment of the Crown	41		Ceuta
José Gamiz (noble) Lieutenant Colonel, Infantry Regiment of New Spain	48	(1804 +)	Castilla la Vieja
Juan Antonio Riaño (noble) Intendant of Guanajuato	42	(1810 +)	Spain
Pedro Alberni (noble) Captain, 2nd Company of Catalonian Volunteers	51	(1803 +)	Catalonia
Juan María Soto (son of a captain) Major, Infantry Regiment of the Crown	64		*Veracruz*
Diego de Oroz (honorable) Captain, Dragoon Regiment of Spain	62		Pamplona
Francisco Norma (noble) Sargento Mayor, Veracruz	53		Aragon

Continued

TABLE 17, *continued*

Bernardo Gallegos (noble)	64		Canary
Captain, Infantry Regiment of the Crown			Islands
Antonio Villamil (noble)	49		Ceuta
Lieutenant Colonel, Infantry Regiment of Mexico			
Antonio Mendivil (hidalgo)	60		Navarre
Captain, Company of Acapulco			
Nicolás Yberri (noble)	49	(1811 +)	*Veracruz*
Captain, Infantry Regiment of the Crown			
Diego García Conde (noble)	38		Barcelona
Captain, Infantry Regiment of Puebla			
Roberto Rollín (noble)	54	(1809 +)	France
Captain, Infantry Regiment of Puebla			
Nicolás Monteagudo (gentleman)	47	(1805 +)	La Mancha
Commander, Lancers of Veracruz			
Antonio Hernández (noble)	60		Almería
Captain, Company of San Blas			

*Officers of Criollo origin are in italics.
 Sp—return to Spain
 Tr—transfer
 +—death
Regular army officers serving in provincial militia units are included in this table rather than in table 18.
Source: Lista por antigüedad de los oficiales veteranos, February 1793, AGN, Historia, vol. 155; Branciforte to Alange, no. 149, January 6, 1795, AGI, México, leg. 1438; Azanza to Alvarez, no. 295, April 26, 1799, AGI, México, leg. 1449; and hojas de servicio, AGS, GM, legs. 7270–7280; and other sources.

more seniority in terms of time spent in the army. Monteagudo made good use of this chance to break through the stifling promotion procedures. Once a captain, he received numerous important viceregal commissions; by the time of his premature death in 1805, he was a lieutenant colonel and commander of the Lancers of Veracruz.[13] In cases like this one, few could criticize the benefits to the army of selling commissions. Unfortunately, however, many other deserving officers simply could not afford to take advantage of the offer. Even though there were individuals prepared to lend fairly large sums to aspirants for commissions, a captain's salary was insufficient to support its holder and to permit repayment of high-interest loans.[14] For the regime, there were immediate gains: the sale of sixteen captaincies and lieutenancies in the regular Infantry Regiments of Mexico and New Spain produced a total of 189,000 pesos. Even after taking into account expenditures for recruiting, uniforms, and other equipment, a surplus of 82,639 pesos remained.[15]

Frequently, the sale of commissions allowed the sons of army officers to follow their fathers into a military career without having to begin as a common soldier or an officer cadet. Most of these candidates were in their late teens or early twenties. Although some were criollo by fate of birth, often the sons of government bureaucrats or the merchant elite, they were more Spanish than Mexican in their outlook. At the same time, wealth alone was not sufficient to guarantee access to the army. When rumors came to Viceroy Flórez that one purchaser, Juan Macali, was not the man of impeccable credentials he claimed to be, he was stricken from the list of captains and his nine thousand pesos were returned. Macali's pretensions to nobility, relationships with Spanish naval officers, and descent from the houses of Macali and Bucheli—described as the most illustrious in Italy—could not be substantiated. Even with the presentation of six testimonials, *Auditor de Guerra* Bataller rejected an appeal. Foreign origins and lack of solid evidence were grounds enough for rejection, but Macali had not held previous positions in the royal service and his reputation in the Mexico City business community was not good.[16]

Once admitted to service, the *oficiales de beneficio,* as they were called, had to prove themselves capable of demonstrating at least minimum military aptitude. Captain Félix Calleja, in charge of officer training, received explicit instructions to select the new officers carefully so that their regiments would not be filled with incompetents who would be difficult to dismiss at a later date.[17] Indeed, three lieutenants were separated from the Infantry Regiment of Puebla for not sufficiently applying themselves during the training program. Generally speaking, however, men who had invested a large amount of money in their commissions were zealous in learning the military profession and responded well to discipline. Maneuvers following the completion of officer training satisfied all observers; only one sublieutenant was sent back to repeat basic drill.[18]

After the beginning of the French Revolution, Spain could not afford the luxury of stationing large numbers of experienced army officers in the colonies. Beginning with the wars of the 1790s, the replacement of officers lost to retirement and natural attrition became a matter for considerable concern. Formerly, it had been the policy to promote distinguished soldiers, NCOs, and cadets from the European army as subaltern officers in the regular training cadres assigned to the Mexican provincial regiments.[19] With the wars against France and Britain occupying full attention, even the regular infantry and dragoon regiments had to turn inward for most promotions. Posts dominated by peninsular officers were filled by criollos whose careers advanced as the mother country encountered greater difficulties in Europe. At the same time, the shortages caused severe pressures upon the small complement of trained officers and NCOs; when, for example, Viceroy Branciforte expanded the provincial army, Colonel Juan Velázquez of the Dragoons of Spain feared that transfers would leave him without sufficient officers and sergeants to put together a trustworthy detachment.[20] By 1800, although sergeants had been posted to vacancies in the artillery companies, ten additional lieutenants and sublieutenants were needed.[21] In all of the regular units it was common to find the ternas for vacant sublieutenancies listing three NCOs.[22] Mexicans, who formed the great majority of the enlisted ranks, were given a larger share of the lieutenancies and captaincies. This was especially true in those regiments assigned to Caribbean stations or to garrison duty at Veracruz where disease opened new opportunities for the survivors.

Despite this trend, the ascent of criollo officers above the rank of captain was by no means assured. One of the real weaknesses of the Mexican army was that old officers refused to retire from their regiments. The average age of brigadiers in 1793 was over sixty years and colonels were well over fifty.[23] The average age of colonels would have been higher, but there were a number of younger officers who held the rank of *coronel graduado*. They were usually company captains who did not receive the salary for their effective rank. As might be expected, some natural attrition occurred among the aged brigadiers; by 1799, some colonels had risen to the rank of brigadier. Even so, the average age of senior officers remained well over fifty-five years. It is interesting that even at this high rank, the transfer of European officers to Mexican commands had stopped almost altogether. Of the six brigadiers who had not held this rank in 1793, all except Governor-Intendant García Dávila of Veracruz, who had been transferred from Havana, received their promotions within the army of New Spain.[24]

The viceroys made frequent reference to the fact that many European officers had reached advanced age and no longer fulfilled their military obligations. Some men, still adjutants and lieutenants stationed with the training cadres of militia units, had come to Mexico with the Villalba expedition of 1764 and remained in their stations without opportunity for advancement.[25] Over the years they became identified with the region in which they served—most developed business interests, married into local families, and became criollo in outlook.[26] It was fear of this fate that caused many Spanish officers to shy away from colonial service or to view it as a form of "involuntary servitude." Viceroy Marquina considered the problem of dead-end assignments of regular officers to be a real impediment to the army's development. No officer could be expected to retain his ambition without at least some opportunity for promotion. The viceroy introduced a system of advancing regular adjutants assigned in training cadres to the important position of major in the provincial regiments. If they were not suitable, captains from the regular regiments were to be encouraged to compete for the rank of major; if they accepted a post in a provincial regiment, there was to be no loss of regular army seniority or promotion.[27]

Old age and senility were most evident in the Dragoon Regiments of Mexico and Spain. Formed during the 1760s, both units lost their dynamism and fighting capacity during years of sedentary garrison duty.[28] Their only challenge was to escort shipments of silver or gangs of criminals from city to city. Most officers were too old or had lost their military vocation—permitting discipline to crumble and abuses to take permanent hold. In 1793, the regimental commanders, Brigadier Agustín Beven and Colonel Juan Velázquez, were, respectively, seventy-three and sixty-six years of age: both were too weak to mount horses without the assistance of servants.[29] Beven could not travel because fluid swelled his ankles. Out of touch with his regiment, he spent most of his time at his hacienda near Jalapa, where he could keep his feet up. Yet he claimed to be fit for duty in a temperate climate and asserted that he had the head and stomach of a twenty-five-year-old.[30] Despite this apparent dedication, Beven had not been in contact with his regiment since 1790. Discipline and subordination declined in all ranks. Officers submitted false receipts for the purchase and feed of horses, mismanaged recruiting, ran up huge debts to the regiment far beyond their capacity to repay, and quite generally turned what was supposed to be an elite unit into a shambles.[31]

Under normal circumstances, the incapacity of a colonel should not have caused the decline of an entire regiment. In the case of the Dragoons of Mexico, however, the rot reached deeper. Lieutenant Colonel José de los Reyes was seventy-one years of age; he suffered a debilitating illness which caused his death in 1794.[32] The third in command, Major Juan María Barrios, rather than stabilizing the regiment, was a disruptive influence. Described by all of his commanders as an officer of reprehensible conduct and malicious ways, Barrios—a peninsular himself—became infamous for siding with the criollos and demonstrating a most profound hatred for Europeans. He contributed much of the antagonism which resulted in the formation of factions within the regiment. Revillagigedo declared the dragoons to have reached the point of total uselessness. While the officers quarreled among themselves, training had been neglected and discipline was nonexistent. To make matters worse, the next officer in order of seniority was Captain Antonio Barrios brother of the major and equally notorious for his bad conduct, devotion to vice, and disrespect for his superiors.[33]

Revillagigedo placed Major Barrios under house arrest in July 1793, while he reported the case to the crown. He requested the immediate transfer of both brothers to Spain, where they could not cause the trouble they generated in Mexico. The question of leadership came up the following year with the death of Lieutenant Colonel Reyes. Sub-Inspector General Gorostiza reviewed the service records of the other officers without discovering a replacement. Another of the senior captains, Joaquín Romo, had a reputation almost as bad as the Barrios brothers. He was known as a malicious gossip against his superiors; on one occasion when he was officer of the guard, he allowed a convicted murderer to obtain pen and paper to write a diatribe against his court-martial.[34] Captain Manuel Rojas was addicted to gambling. Involved with some of the lowest elements in the population, he served a jail term in the castle of San Juan de Ulúa.[35] Not a single officer appeared to deserve promotion. Even the junior subalterns and NCOs emulated their superiors. Few made any effort to fulfill their duties and most were hopelessly in debt. It was exactly this kind of situation that Revillagigedo hoped to cure by his plan for regular rotation of regiments between Mexico and Spain.[36] In this case, little could be done until Brigadier Beven died in 1797. Even then, the new commander, Colonel Antonio Bonilla, spent the most of his time in the viceregal secretariat. Finally, Lieutenant Colonel Casimiro Montero, a good journeyman officer with long experience in New Spain, was given interim command of the regiment. He began the difficult process of eradicating faults which had been allowed to develop for almost a decade.[37]

The attitude of the imperial government toward officer retirement made this kind of regimental breakdown inevitable. Basically, the problem was lack of an adequate pension plan or a plan for the use of officers once they reached a certain age. Revillagigedo believed that old army commanders made fine military governors in Spain, but comparable positions did not exist in Mexico. As a measure to protect the regiments, he proposed retiring officers on full salary. When this solution was rejected, he ordered Pedro Gorostiza to look into the issue. The whole problem stemmed from the poor stipends paid to retired officers. Rather than accept poverty, they did not allow chronic illness or advanced age to dislodge them from their commands. In Gorostiza's opinion, under the regulations of 1780 retired officers were ". . . worse off than a sergeant, drummer, or common soldier." He argued that it was intolerable for men who had devoted more than thirty-five years to the royal service to spend their declining years in abject poverty. To eliminate this weakness, he drafted a new regulation designed to make retirement more attractive and to open the way for promotion of younger officers.[38] Despite the logic of Gorostiza's report, the crown remained adamant in its refusal to improve pensions or to adopt any policy of automatic retirement at a specified age. Royal orders left no room for viceregal interference; those commanders who wished to continue service were to be left in their posts regardless of their physical condition.[39]

By the time younger officers reached the commands occupied by the ancient veterans, they too had passed their most active years. When Brigadier Antonio Bonilla died in 1807, there were five *coroneles graduados* who enjoyed sufficient seniority to command the Dragoons of Mexico. The top three candidates, Colonels Miguel de Emparán, José Muñoz, and Diego García Conde, had served in the army for between thirty-five and fifty years. When Brigadier Vicente Nieto, commander of the Infantry of Puebla, was promoted to the governorship of Montevideo in 1809, the three colonels recommended to replace him—Juan Manuel Bonilla, Manuel de García, and Roberto Rollín—each boasted between forty and fifty years' military service. Bonilla suffered from *"obesidad corporal"* and could not engage in exercise or mount horses; García had reached an advanced age and showed signs of senility; and Rollín, who received the post, died before he could take possession of it.[40]

Despite all of the liabilities connected with assignment to a sedentary colonial army, a few intelligent and capable officers were able to advance their careers. Without much doubt, the greatest success was attained by Félix Calleja, a young infantry officer who accompanied Revillagigedo to Mexico. For his age, Calleja had considerable wartime experience, which gave him an advantage over officers who had not seen action. In 1775, he served in the abortive expedition against Algiers, and during the siege of Gibraltar in 1782 he took part in artillery engagements. Calleja was stationed on one of the floating artillery batteries, where the Conde de Revillagigedo noticed his capacity for command and became his patron. From this point forward, Revillagigedo kept a close watch over Calleja's development. Calleja later served in Minorca and, with the restoration of peace, demonstrated great zeal as the commander of a small army force assigned to destroy contrabandists. Transferred to the Regiment of Savoy, he was placed in charge of training officers and cadets. Then, from 1784 to 1788, he was director of studies at the military college at Puerto de Santa María.[41]

Although he was just over thirty years of age when he joined the Regiment of Puebla, Calleja rose rapidly and managed to retain the favor of all viceroys prior to 1810.[42] In 1790, he began his duties as the regimental training officer, but Revillagigedo assigned him to much more important commissions. The first was to survey the frontier of Colotlán and the province of Nayarit. Besides inspecting the militia forces, Calleja's reports included a wealth of historical, political, and geographical information. Revillagigedo's own curiosity and thirst for scientific knowledge must have been satisfied, for this commission led to others. Between 1792 and 1794, Calleja inspected militia units, prepared census reports, established militia forces in Nueva Galicia, and introduced the new militia system along the Gulf coast. His assignments gave him special competence in northern defense, which Branciforte recognized by giving him wartime responsibility for the coast north of Tampico as well as the northern provinces ruled from Mexico City. By 1799 this enormous command had evolved into what became the Tenth Militia Brigade of San Luis Potosí. From his northern base, Calleja organized one of the best provincial cavalry forces in the viceroyalty; beginning in 1810, he used his northern army to build a reputation that would propel him into the office of viceroy.[43] Unlike many other European officers, Calleja seldom looked back to Spain or attempted to transfer to the metropolitan army. Since he made the rank of full brigadier before 1810, he may well have felt that it was better to lead in Mexico than to rejoin the struggle for promotion in Spain. Although married to a Mexican woman, Calleja did request permission in 1802 for a two-year leave to visit his family, but the outbreak of war against Britain in 1804 prevented his departure. A nineteenth-century Mexican historian, overcome by the irony of this near-removal of the royalist archvillain, wrote on the margin of Calleja's license to visit Spain, "If only he had used it! He would have freed this America from so many evils."[44]

The viceroys who lauded Calleja's intelligence often mentioned Pedro de Alonso as an officer of equally outstanding abilities in an army filled with distinctly mediocre talent.[45] Alonso entered the army as a very young cadet in 1769 and, like so many of the regular officers in New Spain, he gained his battle experience in the campaigns of North Africa. He spent several years in the garrison of Oran and took part in the 1775 expedition against Algiers. During the American Revolution, he fought at Pensacola and again in Santo Domingo. Transferred to New Spain during the formation of the new infantry regiments, he developed a special expertise on the defense of Veracruz. Prior to 1810, Alonso served as interim commander of San Juan de Ulúa, and commanded the Veracruz garrison and the ill-fated 1799 cantonment of Arroyo Moreno. His defense plans and reports on Veracruz formed the basis for coastal defense.[46] In 1800, although he was just forty years of age, he was promoted to the rank of full colonel. Viceroy Marquina thought so much of Alonso that he wanted to appoint him to a regimental command rather than let him waste his talents in charge of a fortress. When the colonelcy of the Infantry of the Crown became vacant, Marquina recommended him for the post. This was not to be, however, for the imperial government transferred Colonel Vicente Muesas from the peninsular Regiment of Zaragoza.[47] Marquina then attempted to have old Brigadier Pedro Garibay promoted to the rank of field marshal and retired to allow Alonso to take command of the Regiment of New Spain. This maneuver failed, but Alonso was given command over the Regiment of Mexico, which was divided between Havana and Veracruz.[48] When war again broke out in 1804, he served as interim governor of Veracruz and in 1808, after the overthrow of Iturrigaray, he became sub-inspector of the troops cantoned at Jalapa. When several other officers were promoted to the rank of brigadier in 1809, Viceroy Lizana wrote a strong commendation on behalf of Alonso's request for a similar promotion.[49]

Another of the intelligent officers attracted to Mexico by Revillagigedo was Carlos de Urrutía. Born in Havana, he was sent to Spain, where he graduated from the military academies of Barcelona and Avila. In the 1780s, he saw action in the sieges of Gibraltar and Minorca. In 1784, he received a commission to arrange various military matters in France; from there he travelled widely throughout Europe. The king of Prussia asked him to assist in doctrinal and field exercises near Berlin and Potsdam, after which he received commendations from Generals Mollendorf and Pretzwitz. He later visited Brunswick, Saxony, Russia, and Austria, where the emperor invited him to dinner and questioned him about some recent reforms in the army of Naples. When Urrutía returned to Spain he submitted a detailed report on European armies and tactics to King Charles III, which was adopted by the Supremo Consejo de Guerra.[50] Urrutía was only forty years of age when he was assigned to the new Regiment of Mexico; as a *coronel graduado,* he had to serve as a company captain until promotion opportunities opened. This happened very quickly when his regiment was transferred into the deadly climate of Havana. Not only did he move into the vacant post of lieutenant colonel, but he was also soon thrust into full command when Colonel Vicente Nieto suffered a series of debilitating illnesses. Nieto became one of Urrutía's greatest supporters; he described him as an officer ". . . possessing profound military knowledge acquired through studies, travel, and field experience."[51] In 1800, upon the strong recommendation of Viceroy Azanza, Urrutía was made commander of the First Militia Brigade of Mexico City. Promotion to the rank of brigadier came only after three unsuccessful attempts, since it was not until 1809, when the provisional government of Spain loosened the promotion structure, that he received the advantage needed. More honors were to follow: in 1810, Brigadier Urrutía became sub-inspector general of the army as well as governor and intendant of Veracruz.[52]

Since rank was the ultimate gauge of success among army officers, perhaps Pedro Garibay should be mentioned even before the three officers that have been discussed. Although he reached the absolute apex of power in New Spain five years before Calleja duplicated the feat, his twilight rise to the viceregency was not so much the result of his own merits as it was the product of the political situation following Iturrigaray's overthrow. Even so, Garibay's army career deserves attention. In 1800, he was sixty-nine years of age, second only in army seniority to Brigadier Pedro Ruiz Dávalos, who was a venerable eighty years. Following family tradition, Garibay had joined the Spanish army in 1742 and he saw action in the wars of Italy, Portugal, and North Africa. According to his service record, he distinguished himself in 1757 during a month of furious Moroccan attacks against the presidio of Ceuta. Transferred to Mexico at the beginning of the military reforms, he spent twenty-one years as the regular army major assigned to the Provincial Regiment of Mexico. It was not until the expansion of the regular infantry that Garibay received command of the Regiment of New Spain. Already, his age and weak health appeared to dictate an early retirement.[53] It came as no surprise that he could not accompany his regiment in 1792 when it was dispatched to bolster the Spanish forces fighting in Santo Domingo. His surgeon advised against any journey into the *tierra caliente* until after he had undergone an operation to cure insect bites on his legs.[54] Recovering sufficiently from this affliction to join his regiment, Garibay led several attacks against French forts before he fell ill once again and returned to Havana.[55] When Branciforte arrived in New Spain, he declared Garibay to be of advanced age and bad health—useful perhaps in an advisory capacity but not as an active commander. Apparently, Branciforte had discussed Garibay's future with officials in the ministry of war before he departed for New Spain; everyone agreed that the old officer should be promoted to field marshal and retired.[56]

No one believed Garibay would live long enough to be much of a drain on the treasury even if he was paid the full salary of a field marshal. While his regiment suffered constant wartime garrison duty at Veracruz through the 1790s, Garibay took up permanent residence in Mexico City. For years he did not even visit his troops.[57] Iturrigaray continued to support the old officer's petitions for a field marshal's salary after the promotion took place in 1802; in his opinion, Garibay should be allowed "... to spend his last days in the decorous manner he deserves."[58] As time would tell, he was not so easily dismissed; long residence in the capital made him the friend or respected acquaintance of the powerful peninsular merchants and administrators who overthrew Iturrigaray in 1808. With the prestige and continuity of high military rank—he was the only field marshal named prior to the overthrow of the

Spanish monarchy—it is not surprising that the reactionary forces turned to him as a kind of figurehead or symbol in the wake of the first *golpe de estado*.[59]

Not all officers could aspire to be viceroys or even colonels. Others saw a far better future in utilizing their hidalgo birth and the social prestige granted to all peninsulares. With a little luck and a great deal of good management, they could achieve at the altar in a few minutes what in the royal service might take a lifetime of honest dedication. Most officers had an abundance of honor and very little money. A good marriage could be the key to escaping what was close to genteel poverty. Pedro de Alonso, for example, complained that he experienced chronic difficulties making ends meet. Numerous trips and other financial liabilities in the line of duty were not possible on a colonel's salary—particularly "... in a country where it costs more to live than anywhere else in the world." Stretched well beyond his capacity to cover his debts, he feared losing his good name.[60] Prices were highest in Veracruz, where many officers lived on credit in order to maintain a modest standard of living. Examining their situation, Colonel Joaquín Gutiérrez de los Ríos described them as "... poorly fed, naked, and depressed by their miserable situation." Prices had doubled over the years since the last salary increase, forcing officers into huge involuntary debts. Gutiérrez quoted the axiom that "little can be expected from a man weakened by hunger and surrounded by wretchedness."[61] Small wonder, then, that marriage to the daughter of some rich miner or merchant became the salvation for honorable but penurious officers.

At the same time, however, the military ordinances governing the marriage of officers were very strict. There was no possibility of an army man rushing out to seek the hand of a *criolla* heiress without long-term planning and considerable patience. Regular army officers and even the provincial militia officers had to obtain royal licenses before they were permitted to contract matrimony. The process was complex, requiring at least several years before the documents might be collected and approval granted by the immediate commander, viceroy, and the king.[62] In addition, marriage was difficult under any circumstances if the woman was not the daughter of an officer or of identifiable noble blood. If she was of the hidalgo class, her quality had to be proven without the slightest challenge to her *limpieza de sangre*. Even so, women had to deposit a dowry of at least twenty thousand reales in the royal treasury—a sum that was raised to fifty thousand reales if they were not of noble or hidalgo origins.[63] Furthermore, all women had to submit their baptismal record, an authorized copy of their father's grade in the army, or full documentation proving the authenticity of their claims to nobility. If the officer wishing to marry did not hold the rank of captain or above at the time of his matrimony, his wife and children would have no claim to survivor benefits paid from the Monte Pío Militar, the military pension fund, unless the husband died in battle.[64] When, for example, Brigadier Antonio Bonilla died not only poor but deeply in debt after years of litigation, he left his widow, Doña Manuela de Torres, absolutely destitute. She had no recourse to the Monte Pío Militar because she married Bonilla when he was only a junior subaltern.[65] The case of Colonel Manuel Vaamonde Villamil, a Galician by origin, demonstrates the degree to which the regime enforced its regulations on unauthorized marriage. He was a knight of the Order of Alcántara, governor of Nuevo León, and an officer with a proven record of service dating back to the 1760s.[66] Yet when Vaamonde fell victim to his emotions and married without securing a royal license, he was stripped of his offices and salary. By 1798, he had been reduced to a state of grinding poverty and was forced to beg for alms in the streets. Viceroy Azanza took pity on his condition and requested a royal pardon and a transfer back to a new post in Spain.[67]

For soldiers willing to play by the rules, the capture of an heiress brought the prospect of enormous wealth. Two officers, Joaquín Gutiérrez de los Ríos and José Antonio Rengel—later the Conde de Alcaraz—married daughters of the great silver mining Fagoaga family.[68] Gutiérrez de los Ríos, a native of Córdoba in Andalusia, began his military career in North Africa during the 1770s, but without showing any outstanding promise. Since he was related to the Conde del Campo de Alange and other powerful figures in the Spanish elite, he experienced little difficulty moving to a civilian job in the colonial bureaucracy. He obtained the position of alcalde mayor of Celaya and Salvatierra, an office he held to his advantage for some years. Indeed, it was as alcalde mayor that Gutiérrez met and courted one of the Fagoaga daughters, thereby changing his military as well as his financial fortunes. To top off this stroke of luck, the Conde del Campo de Alange became imperial minister of war. Viceroy Branciforte, no stranger himself to the usefulness of good connections, wrote to his friend Alange that he planned to confer the command of a provincial infantry regiment upon Gutiérrez.[69] At first there were no openings and he had to be satisfied with the post of lieutenant colonel in the Infantry of Toluca. When the young Conde de Santiago, commander of the Infantry of Puebla, died suddenly, Branciforte transferred Gutiérrez with almost indecent haste.[70] Just how the viceroy gained the acquiescence of the cabildo of Puebla in this appointment is not clear, but the combination of Fagoaga money and executive pressure would have been irresistible. In 1800, Gutiérrez was given command of the provincial infantry column formed in Mexico City and he served in all of the cantonments.[71]

Even more meteoric in his rise to affluence through marriage to a daughter of the Fagoaga family was José Antonio Rengel. A native of Málaga, he joined the army as a cadet in 1763. He fought at Algiers in 1775, participated in numerous North African skirmishes, and was aide-de-camp to the Duque de Crillón during the siege of Gibraltar. In 1784 he was named *comandante inspector* of the Provincias Internas of New Spain, a post he held until it was terminated in 1788.[72] Rengel moved to Mexico City, where he found life much more to his liking than on the northern frontier. Awarded the governorship of New Mexico and Vizcaya, he managed to stay on in the capital, claiming that the climate of the north did not agree with him. Revillagigedo expressed near contempt for this excuse; Rengel was a drain on the treasury, for he continued to draw the governor's salary of eight thousand pesos. In the viceroy's opinion, any officer who behaved in this manner should be returned to Spain as soon as possible.[73] Despite this pressure, Rengel held out; by this point, the wealth he obtained through his wife made him financially independent and able to await an appointment more to his liking. When old Colonel Juan Velázquez of the Dragoons of Spain died in 1797, Rengel was named to the regimental command. In the same year, he was granted the title of Conde de Alcaraz.[74] As has been noted elsewhere, he was now the largest landowner and horse raiser in the *corregimiento* of Querétaro. In the district of Puruándiro he owned the hacienda de Villachuato and held various rural and urban properties elsewhere. Naturally, the management of this landed empire detracted from Alcaraz's dedication to regimental command. Viceroy Iturrigaray complained that he devoted very little time to the army; when the regiment was stationed at the cantonment in 1806, Alcaraz was absent for over a year and a half. Since Iturrigaray recognized that the count suffered from dropsy, he recommended an early retirement.[75] If this proposal made good military sense, it was not a good idea for the viceroy to take on a man who wielded great political and financial power. When Iturrigaray was overthrown, Pedro Garibay did not make the same error; he was quick to appoint Brigadier (soon to be Field Marshal) Alcaraz to command the Jalapa cantonment.[76]

As might be expected, officers did not limit their amorous attentions to the Fagoaga heiresses. Major Juan de Noriega managed one of the greatest conquests when he married twenty-one-year-old Doña María Luisa Martín Vicario, the widow of the wealthy Marqués de Bibanco and daughter of an important Mexico City merchant, Gaspar Martín Vicario. Noriega, a forty-six-year-old native of Abadia in Asturias, had a solid if not outstanding regular army career before he met the *marquesa*. He served with Bernardo de Gálvez in the Louisiana and West Florida campaigns and by 1801 he had risen to the post of *sargento mayor* of the Mexico City garrison. Both Azanza and Marquina commended Noriega for his organizational skills and he commanded the provincial grenadier column at Jalapa in 1801.[77] His matrimony with the marquesa raised more difficulties than usual because of wartime communications difficulties with Spain. Finally, Viceroy Iturrigaray authorized the marriage under special wartime powers. This was fortunate, for the king's final approval was not granted until 1817.[78] Noriega continued to serve in the Mexico City garrison, where he played a key role in maintaining public calm and aiding the transition of power after Iturrigaray's overthrow. As the chief liaison officer between the commanders of army units stationed in the capital and the viceroy, his post became more and more important. Viceroy Lizana submitted glowing testimonials about Noriega's achievements until they had a falling out over how to handle public unrest and policing.[79]

Not all of the romances between regular army officers and wealthy criollas ended happily. Major Vicente Barros de Alemparte, a Galician stationed with the provincial Dragoon Regiment of the Queen, was in the right position to marry well, but he made the wrong choice. He set his sights very high and attempted to marry an aunt of his regimental colonel, land baron Narciso de la Canal. In doing so, Alemparte received far more attention than he anticipated. As soon as Canal learned about the marriage proposal, he did everything in his power to prevent it. While he tolerated the major as a militia colleague, he did not want him as a relative. Alemparte received a public rebuke and was placed under house arrest on the Sunday the matrimonial banns were to have been read. There was little the major could do to counter the position and financial resources of Colonel Canal. Since the dispute made the regiment almost useless, the brigade commander, Ignacio García Revollo, proposed that the major be transferred away from the scene of contention.[80]

With the regulations designed to delay the marriages of young officers, other problems could be anticipated. Casual relationships between regular officers and women of the lower classes were common in spite of official attitudes on correct gentlemanly behavior. In one case, Sublieutenant Manuel Cuvillas of the Infantry of New Spain was charged with grossly immoral behavior and lying to a superior officer. When Cuvillas was transferred from Mexico City to Veracruz, he requested permission to spend a few days visiting his relatives in Puebla. His commander soon learned that the real motivation for the visit was to allow the young officer to live freely with a married woman. Fortunately for Cuvillas, however, he had visited his relatives and was found innocent of lying. On the second charge, the court-martial condemned him for his activities with a low-class woman, but let him off without further punishment.[81] On the other hand, the postponement of marriage sometimes resulted in rather different concerns. Viceroys Azanza and Marquina received numerous denunciations from Presidio del Carmen regarding the policies of the governor, Lieutenant Colonel Agustín Bernardo de Medina. Although he was sixty years of age, Medina had married a young girl from an important local family. Thereafter, he favored his wife's relatives for all positions and contracts. Marquina frowned upon the situation, believing it was poor policy to allow an elderly officer to remain in an office where he was surrounded by rapacious relatives.[82]

The provincial officers' motivations were quite different from those of the regulars. A regimental command or senior commission brought recognition, social prestige, and some power to its holder. Most provincial officers were at least moderately well off prior to their joining the militia and, as has been seen, they were expected to donate large sums of money to the treasury for the privilege of high rank. Viceroy Branciforte went out of his way to make the *fuero militar* appear attractive to potential officers and it remained one of the best means of attracting candidates even after it became quite evident that a militia commission was not always advantageous to the holder.[83] At the same time, the elites' thirst for the fuero, or for tangible gains to offset the donations and time that they were willing to give to the provincial army, should not be overemphasized. Officer status was also a way for wealthy men to extend their activities beyond the cabildo level and fulfill a desire to hold office. It was also a means of manifesting loyalty to the crown, and it guaranteed entry into the society of Mexico City or the provinces. For men who had worked their way to prominence through business, or who were the sons of the criollo landed elite, the opportunities of militia rank were often too much to pass up (see table 18).[84] At the same time, as David Brading has pointed out, this kind of recognition of success was particularly attractive to the Spanish immigrants who had either married wealth or prospered through mining and commercial activities.[85]

Some subjects were almost prodigal in their gifts to the royal service. The family of the millionaire Conde de Valenciana, for example, continued his lavish support for any number of public works and charities. After the count died in 1786, one of his sons and two sons-in-law utilized a part of the family fortune to elevate themselves into senior provincial army commands. The eldest daughter, María Gertrudis, married Antonio Pérez Gálvez, a *malagueño* whose claim to nobility was dubious and who was viewed by the family as a greedy fortune hunter.[86] Whether or not the rumors about his low origins were true, Pérez Gálvez used Valenciana money to expand his own fortune and to propel himself into the status of an imperial benefactor as well as colonel of the local cavalry regiment. He employed nearly nine hundred workers in his mines, smelters, and haciendas.[87] In 1806, his estates produced twenty-six thousand sheep and he purchased another seventy thousand to fill contracts to supply Puebla, Guanajuato, and the Valenciana mines.[88] When the war broke out against France, he donated 3,000 pesos and promised to give the same amount each year for the duration of hostilities. Both Pérez Gálvez and his mother-in-law, the condesa, obligated themselves to levy a personal tax of 3 granos for every mark of silver refined from their mines—which was in itself a generous offer. Between 1770 and 1791, the united houses of Valenciana and Pérez Gálvez—but mostly the former—paid taxes on silver totalling 2,668,845 pesos. From 1791 to 1795, Pérez Gálvez himself had paid another 118,591 pesos.[89] Remarkably, this was only one aspect of the family's support for the state. The condesa donated a full warship of seventy-four cannon, and engaged in philanthropic endeavors such as funding missions in the Provincias Internas and helping the poor during bad harvests. Pérez Gálvez contributed enough to become colonel of the Cavalry Regiment of the Prince, but some of his acts of generosity had strings attached. His wife inherited a claim to a sixth of a debt owed by a merchant named Manuel Ramón de Goya—or 50,000 pesos out of a total of 300,000 pesos. The money was tied up, however, because there were numerous creditors and the Zacatecas miner, Marcelo de Anza, owed a considerable sum to Goya. The matter had been turned over to the courts and was bogged down in competencias between tribunals. With little chance of collecting, Pérez Gálvez donated the 50,000 pesos owed his wife to the crown.[90]

Ignacio de Obregón, possibly the illegitimate son of the Conde de Valenciana,[91] shared his brother-in-law's desire for militia rank. He began by donating sufficient funds to uniform and arm the three cavalry companies from his hometown of León—a sum totaling 7,200 pesos. Already he had given a war contribution of 1,500 pesos through the mining tribunal. For these efforts, Branciforte rewarded Obregón with a company. Not at all satisfied to remain a mere captain, he looked elsewhere for a regimental command. He found the opportunity he was looking for in the Dragoon Regiment of Nueva Galicia based at Aguascalientes. There, donations to raise the militia had not reached anywhere near expectations. Obregón stepped in with an offer to pay whatever sum was not covered through donations and to purchase all of the horses needed by the regiment.[92] This rescue operation was to have cost about 24,000 pesos, but in the end he had to pay almost 33,000 pesos out of the total cost of 47,400 pesos.[93]

The second son-in-law of the Conde de Valenciana, Diego Rul, another *malagueño,* married to María Ignacia,[94] had to look beyond his home province to find a colonelcy. Like Obregón, Rul obtained the rank of captain in the

TABLE 18
Senior Provincial Army Officers* of the Army of New Spain, 1799.†

Name, Quality, Rank, and Posting	Age and Date of Death	Principal Basis of Wealth	Province of Origin
SERVING COLONELS			
José Manuel de Cevallos (hidalgo) Infantry of Tres Villas	60	rural landholding	Córdoba
Marqués de Rivascacho (gentleman) Infantry of Toluca	47 (1800+)	rural landholding	Navarre
Antonio Pérez Gálvez (hidalgo) Cavalry of the Príncipe	39	marriage (Valenciana), landholding, commerce and mining	Málaga
Juan Fernández Munilla (hidalgo) Infantry of Celaya	61 (1802+)	rural landholding	La Rioja
Conde de Peñasco (noble) Dragoons of San Luis	40 (1805+)	mining, rural and urban landing	*San Luis Potosí*
Manuel Rincón Gallardo (hidalgo) Dragoons of San Carlos	41	rural landholding, *mayorazgo*, Ciénega de Mata	*Nueva Galicia*
Joaquín Benito de Medina (noble) Infantry of Mexico	55	inheritance, landholding, and commerce, *regidor* in the cabildo of Mexico	*Mexico*
Conde de la Contramina (noble) Infantry of Tlaxcala	57 (1799+)	silver mining	Santander
Joaquín Gutiérrez de los Ríos (noble) Infantry of Puebla	48	marriage (Fagoaga)	Córdoba
Diego Rul (noble) Infantry of Valladolid	32 (1812+)	marriage (Valenciana), rural landholding, commerce and silver mining	Málaga
Ignacio Obregón (noble) Dragoons of Nueva Galicia	43	inheritance (Valenciana) silver mining	*Guanajuato*
Francisco Menocal (noble) Dragoons of Michoacán	49	rural landholding	*Havana*
Narciso de la Canal (hidalgo) Dragoons of the Queen	42 (1812+)	rural landholding	*San Miguel*
COLONELS BY RANK			
Juan Francisco de Echarrí (hidalgo) Battalion of Oaxaca	52 (1808+)	copper and silver mining, commerce	Navarre

continued

TABLE 18, continued

Name	Age	Source of Wealth	Origin
Mariano Diez de Bonilla (noble) Lieutenant Colonel, Infantry of Puebla	42	Unknown	*Puebla*
LIEUTENANT COLONELS			
Manuel García Quintana (noble) Commander, Battalion of Guanajuato	54	commerce and mining	Santander
Lorenzo Angulo Guardamino (hidalgo) Lieutenant Colonel, Infantry of Tlaxcala	35	commerce, *regidor* of the cabildo of Mexico	Vizcaya
Francisco Septién y Arce (hidalgo) Lieutenant Colonel, Cavalry of the Príncipe	46	marriage, silver mining and smelter operator	Llerena
Manuel Fernández Solano (hidalgo) Lieutenant Colonel, Infantry of Celaya	51	rural landholding, *regidor* of the cabildo Celaya	La Rioja
Marcos González (prominent) Lieutenant Colonel, Infantry of Tres Villas	62	rural landholding	Villa de Cantis
Juan de Lanzagorta (hidalgo) Lieutenant Colonel, Dragoons of the Queen	34	rural landholding, inheritance, *regidor* cabildo of San Miguel	*San Miguel*
Angel Prieto de la Maza (noble) Lieutenant Colonel, Dragoons of San Luis	56	rural landholding	Valle de Penajos
Francisco Miguel Aguirre (noble) Lieutenant Colonel, Dragoons of San Carlos	43	rural landholding	Spain
Miguel de Otero (noble) Lieutenant Colonel, Infantry of Mexico	52	alcalde mayor of Córdoba, officer of the *contaduría general de alcabalas*	*Mexico*
Juan Martínez de Lejarza (noble) Lieutenant Colonel, Infantry of Valladolid	55	rural landholding	Vizcaya
Juan Francisco Calera Lieutenant Colonel, Dragoons of Nueva Galicia	51	?	Spain
Francisco Escovedo y Daza (hidalgo) Commander, Battalion of Guadalajara	58	?	Spain
Manuel García Alonso (noble) Lieutenant Colonel, Infantry of Toluca	48	?	Corivadillo

*Officers of criollo origin are in italics.
†The regular army officers serving in the provincial militia units are listed in table 17.
Source: Azanza to Alvarez, no. 295, April 26, 1799, AGI, México, leg. 1499; Branciforte to Alange, no. 160, January 15, 1795, AGI, México, leg. 1438; Branciforte to Alcudía, no. 29, August 30, 1795, AGI, Estado, leg. 23; and hojas de servicio, AGS, GM, legs. 7272–78.

Cavalry of the Prince on the strength of a thirty-five-hundred-peso donation for the war effort and an offer to uniform and arm one hundred infantrymen.[95] The owner of an enormous empire of haciendas, mines, and businesses, Rul was unwilling to accept a mere captaincy while his relatives commanded their own regiments. Perhaps aware of Obregón's offer to rescue the Regiment of Nueva Galicia, he made the same offer should there be a shortage of donations for the provincial Infantry Regiment of Valladolid. There, only twenty thousand pesos of the needed forty-five thousand pesos had been subscribed. Rul had no difficulty raising the remaining balance of twenty-five thousand pesos. Branciforte awarded him the command, lauding his patriotism and generosity. As far as the viceroy was concerned, Rul had saved the day; funds from the royal exchequer would not be needed to raise the Valladolid militia.[96]

While these arguments and the economic facts convinced the Valladolid cabildo, the appointment of an outsider was not welcomed by the local officers. Juan Martínez de Lejarza, the leading candidate for the colonelcy prior to Rul's appearance, was unwilling to accept the second position. Of Basque origin, Lejarza had been an active member of the Valladolid militias since 1762. He felt that his years of service made him worthy to be colonel.[97] The insult of seeing Rul given the regimental command became more an injury when as lieutenant colonel he had to act as regimental commander. Rul spent very little time in Valladolid looking after routine militia affairs. His life was completely occupied with business interests which demanded part-time residence in Mexico City and a great deal of travel to visit his haciendas, mines, and commercial establishments in the intendancies of Guanajuato, Zacatecas, and Mexico.[98] Rul was aware of the animosity of some officers and before long he suspected that Lejarza was organizing a plot to remove him from his command. Indeed, the lieutenant colonel fanned the potential for trouble by systematically excluding Rul from all decisions concerning the regiment. When Azanza ordered forty soldiers and a lieutenant to reinforce the regular units at Veracruz, Lejarza did not consult the colonel and did not even bother to inform him which men had been sent. Rul's suspicions were aroused further when he learned that Lejarza had requested a promotion to the rank of colonel. His justification for doing so was based upon the weight of duties confronting him since the colonel was always absent.[99]

At this point, Rul challenged the right of any subordinate officer to make decisions without consultation with the colonel. This began a general debate over the rights of commanding officers who were not resident in their units' jurisdiction. Azanza sided with Lejarza, but to make sure of his legal position he asked Colonel Félix Calleja for an opinion. Again supporting Lejarza,

Calleja cited a royal order of August 22, 1797, in which the crown ruled that off-duty militia officers of all ranks could not issue commands once they were separated from the district of their unit. Azanza saw no reason why this order should not apply to Valladolid. Rul was absolutely furious at this decision, which he took as a personal affront and as an act of discrimination against him by the viceroy. Why, he asked, should he be required to reside in his regimental jurisdiction when so many other commanders were permitted to live near to their business interests until such time as their units might be mobilized? He wrote to the viceroy and to the king pointing out that Colonel Joaquín Gutiérrez de los Ríos of the Infantry of Puebla and Colonel Marqués de Rivascacho of the Infantry of Toluca resided in Mexico City. Colonel José Manuel de Cevallos of the Infantry of Tres Villas spent all of his time in Puebla and Colonel Juan Fernández Munilla of the Infantry of Celaya in Querétaro. The senior regular army commanders, Brigadiers Pedro Ruiz Dávalos and Pedro Garibay, spent almost no time with their regiments. Both officers chose to remain in the capital because of their age, physical infirmities, or for other reasons. Even Rul's brother-in-law, Ignacio de Obregón, seldom ventured near his regimental headquarters at Aguascalientes.[100]

Although these examples hardly justified Rul's absenteeism, they pointed out one of the major weaknesses of the provincial army. Félix Calleja, already concerned by the dangers of appointing officers who resided a great distance from their commands, proposed an amendment to military ordinances which authorized promotion based strictly on seniority. In New Spain, two other factors were more crucial—the proximity of an officer to his troops and whether he enjoyed sufficient personal wealth to support the social pressures of an advance in rank. If officers did not maintain personal contact with the men they commanded, the militia units would cease to be of much use when they were mobilized. Calleja had no time for the provincial officer who "... contents himself with enjoyment of the honorific part of his employ and frees himself from anything onerous." If the system of using seniority as the only criterion for promotion continued, within a very few years most officers would live a great distance from their units. Almost as important, Calleja opposed the promotion of officers of limited income such as the hacendados and merchants who commanded the units in his brigade. These men encountered difficulties covering their expenses, but, of greater significance, their rise threatened to weaken class distinctions. Most subaltern officers should be left in their rank and not promoted to captain because of seniority.[101]

The implementation of this scheme proved to be more difficult than either Calleja or the viceroys imagined. To begin with, most men who had sufficient seniority to merit promotion clamored to move up in rank. This was only natural since their reason for joining the militia in the first place was motivated by a desire for status. Provincial officers neglected the military aspects of their commissions and concentrated their full attention on the social rank they hoped to attain. Regular officers complained that they knew nothing about training, inspections, guard duty, subordination, or army discipline. For most local *caballeros* appointed to company command, the only military ordinance that caught their attention was the sentence stating, "the captain always will be respected and punctually obeyed by his subalterns."[102] Haughty militia officers used this regulation to dominate the regular army officers who had been sent to train them. At San Miguel, for example, Major Barros Alemparte of the Dragoon Regiment of the Queen complained that the inexperienced militia officers who had never been out of their home province treated the regular officers with contempt.[103] Because this problem was general throughout the militia system, the regular officers of the training cadres were made dependent upon the brigade commanders without the intervention of the militia officers except as required for the internal management of the barracks.

Among themselves, the prestige-hungry provincial officers behaved little better. They struggled for promotions and sometimes engaged in smear campaigns against their colleagues—describing them in letters to the viceroy as lacking the rank or wealth needed to hold a king's commission.[104] In some instances this sort of behavior led to even more scurrilous attacks against wives and families. In 1778, Colonel Conde de Santiago of the provincial Regiment of Mexico asked for the dismissal of two sublieutenants, José Grajales and José Calapis. According to information he had received, the wives of both officers lacked dignity and social standing. Since both men were known to be good officers, *Auditor de Guerra* Domingo Valcarcel conducted an investigation to find out what the women had done to deserve condemnation. The lieutenant colonel stated that it was public knowledge Grajales's wife had been a "*mujer libertina*" and had been wounded by a common soldier after an affair. He knew less about the wife of Calapis, but said he had heard that she was the daughter of an Indian woman and a friar.[105] Other officers reported having heard similar rumors and hearsay. José Calapis wrote a long defense documenting his wife's hidalgo status and replying to the charges made against her. Even though she had no Indian blood, he saw no reason why mestizo origins should be a sin. Other evidence cleared Grajales's wife and proved that she had been assaulted in the street by a drunken soldier. There was no other relationship. Although the auditor exonerated the wives and banished all charges, some officers continued to keep the case open. Finally, Valcarcel had to order the officers to cease their harassment; he wanted no more harm done to the families and was disgusted by what he described as a stain against the reputation of the regiment.[106]

As might be expected, mobilizations of militia units were not at all what provincial officers had in mind when they obtained their commissions. The cantonments, beginning in 1797 and continuing off and on until 1810, strained many officers' resources and made others reconsider their desire for military rank. With the long interruptions of communications between Mexico and Spain, no promotions could be finalized. Viceroy Iturrigaray saw no alternative to making interim promotions although his powers to do so were uncertain. He feared that Mexican officers of limited resources needed increased army salaries just to live properly after months or even years of active service. Many had been promoted as interim captains, but had not received the pay for the higher rank.[107] Particularly after the activation of the provincial army in 1805, officers sought deferments based on illness, old age, or the pressures of business. Iturrigaray feared that some regiments would be depleted of trained officers. To prevent the poor example of commanders remaining at home for minor reasons, he decided to retire any officer who did not accompany his troops to the cantonment. He began by dismissing seven captains and fifteen lieutenants.[108] By 1808, there was a definite shortage of candidates to fill vacant commissions. In fact, the viceroy had to ask regimental commanders to recommend regular and militia sergeants who were intelligent enough to be promoted into the subaltern ranks.[109]

Even with these measures, Iturrigaray experienced growing difficulties with the officer corps. Brigadier Alcaraz was absent from his regiment for a year and a half under the dubious pretext of illness. Colonel Manuel García Alonso of the Infantry of Toluca had left the cantonment at the end of 1806 because of weak health and was still not back six months later. Lieutenant Colonel Manuel García Quintana, commander of the Battalion of Guanajuato, went to Mexico City for medical treatment and Lieutenant Colonel Juan José de Lejarza of the Infantry of Valladolid had been granted leave to take the thermal baths at Chicandiro. He suffered a chronic urinary ailment which seemed to attack him whenever he was on duty at Jalapa.[110] Diego Rul, now the Conde de Casa Rul, commander of the Valladolid militia, petitioned for a release from service to look after his enormous mining and agricultural interests. He claimed that during the thirty-six months he had been on duty his businesses suffered incalculable damage. Some of his best administrators were ill, leaving his investments in the hands of men in whom he placed no trust.[111]

Clearly, the prestige and opportunity to flaunt an attractive uniform were not worth this burden of inconvenience. Even the much vaunted *fuero militar* brought little advantage and sometimes caused more trouble than it was worth. Relatively minor cases which could have been tried quickly became entangled in competencias between the military jurisdiction and other tribunals. The mining court, merchant consulados, and the ordinary royal judiciary, as well as other tribunals, contested any case in which their vested interests appeared to be challenged.[112] Although these disputes delayed justice for months or even years, the courts eventually settled the question of jurisdiction and the laws were enforced. The army had no desire to protect officers or soldiers from the full weight of the law. On the contrary, they were supposed to set an example for the rest of society. When, for example, Lieutenant Santiago Trasviño of the Battalion of Oaxaca was arrested for running an illegal gambling den in his house where dice, *monte,* and other high-stake card games were played, a dispute developed over which jurisdiction would have the right to prosecute. Trasviño found himself pursued by two adversaries, both of which wanted to impose exemplary punishment. After a lengthy conflict, the ordinary civil courts won the right to try the lieutenant.[113] Other officers found that their obligation to act as the defenders of public morality conflicted with their businesses. Viceroy Garibay, an almost puritanical advocate of the role officers should play, refused to accept the idea of militia Captain Salvador de Benavides operating cock fights and holding bullfights at his home near Tehuacán. These diversions were scandalous at the best of times, but completely unacceptable while the mother country "... groans under the oppression of the common tyrant."[114]

Officers entrusted with the protection of society sometimes ran into difficulties with the clergy. In one of the most bizarre of such cases, Fray Francisco Pérez de Haro, the curate of Tampico, wrote "with tears in his eyes and a trembling hand" about the life and activities of Captain Antonio de la Roca, commander of the local militia division. According to the curate, Roca defied God, the king, and the Church. His evil example perverted the entire town; he lived in an almost constant state of inebriation and when he was not drunk, he was gambling, making love, and making children. During some nights, he toured the streets covered with only a cape and he exposed himself to as many girls as he encountered. In the opinion of the curate, Roca was no better than a monster out of hell who by his cursed life dragged down many others. Already, perverts similar to the captain were flocking to Tampico where they knew that they could escape punishment. Obviously, Roca wanted to introduce "... the unbridled liberty of the French." The voice of the Church was not heeded and few went to confession. If these crimes were not grave enough to attract attention, Pérez added treason. Some months earlier, Roca had ordered the removal of the cannon guarding the waterfront of Tampico.[115]

Considering the severity of the allegations, the response from the military authorities was cool. Branciforte asked Calleja to check into the matter since Tampico came under his command. Calleja rejected the charges as foolish and full of contradictions. Roca was fifty years of age and so ill that his life hung by a thread. The Tampico artillery had been withdrawn on direct orders from Mexico City. Quite generally, the portrait of indolence did not fit the active coastal militia. Instead of sending a special investigator to verify some of the other claims, Calleja laid the blame with the clergy. He attacked the curates of frontier towns as "... arbitrary despots who suffer no opposition to their authority. They shroud themselves with apparent religious zeal and remorselessly denounce anyone who is bold enough to oppose them."[116]

While most army officers seldom if ever became involved in criminal or civil cases, there was one area of exception. Like so many other Spaniards and Mexicans, officers could not resist the temptation of engaging in contraband trade. Particularly in the case of regular army officers who were stationed in Caribbean posts or granted leave to visit their families in Spain, there were ample opportunities to bolster income with smuggling. When customs officers carried out periodic inspections, quite a few officers found themselves caught red-handed and not a little red-faced, attempting to explain why they needed a small mountain of personal baggage. Colonel Juan Velázquez, returning to Mexico from Spain by way of Havana, was caught with seven large chests of sundry goods which were not enumerated in the customs manifests of La Coruña or Havana. The colonel claimed that the problem resulted from an oversight of the customs officers and appealed to the viceroy to remember his good character and military record. The case was tried by the intendant of Veracruz, who found Velázquez guilty of engaging in contraband. The Junta Superior de Real Hacienda expressed concern about the example set by a man of this stature, but let the colonel off with costs that amounted to more than the value of the illegal goods.[117]

The most famous case of an army officer caught with contraband involved Brigadier Antonio Bonilla, commander of the Dragoons of Mexico and secretary of the viceroyalty. Captured with Viceroy Marquina by the British navy off the coast of Yucatan and taken to Kingston, Jamaica, Bonilla attempted to profit from his bad luck. Without the viceroy's knowledge, he arranged to import a cargo of trade goods into New Spain and accepted an offer of transport to Veracruz on a British ship. According to Marquina, Bonilla's first error was to have accepted lodging with "persons of the Jewish sect—not being at all familiar with their devious maxims."[118] While the viceroy suffered during the passage to Veracruz on a small Spanish vessel, Bonilla arrived at the port in comfort with twenty-two bales of goods which were valued at 58,092 pesos. The subsequent scandal forced him to resign from the office of secretary although he did manage to retain his military command.[119] When the audiencia began to investigate the case, Bonilla denied its authority or right to intervene since as a brigadier of the army he possessed the *fuero militar*. He rejected the precedent of any jurisdiction except the army handling his trial. Probably he believed that a court-martial would be more sympathetic, but he used the excuse that his regiment would suffer if he allowed any erosion of the privileges granted to those who underwent the dangers of a military career. While Bonilla did not obtain his demands, he was able to obscure the case in competencias and to drag it out for many years.[120]

As might be expected, the officers did run afoul of the law for breaches of military regulations, negligence, and other minor offenses. Drunkenness, a grave concern in the enlisted ranks, was also a problem in the officer corps—especially in isolated frontier posts and in the unhealthy Veracruz garrison. Lieutenant Andrés de Piedras, a regular army training officer assigned to the Companies of Pardos and Morenos at Veracruz, had to be dismissed because of his addiction to alcohol, gambling, and other scandalous behavior.[121] Lieutenant José María Cuervo of the Battalion of Veracruz was arrested when he went on a wild drinking spree with his company sergeant. He had been warned about his problem with alcohol on several previous occasions and his commander suggested a term of imprisonment at San Juan de Ulúa to dry him out. Cuervo was naturally upset at being described as an "intractable drunk" although he testified, "I do not deny the use of liquor. . . . in this country its consumption is general even amongst the subjects of most distinction."[122]

In more serious cases, where a court-martial by a *junta de generales* was needed, the army experienced difficulty locating seven colonels or more senior officers needed to make up the court. Sub-Lieutenant Francisco González, for example, was brought to trial for possible negligence in allowing the escape of eighteen Apache Indian prisoners who were confined at the Inn of Plan del Río near Veracruz. They were destined for shipment to Havana when they broke loose to murder and maim their way across much of New Spain. González was jailed at the castle of San Juan de Ulúa for over a year before his case came to trial. He named Lieutenant Colonel Juan Manuel de Bonilla, commander of the Battalion of Veracruz, to serve as his defender, which proved to be a wise decision. Bonilla argued that if there had been complicity between the Apaches and the lieutenant, there would be no difficulty deciding the case. But González had done everything within his power to prevent an escape. Although he treated the prisoners well, Apaches spoke a language which no one understood; they prepared their plot over a long period of time and with full knowledge about certain weaknesses in the security system. González had checked the prisoners' manacles and posted adequate numbers of sentries. The escape took place because there were no keys for the rooms in which the Indians were confined and because they were able to break their bonds. If blame was to be assigned, the equipment was at fault and not González. This argument worked, and after almost two years of collecting detailed evidence, González was released.[123] In some other cases, the officers appointed to the court-martial wasted a great deal of time arguing about the composition of the tribunal. When Major Angel Michaus of the Urban Regiment of Commerce was arrested for his behavior in connection with the overthrow of Viceroy Iturrigaray, the court consisted of only two brigadiers and five colonels. No sooner had the officers convened than an angry dispute erupted over seating preference between Colonel Miguel José de Emparán of the Dragoons of Mexico and Colonel Carlos de Urrutía of the First Militia Brigade. Emparán denied the seniority of a commander of sedentary militiamen.[124]

There was a much more positive role played by the army officers. Many were instrumental in introducing and diffusing the ideas of the European Enlightenment. A thoroughly cosmopolitan group of men, they breathed fresh air into the narrow confines of colonial life. The Inquisition recognized the potential danger and at one stage compared the situation to "trusting wolves to watch over sheep."[125] The Marqués de Moncada, commander of the provincial Dragoon Regiment of Puebla, was a devotee of French styles and a supporter of experimental philosophy. Colonel Agustín Beven of the Dragoons of Mexico, originally from Bayonne, France, was denounced to the Inquisition for owning a set of the *Encyclopédie*. Colonel Diego Rul was reported for possessing forbidden books and espousing heretical ideas.[126] Many officers played a role in introducing modern scientific reforms and in expanding scientific curiosity in Mexico. Colonels Francisco Crespo and Miguel Costansó were active in the Real Academia de San Carlos, which was dedicated to teaching architecture, sculpture, painting, and engraving. Costansó planned the botanical gardens in Mexico City.[127] Finally, Colonel Diego García Panes was an unsung scholar of the late eighteenth century. His devotion to historical studies was probably greater than his dedication to the army. Panes obtained royal support and funding for his projected *Historia de Nueva España*. He was one of the first to copy the manuscript of Bernardino de Sahagún[128] and he requested permission to purchase Robertson's *History of America* as well as a number of French works concerned with philosophical and historical investigation of the Americas.[129] Viceroy Flórez granted Panes a leave of absence from military duties to work on his project. Revillagigedo continued the financial support for some time after he named a commission including Miguel Costansó to read the manuscript and to report on its merits.[130] Unfortunately, Panes did not complete his labor and, in 1794, the crown cut off the subsidy because of the war. Even so, the imperial government encouraged Panes to keep working on the history as long as it did not interfere with his military career.[131]

In many respects, the men who managed the defense of New Spain reflected the colony's strengths and weaknesses. For better or worse, however, a large percentage of the officers who had begun their careers in the wars of Europe or the campaigns of North Africa were dead or physically disabled by 1810. They had come to Mexico a few years too early to have much impact upon the wars for independence. There were, of course, some exceptions in the cases of the younger officers. Of the regulars, Colonel Nicolás de Yberri, promoted to command the Infantry of the Crown, died in action during 1811. Others, such as García Dávila, Carlos de Urrutía, and Ignacio García Revollo, commanded forces but were prevented by advanced age from joining the actual fighting. Of the provincial officers, Diego Rul died gloriously in battle against Morelos at the siege of Cuautla, Narciso de la Canal died in jail after an ignominious surrender to the rebels, and Antonio Pérez Gálvez survived the revolutions to continue his business deals and mining pursuits. Very few officers followed the example of the unknown Captain Ignacio de Allende, who joined the side of the revolution.

9
MANPOWER

Raising an army in a province like New Spain tested the mettle of the best recruiters—or perhaps drove them to drink. They had to overcome immense geographical barriers, a diverse population, the danger of social and economic dislocations, and entrenched provincialism. As we have seen, observers such as Viceroy Revillagigedo believed that provincial forces did not repay the time and expenditure needed to raise them. Mexicans could not be moved out of their local economies without damaging the viceroyalty's delicate balance. The small tradesmen and artisans were needed at all times to service their communities. Men who were unemployed or rootless were considered too unreliable for militia duty. Recruitment was particularly damaging in the mining districts where much of the work force consisted of vagrants, delinquents, deserters, and fugitives from militia enlistment in other regions. Revillagigedo proposed a blanket exemption for all mine laborers. They were useless soldiers anyway, but more important, nothing could be permitted to interrupt New Spain's leading industry. This was only the beginning of the process to set deferments. Hacienda managers could not leave the untrustworthy Indian workers for fear of damaging the agricultural and livestock sectors. Muleteers who spent most of their lives on the open road could not be spared from their mission of moving commerce. Even the small farmers played an essential role in producing crops for nearby urban centers. By the time the list was completed, the only classes available for service were the useless vagabonds who were best excluded in the first place.[1]

Compounding these difficulties was the deep mistrust Spanish officers and administrators felt toward the different castas. Mere mention of the Indians or pardos, for example, was sufficient to evoke derogatory terms such as "lazy," "vice-ridden," "corrupt," "devoted to vagabondage," and others.[2]

Since the lower castas paid tribute to the state, military enlistment threatened to reduce tax income as well as awarding pardos or Indians privileges that the regime did not wish to bestow.[3] The army had no intention of serving as a vehicle of social improvement for those who desired to escape the lower racial classifications. Even when there were special pardo battalions in Mexico City and Puebla, the officers complained that recruitment was next to impossible. Few wanted to be identified with the pardos and if there was no other way of escaping this status, men signed up with the provincial militias, which were open in theory to only whites, *castizos,* and mestizos. On some occasions, one brother might be enlisted in the pardo unit and another in a provincial unit.[4]

One of the most belligerent attacks against the castas came from Francisco de Crespo, the architect of the late colonial military system. Enlightened though he was in many respects, Crespo's diatribes against much of the Mexican population would have done credit to the most aggressive exponents of European racial superiority. In his opinion, racial mixture caused degeneration and created bastard groups devoid of proper values: "... they look with deep hatred at the noble Spaniards and with aversion and contempt at the pure Indians." The castas could accept neither the honorable customs of the former nor the humility and hard work of the latter. He compared the products of miscegenation of the New World with the gypsies of the Old: "... the true gypsy has no permanent home, he lives without modesty or pride; to him it is irrelevant whether he is dressed or naked. His science is deceit and lying, his inclination to robbery." Crespo went on to describe the characteristics of gypsies—drunkenness, lasciviousness, vulgarity, obstinacy, and other evils—concluding, "... it seems to me that this is the most accurate portrait of the *coyote, salta atrás, tente en el aire,* and of most men who under different names make up the infinite number of infected *castas.*"[5] Indeed, Crespo believed that these people were more dangerous than the gypsies because they did not live in a relatively small area where they could be controlled and disciplined. In New Spain, the castas formed a hydra of so many heads that they could not be governed. They were everywhere—in the cities, the mining districts, the isolated Provincias Internas, and in the mountains and forests of a truly immense country. While Crespo was convinced that most of this population preferred "their miserable liberty, nakedness, and hunger to an honorable way of life," he saw one possible method of putting them to use. If their children were taken away before they learned the evil customs of their parents, they might be saved. The army would become the vehicle to harness and correct these elements.

Although it is difficult to support Crespo's solutions, one can understand some of his frustrations. For anyone seeking order and reason, the population of Mexico was a nightmare. Large numbers of transients and semitransients further confused the racial picture, making the task of the census taker almost impossible. But this was only the beginning of the problem. The people were well aware that census meant trouble—either taxation or, more frequently, an effort to enlist militia units. The army needed to have accurate population statistics before it could distribute its requirements among the communities assigned to a unit. Beginning in 1764 with the *padrones* (census reports) commissioned by General Villalba, the Mexicans used every means at their disposal to escape enumeration. Writing about the effort to collect data in Mexico City, José Antonio Alzate stated:

> Wives described themselves as widows, mothers neglected to list their sons, sisters left off their brothers, and some families simply disappeared, hiding from house to house or moving into districts of the city that already had been counted.[6]

Viceroy Revillagigedo declared almost all of the existing census data to be useless. Although parish priests submitted annual reports, the lack of method made these figures a useless addition to the viceregal archives. The *padrones* that were to provide a basis for militia enlistment were equally useless and even the general census ordered by the crown in 1776 served no end other than "to produce a large bulky document."[7]

Revillagigedo was convinced that any well-governed province should have an accurate census. Using article 133 of the Ordinance of Intendants, which authorized the intendants to conduct a systematic enumeration of their provinces listing the population by distinction of castas, the viceroy ordered a new census. In fact, none of the intendants up to 1790 had begun the task of producing accurate population statistics. As in the past, they argued that the mere mention of a *padrón* caused the inhabitants to flee, hide, or to lie about their men. To prevent any repetition of previous disasters, Revillagigedo adopted methods which had been proven successful in Spain during the censuses of 1768 and 1787. Great care would be taken not to alarm the population. Wherever possible, parish priests were to accompany the magistrates; they were to calm fears, stop escapes, and to explain the innocuous aspects of enumeration.[8]

Despite improvements, Revillagigedo's record as a census taker was not entirely successful. In 1793, when he came to compiling the total population figure for New Spain, he had to estimate the totals for the important provinces of Veracruz and Guanajuato. As Humboldt noted, "In the new continent, as well as in the old, every enumeration is considered by the people as a sinister presage of some financial operation.' "[9] He estimated an error of a sixth or a seventh in Revillagigedo's total of 4,483,529 inhabitants for New Spain, placing the total closer to 5,200,000. Humboldt discovered that some intendants continued to use the 1793 statistics and made no effort to conduct new enumerations. His own examination of consumption tables, registers of births and deaths, and other figures for Mexico City led him to conclude through comparisons with the great European cities that the total population in 1790 was at least 135,000 persons rather than the published figure of 112,926. In his calculations, the percentage of error increased in the smaller cities. Humboldt's estimate of the population of New Spain in 1808 was 6,500,000.[10]

Although the purpose here is not to examine demographic change and census reports, it is important to understand the potential for error. Since enumeration always preceded the enlistment *sorteo* (lottery), it was little wonder that the people gave incorrect information about the male population. Those who held deferments or knew that they were exempt from militia duty permitted themselves to be counted. In Mexico City, the immensity of the population and the fact that so many lived in a semitransient state baffled those commissioned to make the count. Frustrated officials, who were at a loss about how to enumerate the residents of shanty towns, defended themselves by stating that there was nothing in Europe to compare with the capital of New Spain. The cabildo spent between six thousand and seven thousand pesos from public granary revenues on a census which gave almost no useful information.[11] Men who should have been eligible for militia duty hid themselves until the danger passed. Certainly the census data of 1790 support this evidence. As table 19 illustrates, of all the castas counted, only the European Spanish males outnumbered females. Since they were immigrants, male predominance in numbers was to be expected. Moreover, these men experienced the least difficulty obtaining militia deferment.[12]

Census data were of secondary importance for the regular army. Much to the chagrin of many officers and other observers, the *quintas* (levies) used to obtain manpower for the regular army of Spain were prohibited in the Americas.[13] Until the end of the 1780s, the imperial government attempted to garrison a regiment or as many as three battalions of European troops in New Spain. This policy had the positive advantages of furnishing a strong veteran force and a constant inflow of Spanish soldiers to balance the army, but the numerous disadvantages caused reconsideration even before the wars following the French Revolution. Every Spanish regiment lost at least two-thirds of its manpower by the time it returned to Europe. Deaths, desertions, transfers, and retirements combined to make the enterprise much too costly. Although the Spanish troops who remained in New Spain added weight to the European

TABLE 19
The Population of Mexico City in 1790.*

Secular Population	Men	Women	Total
Europeans	2,185	174	2,359
Spaniards (criollos)	20,925	28,662	49,587
Mestizos	4,255	8,287	12,542
Mulattoes	2,816	4,161	6,977
Indians	10,643	13,100	23,743
Negroes	112	157	269
Other *Castas*	3,836	5,622	9,458
TOTALS	44,772	60,163	104,935
Secular Population			104,935
Male secular employees of monasteries, convents, hospitals and *colegios*			3,610
Female secular employees in the above			3,192
Men in religious communities			588
Women in religious communities			907
TOTAL POPULATION			113,232

*There are slight differences between these figures and Humboldt's.
Source: Estado reducido de los habitantes de México empadronados en el año de 1790, MN, vol. 335.

population, many were deserters and delinquents who ended up in the disease-ridden port garrisons or joined the armies of vagabonds.[14]

With the adoption of the plan to recruit four regular infantry regiments in Mexico, Francisco Crespo suggested a number of potential manpower sources. Hopefully, Mexicans would volunteer for service, but if not, levies of unemployed vagabonds and selections of "clean" criminals from the jails would make up any shortages. At first, Viceroy Flórez rejected the concept of using coercion. He desired a fully volunteer army and sent orders to magistrates and the alcaldes mayores setting out how they should go about recruiting; they were to stress the concepts of glory, duty, and love for the *patria*.[15] Since the Spanish Infantry Regiment of Zamora was still in Mexico, Flórez obtained permission to seek recruits for the new infantry regiments before it was transferred to Havana.[16] This was to be the last source of European NCOs and soldiers until after 1810. To convince the gachupín soldiers to stay in Mexico, Sub-Inspector Mendinueta arranged the payment of incentive allowances—twelve pesos for those who had completed six years' service and eight pesos for the others.[17] From this date forward, reenlistment bonuses became a standard practice to keep trained soldiers in the army. In 1790, for example, European Spaniards received sixteen pesos for reenlistment in the Dragoon Regiment of Mexico while the criollos were given only twelve

TABLE 20
Origins of Enlisted Men in the Regiment of the Crown, 1788.*

Spanish Province	Number	Percent	Foreign Origin	Number	Percent
Castilla la Vieja	59	5.8	Portugal	12	1.2
Castilla la Nueva	32	3.2	Italy	29	2.9
Andalusia	84	8.3	Flanders	11	1.1
Extremadura	11	1.1	Germany	14	1.4
Aragon	6	.6	France	35	3.6
Valencia	10	1.0			
Galicia	42	4.1			
Navarra	10	1.0			
Cataluña	15	1.5			
Asturias	12	1.2			
Enlisted Men of European Origin				382	37.7
Enlisted Men of Mexican Origin				632	62.3
TOTAL ENLISTMENT				1,014	

*Because the figures in these tables are averaged to the nearest tenth of 1 percent, the sum is not always 100 percent.
Source: Documentos de revista de inspección del Regimiento Fixo de Infantería de la Corona, July 26, 1788, AGI, México, leg. 1518.

pesos.[18] Even at this level, petty discrimination and preference for the gachupines accomplished little other than to annoy the Mexican soldiers.

After the expansion of the regular infantry regiments, there was a fairly strong contingent of Europeans in the enlisted ranks[19] (see table 20). Viceroy Revillagigedo wanted to maintain a ratio of at least one-third European troops to two-thirds Mexican, but he could not have been overly concerned with the balance he found at the beginning of his term[20] (see table 21). By as early as 1793, however, he began to express growing alarm at the rapid erosion of

TABLE 21
Ratio of Mexican and *Peninsular* Enlisted Men in the Army of New Spain, 1790.

	MEXICANS		PENINSULARES		
Regular Regiment	Number	Percent	Number	Percent	Total Force
Regiment of the Crown	467	65.9	242	34.1	709
Regiment of New Spain	592	74.5	203	25.5	795
Regiment of Mexico	645	75.4	211	24.6	856
Dragoons of Spain	367	86.8	56	13.2	423
Dragoons of Mexico	362	85.0	64	15.0	426
TOTALS	2,433	75.8	776	24.2	3,209

Source: Documentos de inspección, July 9, 1790, AGN, Historia, vol. 234.

Europeans and consequent increase in Mexicans. Clearly, the peninsular-criollo ratio could not be preserved without European units or a determined imperial commitment to dispatch annual replacements. Although the viceroys petitioned for troops, the balance of the Mexican army became almost irrelevant. This was a difficult reality to accept. Repeatedly, Revillagigedo and his senior commanders stressed the need for Spanish regulars and hammered on the theme that the Mexican army could not function on its own; in Revillagigedo's view, "the criollos lack the vigor, training, or stimulus for command."[21] Spaniards were needed to add *"aire, ardor, y actividad,"* and to implant European martial values in a society that seemed overly permissive.[22]

Without Spanish regiments, the prospects of recruiting gachupines were poor. No legal immigrant wanted to waste his life on the poor salary of a common soldier or an NCO. The only source of European recruits was the occasional ship arriving from Spain which had a few stowaways or *polizones* on board. The dream of a better life in the Americas which had been a major factor in immigration since the sixteenth century still exerted a powerful influence. According to Francisco de Viana, one of the officers of the Malaspina expedition, nothing prevented polizones from boarding vessels bound for New Spain. At Cádiz four men managed to hide themselves and to sail with the expedition. Knowing almost nothing about the Americas, they hoped to find a better and freer life, without hard labor.[23] When Malaspina's ships touched at Acapulco, eleven Spaniards deserted hoping to escape into the interior of New Spain. With rewards of ten pesos offered for each capture, soldiers of the Acapulco garrison soon returned nine of the escapees.[24] In the long run, they were probably more fortunate than the single seaman who gained his freedom. Unless illegal immigrants had relatives, friends, or some money to help them settle, they ended up as unemployed vagabonds. As such, they became the preferred targets for the regular army recruiters. Indeed, the penalty for illegal immigration for the physically fit was eight years' service in one of the regular infantry regiments.

In Mexico City, the army soon located any likely gachupín who lacked regular employment. In a country where simply to be a European conferred considerable social distinction, the resident community helped to stamp out the bad examples. Therefore, in 1791 when Major Tomás Rodríguez of the capital city garrison heard that a gachupín of good appearance yet almost naked appeared daily at a tavern in the plaza de Santo Domingo, he lost no time in arresting the suspect for questioning. The prisoner declared that his name was Fernando Hortiz, age twenty-eight years, a native of Villa de la Vega in the Spanish province of Santander. In Mexico he was a vagabond who went from tavern to tavern looking for odd jobs. Five years before, Hortiz left Santander for Cádiz, where he became a seaman. On a voyage to Veracruz, he landed without a license and when he contracted fever he moved inland to Mexico City to escape the coastal climate. Asked why he travelled about in such an immodest state, he replied that he had suffered many illnesses; if he earned two or three pesos in one week, the next week often passed without employment. Asked whether he would serve in the king's army with pleasure to remove himself from wretchedness, he answered that his first obligation was to look after his old mother and two unmarried sisters in Spain. To improve his image somewhat, Hortiz insisted that while he had been almost naked on the day of his arrest, he did own a shirt. Nevertheless, the army was unimpressed by Hortiz's defense; he was sentenced to eight years in the Infantry Regiment of Puebla.[25]

Although the regular army had to accept the idea of enlisting Mexicans, good quality criollo recruits did not exactly rush to join. The theory of volunteer soldiers attracted by the glory and honor of a military career was soon forgotten. Notwithstanding orders for recruiters to abide by royal ordinances and to enlist only volunteers of the highest quality, compulsion of one kind or another became the general rule. Recruiting teams (*banderas de reclutas*) consisting of a subaltern officer or sergeant, several corporals, and ten to fifteen soldiers visited provincial towns or scoured the capital looking for young men—preferably those uncorrupted by laziness, gambling, and wenching.[26] The recruiters tried to arrive in a town on a market or feast day so that they could display military skills and circulate in the taverns and gathering places where the soldiers could spin tales about the glory and adventure of army life. A few naïve country boys might be taken in momentarily by this method—particularly if well primed by generous use of alcohol. Long before the effects of the hangover had diminished, they found themselves sworn into an eight-year enlistment. Some young outcasts who were in trouble with the law, with the fathers of compromised daughters, or even with their own families were given the opportunity to volunteer or to expect something much worse. Others did not even receive this alternative. Juan de Arellano, collector of alcabalas and pulque taxes of the valley of Coyoacán, petitioned to have his son José Mariano sent either to the army or to some other ''perpetual exile.'' José Mariano, twenty-two years of age, had stolen four thousand pesos from the government funds collected by his father. Although Arellano had made good the money, he had to repay another large sum to recover his possessions from the pawnshop. José Mariano had been in and out of jail on numerous occasions without showing the slightest sign of improvement. In this case, Viceroy Azanza issued orders to the corregidor of Coyoacán to remit the accused to the capital. José Mariano was soon a soldier in the Regiment of New Spain.[27]

In theory, regular army recruits had to be of good health, at least five feet in height, and between sixteen and thirty-six years of age. They were all to come from the *casta limpia* sectors—whites, castizos, and mestizos. Any visible sign of poor racial extraction was supposed to deny a man access to this honorable profession. In reality, few of the regulations were enforced. The physician who certified that all of these conditions had been fulfilled received a flat fee of two reales per recruit inducted. This incentive plus the growing need for any man who could shoulder a musket nullified most of the regulations.[28]

Despite the color and music which heralded the arrival of a *bandera de recluta,* townspeople reacted as if the plague had slipped into their midst. In Querétaro, a frequent target of recruiting missions because it was a central distribution point, the appearance of regular army uniforms caused a general panic among the classes eligible for enlistment[29] (see table 22). Mere rumors of recruiting or, even worse, of levies to locate men for service in Veracruz were sufficient to provoke a flight of young males. In their horror of an unknown fate, many men abandoned their families and possessions. Officers could not understand why the poorest, most miserable resident chose poverty and degradation in preference to regular army service. Even the provincial cavalry regiment lacked popularity. Colonel Ruiz Dávalos enlisted all of the bachelors he could locate, but still had to draw upon the city's married men. The alcalde mayor complained that the best subjects, who considered themselves to be Spaniards and who had families, residences, and good jobs, were addicted to a soft life; they were accustomed to a comfortable existence

TABLE 22
Recruiting Teams Dispatched by the Regiment of the Crown, 1790–99.

1792–93	to Oaxaca
1792–93	to Puebla
1793	to Guadalajara
1793–95	to Puebla
1793–95	to Guadalajara and Querétaro
1794–95	to Guadalajara and Querétaro
1795	to Querétaro
1796	to Querétaro
1797	to Querétaro
1798	to San Luis Potosí
1798	to Mexico City

Source: Report of Pedro de Alonso, May 8, 1799, AGN, IG, vol. 197-A.

without working for their income and they opposed any patriotic sacrifice.³⁰ The opinion notwithstanding, some men of Querétaro who at first failed to evade the recruiters endured incredible hardships to escape at a later date. José Mariano Sánchez, a nineteen-year-old hatter, deserted three times and on each occasion managed to make it back home. On the third attempt, although heavily manacled, he got away from an Acapulco-bound caravan after he had been condemned to service in the Philippine Islands.³¹ Carlos Almaráz not only deserted three times, but also managed to return to Querétaro from Havana, where he had been sentenced to the royal navy.³²

Since volunteers, illegal immigrants, and other recruits were never available in the numbers needed by the regular regiments, the army had to adopt other ways to fill the ranks. One of the most popular was to hold a levy of vagabonds and petty criminals in Mexico City and Puebla. The repugnance of the better classes toward these elements meant that there would be little concerted opposition to what was seen as a police action as well as a good means to satisfy the army. As has been seen in the case of Mexico City during the absence of Viceroy Branciforte, abuses did take place. Generally, however, appeals were sufficient to check corruption or overzealousness. By 1801, the authorities had enough experience with levies to correct the most obvious inequities. Marquina's instructions were quite clear; any man arrested must be given proper access to appeals. Those detained under the most suspicious circumstances were to have ample opportunity to explain their situation. If they could obtain character references from three citizens, they were to be released without further question. In Marquina's view, it would be rare for an honest man to be unable to prove his innocence and explain why he had been arrested late at night or in some suspect location.³³

The intendant of Puebla, Manuel de Flon, stated that he would exercise all of the care necessary to avoid extortion and to punish any law officer who arrested men for personal reasons. Exemptions would be made for men who had wives, children, or widowed mothers. The officers of the levy would apprehend suspects in taverns, gambling dens, and in other places known to be the haunts of vagabonds. The only exception was the cockpit, which fell under special jurisdiction; there, much to Flon's disgust, vagabonds could gather without having to fear the intendant. At the same time, however, Flon worried about the possibility of being deluged by as many as three hundred appeals and declarations from prisoners. Lacking the time or the staff to look into every complaint, he decided to permit the magistrates to exercise full authority within their districts.³⁴

The judges of the Tribunal del Crimen doubted the merits of forced levies, even if pains were taken to protect the rights of subjects. They were quite legal—a reglamento of 1775 sanctioned this method of rounding up unwanted elements and even a bando of May 22, 1799, dealing with nakedness in public places, could be invoked. The problem was the quality of men caught in a dragnet of taverns and gambling dens. After all, Indians, mulattoes, *coyotes*, and other impure castas were excluded from military service. Others might be married, have dependents, and deserve exemptions even if they were guilty of vagabondage or public nudity. Previous experiences confirmed these doubts: in the levies of December and January 1799, of 652 men detained, only 69 were declared fit for service in the regular infantry. Even then, army regulations on height and racial characteristics had to be relaxed.[35]

Experience during the levies of 1801 was no better. Many of the men captured in Mexico City and Puebla appealed their sentences of two to four years in the regular infantry. Some claimed to be Indians even if they did not pay tribute and others stated that they were married with families or septuagenarian parents to support. In the capital, the January and February levies rounded up a motley collection of 162 men, most of whom were ineligible for military service. Those who did "volunteer" to get themselves out of jail were found to be sick—either from chronic ailments or illnesses contracted during their incarceration. Only 63 men were sent to the Infantry of New Spain at Veracruz and even then the health of the recruits was dubious. The surgeon at Perote, José Antonio Castañeda, diagnosed cases of incurable cataracts, ear infections, ruptures, and paralysis.[36] Others perished from fevers in the dungeon of Perote while they awaited assignment to one of the regular regiments.[37]

The forced levies and jail recruitment did not nearly meet the needs of the regiments stationed at Veracruz, Havana, and elsewhere. There were some arrangements made with the courts to have criminals sentenced directly to military duty rather than to jail terms in the presidios, but only a trickle of men ended up in the ranks.[38] In times of crisis and invasion threat, the only possible solution was to utilize the provincial militia structure and to transfer militiamen into the regular regiments. The real difficulty was that the militiamen often refused to cooperate, fleeing their homes or deserting from the columns on the way to the regular regiments. The result was to dislocate the provincial units without appreciably bolstering the regulars. Even so, in less than ten years, the regular army lost its strong European contingent and became almost totally Mexican in enlistment[39] (see tables 23 and 24).

On the surface, the method of recruiting provincial militia units and reserve companies (*compañias sueltas*) lacked the extreme haphazardness of the regulars. Prior to enlistment, a census was taken to furnish data on the number of men eligible within certain boundaries. All suitable males between the ages of

TABLE 23
Ratio of Mexican and *Peninsular* Enlisted Men In the Army of New Spain, 1799–1804.

		MEXICANS		PENINSULARES		
Year	Regular Unit	Number	Percent	Number	Percent	Total Force
1800	Regiment of the Crown	917	95.3	45	4.7	962
1804	Regiment of New Spain	607	95.6	28	4.4	635
1800	Dragoons of Mexico	362	95.5	17	4.5	379
1800	Battalion of Veracruz	550	98.0	11	2.0	561
1800	2nd Company of Cataluña	39	69.6	17	30.4	56
1799	Regiment of Puebla	604	92.8	47	7.2	651
TOTALS		3,079	94.9	165	5.1	3,244

Source: Revistas de inspección, February 26, 1800, AGS, GM, leg. 6981; revista de inspección, Regimiento de Infantería de Nueva España, November 26, 1804, AGI, México, leg. 1468; and Azanza to Alvarez, No. 480, August 30, 1799, AGS, GM, leg. 6980.

sixteen and forty were divided into three categories—bachelors and widowers without children or families to support, married men without children, and finally those who had wives, children, and other dependents. If sufficient bachelors were not available, the selection process moved to the next group until militia requirements were filled. As in the case of the regulars, army commanders hoped to inspire Mexicans to volunteer; if not, there was to be no scouring of the jails or other unsatisfactory method of compelling men to

TABLE 24
Origins of Enlisted Men in the Regiment of New Spain, 1804.

SPAIN AND OTHER COUNTRIES			NEW SPAIN: TOWN OF ORIGIN		
	Number	Percent		Number	Percent
From Spain	23	3.6	Mexico City	206	32.4
Canary Islands	2	0.3	Puebla	203	32.0
Italy	1	0.2	Querétaro	25	3.9
Peru	1	0.2	Valladolid	96	15.1
Caracas	1	0.2	Guanajuato	7	1.1
TOTAL	28	4.4	Tlaxcala	4	0.6
			Veracruz	11	1.7
			Guadalajara	27	4.3
			Oaxaca	26	4.1
			Monterrey	2	0.3
			TOTAL	607	95.6
TOTAL ENLISTMENT	635				

Source: Revista de inspección, November 26, 1804, AGI, México, leg. 1468.

serve. For the militia units, a formal sorteo was used to draft the number of men needed from the available pool of candidates. In a solemn public ceremony, the populace gathered to witness a spectacle that would free some men and enlist others. First, the names of all those eligible for service were written on slips of paper which could be inserted into hollow wooden tablets or ballots. These went into a large urn or sack and into another went similar ballots marked with the word "militiaman" for the number of positions to be filled and the rest were left blank. Then, before a large and nervous crowd, two small boys of about seven years of age drew ballots from each urn. First the name of the candidate was shouted to the assembly, followed by the result of the lottery—militiaman or free from service.[40] Often, the local authorities took the precaution of placing guards around the town to prevent a hasty exodus of those enlisted, but many fled even prior to the lottery.[41]

It should be emphasized that the regime tried to prevent outright corruption in the sorteo procedures. The lottery took place before an impressive array of officials including a *síndico procurador* named by the cabildo, the local militia commander or his adjutant, the regional magistrate, the curate, and the physician, surgeon, or *curandero*. Nevertheless, for those unlucky enough to have been selected, all justice seemed to have disappeared. Exemptions granted prior to the lottery permitted a large number of the most eligible bachelors to avoid service, leaving an assortment of men of the lower social orders who lacked the money or the ability to manipulate the system. Free from service by law were all those of noble or hidalgo status, ministers of the Inquisition, and almost any civil servant including treasury officers, regidores, and scribes. The same privileges extended to the administrators of cities, towns, and haciendas, all churchmen and members of religious communities as well as their salaried employees, and the tenants of haciendas. If these outlets did not permit sufficient avenues of escape, one could seek exemption by becoming the servant of some illustrious personage such as an intendant, corregidor, or any army officer. Merchants and their apprentices were free from provincial militia obligation as were students, muleteers who owned mules, and mine technicians.[42] These possibilities only scratched the surface since men with families and other dependents obtained the lowest priority—usually they were granted exemptions by the board watching over the sorteo. Failing this, the way was open to purchase a discharge for medical reasons from the physician, for racial impurity from the curate, or simply to bribe the local subdelegate. Even the scribes were willing to falsify records for a modest payment.[43] By the end of the elimination procedure, most men of any wealth or quality had their deferments, leaving only the poor to serve in the militia units. In many regions, these men were the most likely to change their domicile or simply to flee into the mountains if called to active service. Often, however, it was the solid artisans and tradesmen with or without dependents who ended up in the militias.[44]

The picture was not entirely negative. In some provinces, particularly in the northern reaches of the viceroyalty, where cavalry and dragoon regiments predominated, the population did not exhibit the level of repugnance to service found in the mining regions, the populated central core of New Spain, and the Indian south. Mounted troops enjoyed several advantages over infantry; to begin with there was prestige and the opportunity to show off. Countrymen dressed in handsome uniforms were given a legitimate reason to ride into the nearby provincial town for militia assemblies. These became almost festive occasions and they generally coincided with religious holidays. Exercises, training sessions, and even the inspections became little more than social gatherings. At the same time, the northerners were close to the Indian frontier and retained a style of life that was compatible with militia duty. It was in this area that Félix Calleja assembled his Brigade of San Luis Potosí. The Dragoon Regiment of San Carlos based at San Luis Potosí was a fully volunteer unit; its racial composition—213 whites, 20 castizos, and 113 mestizos—was a balance the authorities considered almost ideal. More ominous was the fact that the regiment contained only 77 bachelors and 9 widowers. The remaining 260 men were married and unlikely to accept the idea of service outside of their own province.[45] More important than prestige, the mounted regiments seldom served in the Veracruz garrison. The horror stories of death and disease or the family disasters caused by years of service in the cantonments did not have as much impact in the north. It was from this background that Calleja was able to weld together his formidable army and to be ready for the rebellion of 1810.[46]

From the beginning, the enthusiasm generated for the mounted regiments could not be duplicated in the provincial infantry. Some units, such as the Regiment of Tres Villas, based at Jalapa, Córdoba, and Orizaba, were all volunteer when Branciforte reestablished them in 1796, but not all of the soldiers were of *casta limpia* status.[47] In smaller towns and cities, good public relations on the part of the cabildo could generate temporary enthusiasm or at least enough cooperation to hold the lottery and fill the ranks. Very often, however, men fled from their homes as soon as they heard about the plan to raise militias. At Oaxaca, even though the cabildo took precautions to ring the city with police officials and to close all exits, the single bachelors were not to be found. As in the case of the regular regiments, recruiters had to visit the city jails in order to locate men for service.[48] But there were greater obstacles to overcome in the future. Once militiamen tasted military life at the cantonments, experienced firsthand the evil climate at Veracruz, and fretted about abandoned families they left at home, they knew full well that the life of the infantryman was devoid of honor or advantage.

The burden of militia duty fell upon a wider part of the Mexican racial spectrum than the regime cared to admit. Notwithstanding army regulations restricting service to whites, castizos, and mestizos, few units could afford to engage in very rigorous racial selection. Where there were no complaints, almost anyone could be enlisted. Lieutenant Colonel Pedro de Laguna, on an inspection tour of the fourth and fifth Divisions of South Coast Militia, reported from Xamiltepec and Ometepec that the cavalry companies of Spaniards were no such thing. The source of contention was a militia tax of four reales annually levied upon all non-Spaniards. Since all residents considered themselves to be Spaniards, payment of the tax was tacit admission of social inferiority. Laguna saw little if any difference in appearance between those who managed to class themselves as Spaniards and the others who paid the tax. To solve a most unhappy situation, he proposed either the cancellation of the tax based upon race or an extension of the levy to all inhabitants.[49] As might be expected, those who did consider themselves to be of pure European ancestry objected to any effort to integrate them into racially mixed units. Ignacio Patiño, a resident of Papantla, expressed bitter opposition when his three sons were drafted into the local militia. Claiming to be of *casta limpia* status, he rejected any idea that his sons would have to serve alongside mulattoes, *chinos* (mulatto-Indian mixtures), and even Indians. Only the officers were Spaniards and, worst of all, the corporal of the company in which Patiño's sons were enlisted was a pardo.[50] Many officers simply could not be certain about the racial origins of their troops, since even the parish records and tribute registers were unreliable. Apparently, some Spaniards went as far as to claim mulatto status and paid tribute in an effort to evade militia enlistment.[51] This confusion resulting from the process of miscegenation would be solved in part prior to 1810. As the need for manpower increased, racial barriers fell, allowing any man to bear arms.

As we have seen, most of the provincial militiamen were drawn from the artisan, trade, and laboring classes. Racial origins were often less a factor than permanence of residence and health. Tables 25 and 26 illustrate the range of occupations represented among the enlisted ranks in the Battalions of Oaxaca and Guanajuato.[52] Although the different economic pursuits in the two cities become quite evident, militia mobilizations resulted in the same negative impact. By the time new recruits were sent to replace men who had perished on garrison duty, deserted, or served their full enlistments, numerous skilled workers would be removed from their normal tasks. A large percent-

TABLE 25
Occupations of Enlisted Men in the Battalion of Oaxaca, 1796.

Occupation	Number	Occupation	Number
weaver	78	tailor	77
shoemaker	32	carpenter	24
silversmith	21	tanner	18
painter	17	turner	17
blacksmith	15	barber	14
hatter	11	fireworks maker	9
potter	7	buttonmaker	6
stocking refooter	6	pork butcher	5
tallow chandler	5	mason	4
stonecutter	4	saddler	4
farmer	3	guitarmaker	3
baker	3	rosary maker	3
trader	2	fighting cock breeder	2
dyer	2	shopkeeper	2
carriagemaker	2	confectioner	1
clerk	1	traveler	1
muleteer	1	dancer	1
cook	1	cartwright	1
farrier	1	salesman	1
ropemaker	1	gilder	1
soapmaker	1	buttonholemaker	1
unidentified	1		
		TOTAL ENLISTMENT	410

Source: Pie de lista, Batallón de Oaxaca, 1796, AGN, IG, vol. 175-A.

age of the Guanajuato militiamen in 1795 were either directly or indirectly connected with mining. At Oaxaca, the withdrawal of 78 weavers and 77 tailors must have had a damaging effect upon the textile-related industries. Indeed, the mobilization of over 400 tradesmen and artisans combined with the flight of bachelors who feared enlistment cannot help but have caused a reduction in output as well as severe hardship for the militiamen's immediate families. The dire predictions of intendants and subdelegates which descended upon the viceroys after cantonments stretched into years were not without basis. Although 298 of the Oaxaca militiamen were bachelors in their teens, twenties, or early thirties, 112 men were married. This balance changed rather dramatically after 1795 because of the difficulties in locating replacements.

In every respect, militia mobilizations were not to be taken lightly. The viceroys received an avalanche of petitions from all quarters explaining the evil results to society and demanding the return of the militiamen. The Lancers of Veracruz had to be granted special leaves to fish while they were on

TABLE 26
Occupations of Enlisted Men in the Battalion of Guanajuato, 1795.

Occupation	Number	Occupation	Number
laborer	95	mineworker	64
tailor	37	muleteer	28
merchant	24	silversmith	16
crush mill worker	15	carpenter	15
trader	11	stonecutter	10
pork butcher	9	tallow chandler	8
blacksmith	8	finisher	8
farrier	7	musician	6
barber	6	hatter	6
ore-cake mixer	6	quicksilver dealer	5
shoemaker	5	mercury mixer	4
clerk	4	farmer	4
mining whim operator	3	cigarmaker	2
buttonholemaker	2	baker	2
mason	2	painter	2
saddler	2	woodcutter	2
chairmaker	1	refining mill worker	1
dyer	1	buttonmaker	1
field guard	1	carter	1
shopkeeper	1	mining magistral mixer	1
		TOTAL ENLISTMENT	426

Source: Pie de lista, Batallón de Guanajuato, 1796, AGN, IG, vol. 156-B.

active duty because there were not enough men left in their villages to tend crops and care for their families.[53] Viceroy Azanza encountered a great clamor from the families of men serving with the Infantry of Tres Villas. There were few workers available at the best of times in Jalapa, Córdoba, and Orizaba. Militia mobilization skimmed off the best field hands and damaged other branches of industry. With the valuable tobacco crop threatened, the viceroy agreed to release men to their civilian occupations.[54]

Each new demand upon the provincial militiamen hardened resistance and made it more difficult to find new replacements. When Azanza transferred 240 militiamen from the Infantry of Valladolid to bolster the regular units at Veracruz in 1799, Lieutenant Colonel Lejarza simply could not assemble the detachment. In desperation and with his military honor at stake, he asked permission to enlist men who held valid deferments—proposing to begin with members of the *cacique* class and those who were the sole support of septuagenarian parents.[55] Since there were only 5,482 men listed in the census, Azanza suspended Lejarza's proposal and added the towns of Maravatío and Zitácuaro to the regimental jurisdiction. This increased the available manpower potential to 6,700 males of the *casta limpia* sectors. The real difficulty was that men were aware that provincial forces were being sent to Veracruz and assigned to the unsavory regular infantry regiments. At the town of Ario, Lieutenant Manuel González met sullen hostility when he attempted to mobilize his company. His patriotic exhortations fell upon deaf ears until he offered to furnish baggage animals and to pay a bounty of ten pesos to any man who accompanied him. Immediately, the opposition melted and 30 men came forward. The *"terror pánico"* which had been prevalent in the community since word of the Veracruz diaster leaked out now disappeared in an instant. On February 7, 1799, a large crowd gathered to send the men off to their destiny. They marched away, filled with what their officers described as patriotism, shouting *"Viva el Rey."*[56] By the end of May, half of these men were dead in the disaster of the Arroyo Moreno cantonment. Thereafter, recruiting in the intendancy of Valladolid became almost impossible.

If the men of the provincial regiments feared mobilization or assignment to the regular regiments, the doubts of those enlisted in the *compañías sueltas* were even greater. These companies, intended by Revillagigedo to prepare lists of potential recruits in case of invasion or some other similar emergency, were set aside when Branciforte took office. While Revillagigedo had planned sixteen divisions of reserve companies to replace the provincial regiments and battalions, Branciforte expanded the provincial units. It was not until 1797 that the *compañías sueltas* were again brought under active review. Since so much of the population lived in scattered villages and hamlets, making it difficult for them to send companies to provincial regiment assemblies, separate reserve companies were raised under the district subdelegate's command. The intendancy of Mexico with its large population and central location was the first to be organized[57] (see table 27). For men enlisted into these companies in 1794 or 1795, nothing more had taken place after the lottery. There

TABLE 27
Reserve Company Enlistment in 1797.

Intendancy	Men Enlisted
Mexico	3,522
Puebla	919
Valladolid	905
Oaxaca	877
TOTAL	6,223

Source: Branciforte to Alvarez, December 31, 1797, AGI, Estado, leg. 26.

was no uniform or *fuero militar* and few subdelegates bothered to assemble their companies for inspections or training. It came as a sudden shock in 1797 when Branciforte dispatched regular army officers to inspect the companies in the intendancy of Mexico and to mobilize one-third of the men for immediate assignment to the regular infantry. There was little consolation for those selected when they learned that they would be released at the end of the war with the fuero privilege.[58]

In many districts, the subdelegates feared the consequences of publishing Branciforte's orders and did everything possible to seek delays. The acting subdelegate of Tetela del Río, Angel Consul, reported that the people of Real de Tepantitlán, Tetela, and the towns of Asuchitlán and Cuzamala, which made up his province, were very timid when it came to the subject of military service. Isolated from Mexico City and from the mainstream of events, they had never seen troops and feared the prospect of being marched away from their homeland. Consul suspended the viceregal order because he was in the midst of collecting tribute and examining the accounts of the Indian communities.[59] Expecting this sort of inaction, Branciforte played upon the subdelegates' competitive spirit and ambitions. He issued a general letter describing how the subdelegate of Tulancingo had animated his subjects and generated such enthusiasm for the militia that the companies were formed without having to resort to lotteries. All subdelegates were encouraged to inspire the same loyalty so that their inhabitants should not be outdone by the patriots of Tulancingo.[60]

Consul acted with caution, forwarding news of the impending militia enlistment to his subalterns in the four districts of the subdelegation; he appointed a local draft board for each district consisting of the *juez eclesiástico,* a *síndico procurador,* and the local surgeon or *curandero.* Before the public knew anything about the viceregal edict, the *ministros de vara* were given lists of all men who were obligated to appear at the lotteries. Consul chaired the draft board in the district of Tepantitlán; on a given Sunday morning following high mass, the town crier read the viceregal order in the plaza mayor and copies were posted throughout the district. No one was permitted to leave his home neighborhood without express permission of the subdelegate. Any man who did so lost possible rights to deferment and under military ordinances could be punished as a deserter. Throughout the subdelegation, the local magistrates were to conduct an accurate census of Spaniards (whites), castizos, and mestizos. All registered tributarios and others of an *"aspecto indecoroso"* were exempt from the census and from enlistment. In Tepantitlán, Consul enlisted twenty-six "volunteers" from thirty-nine men, mostly mine laborers, who were presented for duty. There were 231 families of *casta limpia* status and on the accepted ratio of one militiaman for every nine families, this was a generous allotment. The same procedure was followed in the other three districts of the subdelegation with local authorities carrying out the enlistment. The subdelegate later toured each district to hear requests for deferment and to look into any complaints resulting from militia formation.[61]

At Zimapán, another mining district in the intendancy of Mexico, Subdelegate Ramón Jáuregui attempted to inspire the same loyalty the viceroy described in Tulancingo. Instead of finding volunteers among the mine and smelter workers, he encountered what he described as "a bold and perverse" dedication to avoid service.[62] All men had to be drafted and even then many fled into the mountains. It was with this background that Jáuregui assembled twenty-four militiamen to serve in the Regiment of New Spain. Determined to impress the viceroy, he did not inform the men of their fate. After an inspection at the treasury office and a four-hour wait in the sun for two men who did not appear, they were marched to the subdelegate's residence and locked up under the guard of their corporals. When the men expressed loud opposition to this treatment, Jáuregui informed them of their destiny and demanded blind obedience.[63] The result was a general uproar. The militiamen, who considered themselves to be "*hombres de bien,*" resented being locked up like criminals and denied even the right to go out to eat. The subdelegate, reluctant to permit the victims out of his custody for an instant until he could turn them over to the regular army, asked the corporals to prevent a general flight. They refused, stating that it would be impossible to keep the men together once they were allowed out of the building.[64]

In the meantime, anger replaced the confusion which had gripped the unfortunate militiamen. Believing that the subdelegate planned to turn them over to the regular army as vagabonds, they demanded to see the viceregal order regarding their disposition. A young refiner named Cayetano Figueroa emerged as the spokesman for the group. Later he testified that he had gone to the assembly as an ordinary citizen fearful that an enemy invasion was taking place. If so, his distress at the prospect of being marched off to regular army duty probably resulted from shock as well as anger.[65] Jáuregui reacted to the militiamen's resistance with unrestrained rage. When Figueroa spoke for the prisoners, the subdelegate shouted, "You are a *pícaro* and seducer of the soldiers."[66] The militiamen defended themselves with even stronger language and Corporal Mariano Muñoz, a mineworker, plunged into the fray, grabbed Figueroa by the hair and punched him in the face. At that point, a mineowner named Fernando Labra came upon the scene and was ordered to fetch all of his workers mounted and armed to quell the tumult. Figueroa, frightened by his own audacity but emboldened from having consumed a quantity of brandy on an empty stomach, drew his dagger and led the militiamen out of their detention and into a corner of the plaza. Unsure of what to do next, they discussed the alternatives while continuing to mock and threaten the subdelegate. Later they fled into the mountains, where they split up to evade capture.[67]

Although Jáuregui was removed from command of the reserve company for his poor conduct and deceit, the image of the militia was tarnished beyond repair. A second assembly, held in September 1797, produced eighteen of the twenty-four recruits Zimapán was to send to the Regiment of New Spain, but the magistrate in charge, José González Retana, found his task to be incredibly difficult. Six of the earlier fugitives were still at large in the mountains and word had spread about the true purpose of the assembly. Mine and hacienda workers stayed well clear of Zimapán, blaming their absences upon the pressure of work or heavy rains. The real fear, of course, was the same *"terror pánico"* encountered by many subdelegates when they attempted to separate men from their *patria chica*.[68] To compound the problem at Zimapán, Branciforte ordered a new batch of militiamen for service in the regular infantry. Retana rounded up eleven victims, but one had to be released because of a large tumor on his backside. The remaining ten were held under constant guard until the day of departure. As they marched out of town, a weeping crowd of women surrounded the small detachment; in the confusion, one of the militiamen escaped and disappeared into the mountains.[69]

The shock and dismay expressed by militiamen assigned to the regular regiments was by no means confined to Zimapán. Anguished petitions flooded into the capital presenting any number of reasons why men wanted to be granted deferments. Nevertheless, a common theme emerged among those sent to the regular army. All were indignant at having been so ill-considered as to be thought fit for the regulars. José Antonio Lascano of Tulancingo attempted to obtain the return of his son Isidro, who had been mobilized from the local reserve company. He employed a number of arguments, from his family's size to his son's poor health, but indicated his own feeling when he concluded, "my son is not a vagabond."[70] José Domingo Pasten, a transporter of pulque from Teotihuacán to Mexico City, stated that without the aid of his son, José Tomás, who had been taken from the local reserve company of the Infantry of New Spain, he could not manage his drove of mules. His health was poor and he needed help to make three or four trips a week to the capital—more so because of the high risk of attacks by thieves. Pasten stressed that his son was neither a vagrant nor a bad man.[71] When Pedro Sarmiento, a resident of Xonacatepec and a militiaman of the Company of Cuautla Amilpas, heard about his assignment to the regular infantry, he fled rather than permitting himself to become a prisoner. During the time Sarmiento made his appeal to the viceroy from his hiding place, the subdelegate arrested and jailed his poor father, threatening to leave him there until such time as the son gave himself up. Sarmiento could not understand why the army was after him since regular army recruits came from "the vagrant and useless population." He concluded that he was a victim of the subdelegate's animosity.[72]

Although petitions from individuals sometimes resulted in special deferments, this pressure did not sway basic policies. Fortunately for the militiamen, however, the mineowners, hacendados, and merchants had much to lose from any dislocation of the labor force. In mining districts like Zimapán, it did not take long before wealthy miners, ore-buyers, and hacendados went to the defense of their skilled and semiskilled mine laborers, ore-buyers, and hacienda managers. Even a vague threat of being marched off to the regular regiments caused semitransient laborers to abandon their jobs and to leave the region for some safer location. In districts where labor shortages were a constant problem, employers refused to be passive witnesses to economic decline. At Zimapán, following the 1797 enlistment tumult, discontented mineworkers had begun to demand more wages than the one-and-a-half reales daily pay they received. The same was true in Pachuca, where a decline in the number of workers was blamed upon militia enlistment. Some mineowners expressed fears that they would not be able to maintain expensive drainage systems if the situation did not improve.[73]

From Taxco, officers of the regional Diputación de la Minería joined their colleagues from other mining districts in a growing protest against the military. Mine laborers fled from their homes, unaware that even if they were not present for the sorteo they could be drafted. Then, after the lottery, the departure of workers accelerated because those who had been selected followed others who had fled earlier.[74] As a matter of fact, the subdelegate of Taxco, Fernando de Mendoza, had done everything within his power to prevent a confrontation similar to the one in Zimapán. While he described his subjects as "a vagrant people by nature and employment," Mendoza attempted to overcome their distaste for the army through gentleness and persuasion. Yet, he agreed with the mineowners that workers had departed from the region, causing labor shortages which threatened to close mines yielding lower-quality ores. His two sorteos accomplished little other than to gather a collection of the chronically ill, crippled, aged, and otherwise exempt. Since the regional economy—already in decline even before the crisis—depended totally upon mining and all of the population was directly or indirectly connected with the industry, he proposed the exemption of all miners from military obligations.[75] The mineowners adopted this proposal completely;

otherwise, they argued, the principal industry of New Spain was threatened. They demanded absolute deferment for all workers who dedicated themselves to the dangerous life of removing precious silver from the earth.

The Mining Tribunal repeated the complaints of the regional mining deputations. The main argument against enlistment was that the subdelegates throughout the mining districts had broken military ordinances concerning racial eligibility. Instead of restricting enlistment to the whites, castizos, and mestizos, most officials were concerned primarily with numbers of militiamen. Miners were of the lower castes—mulattoes, *lobos,* and *coyotes*—men excluded by birth from honorable service because of their high proportion of Indian or African blood. The problem, then, was not the draft but nonobservance of regulations by overzealous officials. In Zimapán, according to information received by the tribunal, all castes had been enlisted without any effort to discriminate between those eligible for the militia and others. If the economic or the racial arguments were not sufficient, the tribunal added that most miners were poor material for the army anyway. Men who labored beneath the ground in the dirty silver mines soon contracted the consumptive lung diseases of *tísica* or *cascado*. In a few years, the most robust youth became a sickly, anemic skeleton.[76] The same was true in the case of refiners and smelter workers who contracted *engraso* or *saturnismo* (lead or metal poisoning) from breathing the oven smoke and crushed ore dust.[77] Apparently some of the mines in the intendancy of Mexico were notoriously dirty and hazardous to the workers' health. In sum, the tribunal strongly endorsed the proposal for a general exemption of all miners. To replace them in the regular regiment, the mining magnates proposed a campaign to round up white, castizo, and mestizo vagabonds who roamed the mining districts.

Even if he did not fully accept these arguments, Branciforte had no wish to enlist people of all races or those with terminal diseases. More important, of course, the viceroy dared not provoke the powerful mining interests of New Spain. Although he suspected that the problems of low caste and disease were magnified, he could not risk economic disruption resulting from the flight of workers whenever army recruiters appeared on the scene. On March 10, 1798, Branciforte issued a general edict excusing mine laborers and those in associated trades from participating in the militia draft.[78]

As a result of this decree, militia formation in most mining districts became a waste of time. Officers of the Regiment of New Spain continued to inspect reserve companies and to look for men suitable for regular army duty, but without the miners and allied workers, most units were empty. In Zimapán, Captain José de Castro reduced the list of men available for enlistment from 150 to 40. Nevertheless, he managed to enroll only 7 militiamen and none were suitable for the regular army. Most of the men he saw were too short, old, chronically ill, or with sufficient impediments of one kind or another that they did not object to presenting themselves for examination. By now the attitude of the populace was so negative toward the military that no amount of threatening changed matters. Branciforte appealed to the men to come forward in a patriotic gesture in defense of their country, and to improve the atmosphere in Zimapán, he ordered the release of those who were still in jail from the first troubles. When this had no effect, he changed his approach, threatening that the heavy hand of viceregal power would fall upon Zimapán. The local curates were told to drum up respect for authority and support for the militia.[79] After their experiences, the people were not swayed by sermons exhorting obedience to legitimate power. Regular officers fulminated against the decree exempting miners and argued that almost any man who had ever heard of a mine used it to avoid the militia. Captain Castro went as far as to propose the utilization of forced Indian labor in the mines in order to free *casta limpia* workers for army service.[80]

By June 1798, Castro had examined 108 individuals and enlisted only eight militiamen. The remainder were unfit for service or able to obtain certification from their employers that they were either miners or worked in some related enterprise. More than fifty men were still absent from the district, but the captain was certain they would claim the miner's exemption when and if they returned. In his opinion, the labor shortage resulted not from the army's activities, but from poor wages and the refusal of some mine operators to permit their employees a share or *partido* of the ore they extracted. Also, workers avoided mines that were poorly situated or inadequately maintained for fear of perishing in a cave-in or some other accident. Castro rejected the Mining Tribunal's contention that most miners were of races inadmissible for military service and too sick to bear arms. Since there were labor shortages in the mines with better health conditions, he saw no reason why men should have to work in dusty mines where they might contract lung ailments.[81] Naturally, an army officer's view of the mine labor situation won no support in Zimapán. In the end, Branciforte had to admit defeat. He suspended formation of the reserve company and recalled Castro and his personnel back to Mexico City.

In other regions, different methods were used to resist enlistment. The subdelegate of Xochimilco, Ignacio Beye y Cisneros, encountered numerous difficulties when he ordered lotteries to select men for the local reserve company. Some residents were members of the Urban Regiment of Commerce of Mexico City; they mocked the efforts of the subdelegate to enlist them and told their friends about this loophole. Service in the sedentary urban militia proved to be an excellent escape from possible assignment from the reserve company to one of the regular regiments. Hacendados resisted presenting their laborers and made it difficult for the census takers to establish how many persons resided on their properties. In one case, Joaquín Romero de Caamaño, whose hacienda, San Juan de Díos, was located on the boundary between the subdelegations of Xochimilco and Coyoacán, avoiding sending his employees to the Company of Xochimilco by saying that they were going to Coyoacán.[82] When it was established that the hacienda did pertain to Xochimilco, Romero de Caamaño insisted he had no white, mestizo, or mulatto workers. His few servants lived in the village of Santa Bárbara Coapa in the territory of the Marquesado del Valle, which had never been controlled from Xochimilco. Further pressed, Romero submitted a list of eleven day laborers whom he claimed were residents of different villages and jurisdictions. They all returned to their homes that night. Since none were forced to work on his estates, they were free to come and go according to their own wish. In most weeks, his labor force changed depending upon the availability of men and the seasonal needs. Only the hacienda administrator and a ten-year-old Indian boy were permanent residents.[83] Similar confusion existed in Cuernavaca, where Subdelegate Antonio de la Landa y Garcés blamed his "inept and disobedient" lieutenants for inactivity in preparing census reports and enlisting the companies. Captain Martín de Medina of the Regiment of New Spain arrived in the town to select a third of the company for his regiment before the lotteries had been held. Delays were still preventing the departure of militiamen in 1798 when a smallpox epidemic raged through the district allowing another rather dubious reprieve from enlistment.[84]

Besides having to wait for the Cuernavaca recruits, Captain Medina was treated to other insults as he pursued his mission to select men from the Companies of Cuernavaca, Xochimilco, and Cuautla Amilpas. On one occasion at Cuautla Amilpas in November 1797, he was in the living room of his quarters with the secretary of the local subdelegate arranging the company register and preparing to march twenty-six local militiamen to the Regiment of New Spain. Suddenly a man entered the room, "without a hat, in shirtsleeves, and with his hair unkempt." Making no effort to introduce himself, he sat down on a bench and demanded, "Are you enlisting Juan Arevalo?" He went on in a loud voice stating, "Arevalo is a madman and must not go to serve the king." Medina was insulted by this uncourteous behavior and upset because the draftees were in a nearby corridor and could hear every word of the dispute. Finally, he had to order two young men he had guarding the militiamen to remove the intruder. He feared that if there was further argument, the militiamen might attempt to escape or to cause some other disorder.[85] The debate continued at the house of the subdelegate in the presence of other persons who happened to be there. The man turned out to be Francisco Díaz de Celís, a retired ensign of the militia who had a reputation for rash behavior.

Resistance to the military by men of the reserve companies and their defenders declined after 1798 because the effort to attach them to the regular regiments ceased. Viceroy Azanza, it will be recalled, decided to transfer men directly from the provincial regiments into the regular units. Nevertheless, by 1804, the threat of war with Britain caused the military to renew its interest in the reserve companies. In 1806, the Mining Tribunal charged that Zimapán and Taxco had been pressed to enlist recruits from classes inadmissible for military service. Although the *auditor de guerra* confirmed Branciforte's ruling of 1798, miners were uneasy because reserve companies from all over the intendancy of Mexico were being attached to the regular and provincial regiments at the cantonment.[86] Indeed, the worst fears of the mine operators appeared to be coming true. Enlistment of miners was in full progress at the northern mining community of Atotonilco near Durango. Nearer to the capital, the subdelegate of Pachuca had issued an order for eighty-five men to form a company. Once again, local mining deputies reiterated their arguments of 1797 against the enlistment of mineworkers. Since two companies from Tulancingo had been activated and those from other subdelegations were in service, the miners had good cause for anxiety.[87] At Zimapán, the *juez eclesiástico,* Father Leandro Cabezas, acted as the spokesman for men who were not engaged in the primary industry. Since miners were exempt, militia enlistment became all the more onerous. The militia turned to the few blacksmiths, tradesmen, and agricultural laborers, which would damage business, commerce, and the harvest.

Iturrigaray could not afford the luxury of allowing resistance and procrastination to slow the creation of an effective defense force. The danger of a British invasion made it more imperative than ever to secure the routes inland rather than to worry about the immediate social and economic consequences of enlistment. While the viceroy agreed to respect the miners' exemption, no other group of workers could expect similar treatment. Beset by army demand for more men, Iturrigaray accepted the alteration of a recruitment policy that had been considered essential since the introduction of the army. Too much of the population had been dismissed as unfit for military duty. On July 8, 1807, the viceroy amended the traditional restrictions and announced a much more flexible policy; if in a given province or district there were not sufficient whites, castizos, and mestizos to fulfill military requirements, other nontributary castes were to be enlisted. If there were still shortages, the non-

Indian tributaries were to be called, and ultimately, when all other sources had been exhausted, the Indians.[88] Since some subdelegates suggested that many men registered as Indians and paid tribute either to obtain use of communal lands or to free themselves from payment of the alcabala, the new approach might have appeared obvious.[89] Yet, the relaxation of the existing policies led to severe social and economic strains—particularly upon the families of men who lived on the margins of Mexican society.

Although the miners were still exempt, the remainder of the population in mining districts came under greatly increased pressure to provide recruits. From Taxco, Subdelegate Antonio del Corral Velasco attacked the new policy as totally impractical. Not only were militia units difficult to raise in his jurisdiction, but he also found that the company formed in 1797 had not respected militia ordinances regarding age, number of dependents, or the health of the recruit. Besides, many of the men enlisted ten years previously now had wives and dependents to support. All of the potentially eligible men of Taxco were employed either directly in the mines or in allied occupations such as refining, smelting, or supply. Others, such as muleteers, conducted ore to the smelters, carried wood and charcoal, and serviced the mines. Even children of only eight or nine years of age performed mine labor as did much of the Indian population from surrounding villages. Those from more distant hamlets in the mountains were so rustic and uncultured that they did not speak Spanish and would be of no use whatsoever to the army. Like a good local administrator, Corral Velasco asked the army to seek its recruits elsewhere— he suggested Iguala, where there must be a surplus of workers and muleteers.[90]

Fear of the army in Taxco continued right up to 1810. Even the possibility of a unit being garrisoned in the town aroused the opposition of both mining and ecclesiastical leaders. In March 1810, a rumor circulated that a battalion made up of reserve companies would be stationed in Taxco. The mining deputation catalogued a list of reasons why this could not take place. Food was scarce and an important staple like maize cost five pesos per *carga* though the season of greatest scarcity had not arrived. Recruitment of miners might result in violence or at least in a general abandonment of the mines by men who feared unknown terrors connected with service. Others did not trust their women, daughters, and sisters to live alone during their absences.[91] The *juez eclesiástico*, Father Manuel Antonio Clavijo, feared the spiritual damage a garrisoned force was certain to cause; he had worked hard to end prostitution and to furnish good moral guidance for his community. Now he saw "the innocence of many virgins sacrificed" and the possibility of new social problems. Like the other leaders of Taxco, he suggested Iguala or Tepecuacuilco as much better locations for the reunion of troops.[92]

After 1807, the pressure for recruits opened the way to a variety of social abuses. Subdelegates, under firm orders to produce soldiers and then replacements for mobilized companies, began to seize any male they could lay their hands on. The results were chaotic to say the least. Pedro Quijada, a recruit presented for duty in Mexico City from the Company of Tula, was forty years of age and had seven children, a widowed sister, and two unmarried sisters to support. He had to be granted a deferment as soon as his case came before the commandant in the capital.[93] This returned responsibility to the subdelegate, who by this time had reached the bottom of the barrel. Elsewhere, conditions were no better; Estéban León, a laborer from Tlaxco in Tlaxcala, went to visit his brother in the town of Coyoacán and was arrested by the subdelegate before he could even locate the house and enlisted in the local militia company. He found himself on active duty in Mexico City, where he was given an opportunity to explain the injustice and to petition for a release.[94] In a similar case, Mariano Castro, an employee of the royal mint, was arrested and incorporated into the Company of Tacubaya. The subdelegate refused to hear his complaint or to look at his identification which proved his connection with the mint.[95] Under the same kind of pressure to locate replacements, the subdelegate of Cuernavaca, Gregorio Joaquín de Castro, stated that he had scoured his district and sent out his lieutenants to look for recruits, but found none. With 220 men from the area on duty in Mexico City, he doubted the ability of his subdelegation to produce more.[96]

Alarmed by the social impact of recruitment, Father Estanislao Segura and postal administrator Valdovinos Blanco, both of Cuernavaca and members of the local draft board, wrote to Iturrigaray:

> We have been eyewitnesses to the miseries of these unfortunates who, with great prejudice to their mothers, wives, and children, are enlisted in the militia and immediately marched from their homes to the capital.

Describing themselves as guardians of the common people, they felt that it was their duty to report that children were having to beg in order to survive and wives were forced to turn to prostitution.[97] There was little Iturrigaray could do about general complaints although he did try to investigate all cases where specific names and other information were available. The letter from Cuernavaca did nothing other than to arouse viceregal resentment. In his view, people everywhere were suffering in the struggle to defend the *patria*. If Segura and Blanco were really the guardians of their town as they claimed, he suggested that they should unburden their own pockets to aid abandoned women and children or take up arms themselves to help defend the kingdom.[98]

Without the racial controls governing enlistment, the lowest income sectors of the population were helpless before subdelegates whose primary concern was to fill their quotas. José Luis Valle, an Indian tributary from Ixtapalapa, the sole support for his old parents and four dependents, was drafted and marched to Mexico City with the Company of Xochimilco. His family operated a grinder for the Ramo de Salitres (the saltpeter monopoly). Unable to run the equipment by himself, his father, Juan Carlos, went to the director of the Ramo de Pólvora (the powder monopoly) to beg the release of José Luis. This official sent him to the intendant of Mexico who, in turn, sent him back to the local subdelegate. Since he refused to take action, Juan Carlos and his wife went to Iturrigaray to ask for viceregal intercession; hearing the evidence from the two poor Indians, the viceroy felt compelled to grant the release.[99] Mariano Ignacio de la Luz, another Indian tributary, was working at his trade as a brickmaker near Cuernavaca when he received a summons to appear before the subdelegate. The moment he arrived before this magistrate, he was sworn into the militia and the next day marched off to Mexico City. He petitioned the viceroy, stating:[100]

> Your Excellency, I am exempt from service for two reasons. First, I am an Indian *tributario* which means that our sovereign excuses me from duty with his troops. Secondly, I am married to María Francesa Tivurcia, who is also a *tributaria*.

Luz enclosed two receipts each for three pesos, signed by the subdelegate, proving that he had paid his tribute for the years 1806 and 1807. He also had a three-year-old son and no family to care for his dependents while he was in the army. In such circumstances, he said, "... even Spaniards [whites] are exempt from militia service." The case went to Subdelegate Gregorio Joaquín de Castro at Cuernavaca, who agreed with most of Luz's statements. Nonetheless, Luz was registered as a mulatto rather than an Indian and he would have to remain in the army.[101]

By 1808, even the backing of a powerful benefactor was of limited help if he happened to be an opponent of the viceroy. In listing men available for the local reserve company which was to go into service with the Infantry of Celaya, the subdelegate of Tacuba included the names of three shepherds employed by Don Gabriel de Yermo. He declared that his men were exempt from the militia, but the subdelegate could not discover any legitimate reason in the militia regulations. On appeal, the *auditor de guerra* recommended deferments in these cases, pointing out that there were royal orders of 1781 and 1800 freeing men engaged in provisioning cities. Iturrigaray overruled this finding with the terse comment, "It is easier to locate good shepherds than good militiamen."[102] Probably this rebuff became one more reason why Yermo was willing to accept leadership of the movement against the viceroy.

For the great majority of militiamen who resigned themselves to active duty, hardships and suffering increased as time passed. In the capital or the cantonment, where the style and cost of living was higher than anything they had experienced, they could not afford to maintain themselves on army pay let alone to have surplus funds to send home. When women and children followed their men, their living conditions were even worse than if they had stayed at home. Sergeant José María Archudía of the Company of Cuernavaca reported that his army pay of four reales daily was not enough to begin feeding and housing his large family. They had accompanied him to Mexico City where poverty exposed them to nakedness and hunger. Archudía had served eight years in his company, but this was his first trip away from his home village of Yautepec. At the time of his original enlistment, he had only a wife to support; now he had four children, his wife, and her old mother.[103] If a sergeant could not survive on his army pay, one can understand the anguished petitions of the common soldiers. Often with as many dependents, they had to get by with daily pay of one-and-a-half reales.

Word of these or similar experiences further hardened attitudes against the army. By 1808, many of the subdelegates were concerned about economic dislocations and the disappearance of workers. Subdelegate Manuel Güemes y Sierra of Huexutla complained that thirty-seven men of the local reserve company deserted the region when they heard about company mobilization.[104] The subdelegate of Izúcar, Francisco Hierro López, had not seen his militiamen for so long that he was sketchy about what they looked like. He sent a census report to the intendant of Puebla enumerating the men he believed to be eligible for duty. Since they were not present, however, he could not describe their racial characteristics or height, or say whether they deserved deferments. When the word had spread that soldiers were coming to remove the company from its *patria chica,* the militiamen and many other individuals who had nothing to do with the militia had departed in what Hierro López described as "a scandalous and tumultuous flight."[105]

Whether or not the reluctant provincials served any useful purpose in the garrisons and cantonments is questionable. Frequent references by the subdelegates to the men's poor appearance and stature and the fact that many did not speak the Spanish language very well raised doubts about how they could fit into an effective fighting force.[106] Although Carlos María Bustamante believed in the inherent abilities of his countrymen to make good soldiers—he said a Mexican became a soldier in a month while a Galician took three months just to learn how to walk with shoes on and how to distinguish between left and right—the evidence does not support his optimism. Adjutant Antonio de Mora, in his instructions for training militiamen, stressed the need for monotonous repetition to teach them how to form a line without looking at their feet. Afterwards, they could begin precision turns and learn how to march so that they would be able to unite with a battalion. For cavalry units, the process was even longer for men had to learn military maneuvers on foot before attempting them on horseback.[107] Few of the provincial regiments let alone the reserve companies followed the kind of training programs necessary to prepare men for the battlefield. One zealous company captain, Juan Antonio de Araujo, attracted viceregal commendation when he attempted to give his men some rudimentary instruction. He hired a drummer at his own cost and, using great restraint to avoid upsetting or threatening the men, he tried to teach them how to march, turn, and quarter-wheel.[108] From a technical point of view, of course, the Mexican soldiers did not have the best equipment in the world. A shipment of supposedly new muskets for the Infantry of Tlaxcala arrived with the barrels blown out of twenty-five weapons. The rest were in dubious condition; when the regiment went on exercises, a sergeant or corporal had to follow the troops in order to pick up the bits and pieces of muskets which fell to the ground.[109]

Perhaps if the army paid better wages and made some provision for the support of families, Mexicans would have felt a little more positive about their patriotic responsibilities. As matters stood, however, a breadwinner had everything to lose and almost nothing to gain. For disabled regular army soldiers there was the Cuerpo de Inválidos, which was a good concept. Stationed at Mexico City, retired or separated soldiers capable of light duties guarded public buildings and performed minor police functions. Unfortunately, low pay and poor conditions caused soldiers to exhibit "an incredible repugnance" to being pensioned off in this manner.[110] For the provincial soldiers, there was not even this limited protection. Men who returned home crippled by diseases or injuries received no pensions from the regime. The best solution was to avoid the army in the first place.

10

DISCIPLINE, PUNISHMENT, AND CONDITIONS OF SERVICE

No eighteenth-century army could have existed without rigid discipline, corporal punishment, and a level of violence unthinkable in the modern military. Throughout Europe, flogging, transportation to overseas colonies, and capital punishment were common tools employed to keep soldiers from preying upon civilian society or each other, or simply deserting from their regiments. Since most men were recruited by some method of force and, as the Duke of Wellington described them, were "the very scum of the earth,"[1] reforms were difficult to introduce and implement upon men hardened by the lash.[2] What was true for the metropolitan armies was even more evident in the colonies, where the level of discipline and the element of patriotism were even less developed. Since many of the regular soldiers and NCOs sent overseas were the unwanted petty criminals, chronic alcoholics, and gamblers of the European regiments, their negative contributions to the colony could be anticipated.

New Spain was no exception to the general pattern. In 1799, when Captain Fernando Villaneuva inspected the regular soldiers assigned to train the frontier militia of Colotlán, he described the twenty-one sergeants and corporals as a gang of "professional drunks, gamblers, and plotters." Sergeant Vicente Nava, a veteran of twenty-six years' service, combined in his person all vices; he gambled, drank to the point where he was stupefied and useless, and sold firearms; when he commanded the barracks it became a "brothel and seedbed of every disorder."[3] Homicides and crimes of passion committed by soldiers were so common as to be scarcely noteworthy, and officers expected such behavior from men whose trade personified violence. Soldier José María

Estrada knifed and killed a comrade after a drinking session in Mexico City at the house of a woman named Margarita. Departing from the house in an intoxicated state, the two men quarreled over whether they should get something to eat.[4] The dragoon Agustín Ledesma, sentenced to hang for having stolen three hundred pesos from his adjutant, managed to slash his own throat a few hours prior to the execution.[5] These were typical of the numerous cases which came before the courts-martial of the viceroyalty. Indeed, when the Cuban regiments requested some Mexicans to fill shortages in 1788, army units divested themselves of almost 200 criminals including "a fine assortment" of murderers, thieves, deserters, pickpockets, and slothful vagabonds. One of these, Manuel Selma, had been sentenced to torture for his role in a murder, but this was suspended when no one could be found to carry out the penalty.[6] In 1810, when the viceroy decided to raise a new battalion for Veracruz and another to send overseas to Santo Domingo, the regular army units of Mexico listed 922 deserters, alcoholics, petty criminals, and sellers of uniforms who were in jail or under arrest and whose departure would be beneficial to the army. The oversize Battalion of Veracruz, long a clearinghouse for unwanted soldiers, had on its rolls a total of 415 deserters, criminals, and habitual drunks who had committed these crimes once or more in Veracruz and another 293 soldiers who had deserted from other regiments before being sentenced to serve at the port.[7] If all of these delinquents had been shipped off to Santo Domingo, the Battalion of Veracruz would have been extinguished. In 1799, when 485 soldiers were transferred from the Regiments of the Crown and New Spain to reinforce the much-depleted Regiment of Puebla stationed at Havana, Colonel Vicente Nieto wrote that the men were of poor appearance and blackish color which repelled the officers and caused them to demand that the new men be rejected for service. But even these bad signs could have been tolerated if the men had shown any indications of being willing to fulfill their duty. A few weeks after their arrival at Havana thirteen were charged with serious crimes and the majority of the others incessantly committed misdemeanors—staying out all night away from the barracks without permission, selling their uniforms, and drinking constantly.[8]

As might be expected, the concentration of criminals and reprobates in the army caused havoc with other sectors of Mexican society. Troops of the Mexico City garrison attacked citizens in parks, theaters, and at other locations where they were supposed to be on guard duty. Viceroy Marquina had to issue specific orders on where and when arms might be employed—noting that theatrical performances and public promenades were not proper occasions. One anonymous but thoroughly outraged citizen wrote to the viceroy that he had been assaulted on his way to the theater by a grenadier of the Regiment of the Crown named Luis Cortés. The incident occurred when he reached into his pocket to give a coin to a poor beggar woman. Without warning, Cortés unleashed a terrible slap with the flat of his sword upon the complainant, almost knocking him out and leaving him with severe bruises on the chest. When, gasping, he asked what prompted this violent behavior, Cortés answered haughtily that he had orders to prevent communication around his sentry post. A report to the officer of the guard resulted in the removal and arrest of the soldier, but no other punishment. The anonymous citizen asked the viceroy to take action against soldiers and officers of the Regiment of the Crown, who were the worst offenders against peaceful citizens. These troops were accustomed to dealing with "the Negroes and other colored castes in Veracruz, whom they control and govern by blows because they do not understand gentle reason."[9]

At night the mounted dragoon patrols were just as hard on the civilian population. Viceroys received frequent complaints of assaults against the keepers of street lamps. In one incident, a corporal discovered a light-keeper sleeping at his post, took away his pike and handlight, administered a severe beating, and then told him to keep quiet about the matter. Viceroy Marquina had to issue special orders to the garrison; even if light-keepers were found sleeping on the job, they were to be reported to the proper authorities and not disciplined on the spot.[10] A few months later the attacks began once more; two light-keepers were arrested and taken to their superiors, one was threatened and sworn at in case he was found sleeping, and another had his light confiscated until he paid a *real* for its return.[11]

Troops in transit or on guard duty over caravans of *presidarios,* Indian deportees, and silver shipments caused trouble and property damage along their routes. Three innkeepers of Querétaro complained to the cabildo that they suffered continuous insults from soldiers—particularly those who travelled under the command of a poorly trained corporal or by themselves. Even when there were officers, abuse, quarrels, and damage to their property could not be avoided.[12] The cabildo sympathized with the innkeepers, but wanted no part of their proposal to house visiting troops in private homes or in the local militia barracks. During a recent visit of the provincial Battalion of Guanajuato on its way to duty in the capital, considerable damage had been done to doors, windows, keys, and anything movable from the barracks. Had they been housed in private dwellings, they would have ruined them in four days. The cabildo proposed an annual subsidy of ten pesos to the innkeepers to cover damages. The brigade commander, Ignacio García Revollo, argued against opening the barracks to visitors because mixing of soldiers from different units always seemed to result in severe disorders and damage. Since the barracks were crammed with the arms, uniforms, and equipment of the militia and were also the living quarters for soldiers and dependents of the training cadre, he opposed any use of the military facilities.[13]

The Indians and castas were the victims of great mistreatment. Living outside of major administrative centers, they lacked the protection of city or provincial authorities. Occasionally, incidents came to light but little was done to protect against recurrence of the same crimes. During the cantonment, for example, soldiers ranged out of Orizaba and Jalapa molesting peaceful Indian farmers, destroying their crops, and disrupting their families. The subdelegate of Orizaba, José Salinas, reported frequent grievances to Viceroy Branciforte. One Indian arrived at home to discover his wife in bed with a corporal of the Regiment of Tlaxcala. Another from the village of Yxhautlancillo reported that he had been robbed of two reales by unidentified soldiers, and a little later an Indian from the same village testified that he had been wounded by a saber slash when he attempted to drive some soldiers away from his orchard. The governor of the *cabildo de naturales,* Eusebio Lucas Ximénez, appeared to lay his own charges against a soldier of the Regiment of Toluca who swore at him and threatened his life. He added further evidence of attacks by soldiers who entered Indian lands to steal fruit, molest women, and engage in other excesses.[14] In one of the most serious incidents, an Indian named Cayetano Sefarino had to be hospitalized for two weeks with head injuries. He had a minor argument with some soldiers on one day and the next afternoon, while he was drinking *tepache* in the local tavern, they attacked and beat him without provocation. Attempts to investigate these complaints produced no convictions, but the *auditor de guerra* warned against further mistreatment of civilians.[15]

Troops invaded Indian towns and appropriated everything they needed without payment—houses, taverns, pack animals, and even the services of the residents. In one instance, soldiers from Toluca carried off pack mules from Apan and did not discard them until they arrived at Jalapa. Wherever they stopped, soldiers left a trail of damaged property which the Indians had to replace out of their community funds. Troops conducting caravans of *presidarios* or Indian prisoners from the north compelled Indian men to serve as watchmen over the prisoners at night and the women to prepare food. Although most Indians did not object to serving the soldiers when stipends were paid, they objected to payment in blows and sword slaps.[16] Two alcaldes had been slashed severely at Almoloya and even the subdelegates experienced little success in preventing incidents. Like the Indian governors, they were mocked by rowdy soldiers. In the opinion of Sub-Inspector General Carlos de

Urrutía, who investigated some of these complaints, much of the trouble resulted when officers did not accompany their troops on marches. Henceforth, soldiers were not to be left on their own.[17]

In their travels, soldiers of the Mexican army as in all armies became involved with women, made promises of marriage in order to seduce them, and then hastened to new conquests. Generally, the military tended to protect men when women or their priests attempted to settle breach of promise and pregnancies through marriage. Officers wanted bachelors in their units if at all possible because married men soon became burdened by families and then neglected their duties. This had been one of the chronic complaints against the Spanish regulars sent to train the Mexican militia regiments since the army was introduced.[18] It was even more essential to maintain a high percentage of bachelors in the regular regiments to facilitate rotation from city to city. In some instances, however, the women prevailed; when María Justa Rey of Puebla failed to obtain permission from the army to marry José Guadencio Gálvez of the Dragoons of Mexico, she carried her case to the capital, where she sought the intervention of the *virreina* Branciforte. The couple had presented themselves for marriage at the cathedral of Puebla, but had been turned away because they lacked the necessary fees. Gálvez's commander, Colonel Gaspar Alvarez de Sotomayor, confirmed the betrothal but opposed the marriage because he had too many useless married men in his regiment.[19] Contrary to the usual result in these cases, Branciforte—probably under pressure from his wife—rejected Alvarez's opposition and ordered that the marriage should take place.

Other cases presented fewer difficulties. When Rafael Blanco reported that his daughter, the wife of a captain in the Urban Regiment of Commerce, was carrying on an adulterous affair with clarinet player José Santiestévan of the provincial Regiment of Mexico, the colonel, some soldiers, and the denunciant went to her house. They caught the pair in her bedroom and Santiestevan was arrested and charged with adultery. He argued that he was merely engaging in conversation, but gave up this defense when informed that having entered the home of a married woman in the absence of her husband was sufficient evidence of guilt. He then confessed to visiting the woman when her husband was away on guard duty although he claimed to have slept with her only one night. For his offense, Santiestevan received a sentence of eight years in the presidio of Havana.[20]

Although these problems could be found in almost any army, conditions in New Spain accentuated certain faults. Since so much of the regular army was made up of men condemned to service for crimes or misdemeanors, it was difficult to eradicate the activities which had caused enlistment in the first place. Furthermore, there was not sufficient money made available in military budgets to pay, house, and uniform the troops. Officers bewailed the lack of patriotism and respect for the law exhibited by their soldiers. Colonel Juan Velázquez mirrored other officers' frustrations when he wrote that punishments prescribed by the royal ordinances of 1776 and 1779 for the Spanish army regarding the crimes of abandonment of guardposts, sale of uniforms, drunkenness, and disrespect for officers were totally ineffective in Mexico. During courts-martial his men showed little shame and he believed that they committed crimes to escape service. Sentence to overseas presidios and the normal healthy fear of courts-martial were no deterrent. Since little or no confidence could be placed in guards, he proposed the addition of twenty-five lashes to every sentence in order to restore at least some intimidation and a modicum of respect for authority.[21]

Education of Mexican soldiers was made doubly difficult because of shortages of good NCOs. Colonel Nemesio Salcedo of the Regiment of the Crown, theoretically the elite infantry unit in New Spain, asked Viceroy Branciforte if he could search the jails of Mexico City for prisoners who knew how to read and write. His regiment suffered a severe shortage of literate sergeants and corporals, let alone soldiers, and he was willing to undertake responsibility for any man who might have these qualifications.[22] For the few soldiers who did wish to improve themselves there was opposition to overcome from their own comrades. The tone of soldier society was described by Captain Manuel Antonio Mora, who had worked himself up from common soldier in the 1764 expedition of Juan de Villalba to major of the Lancers of Veracruz by 1802.[23] Many soldiers were as ignorant about the army years after entering service as they were the day they joined:

> ... if these types saw one of their fellows applied to his obligations in the barracks they called him a Franciscan; if he went to Mass or prayed with his rosary, they called him a hypocrite; if his superiors taught him how to write so that he could learn how to handle papers, they called him a *cagatinta* [stupid clerk]....[24]

The general tendency of NCOs and subaltern officers was to beat whatever they could into Mexican recruits rather than to use more humane methods. Although it is difficult to document the exact level of violence in each regiment, it becomes clear that poor treatment and conditions contributed not a little to the high desertion levels. When soldier José de Aguirre of the Regiment of New Spain was asked why he had deserted from Jalapa, he replied, "I deserted because they treated all of us to blows not as the recruits we were, but as if we were old soldiers."[25] In 1804 Viceroy Iturrigaray issued an order to the commanders of the Mexico City garrison condemning sergeants and corporals for using their sabers on soldiers to make them obey. Some deaths and injuries had been reported and the viceroy refused to accept such excesses in the name of authority.[26]

Soldiers' lives were made even more unpleasant due to the poor facilities provided by the army. Most cities lacked proper barracks and even the regulars had to make do with private houses which were permitted to fall into disrepair. In Veracruz, the one place where good barracks and sanitary conditions were essential to protect the health of the troops, men lived in misery. Colonel Vicente Nieto of the Regiment of New Spain stated that the interior of the house which was his regimental barracks was totally wrecked. One wall in the kitchen seemed ready to fall at any moment and the colonel wrote, "I expect news daily of some men dying there or at least news that half a dozen stewards have suffered head injuries." In their rooms, soldiers faced the full inclemency of the climate for there was no glass in the windows. This was not only dangerous to health, but also detrimental to regimental discipline because there was nothing to prevent men from escaping at night. The jail was insecure and there was no place at all for serious criminals. Not only did Nieto consider the building unserviceable as a barracks, but he also believed it was uninhabitable for any rational human beings. The owners, however, thought that anything was good enough for the troops as long as it had a roof and was closed in— ". . . like the place where the rural hacendado shelters his animals for the night."[27]

Enlisted men very often sold their civilian clothing as soon as they joined the regular army; militiamen did so when they were mobilized for duty. Although they were supposed to be issued sheets and blankets, many had nothing to cover themselves with at night except for their army coat.[28] Poor-quality cloth and constant wearing of the same uniform soon reduced garments to patched-up rags which were hardly impressive during inspections or normal duties. The regime expected uniforms to last six or more years and there was great resistance to replacing garments even if the troops had been stationed where the climate made short work of them. Long before this stage arrived, however, the soldier could convert his uniform, badges, arms, and munitions into ready cash. In Mexico City and other garrison towns there were secondhand dealers, wineshops, and *pulquerías* where soldiers could either sell their uniforms or trade them for other garments. They did this to raise funds for drinking and gambling or to finance their desertion from the army. Often, those who pawned their uniforms had good intentions of redeeming them until their luck failed and they decided to desert. Little of the equipment lost in this manner was ever recovered and numerous royal orders prohibited commerce in military uniforms. Royal orders of 1762 and 1766 established a fifty-peso fine for the offense, but in spite of this there was a ready market for uniforms.[29]

Within the regular regiments soldiers took advantage of any loophole in the regulations to improve their own situation and to make a little extra money. When a soldier died, deserted, or was sent to a presidio, his uniform and equipment were taken over by his corporal or by one of his comrades who left his own worn garments as replacements. Some soldiers had uniforms with three or four names rubbed out and the new recruits whom the officers wished to treat with at least some preference were issued ragged uniforms and broken equipment. Attempts to find methods of indelible marking had limited success: silk thread could be pulled out easily and the juice of the avocado stone, which was indelible, tended to spread with time and to stain the garments. To avoid some of these problems, men of the Regiment of the Crown were ordered to mark their uniforms not with their names but with their musket numbers and company insignia. Despite all regulatory efforts, however, incoming recruits invariably ended up with the worst equipment; this meant that they soon fell into debt to the regiment for repairs and replacements. Sergeants often issued recruits muskets with blown-out barrels and then charged them for the repairs. As a result, many new soldiers found themselves in debt to their regiments for at least three years or more. Fear of greater debts led men to hide defects in their muskets to avoid repair bills inflated by the NCOs. The opportunity for profit was particularly good when new uniforms or shoes were issued. At these times, sergeants were to confiscate old uniforms and to cut the tongues out of old shoes to prevent soldiers from rushing to sell their new ones. Since sales of uniforms and cartridges were endemic, the barracks sergeant had to keep his men's equipment under lock. When a soldier needed to repair his uniform or to change a shirt, he was to be watched to make sure he made no attempt to spirit some item of clothing out of the barracks.[30]

If regimental life was difficult for Mexican soldiers, they encountered even greater problems if they fell ill. As in the case of barracks, the viceroys long reported inadequate army hospital facilities without doing much to solve the shortcomings of existing institutions. In Mexico City, the Hospital General y Militar de San Andrés handled most military patients. From the numbers of complaints from soldiers and verifications from the regimental physicians and surgeons, it is evident that the level of patient care was low even by eighteenth-century standards. Soldiers often emerged from the hospital in worse condition than when they entered. Their certifications of full cure proved to be false because officers reported the same symptoms as early as the day after their men returned to duty. Bitter experience soon taught soldiers to choose jail over the hospital and to keep quiet about their ailments until the last extreme.[31] One problem was that the army paid only two reales per day for army patients—a sum that simply did not cover costs. The hospital staff devoted their attention to other patients who paid higher fees leaving the soldiers to look after themselves as best they could. When the curates of the Regiment of Puebla examined the situation, they reported that food and care for soldiers aggravated rather than cured illnesses. Although these conclusions might be expected from grumbling soldiers in a military hospital, the curates were able to document two recent cases in which soldiers had died without any attention from the hospital staff.[32]

Not all of the blame could be attached to the medical staff. One of the army physicians attached to the hospital, Daniel O'Sullivan, was as good a doctor as any to be found in the Spanish world. Irish-born, he studied philosophy, mathematics, and medicine at Toulouse, Montpellier, and Paris before practicing medicine in London and Edinburgh hospitals and visiting other hospitals in Glasgow and Dublin to increase his knowledge. In 1786 he went to Spain and was commissioned in the new Regiment of Puebla. Serving the army in the Hospital of San Andrés, he was promoted to take charge of the venereal disease department. There, he discovered that local physicians had discontinued the use of mercury treatments, substituting other medicines believed to be more helpful in venereal cases. O'Sullivan studied the situation and decided that the new procedures resulted in deaths and unnecessary suffering. Supported by army commanders, he was able to introduce better methods and to improve conditions in the venereal disease wards. Moreover, O'Sullivan developed new techniques for the treatment of liver ailments and chronic diarrhea, which was a serious problem in the Mexican army.[33]

Despite all of its shortcomings, the Hospital of San Andrés probably provided the best care soldiers could expect. Hospitals in the capital operated by the orders of San Juan de Díos and the Belemitos admitted soldiers during epidemics but never voluntarily. Both orders complained that soldier patients interfered with their charity work and they could not afford patients who paid only two reales daily. Viceroy Revillagigedo agreed to increase the rate to three reales, but the army commanders rejected the proposal. By 1808, the father prior of San Juan de Díos wanted to terminate all connections with the army. His hospital could not afford to subsidize soldiers even if they paid three reales. Inability to offer an acceptable level of food, medicine, and care had resulted in angry disputes with Colonel Francisco Menocal of the Infantry of Michoacán; when a soldier died in the hospital the conflict became intolerable.[34] Viceroy Iturrigaray attempted to shift some of the soldiers to the hospital of the Belemitos, but they refused any new patients. Their institution was primarily for convalescence and they did not have the facilities needed to cure diseased patients. The hospital did not have a resident physician or surgeon and its pharmacy was far from complete. In the end, patients from the Regiment of Michoacán had to be transferred to the Hospital of San Andrés notwithstanding the fact that the soldiers were terrified by its reputation for maltreatment.[35]

Medical conditions at the cantonments during invasion alerts were much more primitive than in the capital. According to army plans, provisional military hospitals were to have been established at Córdoba, Orizaba, and Jalapa under the direction of the intendant of the army, Francisco Rendón. Like so many projects requiring major capital outlay, these plans were dropped and the viceroy decided to utilize existing hospitals for the poor run by the friars of San Hipólito at Jalapa and San Juan de Dios at Orizaba.[36] Like their colleagues in the capital, these friars were dubious about their hospitals being used by the army. The hospital at Jalapa could handle eighty to ninety soldiers and at Orizaba the friars managed to expand their facilities from the regular forty-two beds to about ninety. Both orders made it quite clear that they could not afford to hire physicians or surgeons.[37]

Well before the end of 1797 the cantonment hospitals had become a source of real contention. Soldiers equated hospitalization with terminal illness and the regimental doctors supported all of their grievances. The physician of the Infantry of Tres Villas, Francisco Hidalgo, examined the hospital pharmacy at Jalapa and declared all of the medicines not only useless but also harmful to the patients' health. He recommended that the entire stock be taken out and either burned or buried to prevent the possibility of anyone using the drugs.[38] Other reports condemned the friars of San Hipólito for negligence in patient care, the quality of food served, and even for neglecting the most basic aspects of sanitation and cleanliness. Francisco Rendón ordered Colonel Pedro Garibay to investigate and to submit a full report on hospital conditions. Garibay interviewed a number of officers and sent a captain to visit the hospital—declining to go there himself because ".... my delicate stomach would not permit it."[39]

The patients had nothing positive to say about the hospital or the Christian charity of the good friars. Although the food was not too bad, there were not sufficient physicians, nursing staff, and other attendants. Most medicines were putrefied and administered to patients without any order or method. Many reported "insufferable fetidness caused by filthy conditions," lack of adequate ventilation, and heat that aggravated fevers. Several commanders testified that their men had perished in the hospital without even receiving the last sacraments of the Church.[40] There were temporary improvements, but the outbreak of epidemic smallpox in August and September 1797 sent large numbers of soldiers and civilians into the already understaffed hospital. Colonel José Cevallos could not find walking space in the wards and to protect his men he ordered them removed to private homes. Furthermore, when a soldier had fallen ill, the regimental physician and chaplain accompanied the sick man to the hospital only to discover that they could not begin emergency treatment or prescribe medicine because there was no friar in the pharmacy and none was to be found looking after the wards. Since the regiment paid two reales and the treasury an additional two-and-a-half reales, Rendón saw no reason for this abandonment of patients.[41]

Colonel Cevallos was so upset by hospital conditions that he proposed to establish a regimental hospital—offering to fund it himself if the sum provided by the regiment and treasury was not sufficient. He planned to operate the hospital by utilizing his officers, chaplains, and surgeons, and by employing some of his soldiers as nursing staff and orderlies.[42] Although this idea was dismissed by Rendón, who did not think the regiment capable of running a full hospital, it demonstrates the weight of feeling by officers and soldiers. Branciforte censured the prior of San Hipólito and insisted on immediate improvements. Even with this, however, the dispute continued; on November 8, Dr. Hidalgo, accompanied by the major of the Regiment of Tres Villas, an adjutant, the surgeon, and a number of soldiers, pushed his way into the hospital, shoving the friars aside and shouting insults. The prior reported the incident to the viceroy, who ordered Hidalgo to stay away from the hospital.[43] Despite all of this evidence, the Hospital of San Hipólito was still in use during Viceroy Iturrigaray's cantonments in 1805. Rendón, upset by the horror stories concerning treatment and conditions, visited the hospital himself to verify the true situation. He found only the prior and three monks on duty to care for 120 patients. The wards and rooms were dirty and the patients' beds were equally filthy; no attempt was being made in the hospital to scrub with vinegar and to perfume with aromatic herbs necessary to prevent "stench and contagion." Since there were troops from six regiments arriving in Jalapa, the intendant wanted at least twelve friars on duty at all times. He saw the possibility of there being as many as 500 hospitalized soldiers at any given time and once again renewed his proposal for the creation of a provisional military hospital.[44]

The only permanent military hospital in New Spain, the Hospital Real de San Carlos, was located in Veracruz, the disease capital as well as the most important permanent garrison guarding the entry to the viceroyalty. If soldiers feared the hospitals of the interior, they had even more cause for terror when confronted with the prospects of hospitalization at Veracruz. Epidemics of *vómito negro* (yellow fever) and other tropical diseases swept through the port city, attacking the highland soldiers, who lacked any resistance. Recent arrivals huddled in their barracks for several days attempting to convince themselves that the sick soldiers around them were suffering from what was generally believed to be the result of too much brandy and eating bananas. Soon, however, they were hauled off to the army hospital or, during severe epidemics, to provisional hospitals, where a large number died the same day. In the Regiment of the Crown, 853 soldiers died between 1797 and 1800.[45] Between 1791 and 1796 over 80 men of the Dragoon Regiment of Mexico died of illnesses contracted during short visits to Veracruz to deliver shipments of silver and presidarios and 200 men perished while garrisoned at the port.[46] Little wonder that soldiers equated orders to serve at Veracruz with a sentence of death!

The high death rates resulted in large part from the primitive state of medical science and the still insuperable problems with understanding the causes of yellow fever and other tropical diseases. At the same time, conditions in the port hospitals aggravated other difficulties. The Hospital of San Carlos was supposed to hold about 350 patients, but there were often as many as 500 to 600 crammed into its wards.[47] To make matters worse, the building was originally a house rather than a hospital, which made it difficult to adequately use the available space. It was located beside a large, foul-smelling swamp near the city walls. As a result, rooms were always damp and without adequate ventilation. The two surgeries handled all types of operation which meant that the utensils, equipment, and even the walls were impregnated with the mercury used in the treatment of venereal disease. Conditions were even worse when overflow patients were placed in private homes near the hospital. There they were forgotten by the physicians and received no care from the *presidarios* who were supposed to look after them. Hospital food was prepared in the same room used by the dispensary where filthy containers, basins, and old utensils were stored. There was no pharmacy and all drugs were furnished on contract by an *asentista* who received a flat rate of one real daily to prepare medicines for each patient.[48]

The hospital staff demonstrated little dedication to healing the sick. The *practicantes,* assistants to the physicians and surgeons, earned only six reales daily, less than stonemasons in the port city. Nursing staff and orderlies received even less for their services, which meant that the quality of employees was low. Few cared at all about the patients and the staff made little attempt to discharge their duties. When threatened with punishment they deserted, and when left on their own the patients suffered.[49] The use of forced *presidario* labor in the hospital further complicated the situation, and did little to alleviate the poor conditions. The physicians and surgeons, while more dedicated to curing the sick, could not be expected to solve the basic failures of the hospital. In 1796, not a bad year for yellow fever, the two physicians and one surgeon had a caseload of well over one hundred patients rather than the average of forty common in Spain. To assist the doctors there were only two senior assistants, two chaplains, eight staff members, and forty *presidarios*. The surgeon, Juan de la Puerta, excellent in his day, was old and, worst of all, exceptionally nearsighted.[50] When Viceroy Marquina examined the Veracruz hospitals, he could not understand why, in a country of such terrible disease, the hospitals were so poor.[51]

Fear of losing the garrison of Veracruz to disease without a shot being fired at an enemy caused some viceroys to experiment in order to find some means of saving soldiers. Branciforte attempted to keep his troops out of the port altogether, but as Viceroy Iturrigaray discovered, the powerful merchants and residents of the coast refused to submit to this solution. Azanza made a tragic error when he adopted the plan to establish a cantonment at Arroyo Moreno, about two leagues from the port, where the climate was believed to be less punishing to men from the interior. The lessons learned in this experience were expensive in every way. Barracks, kitchens, barns, hospitals, and other buildings for six hundred infantrymen and two hundred lancers cost the treasury over 110,000 pesos.[52] Then, contractors were unwilling to provide meat and other food for the cantonment without a guaranteed monopoly and additional fees as high as 60 pesos per day.[53]

Much worse than these annoyances, it rapidly became evident that the move from Veracruz to an uninhabited site complicated rather than solved the disease problem. High costs caused Azanza to reduce the amount budgeted for hospitals, particularly since he believed no more than 80 to 90 soldiers could possibly be sick at one time.[54] The viceroy was all for rushing the regular and provincial infantry units to the cantonment although many of the buildings were not completed. The plaster was so wet in the barracks that the pins holding hammocks to the walls popped out. The commander, Colonel Pedro de Alonso, warned against excessive haste in settling the troops. Until the hospital was ready, ovens constructed, and furniture arrived for the barracks, he opposed sending 600 men to Arroyo Moreno. By mid-May 1799, Alonso had begun to doubt the wisdom of sending any men at all to the cantonment; the climate appeared to be the same or perhaps even worse than that of the port. Despite all efforts to protect the troops from *vómito negro,* 124 men from the provincial Regiments of Toluca and Celaya had perished.[55] Azanza overruled the "minor obstacles" raised by Alonso and sent provincial troops from the Regiment of Valladolid and the Battalion of Guanajuato from Jalapa and regulars from the Regiments of the Crown and New Spain.

By the end of August, Arroyo Moreno was a disaster area. The hospital was full to overflowing and another building, which was to have been the officers' quarters, had to be used to house the sick.[56] Heavy rains during the summer left the cantonment in the midst of large pools of stagnant water: according to accepted medicial beliefs it was the "exhalations of the putrid waters" that caused the high death rate.[57] Indeed, the moisture did accentuate problems resulting from haste and poor construction. The cement floors broke up so that it was impossible to scrub the surface without forming a mass of mud. In the hospitals where patients spilled feces, urine, and vomit, the horrible odor could not be removed without actually taking up the floor.[58]

With nearly half of the soldiers sent to Arroyo Moreno either dead or dying, Azanza had no alternative other than to order an immediate withdrawal to Veracruz. A junta of physicians, officers, and engineers met to hold a post-mortem into the causes of the tragedy and to recommend ways of making the cantonment habitable. They proposed an expenditure of 50,000 pesos to disinfect the buildings, replace ceilings and floors, and drain swamps. Even so, they did not promise that the contagion could be controlled.[59] A few troops remained on the site to guard abandoned equipment, but no use was discovered for the buildings. By July 1800, only a year after the original construction, the thatched roof of one building had collapsed. There was no alternative to tearing down the remaining edifices for scrap. Military expenditure has changed little over the years. What cost 110,000 pesos in 1799 returned a mere 4,600 pesos for the contract to collect lumber, nails, doors, and other materials.[60]

As we have seen, the yellow fever epidemic of 1799 killed a total of 891 soldiers in the Hospital of San Carlos alone.[61] The Regiments of the Crown and New Spain, which each had a total enlistment of 1,350, lost 875 men—an annual death rate of 32 percent. Including the mortality figures from the Battalion of Veracruz, the regular army garrison lost 928 soldiers. Confronted with the obvious reality of these grim statistics, the survivors—many of them activated provincial militiamen assigned to the regular units—saw desertion as their sole salvation. Although only 394 men were able to make good their flight from Veracruz in 1799, it was not for lack of trying.[62] Many more would have escaped if it had not been for the tough Lancers of Veracruz, who set up posts on the roads and trails inland to intercept deserters. Patrols of militiamen, who knew the country better than anyone else, worked out of Xamapa, San Diego, Antigua, and at the mouth of the Xamapa river, proving themselves to be formidable obstacles to the fleeing soldiers.[63] Many deserted only to find themselves back in their units under much worse conditions after days of exhausting flight without food or rest. Whatever the barriers or the penalties, men continued to seek ways to desert. Even after the disease deaths began to decline, the survivors showed no more willingness to accept duty at the port. As table 28 illustrates, desertion became a greater drain of manpower than yellow fever.[64] Even though many deserters were recovered, they had to be punished and were not available for normal duties. Officers were not exaggerating when they insisted that desertion and disease had destroyed the effectiveness of the regular infantry regiments.

The propensity to desert or "the epidemic of desertion," as officers described it, increased but was by no means caused entirely by hospital conditions and fear of untimely death to yellow fever. Desertion had been a chronic problem ever since the formation of the army in the 1760s. The geography of New Spain permitted men to disappear into isolated regions or frontier zones where they were seldom apprehended. Although monthly lists of deserters were circulated to alcaldes mayores and the agents of the acordada,[65] the regime lacked the machinery needed to watch over society. As a result, legislation designed to prevent desertion and general amnesties for deserters who would return to serve out their enlistments were repeated time after time.[66] It was the carrot and stick approach. Deserters who had settled down and had families and property might send one or two replacements in their places and those who returned themselves received no further penalties. Those who spurned the king's clemency would be prosecuted with the full vigor of

TABLE 28
Deaths and Desertions in the Regiments of the Crown and New Spain, 1800–1802.

Unit	Year	Dead	Deserters	Recaptured Deserters
Regiment of the Crown				
1st battalion at Perote and Veracruz	1800	218	233	82
2nd battalion at Veracruz	1800	95	26	28
1st battalion at Jalapa	1801	29	350	214
2nd battalion at Veracruz	1801	42	27	28
1st and 2nd battalions at Mexico City	1802	34	266	188
Regiment of New Spain at Veracruz	1800–02	802	656	?
TOTALS		1,220	1,558	540

Source: Vicente María de Muesas to Marquina, October 19, 1802, AGI, México, leg. 1465, and Iturrigaray to Caballero, no. 215, August 27, 1803, AGN, CV, series 1, vol. 215.

the law. Anyone convicted of counseling soldiers to desert or giving them civilian clothing, horses, or any other help would be sentenced to six years in the Havana presidios if of noble status, and to the same term in the arsenals or public works if a plebeian. Women were to be fined fifty pesos or exiled from their hometowns for five years. Furthermore, these people would be liable for fines of twelve pesos to cover the regiment's expenses in apprehending the deserter, and the costs of his uniform, horse, and any equipment lost or sold. Those civilians who knew about and did not report deserters were liable to pay the same fines and, in the case of plebeian males, they could be condemned to serve out the deserter's enlistment. To reward civilians who helped prosecute deserters, bounties of ten pesos were paid for capture and four pesos for denunciation. This last initiative sometimes proved too successful; men who were neither soldiers nor deserters were turned in by those to whom they owed money.[68]

There was little the army could do to prevent desertion. Colonel Rafael Vasco, commander of the Infantry Regiment of Mexico during its formation in 1788, became nearly apoplectic when he considered the trials of officers encharged with regimental formation. At Perote in May 1788, he lost two transferees from other regiments, six pardoned deserters, fourteen recent recruits from Valladolid, and five from other cities.[69] He explained some of this desertion as the normal reaction of men removed from the liberty of their home provinces exposed for the first time to military discipline, and he thought that the disagreeable climate and gloomy location of Perote affected others. The Valladolid men, however, were influenced by eighteen *malas mujeres* who incited them to desert. On one occasion seven soldiers departed with one woman. Although the lieutenant of Perote rounded up twenty-two women in connection with the deserters, all were released after warnings. Vasco sent out patrols to chase down deserters, but the mountainous wild country frustrated their efforts. The only authority respected by the soldiers was the Tribunal of the Acordada and Vasco felt that it had not acted with accustomed vigor.[70]

When the Regiment of Mexico was sent to garrison Mexico City in January 1789, Vasco continued to complain about unacceptable desertion rates. Now it was not the isolation of Perote but the urban jungle that permitted deserters to remain hidden from the law. Men adopted the bad customs of their comrades or found their own way to the array of vices available in the city. Vasco proposed a better system to circulate names and descriptions of deserters to all law officers. Even more important, he formulated what he believed to be a permanent solution to the problem. Any soldier who deserted even for the first time must be deported from the viceroyalty to Cuba to complete his enlistment there. This would avoid the high costs of jailing deserters and at the same time remove a source of discredit and embarrassment to the regular army. Since the Cuban regiments always needed recruits, the plan would serve the royal interest. At the same time, the deserter would be helped because if he repeated his crime in Mexico he could expect a long term in overseas presidios. If this rather severe step ended desertion, it would save an enormous drain of regimental funds to cover losses of uniforms, weapons, and the unpaid debts of soldiers.[71]

Sub-Inspector General Pedro de Mendinueta supported Vasco's recommendations although he wanted a ruling from the imperial government since the sentence of deportation to Cuba was more severe than the existing penalty for first-offense desertion. A royal order of June 11, 1778, punished first-time deserters with four months in jail followed by eight years' service in their regiments counted from the day of their apprehension.[72] Viceroy Flórez forwarded the proposal to Spain, where it was adopted with uncharacteristic haste.[73] The imperial cabinet had recently completed a review of disastrous losses of Spanish soldiers from regiments stationed in the Indies. Already proposals had been made to the viceroy and the captain general of Cuba to set up a reciprocal exchange of deserters, vagabonds, idlers, and other criminals who might be employed in the respective defense forces. Flórez rejected this idea because he knew very well that the criminal elements of the islands would lose little time in deserting from the Mexican regiments. They would add their numbers to the existing armies of delinquents and vagabonds at a time when the regime was attempting to stamp them out. In the viceroy's opinion, one way to prevent the spread of criminality in New Spain was to keep the outcasts of other provinces away.[74] The captain general of Guatemala expressed similar sentiments when confronted with the prospect of receiving criminals from Mexico to bolster the Regiment of Guatemala.[75] It was one thing to deport unwanted individuals and quite another to face the prospect of receiving the delinquents of other provinces.

The deportation scheme proved to be something of a disaster for the regular army. The deterrent of Cuba did nothing to lower desertion rates and it became quite obvious that the approach was wrong.[76] Sub-Inspector General Pedro Gorostiza discovered that after two years' operation and the deportation of deserters, petty thieves, soldiers who abandoned guardposts, and other offenders, the army lost nearly a quarter of its strength annually. All of this resulted from Colonel Vasco's poorly conceived proposal. Gorostiza wrote, "If that officer [Vasco] had any idea of the considerable loss of men to this small army, and the multiplicity of causes that produce it, I am convinced that such a thought would not have entered his imagination." In the sub-inspector's opinion, the propensity to desert was strong in all armies and it simply could not be avoided in Mexico, where the majority of soldiers were natives of the country, raised in a state of anarchy, without any education. For such men military discipline was a shock that caused them to desert without really considering the gravity of their act. Often it was for pure whim in order to enjoy some momentary pleasure. Punishment was not particularly severe on first offenses and deserters were indifferent about loss of time if they were recent recruits. However, once having been captured or surrendering themselves voluntarily, soldiers shunned repetition of the crime for fear of severe punishment.[77]

The error then was to deport soldiers before they had a chance to realize the severity of their crime. A similar mistake had been made in Spain in 1773 when the king ordered first-time deserters to be sent to the regiments of Oran and Ceuta. The outflow of troops had been so great that the order was suspended shortly after its implementation. In Gorostiza's opinion, "... the soldier always is a lover of novelty and his slowness to comprehend does not permit him to reflect upon what would be good or bad." Viceroy Revillagigedo agreed with the sub-inspector and suspended the deportation until clarification of the matter by the crown.[78] From this time on, Cuba received only the chronic deserters and the more dangerous variety of criminals. To replace deportation, the viceroy proposed sentencing deserters to terms laboring in the public works of New Spain. Other soldiers would see them performing degrading tasks and be deterred by fear or shame from sharing this fate. Such a solution would halt the population drain and save New Spain from having to assimilate the incorrigible criminals who returned from the Cuban presidios.[79]

Revillagigedo's request for modification of the penalty for first-offense desertion went to the imperial Consejo Pleno de Guerra in June 1793. There was no support for modifying the military ordinances. Soldiers could commit two types of crimes: ordinary offenses the same as any subject, and military offenses. The latter were always more serious because of the solemn oath soldiers had sworn and the contract they had sealed with the crown and *patria*. The gravity of these crimes caused invocation of the full severity of the law and it was for this reason that in military discipline there were so many capital punishments, mutilations of limbs, tortures, and other penalties. The council was loath to make any changes in military law that might make the penal code for soldiers of Mexico different than elsewhere in the empire, but at the same time if deportation of offenders caused difficulties for the army and even depopulation, it was better to sentence men to the public works of New Spain. In crimes which soldiers shared with the civilian population—

drunkenness, prohibited use of firearms, sale of uniforms, and mismanagement of mess money—the viceroy was given authority to levy fitting punishments.[80]

Before long the Mexican army needed its chronic offenders and murderers to keep the ranks of the regular units filled. The transfer of three infantry regiments from New Spain to serve in Cuba, Santo Domingo, and Louisiana forced the army commanders to conserve remaining manpower. When Revillagigedo formed the new regular Infantry Battalion of Veracruz in 1793, deserters guilty of up to three offenses were asked to come forward to serve eight years and thereby earn a full pardon.[81] Although the viceroyalty was still willing to divest itself of 186 dangerous murderers, deserters, and vagabonds,[82] Cuban officers expressed great repugnance at having to receive the incorrigible criminals of New Spain.[83] In 1795 Viceroy Branciforte solved part of the problem when he decided to retain all deserters for use in Mexico.[84]

As has been seen, desertion became even more a concern as the army mobilized forces to meet potential invasion threats. Delinquents from both regular and militia units appeared with alarming frequency in the gangs of highwaymen that plagued isolated regions, and among the criminal elements of the cities. Acordada officials found that these men managed to impede justice even after their capture by claiming the *fuero militar*. Because of the problem's urgency, Branciforte authorized the Acordada to proceed freely against any criminals until testimony was taken and the offenders might be sent to their commanders for punishment.[85] Within the army, since deserters were no longer being shipped to Havana, the regimental majors and adjutants found themselves bogged down with enormous numbers of cases to prepare against chronic delinquents. To compound the confusion, different punishments were prescribed depending upon the exact circumstances of the crime. Deserters who sought asylum in a church or surrendered themselves received lighter sentences than those who were captured by the police.

Cumbersome legal procedures had long been a matter for concern among senior officers. The length and high costs of courts-martial as well as the difficulty in assembling officers to serve in them led to concerted pressures to seek more rapid and less formal methods of dealing with criminals.[86] Frequent complaints to the crown about chronic deserters clogging the jails and causing severe embarrassment as well as administrative problems for their regiments led to legislation designed to speed the legal process. Instead of convening a formal court-martial, the regimental adjutants were empowered to receive the declarations of second-offense deserters, to examine the motives that caused repetition of the crime, and to see whether there were extenuating circumstances that might weigh in favor of the accused. If not, he was to be destined for a presidio without delay—accompanied by copies of his regimental record, a statement of the nature of his crime, and the sentence signed by the commander and indicating the term of punishment. If there were any good reasons for further judicial process, a normal court-martial would be convened.[87]

Another area of potential jurisdictional conflict and administrative delay occurred when deserters and other military criminals sought the asylum of the Church. Viceroy Revillagigedo had become involved in this question when an officer was refused permission by a curate to remove a deserter from Church sanctuary. The issue had been whether the officer upon receiving the prisoner should give his word of honor or the formal *caución juratoria* not to endanger the life or limb of the prisoner.[88] In the latter case, a notary and representative of the vicar general's office had to be present at the church door where the ceremonial exchange took place. This matter went to the archbishop of Toledo, Antonio Ventura de Taranco, who supported the requirement of the formal pledge before offenders might be turned over to the army.[89] Although the privilege of asylum had been restricted by this date,[90] the continuation of jurisdictional and procedural disputes permitted some criminals to escape and others to commit new crimes before they might be extracted from sanctuary. In 1797 a new royal *cédula* streamlined the steps necessary to remove military men and to speed the course of justice.[91]

The question of asylum was more important to deserters than might first meet the eye because capture outside of the Church often meant greater punishment. The penalty of *carreras de baquetas,* or running the gauntlet between two files of one's comrades who whipped the victim with their wooden or metal ramrods, was unquestionably the greatest fear of deserters and other army offenders. The penalty for second offenses or recurrent desertion without Church immunity was six *carreras de baquetas* between two hundred men and ten years in a presidio.[92] There was, however, considerable opposition to this punishment which often maimed and was believed to be responsible for the deaths of some soldiers. The psychological damage was quite clear: once a man had been scourged by this ignominious chastisement, he was not considered fit to remain in his regiment.[93] Appeals to the crown for sentence reductions often resulted in removal of the *baquetas* and there was some doubt about its legality since a royal order in 1788 had ruled that incorrigible deserters sentenced to ten years in the Philippine presidios should not be scourged by their comrades-at-arms.[94] In 1803 the imperial government suspended the baquetas until an investigation could be completed into whether or not the lives of victims were endangered. Physicians and others who possessed information on the potential for maiming or even for death through the baquetas were to give their opinions for or against the penalty. Iturrigaray investigated, but considered the threat of baquetas to be the best deterrent to would-be deserters.[95] By 1805, however, the crown had collected sufficient data to decree the permanent suppression of baquetas for deserters who had not obtained Church immunity. Instead, all second offenders with or without Church sanctuary were to be sentenced to six months in fetters during which they would clean barracks and perform the most degrading tasks of regimental sanitation; after that they were to be sent for ten years to a presidio.[96]

It was one thing to treat the hardened regulars with the full vigor of military law, but quite another when green countrymen of the provincial units committed the same offenses. Nothing could be done to soften penalties imposed upon militiamen temporarily assigned to the regular regiments, but when the provincial militias were mobilized and marched away from their home districts, shock at being away from home, anxiety about abandoned families, and ignorance about the penalties imposed upon deserters caused many men to flee. Viceroy Branciforte saw little purpose in filling jails and presidios with men who otherwise were peaceful citizens. He reviewed the laws on desertion and found a number that could apply in the cases of mobilized militia units.[97] The least harsh was the penalty invoked in the Militia Ordinance of Cuba (1769), and the harshest in a royal order of 1794. The first condemned deserters to two years in public works as a presidario and the second to six years in the royal arsenals. Although the ministry of war accepted the lesser penalty,[98] most viceroys were unwilling to impose even this upon militiamen. Deserters from the provincial Regiment of Mexico at Córdoba in 1797 were released with notations on their service records even though they had been found guilty by courts-martial.[99]

There were dangers in exercising too much leniency with militiamen for they were the most adept at making good their escape and then avoiding capture. In 1807 Corporal Manuel Merino and two soldiers of the Company of Xilotepec deserted from the cantonment and returned to their home provinces. Since all three were musicians, they appeared at fandangos in and around Xilotepec where everyone could see that they had not been apprehended. Others of their company still at the cantonment became restless and annoyed—particularly because they had wives and children to support while the three deserters were bachelors. Before long, other men, encouraged by the musicians' successful escape, also began to desert.[100]

With the increased use of provincial soldiers in the cantonments and in the Veracruz garrison, it was not long before Mexicans from all provinces felt the implications of mobilization. Without even considering the social and economic impact of removing farmers, workers, and tradesmen from their homes, so many died in places such as Arroyo Moreno and Veracruz, or returned home permanently disabled, that it is hardly surprising that those who could not avoid enlistment looked for other escapes. In 1797 the provincial Regiment of Mexico stationed at Córdoba lost 106 men to desertion— about an eighth of the total enlistment. By 1801, however, Viceroy Marquina experienced difficulties keeping together even an elite force of provincial militiamen. Concerned by the consequences of removing entire regiments from their home provinces, he mobilized only the twelve grenadier companies of six infantry regiments, about eight hundred men, and stationed them in Mexico City.[101] In a three-month period, eighty-one grenadiers deserted and another forty-nine were absent without permission for more than three days and supposed to be deserters. The officers tried every method to reduce desertion—warnings of severe penalties, patriotic speeches to stimulate love for honor and duty, and even mild treatment—without notable success. When the troops were told that they were to be marched to Jalapa, they feared this meant Veracruz and thirteen deserted the same night. More left on subsequent days and Marquina had to take the rather exceptional step of appearing before the troops to promise that he would not send them to the port unless an actual invasion occurred.[102] Exactly the same experience confronted officers when twelve additional companies were ordered to the capital to form a one-thousand-man light infantry column. In only four months 20 percent of the soldiers deserted.[103] Some officers became so frustrated by their inability to prevent the disappearance of their militiamen that they recommended increasing punishments the same as those meted out to regular soldiers.[104]

Remarkably, the officers' constant frustrations over the behavior of their troops resulted in few major breaches of army ordinances. Generally speaking, Spanish military law and procedures carried impartial if rigorous justice. There were, of course, cases of officers who used the *fuero militar* to protect their men against local magistrates and other justices, but the army authorities always were quite clear that privileges encompassed in the *fuero militar* were to honor and not to grant special exemptions of any kind from existing laws.[105] Even during the worst disputes over whether military or royal justices held jurisdiction over militiamen, the *auditor de guerra* insisted that the crown had no intention of releasing these individuals from the law or of pardoning their crimes. The only change would be that military judges were the ones to apply the law in the cases of their men.[106] As Manuel Antonio de Mora pointed out, "... the royal service has no intention through the *fuero* to authorize delinquents in their vices and joining the militia excuses no one from good behavior and respect for parents and betters."[107] Indeed, it was held that men who enjoyed the *fuero militar* were under an even greater obligation than ordinary citizens to abide by the law and to go out of their way to assist in helping to defend the law.[108]

Abuses were not permitted to go far before militiamen were brought back under control. When, for example, soldiers of the provincial Cavalry Regiment of Querétaro employed in the tobacco factory used their military affiliation to disobey their foremen or justify shoddy workmanship and wastage of tobacco, the tobacco factory officials attempted to invoke their own judicial powers to quell the *cigarreros milicianos*. One worker had punched an overseer and all of the militiamen wore the red cockade on their hats identifying them as soldiers. Whenever they were reproached or given orders, they shouted that they had no other chiefs than their officers.[109] Although the militiamen had been ordered to wear the cockade to identify their militia affiliation and to keep them out of trouble with the local *justicias* and *ministros de vara,* the factory overseers wanted them to check their hats upon arriving at work so they would not be distinguishable from other workers. Tobacco factory workers belonging to the militia in Mexico City had been similarly haughty and insubordinate until Viceroy Branciforte ordered them to subject themselves to the regulations governing their duties or to expect suitable corrective punishment by their superiors at the factory.[110] Viceroy Iturrigaray rejected the argument that militiamen should be commanded to remove their badges and cockade, but at the same time he refused to condone any misdemeanors, shoddy work, or lack of subordination to their superiors committed under protection of the *fuero militar*. If further breaches of discipline arose in the Querétaro factory, he promised to take immediate steps to inflict exemplary punishment.[111]

If the viceroys had to intervene in relatively minor incidents or to discipline the occasional officers who permitted their men to abuse other jurisdictions, there was no similar room for error in cases where the court-martial was used. The *consejos de guerra* left no stone unturned in their effort to gather evidence for or against the accused. When, for example, first-time deserter José de Aguirre of Toluca testified that he was illiterate and no one had informed him about the punishment for his crime, no decision could be reached until it was settled whether or not the regulations had been read to the recruit at the time he entered the army. When the seven officers of the court-martial voted four to three for conviction and a six-year term in a presidio, the *auditor de guerra* found sufficient doubts to overturn the decision and return Aguirre to his regiment.[112] In the case of soldier José Joaquín Contreras of the Regiment of New Spain, the court-martial went to considerable trouble to gather evidence. Contreras, originally a militiaman from the Battalion of Oaxaca, deserted first from Orizaba in 1797 and was sentenced to serve in the regular army for the duration of the war. He deserted twice from Veracruz—the last time from the hospital—he threw away his uniform to avoid detection. The case appeared to be simple and the prosecutor demanded the penalty of six *carreras de baquetas* followed by ten years in a presidio. Contreras's defender (attorney), Lieutenant Félix Olla of the Regiment of Tlaxcala, who was serving with the Infantry of New Spain, was able to turn the case around by arguing that Contreras was the only son of a widowed mother who had three daughters to support and therefore he never should have been inducted in the first place. The court sent to Oaxaca to obtain information on this claim and learned from Major Luis de Zárate that Contreras had entered the army because of poor behavior and that his mother had remarried. Although these facts renewed the prosecution's demand for conviction, evidence from soldiers of Oaxaca suggested that there were grounds for a pardon. They testified that Contreras's mother worked herself to exhaustion as a seamstress to support her three daughters. In the end, the court-martial officers voted unanimously to pardon Contreras and to release him from the army.[113]

Just or not, the army of New Spain failed to perform as its planners had intended. In establishing the army in Mexico, Spain was all too successful in transplanting the weaknesses rather than the strengths of European armies. Very often it was the dregs, rather than the stout artisans, tradesmen, and laborers, who filled the ranks and suffered duty in the hostile environment of Veracruz. Although part of the failure may be attributed to the small amount spent on colonial defense, it is clear that the martial virtues Spain hoped to inculcate did not take root. Faced with the very real terrors of having to serve in the Veracruz garrison or outside the narrow confines of their home provinces, Mexicans deserted, risked the lash, and even took a chance on being deported to an overseas presidio from which there was little likelihood of return. When all was said and done, there was little advantage to service in the regular army and, as time passed, the provincial militiamen adopted the same view. Frederick the Great once remarked, "If my soldiers began to think, no one would remain in the ranks."[114] Mexicans did not even have to think to see the disadvantages of army life.

11
CAST ADRIFT

Despite all of the difficulties in raising military forces and creating a defense for Spain's most valuable American possession, officers were fairly confident about the future until the disasters which began to rock the empire in 1808. Using hindsight, it is easy to conclude that internal weaknesses should have caused much more self-examination on the part of both army planners and civilian bureaucrats. But all of the storms of the eighteenth century had been weathered without untoward results; Indian conspiracies, criollo discontent, and even the possibility of an enemy invasion had come and gone. The army had improved at least to the degree that it was able to field a force of almost sixteen thousand men and to keep them under arms for over a year. Yet no one was prepared for the shock of the Napoleonic invasion of Spain and the Bourbons' ignominious surrender and abdication. As the pillar of absolutism crumbled, it left its supporters clinging to an increasingly precarious position beset by what appeared to be a multitude of enemies. Efforts to shore up the regime and to prevent further erosion brought momentary hopes, but defeats lowered expectations and resulted in a general spirit of defeatism. The "desired one," Ferdinand VII, was not present to rally the imperial cause; the general uprising of the Spanish population, the alliance with Britain, and momentary victories at Bailén and Zaragoza gave cause for optimism until the even greater inundation of Iberia by French armies. Although the gestures continued, it was difficult to believe the propaganda generated to whip up the patriotism of Mexicans and to make them believe that national salvation against Napoleon was possible. As we have seen in the August 1808 incident with the French schooner *Vaillant* at Veracruz, no one behaved very well when confronted with a small example of the French menace. And since the United States refused to recognize the provisional governments in Spain, many Mexicans came to believe in the possibility of their northern neighbors joining with the French in a joint invasion to further the cause of Bonaparte.

By the beginning of 1810, the regime in New Spain had suffered a series of grave blows to its depleted morale. There were new rumors of a French expeditionary force being formed at Brest, and three months' silence from any vestigial independent Spanish government caused fears that the patriots had been crushed once and for all. In the north, incidents along the Texas border with Louisiana tended to confirm the hostility of the Americans. Confronted with the unknown and depressed far more than they cared to admit, army officers fixed their vision upon the international situation and the danger of invasion. For these men, most of whom were patriotic Spaniards, the ordeal of witnessing the cataclysm which rolled over their homeland was a tragedy of immeasurable proportions. Instead of being able to join the struggle to the death, they found themselves stationed in a colony where the criollos expressed only superficial patriotism and the rest of the population was cavalier in its disrespect for the imperial cause. The only consolation was that America remained Spanish during the ruin and desolation of the mother country. While some officers doubted the possibility of restoring the Spanish Bourbons, others saw the New World colonies remaining as the beacon of Spanish civilization. As Brigadier Pedro de Alonso wrote:

> Mexico must become the refuge, shelter, and haven for all families who escape the slavery of the Continent and emigrate to this New Spain. It is rich, abundant, and free of the quixotic ideas of the tyrant who wants to seduce us in an attempt to conquer us.[1]

Many of the senior officers, members of the audiencia and other tribunals, and Viceroy Lizana shared these preoccupations. Even the bulwark of the British navy was not sufficient to allay pessimism. Ironically, neither Alonso nor other officers who saw Mexico as a haven for Spanish refugees were able to foresee their own struggle. Within a few months, their dreams and fears would be shattered by the near-spontaneous uprising of Father Miguel Hidalgo's Indian and casta hordes.

In many respects, the gachupines who governed New Spain engineered their own downfall. Instead of making the most of a minority position, the Spaniards pursued a course of precipitous confrontation. The army was dragged into most of the events as a horrified but immobile spectator. The parade of calamities began with news of the mutiny of Aranjuez and the March 18, 1808, abdication of Charles IV in favor of Ferdinand VII. The *Gazeta de México* reported the unusual story in some detail and Mexico celebrated the royal accession. The fiestas were still going on when at the end of June, the merchant vessel *Ventura* brought news of the degrading pilgrimage to Bayonne and the Bourbon abdication in favor of a regent, the Duke of Berg.² Immediately, the European Spanish minority suspected a criollo conspiracy to take power. Wealthy merchants, members of the audiencia, and others pressed Iturrigaray to recognize any remaining authority in Spain rather than to create a provisional government for the viceroyalty. When in August two delegates arrived from the Junta Suprema of Seville—Juan Jabat, an old enemy of Iturrigaray, and Manuel Francisco de Jáuregui, the viceroy's brother-in-law—the gachupines were given a new lease on life. After receiving a jubilant welcome in Veracruz, the junta's agents were able to strengthen the European faction in Mexico City.³

Confronted by a situation which confounded Bourbon administrators throughout the Americas, Iturrigaray had begun to build a political base. One of the most important steps was to overcome unpopularity resulting from the infamous 1804 Consolidation Decree. Seeking new sources of funds to finance the imperial war effort, the crown had confiscated the Church's invested capital. In fact, however, the attack on Church wealth was much more a blow to those who had borrowed the money. The recall of mortgages and other loans caused severe hardships and has been identified by historians as a primary source of criollo disenchantment.⁴ Like many others, Iturrigaray appears to have believed that Spain would not be able to resist the domination of Napoleon. Seeking the most viable constituency, he began to court the criollo faction centered in the cabildo of Mexico City. When he supported the concept of convoking a *junta de gobierno* to discuss the important issues of the day and to advise him in case he had to exercise personal command over the army of operations, the gachupín faction cried treason and began to plot their own course of action.⁵

Already by the beginning of August, Iturrigaray was in grave political jeopardy. No matter what he did to extricate himself from one crisis, he sank deeper into the growing turmoil. Some sectors of the population attributed his every move to a plot to weaken ties with Spain or even to declare himself the emperor of an independent Mexico.⁶ Others hoped that this was an accurate description of the situation. Looking back upon these events, José María Luis Mora, the nineteenth-century liberal historian, condemned Iturrigaray for not exerting his leadership to proclaim a bloodless declaration of independence.⁷ Certainly the viceroy was fully aware of the growing danger and had some premonition of the fate that was to befall him in mid-September. The consulado and other tribunals reported increasing numbers of seditious papers appearing in Mexico City and elsewhere.⁸ Rumors reached Iturrigaray about the formation of parties and he was convinced that Juan Jabat either carried instructions to discredit him or was acting on his own.[9] Finally, on September 5, 1808, Iturrigaray informed the audiencia he intended to depart from New Spain; he would relinquish interim command to Field Marshal Pedro Garibay until the document signifying his successor could be opened. Whether or not the threatened resignation was a political ploy to gain support, Iturrigaray's arguments made good sense. He insisted that he had done everything within his power to prove his loyalty, but could not recognize the Junta Suprema of Seville when he received similar representations from the juntas of Asturias, Valencia, Aragón, and Mallorca. All of these groups claimed to be sovereign and he saw no legal case to accept such pretensions. Instead of selecting a favored junta, he dispatched a schooner to Cádiz with funds to assist all groups resisting Napoleon.[10]

The actual overthrow of Iturrigaray appears to have been provoked more by the prevailing spirit of fear and mistrust rather than by any single event. In their imaginations, the European Spaniards were able to manufacture a full-blown conspiracy from a number of rather innocuous viceregal measures to shore up the government. Besides convoking the advisory juntas, Iturrigaray made appointments in the royal exchequer, and promoted six officers to the rank of brigadier and García Dávila to field marshal. These acts were taken as outright preemptions of sovereignty rather than attempts to stabilize the administration and army during a period of interrupted communications with the mother country.[11] If these charges were not sufficient proof, the Europeans believed rumors that Iturrigaray planned to cement his alliance with the criollos by naming confirmed enemies of the gachupines to the audiencia—lawyers Juan Francisco de Azcárate and José Antonio Cristo, Friar Melchor de Talamantes, and others. Iturrigaray's difficulties with powerful elements at Veracruz, his apparent refusal to defend the port, and his threat to send regular troops to chastise unruly citizens of the coast added to the general suspicions.

A major factor in the actual timing of the coup was that the Europeans learned about troop movements which could be taken as further proof of viceregal plotting. The Infantry of Celaya and the Dragoons of Nueva Galicia, commanded by Colonels Manuel Fernández Solano and Ignacio Obregón, known friends and supporters of Iturrigaray, were on the road to Mexico City. While the mobilization of these troops was merely a precaution to bolster the capital's garrison, the Europeans believed that Iturrigaray intended to use them in his evil machinations. If they did not move quickly, they would lack the numerical strength and force of arms to halt what now seemed to be an independence movement headed by the viceroy. According to another rumor, Iturrigaray planned to move the troops from the cantonment to Mexico City so that he could convince them to support him and to demand his coronation.

This event was believed to be slated for October 14, 1808, the holiday of San Calexto and Ferdinand VII's birthday. On the same day, the plotters were to burn the Basilica of the Virgin of Guadalupe and to begin a general insurrection. Talamantes and others in the criollo party would blame the Europeans for this act so that they could crush all gachupines. Finally, the French crew of the schooner *Vaillant* detained in August was to be freed and sent to the island of Guadeloupe to request troops for New Spain.[12]

Although Carlos María de Bustamante and others continued to warn Iturrigaray about the possibility of a conspiracy to overthrow him and questioned the advisability of placing trust in a viceregal guard made up of mercenaries from the Regiment of Commerce, the viceroy did not realize the true gravity of the situation.[13] Having obtained the audiencia's acquiescence, Gabriel Yermo and 232 European merchants and *cajeros* accomplished their plan with shocking ease. They carried out a swift assault upon the viceregal palace after midnight on September 16, 1808. One guard was killed when he attempted to resist. Iturrigaray and his family were arrested. The experience was traumatic not only for the colony; Vicente de Iturrigaray recalled, "I was only 6 years old, but I can still see those men, most of them drunk, enter our palace uttering atrocious threats."[14]

Mexico City awoke to find Iturrigaray in custody and the criollo leadership jailed. The gachupín conspirators were so thorough in their operations that the city was stunned into temporary silence. Garibay was sworn in as viceroy the same day despite the fact that there was no legal precedent for such a step. The new regime lost no time in convoking all available army officers, civil leaders, and ecclesiastical authorities. They heard an explanation of the events and were required to swear allegiance to Garibay. The octogenarian field marshal, hardly the decrepit weakling some historians have described, took his seat at the head of the audiencia. His first major acts concerned the disposition of the army and sought to solve some of the major defensive issues. As has been mentioned, he made a gesture of good will to Veracruz by returning Governor-Intendant García Dávila and transferring artillery companies to bolster the port defenses. García Dávila was most anxious to please since his controversial promotion to field marshal was still very much on the minds of the victors. Garibay revoked the rank, but made a strong appeal to the Junta Central of Spain for its return.[15] Command of the army of operations was awarded to Brigadier Conde de Alcaraz, who was highly critical of Iturrigaray's policies and could be trusted to welcome the change. His orders were to exercise "prudence and in case of trouble use caution corresponding to the circumstances." Quite generally, Garibay brought a feeling of legality and continuity to what could have been a much more difficult transition. His rather laconic interpretation of the events surrounding the coup for the Junta Central underlined his own desire to prevent a massive purge against criollo leaders.[16]

Much to the surprise of many historians and some contemporary observers, the army accepted the overthrow of Iturrigaray without apparent concern. There was none of the resistance which characterized later Mexican armies confronted with the political removal of a popular chief of staff. Lucas Alamán mentioned some discussions about plots within the cantonment to free the ex-viceroy, but nothing came of them.[17] Colonel Joaquín Colla and Major Martín Angel Michaus of the Regiment of Commerce were removed from their commands for inflammatory statements, but merchant politics appear to have been the primary reason. Since the senior officers belonged to the gachupín minority, they shared the fears of the Mexico City conspirators about the criollo menace.[18] Equally important, the army had no tradition of interference in the political life of New Spain. Confronted with the successful coup, the officers had no taste for intervention against Pedro Garibay, who was one of the most senior commanders.

Despite differences of opinion, most observers agreed that the overthrow of Iturrigaray resulted from the criollo-gachupín rivalry. One angry criollo account—an anonymous letter said to have originated in New York—appeared in California during November 1808. The author described the "most inflamed division and hostility" between the two factions. The Europeans had arrested the viceroy because the criollos wanted to crown him king. Even after the coup, the gachupín residents of the capital were said to be afraid to leave their homes. In the letter writer's opinion, the Europeans would say:

> Now we will inflict exemplary punishment upon this vile criollo scum and we will make them recognize our superiority: not a count nor a marqués will remain, few clerics will escape, and even fewer lawyers. America will receive the destiny we wish to give it.[19]

He went on to condemn the criollo elite for their lack of patriotism, enlightenment, and energy. They were uneducated and could seldom think of anything more than eating and sleeping. And the rest of the population was even worse. How else could three hundred or so Europeans instill such terror and fright? He described the army as a "heap" of men and concluded:

> What are the talents of soldiers, officers, and commanders who in cold blood stand aside while their general is arrested and conducted to a castle by 40 merchants who never have handled muskets? These are the

men some call an army and even a respectable army. Of course this must be in irony because they do not feel the impulses of valor, the fire of honor, and the fury that such shameful arrogance should arouse in the hearts of the most peaceful. These men are not soldiers nor do they deserve the name. Each is a painted pasteboard box that cannot breathe or become inflamed unless it is put in a bonfire.[20]

These were bitter words but they explained the frustrations of those who saw their own plans dashed to pieces by a small minority. Indeed, the new regime did not expect any interference from the troops of the Jalapa cantonment. Iturrigaray and his family were conducted to Veracruz through Jalapa, where the army could have made its move. Only fifty militiamen of the Dragoons of Michoacán, replaced by an equal number of the Dragoons of the Príncipe at Perote, accompanied the merchant volunteers and men of the Urban Cavalry Squadron guarding the ex-viceroy. At the cantonment, regular dragoons of the Regiment of Spain took over and delivered the prisoners to the Castle of San Juan de Ulúa.[21] Garibay was anxious to dispatch Iturrigaray for Spain; he ordered Governor García Dávila to arrange with the captain of the British frigate *Melpomene* or any other vessel in the vicinity of Veracruz to transport the prisoner to Cádiz. In fact, however, it was not until December 9, 1808, that Iturrigaray sailed on the vessel *San Justo*.[22]

There were a few men who, recognizing the true dangers for the future, dared to protest against the gachupín conspirators and to speak in favor of Iturrigaray. Manuel de Jáuregui defended his relative against the charge of treason: he said a sixty-eight-year-old officer with more than fifty years' noble service to Spain was not likely to turn traitor to his fatherland. If Iturrigaray made mistakes and was gullible in accepting advice from elements in the cabildo of Mexico, his policy had been to reduce the level of rivalry between the Europeans and Americans. Since force did not seem possible as a means of retaining control over Mexico, Iturrigaray sought to obtain the cooperation of the competing factions. The advisory juntas had been created to discuss defense, raise loans for the mother country, and allow Mexicans to participate in other areas. He believed that the criollos would be flattered by this method; they would see New Spain raised from a colonial position into that of a Spanish province.[23] Another friend of the deposed viceroy, the Marqués de Casa Alta, dismissed all of the charges made by Yermo and his party. In his opinion, "there are always those who are opposed to policies for private ends and even more so here where interest governs everything."[24] Like Jáuregui, the marqués condemned both the Mexico City and Veracruz merchants for manipulating the truth to serve their own private concerns. In the coup's aftermath, the inhabitants of New Spain were more divided than ever before. While the country was surrounded by external enemies, the gachupines, criollos, and Indians refused to cooperate. Casa Alta saw an exceedingly bleak future for both Mexico and Spain.[25]

Even a detailed investigation by the audiencia failed to turn up any hard evidence to support the conspirators' actions. Witnesses from Veracruz attempted to prove that Iturrigaray wanted an assembly in Mexico City in order to punish the patriotic population of the port and suggested that the viceroy desired to be king.[26] Others attacked Iturrigaray for having permitted a relaxation of military discipline at the cantonment and for releasing officers who wanted to return to their homes. Every promising bit of dirt was exposed and discussed at length. Nonetheless, once hearsay, rumor, and innuendo had been set aside, there was nothing left of the case. Those who knew the facts had no difficulty challenging the detractors. Manuel Velázquez de Léon, secretary of the viceroyalty under Iturrigaray, pointed out that in the area of defense policy, the viceroy had been governed by royal orders and the decisions of *juntas de guerra*. The suspicions of the Veracruz merchants and others simply were not correct.[27]

As many observers realized, the calm of colonial Mexico would not be restored. Those who were the strongest in their support of the Spanish cause against Napoleon condemned any criticism of the gachupín faction. Their extremism drove away many patriotic Mexicans whose first impulse had been to defend the mother country. From the arrival of the first news describing the mother country's agony, a call to arms resulted in the formation of large unorganized militia units throughout New Spain called Volunteers of Ferdinand VII. In the intendancy of Puebla, 1,782 men volunteered although many were found to be overage or of poor racial extraction. From Texcoco, 6,000 Indians offered their services and in San Luis Potosí the employees of merchants formed a company and offered to pay for mounts, uniforms, and arms.[28] The Mining Tribunal offered to manufacture one hundred cannon with carriages and to raise eight artillery companies. Students from the school of mining who were trained in mathematics were to serve as subaltern officers.[29]

While many of these volunteers either lost interest or were dismissed prior to September 1808, others became an impediment to the cause they claimed to serve. In Mexico City, for example, they ran wild after the overthrow of Iturrigaray. They took the law into their own hands and refused to obey orders from army officers. Bustamante, a witness to their activities, wrote, "they gambled, drank, and committed excesses in the patio of the viceregal palace as if it was the foulest brothel."[30] Even Garibay condemned the Volunteers of Ferdinand VII. As far as he could see, they came from all classes and conditions; they lacked discipline, seldom were led by trained officers, and dressed in cast-off portions of uniforms according to their tastes. Most were ignorant of the most elementary military knowledge. Fearing that these vigilantes would cause irreparable harm, Garibay retired them from active duty and sought to reorganize the militia companies.[31]

In order to rationalize enlistment and to begin a training program, Garibay ordered Félix Calleja and Joaquín Gutiérrez de los Ríos to weed out troublemakers and to make the volunteers more useful.[32] Since the consulado of Mexico was a main pillar of the new regime, the viceroy approved a merchant plan to raise ten companies of one hundred men each which would take the name "Volunteers of Ferdinand VII." This time, care was to be taken to bar noxious plebeian elements and other troublemakers from participation. Instead of enlisting any volunteers, only the merchants, their employees, and their sons would be admitted. If there were not sufficient men in these categories, genuine volunteers from the guilds could make up the shortages. All men had to be whites although there was to be no discrimination between gachupines and criollos. To prove this point, the viceroy insisted upon equal division of the officer commissions. There must be five American captains, lieutenants, and sublieutenants to match the five Europeans of each rank. The officers were to be mixed in the companies and wherever possible the NCOs were to be divided along the same lines.[33] Similar difficulties with the Volunteers of Ferdinand VII in Puebla resulted in the same kind of reorganization and dismissal of those who had enlisted for less than patriotic reasons. Intendant Conde de la Cadena created two battalions of five hundred men each. While few men of the local elite were enthusiastic about serving as officers, the units were ready to defend the city by the time of the Hidalgo revolt.[34]

Despite enthusiasm for the deposed monarch, Garibay was not given a moment of peace. There were enemies everywhere and the question was to identify which ones posed the greatest dangers. Along the coasts and northern frontier, both France and the United States threatened to invade Mexico during Spain's weakness. Even more alarming, however, the signs of internal unrest did not disappear. In Mexico City, the removal of the leading criollo politicians provoked rather than silenced the bitterness between the factions. Almost every day, seditious pamphlets, broadsides, and crude slogans appeared on the walls of public buildings, churches, cemeteries, and in other locations. On April 1, 1809, for example, signs reading *"Libertad cobardes criollos"* were put up in the church of La Merced and in the cathedral. Identification of the culprit was impossible because so many people passed through the churches. The watchmen and janitors were of no help since they were illiterate members of the *"ínfima plebe."* Often they washed down the slogans with other announcements and threw away seditious posters with the other garbage. When the priests proved incapable of preventing the appearance of prorevolutionary statements, Chief Inquisitor Isidro Sainz de Alfaro stepped up the level of security. Spies were stationed in the cathedral and in other buildings used by those who wished to stir up public dissension.[35]

At the same time, anonymous letters from the provinces were mailed to members of the audiencia, the viceroy, and to other leading figures. *Oidor* Guillermo Aguirre received information about a new criollo conspiracy said to be directed by the anti-European Marqués de Rayas. Garibay was to be assassinated and Colonel Miguel de Emparán of the Dragoons of Mexico was supposed to take military command of the movement.[36] As will be seen, there was sufficient truth in this report to support other rumors circulating through the capital. Garibay responded by concentrating troops from the cantonment and other garrisons in Mexico City. Gabriel Yermo and the gachupín leaders opposed this approach; in their view, the appearance of so many troops caused the increase in seditious conversations. Yermo condemned the new administration for not having dealt severely enough with subversive elements.[37] Clearly, there was a falling out among the victors which could not help but weaken the regime.

By the beginning of 1809, rebellious mutterings and slogans had given way to a number of more frightening plans to declare independence or to establish a provisional government to rule in the absence of Ferdinand VII. One broadside, sent to a number of priests and government officials, outlined some major economic issues as well as attacking the gachupín faction. The author, Manuel Palacio, curate of Huichapán, informed Mexicans that every year they lost a total of 18,000,000 pesos which flowed out of the colony. In a single decade, 180,000,000 pesos left Mexico for Spain. If this was not enough to impoverish the Mexicans, the imperial government had introduced the Consolidation Decree expropriating Church funds and other repressive levies. Viceroys sold subdelegations and other offices "to satiate their greed and to make every one of the purchasers into an enemy of the people." As for the Junta Central which claimed to rule America, what right, he asked, did they have to reduce Mexicans into the vassals of the vassals of Spain?[38] Another letter, signed with the pseudonym Justo Patricio Paiseron, ordered Mexicans to "open your eyes and know the terrible evils that threaten if you do not prepare right now to counter them." Napoleon had crushed Spain and it was up to New Spain to declare independence in order to save itself and the Catholic faith for Ferdinand VII. Garibay, the audiencia, and representatives from the provinces should form a sovereign representative junta just as the people of the peninsula had done.[39] The author of this letter, an audiencia lawyer named Julián

Castillejos, was soon under arrest for his proposal. With several others charged with writing or circulating seditious materials, he was sent to Cádiz for trial.[40]

Of much more concern to Garibay than the occasional seditious letter, the general level of unrest began to shake the regime's confidence in its ability to restore order. Censorship of private correspondence in and out of Mexico City produced some candid remarks about how literate Mexicans viewed the situation. Luis Lozano, for example, wrote to his brother José Ignacio, curate of Mexquitic near San Luis Potosí, stating that he had not heard any news from the north for two mails and he was very concerned. While Lozano made a point of describing himself as apolitical, he did express shock at the poor reasons the police had given for jailing some individuals. He reported rumors of tension and revolt from the province of Tepeaca near Puebla and from Tlaxcala. The capital was not calm, but the viceroy was taking every precaution to maintain full security. Lozano stated:

> Never have I seen this city guarded by so many troops. The double patrols of infantry and cavalry do not leave the *barrios* for a moment and they do not neglect the center of the city. Artillery and the grenadier column garrison the palace and there are a great number of secret spies observing malcontents...[41]

Lozano did not believe that an insurrection was imminent, but he was worried enough to consider departing from Mexico City before very long. He found himself in real trouble because he enclosed a copy of Justo Patricio Paiseron's inflammatory letter.

In another intercepted personal communication, Julián Carbonel of Guanajuato, writing to Julián Rivero in Mexico City, pointed out the real thirst of educated men for hard news. In his view:

> ... the gazette of that city vexes me more and more because of its poor selection of news and lack of discussion of the events. It would be tolerable in another type of publication, but not in one dedicated to informing the public about occurrences of which for their advantage they must be informed.[42]

Censorship of news or the falsification of some aspects of important stories were poor techniques since no one could develop a true picture of the political situation. Carbonel concluded:

> The illnesses of the body politic are the same as those suffered by an individual. If this person cannot hide his true condition so that the

symptoms are known for his cure, neither must it be done with the former and with greater reason since so many are involved; in the case of the individual only he is prejudiced.[43]

This material in itself did not attract the censor, but Carbonel referred to a reference Rivero had made in a previous letter to the *Moniteur Français*. Although he did not accept Napoleonic propaganda—"we are not as superficial as the French or as weak as the Italians"—mere contact with a French publication was a serious matter. Besides, Carbonel had been in contact with the Marqués de Rayas, who had recently arrived in Guanajuato. He mentioned his support for the defense made by the marqués on behalf of Iturrigaray.

As the atmosphere of suspicion deepened, casual comments or remarks were sufficient to cause individuals to report what they interpreted to be examples of dangerous sedition. On one occasion, the commander of the Nuevo Santander cavalry, José Florencio Barragán, let his tongue slip in a simple conversation with Father Bernardo de Oca of the Divina Pastora mission near Rioverde. Barragán arrived at the mission from Querétaro and when asked to relate any news, he said that while nothing had been heard from Spain since January, it was fruitless to hope that Bonaparte had faltered. He blamed the disasters in Spain upon Ferdinand VII for having quarreled with his father. If this was not enough evidence to cause denunciation, Barragán went on to dismiss the Volunteers of Ferdinand VII in New Spain as "a multitude without leadership or determined direction."[44] Barragán received a severe reprimand for his indiscretion. In another instance, a retired army captain, Francisco Blanco, reported from Perote that, during a recent night of theatrical comedies, one of the players stated, "*Señores,* do they say that a new viceroy is coming to govern us? Will we have to permit the gachupines to rule us?" Despite the dangerous nature of these statements, the audience, including the local *teniente de justicia,* remained quiet. As a good European, Blanco believed that it was his duty to report the matter. An investigation followed in which witnesses identified an actor of medium build, dark complexion, dressed in white trousers, a palmetto hat, and with bare legs and feet. It was assumed that he was a traveller from Veracruz who was heading into the interior.[45]

In response to the criticism and antagonism between the factions, Garibay announced his determination to publish all of the news—good or bad. He begged the people of New Spain to "forget for now and forever the sobriquets criollo and gachupín." All were Spanish subjects and elements of the same nation. He reminded Mexicans that the Consolidation Decree had been suspended definitively. Rather than continuing to squabble over old issues, he asked all sectors to denounce real traitors and to turn in seditious papers.[46] Church leaders dealt with the same themes, exhorting the populace to resist the spirit of anarchy which gripped New Spain. The bishop of Puebla published his sermons in which he warned Mexicans against the concept that sovereignty returned to the people with the imprisonment of the king. Spain's troubles were no reason to establish an independent kingdom or a republic. Like Garibay, he entreated them to throw off narrow allegiance to party or faction—criollo or gachupín—and to unite against the foreign enemy.[47]

For Garibay, however, increasing signs of discord and disunity pointed toward something more than the work of a few unrelated extremists. He was not certain how much of the trouble resulted from the activities of foreign agents, but the capture of General Gaëten d'Alvimart at Nacogdoches, on the northern frontier, pointed toward some direct Napoleonic meddling.[48] There was even the fear that ex-king Charles IV might appear in Mexico as a part of some diabolical French plan. If so, he was to be shown great respect and returned to Spain on the first available ship. In the event that he arrived with a French expeditionary army, he was to be treated like any other enemy.[49] To crush any unified conspiracy before it matured, Garibay expanded his own intelligence network and took steps to streamline judicial proceedings. He appointed *Alcalde del Crimen* Juan Collado to devote his full attention to the task of identifying and prosecuting offenders. Collado pursued his mission with "ardor and zeal," but the duties proved to be too much for just one official. Before long, the audiencia had to expand its activities and to create a special tribunal to investigate cases of treason. This court, named the Junta de Seguridad y Buen Orden, set into motion the machinery needed to deal with more general insurrection.[50]

Although Garibay was motivated by the most patriotic sentiments, he was not able to restore peace. The gachupín leaders who had chosen him as their malleable mouthpiece soon discovered to their sorrow that the old general pursued his own policies. Fearing repetition of the events of September 1808, he kept his palace under heavy guard. The Spaniards pressed for the appointment of an energetic military viceroy who would arrive with up to six thousand European troops and end further talk of independence. This of course was pure fantasy in 1809 since the Junta Central could not spare a single soldier. After lengthy discussions about the Mexican situation, the provisional government decided to appoint a peacemaker rather than an army officer. Archbishop Francisco Javier de Lizana y Beaumont was ordered to replace Garibay.[51]

The archbishop-viceroy took office on July 16, 1809, but there was little expectation in any circle that he could end the crisis. Although Lizana was certain that Mexicans welcomed his government,[52] there was to be no honeymoon. Before the month was out, he expressed concern about the existence of a small opposition faction in the capital which had harassed the government since the overthrow of Iturrigaray. While these men were not strong enough to pose a threat on their own, they could act as agents to arouse the populace. It came as no surprise to Lizana when pamphlets and letters maligning his policies began to appear. Numerous rumors were spread including one which stated that the appointment of the archbishop resulted from direct intrigue with the French.[53] Like Garibay, Lizana seemed to fear the gachupín faction much more than the criollos. He continued to garrison artillery and troops around the viceregal palace to deter a possible coup. One of his first measures to weaken the opposition was to transfer the Dragoons of Mexico out of the capital. Colonel Miguel de Emparán and some of his officers continued to be identified as major troublemakers. Lizana reprimanded other officials, including Francisco Bernal, director of the Powder Monopoly, for disseminating rumors. Equally unhappy about the behavior of some of his immediate subordinates, he dismissed the secretary of the viceroyalty, Manuel Merino Moreno, whom he described as Garibay's henchman, and replaced him with Manuel Velázquez de León, who had held the office under Iturrigaray.[54]

The opposition Lizana feared more than any other came from two members of the audiencia—Guillermo de Aguirre and Ciriaco González Carvajal. Both disputed Emparán's removal from the capital and were blamed for supporting the opposition of Francisco Bernal. It is difficult to understand exactly why Lizana distrusted two oidores who should have been his strongest supporters, but both were known to have been involved in the overthrow of Iturrigaray. Rumors that they were *afrancesados* and would not have opposed a transition to Napoleonic rule seem to lack any real substance.[55] Whatever the source of the division, Lizana was determined to remove both men as soon as possible. Carvajal posed less of a danger because of his advanced age, poor health, and weak character; nevertheless, others in the opposition faction were able to make good use of his prestigious position. Aguirre was identified as the real threat. He was young, healthy, and a natural leader of men. He had numerous friends, which caused Lizana to want him sent back to Spain before he caused any further trouble.[56]

Uncertain of just who was friend or foe in official circles, Lizana was unable to forge a clear policy to govern New Spain. He vacillated and fretted as the news from Iberia turned from bad to worse. In the deepening atmosphere of confusion, rumors of plots hatched by the more violent gachupín and criollo factions swept through Mexico City. These became more and more persistent as the rule of the Junta Central—always questionable from a constitutional point of view—crumbled before the advancing French armies. Crowded into a small enclave around Cádiz, the provisional government lost its small reserve of respectability. For many Mexicans as well as for other Spanish Americans, it was time to discuss the formation of alternative regimes. Even though more than three million pesos could still be raised in New Spain to support the Spanish cause, many doubted the ability of the mother country to survive as an independent power.[57]

In Valladolid, a small group of criollos met to analyze the implications of the news from Europe and the plots thought to be afoot in Mexico. Some had heard that the gachupines planned a campaign of genocide or to turn the province over to either France or Britain. The local infantry battalion had been returned from duty in the cantonment, leaving some young officers perplexed by inaction and anxious to prevent their country from falling easy victim to any enemy. Militia Captain José María Obeso played a major role in the debates over solutions, which touched upon the possibility of a declaration of independence for New Spain. This idea gained impetus with the arrival of Ensign José María de Michelena, a native of Valladolid, on a recruiting mission for the Infantry Regiment of the Crown.[58] Michelena was more successful at hatching plots than he was in finding recruits. He added a few militia officers to the existing group and turned the discussions to the idea of a military uprising. According to the plan, the militia of the intendancies of Valladolid and Guanajuato would lead an army of between eighteen thousand and twenty thousand men. To gain the support of such large numbers, Indians were to be recruited on the promise of permanent exemption from tribute payment and other oppressive taxes. Before the plan could mature into action, it was exposed and its proponents arrested.[59]

Although the Valladolid conspiracy has often been isolated as a clear precursor movement to the Hidalgo revolt, it was one manifestation of the state of unrest which gripped New Spain. Despite later claims of Carlos María de Bustamante and some of the conspirators themselves, the testimony they gave at their trials probably summarizes their motivations quite closely. Michelena, only twenty-eight years of age, argued that his behavior had been inspired by the constant rumors of treachery which followed Iturrigaray's overthrow. He heard that the Mining Tribunal and the consulado of Mexico were in revolt, an Englishman was said to be mapping Guanajuato, and a British fleet was supposed to be standing by off the coast of Veracruz. Many spoke of plots to depose Viceroy Garibay and, since the news of the imprisonment of Ferdinand VII, there had been persistent talk of a negotiated surrender to the French. While Michelena agreed with the concept of forming a national junta to govern in the absence of Ferdinand VII, his own actions had been influenced by a report that Europeans of the consulado were plotting to behead the principal criollos. Michelena was well aware that there had been threats against Viceroy Lizana; the heavy guard surrounding the viceregal palace was proof enough to convince the Valladolid group of this danger.[60] Finally, the incapacity of the provincial intendants or, even worse, their *afrancesado* tendencies caused Michelena and the others to look for alternatives. This was no rumor; as early as July 22, 1808, Intendant Felipe Díaz de Ortega of Valladolid, believing that Spain was vanquished, began to direct routine appeals to the Napoleonic regent, the Duke of Berg.[61] Bustamante, the lawyer for the defense, was able to argue that Michelena and his cohorts were patriots rather than revolutionaries. Since Lizana had no wish to create martyrs of any description, the conspirators escaped rigorous punishment.

For the traditional authorities—civil, military, and religious—the multitude of plots and counterplots obscured the immediate dangers to the regime. Lizana spent much of his time trying to deal with the possibility of a French invasion. He issued patriotic proclamations furnishing lurid details on how Napoleon permitted his troops to desecrate churches, sack towns, and rape Spanish virgins. If the French dared to invade New Spain, they would be met as David met Goliath: "You were bold to come to me with powerful troops. I meet you in the name of the Lord."[62] To prepare for the confrontation, he renewed the cantonment at Jalapa, issued a flood of orders for the formation of new militia battalions, expanded the Veracruz garrison, and even sought to locate some cast-off soldiers to reinforce the Spanish forces in Santo Domingo.[63] Similar fears of an American invasion from the north led to the concentration of troops at San Luis Potosí.

This frenetic activity accomplished little other than to reinforce existing doubts and to weaken the defenses of the interior. From Querétaro, for example, the cabildo and *Corregidor* Miguel Domínguez worried about their ability to contain the plebeian masses after the provincial cavalry regiment was transferred to garrison Mexico City. They proposed the immediate enlistment of an urban battalion to prevent jailbreaks, to guard the untrustworthy tobacco factory workers, and to prevent violence caused by crop failures and a growing shortage of maize. Although the local authorities had managed to distribute sufficient food up to the end of 1809, they were apprehensive about the situation for 1810.[64] Lizana authorized organization of the urban militia of Querétaro and issued orders to other major cities calling for similar militias to maintain internal calm while the provincial troops were guarding the coasts and frontiers.[65]

Throughout the fertile plains of the Mexican Bajío, crop failures caused officials to express similar concerns about their ability to prevent outbreaks of violence. By the end of 1809, troops were needed in both Querétaro and Celaya to accompany maize to the granaries if robberies were to be prevented. As Enrique Florescano has pointed out, poor crops and consequent high grain prices in 1809 and 1810 increased social tensions on the eve of the Hidalgo revolt.[66] These pressures, combined with the mobilization of provincial militia units and efforts to raise new militias, placed an added burden upon local governments. In Silao, the cabildo resisted the mobilization of any residents who were connected with the provision of food. Threatened by a very poor harvest in 1809, the cabildo set up a fund to purchase maize in advance of the worst crisis. They collected twenty-two thousand pesos and placed the fund under the control of militia captain Martín del Collado, who was a leading supporter of poor relief and other philanthropic projects. He sold 2,700 *fanegas* of maize at three pesos per fanega rather than at the price of four pesos current elsewhere in the province. This plan was so successful in protecting Silao from market fluctuations that Collado expanded his operations. As *depositario,* he introduced a systematic program to advance money to farmers in return for crops to be delivered in February and March 1810. In fact, Collado appears to have earned profits from grain sales and he did have eight thousand pesos of his own money invested. When the local militia was mobilized, the cabildo requested an exemption for Collado to continue his good works.[67] The intendant of Guanajuato, Antonio Riaño, was less than enthusiastic about the Silao project. He was upset about Collado's method of cornering the futures market in essential food commodities. This was nothing short of interference with the free market or an effort to monopolize production and to deny the export of grain to Guanajuato. Farmers who sold future crops at current prices would not receive a just price. More important, of course, Riaño feared food shortages in Guanajuato—particularly if other communities adopted the methods of Silao. Before long, the city would be reduced to the brink of ruin. As provincial intendant, he warned that he might have to employ the army to requisition maize.[68]

Lizana had little time to devote to any single source of irritation. Preoccupied by the external threat, internal unrest, and the economic situation, he could not respond to each new sign of impending crisis. Despite a constant flow of new information during the first months of 1810, the regime was paralyzed. From Guadalajara, the cabildo warned of increasing unrest which appeared to be incited by hidden enemies. No one could be quite certain what impact this unknown leadership might exert upon "... an ignorant and gullible mass which is inclined to fads and susceptible to seduction." Members of the cabildo feared a popular insurrection resulting from the delicate situation caused by the fall of Spain. The appearance of a letter signed by Napoleon offering the Indians freedom from tribute was bad enough, but as a kind of sign of the times, small clay pots were appearing from Tonalá bearing the inscription *"Viva Nuestro Rey Buenparte [sic]."*[69] Although the better plebeian elements showed some signs of loyalty, the municipal governors of Guadalajara dared not even guess at the true state of Indian opinion.

Similar signs were evident in the city of Zacatecas. The cabildo reported unexpected turbulence from the populace and several seditious sheets had been posted throughout the town. One of these, signed by a Rosalio Casteras, proposed the expulsion of all gachupines from New Spain; those who delayed beyond a specified one-month period were to be systematically exterminated.[70] Cabildo members warned that the French were an astute and untiring foe who were doing everything within their power to promote disorder and anarchy in Mexico. To add strength to the police forces available in Zacatecas, a number of voluntary militia units were being raised.

Even in the capital, the heavily reinforced garrison and numerous Inquisition spies did not slow the deluge of rumors or the appearance of slogans on public buildings. With so many potential enemies, Lizana grew somewhat inured to the possibility of either a gachupín or criollo attempt against his government. Gossip seemed to be confirmed at the end of January 1810, when a resident named José María Herrera reported that he had overheard a group of Europeans plotting the overthrow of the archbishop-viceroy. Herrera claimed to have left his house late at night following a quarrel with his wife; around 1:00 A.M., he was at the gate of Puente de Alvarado when he saw a group of men coming toward him. Frightened that they must be members of the Acordada patrol, he hid himself behind the gate. The men stopped close by and although much of their conversation took place in a language he did not understand, he identified them as Basques. From what was said in Spanish, Herrera learned that they were discussing a coup against Lizana. Two newcomers rejected any attempt, arguing that the royal palace was too well guarded for the ninety-nine men in their party. This testimony was accepted at first, but after a series of interrogations, Herrera admitted that he had concocted the entire story hoping to profit from the sale of information.[71]

The arrival of the brig *San Francisco de Paula* at Veracruz on April 25, 1810, crushed any lingering faith in the revival of Spanish fortunes. Mexico learned of the fall of Málaga, the entry of the French into Seville, and the siege of Cádiz. Most of Andalusia was now under enemy control and delegates of the Junta Central had fled on vessels of the Spanish squadron at Cádiz.[72] Shaken by these reports, the viceroyalty was plunged into further perplexity when Lizana received an order of February 22, 1810, removing him from the viceregency and appointing the audiencia to exercise interim command.⁷³ Before the new government could evaluate its situation, on May 10, 1810, the frigate *Concepción,* alias the *Veloz,* arrived from Puerto Cabello with news of the Venezuela insurrection. Although Caracas claimed to maintain its loyalty to Ferdinand VII, additional news that the Junta Central had disbanded and been replaced by a small Council of Regency seemed to portend the death knell of an independent Spain. As far as Caracas was concerned, Spain was beaten.⁷⁴

The audiencia broke communications with the rebellious province and appointed venerable Field Marshal Pedro Garibay to chair yet another *junta de guerra* dedicated toward proposing solutions to the various threats.⁷⁵ By this time, however, observers outside of the army began to propose far-reaching reforms beyond the mere mobilization of militia units or the reinforcement of the Jalapa cantonment. To strengthen Mexico, basic social inequities had to be ended. The most famous of these representations were written by Manuel Abad y Queipo, the bishop elect of Michoacán. Beginning in 1809, he warned Garibay about the possibility of a Franco-American invasion force of up to thirty thousand troops which might attack New Spain. Against such an enemy, the Mexican army could field between ten thousand and twelve thousand ill-disciplined troops drawn from the "scum of the population."⁷⁶ The only logical solution was to end restrictive enlistment policies and to recruit those who belonged to the tributary castas. These people would be attracted to service if granted permanent exemption from tribute payment. The bishop had visited France, where he was impressed by the organizational superiority of the revolutionary armies. French methods should be adopted in Mexico employing active officers such as Calleja, Costansó, Flon, Alonso, Urrutía, Emparán, and others. If the regime feared a loss of tax income, he proposed raising tobacco taxes or opening commerce with foreign nations, which would eliminate contraband as well as increase revenues.⁷⁷

By May 1810, Abad y Queipo demanded immediate action to halt the slide into revolution and independence. He rejected the defeatist attitudes of those who believed that Napoleon had extinguished the Spanish nation. In Mexico, the interim regimes of Garibay and Lizana had exacerbated rather than calmed the passions between gachupines and criollos. News of the fall of Andalusia and the collapse of the Junta Central was quite enough to popularize seditious movements without the added disaster of the Venezuelan uprising. Only social reforms would forestall revolution. Since the 80 percent of the population comprising Indians and castas lived in misery, it was natural that they would side with the Spanish Americans against the Europeans—if only because the gachupines were a symbol of dominance. In this event, Abad y Queipo predicted a devastating social revolution similar to the one which had ruined Saint Domingue.⁷⁸

Others predicted similar disasters if basic social reforms were not implemented. A well-known criollo lawyer, Juan Nazario Peimbert, later a member of the prorevolutionary Guadalupes,[79] prepared his own defense plan for New Spain. In his opinion, the Indians should be recruited into a two-hundred-thousand-man army which was to be named "El Irresistible de Naturales Voluntarios del Fernando VII." Like Abad y Queipo, Peimbert planned to offer freedom from tribute as an incentive to enlistment. He rejected the general belief that Indians were pusillanimous as they had been during the sixteenth-century conquest. Most were mixed with Spaniards and with other castas as their color and appearance demonstrated. To prove this point, Peimbert stated that pure Indians did not grow beards or spit. Since the present population did both, it was easy to identify the role played by Spaniards, Negroes, and mulattoes in confusing the Indian lineages. The basic submissiveness of the Indians made them apt candidates for military discipline. Subdelegates, curates, and even their own Indian governors and officials whipped and punished them without distinction. They spent their lives on haciendas or at other labor without questioning the source of authority that ordered them to work.[80] Peimbert condemned the "impiety, ingratitude, and insatiable greed" motivating Spaniards, mulattoes, and even Negroes to mistreat the humble Indians. Magistrates threw them into jail and ordered them lashed on the pillory without a second thought. He was quite certain that if Indians withheld their labor for eight days, society would be forced to recognize their essential role.

The army called "El Irresistible" would overcome hardships more easily than any other. Indians were accustomed to sleeping out in the open and their food and dress were most ordinary. They would cost very little in comparison with other soldiers because they needed nothing more than a coarse cotton shirt and pair of breeches for underclothing. A cotton cloak and pair of goat-leather leggings were sufficient to protect them from the elements. Their equipment would be complete with a straw hat, pair of sandals, a sisal mat, and a gourd for water. Provisions of tortillas and jerked beef would be quite sufficient for a ten-day march. Armed with muskets and machetes in place of sabers, this army could frighten any enemy.[81]

Although Peimbert was quite correct in his assessment of Indian fighting potential, it was too late to harness their energies for the existing regime. Yet, the idea of seeking Indian support was not as farfetched as it might at first seem. From many parts of New Spain, Indian leaders expressed similar concerns to criollos when they discussed the crises of the Spanish world. Dionisio Cano y Moctezuma, Indian governor of Tecpan, insisted that his subjects were quite prepared to take up their slings and even to learn how to use muskets in the king's defense. While his people had suffered from the recent crop failures and could not make financial donations, they offered their personal services.[82]

The downward spiral into violence which had begun with the overthrow of Iturrigaray continued without interruption. The feeble attempts of the audiencia to improve the record of the two previous interim viceroys produced no solid results. In Cádiz, despite the fact that the fortunes of the Council of Regency were at a low ebb, steps were taken to prevent the loss of New Spain and its silver wealth. Since a dynamic military governor was needed, Francisco Javier de Venegas, the hero of the battle of Bailén, was transferred to Mexico City. He had been appointed to take command of the viceroyalty of New Granada, but this new commission took precedence. He rushed to Mexico, arriving in Veracruz on August 25, 1810. Immediately, he began to hear rumors of unrest and possible insurrection. After an inspection of the army cantoned at Jalapa, Venegas took office in Mexico City on September 14, 1810.[83] Two days later, Miguel Hidalgo y Costilla unleashed the Indian and casta masses upon the viceroyalty.

CONCLUSION

The shock resulting from the realization that a massive social upheaval was taking place galvanized the regime into a determined response. Before many weeks had passed, few could challenge the importance of the army Spain implanted in Mexico. Although several units went over to the rebel side, the great majority of the regular and provincial forces remained loyal. With the atrocities in Guanajuato and other towns and the growing racist attitudes exhibited by the revolutionary soldiers, there was good reason to suspend the criollo-gachupín animosity long enough to destroy the common enemy. The cry of *"Viva la Virgen de Guadalupe y el Rey Fernando VII y muera el mal gobierno"*[1] fell upon deaf ears as Viceroy Venegas dispatched Brigadier Calleja, the Conde de la Cadena, and other officers to undertake the systematic destruction of Hidalgo's masses. From the very first major military engagement at Monte de las Cruces, the weaknesses of the rebels became painfully evident. Even when soldiers of militia units from insurgent territories were available, the shortage of experienced officers made them almost as useless as the untrained Indians.[2] Outnumbered at Las Cruces by at least twenty to one, the royalists were able to prevent the capture of Mexico City and to breath confidence and spirit into their cause. At Aculco on November 3, 1810, Calleja sent into battle seven thousand troops of the disciplined colonial army. The huge rebel forces, estimated at up to forty thousand men, broke and fled despite their numerical advantages, and were incapable of rallying. For the royalists, the muskets and other arms purchased to resist a possible French invasion were turned on the poorly armed Indians. The major mission for Venegas and Calleja was to recover rebel towns and to capture the leaders of the first insurrection.[3]

In many respects it might be argued that the army of New Spain did not pose the dangers historians have identified. The army saved Mexico City from the revolutionaries in 1810 and it crushed all opposition before turning to support the criollo view of independence. Nonetheless, years passed until young officers such as Agustín de Iturbide reached senior rank and were able to take control over the military. Certainly until 1810, the army showed no tendency to intervene in political affairs. Since the interests of the regime and the officers were similar, few problems could be anticipated. Even with the challenge caused by Iturrigaray's overthrow, the senior gachupín officers identified themselves with the provisional government of Pedro Garibay. Indeed, the martial spirit and creation of an autonomous praetorian tradition which Mora, McAlister, and other historians have attributed to the late eighteenth century were not present.[4] The checks and balances imposed by other elements of the Bourbon bureaucracy, as well as privileged sectors such as the merchant and mining jurisdictions, served to impede any pretensions by army officers. Besides, it was not the policy of Spain to produce an irresponsible institution—military or otherwise. For Mora as well as for other historians, the postindependence experience colored their view of the late colonial period.

The rage for offices and titles which characterized Bourbon Mexico explains the popularity of provincial militia commissions and the *fuero militar*. For Mexican criollos or for Spanish immigrants who had made fortunes in mining, business, or through marriage, there were few opportunities to exercise the social prerogatives of success. The Bourbon reformers who did so much to close off access to important offices granted flashy uniforms and minor privileges to those who wished to parade their wealth. In exchange, these men would have to devote their service and perhaps give their lives if an invasion occurred. As might be expected, little was said about these latter ramifications of holding militia commissions. After months or even years of active duty in cantonments and the consequent interference with family and business concerns, the *fuero militar* lost much of its luster.

For Mexicans who served in the ranks, the military brought many more liabilities than advantages. Guildsmen, artisans, and laborers tended to be less impressed with possible social distinctions. The prospect of separation from their families and low pay in the army caused them to avoid enlistment or to escape mobilization. Particularly in the case of the regular army, enlistment was looked upon with abhorrence, similar to a prison sentence. The possibility of an untimely death of yellow fever or some other tropical disease in Veracruz, Havana, Santo Domingo, Florida, or Louisiana meant that few volunteered for a military career. Pressed to fill the ranks, the army took to rounding up vagabonds, commuting the jail terms of criminals, and raiding the provincial militia regiments. In the more accessible provinces, twenty years of forced recruitment and knowledge that any commoner could be taken despite legitimate exemptions tended to alienate much of the laboring population. Combined with numerous grievances against the subdelegates and other officials, many would see the revolutionary proclamations of Hidalgo and

Morelos as a way to rid themselves of predatory governors, taxes, and army levies. As many historians have pointed out, the real weakness of the Bourbon reforms was at the local level, where minor officials had to implement imperial readjustments. Even where the subdelegates and urban officials were not primarily motivated by profit, it was difficult to serve the people at the same time as the state.

As we have seen throughout this study, the regime failed to perceive the complexity of the society it governed. The basic motivations of the Indian and casta majority and their desire to escape tribute payment, forced labor, and other oppression were not recognized. The army, often the agency of police power, continually suspected the Indian population; minor unrest directed against a local governor or an unpopular tax resulted in heavy-handed repression. Similarly, many officers suspected the motivations of mulattoes who might be inspired by the social revolution in Haiti. Yet, if the army served to alienate some sectors of the population, it also exerted pressure to assimilate others to European society. The movement of large numbers of men from their small towns and villages into garrison duty in the larger cities opened their eyes to the changes which had been going on in New Spain. Many saw the possibility of escaping their social or racial origins. The rigidity of casta society was crumbling anyway, and the movement of people merely hastened this process.

Because the army of New Spain was not called upon to perform its primary task of repelling external invasion, one may only speculate upon what might have happened if, for example, Britain had dispatched Arthur Wellesley to attack Veracruz. On the one hand, the Mexicans exhibited few signs of wanting to achieve martial glory. Desertion levels and low morale were general problems, even apart from the horrible conditions in the coastal garrisons. Even the acclimatized militiamen preferred flight to resistance. In many incidents, the militiamen abandoned their muskets and their watchtowers when they sighted a strange sail.[5] At the same time, however, the strategy of concentrating the main force of the Mexican army inland was an excellent alternative to coastal defense. Not only was the health of the troops maintained, but a potential invading force would have encountered epidemic yellow fever as well as other tropical illnesses. If other Caribbean expeditions of the period can be used as an indication, a successful invasion of New Spain would have been exceptionally difficult.

The history of the army of New Spain forms an important chapter of Bourbon reform policy. Since the military emerged after independence to fill part of the vacuum left by the Spanish regime, it is essential to understand the earlier period. Beginning with the disruption of the Bourbon state, the army was able to expand its privileges at the expense of other institutions.

APPENDIX 1

Troops Cantoned at Córdoba, Orizaba, Perote, and Jalapa in August 1806

Córdoba

Provincial Infantry Regiment of Puebla	845
reinforced by the Reserve Companies of Acatlán and Tlapa	91
Provincial Infantry Regiment of Tres Villas	845
reinforced by the Reserve Company of Xochimilco	60
Provincial Infantry Battalion of Oaxaca	425
reinforced by the Reserve Company of San Cristóval	60
TOTAL	2,326

Orizaba

Provincial Infantry Regiment of Mexico	845
Provincial Infantry Regiment of Tlaxcala	845
reinforced by the Reserve Companies of Chiautla and Chietla	178
TOTAL	1,868

Perote

Provincial Infantry Regiment of Celaya	845
reinforced by the Reserve Companies of Tacuba, Guautitlán, and Huichapán	183
Provincial Infantry Battalion of Guanajuato	425
reinforced by the Reserve Company of Actopán	60
Provincial Dragoon Regiment of the Príncipe	361
Regular Dragoon Regiment of Mexico	364
TOTAL	2,238

Jalapa

Regular Infantry Regiment of the Crown	1,031
Regular Infantry Regiment of New Spain	834
Provincial Infantry Regiment of Toluca	845
reinforced by the Reserve Companies of Cuernavaca and 2 Companies of Tluajuapán	232
Provincial Infantry Regiment of Valladolid	845
reinforced by the Reserve Companies of Nochistlán, Teposcolula, Yanhuitlán, and Tlaxiaco	188
Regular Dragoon Regiment of Mexico	492
Infantry artillery	114
TOTAL	4,581
TOTAL INFANTRY	9,796
TOTAL CAVALRY	1,217
TOTAL MANPOWER	11,013

APPENDIX 2

List of the Viceroys of New Spain, 1760–1810

Joaquín de Monserrat y Cruillas, Marqués de Cruillas, October 6, 1760, to August 23, 1766.
Carlos Francisco de Croix, Marqués de Croix, August 23, 1766, to October 22, 1771.
Antonio María Bucareli y Ursúa, October 22, 1771, to April 9, 1779.
Martín Díaz de Mayorga, August 23, 1779, to April 28, 1784.
Matías de Gálvez, April 28, 1784, to November 3, 1784.
Audiencia Gobernadora, November 3, 1784, to June 16, 1785.
Bernardo de Gálvez, Conde de Gálvez, June 16, 1785, to November 8, 1786.
Audiencia Gobernadora, November 8, 1786, to May 8, 1787.
Alonso Núñez de Haro y Peralta, Archbishop of Mexico, interim viceroy, May 8, 1787, to August 16, 1787.
Manuel Antonio Flórez, August 6, 1787, to October 17, 1789.
Juan Vicente de Güemes Pacheco y Horcasitas, Conde de Revillagigedo, October 17, 1789, to July 12, 1794.
Miguel de la Grúa Talamanca, Marqués de Branciforte, July 12, 1794, to May 31, 1798.
Miguel José de Azanza, May 31, 1798, to April 29, 1800.
Félix Berenguer de Marquina, April 29, 1800, to January 5, 1803.
José de Iturrigaray, January 5, 1803, to September 16, 1808.
Pedro de Garibay, September 16, 1808, to July 16, 1809.
Javier Lizana y Beaumont, Archbishop of Mexico, July 16, 1809, to April 25, 1810.
Audiencia Gobernadora, April 25, 1810, to September 4, 1810.
Francisco Javier de Venegas, September 4, 1810, to February 1813.

GLOSSARY

acordada: law enforcement tribunal and agency
afrancesado: Francophile; a name given to those who supported France
alcabala: sales tax
alcalde: magistrate and cabildo member
alcalde de barrio: city district magistrate
alcalde de corte: magistrate attached to the government
alcalde del crimen: audiencia judge attached to the sala del crimen
alcalde de cuartel: city district magistrate
alcalde mayor: district magistrate
alcalde ordinario: municipal magistrate
alguacil: constable or police official
alguacil mayor: chief constable
almacén: warehouse
almacenero: the owner of an important merchant house
alquilones: persons hired to serve as replacements in the Urban Regiment of Commerce of Mexico
apoderado general: attorney
arbitrios: taxes
arribeño: person from the highlands
asentista: contractor or monopolist
audiencia: high court and governing body under the viceroy
auditor de guerra: judge advocate of the army, audiencia judge responsible for army affairs
bandera de recluta: recruiting team
bando: proclamation
barrio: town or city district
caballero: gentleman
cabildo: municipal council
cabildo extraordinario: a cabildo convened for an important reason
cabildo de naturales: Indian governing council
cacique: Indian chief or local ruler
cajero: apprentice or merchant assistant
campesino: rural worker or resident, peasant
carga: load
carreras de baquetas: military punishment of running the gauntlet between two files of soldiers
castas: castes, racial mixtures
casta de razón: acceptable castes; usually whites, castizos, and mestizos
castizo: a mixed-blood of Spanish and mestizo ancestry
chichique: a fermented beverage made with sugar
chinguirito: inferior grade rum
comandante general: commander general of the army
comisario: peace officer
comisario de guerra: official in charge of fiscal matters relating to the army

compañía suelta: reserve company of militia
competencia: conflict of jurisdiction
consejo de guerra: court-martial
consejo pleno de guerra: full war council of the imperial government
consul: consulado judge
consulado: merchant guild and commercial court
coronel graduado: colonel by rank, but without pay or effective command
corregidor: district magistrate
corregimiento: jurisdiction of a corregidor
coyote: a mixed-blood of mulatto and mestizo ancestry
criollo: creole, a Spaniard born in America
conquistador: conqueror, generally applied to the sixteenth-century soldiers-of-fortune who acquired Spain's New World territories.
cuadrillero: police official
curandero: medical practitioner without official degree
depositario: receiver or trustee
diputación de la minería: regional mining board under the Mining Tribunal
espíritu militar: esprit de corps or martial spirit
expediente: file of papers bearing on a case
fandango: a lively dance accompanied by guitars and other instruments
fanega: unit of dry measure, about 1.5 bushels
fiscal: legal official
fiscal de lo civil: crown attorney attached to the audiencia
flota: fleet of ships
fuero: corporate privileges, right to trial by members of the same profession
fuero criminal: right to trial by the military in criminal cases
fuero militar: corporate privileges and the right of soldiers to trial by the military jurisdiction
gachupín: a Spaniard born in Europe, resident in New Spain
gente de razón: people of reason or acceptable non-Indian castes; also, Hispanicized Indians
golpe de estado: coup d'état
grano: monetary value, one-twelfth of a real
guachinango: term used at Veracruz to describe a person from overseas
hacienda: large landed estate; hacendado, owner of the estate
hidalgo: person of genteel birth
intendente de ejército: intendant of the army
jefe militar: military commander
juez de alzadas: judge in appeal cases
juez eclesiástico: ecclesiastical judge
juez de gremios: guild judge
junta de comercio: council of merchants
junta de generales: council of senior army officers
junta de guerra: council of war
junta de marina: naval war or planning council
junta de seguridad y buen orden: tribunal established to look into suspicious political behavior and unrest
junta superior de real hacienda: chief finance committee after the creation of the intendancies
justicia: officer of the law
limpieza de sangre: purity of blood; in Spain indicated absence of Jewish or Moorish ancestry—in the Americas, that the individual was free of nonwhite ancestry
lobo: a mixed-blood of Indian and mestizo ancestry
malagueño: a native of Malaga, Spain

maravedí: monetary unit, one thirty-fourth of a real
marqués: marquis
mayordomo: majordomo
mestizaje: miscegenation
ministro de vara: constable
monte: a card game
monte pío militar: military pension fund
moreno: free Negro
milpa: plot of land, usually a cornfield
no le entiendo: a person of unclear racial ancestry
norte: norther, a strong wind from the north
obraje: textile workshop
oficial de beneficio: an officer who purchases his commission
oidor: a judge of the audiencia
ordenanza general: general ordinance
padrón: census
pardo: mulatto, of mixed white and Negro ancestry
partido: share of ore taken by mine workers; or the districts of an intendancy administered by a subdelegate
patria: fatherland
patria chica: literally, small fatherland; refers to province or district from which a person came and to which he often remained loyal
peninsular: a Spaniard born in Europe, resident in New Spain
peso: monetary unit worth eight reales
pícaro: rascal or knave
polizón: an illegal immigrant
practicante: an assistant to a physician or surgeon
presidario: a criminal sentenced to labor in a presidio or fortress
prior: head of the consulado
procurador síndico del común: town official responsible for guarding the public interest
pulquería: a tavern which served pulque, the beverage made from the fermented juice of the maguey plant
purga de jalapa: purgative drug obtained from a tuberous root plant
quintal: a hundred pounds
quintas: levy of men for the army
real: monetary unit worth one eighth of a peso
real acuerdo: resolution of the audiencia in executive session presided over by the viceroy
real cédula: royal order or decree
regidor: councilman in a cabildo
reglamento: regulation
renta de tabaco: the tobacco monopoly
repartimiento: forced distribution of money or goods by a district magistrate or governor such as a subdelegate, often in association with an important merchant.
residencia: judicial review of an official's conduct at the end of his term of office
sala del crimen: audiencia court which heard criminal cases
salta atrás: a mixed-blood of mulatto and Spanish ancestry
sargento mayor: major or third-in-command of a regiment
síndico procurador: attorney or official in charge of the military draft named by the cabildo
situados: subsidies sent to less wealthy Spanish possessions
sorteo: lottery for selecting army recruits
supremo consejo de guerra: supreme war council in Madrid

teniente: lieutenant
teniente de justicia: deputy of a subdelegate
tente en el aire: a person of unclear racial ancestry
tepache: mixed drink made with pulque, pineapple, water, and cloves
terna: three names presented as candidates for promotion
tierra caliente: the lowlands
tísica: a consumptive lung ailment suffered by miners
tributario: a person of Indian or caste origin who paid the head tax
vaquero: cowboy
veracruzano: resident of Veracruz
visitador general: official in charge of general inspection of a kingdom or province
vómito negro: yellow fever

NOTES

Preface

1. Carlos María de Bustamante, *Suplemento a la historia de los tres siglos de México durante el gobierno español escrita por el Padre Andrés Cavo,* 3 vols. (Mexico, 1836), 3:74.
2. Lucas Alamán, *Historia de Méjico desde los primeros movimientos que preparon su independencia en el año de 1808, hasta la época presente,* 5 vols. (Mexico, 1849), 1:147; and José María Luis Mora, *México y sus revoluciones,* 3 vols. (Mexico: Editorial Porrúa, 1965), 2:239.
3. Mora, *México y sus revoluciones,* 1:92, 120, 351–77; idem, *Obras sueltas* (Mexico: Editorial Porrúa, 1963), pp. 71–72, 549–56. Also see Charles A. Hale, *Mexican Liberalism in the Age of Mora, 1821–1853* (New Haven: Yale University Press, 1968), pp. 141–44. Lorenzo de Zavala, while not as specific in his attacks, identified military privileges as one of the evils of the conservative sector. See Lorenzo de Zavala, *Obras: Ensayo crítico de las revoluciones de México desde 1808 hasta 1830,* 2 vols. (Mexico: Editorial Porrúa, 1969), 2:22.
4. María del Carmen Velázquez, *El estado de guerra en Nueva España, 1760–1808* (Mexico: El Colegio de México, 1950); and Lyle N. McAlister, *The "Fuero Militar" in New Spain, 1764–1800* (Gainesville: University of Florida Press, 1957).
5. Enrique Florescano, *Precios del maíz y crisis agrícolas en México, 1708–1810* (Mexico: El Colegio de México, 1969); and Romeo Flores Caballero, *La contrarevolución en la independencia: los españoles en la vida política, social y económica de Mexico, 1804–1838* (Mexico: El Colegio de México, 1969).
6. See José Antonio Calderón Quijano, ed., *Los virreyes de Nueva España en el reinado de Carlos III,* 2 vols. (Seville: Escuela de Estudios Hispano-Americanos, 1967, 1968), and idem, *Los virreyes de Nueva España en el reinado de Carlos IV,* 2 vols. (Seville: Escuela de Estudios Hispano-Americanos, 1972).
7. Herbert I. Priestley, *José de Gálvez, Visitador General of New Spain 1765–1771* (Berkeley: University of California Press, 1916), p. 279.
8. Alexander von Humboldt, *Political Essay on the Kingdom of New Spain,* 4 vols. (London, 1811).
9. Ibid., 1:127.
10. Florescano, *Precios del maíz;* Nancy M. Farriss, *Crown and Clergy in Colonial Mexico, 1759–1821* (London: Athlone Press, 1968); David A. Brading, *Miners and Merchants in Bourbon Mexico, 1763–1810* (Cambridge: Cambridge University Press, 1971); Brian R. Hamnett, *Politics and Trade in Southern Mexico, 1750–1821* (Cambridge: Cambridge University Press, 1971).

Introduction

1. Consulado of Mexico to the Marqués de Branciforte, August 8, 1794, AGN, IG, vol. 60-B.
2. José Miguel de Azanza to José Alvarez, no. 100, September 27, 1798, AGI, México, leg. 1447; and José Caballero to Pedro Cevallos, Aranjuez, May 18, 1804, AGI, Estado, leg. 39. For background on the Provincias Internas see Luis Navarro García, *José de Gálvez y la Comandancia General de las Provincias Internas* (Seville: Escuela de Estudios Hispano-Americanos, 1964).

3. José Antonio Calderón Quijano, *Fortificaciones en Nueva España* (Seville: Escuela de Estudios Hispano-Americanos, 1953), p. 230.

4. See Richard Pares, *War and Trade in the West Indies, 1739-1763* (Oxford: Oxford University Press, 1936).

5. Instructions for Lieutenant General Juan de Villalba, 1765, AGI, leg. 2422.

6. Plan de defensa de Veracruz, 1775, AGI, México, leg. 2418; Branciforte to the Prince of the Peace, December 28, 1796; and the Conde de Revillagigedo to Antonio Valdés, no. 296, February 9, 1790, AGS, GM, leg. 6959.

7. Brading, *Miners and Merchants*, pp. 33-92.

8. Jean Sarrailh, *La España ilustrada de la segunda mitad del siglo XVIII* (Mexico: Fondo de Cultura Económica, 1957); and Richard Herr, *The Eighteenth Century Revolution in Spain* (Princeton: Princeton University Press, 1958).

Chapter 1

1. Conde de Revillagigedo to the provincial intendants, January 3, 1792; and Manuel de Terán to the intendant of San Luis Potosí, Bruno Díaz de Salcedo, Río Verde, January 20, 1792, AGN, IG, vol. 100-A.

2. Juan Juárez Moreno, *Corsarios y piratas en Veracruz y Campeche* (Seville: Escuela de Estudios Hispano-Americanos, 1972), pp. 230-33.

3. Alonso Basco y Vargas to the Marqués de Cruillas, Alvarado, September 30, 1762, and November 13, 1762, AGN, IG, vol. 532-A.

4. Antonio López Matosso to Cruillas, Tlaxcala, October 28, 1762, and López Matosso to Cruillas, Huamantla, September 24, 1762, AGN, IG, vol. 532-A.

5. Relación de los gastos en los preparativos de la guerra en el año 1762, AGN, IG, vol. 247-A.

6. Lyle N. McAlister, "The Reorganization of the Army of New Spain, 1763-1766," *Hispanic American Historical Review* 23(1953):8.

7. Juan de Villalba y Angulo to Cruillas, November 1, 1764, AGN, IG, vol. 304-A.

8. Instrucción de 1 Agosto 1764 para gobierno y comandancia general de las armas é instrucción de las tropas del reino, AGN, IG, vol. 224-A.

9. Velázquez, *El estado de guerra,* p. 69.

10. Cruillas to Villalba, April 18, 1765, and Villalba to Cruillas, April 12, 1765, AGN, IG, vol. 304-A.

11. Cruillas to Villalba, March 14, 1765, AGN, IG, vol. 304-A.

12. Instrucción de 1 Agosto 1764, AGN, IG, vol. 224-A.

13. AGI, México, leg. 2422.

14. Proyecto militar de 1784, AGI, México, leg. 2418.

15. Velázquez, *El estado de guerra,* pp. 105-9; and Priestley, *José de Gálvez,* p. 223.

16. Noticias venidas de Londres con fecha de 8 Agosto de 1766, AGN, IG, vol. 224-A.

17. Ibid.

18. Julián de Arriaga to the Marqués de Croix, San Ildefonso, September 18, 1766, AGN, IG, vol. 224-A.

19. Calderón Quijano, ed., *Los virreyes de Nueva España en el reinado de Carlos III,* I:190-94, and Arriaga to Croix, Aranjuez, June 24, 1767, AGN, IG, vol. 224-A.

20. Calderón Quijano, ed., *Los virreyes de Nueva España en el reinado de Carlos III, 1757-1779,* 1:III.

21. The Marqués de Torre to Croix, September 7, 1768, and September 12, 1768, AGN, IG, vol. 36-B.

22. Report of Torre, October 24, 1768, AGN, IG, vol. 36-B.

23. Ibid.

24. Arriaga to Croix, El Pardo, March 15, 1771, AGN, IG, vol. 224-A.
25. Joaquín de Llano y Villaurrutia to Antonio María Bucareli, San Luis Potosí, February 1, 1775, AGN, IG, vol. 202-B.
26. Arriaga to Croix, July 18, 1769, AGN, IG, vol. 224-A.
27. Diego García Panes to the Prince of the Peace, October 19, 1792, AGI, Estado, leg. 25.
28. Bernard E. Bobb, *The Viceregency of Antonio María Bucareli in New Spain, 1771–1779* (Austin: University of Texas Press, 1962), p. 93. Cisneros had been the *teniente del rey* under Bucareli at Havana.
29. Cisneros to Bucareli, July 13, 1778, AGN, IG, vol. 361-A.
30. Cisneros to Conde de Santiago, colonel of the Provincial Infantry Regiment of Mexico, October 21, 1778, AGN, IG, vol. 361-A.
31. Reflexiones sobre el reino de Nueva España, y algunos otros puntos deducidos del dictamen dado por el Fiscal de Real Hacienda el Señor Areche en 1774... sobre proposiciones que hizo el Exmo. Señor Inspector Don Pascual de Cisneros, punto a formación de milicias provinciales en el reino, MN, vol. 568.
32. Report of Martín Merino, September 8, 1780, and Cisneros to Martín de Mayorga, September 18, 1780, AGN, IG, vol. 104-B.
33. Priestley, *José de Gálvez*, p. 224.
34. Pedro Gorostiza to José de Galvez, Madrid, August 19, 1776, AGI, Indiferente General, leg. 1565.
35. Proyecto sobre tropas para Nueva España, 1776, AGI, Indiferente General, leg. 1565.
36. Ibid.
37. Velázquez, *El estado de guerra*, pp. 134–35.
38. Mayorga to Joseph de Carrión y Andrade, February 6, 1781, AGI, México, leg. 1510.
39. Calderón Quijano, ed., *Los virreyes de Nueva España en el reinado de Carlos III*, II:77.
40. Pedro de Gorostiza to Revillagigedo, July 16, 1792, AGN, Historia, vol. 248.
41. Manuel Antonio Flórez to Valdés, no. 315, May 24, 1788, AGI, México, leg. 1516.
42. Instrucción reservada of Viceroy Flórez, no. 1180, August 27, 1789, AGI, México, leg. 1293.
43. Calderón Quijano, ed., *Los virreyes de Nueva España en el reinado de Carlos IV*, I:33.
44. Proyecto militar de 1784, AGI, México, leg. 2418.
45. Ibid., Resumen general de los gastos que deben causar anualmente los cuerpos de milicias provinciales.
46. Ibid., Resumen de fuerzas de los cuerpos provinciales que se proponen.
47. Ibid.
48. Flórez to Valdés, no. 42, November 26, 1787, AGI, México, leg. 1514.
49. Mendinueta, colonel of the peninsular Infantry Regiment of the King, became subinspector general of the Mexican army in June 1785. He replaced José de Ezpeleta, who held the office after Cisneros's departure in 1783, but who did not serve long before his promotion to the captaincy general of Cuba. See AGI, leg. 2424.
50. Mendinueta to Flórez, November 23, 1787, AGN, Archivo Provisional de Temporalidades, caja 4.
51. Flórez to Valdés, no. 27, November 23, 1787, AGI, México, leg. 1514.
52. Mendinueta to Flórez, November 23, 1787, and Flórez to Mendinueta, December 6, 1787, AGN, Archivo General de Temporalidades, caja 4.
53. Royal Order, San Ildefonso, September 25, 1787, AGN, Historia, vol. 249.
54. Flórez to Valdés, no. 92, January 23, 1788, AGI, México, leg. 1515, and Flórez to Mendinueta, January 11, 1788, and Mendinueta to Flórez, February 2, 1788, AGN, Historia, vol. 249.
55. Benito Pérez to Mendinueta, April 22, 1788, AGN, Historia, vol. 249.
56. Flórez to Ezpeleta, February 24, 1788, AGI, section 11-A, Cuba, leg. 1408, and Flórez to Valdés, no. 166, February 25, 1788, AGN, CV, series 2, vol. 19.

57. Flórez to Valdés, no. 94, January 24, 1788, AGI, México, leg. 1515. The figure of 979 troops for the regular infantry regiments resulted from minor adjustments in the Crespo Plan.
58. Branciforte to Alange, no. 20, July 30, 1794, and Branciforte to Alange, October 5, 1794, AGI, Estado, leg. 22. For a printed copy of the royal order of October 20, 1788, see Velázquez, *El estado de guerra*, pp. 243–45.
59. Instrucción reservada que de orden del Rey debe observer el teniente general Conde de Revillagigedo nombrado por S.M. Virrey de Nueva España, AGS, GM, leg. 7011.
60. Calderón Quijano, ed., *Los virreyes de Nueva España en el reinado de Carlos IV*, I:93, and J. Ignacio Rubio Mañé, "Síntesis histórica de la vida del II Conde de Revillagigedo, virrey de Nueva España," *Anuario de Estudios Americanos* 6(1949):451–96. Floridablanca managed to find a post for Revillagigedo during the siege of Gibraltar in 1779. Charles IV named him viceroy of La Plata, but the early resignation of Flórez moved him to New Spain.
61. Revillagigedo in a private letter to the Conde de Aranda, July 31, 1792, AHN, Estado, leg. 4287.
62. Revillagigedo to Alejandro Malaspina, October 26, 1791, MN, vol. 280.
63. Revillagigedo to Malaspina, October 31, 1791, MN, vol. 280.
64. Sobre extinción y reforma de los dos batallones de pardos de México y Puebla, 1792–1794, AGN, IG, vol. 197-B.
65. Revillagigedo to Valdés, Madrid, April 13, 1789, AGS, GM, leg. 7011.
66. Revillagigedo to Alange, no. 875, May 29, 1793, AGI, México, leg. 1437.
67. Gorostiza to Branciforte, October 3, 1794, AGS, GM, leg. 6970.
68. Revillagigedo to Valdés, no. 296, February 6, 1790, AGS, GM, leg. 6959.
69. Revillagigedo to Valdés, no. 528, April 30, 1790, AGI, México, leg. 1538, and Revillagigedo to Alange, no. 177, February 7, 1791, AGS, GM, leg. 6966.
70. Revillagigedo to Valdés, November 12, 1789, AGI, México, leg. 1531.
71. Revillagigedo to Valdés, no. 50, July 12, 1790, AGN, CV, series 2, vol. 30.
72. Revillagigedo to Alange, no. 296, February 6, 1790, AGS, GM, leg. 6959.
73. Reglas que deberán observarse para la formación y alistamiento de las milicias de lo interior del reino, May 29, 1794, AGI, Estado, leg. 22.
74. Reglamento provisional para el régimen, gobierno y nueva planta de las milicias mixtas del seno que comprehende la provincia de Tampico y Panuco hasta el río Guazacualco, costas laterales de Veracruz, May 19, 1793, AGN, IG, vol. 21-A.
75. Revillagigedo to Alange, January 3, 1792, AGS, GM, leg. 6955.
76. José Bravo Ugarte, ed., *Instrucción reservada al Marqués de Branciforte* (Mexico: Editorial Jus, 1966), p. 228.
77. Revillagigedo to Alange, January 3, 1792, AGS, GM, leg. 6955, and Gorostiza to Revillagigedo, June 30, 1792, AGN, CV, series 1, vol. 167.
78. Revillagigedo to Alange, no. 302, August 2, 1791, AGS, GM, leg. 6963, Revillagigedo to Alange, no. 470, January 3, 1792, AGS, GM, leg. 6964, Revillagigedo to Alange, no. 1089, December 31, 1793, and no. 1131, February 28, 1794.
79. Alange to Revillagigedo, San Lorenzo, November 23, 1791, AGS, GM, leg. 6963.
80. Revillagigedo to Aranda, no. 117, October 31, 1792, and Duque de Alcudía to Alange, Aranjuez, March 29, 1793, AGS, GM, leg. 6965. Also see AHN, leg. 4288, for copies of this correspondence.
81. Luis de las Casas to Revillagigedo, June 30, 1792, AGN, Historia, vol. 248, and Las Casas to Alange, no. 434, June 30, 1792, AGI, section 11-A, Cuba, leg. 1486.
82. Revillagigedo to Las Casas, May 29, 1793, AGI, section 11-A, Cuba, leg. 1473, Revillagigedo to Las Casas, December 12, 1793, AGI, section 11-A, Cuba, leg. 1487, and Las Casas to Revillagigedo, April 7, 1794, AGI, section 11-A, Cuba, leg. 1488.
83. Revillagigedo to Alange, May 29, 1793, AGS, GM, leg. 6966.
84. Revillagigedo to Alange, no. 875, May 29, 1793, AGI, México, leg. 1437.

85. The remaining provincial militia units were the Provincial Infantry Regiment of Mexico, the Provincial Infantry Battalion of Puebla, the Lancers of Veracruz, and the Pardo and Moreno Companies of Veracruz.
86. Revillagigedo to Alange, no. 1086, December 31, 1793, AGI, México, leg. 1435, Revillagigedo to Alange, no. 1225, June 28, 1794, AGN, CV, series 1, vol. 175, and Gorostiza to Revillagigedo, May 29, 1794, AGN, IG, vol. 407-A.
87. Alange to Revillagigedo, San Ildefonso, September 1, 1793, AGS, GM, leg. 6966, and Revillagigedo to Alange, no. 1065, November 30, 1793, AGN, CV, series 2, vol. 36.
88. Revillagigedo to Pedro de Acuña, November 6, 1793, AGI, México, leg. 1885.
89. Revillagigedo to Alange, no. 1166, March 31, 1794, and ministry of war memorandum, September 29, 1794, AGS, GM, leg. 6967.
90. Revillagigedo to Valdés, February 6, 1790, AGS, GM, leg. 6959.
91. Revillagigedo to Malaspina, October 31, 1791, MN, vol. 280.
92. Juan Vicente (Revillagigedo) to Floridablanca, May 1, 1792, AHN, Estado, leg. 4288.
93. Branciforte to Eugenio de Llaguno, July 29, 1794, AGI, México, leg. 1439.
94. Branciforte to Alange, no. 22, July 3, 1794, AGI, México, leg. 1439.
95. Gabriel de Aristizabal to Branciforte, August 29, 1794, AGS, GM, leg. 6970.
96. Branciforte to Alange, no. 205, February 28, 1795, AGS, GM, leg. 6971, and Branciforte to Alcudía, no. 37, October 5, 1794, AGI, Estado, leg. 22.
97. Ibid., and Branciforte to Alange, October 5, 1794, AGI, México, leg. 1438.
98. Mora, *México y sus revoluciones,* I: 226; Carlos Bustamante, *Suplemento,* III: 169. Lucas Alamán, *Disertaciones sobre la historia de la república mexicana,* 3 vols. (México, 1849), III: 83, and Brading, *Miners and Merchants,* pp. 81, 238.
99. Calderón Quijano, ed., *Los virreyes de Nueva España en el reinado de Carlos IV,* I:549.
100. Branciforte to Alange, no. 205, February 28, 1795, AGS, GM, leg. 6971, and Branciforte to Azanza, December 28, 1796, AGI, Estado, leg. 25.
101. Gorostiza to Branciforte, Jalapa, August 24, 1794, AGS, GM, leg. 6970.
102. Branciforte to Gorostiza, September 9, 1794, AGS, GM, leg. 6970.
103. Gorostiza to Branciforte, September 18, 1794, AGS, GM, leg. 6970, and Branciforte to Alange, no. 81, October 5, 1794, AGI, México, leg. 1438.
104. Branciforte to Alange, no. 109, November 3, 1794, AGI, México, leg. 1438.
105. Branciforte to Alcudía, no. 58, December 1, 1794, AGI, Estado, leg. 22.
106. Branciforte to Azana, no. 709, November 28, 1796, AGS, GM, leg. 6974, and Branciforte to the Prince of the Peace, October 29, 1796, AGN, CV, series 2, vol. 33.

Chapter 2

1. Diego García Panes to the king, October 30, 1792, AGI, Estado, leg. 35. Also see Christon I. Archer, "The Key to the Kingdom: the Defense of Veracruz, 1780-1810," *The Americas* 27 (April 1971):426-49.
2. Philip Henry Stanhope, *Conversations with the Duke of Wellington* (London, 1889), p. 116.
3. Humboldt, *Political Essay,* I: 83-85.
4. Flórez to Valdés, no. 793, January 27, 1789, AGI, México, leg. 1529.
5. Humboldt, *Political Essay,* IV: 8.
6. Branciforte to Miguel Costansó, January 12, 1797, and Costansó to Branciforte, January 18, and February 8, 1797, AGN, IG, vol. 328-A.
7. Peter Gerhard, *México en 1742* (Mexico: Editorial Porrúa, 1962), p. 13.
8. Proyecto del fuerte de San Miguel de Perote, 1769, AGI, México, leg. 2422; Bobb, *The Viceregency,* pp. 122-23.

9. Propuesto general de los gastos que ocasionarían los preparativos precisos para en caso que las tropas acantonadas hubieron de trasladarse a los puntos de la costa de Veracruz..., 1798, AGN, IG, vol. 328-A.

10. Representación del ayuntamiento de Veracruz sobre que los bagajes para la tropa se provean por contrata con asentista, 1792, AGN, IG, vol. 35.

11. Revillagigedo to Valdés, March 27, 1790, AGI, México, leg. 1536.

12. Plan de defensa de Veracruz, 1775, AGI, México, leg. 2418.

13. Revillagigedo to Pedro López de Lerena, no. 301, March 31, 1791, and Instrucción que han de observar los comandantes de los buques del Rey guardacostas del seno mexicano, AGI, Mexico, Leg. 1541; and Revillagigedo to Lerena, June 26, 1791, AGI, Mexico, leg. 1543.

14. Marquina to Mariano Luis de Urquijo, no. 109, October 30, 1800, AGI, Estado, leg. 28.

15. Hamnett, *Politics and Trade,* p. 99.

16. Revillagigedo to Valdés, August 31, 1789, AGI, México, leg. 1531.

17. Report of Diego García Panes, November 13, 1798, AGN, IG, vol. 508-A.

18. Humboldt, *Political Essay,* II:265.

19. Visita y reconocimiento hecho al hospital común nombrado de San Juan de Montesclaros, October 10, 1795, AGN, Hosp, vol. 36.

20. Mora, *México y sus revoluciones,* I:17.

21. Gorostiza to Revillagigedo, April 29, 1790, AGN, Historia, vol. 237.

22. Humboldt, *Political Essay,* IV:11.

23. Marquina to García Dávila, April 29, 1801, AGN, IG, vol. 70-B.

24. Francisco de Ajofrín, *Diario del viaje que hizo a la América en el siglo XVIII,* 2 vols. (Mexico: Editorial Porrúa, 1964), 1:36.

25. Humboldt, *Political Essay,* IV:177.

26. Ibid., p. 189.

27. Ibid., p. 190.

28. Método con que se curan las fiebres epidémicas que acometan a los Europeos por primera vez que pasan a aquellos climas nombradas por los ingleses, yellow fever, por los franceses, maladie asian, y por los españoles, vómito prieto, MN, vol. 2202.

29. *Gazeta de México,* 19 November 1800.

30. Azanza to Antonio Cornel, no. 35, May 31, 1800, AGI, México, leg. 2473.

31. Expediente sobre haberse contagiado los milicianos de Valladolid con los uniformes de aquellos que murieron en Veracruz de fiebres pútridas, 1801, AGN, Hosp, vol. 54.

32. Iturrigaray to José Antonio Caballero, no. 327, November 26, 1803, AGN, CV, series 1, vol. 215.

33. Miguel Lerdo de Tejada, *Apuntes históricos de la heroica ciudad de Veracruz,* 2 vols. (Mexico: Secretaría de Educación Pública, 1945), I: 367.

34. Branciforte to Azanza, January 29, 1797, AGN, CV, series 2, vol. 34.

35. García Panes to Branciforte, no. 3724, November 16, 1796, AGN, Historia, vol. 367.

36. Francisco Rendón to Branciforte, February 26, 1797, AGI, Estado, leg. 37.

37. Branciforte to Alvarez, no. 845, June 30, 1797, AGI, México, leg. 1444, and Pedro de Nava to the Prince of the Peace, March 31, 1797, AGI, Estado, leg. 37.

38. Marqués de Santa Clara to Branciforte, May 9, 1797, AGI, section 11-A, Cuba, leg. 1517-B.

39. Branciforte to Ramón de Castro, July 14, 1797, AGI, Estado, leg. 26, and Branciforte to Alvarez, August 27, 1797, AGI, México, leg. 1444.

40. Branciforte to Alvarez, no. 911, October 30, 1797, AGS, GM, leg. 7028.

41. Branciforte to the Prince of the Peace, no. 475, March 30, 1797, AGN, CV, series 2, vol. 34, and Branciforte to the Prince of the Peace, no. 11, June 30, 1797, AGI, Estado, leg. 26.

42. Dictamen del Teniente Coronel de Artillería Don Pedro de Laguna sobre defensa de la plaza de Veracruz, November 24, 1798, AGN, IG, vol. 508-A.

43. Branciforte to Alvarez, no. 281, May 31, 1797, AGN, CV, series 2, vol. 34.
44. García Panes to Branciforte, no. 4060, March 4, 1797, AGN, Historia, vol. 367.
45. Branciforte to the Prince of the Peace, September 30, 1797, AGI, Estado, leg. 26.
46. Cabildo of Veracruz to García Panes, December 2, 1797, AGN, Hosp, vol. 19.
47. Santa Clara to Alvarez, no. 346, December 12, 1797, AGI, section 11-A, Cuba, leg. 1527, and Branciforte to Santa Clara, December 16, 1797, AGI, section 11-A, Cuba, leg. 1517-B.
48. Branciforte to the Prince of the Peace, no. 93, December 30, 1797, AGI, Estado, leg. 26.
49. Report of the junta de oficiales generales, Orizaba, January 26, 1798, AGI, Estado, leg. 27.
50. Branciforte to García Panes, April 13, 1798, AGN, Historia, vol. 367.
51. García Panes to Branciforte, no. 5058, April 18, 1798, AGN, Historia, vol. 367.
52. Branciforte to the Prince of the Peace, no. 72, April 29, 1798, AGI, Estado, leg. 27.
53. Instrucción reservada del Virrey Branciforte al Señor José Miguel de Azanza, 1798, AGN, CV, series 2, vol. 36.
54. Unsigned report from Veracruz, 1804, AGN, Archivo Provisional, Hospitales Militares, Caja 1; Humboldt, *Political Essay,* IV: 157.
55. Dictamen del Teniente Coronel Don Pedro de Laguna, November 24, 1798, AGN, IG, vol. 508-A.
56. Reports of García Panes, October 5, 1798, and November 13, 1798, AGN, IG, vol. 508-A.
57. Hamnett, *Politics and Trade,* p. 100.
58. Sobre la ausencia del Sr. Ciriaco de Cevallos, 1808–1810, AGN, Infidencias, vol. 30.
59. Branciforte to Azanza, May 30, 1798, AGN, CV, series 2, vol. 36.
60. Azanza to Alvarez, June 3, 1798, AGI, México, leg. 1447.
61. Propuesto general para en caso de que las tropas acantonadas hubieron de trasladarse a los puntos de la costa de Veracruz, 1798, AGN, IG, vol. 328-A.
62. Ibid., and Azanza to Francisco de Saavedra, no. 91, September 3, 1798, AGI, Estado, leg. 27.
63. Royal Order, Aranjuez, April 10, 1798, AGI, Estado, leg. 27.
64. Azanza to Alvarez, no. 76, September 3, 1798, AGI, México, leg. 1447.
65. Azanza to Alvarez, no. 181, January 10, 1799, AGN, CV, series 2, vol. 38, and Alvarez to Azanza, Madrid, July 24, 1798, AGS, GM, leg. 6977.
66. Azanza to Alvarez, no. 182, January 8, 1799, AGN, CV, series 2, vol. 38.
67. Azanza to Santa Clara, February 10, 1799, AGI, section 11A, Cuba, leg. 1517-B.
68. Azanza to Alvarez, January 16, 1799, and February 28, 1799, Prevenciones para la saca de gente de los cuerpos provinciales, AGI, México, leg. 1450.
69. Instrucción para la defensa de Veracruz, January 20, 1799, AGN, IG, vol. 508-A.
70. Azanza to Alvarez, no. 279, April 6, 1799, AGI, México, leg. 1449, and Informe del Teniente Coronel Pedro de Alonso sobre la defensa de San Juan de Ulúa, June 30, 1798, AGN, IG, vol. 508-A.
71. Azanza to Alvarez, no. 349, May 31, 1799, AGI, México, leg. 1449.
72. Padrón formado por el comandante del cuerpo provincial de lanceros de Veracruz, January 26, 1799, AGN, IG, vol. 47-B. The total population of the Veracruz coastal zone was 654 Spaniards, 1,614 mestizos, and 5,841 pardos and morenos.
73. Branciforte to Cornel, San Lorenzo, October 28, 1799, AGS, GM, leg. 6981.
74. Alonso to the cabildo of Veracruz, June 6, 1800, AGN, Historia, vol. 361.
75. Azanza to Alvarez, no. 352, June 2, 1799, AGI, México, leg. 1449.
76. Azanza to Saavedra, no. 12, March 10, 1799, AGI, Estado, leg. 28, and Azanza to Alvarez, no. 250, March 10, 1799, AGI, México, leg. 1450.
77. Dionisio Alcalá Galiano to Azanza, Veracruz, March 2, 1799, AGI, Estado, leg. 28.

78. Azanza to Cornel, no. 663, February 26, 1800, AGI, Mexico, leg. 2473.
79. Azanza to Cornel, no. 669, February 26, 1800, AGI, México, leg. 2473, and Ordenes y providencias sobre la saca de gente de los cuerpos provinciales para reforzar segunda vez los regimientos veteranos de la Corona y Nueva España, 1800, AGN, IG, vol. 147-A.
80. Unsigned report from Veracruz, 1804, AGN, Archivo Provisional, Hospitales Militares, Caja 1; Humboldt, *Political Essay,* IV:157.
81. Marquina to Cornel, no. 35, May 31, 1800, AGI, México, leg. 1453.
82. Cabildo of Veracruz to Marquina, July 12, 1800, AGN, Historia, vol. 358.
83. Marquina to Cornel, no. 78, July 27, 1800, AGI, México, leg. 1453.
84. Marquina to Caballero, no. 22, July 27, 1800, AGN, CV, series 1, vol. 204, and Marquina to Cornel, August 28, 1800, AGN, CV, series 1, vol. 203.
85. Marquina to Cornel, no. 211, February 26, 1801, AGI, México, leg. 1458.
86. Marquina to García Dávila, February 2, 1801, García Dávila to Marquina, February 7, 1801, and Marquina to Caballero, no. 578, March 27, 1802, AGI, México, leg. 1464.
87. Marquina to García Dávila, July 16, 1800, García Dávila to Marquina, no. 2326, February 6, 1801, and no. 2322, February 6, 1801, AGN, Historia, vol. 358.
88. Marquina to Caballero, July 27, 1801, AGI, México, leg. 1459, and Costansó to Marquina, February 16, 1801, AGN, Historia, vol. 521.
89. Marquina to the junta de guerra, Veracruz, March 12, 1801, AGI, México, leg. 1464. The members of the junta were García Dávila, Diego García Panes, Miguel Costansó, José Gómez, Juan Manuel Bonilla, Pedro de Laguna, Nicolás de Monteagudo, the Conde de Alcaraz, Joaquín Gutíerrez de los Ríos, Pedro de Alonso, Manuel de Flon, and José Fonnegra.
90. Instructions to the junta de guerra, Veracruz, March, 1801, AGN, Historia, vol. 358.
91. Report of Manuel de Flon, March 15, 1801, AGN, Historia, vol. 358.
92. Marquina to Caballero, no. 314, July 27, 1801, AGI, México, leg. 1459.
93. Marquina to Caballero, no. 755, September 26, 1802, AGI, México, leg. 1464.
94. Marquina to Caballero, no. 670, June 26, 1802, AGI, México, leg. 1464.
95. Marquina to Caballero, no. 635, May 27, 1802, AGN, CV, series 1, vol. 210.
96. Marquina to Someruelos, July 9, 1802, Someruelos to Marquina, September 22, 1802, November 20, 1802, and December 6, 1802, AGI, section 11-A, Cuba, leg. 1711.

Chapter 3

1. José de Iturrigaray to Caballero, no. 251, August 23, 1803, and no. 327, November 26, 1803, AGN, CV, series 1, vol. 215.
2. Report of the consulado of Veracruz to the consulado of Havana, National Archives of the United States, Dispatches from United States Consuls in Havana, 1783–1906, vol. 1.
3. García Dávila to Iturrigaray, February 10, 1803, AGN, IG, vol. 47-B.
4. García Dávila to Iturrigaray, March 9, 1803, AGN, Historia, vol. 367.
5. Iturrigaray to Caballero, no. 370, January 24, 1804, AGN, CV, series 1, vol. 220.
6. Iturrigaray to Caballero, no. 327, November 26, 1803, AGN, CV, series 1, vol. 215.
7. Iturrigaray to Caballero, no. 814, May 7, 1805, AGN, CV, series 1, vol. 225.
8. Royal order, May 8, 1804, AGN, Historia, vol. 521.
9. Miguel Costansó to Iturrigaray, January 16, 1805, and Iturrigaray to the consulado of Veracruz, March 14, 1805, AGN, Historia, vol. 521.
10. Cabildo of Veracruz to Iturrigaray, March 18, 1805, AGN, Historia, vol. 521.
11. Ibid.
12. Iturrigaray to the consulado of Veracruz, March 24, 1805, AGN, Historia, vol. 521.
13. Ibid.
14. Iturrigaray to the consulado of Veracruz, September 21, 1805, AGN, Historia, vol. 521.

Notes 317

15. The Marqués de Someruelos to Iturrigaray, Havana, February 19, 1805, AGI, section 11A, Cuba, leg. 1711; Iturrigaray to Ciriaco Cevallos, April 16, 1805, MN, vol. 149; Iturrigaray to Caballero, no. 199, July 27, 1803, AGN, CV, series 1, vol. 215; and Iturrigaray to Caballero, no. 370, January 27, 1804, AGN, CV, series 1, vol. 220.

16. Plan sobre el sistema de armamento y operaciones de guerra más adequado al puerto de Veracruz presentado por el comandante del apostadero, Ciriaco Cevallos, April 6, 1805, MN, vol. 149.

17. Iturrigaray to Caballero, no. 816; May 7, 1805, and August 27, 1805, AGN, CV, series 1, vol. 225.

18. Diputación de comercio de Oaxaca, Antonio Sánchez, Francisco Antonio de Goytía, and Manuel del Solar Campero to Iturrigaray, February 7, 1806, AGN, Historia, vol. 521; and expediente 17, AGN, Archivo de Hacienda, leg. 664.

19. Consulado of Veracruz to Iturrigaray, September 10, 1805, AGN, Historia, vol. 521.

20. Diputación de comercio de Campeche to Miguel Cayetano Soler, no. 272, April 23, 1808, AGI, México, leg. 1975.

21. Iturrigaray to the consulado of Veracruz, September 21, 1805, AGN, Historia, vol. 521.

22. Cevallos to Iturrigaray, October 6, 1805, AGN, Historia, vol. 521.

23. Prince of the Peace to Iturrigaray, Madrid, September 24, 1805, AGN, Historia, vol. 361.

24. Iturrigaray to the cabildo of Veracruz, September 14, 1807, and Iturrigaray to Caballero, no. 1357, September 2, 1807, AGN, Historia, vol. 361.

25. Marqués de Casa Irujo to Someruelos, Philadelphia, November 20, 1805, December 10, 1805, February 4, 1806, and March 4, 1806, AGI, section 11A, Cuba, leg. 1708; and Pedro de Alonso to Iturrigaray, August 14, 1806, AGN, Historia, vol. 521.

26. Casa Irujo to Someruelos, February 4, 1806, November 20, 1806, and December 10, 1806, AGI, section 11A, Cuba, leg. 1708.

27. Charles William Vane, Marquess of Londonderry, ed., *Correspondence Despatches, and other Papers of Viscount Castlereagh, Second Marquess of Londonderry: Second Series: Military and Miscellaneous,* 12 vols. (London, 1851), VII:293–97.

28. Duke of Wellington, *Supplementary Despatches, Correspondence, and Memoranda of Field Marshal Arthur, Duke of Wellington, K. G.,* 15 vols. (London, 1860), VI:61–66; and in VII, Memorandum, November 2, 1806, 35–38; Memorandum, no. 4, November 20, 1806, 45–47, and "Result of Conversation with Mr. Fraser on the 6th and 7th of November, 1806," 38–39.

29. Estado que manifiesta las tropas que hay puestas sobre las armas y se hallan acantonadas en las villas de Córdoba, Orizaba, Perote, y Jalapa, August, 1806, AGN, Historia, vol. 521.

30. Prince of the Peace to Iturrigaray, Madrid, December 4, 1806, AGN, Historia, vol. 40 and vol. 261; Iturrigaray to the Prince of the Peace, no. 29, March 3, 1807, AGN, CV, series 2, vol. 50; Resumen del numero de tropas efectivas que se hallan sobre las armas para oponerse a cualquiera invasión del enemigo, March 29 and October 14, 1807, AGN, Historia, vol. 361.

31. Diario militar del exército acampado en el Llano del Encero por Capitán Cristóbal Domínguez, ayudante del Regimiento de Valladolid, *Gazeta de México,* 23 March 1806, and 23 December 1806.

32. Cabildo of Veracruz to Iturrigaray, August 16, 1806, and Iturrigaray to Juan Manuel de Bonilla, August 19, 1806, AGN, Historia, vol. 521.

33. Cabildo of Veracruz to Iturrigaray, August 23, 1806; Iturrigaray to the cabildo, August 29, 1806, and the cabildo to Iturrigaray, September 6, 1806, AGN, Historia, vol. 521.

34. Iturrigaray to the Cabildo of Veracruz, October 7, 1807, AGN, Historia, vol. 361, and *Gazeta de México,* 18 April 1807.

35. Caballero to Iturrigaray, Aranjuez, April 20, 1807, AGN, Historia, vol. 367, and Cabildo of Veracruz to the Junta Suprema, August 26, 1808, AGN, Historia, vol. 50.

36. Iturrigaray to the cabildo of Veracruz, September 14, 1807, AGN, Historia, vol. 361.

37. Cabildo of Veracruz to Iturrigaray, September 30, 1807, AGN, Historia, vol. 361.
38. Iturrigaray to the cabildo of Veracruz, October 7, 1807, and Iturrigaray to Caballero, October 8, 1807, AGN, Historia, vol. 361.
39. Cabildo of Veracruz to Iturrigaray, October 31, 1807, AGN, Historia, vol. 361.
40. Iturrigaray to Pedro de Alonso, November 10, 1807, and Iturrigaray to Caballero, no. 1468, December 27, 1807, AGN, Historia, vol. 361.
41. Pedro Telmo de Landero to Iturrigaray, January 9, 1808, AGN, Historia, vol. 361.
42. Order of Colonel Pedro de Alonso, March 8, 1808, AGN, Historia, vol. 361.
43. Iturrigaray to Antonio Olaguer Felin, no. 1599, May 24, 1808, AGN, CV, series 1, vol. 237.
44. Ambrosio de Sagarzurieta to Iturrigaray, November 30, 1807, AGN, Historia, vol. 361.
45. Marquess of Londonderry, ed., *Correspondence,* VII:429–40.
46. Duke of Wellington, *Supplementary Despatches,* VII:65.
47. Iturrigaray to Pedro de Cevallos, June 21, 1808, AGI, México, leg. 1320, and *Gazeta de México,* 21 June 1808.
48. Pedro de Alonso to Iturrigaray, July 21, 1808, AGN, Historia, vol. 46; J. E. Hernández y Dávalos, *Colección de documentos para la historia de la guerra de independencia de México de 1808 a 1821,* 6 vols. (Mexico, 1877), I:527.
49. Pedro de Alonso to Iturrigaray, no. 2181, August 10, 1808, AGI, Mexico, leg. 1321; Lerdo de Tejada, *Apuntes históricos,* II:28–30.
50. Order of Cevallos, August 10, 1808, and Cevallos to Pedro Garibay, October 15, 1809, AGN, Infidencias, vol. 30.
51. Alonso to Iturrigaray, no. 2181, August 10, 1808, AGI, México, leg. 1321, and petition of Antonio Ortiz to the Junta de Seguridad y Buen Orden, October 17, 1809, AGN, Infidencias, vol. 30.
52. José María Migoni to Carlos María de Urrutía, June 7, 1810, AGN, Infidencias, vol. 30.
53. Garibay to Pedro de Cevallos, no. 2, February 20, 1809, AGN, CV, series 1, vol. 241.
54. Lerdo de Tejada, *Apuntes históricos,* II:36; Alamán, *Historia de Méjico,* I:185.
55. Iturrigaray to Alonso, August 14, 1808, AGI, México, leg. 1321.
56. Cevallos to Iturrigaray, October 15, 1809, and testimony of José Ignacio de la Torre, Manuel Antonio de Ysassi, José Ignacio Pavón y Muñoz, and Félix Aguirre, May and June, 1810, AGN, Infidencias, vol. 30.
57. Alamán, *Historia de Méjico,* I:185; Noticia del comercio que han hecho los buques neutrales desde 26 de Septiembre de 1805 hasta fin de Abril de 1807, MN, vol. 317.
58. Pedro Telmo de Landero to Iturrigaray, no. 668, September 5, 1808, AGN, Historia, vol. 50.
59. Cabildo of Veracruz to the Junta Suprema, August 26, 1808, AGN, Historia, vol. 50.
60. Iturrigaray to Calleja, August 21, 1808, Iturrigaray to García Dávila, September 10, 1808, and Iturrigaray to Calleja, September 14, 1808, AGN, Historia, vol. 50.
61. Oficio del ayuntamiento de Veracruz al Virrey Garibay en que se manifiesta el júbilo con que esa ciudad ha recibido la noticia de la deposición de Iturrigaray, September 18, 1808, in Genaro García, *Documentos históricos mexicanos, obra conmemorativa del primer centenario de la independencia de México,* 7 vols. (Mexico, 1910), II:211. The effort to discredit Iturrigaray's defense plans and policies regarding Veracruz came to nothing. See Genaro García, *Documentos,* II:239–41, and Hernández y Dávalos, *Colección de documentos,* I:624–26.
62. Cabildo of Veracruz to Garibay, September 23, 1808, AGN, Historia, vol. 50, and report of Garibay, no. 25, November 26, 1808, AGN, CV, series 2, vol. 52.
63. Garibay to García Dávila, October 26, 1808, and Pedro de Laguna to Garibay, December 24, 1808, and January 24, 1808, AGN, IG, vol. 166-A.
64. Garibay to the Junta Central de Sevilla, September 24, 1808, AGI, México, leg. 1319, and Garibay to García Dávila, September 16, 1808, AGN, Historia, vol. 46.
65. García Dávila to Garibay, October 15, 1808, AGN, IG, vol. 166-A.

Notes 319

66. Cabildo of Veracruz to Garibay, November 4, 1808, AGN, IG, vol. 166-A.
67. Garibay to García Dávila, February 20, 1809, AGN, IG, vol. 166-A.
68. Garibay to Manuel Merino, July 1, 1809, and García Dávila to Garibay, July 7, 1809, AGN, IG, vol. 166-A.
69. García Dávila to the king, July 17, 1809, AGN, IG, vol. 166-A.
70. Lizana to Calleja, May 2, 1810, and Carlos de Urrutía to Lizana, April 24, 1810, AGN, IG, vol. 410-A.
71. Lizana to Cornel, no. 314, May 1, 1810, AGN, CV, series 1, vol. 243, and Audiencia to Francisco de Eguía, secretary of war in the Council of Regency, June 1, 1810, AGN, CV, series 1, vol. 246.
72. Estado que manifiesta el número de enfermos entrados, curados, y muertos y existentes en el Hospital de San Sebastián, May and June, 1810, AGN, IG, vol. 410-A.
73. José Luyando to Pedro Catini, regent of the audiencia of Mexico, May 15, 1810, and Audiencia to the Marqués de Hormazas, no. 10, June 6, 1810, AGI, México, leg. 1475.

Chapter 4

1. Warren G. Cook, *Flood Tide of Empire: Spain and the Pacific Northwest, 1543–1819* (New Haven: Yale University Press, 1973), p. 200.
2. Marqués del Campo to Floridablanca, London, November 26, 1790, AHN, Estado, leg. 4291.
3. Royal Order, Aranjuez, May 18, 1791, AGI, IG, leg. 662.
4. Revillagigedo to Pedro de Lerena, no. 605, October 29, 1791, AGI, México, leg. 1544, and Revillagigedo to Floridablanca, no. 88, September 30, 1791.
5. Humboldt, *Political Essay*, IV:263.
6. Revillagigedo to Alange, no. 857, April 30, 1793, AGI, México, leg. 1435.
7. Revillagigedo to Aranda, no. 18, May 31, 1792, and no. 28, August 30, 1792, AGI, Estado, leg. 21.
8. Revillagigedo to Floridablanca, no. 88, September 30, 1791, and no. 91, November 30, 1791, AGI, Estado, leg. 20.
9. Revillagigedo to Valdés, no. 112, February 6, 1790, AGS, GM, leg. 6960.
10. Revillagigedo to Floridablanca, no. 88, September 30, 1791, AGI, Estado, leg. 20.
11. José Miranda, *Humboldt y México* (Mexico: UNAM, 1961), p. 19, and Flórez to Valdés, no. 449, July 26, 1788, AGI, México, leg. 1518.
12. Branciforte to Alcudía, no. 30, September 30, 1794, AGI, Estado, leg. 22.

> The French are the wisest
> It is not absurd to follow them in their opinions.
> However many may make the laws
> They will never be able to suffocate the cries
> That Nature inspires.

13. Branciforte to Alcudía, no. 36, October 3, 1794, AGI, Estado, leg. 22, and Calderón Quijano, ed., *Los Virreyes de Nueva España en el reinado de Carlos IV*, I:390–95.
14. Juan Ignacio de Bejarno y Frías to Alcudía, January 10, 1795, AGI, Estado, leg. 39. Similar reports had reached the archbishop of Mexico from a priest in the capital. See Archbishop to Alcudía, no. 22, October 4, 1794, AGI, Estado, leg. 41.
15. Miranda, *Humboldt y México*, p. 21.
16. Branciforte to Alcudía, no. 59, December 3, 1794, AGI, Estado, leg. 22.
17. Francisco Javier de Borbón to Branciforte, no. 59, November 11, 1794, AGI, Estado, leg. 22.

18. Dictamen de los ministros de la Real Sala del Crimen, November 12, 1794, AGI, Estado, leg. 22.
19. Alcudía to Branciforte, no. 59, Aranjuez, March 22, 1795, AGI, Estado, leg. 22; Audiencia to Llaguno, February 28, 1795, AGI, Estado, leg. 36; and Branciforte to Alcudía, no. 33, August 30, 1796, and no. 45, October 23, 1796, AGI, Estado, leg. 23. Of the French prisoners, 21 were sent to Cádiz and another small group was to be dispatched at a later date.
20. Branciforte to Alcudía, no. 115, AGN, CV, series 2, vol. 32; John Rydjord, *Foreign Interest in the Independence of New Spain* (Durham, N.C.: Duke University Press, 1935), p. 128. The book *Desengaño del hombre* was written by James (Santiago) Puglia, a Spanish instructor in Philadelphia.
21. Branciforte to Alcudía, no. 36, October 30, 1794, AGI, Estado, leg. 22.
22. Azanza to Alvarez, no. 58, August 27, 1798, AGI, México, leg. 1447.
23. Irujo to the Marqués de Santa Clara, October 2, 1798, AGI, section 11-A, Cuba, leg. 1518-B: and Irujo to Santa Clara, February 6, 1799, AGI, section 11-A, Cuba, leg. 1518-A.
24. Azanza to Alvarez, no. 181, January 10, 1799, AGI, México, leg. 1446.
25. Noel M. Loomis, "Philip Nolan's Entry into Texas in 1800," in John F. McDermott, ed., *The Spanish in the Mississippi Valley, 1762-1804* (Urbana: University of Illinois Press, 1974), p. 129.
26. Pedro de Nava to Azanza, September 25, 1798, and José Blanco, interim governor of Nuevo Santander to his commanders, November 20, 1800, AGN, Historia, vol. 413.
27. Declaration of Mordecai Richards to José Vidal, December 13, 1800, AGN, Historia, vol. 413.
28. Marquina to Cornel, no. 252, June 26, 1801, AGI, México, leg. 1459.
29. Exposición hecha reservadamente al Ministro de Estado en 1801 por Don Ramón López de Angulo, demonstrando el riesgo que con la independencia de los Estados Unidos corrían nuestras posesiones vecinas a ellos y hasta México... , New Orleans, May 15, 1801, MN, vol. 315.
30. Casa Irujo to Someruelos, Philadelphia, November 20, 1805, December 10, 1805, February 4, 1806, February 14, 1806, and March 4, 1806, AGI, section 11-A, Cuba, leg. 1708.
31. Casa Irujo to Someruelos, November 16, 1806, and December 10, 1806, AGI section 11-A, Cuba, leg. 1708.
32. Iturrigaray to the Prince of the Peace, January 20, 1807, AGN, CV, series 2, vol. 50.
33. James Wilkinson to Iturrigaray, Natchez, November 17, 1806, AGI, México, leg. 1471.
34. Iturrigaray to Wilkinson, January 21, 1807, and Iturrigaray to the Prince of the Peace, March 12, 1807, AGI, México, leg. 1471. Also see Enrique Lafuente Ferrari, *El Virrey Iturrigaray y los orígenes de la independencia de Méjico* (Madrid: La Semana Gráfica, 1941), p. 59.
35. *The American Register*, II:87, quoted in Rydjord, *Foreign Interest*, p. 217.
36. Garibay to Pedro de Cevallos, May 12, 1809, AGN, CV, series 1, vol. 241.
37. Instrucción para el Teniente Coronel Don Julián Bustamante, April 4, 1809, AGI, México, leg. 1633.
38. Garibay to Francisco de Saavedra, no. 109, June 30, 1809, AGN, CV, series 1, vol. 239.
39. Luis de Cloves to Pedro de Cevallos, Madrid, December 7, 1814, AGI, IG, leg. 1603.
40. José Vidal to Garibay, New Orleans, December 17, 1808, AGI, section 11-A, Cuba, leg. 1712.
41. Ciriaco Cevallos to Benito Pérez, governor of Yucatan, New Orleans, July 20, 1809, AGN, Infidencias, vol. 30.
42. Luis de Onís to Garibay, Philadelphia, no. 1, October 31, 1809, AGI, IG, leg. 1566.
43. Ignacio Pérez de Lema to Garibay, May 30, 1809, AGI, México, leg. 1634.
44. Garibay to Martín de Garay, no. 21, June 30, 1809, AGN, CV, series 1, vol. 241.
45. H. I. Priestley, *José de Gálvez*, p. 228.
46. Juan Francisco de Echarri to Azanza, April 24, 1799, AGN, IG, vol. 176-A.
47. Audiencia of Guadalajara to Revillagigedo, November 20, 1789, and Revillagigedo to the audiencia, December 2, 1789, AGN, Historia, vol. 226.
48. Branciforte to Alcudía, no. 111, May 30, 1795, AGN, CV, series 2, vol. 32.

Notes 321

49. Branciforte to Alcudía, no. 15, August 3, 1795, AGI, Estado, leg. 23.
50. Branciforte to the Prince of the Peace, no. 220, November 30, 1795, AGN, CV, series 2, vol. 32.
51. Francisco Saavedra to Francisco de Escovedo, Guadalajara, September 2, 1799, and Escovedo to Vicente Llorena, September 3, 1799, AGN, IG, vol. 370-A.
52. Azanza to the audiencia, September 14, 1799, AGN, IG, vol. 370-A.
53. Bernardino Bonavía to Iturrigaray, March 11, 1803, AGN, IG, vol. 175-A.
54. Ordenes que deben observarse en los paseos de la Alameda y Bucareli por la tropa que se destine a ellos los días de fiesta, 1791, MN, vol. 335.
55. Revillagigedo to Valdés, November 30, 1789, AGI, Mexico, leg. 1531.
56. Branciforte to the Prince of the Peace, no. 20, August 19, 1797, and no. 7, July 3, 1797, AGI, Estado, leg. 26.
57. Azanza to Saavedra, no. 53, July 27, 1798, AGI, Mexico, leg. 1448; Marquina to Miguel Cayetano Soler, Santander, May 13, 1803, AGI, México, leg. 1319.
58. Iturrigaray to Cayetano Soler, no. 1012, June 26, 1806, AGN, CV, series 1, vol. 229.
59. Humboldt, *Political Essay,* II:106, and Priestley, *José de Gálvez,* p. 217.
60. Calderón Quijano, ed., *Los Virreyes de Nueva España en el reinado de Carlos III,* II:175.
61. Humboldt, *Political Essay,* I:149.
62. Flórez to Valdés, no. 817, February 26, 1789, AGI, México, leg. 1528.
63. Flórez to Valdés, no. 27, November 23, 1787, AGI, México, leg. 1514, and Flórez to Valdés, no. 731, December 27, 1788, AGI, México, leg. 1523.
64. Esteban Tizón to Flórez, Papantla, July 29, 1788, AGN, IG, vol. 414-A.
65. Ibid.
66. Juan García Amoroso to Bernardo de Troncoso, Tlacotalpan, October 23, 1787, AGN, Historia, vol. 326.
67. Report of Manuel Sabón de Oliveros, Acayucan, October 22, 1787, AGN, Historia, vol. 326.
68. Report of the junta de guerra, October 24, 1787, and Troncoso to Flórez, no. 175, October 24, 1787, AGN, Historia, vol. 326.
69. Miguel Corral to Troncoso, November 15, 1787, AGN, Historia, vol. 326.
70. Corral to Flórez, December 12, 1787, AGN, Historia, vol. 326.
71. Report of the Council of Indies, 1805, AGI, Estado, leg. 30.
72. Conjuración: acerca del cierto señor de que el Comandante del Departamento de San Blas dió parte al Exmo. Virrey de Nueva España, 1801, AGN, Historia, vol. 428; Marquina to Caballero, no. 113, June 26, 1801, AGN, CV, series 1, vol. 207.
73. Marquina to Urquijo, no. 10, February 26, 1801, AGI, Estado, leg. 29.
74. José Abascal to Marquina, January 5, 1801, and Marquina to Abascal, January 9, 1801, AGI, México, leg. 1456.
75. Report of the Council of Indies, 1805, AGI, Estado, leg. 30.
76. Marquina to Urquijo, no. 10, February 26, 1801, AGI, Estado, leg. 29.
77. García Dávila to Marquina, no. 1449, February 25, 1801, and Marquina to García Dávila, March 7, 1801, AGN, IG, vol. 396-A.
78. Marquina to Caballero, no. 113, June 26, 1801, AGI, México, leg. 1456.
79. Testimony of Simón Pascual and Miguel Aparicio, April 4, 1801, AGN, IG, vol. 396-A.
80. Calleja to Marquina, December 5, 1801, and Report of the Fiscal de lo Civil, Borbón, June 30, 1803, AGN, Historia, vol. 413.
81. Testimony of Juan José García, January to April, 1802, Report of the Tribunal del Protomedicato, June 21, 1802, and Report of the Fiscal de lo Criminal, June 30, 1803, AGN, Historia, vol. 413.
82. Marquina to Caballero, no. 113, June 26, 1801, AGN, CV, series 1, vol. 207.
83. Iturrigaray to Cevallos, no. 175, July 27, 1803, AGI, Estado, leg. 30.
84. Cuentas de los gastos causados con motivo de la intentada sublevación de Tepic, 1801, AGN, IG, vol. 46-A.

85. Report of the Council of Indies, 1805, AGI, Estado, leg. 30. The minister of war agreed with the Council of Indies, but declined to issue reprimands.
86. Marquina to Urquijo, no. 85, June 11, 1800, AGI, Estado, leg. 28.
87. Ibid.
88. Marquina to Urquijo, no. 87, June 25, 1800, no. 91, July 27, 1800, and no. 97, August 27, 1800, AGI, Estado, leg. 28.
89. Marquina to Cevallos, no. 28, July 28, 1801, and Manuel del Castillo Negrete to Marquina, June, 1801, AGI, Estado, leg. 29.
90. Azanza to Urquijo, November 30, 1799, AGI, Estado, leg. 28; and Hugh M. Hamill, *The Hidalgo Revolt: Prelude to Mexican Independence* (Gainesville: University of Florida Press, 1966), p. 93.
91. Azanza to Urquijo, November 30, 1799, AGI, Estado, leg. 28. Also see AGN, CV, series 2, vol. 38, for a copy of this document and a list of those arrested.
92. Silvestre Díaz de la Vega to Marquina, September 19, 1800, and Manuel de Santa María to Marquina, October 27, 1800, AGI, Estado, leg. 28.
93. Report of the Council of Indies, January 24, 1801, AGI, Estado, leg. 28.
94. Marquina to Urquijo, October 27, 1800, AGI, Estado, leg. 28.
95. Cevallos to the cabildo of Veracruz, August 10, 1808, AGN, Infidencias, vol. 30.

Chapter 5

1. Brading, *Miners and Merchants*, p. 42. Also see Brading, "Government and Elite in Late Colonial Mexico," *HAHR* 53 (1973):389–414; Mark A. Burkholder, "From Creole to *Peninsular:* The Transformation of the Audiencia of Lima," and Jacques A. Barbier, "Elites and Cadres in Bourbon Chile," *HAHR* 52 (1972):395–415, 416–435; and Leon G. Campbell, "A Colonial Establishment: Creole Domination of the Audiencia of Lima during the Late Eighteenth Century," *HAHR* 52 (1972):1–25.
2. Títulos de Intendentes, 1787, AGI, México, leg. 1973. For studies of the other viceroyalties see John Lynch, *Spanish Colonial Administration, 1782–1810* (London: Athlone Press, 1958), pp. 291–301, and J. R. Fisher, *Government and Society in Colonial Peru: The Intendant System, 1784–1814* (London: Athlone Press, 1970), pp. 240–50.
3. Revillagigedo to Valdés, no. 349, February 26, 1790, AGI, México, leg. 1537.
4. Títulos de Inspectores y Sub-Inspectores, June 22, 1785, AGI, México, leg. 2424.
5. Testimonio... del Exmo. Señor Virrey Conde de Gálvez, November 26, 1786, AGI, México, leg. 1512.
6. Revillagigedo to Antonio Porlier, no. 63, January 8, 1790, AGN, CV, series 2, vol. 30.
7. Royal Order, March 7, 1789, AGI, México, leg. 1182; and Revillagigedo to Valdés, no. 649, July 3, 1790, AGI, México, leg. 1532.
8. Revillagigedo to Valdés, no. 648, July 2, 1790, AGI, México, leg. 1300.
9. Branciforte to Alcudía, no. 58, December 1, 1794, AGI, Estado, leg. 22.
10. Branciforte to Alange, no. 132, December 1, 1794, AGI, México, leg. 1438.
11. Branciforte to Alvarez, no. 912, October 30, 1797, AGN, CV, series 2, vol. 34.
12. Flórez to Valdés, no. 547, September 23, 1788, AGI, México, leg. 1520, and Flórez to Valdés, no. 617, October 27, 1788, AGI, México, leg. 1521. The previous secretary, Fernando de Córdoba, was transferred to the secretaría del despacho universal in Spain.
13. Manuel Pastor to Azanza, August 14, 1798, and Azanza to Alvarez, no. 121, November 6, 1798, AGI, México, leg. 1446.
14. Marquina to Caballero, no. 352, August 27, 1801, AGI, México, leg. 1459.
15. Branciforte to Alvarez, no. 912, Orizaba, October 30, 1797, AGI, Estado, leg. 26.
16. Noticia que manifiesta el número de tropas de que constar los Cuerpos provinciales, urbanos, y demas milicias del reino de Nueva España con algunas veteranas fixas, su reparto en divisiones ó brigadas... , March, 1800, AGN, IG, vol. 386-A.

17. Azanza to Cornel, no. 684, March 27, 1800, AGN, CV, series 1, vol. 200.
18. Azanza to Cornel, no. 685, March 27, 1800, AGI, México, leg. 1452.
19. Royal Order, March 27, 1800, AGI, México, leg. 1459.
20. Instrucción que deben arreglar sus funciones los comandantes de brigada, March 26, 1800, AGN, IG, vol. 386-A.
21. Marquina to Urquijo, no. 23, August 30, 1800, AGI, Estado, leg. 29; and Marquina to Miguel Cayetano Soler, no. 61, July 27, 1800, and Royal Order, July 27, 1800, AGI, México, leg. 1319.
22. Marquina to Caballero, no. 270, July 27, 1801, AGI, México, leg. 1459.
23. Marquina to Cornel, no. 57, July 27, 1800, AGI, México, leg. 1453; Instrucción reservada de Marquina, 1801, AGN, Historia, vol. 282; and Iturrigaray to Caballero, no. 679, November 26, 1804, AGI, México, leg. 1468.
24. Azanza to Alvarez, no. 91, September 27, 1798, AGI, México, leg. 1447.
25. Revillagigedo to Las Casas, November 26, 1793, AGI, section 11-A, Cuba, leg. 1473.
26. Azanza to the captain general of Cuba, September 26, 1798, AGI, section 11-A, Cuba, leg. 1517-B; and Azanza to Alvarez, August 30, 1799, AGS, GM, leg. 6980.
27. Iturrigaray to Caballero, no. 679, November 26, 1804, AGI, México, leg. 1468.
28. Conde de Alcaraz to Iturrigaray, October 22, 1804, AGI, México, leg. 1468.
29. Lizana to Cornel, no. 92, November 19, 1809, AGN, CV, series 1, vol. 243; and Cornel to Lizana, December 4, 1809, AGI, México, leg. 1320.
30. Flórez to Valdés, no. 821, February 26, 1789, AGI, México, leg. 1528.
31. Revillagigedo to the Marqués de Bexmar, no. 362, January 31, 1792, AGI, Mexico, leg. 1432.
32. One example was Revillagigedo's interpretation of the royal order of February 9, 1793, extending the *fuero militar*. Bataller formed an opinion supporting a narrow view of the decree while Cacho Calderón furnished the arguments Branciforte needed to expand the decree. See AGN, IG, vol. 13-B.
33. Branciforte to Alange, no. 106, October 31, 1794, AGI, México, leg. 1438.
34. Azanza to Alvarez, no. 138, November 26, 1798, AGI, México, leg. 1446; Marquina to Caballero, no. 515, February 26, 1802, AGI, México, leg. 1464; and memorandum of Iturrigaray, December 14, 1803, AGN, IG, vol. 10.
35. Guillermo de Aguirre to Iturrigaray, December 14, 1803, AGN, IG, vol. 10.
36. Iturrigaray to Caballero, no. 347, December 27, 1803, AGN, CV, series 1, vol. 215.
37. Iturrigaray to Caballero, no. 357, November 26, 1805, AGN, CV, series 1, vol. 226.
38. Iturrigaray to Caballero, no. 1024, May 27, 1806, AGN, CV, series 1, vol. 230; and Lizana to Cornel, no. 93, November 16, 1809, AGN, CV, series 1, vol. 243.
39. Lynch, *Spanish Colonial Administration*, pp. 47–48.
40. Brading, *Miners and Merchants*, pp. 46–48.
41. Conde de Tepa to Bucareli, July 1, 1775, AGI, México, leg. 1973.
42. *Ordenanza para el establecimiento é instrucción de intendentes de exército y provincia en el reino de Nueva España* (Madrid, 1786), articles 250–302.
43. Dispatches of Mangino, July to November, 1787, AGI, México, leg. 1978; and Mangino to the Marqués de Sonora, no. 171, August 27, 1787, AGI, México, leg. 1979.
44. Flórez to Valdés, no. 132, February 8, 1788, AGI, México, leg. 1973.
45. Ibid.
46. Instrucción reservada que de orden del Rey debe observar el Teniente General Conde de Revillagigedo nombrado por S.M. Virrey de Nueva España, 1789, AGS, GM, leg. 7011.
47. Revillagigedo to Alange, no. 22, July 27, 1790, AGS, GM, leg. 6966.
48. Revillagigedo to Valdés, no. 648, July 2, 1790, AGI, México, leg. 1300.
49. Revillagigedo to Valdés, no. 649, July 3, 1790, AGI, México, leg. 1532.
50. Revillagigedo to Pedro de Lerena, no. 40, July 31, 1790, and no. 380, May 5, 1791, AGI, México, leg. 1300.

51. Flórez to Valdés, no. 524, August 28, 1788, AGI, México, leg. 1531.
52. Revillagigedo to Valdés, no. 18, October 27, 1789, AGS, GM, leg. 7019.
53. Revillagigedo to Pedro de Acuña, no. 653, September 30, 1793, AGI, México, leg. 1436. Flon had 32 years' army service in North Africa and in the Americas. In 1784 he was named interim governor of Nueva Vizcaya. He was interim governor of Puebla when he received the intendancy in 1787.
54. Revillagigedo to Valdés, no. 107, November 26, 1789, AGI, México, leg. 1531.
55. Revillagigedo to Alange, July 29, 1790, AGN, CV, series 1, vol. 159.
56. Azanza to Alvarez, no. 84, September 27, 1798, AGI, México, leg. 1447.
57. Marquina to Caballero, no. 652, June 26, 1802, AGI, México, leg. 1464; Pérez Gálvez to Lizana, October 18, 1809, AGN, IG, vol. 158-B.
58. Branciforte to Pérez Gálvez, May 7, 1796, AGN, IG, vol. 384-A.
59. Pérez Gálvez to Branciforte, May 13, 1796, AGN, IG, vol. 384-A.
60. Juan Francisco de Echarrí to Azanza, April 24, 1799, AGN, IG, 175-A.
61. Antonio de Mora y Peysal to Azanza, December 31, 1799, AGN, IG, vol. 175-A.
62. Bernardo Bonavía to Iturrigaray, March 11, 1803, AGN, IG, vol. 175-A.
63. Luis Ortiz de Zárate to Marquina, September 14, 1801, and Bonavía to Iturrigaray, October 26, 1807, AGN, IG, vol. 175-A.
64. Mora y Peysal to Iturrigaray, December 22, 1807, AGN, IG, vol. 175-A; and Hamnett, *Politics and Trade,* pp. 77.
65. Francisco Rendón to Branciforte, February 26, 1797, AGI, Estado, leg. 37.
66. Rendón was well qualified to handle the new post. In 1779, he served as secretary to the commission of Juan de Miralles to the United States. After numerous important assignments, he became intendant of Louisiana and West Florida, and then accepted the intendancy of Zacatecas in 1796. See Rendón to Iturrigaray, March 16, 1808, AGI, México, leg. 1631.
67. Rendón to Branciforte, January 30, 1797, AGN, IG, vol. 391-A; and Branciforte to Azanza, no. 783, February 26, 1797, AGN, CV, series 2, vol. 34.
68. Rendón to Branciforte, February 26, 1797, AGI, Estado, leg. 37.
69. Marquina to Flon, February 3, 1801, AGN, Historia, vol. 358.
70. Estado que manifiesta las tropas . . . en las villas de Córdoba, Orizaba, Perote, y Jalapa, 1806, AGN, Historia, vol. 521; and Rendón to Lizana, August 4, 1809, AGI, México, leg. 1473.
71. Rendón to Iturrigaray, March 16, 1808, AGI, México, leg. 1631; Pedro Garibay to Saavedra, May 12, 1809, AGI, México, leg. 1633; and Audiencia Gobernativa to Eguía, no. 35, June 5, 1810, AGN, CV, series 1, vol. 246.
72. Hamnett, *Politics and Trade,* p. 7.
73. Humboldt, *Political Essay,* I:195; Brading, *Miners and Merchants,* p. 75; and Revillagigedo to Lerena, no. 402, June 1, 1791, AGI, México, leg. 1540.
74. Luis Navarro García, *Intendencias en Indias* (Seville: Escuela de Estudios Hispano-Americanos, 1959), p. 109; Fisher, *Government and Society,* p. 99; and Calderón Quijano, ed., *Los Virreyes de Nueva España en el reinado de Carlos IV,* I:71.
75. Manuel Antonio de Mora to Gálvez, May 25, 1784, AGN, IG, vol. 14.
76. Pedro de Laguna to Branciforte, Ometepec, March 28, 1796, AGN, IG, vol. 289-B.
77. Basilio Mazas, administrador de alcabalas, to Revillagigedo, Tehuacán, April 29, 1790, AGN, IG, vol. 103-A.
78. Baltasar Ruiz to the intendant of Veracruz, January 2, 1796, AGN, IG, vol. 384-A.
79. Diego García Panes to Ruiz, no. 58, January 9, 1796, AGN, IG, vol. 384-A.
80. Ruiz to Captain Juan Baptista de la Torre, April 14, 1796, AGN, IG, vol. 384-A.
81. Torre to Ruiz, April 14, 1796, and Report of *Auditor de Guerra* Cacho Calderón, May 14, 1796, AGN, IG, vol. 384-A.
82. José Bailio Medillín to Captain Antonio Ynguanzo, January 1803, AGN, IG, vol. 32-A.
83. Ynguanzo to Tómas de Anteparaluzeta, January 7, 1803, and Anteparaluzeta to Ynguanzo, December 26, 1802, AGN, IG, vol. 32-A.
84. Anteparaluzeta to Ynguanzo, February 8, 1803, AGN, IG, vol. 32-A.

Notes 325

85. Anteparaluzeta to Ynguanzo, December 28, 1802, and Ynguanzo to Major Manuel de Santa María, December 29, 1802, AGN, IG, vol. 32-A.
86. Santa María to Marquina, San Luis Potosí, March 14, 1803, AGN, IG, vol. 32-A.
87. Calleja to Iturrigaray, San Luis Potosí, March 21, 1803, and Report of Cacho Calderón, April 19, 1803, AGN, IG, vol. 32-A.
88. Hamnett, *Politics and Trade,* pp. 75–82.
89. Petitions of Mextitlán militiamen, October 1807, AGN, IG, vol. 60-A.
90. Petition of José Antonio Fernández, October 1807, AGN, IG, vol. 60-A.
91. Petitions of Antonio and Rafael Castillo, November 1807, AGN, IG, vol. 63-B.
92. Petition of Jueces Eclesiásticos Joaquin Ugalde, Pedro Ugalde, and José Leandro Cabezas to Iturrigaray, September 18, 1807, AGN, IG, vol. 28-A.
93. Report of Major Juan de Noriega, México, November, 1807, AGN, IG, vol. 63-B.
94. Ignacio Muñoz to Iturrigaray, October 7, 1807, AGN, IG, vol. 28-A.
95. Muñoz to Iturrigaray, October 14, 1807, AGN, IG, vol. 402-A.
96. Petition of 18 militiamen of the Company of Mextitlán, México, October 9, 1807, AGN, IG, vol. 331-A.
97. Petition of Rafaela Manuela Hernández, 1808, AGN, IG, vol. 331-A.
98. Testimony of witnesses to Joaquín Miramón, *Partido* of Mextitlán, January-February 1808, AGN, IG, vol. 331-A.
99. Miramón to Manuel Francisco de Arce, February 8, 1808, AGN, IG, vol. 331-A.
100. Reglas que deberán observarse para la formación y alistamiento de milicias en lo interior del Reino de Nueva España, July 1794, AGI, México, leg. 1439.
101. Miguel Lerdo de Tejada, *Comercio exterior de México desde la conquista hasta hoy* (Mexico, 1853), tables; and Ajofrín, *Diario del viaje* 1964, II:23. The purgative Jalap was well known and respected throughout Europe and the Americas. Between 1802 and 1804 for example, New Spain exported 5,202 pounds, worth a total of 130,731 pesos.
102. Petition of Mariano Morales and Felipe Razo (alias Felipe Calva), 1808, AGN, IG, vol. 331-A.
103. Testimony of Mariano Morales, Zacualtipán, June 21, 1808, AGN, IG, vol. 331-A. Razo also refused to name their correspondent, but said he was a gentleman who had advised them to report the abuses of Mextitlán.
104. Arce to Lavin, July 6, 1808, and Lavin to Arce, July 19, 1808, AGN, IG, vol. 331-A.
105. Testimony of witnesses, Zacualtipán, July, 1808, AGN, IG, vol. 331-A.
106. Testimony of Guadalupe Gómez, Zacualtipán, July 19, 1808, AGN, IG, vol. 331-A.
107. Testimony of Josefa Hernández, Zacualtipán, July, 1808, AGN, IG, vol. 331-A.
108. Testimony of Paula Gertrudis Olivares, Zacualtipán, July, 1808, AGN, IG, vol. 331-A.
109. Petition of Miguel Angeles, Felipe Razo (alias Felipe Calva), Mariano Morales, and Miguel Solís, December 11, 1807, and Lavin to Iturrigaray, July 22, 1808, AGN, IG, vol. 331-A.
110. Testimony of Manuel Mateos, Zacualtipán, July 1808, AGN, IG, vol. 331-A.
111. Juan de Bustamante to Lavin, Tianguistengo, July 23, 1808, AGN, IG, vol. 331-A.
112. Testimony of Mariano Cuello, Zacualtipán, July 1808, AGN, IG, vol. 331-A.
113. Testimony of José Martín, July, 1808, AGN, IG, vol. 331-A.
114. Testimony of Antonio Mercado, July, 1808, AGN, IG, vol. 331-A.

Chapter 6

1. For material on the cabildos in the eighteenth century see John P. Moore, *The Cabildo in Peru under the Bourbons: A Study in the Decline and Resurgence of Local Government in the Audiencia of Lima, 1700–1824* (Durham: Duke University Press, 1966); Lynch, *Spanish Colonial Administration,* chapter 9; and Fisher, *Government and Society,* chapter 8.
2. Cabildo of Celaya to Revillagigedo, December 23, 1789, AGN, Historia, vol. 226.

3. Pascual Cisneros to Mayorga, September 18, 1780, AGN, IG, vol. 104-B.
4. Manuel Antonio de Mora to Gálvez, Valladolid, May 25, 1784, AGN, IG, vol. 14.
5. Branciforte to the Prince of the Peace, no. 80, December 30, 1794, AGI, Estado, leg. 23.
6. One *carga* weighs 225 pounds.
7. In 1799, 12,264.5 *cargas* of flour and 6,159 *cargas* of wool entered Querétaro. The flour paid 1,533.0.6 pesos and the wool 1,539.6.0 for a total income of 3,072.6.6 pesos. See Cuenta general de cargo y data, AGN, IG, vol. 35-A.
8. Cisneros to Mayorga, September 18, 1780, AGN, IG, vol. 104-B. According to Crespo's estimate, the full cost for regular army salaries would be about 27,000 pesos. The bulk of this came from the royal treasury. See Proyecto de Crespo, AGI, Mexico, leg. 2418.
9. Testimony of hacendados to the cabildo of Querétaro, April, 1780, AGN, IG, vol. 104-B.
10. Testimony of José González Roxo, April, 1780, AGN, IG, vol. 104-B.
11. Ruiz Dávalos to Mayorga, March 28, 1783, AGN, IG, vol. 104-B; and Cabildo of Querétaro to Branciforte, October 4, 1794, AGI, Estado, leg. 23.
12. Ruiz Dávalos to Mayorga, May 26, 1780, AGN, IG, vol. 104-B.
13. Nicolás Rivera to the king, Madrid, August 2, 1798, AGN, IG, vol. 155-B.
14. Cisneros to Mayorga, August 31, 1780, and Ruiz Dávalos to Matías de Gálvez, September 2, 1783, AGN, IG, vol. 104-B. For material on the Septién family, see Brading, *Miners and Merchants,* pp. 312–16.
15. Ruiz Dávalos to Mayorga, August 23, 1780, AGN, IG, vol. 104-B.
16. Ruiz Dávalos to Matías de Gálvez, June 27, 1783, AGN, IG, vol. 104-B. The cabildo was in fact enlarged during 1783.
17. For information on the climate disasters of 1785, see Florescano, *Precios del maíz,* p. 133, 148–49; Charles Gibson, *The Aztecs under Spanish Rule: A History of the Indians of the Valley of Mexico, 1519–1810* (Stanford: Stanford University Press, 1964), p. 316; and Hamnett, *Politics and Trade,* p. 63.
18. Apoderados de los dueños de haciendas en junta de guerra, October 5, 1784, AGN, IG, vol. 104-B.
19. Proposiciones para el establecimiento de caballos, April 15, 1780, AGN, IG, vol. 104-B.
20. Mendinueta to Conde de Gálvez, April 28, 1786, AGN, IG, vol. 104-B.
21. Ruiz Dávalos to Matías de Gálvez, June 27, 1783, AGN, IG, vol. 104-B.
22. Branciforte to the Prince of the Peace, no. 80, December 30, 1795, AGI, Estado, leg. 23; and José Ignacio Ruiz Calado to Branciforte, February 14, 1797, AGN, IG, vol. 155-B.
23. Report of Fiscal de lo Civil Ramón Posada, November 14, 1783, AGN, IG, vol. 104-B. The administrator of *alcabalas* received a commission of 3 percent for looking after the militia tax fund.
24. Revillagigedo to the Council of Indies, February 28, 1792, AGN, CV, series 2, vol. 26.
25. Sobre arbitrios para la plateación y subsistencia del Batallón Urbano de Querétaro, 1810, and Cabildo report, August 16, 1810, AGN, IG, vol. 240-A. Humboldt counted 20 *obrajes* and 300 *trapiches* in the city. See Humboldt, *Political Essay,* III: 462.
26. Juan de Villalba y Velázquez to Matías de Gálvez, September 2, 1783, AGN, IG, vol. 104-B.
27. Cabildo to Branciforte, October 4, 1794, AGI, Estado, leg. 23.
28. Branciforte to the cabildo, January 4, 1797, AGN, IG, vol. 155-B.
29. Cabildo to Branciforte, January 13, 1797, AGN, IG, vol. 155-B.
30. Branciforte to the cabildo, January 31, 1797, AGN, IG, vol. 155-B.
31. Report of Auditor de Guerra Cacho Calderón, September 28, 1797, AGN, IG, vol. 155-B.
32. Condiciones bajo de las cuales han de entregar los dueños de las haciendas ... los caballos para el Regimiento Provincial de esta ciudad, August 3, 1797, AGN, IG, vol. 155-B.
33. See Brading, *Miners and Merchants,* p. 183.
34. Report on haciendas and the number of horses in use on each, 1799, AGN, IG, vol. 155-B.
35. Junta de hacendados de Querétaro, San Juan del Río y Tolimanejo, AGS, GM, leg. 6981.

The three *apoderados* were the Marqués de Villa del Villar del Aguila, Pedro Alonso Martínez Tendero, and Francisco Antonio Diez Marina. These men were not opposed to the army as much as to what they identified as abuses. Villar del Aguila donated 2,000 pesos to the regiment and Diez de Marina donated 1,100 pesos.

36. Nicolás Rivera to the king, Madrid, August 2, 1798, and Petition of Mariano Pérez de Tagle, 1799, AGN, IG, vol. 155-B.
37. Ibid.
38. Royal order, February 10, 1799, AGI, México, leg. 1452.
39. Ruiz Dávalos to Azanza, September 24, 1799, AGN, IG, vol. 155-B.
40. Ruiz Dávalos to Branciforte, April 26, 1797, AGN, IG, vol. 155-B.
41. Petition of Ignacio García Revollo and 22 officers of the Querétaro cavalry, July 16, 1799, AGN, IG, vol. 155-B.
42. Azanza to Alvarez, April 22, 1800, AGS, GM, leg. 6981. The problems experienced in Querétaro were duplicated wherever there were mounted militia units. See Caballos para el Regimiento Provincial de Puebla y los problemas resultantes, 1795, AGN, IG, vol. 99-A, and for the Dragoon Regiment of Nueva Galicia, AGN, IG, vol. 157-B.
43. José Ignacio Ruiz Calado to Azanza, September 7, 1799, AGN, IG, vol. 155-B.
44. Royal order, San Lorenzo, November 18, 1800, AGS, GM, leg. 6981.
45. Pedro de Laguna to Branciforte, Oaxaca, February 9, 1796, AGN, IG, vol. 175-A.
46. Hamnett, *Politics and Trade*, pp. 156–64.
47. Instrucción para el comandante del nuevo Batallón Provincial de Oaxaca, el Coronel Juan Francisco Echarrí, February 9, 1796, and Laguna to the alcaldes of Oaxaca, February 9, 1796, AGN, IG, vol. 175-A.
48. Luis Ortiz de Zárate to Mora y Peysal, December 31, 1796, AGN, IG, vol. 3-A.
49. Cabildo to Zárate, August 22, 1797, Branciforte to the cabildo, November 8, 1797, and Zárate to Branciforte, November 22, 1797, AGN, IG, vol. 3-A.
50. Laguna to Branciforte, Orizaba, December 22, 1797, AGN, IG, vol. 3-A.
51. Branciforte to the cabildo of Oaxaca, January 20, 1798, AGN, IG, vol. 3-A.
52. José de Gálvez to Bucareli, El Pardo, March 19, 1777, AGN, IG, vol. 53-B.
53. Sugar and Cacao Tax Income, AGN, IG, vol. 126-B.

| 1786 | 1,759 pesos | 1789 | 2,528 pesos |
| 1788 | 1,918 pesos | 1790 | 2,299 pesos |

In 1786 for example the militia picket cost 1,601 pesos, 6 reales leaving a small surplus of 157 pesos, 2 reales.

54. Antonio de San José Muro to Branciforte, August 5, 1794, AGN, IG, vol. 289-B. According to Muro, a poor woman considered 1 real worth of cacao and some maize as a splendid banquet for a family of four children. The cacao of Guayaquil used by the poor was somewhat bitter but cheaper than that of Guatemala. It was mixed in a ratio of 1 spoon of chocolate to 12 spoons of sugar.
55. Relación de los gremios, artes, y oficios que hay en la nobilísima ciudad de México..., 1788, MN, vol. 568.
56. Revillagigedo to Alange, no. 869, May 29, 1793, AGS, GM, leg. 6970.
57. Cabildo of Mexico to Revillagigedo, May 6, 1793, AGS, GM, leg. 6970.
58. Branciforte to Alange, no. 82, October 5, 1794, AGI, México, leg. 1438.
59. Cabildo of Mexico to Revillagigedo, October 31, 1793, AGI, México, leg. 1437.
60. Captains José de la Pera y Casa and Francisco de Paula de Luna, representatives of the *junta de capitanes* to the king, July 19, 1793, AGS, GM, leg. 6969.
61. Branciforte to Alange, no. 271, April 28, 1795, AGS, GM, leg. 6969. During mobilization in 1781, full salaries had been paid.
62. Revillagigedo to the captains, July 24, 1793, AGS, GM, leg. 6969.
63. Ministry of War memorandum, 1795, and Royal Order, Aranjuez, March 21, 1795, AGS, GM, leg. 6970.
64. Branciforce to Alange, no. 82, October 5, 1794, AGI, México, leg. 1438.

65. *Gazeta de México,* 19 August 1797.
66. José Antonio Alzate to Branciforte, December 16, 1796, AGN, Historia, vol. 44.
67. Alzate to Branciforte, July 8, 1797, AGN, Historia, vol. 44.
68. Branciforte to Pedro Ruiz Dávalos, July 12, 1797, AGN, Historia, vol. 44. Branciforte ordered an investigation into these charges. Although it was difficult to verify individual cases, Salazar and Cristalinas lost their commission to arrest vagabonds.
69. Colonel Joaquín Benito de Medina to Branciforte, Córdoba, August 9, 1797, AGN, IG, vol. 49.
70. Medina to Branciforte, November 8, 1797, AGN, IG, vol. 49.
71. Medina to Branciforte, January 27, 1798, AGN, IG, vol. 49.
72. Tomás Rodríguez de Biedma to Branciforte, February 22, 1798, and Medina to Azanza, September 3, 1798, AGN, IG, vol. 49. Because of what was described as an oversight, the 72 men were not marched to Orizaba. The colonel asked the surgeon and regimental major from the Infantry of Toluca to conduct a reexamination. Their report verified the uselessness of 56 men and stated that the remaining 16 could stay on duty even though they did have definite disabilities.
73. Medina to Azanza, September 3, 1798, and Azanza to Medina, October 1, 1798, AGN, IG, vol. 49.
74. Estados que manifiesta los soldados que se hallan inútiles, Regimiento Provincial de México, February 9, 1798, and August 11, 1798, AGN, IG, vol. 49.
75. Marquina to Urquijo, October 20, 1800, AGI, Estado, leg. 29. Marquina dismissed the second battalion except for the grenadier company when he found it "in an imaginary state."
76. Marquina to Cornel, no. 131, October 27, 1800, Cabildo to Marquina, July 14, 1800, September 10, 1800, and Marquina to the cabildo, September 22, 1800, AGI, México, leg. 1453.
77. Branciforte to Costansó, January 8, 1797, and Costansó to Branciforte, January 28, 1797, AGN, IG, vol. 328-A.
78. Costansó to Branciforte, February 15, 1797, AGN, IG, vol. 328-A.
79. Rendón to Branciforte, January 12, 1797, and Francisco del Puy y Ochea to Branciforte, Orizaba, June 26, 1797, AGN, IG, vol. 134-B. For similar problems in Córdoba, see Joaquín Benito de Medina to Branciforte, Córdoba, August 9, 1797, AGN, IG, vol. 49.
80. Sobre formación de tarifa de los víveres en la villa de Orizaba con motivo de acantonamiento, AGN, IG, vol. 134-B.
81. Puy y Ochea to Branciforte, June 26, 1797, and Branciforte to Puy y Ochea, July 8, 1797, AGN, IG, vol. 134-B. Branciforte denied any connection with the accused.
82. El cabildo... manda que por ahora y hasta nueva orden los dueños de tienda y demas personas que les comprehende, observen y guarden la postura siguiente, March 16, 1797, AGN, IG, vol. 134-B.
83. Order of the cabildo of Orizaba, March 16, 1797, AGN, IG, vol. 134-B.
84. Order of Pedro Andrés Marín, February 13, 1797, AGN, IG, vol. 134-B.
85. Petition of Doña María Catarina Baptista, 1797, AGN, IG, vol. 164-A.
86. Juan Antonio Carrera and José Manuel de Rayas to Branciforte, Jalapa, August 14, 1797, AGN, IG, vol. 134-B.
87. Marquina to the subdelegate of Jalapa, February 4, 1801, AGN, Historia, vol. 358; and Consulta del ayuntamiento de Jalapa sobre alojamiento de tropas, April 20, 1801, AGN, IG, vol. 61-A.
88. Costansó to Iturrigaray, Jalapa, April 1, 1805, AGN, IG, vol. 477-A.
89. Ayuntamiento of Querétaro to Iturrigaray, April 21, 1808, AGN, IG, vol. 80.
90. Ana María de Leyra to the *administrador de alcabalas,* Orizaba, January 2, 1809, AGN, IG, vol. 462-A.
91. Jaime Tutzó to the *diputación capitular* of Jalapa, May 11, 1805, AGN, IG, vol. 477-A. The house belonged to José María Becerra.
92. Costansó to Iturrigaray, May 12, 1805, AGN, IG, vol. 477-A; and Costansó to Iturrigaray, November 2, 1806, AGN, Historia, vol. 358.

93. See chapter 7.
94. Herr, *The Eighteenth Century Revolution*, p. 444.
95. Revillagigedo to Malaspina, January 19, 1791, MN, vol. 280.
96. Juan Vicente (Revillagigedo) to Aranda, July 31, 1792, AHN, Estado, leg. 4287.
97. Branciforte to Alange, no. 204, February 28, 1795, AGN, CV, series 2, vol. 32.
98. Order of Branciforte, November 25, 1794, and Branciforte to Juan Velázquez, December 27, 1794, AGN, IG, vol. 211-B.
99. Branciforte to the commissioned officers, December 27, 1794, AGN, IG, vol. 270-A.
100. Instructions for Colonel José Antonio Rengel, 1795, AGN, IG, vol. 156-B.
101. Estado que manifiesta el numero de milicianos establecidos en las jurisdicciones de Guanajuato, Silao, Irapuato, León, and Pénjamo, January 29, 1795, AGN, IG, vol. 156-B.
102. Branciforte to Alange, no. 204, February 20, 1795, AGN, CV, series 2, vol. 32.
103. Cabildo of Guanajuato to Branciforte, January 26, 1795, and Rengel to Branciforte, May 13, 1795, AGN, IG, vol. 156-B.
104. Cabildo to Branciforte, May 25, 1795, AGN, IG, vol. 157-B.
105. Noticia de las ofertas y gastos en el Batallón de Guanajuato y Regimiento de Caballería del Príncipe, August 1795, AGN, IG, vol. 157-B.
106. Pérez Gálvez to Branciforte, August 16, 1795, and renunciations of José Miguel Muzquiz, Manuel Ignacio de Muzquiz, Martín del Collado, and José María Uribarren, AGN, IG, vol. 156-B.
107. Julián Pablo de la Peña to Branciforte, Irapuato, August 2, 1795, AGN, IG, vol. 156-B.
108. José María de Lanuza to Branciforte, Irapuato, August 8, 1795, AGN, IG, vol. 156-B.
109. Petition of Ignacio Navarro Caziño, 1795, AGN, IG, vol. 156-B.
110. Pedro Salinas Medilla to Branciforte, Pénjamo, February 9, 1795, AGN, IG, vol. 156-B.
111. Anonymous letter to Branciforte, January 13, 1795, AGN, IG, vol. 156-B.
112. Cabildo of Guanajuato to Branciforte, March 23, 1795, AGN, IG, vol. 156-B.
113. Velázquez was no stranger to the province of Michoacán. During the War of American Independence, he had formed a number of militia units. Later, while lieutenant colonel of the Dragoons of Spain, he attempted to maintain his command of the Michoacán militia. Viceroy Flórez ended his effort when the regular cadre in the Michoacán militias lost all military usefulness. See Flórez to Valdés, March 23, 1788, AGI, Mexico, leg. 1515.
114. Relación de los hombres útiles de las tres clases . . . , December 10, 1794, AGN, IG, vol. 211-B.
115. Anónimo contra el establecimiento de milicias, January 1795, AGN, Historia, vol. 155.
116. Antonio Bonilla to Velázquez, México, January 24, 1795, and Velázquez to Bonilla, January 19, 1975, AGN, IG, vol. 211-B.
117. Velázquez to Branciforte, January 1795, AGN, IG, vol. 211-B.
118. Lista de las personas por el ayuntamiento de la villa de Zamora para jefes y oficiales del Regimiento de Dragones de Michoacán, January 25, 1795, AGN, IG, vol. 211-B.
119. Velázquez to Branciforte, January 1795, AGN, IG, vol. 211-B.
120. Listas de los sujetos de este vecindario que contribuyeron graciosamente para el vestuario de las dos compañias de milicias de esta villa . . . , 1795, AGN, IG, vol. 374-A.
121. Humboldt, *Political Essay*, IV:258.
122. Alamán, *Disertaciones*, III:83; Bustamante, *Suplemento a la historia*, III:169; and McAlister, *The "Fuero Militar,"* p. 68.
123. Branciforte to Alcudía, April 8, 1794, AGI, Estado, leg. 23.
124. Branciforte to Alange, no. 205, February 28, 1795, AGS, GM, leg. 6971.
125. Instrucción reservada de Branciforte, May 30, 1798, AGN, CV, series 2, vol. 36.
126. *Reglamento para las milicias de la Isla de Cuba* (Madrid, 1769).
127. Reglamento para las milicias disciplinadas de infantería y dragones del Nuevo Reino de Granada, July 13, 1794, AGI, IG, leg. 663. For detailed discussion on whether this *reglamento* applied to New Spain, see AGN, IG, vol. 158-B.

128. Calleja to Iturrigaray, September 6, 1805, AGN, IG, vol. 315-A.
129. Instrucción a que deben arreglar sus funciones los comandantes de brigada, March 26, 1800, AGN, IG, vol. 336-A.
130. Report of Bataller, February 8, 1806, AGN, IG, vol. 315-A.
131. Azanza to Alvarez, no. 310, April 28, 1799, and the cabildo of Tlaxcala to Azanza, June 25, 1799, AGI, México, leg. 1449.

Chapter 7

1. Rosa Feijoo, "El tumulto de 1692," *Historia Mexicana* 14 (1965):661.
2. Consulado to Branciforte, August 8, 1794, AGN, IG, vol. 60-B.
3. Revillagigedo to Alange, no. 1129, March 4, 1794, AGS, GM, leg. 6967; and consulado to Revillagigedo, October 24, 1791, AGN, IG, vol. 122-A. There was also an Urban Battalion of Commerce of Puebla formed in 1742. See Revillagigedo to Alange, no. 1017, September 30, 1793, AGS, GM, leg. 6968.
4. Consulado to Conde de Gálvez, December 1783, AGN, IG, vol. 122-A.
5. Revillagigedo to Alange, no. 1129, March 4, 1794, AGS, GM, leg. 6967. In 1652, the king granted the consulado of Mexico the right to tax merchandise imported into New Spain at a rate of .006 percent. Not needing the full amount, the merchants collected half of the tax until 1722 when the militia regiment began to absorb more money.
6. Report of Francisco Crespo, December 22, 1784, AGN, IG, vol. 122-A.
7. Consulado to Azanza, February 26, 1800, AGN, IG, vol. 19.
8. Consulado to Branciforte, August 8, 1794, AGN, IG, vol. 60-B.
9. Consulado to Azanza, February 26, 1800, AGN, IG, vol. 19.
10. Order of Viceroy Bucareli, May 10, 1774, AGN, IG, vol. 42-A.
11. Consulado to Branciforte, August 8, 1794, AGN, IG, vol. 60-B.
12. Juan Velasco to the *auditor de guerra,* April 25, 1782, AGN, IG, vol. 122-A; and McAlister, *The "Fuero Militar,"* pp. 34–38.
13. Consulado to the *auditor de guerra,* April 25, 1782, AGN, IG, vol. 122-A.
14. *Junta general* of officers, September 30, 1783, AGN, IG, vol. 122-A.
15. Report of Lorenzo José Cabrera, *apoderado* of the sergeants, April 22, 1784, AGN, IG, vol. 122-A.
16. Consulado to Gálvez, December 17, 1783, AGN, IG, vol. 122-A.
17. Consulado to Gálvez, September 1, 1783, AGN, IG, vol. 122-A.
18. Juan José Pérezcano to the consulado, April 16, 1782, AGN, IG, vol. 122-A. Pérezcano succeeded Agustín de Iglesias Cotillo in the regimental command.
19. Consulado to Gálvez, July 12, 1783, AGN, IG, vol. 122-A.
20. Consulado to Gálvez, December 17, 1783, AGN, IG, vol. 122-A.
21. Report of Inspector General Pascual de Cisneros, June 20, 1783, and Pérezcano to the king, February 20, 1786, AGN, IG, vol. 122-A.
22. Pérezcano to Gálvez, August 9, 1783, and Cisneros to Gálvez, August 30, 1783, AGN, IG, vol. 122-A.
23. Report of *Auditor de Guerra* Félix del Rey, October 24, 1783, AGN, IG, vol. 122-A.
24. Consulado to Gálvez, December 17, 1783, AGN, IG, vol. 122-A.
25. Order of Gálvez, March 18, 1784, AGN, IG, vol. 122-A. Ordinary royal justices and other tribunals were given the right to try cases of merchant militiamen which fell under their respective jurisdictions. For subsequent reiteration of this ruling see Flórez to Valdés, January 5, 1789, AGI, México, leg. 1523; and Mining Tribunal to Marquina July 3, 1802, AGN, IG, vol. 30.
26. Report of Francisco Crespo, December 22, 1784, AGN, IG, vol. 122-A.
27. Proyecto militar de 1784, AGI, México, leg. 2418.

28. Report of Crespo, December 22, 1784, AGN, IG, vol. 122-A.
29. Proposiciones para el arreglo del Regimiento Urbano de Comercio, 1784, AGN, IG, vol. 122-A.
30. José de Gálvez to Viceroy Gálvez, November 8, 1784, AGN, IG, vol. 122-A; and royal order, San Ildefonso, August 17, 1786, AGS, GM, leg. 6967.
31. See Brading, *Miners and Merchants,* pp. 107–108. Pérezcano was referring to the parties of Basques and Montañeses.
32. Pérezcano to the king, February 20, 1786, AGN, IG, vol. 122-A.
33. Ibid., and Report of Crespo, March 20, 1786, AGN, IG, vol. 122-A. Asked to comment on Pérezcano's letter, Crespo stated that an exaggerated view was to be expected from a regimental partisan. He did agree that much of the criticism by the consulado had been unnecessarily offensive.
34. Gorostiza to Revillagigedo, October 8, 1791, AGN, IG, vol. 122-A. Also see Velázquez, *El estado de guerra,* p. 150.
35. Gorostiza to Revillagigedo, October 1791, AGS, GM, leg. 6967; José Bravo Ugarte, ed., *Instrucción Reservada al Marqués de Branciforte, 1794* (Mexico: Editorial Jus, 1966), p. 233; and McAlister, *The "Fuero Militar,"* p. 65.
36. Gorostiza to Revillagigedo, October 1791, AGS, GM, leg. 6967.
37. Revillagigedo to Alange, no. 296, February 6, 1790, AGS, GM, leg. 6959.
38. Revillagigedo to Alange, no. 1129, March 4, 1794, AGS, GM, leg. 6967.
39. Revillagigedo to Alange, no. 296, February 6, 1790, AGS, GM, leg. 6959.
40. Consulado to Revillagigedo, October 24, 1791, AGS, GM, leg. 6967; and *Real declaración sobre puntos esenciales de la Ordenanza de milicias provinciales de España* (Madrid, 1767), art. 39.
41. Brading, *Miners and Merchants,* p. 110.
42. Petition of 72 merchants to Azanza, 1800, AGN, IG, vol. 19.
43. Petition of 54 merchants, June 14, 1794, AGN, IG, vol. 60-B.
44. Sumaria sobre averiguar cual fue el motivo que una patrulla del Regimiento del Comercio... mandará abrir una acesoria del puente de las Ratas, 1794, AGN, IG, vol. 164.
45. Revillagigedo to Alange, no. 1129, March 4, 1794, AGS, GM, leg. 6967.
46. Nueva planta del Cuerpo de Comercio, November 8, 1791, AGS, GM, leg. 6967.
47. Consulado to Revillagigedo, November 28, 1791, AGS, GM, leg. 6967.
48. Ibid.
49. Gorostiza to Revillagigedo, December 21, 1791, AGS, GM, leg. 6967.
50. Reglamento provisional para el régimen, gobierno, y subsistencia del Regimiento Urbano del Comercio, May 18, 1793, AGS, GM, leg. 6967.
51. Gorostiza to Revillagigedo, January 18, 1794, and Revillagigedo to Alava, February 27, 1794, AGN, IG, vol. 122-A; and Department of War memorandum, April 7, 1794, AGS, GM, leg. 6979.
52. Consulado to Branciforte, August 8, 1794, AGN, IG, vol. 60-B.
53. McAlister, *The "Fuero Militar,"* pp. 76–89; and Velázquez, *El estado de guerra,* pp. 154–55.
54. Manuel Antonio de Santa María y Escovedo to Revillagigedo, June 17, 1793, and Ravago to Revillagigedo, June 22, 1793, AGN, IG, vol. 13-B.
55. Report of *Fiscal de Real Hacienda* Ramón Posada, September 13, 1793, AGN, IG, vol. 13-B; and Branciforte to Alange, no. 277, May 29, 1795, AGN, CV, series 1, vol. 181.
56. Revillagigedo to the consulado, June 3, 1794, AGN, IG, vol. 13-B.
57. Consulado to Revillagigedo, May 26, 1794, AGN, IG, vol. 60-B.
58. Ibid.
59. Mining Tribunal to Branciforte, January 16, 1795, AGN, IG, vol. 13-B.
60. Cacho Calderón to Branciforte, March 17, 1795, AGN, IG, vol. 13-B.
61. Branciforte to the Prince of the Peace, Orizaba, July 30, 1797, AGI, Estado, leg. 26.

62. Cacho Calderón to Branciforte, March 17, 1795, AGN, IG, vol. 13-B.
63. Branciforte to the Prince of the Peace, Orizaba, July 30, 1797, AGI, Estado, leg. 26.
64. Consulado to Branciforte, December 3, 1794, AGN, IG, vol. 13-B.
65. Bernardino Bonavía to Branciforte, December 30, 1794; and *Gazeta de México,* 18 January 1795. Branciforte published a *bando* to clarify the situation. The *fuero criminal,* and never the *fuero civil,* was granted to the merchant and not to the substitute. Later, the *cajeros* were permitted to hold the *fuero criminal.*
66. Mining Tribunal to Branciforte, January 16, 1795, AGN, IG, vol. 13-B.
67. Audiencia to Branciforte, January 20, 1795, AGN, IG, vol. 13-B.
68. Revillagigedo to the Marqués de Bajamar, no. 362, January 31, 1792, AGI, México, leg. 1432.
69. Cacho Calderón to Branciforte, March 17, 1795, AGN, IG, vol. 13-B; and Tomás de Urizar to Branciforte, April 2, 1796, AGN, IG, vol. 384-A.
70. Ibid.
71. Pedro Varela to Branciforte, March 20, 1797, AGN, IG, vol. 336-A.
72. Branciforte to Alvarez, July 30, 1797, AGN, CV, series 2, vol. 34.
73. Alvarez to Gaspar Melchor de Jovellanos, January 31, 1798, AGN, IG, vol. 336-A.
74. Francisco de Saavedra to Branciforte, May 16, 1798, AGN, IG, vol. 336-A; Bando en que S.M. se ha servido derogar el Fuero Militar concedido a los comerciantes y mineros alistados en los Cuerpos de Milicias Provinciales y Urbanos, October 20, 1798, AGN, IG, vol. 17-B; and *Gazeta de México,* 16 November 1798.
75. Padrón del Regimiento de Comercio, 1800, AGN, IG, vol. 19.
76. Urizar to Branciforte, April 2, 1796, AGN, IG, vol. 384-A.
77. Consulado to Urizar, October 4, 1797, and October 27, 1797, AGN, IG, vol. 3-A.
78. Urizar to the consulado, November 27, 1797, AGN, IG, vol. 3-A.
79. Antonio de Bassoco to Branciforte, January 8, 1798, AGN, IG, vol. 3-A.
80. Petition of 72 merchants to Azanza, 1800, and Consulado to Azanza, February 26, 1800, AGN, IG, vol. 19.
81. Petition of 109 merchants to Marquina, 1801, AGN, IG, vol. 42-A.
82. Azanza to the consulado, March 15, 1800, AGN, IG, vol. 19.
83. Joaquín Colla to Azanza, February 9, 1800, AGN, IG, vol. 19.
84. Azanza to Cornel, no. 730, April 22, 1800, AGI, México, leg. 1452. Colla became the acting colonel on the death of Tomás de Urizar. At the time of his promotion, he was 64 years of age and had 42 years' military service.
85. Joaquín de Caamaño to Marquina, February 5, 1801, AGN, IG, vol. 42-A.
86. Colla to Azanza, March 14, 1800, AGN, IG, vol. 19; Marquina to Cornel, no. 131, October 27, 1800, AGI, México, leg. 1453; and Colla to Marquina, February 7, 1801, AGN, IG, vol. 42-A.
87. Colla to Marquina, May 7, 1801, AGN, IG, vol. 42-A.
88. Consulado to Azanza, February 26, 1800, AGN, IG, vol. 19.
89. Razón y lista de toda la gente comerciante que gozan fuero en el Regimiento del cargo del Señor Coronel... , 1801, AGN, IG, vol. 42-A.
90. Colla to Marquina, May 10, 1801, AGN, IG, vol. 42-A.
91. Marquina to Caballero, no. 482, January 27, 1802, AGI, México, leg. 1462.
92. Consulado to Azanza, March 8, 1800, AGN, IG, vol. 1465; and Marquina to Caballero, no. 792, September 26, 1802, AGI, México, leg. 1465.
93. Consulado to Azanza, February 26, 1800, AGN, IG, vol. 19.
94. Petition of 109 merchants, 1801, AGN, IG, vol. 42-A; and Reports on the probate of the will of Martín de Arriva, 1801, AGN, IG, vol. 93.
95. Marquina to Caballero, no. 518, February 26, 1802, AGI, México, leg. 1464.
96. Consulado to Iturrigaray, November 23, 1807, AGN, IG, vol. 98; and *expediente* 28, AGN, Archivo de Hacienda, leg. 664.
97. Colla and Angel Michaus to Iturrigaray, December 19, 1807, AGN, IG, vol. 98.

98. Consulado to Iturrigaray, March 15, 1808, AGN, IG, vol. 98.
99. Petition of 60 merchants, September 17, 1808, AGN, IG, vol. 87-B.
100. Alamán, *Historia de Méjico* I: 57.
101. Garibay to Cornel, no. 90, July 16, 1809, AGN, CV, series 1, vol. 239.
102. Colla to Francisco Venegas, January 13, 1812, AGN, IG, vol. 93.
103. Colla to Garibay, October 5, 1808, AGN, IG, vol. 87-B.
104. Consulado to all merchants, September 27, 1808, and Petition of 13 merchants to Garibay, September 27, 1808, AGN, Archivo de Hacienda, leg. 663.
105. Gabriel Yermo, José Martínez Barenque, and Mateo Mosso to the consulado, October 7, 1808, AGN, Archivo de Hacienda, leg. 663.

Chapter 8

1. Humboldt, *Political Essay,* IV: 259.
2. Mora y Peysal to Azanza, December 31, 1799, AGN, IG, vol. 175-A.
3. Calleja to Azanza, October 8, 1798, AGN, IG, vol. 157-B.
4. Captain José Zambrano and Sublieutenant Joaquín Medina to the king, November 26, 1793, AGN, IG, vol. 197-B; and Los pardos de Puebla sobre que se le haga saber la real orden que mando su reforma, 1792, AGN, IG, vol. 100-A.
5. Patentes, nombramientos militares, AGI, México, leg. 2427; and hojas de servicio, AGS, GM, legs. 7270–7278.
6. Documentos de revista de inspección del Regimiento Fixo de Infantería de la Corona, July 26, 1788, AGI, México, leg. 1518.
7. Lista por antigüedad de los oficiales veteranos, February 1793, AGN, Historia, vol. 155; Branciforte to Alange, no. 149, January 6, 1795, AGI, México, leg. 1438; Azanza to Alvarez, no. 295, April 26, 1799, AGI, México, leg. 1449; and hojas de servicio, AGS, GM, legs. 7270–7278; and other sources.
8. Patentes y nombramientos militares, Regimiento de Puebla, 1788–1800, AGI, México, leg. 2427.
9. Revillagigedo to Alange, no. 989, August 31, 1793, AGN, CV, series 2, vol. 26. This was not a new practice in New Spain. The Dragoon Regiment of Mexico was funded in 1767 through the sale of commissions.
10. Valdés to Flórez, San Ildefonso, September 24, 1787, AGN, Historia, vol. 249.
11. Flórez to Valdés, no. 95, January 24, 1788, AGI, México, leg. 1515.
12. Flórez to Valdés, no. 391, June 24, 1788, AGI, México, leg. 1517; and Mendinueta to Flórez, April 15, 1788, AGN, Historia, vol. 155.
13. Nicolás Monteagudo to Branciforte, October 26, 1796, AGI, Estado, leg. 25; and Iturrigary to Caballero, no. 757, February 26, 1805, AGN, CV, series I, vol. 225.
14. Flórez to Valdés, no. 391, June 24, 1788, AGI, México, leg. 1517.
15. Revillagigedo to Alange, no. 328, February 26, 1790. AGI, México, leg. 1537.
16. Relación de los sugetos que solicitan beneficiar empleos de capitanes y tenientes en los cuerpos de nueva leva, 1788, AGN, Historia, vol. 250.
17. Revillagigedo to José de Alava, December 11, 1789, AGN, Historia, vol. 257.
18. Calleja to Alava, December 17, 1789, AGN, Historia, vol. 257.
19. Relación de tenientes veteranos que de real orden vinieron de Europa y se han destinado a este Regimiento de México, 1778, AGN, IG, vol. 361-A.
20. Velázquez to Antonio Bonilla, January 8, 1795, AGN, IG, vol. 211-B.
21. Azanza to Cornel, no. 707, April 22, 1800, AGI, México, leg. 1452.
22. Marquina to Caballero, no. 376, July 27, 1801, AGI, México, leg. 1459. The *terna* was the list of three candidates, in order of seniority, who were considered most apropos for the vacancy.
23. Lista por antigüedad de los oficiales, February 4, 1793, AGN, Historia, vol. 155.

24. Lista por antigüedad de los oficiales, April 26, 1799, AGI, México, leg. 1449.
25. Flórez to Valdés, no. 94, January 24, 1788, AGI, México, leg. 1515; and Revillagigedo to Valdés, no. 9, November 12, 1789, AGN, CV, series 2, vol. 30.
26. Revillagigedo to Valdés, no. 508, April 30, 1790, AGI, México, leg. 1538; and Revillagigedo to Alange, no. 177, February 7, 1791, AGS, GM, leg. 6966.
27. Marquina to Caballero, no. 584, April 26, 1802, AGI, México, leg. 1464.
28. Revillagigedo to Alange, no. 989, August 31, 1793, AGN, CV, series 2, vol. 26.
29. Revillagigedo to Valdés, November 30, 1789, AGS, GM, leg. 6959. Beven had served the army for 51 years and Velázquez for 49 years.
30. Beven to Branciforte, Jalapa, October 16, 1794, AGN, IG, vol. 282-A.
31. Revillagigedo to Alange, no. 989, August 31, 1793, AGN, CV, series 2, vol. 26. This was not the first time that there had been financial chaos in the Regiment of Mexico. Previously, officers had been forced to live on half or even third pay to make up a regimental debt of 16,000 pesos.
32. Revillagigedo to Alange, no. 1126, February 28, 1794, AGS, GM, leg. 6967.
33. Branciforte to Alange, no. 153, January 15, 1795, AGI, México, leg. 1438.
34. Revillagigedo to Alange, no. 1126, February 28, 1794, AGS, GM, leg. 6967; and hoja de servicio, 1800, AGS, GM, leg. 7277.
35. Branciforte to Alange, no. 153, January 15, 1793, AGI, México, leg. 1438.
36. Revillagigedo to Alange, no. 990, August 23, 1793, AGN, CV, series 2, vol. 26; and Revillagigedo to Valdés, nos. 9 and 921, November 12, 1789, and July 12, 1790, AGN, CV, series 2, vol. 30.
37. Branciforte to Alvarez, no. 921, October 27, 1797, AGI, México, leg. 1445; and hoja de servicio, 1800, AGS, GM, leg. 7277.
38. Gorostiza to Revillagigedo, January 25, 1790, AGN, IG, vol. 66-B.
39. Revillagigedo to Valdés, November 30, 1789, and royal order, March 12, 1790, AGS, GM, leg. 6959.
40. Lizana to Cornel, no. 19, August 19, 1809, AGN, CV, series 1, vol. 243.
41. Hoja de servicio, December 28, 1798, AGS, GM, leg. 7275. A notation on Calleja's service record stated, *"este oficial es uno de los mejores que hay en este Exército por su instrucción y por el celo con que sirve S.M."*
42. Branciforte to the Prince of the Peace, no. 61, October 30, 1797, AGI, Estado, leg. 26; Azanza to Cornel, no. 685, March 27, 1800, AGI, México, leg. 1452; and Iturrigaray to Caballero, no. 1022, May 27, 1806, AGN, CV, series 1, vol. 230.
43. Marquina to Caballero, no. 755, September 26, 1802, AGI, México, leg. 1465; "Don Félix María Calleja del Rey: Actividades anteriores a la guerra de independencia," *Boletín del Archivo General de la Nacón,* series two, no. 1 (1960):57–86, no. 2 (1960):253–97, and no. 4 (1960):553–81 (Mexico: AGN).
44. Iturrigaray to Caballero, no. 324, November 26, 1803, AGN, CV, series 1, vol. 215.
45. Marquina to Caballero, no. 478, January 27, 1802, AGI, México, leg. 1462.
46. Hoja de servicio, AGS, GM, leg. 7277; Azanza to Alvarez, no. 93, September 28, 1798, AGI, México, leg. 1447; Informe del Teniente Coronel Alonso sobre la defensa de San Juan de Ulúa, June 30, 1798, AGN, IG, vol. 508-A; Azanza to Alvarez, no. 349, May 31, 1799, AGI, México, leg. 1449; Marquina to Caballero, no. 751, August 27, 1802, AGI, México, leg. 1464; and Lizana to Cornel, no. 90, November 16, 1809, AGN, CV, series 1, vol. 243.
47. Marquina to Caballero, no. 478, January 27, 1802, AGI, México, leg. 1463; Garibay to Cornel, no. 4, February 20, 1809, AGN, CV, series 1, vol. 239; Cornel to Lizana, December 19, 1809, AGI, Mexico, leg. 1320. Muesas was one of the few officers to arrive in Mexico after 1800. He displaced Alonso on this occasion and a feud developed between the two men that did not end until Muesas was transferred to Montevideo.
48. It will be recalled that more than half of the Infantry of Mexico remained in Havana.
49. Azanza to Alonso, no. 349, May 31, 1799, AGI, México, leg. 1449; and Lizana to Cornel, no. 90, November 16, 1809, AGN, CV, series 1, vol. 243.

50. Carlos de Urrutía to Marquina, September 26, 1801, AGI, México, leg. 1459; and hoja de servicio, 1795, AGS, GM, leg. 7272.
51. Patentes de comandantes, September 1800, AGI, México, leg. 2424.
52. Garibay to Cornel, no. 15, February 20, 1809, AGN, CV, series 1, vol. 239; Cornel to Lizana, Seville, December 4, 1809, AGI, México, leg. 1320; and Lizana to Cornel, no. 212, February 20, 1810, AGN, CV, series 1, vol. 243.
53. Flórez to Valdés, no. 1152, July 27, 1789, AGI, México, leg. 1524; and Azanza to Alvarez, no. 86, September 27, 1798, AGI, México, leg. 1447.
54. Garibay to Revillagigedo, August 12, 1792, AGN, Historia, vol. 248.
55. Garibay to Branciforte, July 18, 1794, AGN, IG, vol. 30-B.
56. Branciforte to Alange, no. 91, October 13, 1794, AGI, México, leg. 1438.
57. Marquina to Caballero, no. 478, January 27, 1802, AGI, México, leg. 1462.
58. Iturrigaray to Caballero, no. 173, July 27, 1803, AGN, CV, series 1, vol. 215.
59. Garibay to Lizana, July 21, 1809, and Cornel to Lizana, Seville, January 1, 1810, AGN, IG, vol. 358-A. Garibay was rewarded by a promotion to the rank of lieutenant general.
60. Alonso to Iturrigaray, Veracruz, December 3, 1806, AGN, IG, vol. 165-A.
61. Joaquín Gutiérrez de los Ríos to Lizana, November 5, 1809, AGN, IG, vol. 166-A.
62. See Santiago Gerardo Suárez, *El ordenamiento militar de indias* (Caracas: Academia Nacional de la Historia, 1971), pp. xlii–lxxviii.
63. *Reglamento para las milicias de la Isla de Cuba* (Madrid, 1769), chapter 7.
64. Reglamento del Monte Pío de viudas, huérfanos, y madres de oficiales militares, 1761, y Real Declaración de 17 de junio de 1773 del mismo reglamento para el gobierno y régimen del Monte, AGN, IG, vol. 23-A.
65. Iturrigaray to Cayetano Soler, no. 1445, February 13, 1808, AGN, CV, series 1, vol. 231; and Garibay to Saavedra, no. 25, February 20, 1809, AGI, México, leg. 1633.
66. Hoja de servicio, AGS, GM, leg. 7278; and Revillagigedo to Alange, no. 825, March 31, 1793, AGI, México, leg. 1435.
67. Azanza to Alvarez, no. 55, August 27, 1798, AGI, México, leg. 1447.
68. For excellent background see Brading, *Miners and Merchants*, pp. 173–83.
69. Marquina to Caballero, no. 480, January 26, 1802, AGI, México, leg. 1462; and Hoja de servicio, AGS, GM, leg. 7276.
70. Personal letter of Branciforte to Alange, November 3, 1794, AGI, México, leg. 1438; Branciforte to Alvarez, no. 813, May 27, 1797, AGI, México, leg. 1444; and Branciforte to Alvarez, no. 806, April 27, 1797, AGI, México, leg. 1445.
71. Garibay to Cornel, no. 29, May 12, 1809, AGN, CV, series 1, vol. 239; and Audiencia to Francisco Eguía, no. 53, June 26, 1810, AGN, CV, series 1, vol. 246.
72. Hoja de servicio, AGS, GM, leg. 7277. For background on Rengel's career in the Provincias Internas see Max L. Moorhead, *The Apache Frontier: Jacobo Ugarte and Spanish-Indian Relations in Northern New Spain, 1769–1791* (Norman: University of Oklahoma Press, 1968), p. 68.
73. Revillagigedo to Alange, no. 3, July 27, 1790, AGS, GM, leg. 6959.
74. Patentes y nombramientos militares, AGI, México, leg. 2425.
75. Iturrigaray to Caballero, no. 1322, July 16, 1807, AGN, CV, series 1, vol. 234.
76. Garibay to the Conde de Alcaraz, September 16, 1808, AGN, Historia, vol. 48.
77. Hoja de servicio, AGS, GM, leg. 7277; and Marquina to Caballero, no. 680, July 7, 1802, AGI, Mexico, leg. 1464. For background on Bibanco and Vicario, see Brading, *Miners and Merchants*, pp. 188–91.
78. Juan de Noriega sobre licencia para casarse con Doña María Luisa Martín Vicario, 1805–1817, AGN, IG, vol. 165-A.
79. Lizana to Cornel, no. 38, September 26, 1809, and no. 88, November 15, 1809, AGN, CV, series 1, vol. 243.
80. Vicente Barros de Alemparte to Ignacio García Revollo, August 23, 1804, and García Revollo to Iturrigaray, September 19, 1804, AGN, IG, vol. 32-A.

81. Azanza to Alvarez, no. 256, October 10, 1799, AGS, GM, leg. 6979.
82. Marquina to Cornel, no. 131, October 27, 1800, AGI, México, leg. 1453.
83. Conde de la Cadena to Carlos de Urrutía, March 29, 1810, AGN, IG, vol. 92-A.
84. Azanza to Alvarez, no. 295, April 26, 1799, AGI, México, leg. 1499; Branciforte to Alange, no. 160, January 15, 1795, AGI, México, leg. 1438; Branciforte to Alcudía, no. 29, August 30, 1795, AGI, Estado, leg. 23; and hojas de servicio, AGS, GM, legs. 7272–7278.
85. D. A. Brading, "Government and Elite in Late Colonial Mexico," *HAHR* 53, no. 3 (August 1973): 409–10.
86. Brading, *Miners and Merchants*, 308–309.
87. Pérez Gálvez to Branciforte, August 30, 1795, AGN, IG, vol. 156-B.
88. Doris Ladd, "The Mexican Nobility at Independence, 1780–1836," (Ph.D. diss., Stanford University, 1972), p. 82.
89. Pérez Gálvez to Branciforte, August 30, 1795, AGN, IG, vol. 156-B.
90. Pérez Gálvez to Branciforte, May 8, 1795, AGN, IG, vol. 156-B.
91. Brading, *Miners and Merchants*, p. 310.
92. Branciforte to Alvarez, no. 589, February 28, 1798, AGI, Estado, leg. 27.
93. Resumen general de cuestas, Regimiento de Dragones de Nueva Galicia, Aguascalientes, September 1, 1799, AGN, IG, vol. 157-B.
94. Brading, *Miners and Merchants*, p. 309.
95. Rul to Branciforte, January 14, 1795, AGN, IG, vol. 156-B.
96. Branciforte to Alvarez, no. 870, July 30, 1797, AGN, CV, series 2, vol. 34.
97. Hoja de servicio, AGN, IG, vol. 392-A; and Velázquez to Branciforte, January 1795, AGN, IG, vol. 211-B.
98. Rul to Azanza, August 25, 1799, AGI, México, leg. 1453.
99. Azanza to Rul, March 3, 1800, AGI, México, leg. 1453.
100. Rul to Azanza, April 28, 1800, and Rul to the king, May 12, 1800, AGI, México, leg. 1453.
101. Calleja to Marquina, no. 878, June 29, 1802, AGI, México, leg. 1465.
102. Proposiciones del Ayudante Mayor Manuel Antonio de Mora, May 25, 1785, AGN, IG, vol. 14.
103. Barros Alemparte to García Revollo, August 23, 1805, AGN, IG, vol. 32-A.
104. Marquina to Caballero, no. 794, September 26, 1802, AGI, México, leg. 1465.
105. Conde de Santiago to Cisneros, November 10, 1778, and testimony of Lieutenant Colonel Luis de Luyando, AGN, IG, vol. 392-A.
106. Report of *Auditor de Guerra* Domingo Valcarcel, May 31, 1779, AGN, IG, vol. 392-A.
107. Garibay to Cornel, no. 1, February 20, 1809, AGN, CV, series 1, vol. 239.
108. Iturrigaray to Caballero, no. 934, November 26, 1805, AGN, CV, series 1, vol. 225.
109. Iturrigaray to Olaguer Felín, no. 1592, April 30, 1808, AGN, CV, series 1, vol. 237.
110. Iturrigaray to Caballero, no. 1322, July 16, 1807, AGN, CV, series 1, vol. 234.
111. Rul to Iturrigaray, Jalapa, August 25, 1808, AGN, IG, vol. 301-B.
112. Queja del Real Tribunal de Minería, 1802, AGN, IG, vol. 50; and Expediente promovido por el Señor Fiscal Protector de Naturales sobre el fuero de los individuos de milicias provinciales, 1798, AGN, IG, vol. 336-A.
113. Sobre concurrencia a juego prohibido de varios individuos del fuero de guerra, 1797–1798, AGN, IG, vol. 370-A.
114. Garibay to the subdelegate of Tehuacán, July 12, 1809, AGN, IG, vol. 205-B.
115. Fray Francisco Pérez de Haro to Branciforte, April 20, 1798, AGN, IG, vol. 72-A.
116. Calleja to Branciforte, May 26, 1798, AGN, IG, vol. 72-A.
117. Flórez to Valdés, no. 931, April 26, 1789, AGI, México, leg. 1526.
118. Marquina to Urquijo, June 13, 1800, AGN, CV, series 2, vol. 41.
119. Marquina to Cornel, no. 38, June 13, 1800, AGI, México, leg. 1453; and Report of the Audiencia, July 30, 1800, AGI, México, leg. 1319.

120. Audiencia to Marquina, February 15, 1801, AGI, México, leg. 1319.
121. Report of Cisneros, November 16, 1778, AGN, IG, vol. 361-A.
122. Juan Manuel de Bonilla to Branciforte, September 20, 1796, and José María de Cuervo to Branciforte, San Juan de Ulúa, August 10, 1796, AGN, IG, vol. 216-B.
123. Condución de Apaches en cuerda para Veracruz, 1796, AGN, IG, vol. 77.
124. Lizana to Cornel, no. 77, November 10, 1809, AGN, CV, series 1, vol. 243.
125. Miranda, *Humboldt y México* p. 28.
126. Hamill, *The Hidalgo Revolt,* p. 8; and Brading, *Miners and Merchants,* p. 309.
127. Calderón Quijano, ed., *Los virreyes de Nueva España en el reinado de Carlos IV,* 1:32.
128. Francisco Esteve Barba, *Historiografía Indiana* (Madrid: Editorial Gredos, 1964), p. 187.
129. García Panes to Aranda, July 5, 1792, AGI, Estado, leg. 25.
130. Flórez to Antonio Porlier, no. 164, February 26, 1789, AGI, Mexico, leg. 1426; and Revillagigedo to Porlier, no. 29, December 27, 1789, AGI, México, leg. 1465.
131. Pedro Acuña to Revillagigedo, Madrid, August, 1792, and Branciforte to Alange, no. 55, August 29, 1794, AGI, México, leg. 1438. A copy of García Panes's manuscript is filed in the Biblioteca Nacional in Mexico City.

Chapter 9

1. Revillagigedo to Valdés, no. 296, February 9, 1790, AGS, GM, leg. 6959.
2. Antonio de Llano y Villaurrutía to Bucareli, February 1, 1775, AGN, IG, vol. 202-B.
3. Branciforte to Alange, no. 55, September 20, 1794, AGI, México, leg. 1438.
4. Pedro Camuñez to Pascual de Cisneros, August 30, 1777, AGN, IG, vol. 42-B.
5. Proyecto de 1784, AGI, México, leg. 2418.
6. Discurso de Alzate acerca de la población de México, MN, vol. 568.
7. Revillagigedo to Lerena, no. 73, September 26, 1790, AGI, México, leg. 1533.
8. Revillagigedo to Valdés, no. 204, January 11, 1790, AGI, México, leg. 1530.
9. Humboldt, *Political Essay,* I:97.
10. Ibid., IV: 291–98. Also see Fernando Navarro y Noriega, *Memoria sobre la población del reino de Nueva España* (Mexico: Editorial Porrúa, 1954).
11. Cabildo of Mexico to Marquina, July 14, 1800, AGI, México, leg. 1453.
12. Estado reducido de los habitantes de México empadronados en el año de 1790, MN, vol. 335.
13. See Antonio Xavier Pérez y López, *Teatro de la legislación universal de España é Indias,* 28 vols. (Madrid, 1798), XXV:170–280.
14. Proyecto de 1784, AGI, México, leg. 2418.
15. Flórez to Mendinueta, January 11, 1788, AGN, Historia, vol. 249; and Flórez to Valdés, no. 92, January 23, 1788, AGI, México, leg. 1515.
16. Flórez to Ezpeleta, February 24, 1788, AGI, section 11-A, Cuba, leg. 1408.
17. Mendinueta to Flórez, January 19, 1788, AGN, Historia, vol. 249.
18. Gorostiza to Beven, October 7, 1790, AGN, Historia, vol. 155.
19. Documentos de revista de inspección del Regimiento Fixo de Infantería de la Corona, July 26, 1788, AGI, México, leg. 1518.
20. Documentos de inspección, July 9, 1790, AGN, Historia, vol. 234.
21. Revillagigedo to Alange, no. 302, August 2, 1791; and Revillagigedo to Alange, no. 177, February 7, 1791, AGS, GM, leg. 6966.
22. Revillagigedo to Alange, no. 1065, November 30, 1793, AGN, CV, series 2, vol. 26.
23. Francisco Xavier de Viana, *Diario de viaje,* 2 vols. (Montevideo: Ministerio de Instrucción Pública, 1958), I: 19.
24. Ibid., I:286.

25. Tomás Rodríguez de Biedma to Revillagigedo, March 6, 1793, AGN, Historia, vol. 258; and Case of Juan de Vega Puertas, 1791, AGN, Historia, vol. 241.
26. Orders of Colonel José Manuel de Alava, November 27, 1789, AGN, Historia, vol. 257.
27. Solicitud de Juan de Arellano, October, 1798, and Azanza to the *corregidor* of Coyoacán, March 13, 1799, AGN, IG, vol. 392-A.
28. Establecimiento de banderas de reclutas, November 27, 1789, AGN, Historia, vol. 257.
29. Report of Pedro de Alonso, May 8, 1799, AGN, IG, vol. 197-A.
30. Juan de Villalba y Velázquez to Flórez, February 7, 1788, AGN, Historia, vol. 255.
31. Case of Mariano Sánchez, 1790, AGN, Historia, vol. 233.
32. Case of Carlos Almaraz, 1788, AGN, Historia, vol. 237.
33. Marquina to tribunals and magistrates in Mexico City, February 4, 1801, and Marquina to Flon, January 31, 1801, AGN, IG, vol. 275-B.
34. Flon to Marquina, February 4, 1801, AGN, IG, vol. 275-B.
35. Dictamen del Real Acuerdo, February 6, 1801, and Tribunal del Crimen to Marquina, February 8, 1801, and April 30, 1801, AGN, IG, vol. 275-B.
36. Sobre inutilidad de 5 de los 63 vagos remitidos a Perote, September 8, 1801, AGN, IG, vol. 289-A.
37. Governor of Perote to Lizana, May 3, 1810, AGN, IG, vol. 410-A.
38. Gorostiza to Revillagigedo, April 22, 1790; and Colin M. McLachlan, *Criminal Justice in Eighteenth Century Mexico: A Study of the Acordada* (Berkeley: University of California Press 1974), p. 76.
39. Revistas de inspección, February 26, 1800, AGS, GM, leg. 6981; revista de inspección, Regimiento de Infantería de Nueva España, November 26, 1804, AGI, México, leg. 1468; and Azanza to Alvarez, no. 480, August 30, 1799, AGS, GM, leg. 6980.
40. Reglas que deberán observarse para la formación y alistamiento de las milicias en lo interior del reino, May 29, 1794, AGI, Estado, leg. 22.
41. Testimonio de las diligencias practicadas en el establecimiento de una compañía suelta de milicias, Tetela del Río, 1797, AGN, IG, vol. 185.
42. Cabildo of Mexico to Marquina, October 27, 1800, AGI, México, leg. 1453.
43. Pedro Vicente Ormigo, subdelegate of Huejozingo, to Branciforte, August 1, 1797, AGN, IG, vol. 3-A.
44. Mendinueta to Flórez, November 23, 1787, AGN, Archivo Provisional de Temporalidades, caja 4.
45. Branciforte to the Prince of the Peace, no. 43, March 27, 1796, AGI, Estado, leg. 24.
46. Mora, *México y sus revoluciones,* III:54–55.
47. Branciforte to Alange, March 27, 1796, AGS, GM, leg. 6972.
48. Luis Ortiz de Zárate to Branciforte, November 22, and December 31, 1796, AGN, IG, vol. 3-A.
49. Laguna to Branciforte, July 1, 1796, and Francisco París to Branciforte, July, 1796, AGN, IG, vol. 289-B.
50. Ignacio Patiño to Revillagigedo, May, 1792, AGN, IG, vol. 100-A.
51. Pérez Gálvez to Branciforte, May 13, 1796, AGN, IG, vol. 384-A.
52. Pie de lista, Batallón de Oaxaca, 1796, AGN, IG, vol. 175-A; and Pie de lista, Batallón de Guanajuato, 1796, AGN, IG, vol. 156-B.
53. Flórez to Valdés, no. 144, February 23, 1788, AGI, México, leg. 1515; and Nicolás de Monteagudo to García Dávila, February 23, 1802, AGN, IG, vol. 315-A.
54. Azanza to Alvarez, no. 22, July 27, 1798, AGI, México, leg. 1447.
55. Lejarza to Azanza, February 22, 1799, AGN, IG, vol. 211-B.
56. Report of Lejarza, February 15, 1799, AGN, IG, vol. 147-A.
57. Branciforte to Alvarez, December 31, 1797, AGI, Estado, leg. 26.
58. Sobre la comisión dada a los oficiales nombrados por el perfecto arreglo de dichas compañías y saca de gente por Nueva España y Corona, 1797, AGN, IG, vol. 407-A.

Notes 339

59. Instrucción que debe observar el subdelegado para la creación de compañías sueltas de milicias en el distrito de su jurisdicción, January 7, 1797, AGN, IG, vol. 312-A; and Consul to Branciforte, Tepantitlán, February 4, 1797, AGN, IG, vol. 185.
60. Consul to Branciforte, March 14, 1799, AGN, IG, vol. 185.
61. Consul to Branciforte, April 17, April 23, and May 23, 1797, AGN, IG, vol. 185.
62. Jáuregui to Branciforte, February 16, 1797, AGN, IG, vol. 185.
63. Jáuregui to Captain José de Castro, September 2, 1797, and Testimony of Corporal Campos, November 7, 1797, AGN, IG, vol. 102-B.
64. Testimony of Corporal Mariano Muñoz, November 6, 1797, AGN, IG, vol. 102-B.
65. Testimony of Cayetano Figueroa, January 28, 1798, AGN, IG, vol. 102-B.
66. Testimony of Fernando Labra, November 17, 1797, and Corporal Matías Barrera, November 8, 1797, AGN, IG, vol. 102-B.
67. Testimony of José Mariano Campos, November 6, 1797, and of Figueroa, January 29, 1798, AGN, IG, vol. 102-B.
68. Retana to Branciforte, September 14, 1797, and October 12, 1797, AGN, IG, vol. 102-B.
69. Retana to Branciforte, October 29, 1797, and Report of Pedro Juñón, *oficial real* of Zimapán, October 19, 1797, AGN, IG, vol. 102-B.
70. Solicitud de José Antonio Lascano, Orizaba, August 12, 1797, AGN, IG, vol. 102-B.
71. Solicitud de José Domingo Pasten, San Juan Teotihuacán, October 5, 1797, AGN, IG, vol. 102-B.
72. Solicitud de Pedro Sarmiento, Cuautla Amilpas, 1797, AGN, IG, vol. 102-B.
73. Diputación Territorial de Zimapán to Branciforte, February 1, 1797, and Diputación Territorial de Pachuca to Branciforte, October 18, 1797, AGN, IG, vol. 297-B.
74. Diputación Territorial de Taxco to Branciforte, May 27, 1797, AGN, IG, vol. 297-B.
75. Mendoza to Branciforte, Taxco, January 2, 1798, AGN, IG, vol. 185.
76. Real Tribunal de la Minería to Branciforte, November 8, 1797, AGN, IG, vol. 289-B.
77. Castro to Branciforte, June 7, 1798, AGN, IG, vol. 314-A.
78. Branciforte to the Real Tribunal de la Minería, March 10, 1798, AGN, IG, vol. 289-B; and Branciforte to Alvarez, no. 1000, January 30, 1798, AGS, GM, leg. 6976.
79. Branciforte to Retana, May 4, 1798, AGN, IG, vol. 314-A.
80. Castro to Branciforte, Zimapán, June 7, 1798, AGN, IG, vol. 314-A; and Captain Martín de Medina to Branciforte, February 17, 1798, AGN, IG, vol. 297-B.
81. Castro to Branciforte, June 7, 1798, AGN, IG, vol. 314-A.
82. Ignacio Beye y Cisneros to Branciforte, April 23, 1797, AGN, IG, vol. 185.
83. Caamaño to Cisneros, May 12, 1797, and Caamaño to Branciforte, June, 1797, AGN, IG, vol. 102-B.
84. Landa y Garces to Branciforte, August 23, 1797, and February 10, 1798, AGN, IG, vol. 185.
85. Medina to Branciforte, November 8, 1797, AGN, IG, vol. 102-B.
86. Real Tribunal de la Minería to Iturrigaray, August 27, 1806, and Report of *Auditor de Guerra* Bataller, October 13, 1806, AGN, IG, vol. 297-B.
87. Diputación Territorial de Pachuca to Iturrigaray, October 18, 1807, and Cabezas to the Archbishop of Mexico, December 7, 1807, AGN, IG, vol. 297-B.
88. Pedro Telmo de Landero to Iturrigaray, no. 1594, July 20, 1807, and Antonio del Corral Velasco to the Intendant of Mexico, Taxco, November 28, 1807, AGN, IG, vol. 60-A.
89. Ignacio Muñoz to Iturrigaray, Mextitlán, October 14, 1807, AGN, IG, vol. 402-A. It will be recalled that this subdelegate was one of the worst offenders in the sale of militia exemptions.
90. Corral Velasco to Francisco Manuel de Arce, November 28, 1807, AGN, IG, vol. 60-A.
91. Diputación Territorial de Taxco to Lizana, March 31, 1810, AGN, IG, vol. 410-A.
92. Clavijo to Lizana, March 31, 1810, AGN, IG, vol. 410-A.
93. Pie de lista de la Compañía Suelta de Milicias de Tula, July 12, 1807, AGN, IG, vol. 60-A.

94. Petition of Juan Estevan León, 1807, AGN, IG, vol. 28-A.
95. Petition of Mariano Castro, June, 1807, AGN, IG, vol. 28-A.
96. Castro to Iturrigaray, May 6, 1807, AGN, IG, vol. 402-A; and Castro to Arce, August 7, 1807, AGN, IG, vol. 60-A.
97. Segura and Blanco to Iturrigaray, March 10, 1807, AGN, IG, vol. 402-A.
98. Iturrigaray to Segura and Blanco, April 25, 1807, AGN, IG, vol. 402-A.
99. Petition of Juan Carlos, July, 1807, AGN, IG, vol. 28-A.
100. Petition of Mariano Ignacio de la Luz, 1807, AGN, IG, vol. 28-A.
101. Castro to Iturrigaray, May 21, 1807, AGN, IG, vol. 28-A.
102. Ezequiel de Lizara to Iturrigaray, April 8, 1808, and Report of Iturrigaray, April 25, 1808, AGN, IG, vol. 297-B.
103. Archudía to Iturrigaray, May, 1807, AGN, IG, vol. 28-A.
104. Güemes y Sierra to Iturrigaray, August 30, 1808, AGN, IG, vol. 92-A.
105. López to the Conde de la Cadena, Izucar, April 20, 1807, AGN, IG, vol. 28-A.
106. José Mariano de la Peza y Casas to Branciforte, Actopan, February 10, 1797, AGN, IG, vol. 185.
107. Bustamante, *Suplemento a la Historia,* III:104; and Método que propone el Ayudante Mayor Don Manuel Antonio Mora, October 20, 1781, AGN, IG, vol. 14.
108. Araujo to Iturrigaray, March 31, 1807, AGN, IG, vol. 60-A.
109. Juan Rubio and Pedro de Quevedo to the Conde de la Contramina, February 14, 1797, AGN, IG, vol. 177-B.
110. Gorostiza to Revillagigedo, July 25, 1790, AGN, IG, vol. 66-B.

Chapter 10

1. Philip Henry Stanhope, *Notes of Conversations with the Duke of Wellington* (London, 1889), p. 18.
2. E. Christiansen, *The Origins of Military Power in Spain, 1800–1854* (Oxford: Oxford University Press, 1967), p. 6; and Richard Glover, *Peninsular Preparation: the Reform of the British Army, 1795–1809* (Cambridge: Cambridge University Press, 1963), pp. 176–77.
3. Fernando Villaneuva to Azanza, January 10, 1799, AGN, IG, vol. 157-B.
4. Case of José María Estrada, 1788, AGN, Historia, vol. 225.
5. Revillagigedo to Alange, no. 989, August 31, 1793, AGN, CV, series 2, vol. 26.
6. List of Criminals, 1788, AGN, Historia, vol. 225.
7. Sobre envio de tropa a la Isla de Santo Domingo, 1810, AGN, IG, vol. 71-A.
8. Vicente Nieto to Azanza, Havana, July 2, 1799, AGN, IG, vol. 197-A.
9. Marquina to Juan de Noriega, April 21, 1802, Marquina to Pedro de Alonso, July 1, 1802, and anonymous letter to Marquina, June 25, 1802, AGN, IG, vol. 165-A.
10. Pedro de Basave, guarda mayor de México to Marquina, September 25, 1802, AGN, IG, vol. 165-A.
11. Cayetano Candalejo to Manuel Cuevas y Luyando, February 7, 1803, and Cuevas y Luyando to Iturrigaray, February 8, 1803, AGN, IG, vol. 165-A.
12. Petition of Ignacio Reyes, Tómas Rodríguez, and Francisco Varela (with José Sarías who did not sign) to the cabildo of Querétaro, 1806, AGN, IG, vol. 80.
13. Testimony of various officials, November, 1806, AGN, IG, vol. 80. In the end it was decided to use the barracks rather than private houses or the inns. The local militia tax would pay for damages.
14. José Salinas to Branciforte, Orizaba, August 29, 1797, AGN, IG, vol. 134-B.
15. Declarations of Eusubio Lucas Ximénez, Cayetano Seferino, and others, and report of Cacho Calderón, September 9, 1797, AGN, IG, vol. 134-B.

16. Petitions of Indians, May, 1810, AGN, IG, vol. 410-A.
17. José Antonio Méndez, subdelegate of Apan, to Marquina, May 25, 1801, Audiencia Gobernativa to Urrutía, June 25, 1810, and Urrutía's report, July 11, 1810, AGN, IG, vol. 410-A.
18. Marqués de Torre to Croix, September 7, 1768 AGN, IG, vol. 36-B, and Manuel Antonio Mora to Matías de Gálvez, May 25, 1784, AGN, IG, vol. 14.
19. Petition of María Justa Rey Mires y Areyano, and report of Colonel Gaspar Alvarez de Sotomayor, August 17, 1794, AGN, IG, vol. 282-A.
20. Case of José Santiestevan, 1794, AGN, Historia, vol. 155.
21. Colonel Juan Velázquez to Revillagigedo, October 21, 1793, AGN, IG, vol. 3-A.
22. Nemesio Salcedo to Branciforte, May 27, 1796, AGN, IG, vol. 216-B.
23. Marquina to Caballero, no. 568, March 27, 1802, AGI, México, leg. 1464.
24. Mora to Gálvez, May 25, 1784, AGN, IG, vol. 14.
25. Court-martial of José de Aguirre, January, 1801, AGI, México, leg. 165-A.
26. Iturrigaray to Noriega, August 16, 1804, AGN, IG, vol. 165-A.
27. Vicente Nieto to Pedro Corvalán, January 13, 1791, AGN, IG, vol. 470-A.
28. Sobre haberse contagiado los milicianos de Valladolid con los uniformes de aquellos que murieron en Veracruz de fiebres pútridas, 1801, AGN, Hosp, vol. 54.
29. Bando, prohibiendo se reciban a empeño en las tiendas de pulpería, vinaterías, pulquerías, etc. prendas de vestuario ni armas a la tropa, 1790, AGN, Historia, vol. 234; *Gazeta de México,* 13 April 1790, and Nemesio Salcedo to Branciforte, July 16, 1795, AGN, Historia, vol. 263.
30. Regiment of the Crown, Disposiciones que se necesitan dar, para establecer en este regimiento, un bien sistema de gobierno interior. . . . , Pedro de Alonso, May 9, 1799, AGN, IG, vol. 197-A.
31. Report of surgeons Cayetano Muns and Daniel O'Sullivan of The Regiment of Puebla, January 7, 1790, AGN, Historia, vol. 257.
32. Petition of the chaplains of the Regiment of Puebla, Pedro Peña and Antonio Paulo, January 8, 1790, AGN, Historia, vol. 257.
33. Daniel O'Sullivan to Revillagigedo, September 25, 1793, AGN, IG, vol. 385-A.
34. Juan Nepomuceno de Abreu to Iturrigaray, convento de San Juan de Díos, May 23, 1808, AGN, IG, vol. 356-A.
35. Bernardo Esferesa to Iturrigaray, Hospital Belemitico, May 30, 1808, and Archbishop Francisco Javier Lizana y Beaumont to Iturrigaray, July 2, 1808, AGN, IG, vol. 356-A. Lizana who was responsible for operation of the hospital insisted that it gave excellent care. The negative view is substantiated by an earlier report of Archbishop Alonso Núñez de Haro. See Donald B. Cooper, *Epidemic Disease in Mexico City, 1761–1813* (Austin: University of Texas Press, 1965), p. 58.
36. Francisco Rendón to Branciforte, January 30, 1797, and Branciforte to Rendón, February 6, 1797, AGN, IG, vol. 391-A.
37. José de Torres, convento de San Hipólito, to Rendón, February 8, 1797, and José Hernández to Rendón, convento principal de San Juan de Dios, February 8, 1797, AGN, IG, vol. 391-A.
38. José Manuel de Cevallos to Pedro Garibay, n.d., 1797, AGN, IG, vol. 44-B.
39. Garibay to Rendón, July 13, 1797, AGN, IG, vol. 134-B.
40. Cevallos to Rendón, July 13, 1797, AGN, IG, vol. 134-B. There was some suspicion that the hospital pharmacist, José Sánchez, was shortchanging patients. See Rendón to Branciforte, March 12, 1797, AGN, IG, vol. 391-A.
41. Cevallos to Branciforte, September 23, 1797, AGN, IG, vol. 134-B; and Rendón to Branciforte, March 12, 1797, AGN, IG, vol. 391-A. The regiments also paid for clothing, utensils, and straw bedding.
42. Cevallos to Branciforte, October 22, 1797, AGN, IG, vol. 134-B.
43. Branciforte to Francisco Hidalgo, January 27, 1798, AGN, IG, vol. 44-B.

44. Rendón to Iturrigaray, May 30, 1805, AGN, Archivo Provisional, Hospital Militar, caja 2.
45. Pedro de Alonso to Calleja, December 21, 1799, AGS, GM, leg. 6981.
46. Agustín Beven to Branciforte, January, 1796, and Casimiro Montero to Azanza, June 17, 1798, AGN, IG, vol. 315-A.
47. Revillagigedo to Valdés, August 31, 1789, AGI, México, leg. 1531.
48. José María de Zavaleta y Moreno, hospital controller, to Azanza, November 20, 1799, and Zavaleta to the Prince of the Peace, August 4, 1802, AGN, Hosp, vol. 2.
49. AGN, Hosp, vol. 50. Also see Josefina Muriel, *Hospitales de la Nueva España*, 2 vols. (Mexico: Editorial Jus, 1960), II:210–44.
50. García Panes to Branciforte, no. 3724, November 16, 1796, AGN, Historia, vol. 367.
51. Instrucción reservada de Félix Berenguer de Marquina, 1803, AGN, Historia, vol. 282.
52. Azanza to Miguel Costansó, February 26, 1799, AGN, IG, vol. 477-A.
53. Felipe Vivanco to the intendant of Veracruz, May 17, 1799, and reports on Vivanco's proposals, May and June, 1799, AGN, IG, vol. 146-A.
54. Azanza to García Dávila, May 21, 1799, AGN, IG, vol. 147-A.
55. Pedro de Alonso to Azanza, May 15, 1799, AGN, IG, vol. 477-A.
56. García Dávila to Azanza, August 31, 1799, AGN, IG, vol. 477-A.
57. Azanza to Antonio Cornel, no. 663, February 26, 1800, AGI, México, leg. 2473.
58. Pedro de Alonso to García Dávila, Arroyo Moreno, August 2, 1799, AGN, Hosp. vol. 35.
59. Azanza to Cornel, no. 663, February 26, 1800, AGI, México, leg. 2473.
60. García Dávila to Marquina, no. 1865, July 18, 1800, AGN, Hist, vol. 358, and Consulta del Señor governador de Veracruz sobre destino de los galerones que sirvieron a las tropas acantonadas en Arroyo Moreno, May, 1801, AGN, IG, vol. 164.
61. Hospital statistics, 1801, AGN, Archivo Provisional, Hospital Militar, caja 1.
62. Azanza to Cornel, no. 669, February 26, 1800, AGI, México, leg. 2473.
63. Nicolás de Monteagudo to Dávila, August 14, 1799, AGN, IG, vol. 477-A.
64. Vicente María de Muesas to Marquina, October 19, 1802, AGI, México, leg. 1465, and Iturrigaray to Caballero, no. 251, August 27, 1803, AGN, CV, series 1, vol. 215.
65. Gaspar Alvarez de Sotomayor to Revillagigedo, April 29, 1794, AGN, IG, vol. 282-A.
66. Florez to Valdés, no. 91, January 23, 1788, AGI, México, leg. 1515, Revillagigedo to Alange, no. 895, May 29, 1793, AGS, GM, leg. 6966, Revillagigedo to Valdés, no. 1050, June 26, 1789, AGI, México, leg. 1527, and Juan E. Hernández y Dávalos, ed., *Colección de documentos para la historia de la guerra de independencia de México de 1808 a 1821*, 6 vols. (Mexico, 1877–82), I:532.
67. Bando, May 2, 1788, AGN, Historia, vol. 235.
68. Pedro Gorostiza to Revillagigedo, September 13, 1791, AGN, Historia, vol. 246.
69. Rafael Vasco to Pedro de Mendinueta, July 3, 1788, AGN, Hist, vol. 235.
70. Vasco to Mendinueta, June 26, 1788, and August 21, 1788, AGN, Hist, vol. 235.
71. Vasco to Flórez, January 9, 1789, AGN, Hist, vol. 235.
72. Flórez to Valdés, no. 1009, May 27, 1789, AGI, México, leg. 1527.
73. Royal order, November 1, 1789, AGN, Hist, vol. 235.
74. Flórez to Valdés, no. 202, March 23, 1788, AGI, México, leg. 1515, and Flórez to José de Ezpeleta, March 10, 1788, AGI, Section 11-A, Cuba, leg. 1408.
75. Revillagigedo to Alange, no. 308, July 27, 1791, AGN, CV, series 1, vol. 163, and Revillagigedo to Alange, no. 518, March 31, 1792, AGN, CV, series 1, vol. 167.
76. Revillagigedo to Alange, no. 642, July 30, 1792, AGS, GM, leg. 6965.
77. Revillagigedo to Alange, no. 523, March 31, 1792, and Gorostiza to Revillagigedo, October 26, 1790, AGS, GM, leg. 6973.
78. Gorostiza to Revillagigedo, February 21, 1792, AGS, GM, leg. 6973.

79. Revillagigedo to Alange, nos. 1048 and 642, July 30, 1792, AGS, GM, leg. 6965.
80. Notes of the *Consejo Pleno de Guerra,* June 18, 1793, and royal order, September 7, 1793, AGS, GM, leg. 6966.
81. *Gazeta de México,* 24 May 1793; report of the *junta de guerra,* Jalapa, April 3, 1801, AGN, Hist, vol. 358.
82. Governor of Havana to governor of Veracruz, Havana, February 9, 1793, AGI, Section 11-A, Cuba, leg. 1474.
83. Branciforte to Alange, no. 350, August 31, 1795, AGN, CV, series 1, vol. 181.
84. Branciforte to the governor of Havana, July 15, 1795, AGI, Section 11-A, Cuba, leg. 1473. A royal order of September 6, 1796, approved the termination of deportation. See AGS, GM, leg. 6973.
85. Order of Branciforte, June 30, 1796, AGN, IG, vol. 171-A.
86. Revillagigedo to Alange, no. 81, October 27, 1790, AGN, CV, series 1, vol. 159.
87. Cumplimiento a Real Orden de 20 de Abril 1800 sobre que a los desertores de segunda se les destine sin la formalidad de proceso, AGN, IG, vol. 152.
88. Revillagigedo to Alange, no. 281, May 7, 1791, AGI, Mexico, leg. 1298.
89. Report of the Archbishop of Toledo, March 12, 1792, AGI, México, leg. 1298, and Revillagigedo to Alange, no. 813, February 28, 1793, AGI, México, leg. 1437.
90. Farriss, *Crown and Clergy,* pp. 97–98.
91. Real Cédula, April 1, 1797, AGN, IG, vol. 72-A.
92. Revillagigedo to Valdés, no. 642, June 26, 1790, AGI, México, leg. 1539.
93. Marquina to Caballero, no. 686, July 27, 1802, AGI, México, leg. 1464.
94. Marquina to Caballero, no. 540, March 27, 1802, AGI, México, leg. 1464, and Revillagigedo to Alange, no. 145, January 31, 1791, AGN, CV, series 1, vol. 163.
95. Iturrigaray to Caballero, no. 78, April 26, 1803, AGN, CV, series 1, vol. 215.
96. Iturrigaray to Caballero, no. 841, June 26, 1805, AGN, CV, series 1, vol. 225.
97. Branciforte to Alvarez, no. 886, August 28, 1797, AGS, GM, leg. 6976, and Branciforte to the Prince of the Peace, no. 75, April 29, 1798, AGI, Sección de Estado, leg. 27.
98. Alvarez to Branciforte, January 21, 1798, AGN, IG, vol. 158-B.
99. Joaquín Benito Medina y Torres to Branciforte, Córdoba, August 9, 1797, AGN, IG, vol. 49.
100. José Ruiz to Iturrigaray, April 30, 1807, AGN, IG, vol. 402-A.
101. Tómas Rodríguez de Biedma to Branciforte, February 22, 1798, AGN, IG, vol. 49, and Marquina to Cornel, no. 132, October 27, 1800, AGN, CV, series 1, vol. 203.
102. Juan de Noriega to Marquina, February 9, 1801, AGN, IG, vol. 70-B, and monthly statistics, January to September 1801, AGI, México, leg. 1458.
103. Monthly reports, March to August, 1801, AGN, IG, vol. 70-B.
104. Bernardino Bonavía to Iturrigaray, August 9, 1803, AGN, IG, vol. 158-B.
105. Conde de la Cadena (Manuel de Flon) to Carlos de Urrutía, March 29, 1810, AGN, IG, vol. 92-A.
106. Report of Cacho Calderón, March 17, 1795, AGN, IG, vol. 13-B.
107. Proposiciones del ayudante mayor Manuel Antonio de Mora, Vallodolid, May 25, 1784, AGN, IG, vol. 14.
108. Report of Miguel Bataller, February 9, 1805, AGN, IG, vol. 13-B.
109. Feliciano de Pando to Ignacio García Revollo, July 4, 1803, AGN, IG, vol. 50.
110. Ignacio García Revollo to Iturrigaray, July 5, 1803, and report of the administrator of the Mexico City factory, July 8, 1803, AGN, IG, vol. 50.
111. Order of Viceroy Iturrigaray, July 18, 1803, AGN, IG, vol. 50.
112. Court-martial transcript, trial of José Aguirre, 1800–1801, AGI, México, leg. 1456.
113. Court-martial transcript, trial of José Contreras, 1800, AGI, Mexico, leg. 1453.

114. John U. Nef, *War and Human Progress: an Essay on the Rise of Industrial Civilization* (London: Routledge, 1950), p. 307.

Chapter 11

1. Report of Pedro de Alonso, January 13, 1810, AGN, IG, vol. 166-A.
2. Iturrigaray to Cevallos, June 21, 1808, AGI, México, leg. 1320, and *Gazeta de México* 15 (June 9, 1808).
3. Enrique Lafuente Ferrari, *El Virrey Iturrigaray* (Madrid: La semana gráfica, 1941), p. 191.
4. Michael P. Costeloe, *Church Wealth in Mexico: A Study of the "Juzgado de Capellanías" in the Archbishopric of Mexico, 1800–1856* (Cambridge: Cambridge University Press, 1967), p. 111; and Romeo Flores Caballero, *La contrarevolución en la independencia* (Mexico: El Colegio de México, 1969), pp. 28–65.
5. Genaro García, *Documentos,* II:56–59; Hamill, *The Hidalgo Revolt,* p. 95; and Ladd, "The Mexican Nobility," pp. 191–92.
6. Propósitos que se atribuían al virrey de México D. José de Iturrigaray y por los que fue enviado a España, MN, vol. 1429; and Relación de los acontecimientos de Septiembre de 1808, hecha por el Marqués de Casa Alta al Conde de Floridablanca, November 26, 1808, in Genero García, *Documentos,* II: 290.
7. Mora, *México y sus revoluciones,* II:295.
8. Consulado to Iturrigaray, August 6, 1808, in Hernández y Dávalos, *Colección de documentos,* I:510.
9. Iturrigaray to the junta of Seville, September 5, 1808, AGI, México, leg. 1319.
10. Iturrigaray to the junta of Seville, September 6, 1808, AGI, Mexico, leg. 1319.
11. Alamán, *Historia de Méjico* I:234.
12. Propósitos que se atribuían al virrey de México, MN, vol. 1429, and Lafuente Ferrari, *El Virrey Iturrigaray,* pp. 228–44.
13. Bustamante, *Suplemento,* III:237.
14. Genaro García, *Documentos,* II:413; and Jáuregui to Francisco de Saavedra, September 23, 1810, AGI, México, leg. 1319.
15. Iturrigaray to García Dávila, September 9, 1808; García Dávila to Iturrigaray, September 11, 1808; and Garibay to García Dávila, September 17, 1808, AGN, Historia, vol. 48. The rank was awarded in 1809.
16. Garibay to Alcaraz, September 16, 1808, AGN, Historia, vol. 48.
17. Alamán, *Historia de Méjico,* I:257.
18. Oficio del comandante de las tropas acantonadas en Jalapa felicitando a Garibay por haberse encargado del mando del virreinato, September 22, 1808, in Hernández y Dávalos, *Colección de documentos,* I:598.
19. Carta escrita de Nueva York por F.G. a un amigo de Veracruz con fecha de 10 de Noviembre de 1808, AGN, IG, vol. 77.
20. Ibid.
21. Garibay to Alcaraz, September 20, 1808; and Vicente Barros de Alamparte to Garibay, Perote, September 26, 1808, AGN, Historia, vol. 48.
22. Garibay to Francisco de Saavedra, no. 30, September 22, 1808, AGI, México, leg. 1633.
23. Jáuregui to Saavedra, September 23, 1808, AGI, México, leg. 1319.
24. Relación de los acontecimientos de Septiembre, 1808, in Genaro García, *Documentos,* II:285.
25. Ibid., p. 290.
26. Tomás Calderón a nombre de la Real Audiencia pide informes a Juan Martín de Juanmartiñena sobre la conducta de Iturrigaray, October 31, 1808, in Hernández y Dávalos, *Colección de documentos,* I:628.

27. Por orden del Real Acuerdo se pide informe al secretario del virreinato sobre los 5 puntos que se señalan, de la conducta de Iturrigaray, y la contestación, in ibid., p. 624.
28. *Gazeta de México,* August and September 1808.
29. Mining Tribunal to Iturrigaray, August 1, 1808, AGN, Historia, vol. 46.
30. Bustamante, *Suplemento,* III:243.
31. Garibay to Pedro Cevallos, May 12, 1809, AGN, CV, series 1, vol. 241; and Garibay to Cevallos, no. 4, November 13, 1808, AGI, México, leg. 1633.
32. Garibay to Calleja, September 23, 1808, AGN, Historia, vol. 48.
33. Consulado of Mexico to Garibay, September 19, 1808, AGN, Archivo de Hacienda, leg. 663.
34. Conde de la Cadena to Lizana, February 1810, AGN, IG, vol. 200-A.
35. Padre Andrés Bonilla to Garibay, April 6, 1809, and Isidro Sainz de Alfaro to Garibay, April 9, 1809, AGN, Historia, vol. 415.
36. Guillermo Aguirre to Garibay, February 1809, AGI, México, leg. 1472.
37. Representación que dirigió a la Junta de España, Don Gabriel Yermo, November 12, 1808, in Hernández y Dávalos, *Documentos,* I:655–58.
38. Anónimos esparcidos desde Huichapán, 1809, AGI, México, leg. 1472.
39. Carta de Justo Patricio Paiseron, February 5, 1809, AGI, México, leg. 1472.
40. Garibay to Martín Garay, no. 20, June 30, 1809, AGI, México, leg. 1472; and Extracto de la causa instuída contra el Licenciado D. Julían Castillejos, 1809, in Genaro García, *Documentos,* I:101–83.
41. Luis Lozano to José Ignacio Lozano, February 12, 1809, AGI, México, leg. 1472.
42. Julían Carbonel to Julián Rivero, February 20, 1809, AGI, México, leg. 1472.
43. Ibid.
44. Bernardo de Oca to Garibay, May 31, 1809, AGN, IG, vol. 188-B.
45. Francisco Villalba to Garibay, April 7, 1809, and Antonio José de Salazar to Garibay, May 18, 1809, AGN, Historia, vol. 415.
46. Proclama del Virrey Garibay, April 20, 1809, AGN, IG, vol. 276-B.
47. Exhortación del ilustrísimo Señor Obispo de Puebla a sus Diocesanos, October 12, 1808, Bodleian Library, Oxford University, Collection of Spanish Tracts, 1808–1840.
48. Garibay to Cevallos, no. 7, February 20, 1809, AGN, CV, series 1, vol. 241; Hamill, *The Hidalgo Revolt,* p. 103; and Jacques Houdaille, "Gaëtan Souchet D'Alvimart, the Alleged Envoy of Napoleon to Mexico, 1807–1809," *The Americas* 16(1959):109–31.
49. Garibay to Garay, no. 24, June 30, 1809, AGI, México, leg. 1633.
50. Garibay to Benito de Hermida, no. 46, July 16, 1809, AGN, CV, series 1, vol. 241; Farriss, *Crown and Clergy,* pp. 206–9.
51. Alamán, *Historia de Méjico,* I: 300–302.
52. Garibay to Cornel, no. 103, July 17, 1809, AGN, CV, series 1, vol. 240.
53. Lizana to Hermida, no. 13, August 30, 1809, AGI, México, leg. 1472.
54. Lizana to Hermida, no. 17, September 26, 1809, AGI, México, leg. 1321.
55. Mora, *México y sus revoluciones,* II:295–96; and Hamill, *The Hidalgo Revolt,* p. 108.
56. Lizana to Hermida, no. 13, August 30, 1809, AGI, México, leg. 1472.
57. Lizana to Saavedra, no. 33, August 19, 1809, AGI, México, leg. 1473.
58. Abraham López de Lara, "Los denunciantes de la Conspiración de Valladolid en 1809," *Boletín del Archivo General de la Nación,* series two, no. 6 (1965):23.
59. Hamill, *The Hidalgo Revolt,* pp. 97–99.
60. Cuaderno tercero de la causa instruída en Valladolid, December 21, 1809, to May 1810, in Genaro García, *Documentos,* I:340–46.
61. Felipe Díaz de Ortega to the Duque de Berg, July 22, 1808, and Iturrigaray to Díaz de Ortega, July 27, 1808, AGN, Historia, vol. 46.
62. Proclama de Lizana, January 23, 1810, AGI, México, leg. 1321.
63. Sobre el envio de tropa a la Isla de Santo Domingo, 1810, AGN, IG, vol. 71-A.

64. Miguel Domínguez to Lizana, November 11, 1809, and the cabildo of Querétaro to Lizana, November 10, 1809, AGN, IG, vol. 240-A.
65. Ignacio García Revollo to the audiencia, September 1810, AGN, IG, vol. 240-A.
66. Florescano, *Precios del maíz,* p. 179.
67. Cabildo of Silao to Lizana, December 28, 1809, AGN, IG, vol. 158-B.
68. Juan Antonio Riaño to Lizana, January 19, 1810, AGN, IG, vol. 158-B.
69. Cabildo of Guadalajara to Lizana, May 1, 1810, AGN, IG, vol. 410-A.
70. Cabildo of Zacatecas to Lizana, May 8, 1810, AGN, IG, vol. 410-A.
71. Tribunal of the Inquisition to Lizana, February 1, 1810, AGN, IG, vol. 53-B.
72. Letter of Martín de Revilla, Veracruz, April 15, 1810, AGI, section 11-A, Cuba, leg. 1716.
73. Audiencia to the Minister of Gracia y Justicia, no. 10, May, 1810, AGI, México, leg. 1474.
74. Audiencia to the Secretary of State, May 31, 1810, AGI, México, leg. 1474; and Edgar Gabaldón Marquez, *El México virreinal y la "sublevación" de Caracas, 1810* (Caracas: Archivo General de la Nación, 1971), p. 43.
75. Audiencia to Francisco Eguía, Secretary of War, Council of Regency, June 1810, AGN, CV, series 1, vol. 246.
76. Manuel Abad y Queipo, *Colección de los escritos más importantes que en diferentes épocas dirigió al gobierno Don Manuel Abad y Queipo* (Mexico, 1813), p. 126.
77. Ibid., p. 127.
78. Ibid., pp. 155–58.
79. Wilbert H. Timmons, "Los Guadalupes: A Secret Society in the Mexican Revolution for Independence," *HAHR* 30 (1950):457–58.
80. El Licenciado Don Juan Nazario Peimbert propone un arbitrio para la formación de un exército de 200,000 hombres a poco costo, April 13, 1810, AGN, IG, vol. 410-A.
81. Ibid.
82. Dionisio Cano y Montezuma to Lizana, April 27, 1810, AGN, IG, vol. 410-A.
83. Francisco Javier de Venegas to Nicolás María de Sierra, no. 1, September 18, 1810, AGI, México, leg. 1474.

Conclusion

1. Tribunal de la Contaduría to the Council of Regency, November 27, 1810, AGI, México, leg. 1321.
2. Mora, *México y sus revoluciones* II:77.
3. Audiencia to the Council of Regency, AGI, Mexico, leg. 1321.
4. Mora, *México y sus revoluciones* II:239; McAlister, *The "Fuero Militar,"* p. 15; and Charles A. Hale, *Mexican Liberalism in the Age of Mora, 1821–1853* (New Haven: Yale University Press, 1968), p. 141.
5. Pedro de Alonso to Iturrigaray, July 26, 1806, AGN, IG, vol. 294-A.

BIBLIOGRAPHY

A. Primary Sources*

Spain

AGI———Archivo General de Indias, Sevilla.
  Mexico, Audiencia de México, legajos 1293, 1298, 1300, 1319–21, 1426, 1432, 1435–40, 1444–50, 1452–53, 1456–59, 1462–65, 1468, 1471–75, 1510, 1512, 1514–18, 1520–21, 1523–24, 1526–33, 1536–39, 1540, 1541–44, 1603, 1631, 1633–34, 1973, 1975, 1978, 1979, 2418, 2422, 2424–27, 2473.
  Estado, legajos 20–30, 35–41.
  Indiferente General, legajos 662–63, 1565–66, 1885.
  Sección 11-A, Cuba, legajos 1408, 1473–74, 1486–88, 1517-B, 1518-A, 1518-B, 1527, 1708, 1711–12, 1716.
AGS———Archivo General de Simancas
GM———Guerra Moderna, legajos 6955, 6959, 6961, 6963–74, 6976–77, 6979–81, 7011, 7019, 7028, 7270–78.
AHN———Archivo Histórico Nacional, Madrid.
  Estado, legajos 4287–88, 4291.
MN———Museo Naval, Madrid.
  Vols. 149, 280, 315, 317, 335, 568, 1429, 2202.

Mexico

AGN———Archivo General de la Nación.
  Archivo de Hacienda, legajos 663–64.
  Archivo Provisional: Hospitales Militares, caja 1, caja 2.
  Archivo Provisional de Temporalidades, caja 4.
  CV, Correspondencia de los Virreyes, series 1, Vols. 159, 163, 167, 175, 181, 203–4, 207, 210, 215, 225, 229–31, 234, 237, 239, 240–41, 243, 246.
  CV, Correspondencia de los Virreyes, series 2, Vols. 19, 26, 30, 32–34, 36, 38, 41, 50, 52.
  Hist, Historia, Vols. 40, 44, 46, 48, 50, 155, 159, 200, 215, 220, 225–26, 230, 233–35, 237, 241–43, 246, 248–49, 250, 255, 257–58, 261, 263, 282, 326, 358, 361, 367, 413, 415, 428, 521.
  Hosp, Hospitales, Vols. 2, 19, 35–36, 50, 54.
  Infidencias, Vol. 30.
  IG, Indiferente de Guerra, Vols. 10, 14, 19, 35, 49, 50, 77, 80, 93, 98, 152, 164, 185, 3-A, 21-A, 23-A, 28-A, 32-A, 35-A, 42-A, 46-A, 60-A, 61-A, 71-A, 72-A, 92-A, 99-A, 100-A, 103-A, 122-A, 146-A, 147-A, 164-A, 165-A, 166-A, 171-A, 175-A, 176-A, 197-A, 200-A, 224-A, 240-A, 247-A, 270-A, 282-A, 289-A, 294-A, 304-A, 312-A, 314-A, 315-A, 328-A, 331-A, 336-A, 356-A, 358-A, 362-A, 370-A, 374-A, 384-A, 385-A, 386-A, 391-A, 392-A, 396-A, 402-A, 407-A, 410-A, 414-A, 462-A, 470-A, 477-A, 508-A, 532-A, 13-B, 17-B, 30-B, 36-B, 40-B, 42-B, 44-B, 47-B, 53-B, 60-B, 63-B, 66-B, 67-B, 70-B, 87-B, 102-B, 104-B, 126-B, 134-B, 155-B, 156-B, 157-B,

*Only those cited in the text

158-B, 177-B, 188-B, 197-B, 202-B, 205-B, 211-B, 216-B, 275-B, 276-B, 289-B, 297-B, 301-B.

United States

National Archives of the United States, Dispatches from United States Consuls in Havana, 1783–1906, Vol. 1.

B. Unpublished Regulations, Ordinances, and Rules Governing the Army of New Spain.

Reglamento del Monte Pío de Viudas, Huérfanos y Madres de Oficiales Militares Aprobado de S.M. en Real Orden de 20 Abril de 1761, AGN, IG, vol. 23-A.

Instrucción de 1 Agosto 1764 para gobierno y comandancia general de armas é instrucción de las tropas del reino. AGN, IG, vol. 224-A.

Privilegios, obligaciones y orden que deberán observar las milicias de Veracruz, 1767, AGN, IG, vol. 40-B.

Dictamen del Marqués de la Torre, Inspector General de Infantería en punto de milicias del Reino de Nueva España, y otros relativos a su conservación, seguridad, y defensa, October 24, 1768, AGN, IG, vol. 36-B.

Real Declaración de 17 de Junio de 1773 del Monte Pío de Viudas, Huérfanos y Madres de Oficiales Militares y otras Reales Ordenes del mismo tratan, AGN, IG, vol. 23-A.

Plan de defensa de Nueva España por las costas colaterales a Veracruz comprehendidas entre Alvarado y Zempoala, 1775, AGI, México, leg. 2418.

Plan de tropas que se propone para el Reino de Nueva España por Pedro de Gorostiza, 1776, AGI, Indiferente General, leg. 1565.

Reglamento para la tropa de Infantería Veterana Fixa de la Provincia de Yucatán y Campeche, 1778, AGI, Indiferente General, leg. 1885.

Reglamento de los Sueldos Mensuales que el Rey se ha servido señalar a los Oficiales de los Regimientos de Infantería, Caballería, y Dragones, que obtengan su retiro en América, January 17, 1780, AGN, IG, vol. 66-B.

Proyecto Militar de 1784 por Francisco Crespo, AGI, México, leg. 2418.

Reglamento de Sueldos, y Prest asi para la Tropa Veterana de Infantería y Caballería, como para las Milicias de una y otra clase quando se pone sobre las Armas, 1787, AGI, Indiferente General, leg. 662.

Proyecto Militar del Conde de Revillagigedo, no. 296, February 6, 1790, AGS, GM, leg. 6959.

Reglamento que propone para el Cuerpo de Inválidos en el Reino de Nueva España, July 24, 1790, Pedro de Gorostiza, AGN, IG, vol. 66-B.

Reglamento Provisional para el régimen, gobierno y subsistencia de las Milicias de la Frontera de San Luis Colotlán, establecidas con objeto a la defensa interior y exterior de esta Provincia, y la del Nayarit, October 12, 1791, AGS, GM, leg. 6961.

Reglamento y Ordenanza que deben observar los Ministros empleados en los Hospitales que estan establecidos, y se establecen en las Plazas, y asimismo en los que se ofrecieron formar el Exército, cuyo método y régimen manda S.M. se practique con la mayor observancia, para el mejor desempeño de su Real Servicio, 1792, AGN, Hosp, vol. 50.

Reglamento para el régimen y gobierno de las dos Compañías de Infantería ligera de Nueva España, 1792, AGS, GM, leg. 6966.

Reglamento Provisional para el régimen, gobierno, y substancia del Regimiento de Infantería Urbano del Comercio de esta Capital, 1793, AGN, IG, vol. 122-A.

Reglamento Provisional para el Cuerpo de Caballería de la Frontera de la Provincia de Nueva Santander, 1793, AGI, México, leg. 1453.

Reglamento Provisional para el régimen, gobierno y nueva planta de las Compañías de Milicias Mixtas de Seno que comprehende la Provincia de Tampico y Pánuco hasta Río Guazacualco, Costas laterales de Veracruz, 1793, AGN, IG, vol. 21-A.

Reglamento para el régimen, gobierno y nueva planta de las Milicias de Tabasco, 1793, AGI, México, leg. 1453.

Reglas que deberán observarse para la formación y alistamiento de las milicias de lo interior del Reino, 1794, AGN, IG, vol. 407-A.

Reglamento para las Milicias Disciplinadas de Infantería y Dragones del Nuevo Reino de Granada y Provincias agregadas a este Virreinato, 1794, AGI, Indiferente General, leg. 663.

Reglamento formado para el Cuerpo de Inválidos de Nueva España por el Exmo. Señor Marqués de Branciforte, Virrey, Governador y Capitán General consecuencia de Real Orden de 29 de Abril de 1795, AGN, IG, vol. 40-B.

Instrucción para el arreglo del Cuerpo de Lanceros de Veracruz, 1798, AGI, México, leg. 1449.

Bando en que S. M. se ha servido derogar el Fuero Militar concedido a los comerciantes y mineros alistados en los cuerpos de milicias provinciales y urbanos, 1798, AGN, IG, vol. 17-B.

Reglamento del Cuerpo de Inválidos de Nueva España, 1799, AHN, IG, vol. 66-B.

Reglamento de los sueldos, prest y gratificaciones que libres del descuento de inválidos, se han de abonar mensualmente a los Oficiales, Tropa, y fondos de los diferentes Cuerpos de Exército, 1803, AGN, IG, vol. 67-B.

Sobre arbitrios para la planteación y subsistencia del Batallón Urbano de Querétaro, 1810, AGN, IG, vol. 240-A.

C. Bibliographical Aids and Guides to Archives

Carrera Stampa, Manuel. *Archivalia mexicana*. Mexico: UNAM, 1952.

Esteve Barba, Francisco. *Historiografía indiana*. Madrid: Editorial Gredos, 1964.

Gerhard, Peter. *A Guide to the Historical Geography of New Spain*. Cambridge: Cambridge University Press, 1972.

Greenleaf, Richard E., and Michael C. Meyer, eds. *Research in Mexican History: Topics, Methodology, Sources, and a Practical Guide to Field Research*. Lincoln: University of Nebraska Press, 1973.

Handbook of Latin American Studies (1936–). Gainesville: University of Florida Press.

Hojas de servicios de América, catálogo XXII del Archivo de Simancas, Secretaría de Guerra, Siglo XVIII. Valladolid: Patronato Real de Archivos Históricos, 1958.

Indice histórico español (1953–). Barcelona: Centro de Estudios Históricos Internacionales, Universidad de Barcelona.

Millares Carlo, Agustín. *Repertorio bibliográfico de los archivos mexicanos y de los europeos y norteamericanos para la historia de México*. Mexico: Biblioteca Nacional, 1959.

Peña y Cámara, José María de la. *Archivo General de Indias de Sevilla. Guía del visitante*. Madrid: Dirección General de Archivos y Bibliotecas, 1958.

Plaza, Angel de la. *Archivo General de Simancas. Guía del investigador*. Valladolid: Dirección General de Archivos y Bibliotecas, 1962.

Ramos, Roberto. *Bibliografía de la historia de México*. Mexico: Instituto Mexicano de Investigaciones Económicas, 1956.

Secretaría de Guerra y Marina, México. *Apuntes para una bibliografía militar de México, 1536–1936*. Mexico: Secretaría de Guerra y Marina, 1937.

D. Printed Documents and Contemporary Works

Abad y Queipo, Manuel. *Colección de los escritos más importantes que en diferentes épocas dirigió al gobierno Don Manuel Abad y Queipo.* Mexico, 1813.
Ajofrín, Francisco de. *Diario del viaje que hizo a la América en el siglo XVIII,* 2 vols. Mexico: Editorial Porrúa, 1964.
Alamán, Lucas. *Disertaciones sobre la historia de la república mexicana,* 3 vols. Mexico, 1849.
———. *Historia de Méjico desde los primeros movimientos que preparon su independencia en el año de 1808 hasta la época presente,* 5 vols. Mexico, 1849.
Azanza, Miguel José de. *Instrucción reservada que dio el Virrey Don Miguel José de Azanza a su sucesor Don Félix Berenguer de Marquina,* prólogo y notas de Ernesto de la Torre. Mexico: Editorial Jus, 1960.
Bustamante, Carlos María de. *Cuadro histórico de la revolución mexicana,* 3 vols. Mexico: Ediciones de la Comisión Nacional, 1961.
———. *Suplemento a la historia de los tres siglos de México, durante el gobierno español,* escrita por el Padre Andrés Cavo, 3 vols. Mexico, 1836.
"Conjura de los machetes." *Boletín del Archivo General de la Nación* 4(1933):76–86.
Collection of Spanish Tracts in the Bodleian Library, Oxford University, 8 vols.
"El Ejército de Nueva España a fines del siglo XVIII," *Boletín del Archivo General de la Nación* 9(1938):236–75.
Croix, Marqués de. *Instrucción del Virrey Marqués de Croix que deja a su sucesor Antonio María Bucareli,* prólogo y notas de Norman F. Martin. Mexico: Editorial Jus, 1960.
García, Genaro. *Documentos históricos mexicanos, obra conmemorativa del primer centenario de la independencia de México,* 7 vols. México, 1910.
Gemelli Carreri, Juan F. *Viaje a Nueva España,* 2 vols. México: Libro-Mex, 1955.
Gerardo Suárez, Santiago. *Las instituciones militares venezolanas del período hispánico en los archivos.* Caracas: Biblioteca de la Academia Nacional de la Historia, 1969.
———. *El ordenamiento militar de Indias.* Caracas: Biblioteca de la Academia Nacional de la Historia, 1971.
Hernández y Dávalos, Juan E., ed. *Colección de documentos para la historia de la guerra de independencia de México de 1808 a 1821,* 6 vols. Mexico, 1877–82.
Humboldt, Alexander von. *Political Essay on the Kingdom of New Spain,* 4 vols. London, 1811.
Instrucciones que los virreyes de Nueva España dejaron a sus sucesores, 2 vols. Mexico, 1873.
Lerdo de Tejada, Miguel. *Comercio exterior de México desde la conquista hasta hoy.* Mexico, 1853.
López de Lara, Abraham. "Los denunciantes de la conspiración de Valladolid en 1809." *Boletín del Archivo General de la Nación* 1(1965):7–41.
Mier, Fray Servando Teresa de. *Historia de la revolución de Nueva España,* 2 vols. London, 1813.
———. *Memorias,* 2 vols. Mexico: Editorial Porrúa, 1946.
Mora, José María Luis de. *México y sus revoluciones,* 3 vols. Mexico: Editorial Porrúa, 1965.
———. *Obras sueltas.* Mexico: Editorial Porrúa, 1963.
Morfi, Fray Agustín de. *Viaje de Indias y diario del Nuevo México.* Mexico: Bibliófilos Mexicanos, 1935.
Navarro y Noriega, Fernando. *Memoria sobre la población de Nueva España.* Mexico: José Porrúa, 1954.
O'Crouley, Pedro Alonso. *A Description of the Kingdom of New Spain, 1774.* San Francisco: John Howell, 1972.
"La organización del ejército en Nueva España." *Boletín del Archivo General de la Nación* 11 (1940):617–63.
"La organización de milicias provinciales en Nueva España." *Boletín del Archivo General de la Nación* 9(1938):408–38.

Ordenanza general formada de orden de S.M. y mandada imprimir y publicar para el gobierno y instrucción de Intendentes, Subdelegados, y demás empleados en Indias. Madrid, 1803.

Pérez y López, Antonio Xavier. *Teatro de la legislación universal de España é Indias,* 28 vols. Madrid, 1791–98.

Real declaración sobre puntos esenciales de la ordenanza de milicias provinciales de España. Madrid, 1767.

Real ordenanza para el establecimiento é instruccion de Intendentes de Exército y Provincia en el reino de Nueva España. Madrid, 1786.

Reglamento para las milicias de la Isla de Cuba, aprobada por S.M. y mandado que se observen inviolablemente todos sus artículos por Real Cédula expedida en el Pardo a 19 de enero de 1769. Madrid, 1769.

Revillagigedo, Conde de. *Informe sobre las misiones, 1793, é Instrucción reservada al Marqués de Branciforte, 1794.* Mexico: Editorial Jus, 1966.

Rubio Mañé, J. Ignacio. "Don Félix María Calleja del Rey: Actividades anteriores a la guerra de independencia," *Boletín del Archivo General de la Nación,* series two, no. 1 (1960):57–86, 253–97, and 553–81, and no. 2 (1961):79–108.

———. "Don Félix Berenguer de Marquina, Virrey electo de Nueva España, prisionero de los ingleses en Jamaica." *Boletín del Archivo General de la Nación* 30(1959):165–220.

Stanhope, Philip Henry. *Notes of Conversations with the Duke of Wellington.* London, 1889.

Vane, Charles William, Marquess of Londonderry, ed. *Correspondence, Despatches, and other papers of Viscount Castlereagh, Second Marques of Londonderry: Second Series: Military and Miscellaneous,* 12 vols. London, 1848–1853.

Velasco Ceballos, Rómulo. *La administración de D. Frey Antonio María de Bucareli y Ursúa,* 2 vols. Mexico: Talleres Gráficos de la Nación, 1936.

Viana, Francisco Xavier de. *Diario de viaje,* 2 vols. Montevideo: Ministerio de Instrucción Pública, 1958.

Ward, H. G. *Mexico in 1827,* 2 vols. London, 1828.

Wellington, Duke of. *Supplementary Despatches, Correspondence and Memoranda of Field Marshal Arthur, Duke of Wellington,* 15 vols. London, 1858–1872.

Zavala, Lorenzo de. *Obras,* 2 vols. Mexico: Porrúa, 1969.

E. Secondary Works

Aguirre Beltrán, Gonzalo. *La población negra de México, 1519–1810: estudio etnohistórico.* Mexico: Ediciones Fuente Cultural, 1946.

Alden, Dauril. *Royal Government in Colonial Brazil, with Special Reference to the Administration of the Marquis of Lavaradio, Viceroy, 1769–1779.* Berkeley: University of California Press, 1968.

Alessio Robles, Vito. *Acapulco en la historia y en la leyenda.* Mexico: Imprenta Mundial, 1932.

Al'perovich, Moisei S. *Historia de la independencia de México, 1810–1824,* trans. Adolfo Sánchez Vázquez. Mexico: Editorial Grijalbo, 1967.

Anna, Timothy E. "Mexico City during the War of Independence, 1810–1821." Ph.D. diss., Duke University, 1969.

Archer, Christon I. "The Deportation of Barbarian Indians from the Internal Provinces of New Spain, 1789–1810." *The Americas* 29(1973):376–85.

———. "The Key to the Kingdom: The Defense of Veracruz, 1780–1810." *The Americas* 27(1971):426–49.

———. "Pardos, Indians, and the Army of New Spain: Inter-Relationships and Conflicts, 1780–1810." *Journal of Latin American Studies* 6(1974):231–55.

———. "To Serve the King: Military Recruitment in Late Colonial Mexico." *HAHR* 55(1975):226–50.

Arcila Farías, Eduardo. *El siglo ilustrado en América: reformas económicas del siglo XVIII en Nueva España*. Caracas: Ediciones del Ministerio de Educación, 1955.

Arías Divito, Juan Carlos. *Las expediciones científicas españolas durante el siglo XVIII: Expedición botánica de Nueva España*. Madrid: Ediciones Cultura Hispánica, 1968.

Arrangoiz, Francisco de Paula de. *Méjico desde 1808 hasta 1868: relación de los principales acontecimientos que han tenido lugar desde la prisión del Virrey Iturrigaray hasta la caída del segundo empirio,* 4 vols. Madrid, 1871–72.

Arroniz, Joaquín. *Ensayo de una historia de Orizaba*, 2 vols. Mexico: Editorial Citlatépetl, 1959.

Bakewell, P. J. *Silver Mining and Society in Colonial Mexico, Zacatecas, 1546–1700*. Cambridge: Cambridge University Press, 1971.

Barbier, Jacques A. "Elites and Cadres in Bourbon Chile." *HAHR* 52(1972):416–35.

Benson, Nettie, L., ed. *Mexico and the Spanish Cortes, 1810–1822: Eight Essays*. Austin: University of Texas Press, 1966.

Bernstein, Harry. *Origins of Interamerican Interest, 1700–1812* Philadelphia: University of Pennsylvania Press, 1945.

Bobb, Bernard E. *The Viceregency of Antonio María Bucareli in New Spain, 1771–1779*. Austin: University of Texas Press, 1962.

Brading, David A., and Celia Wu. "Population Growth and Crisis: León, 1720–1860." *Journal of Latin American Studies* 5(1973):1–36.

Brading, David A. "Creole Nationalism and Mexican Liberalism." *Journal of Interamerican Studies and World Affairs* 15(1973):139–90.

———. "Los españoles en México hacia 1792." *Historia mexicana* 23(1973):126–44.

———. "Government and Elite in Late Colonial Mexico," *HAHR* 53(1973):389–414.

———. "Grupos étnicos; clases y estructura ocupacional en Guanajuato, 1792." *Historia Mexicana* 21(1972):460–80.

———. *Miners and Merchants in Bourbon Mexico, 1763–1810* (Cambridge: Cambridge University Press, 1971).

Brinckerhoff, Sidney B., and Odie B. Faulk. *Lancers for the King: A Study of the Frontier Military System of New Spain*. Phoenix: Arizona Historical Foundation, 1965.

"British Schemes against Spanish America in 1806." *HAHR* 28(1947):269–78.

Burkholder, Mark A. "From Creole to *Peninsular:* The Transformation of the Audiencia of Lima." *HAHR* 52(1972):395–415.

Calderón Quijano, José Antonio. *Historia de las fortificaciones en Nueva España*. Seville: Publicaciones de la Escuela de Estudios Hispano-Americanos, 1953.

———. "Ingenieros militares en Nueva España." *Anuario de Estudios Americanos* 6(1949):1–71.

———. ed. *Los virreyes de Nueva España en el reinado de Carlos III,* 2 vols. Seville: Publicaciones de la Escuela de Estudios Hispano-Americanos, 1967–68.

———. ed. *Los virreyes de Nueva España en el reinado de Carlos IV,* 2 vols. Seville: Publicaciones de la Escuela de Estudios Hispano-Americanos, 1972.

Campbell, Leon G. "The Changing Racial and Administrative Structure of the Peruvian Military under the Later Bourbons." *The Americas* 33(1975):117–33.

———. "A Colonial Establishment: Creole Domination of the Audiencia of Lima during the Late Eighteenth Century. *HAHR* 52(1972):1:25.

Cartright, F. F. *Disease and History*. London: Hart-Davis 1973.

Casarrubias, Vicente. *Rebeliones indígenas en la Nueva España*. Mexico: Secretaría de Educación Pública, 1963.

Castañeda, Carlos E. "The Corregidor in Spanish American Colonial Administration." *HAHR* 9(1929):446–70.

Christiansen, E. *The Origins of Military Power in Spain, 1800–1854*. Oxford: Oxford University Press, 1967.

Cook, Sherburne F. "The Smallpox Epidemic of 1797 in Mexico." *Bulletin of the History of Medicine* 7(1939):937–69.
Cook, Warren L. *Flood Tide of Empire: Spain and the Pacific Northwest, 1543–1819*. New Haven: Yale University Press, 1973.
Cooper, Donald B. *Epidemic Disease in Mexico City, 1761–1813*. Austin: University of Texas Press, 1965.
Corona Baratech, Carlos. *Revolución y reacción en el reinado de Carlos IV*. Madrid: Ediciones Rialp, 1957.
Costeloe, Michael P. *Church Wealth in Mexico: A Study of the "Juzgado de Capellanías" in the Archbishopric of Mexico*. Cambridge: Cambridge University Press, 1967.
Cotner, Thomas E., and Carlos E. Castañeda. *Essays in Mexican History*. Austin: University of Texas Press, 1958.
Di Tella, Torcuato S. "The Dangerous Classes in Early Nineteenth Century Mexico." *Journal of Latin American Studies* 5(1973):79–105.
Domínguez Ortiz, Antonio. *La sociedad española en el siglo XVIII*. Madrid: Consejo Superior de Investigaciones Científicas, 1955.
Farriss, Nancy M. *Crown and Clergy in Colonial Mexico, 1759–1821: The Crisis of Ecclesiastical Privilege*. London: Athlone Press, 1968.
Faulk, Odie B. *The Last Years of Spanish Texas, 1778–1821*. The Hague: Mouton, 1964.
Feijoo, Rosa. "El tumulto de 1692." *Historia Mexicana* 14(1965):656–79.
Fisher, J. R. *Government and Society in Colonial Peru: The Indendant System, 1784–1814*. London: Athlone Press 1970.
Fisher, Lillian E. *The Background of the Revolution for Mexican Independence*. Boston: The Christopher Publishing House, 1934.
———. *Champion of Reform: Manuel Abad y Queipo*. New York: Library Publisher, 1955.
———. *The Intendant System in Spanish America*. Berkeley: University of California Press, 1929.
Flores Caballero, Romeo. *La contrarevolución en la independencia: los españoles en la vida política, social y económica de México, 1804–1838*. Mexico: El Colegio de México, 1969.
Florescano, Enrique. "El problema agrario en los últimos años del virreinato, 1800–1821." *Historia Mexicana* 20(1971):477–510.
———. *Precios del maíz y crisis agrícolas en México*. Mexico: El Colegio de México, 1969.
Gabaldón Marquez, Edgar. *El México virreinal y la "sublevación" de Caracas, 1810*. Caracas: Archivo General de la Nación, 1971.
García, Genaro. "El plan de independencia de la Nueva España en 1808." *Anales del Museo Nacional de México* (1904): 85–151.
García Martínez, Bernardo. *El marquesado del valle: tres siglos de régimen señorial en Nueva España*. Mexico: El Colegio de México, 1969.
Gerhard, Peter. *México en 1742*. Mexico: Editorial Porrúa, 1962.
Gibson, Charles. *The Aztecs under Spanish Rule: A History of the Indians of the Valley of Mexico, 1519–1810*. Stanford: Stanford University Press, 1964.
———. "Writings on Colonial Mexico." *HAHR* 55(1975):287–323.
Glover, Richard. *Peninsular Preparation: The Reform of the British Army, 1795–1809*. Cambridge: Cambridge University Press, 1963.
Gutiérrez Santos, Daniel. *Historia militar de México, 1325–1810,* 3 vols. Mexico: Ediciones Ateneo, 1961.
Hale, Charles A. *Mexican Liberalism in the Age of Mora, 1821–1853*. New Haven: Yale University Press, 1968.
Hamill, Hugh M. *The Hidalgo Revolt: Prelude to Mexican Independence*. Gainesville: University of Florida Press, 1966.

———. "Royalist Counterinsurgency in the Mexican War for Independence: The Lessons of 1811." *HAHR* 53(1973):470–89.
Hamnett, Brian R. "The Appropriation of Mexican Church Wealth by the Spanish Bourbon Government—the "Consolidación de Vales Reales." *Journal of Latin American Studies* 1(1969):85–113.
———. *Politics and Trade in Southern Mexico, 1750–1821*. Cambridge: Cambridge University Press, 1971.
Haring, Clarence H. *The Spanish Empire in America*. New York: Oxford University Press, 1947.
Harris, Charles H. *A Mexican Family Empire: The Latifundio of the Sánchez Navarros, 1765–1867*. Austin: University of Texas Press, 1975.
Hellwege, Johann. *Die spanischen Provinzialmilizen in 18. Jahrhundert*. Boppard Am Rhein: Harald Boldt Verlag, 1969.
Herr, Richard. *The Eighteenth Century Revolution in Spain*. Princeton: Princeton University Press, 1958.
———. "Good and Evil, and Spain's Rising against Napoleon." In *Ideas in History, Essays Presented to Louis Gottschalk by his Former Students*, edited by Richard Herr. Durham: Duke University Press, 1965.
Houdaille, Jacques. "Gaëten Souchet D'Alvimart, the Alleged Envoy of Napoleon to Mexico, 1807–1809." *The Americas* 16(1959):109–31.
Howe, Walter. *The Mining Guild of New Spain and its Tribunal General, 1770–1821*. Cambridge, Mass.: Harvard University Press, 1949.
Jiménez Rueda, Julio. *Herejías y supersticiones en la Nueva España*. Mexico: Imprenta Universitaria, 1946.
Johnson, John J. *The Military and Society in Latin America*. Stanford: Stanford University Press, 1964.
Juárez Moreno, Juan. *Corsarios y piratas en Veracruz y Campeche*. Seville: Publicaciones de la Escuela de Estudios Hispano-Americanos, 1972.
Juretschke, Hans. *Los afrancesados en la guerra de la independencia*. Madrid: Ediciones Rialp, 1962.
Kahle, Günter. *Militär und Staatsbildung in den Anfängen der Unabängigkeit Mexikos*. Wien: Böhlav Verlag, 1969.
Kaufmann, William W. *British Policy and the Independence of Latin America, 1804–1828*. New Haven: Yale University Press, 1951.
Kuethe, Allan J. "The Status of the Free Pardo in the Disciplined Militia of New Granada." *Journal of Negro History* 36(1971):105–17.
Ladd, Doris Maxine. "The Mexican Nobility at Independence, 1780–1826." Ph.D. diss., Stanford University, 1971.
Lafuente Ferrari, Enrique. *El Virrey Iturrigaray y los orígenes de la independencia de Méjico*. Madrid: La Semana Gráfica, 1941.
Lavrin, Asunción. "The Execution of the Law of *Consolidación* in New Spain: Economic Aims and Results." *HAHR* 53(1973):27–49.
Lay, Bennett. *The Lives of Ellis Bean*. Austin: University of Texas Press, 1960.
Lerdo de Tejada, Miguel, *Apuntes históricos de la heroica ciudad de Veracruz*, 2 vols. Mexico: Secretaría de Educación Pública, 1945.
Lieuwen, Edwin. *Arms and Politics in Latin America*. Rev. ed. New York: Praeger, 1961.
Lockhart, James. "The Social History of Colonial Spanish America: Evolution and Potential." *Latin American Research Review* 7(1972):6–45.
Lynch, John. "British Policy and Spanish America." *Journal of Latin American Studies* 1(1969):1–30.
———. *The Spanish American Revolutions, 1808–1826*. New York: Norton, 1973.
———. *Spanish Colonial Administration, 1782–1810: The Intendant System in the Viceroyalty of Río de la Plata*. London: Athlone Press, 1958.

McAlister, Lyle N. *The "Fuero Militar" in New Spain, 1764-1800.* Gainesville: University of Florida Press, 1957.

———. "Recent Research and Writings on the Role of the Military in Latin America." *Latin American Research Review* 2(1966):5-36.

———. "The Reorganization of the Army in New Spain, 1763-1765." *HAHR* 33(1953):1-32.

———. "Social Structure and Social Change in New Spain." *HAHR* 43(1963):349-70.

McDermott, John F. ed. *The Spanish in the Mississippi Valley, 1762-1804.* Urbana: University of Illinois Press, 1974.

MacLachlin, Colin M. *Criminal Justice in Eighteenth Century Mexico.* Berkeley: University of California Press, 1974.

MacLeod, Murdo J. *Spanish Central America: A Socioeconomic History 1520-1720.* Berkeley: University of California Press, 1973.

Macías, Anna. *Génesis del gobierno constitucional en México, 1808-1821.* Mexico: Secretaría de Educación Pública, 1973.

Madariaga, Salvador. *The Fall of the Spanish American Empire.* London: Macmillan, 1947.

Manning, William R. *The Nootka Sound Controversy.* Washington, 1905.

Martin, Norman F. "La desnudez en la Nueva España del siglo XVIII." *Anuario de Estudios Americanos* 29(1972):24-32.

Miranda, José. *Humboldt y México.* Mexico: UNAM, 1962.

———. *Las ideas y las instituciones políticas mexicanas 1520-1820.* Mexico: Imprenta Universitaria, 1952.

Moore, John P. *The Cabildo in Peru under the Bourbons: A Study in the Decline and Resurgence of Local Government in the Audiencia of Lima, 1700-1824.* Durham: Duke University Press, 1966.

Moorhead, Max. *The Apache Frontier: Jacobo Ugarte and Spanish Indian Relations in Northern New Spain, 1769-1791.* Norman: University of Oklahoma Press, 1968.

Morazzani de Pérez Enciso, Gisela. *La intendencia en España y en América.* Madrid: Imprenta Universitaria, 1966.

Motten, Clement G. *Mexican Silver and the Enlightenment.* Philadelphia: University of Pennsylvania Press, 1950.

Muriel, Josefina. *Hospitales de la Nueva España*, 2 vols. Vol. 1, *Fundaciones del siglo XVI.* Mexico: Editorial Jus, 1956; Vol. 2, *Fundaciones de los siglos XVII y XVIII.* Mexico: Editorial Jus, 1960.

Nava Oteo, Guadalupe. *Cabildos y ayuntamientos de la Nueva España en 1808.* Mexico: Secretaría de Educación Pública, 1973.

Navarro García, Luis. *Intendencias en Indias.* Seville: Escuela de Estudios Hispano-Americanos, 1959.

———. *José de Gálvez y la comandancia general de las Provincias Internas.* Seville: Escuela de Estudios Hispano-Americanos, 1964.

Nef, John U. *War and Human Progress: An Essay on the Rise of Industrial Civilization.* Cambridge, Mass.: Harvard University Press, 1950.

Ocampo, Javier. *Las ideas de un día: el pueblo mexicano ante la consumación de su independencia.* Mexico: El Colegio de México, 1969.

Osborn, Wayne S. "Indian Land Retention in Colonial Metztitlán." *HAHR* 53(1973):217-38.

Pagliaro, Harold E., ed. *Racism in the Eighteenth Century Culture.* Cleveland: Case Western Reserve University, 1973.

Pan-American Institute of Geography and History. *Seminar on Colonial Institutions in the 18th Century.* Mexico: P.A.I.G.H., 1974.

Pares, Richard. *War and Trade in the West Indies, 1739-1763.* Oxford: Oxford University Press, 1936.

Priestley, Herbert I. *José de Gálvez, Visitador General of New Spain 1765-1771.* Berkeley: University of California Press, 1916.

Riva Palacio, Vicente. *México a traves de los siglos,* 5 vols. Barcelona, 1888–1889.
Rivera Cambas, Manuel. *Los gobernantes de México.* Mexico, 1872.
Robertson, William S. *The Life of Miranda,* 2 vols. Chapel Hill: University of North Carolina Press, 1929.
Rubio Mañé, Ignacio. "Síntesis histórica de la vida del II Conde de Revillagigedo, Virrey de Nueva España." *Anuario de Estudios Americanos* 6(1949):451–96.
Rydjord, John. *Foreign Interest in the Independence of New Spain.* Durham: Duke University Press, 1935.
Sánchez Agesta, Luis. *El pensamiento político del despotismo ilustrado.* Madrid: Instituto de Estudios Políticos, 1953.
Santiago Cruz, Francisco. *El Virrey Iturrigaray: Historia de una conspiración.* Mexico: Editorial Jus, 1965.
Sarrailh, Jean. *La España ilustrada de la segunda mitad del siglo XVIII.* Mexico: Fondo de Cultura Económica, 1957.
Schendel, G. *Medicine in Mexico: From Aztec Herbs to Betatrons.* Austin: University of Texas Press, 1968.
Sierra, Catalina. *El nacimiento de México.* Mexico: UNAM, 1960.
Sierra, Justo. *Evolución política del pueblo mexicano.* Mexico, 1900.
Smith, Robert S. "The Institution of the Consulado in New Spain." *HAHR* 24(1944):62–85.
Syrett, David. *The Siege and Capture of Havana, 1762.* London: Navy Records Society, 1970.
Thurman, Michael E. *The Naval Department of San Blas: New Spain's Bastion for Alta California and Nootka, 1767–1798* (Glendale: Arthur Clark Co., 1967).
Timmons, Wilbert H. "Los Guadalupes: A Secret Society in the Mexican Revolution for Independence." *HAHR* 30(1950):453–79.
Velázquez, María del Carmen. *El estado de guerra en Nueva España, 1760–1808.* Mexico: El Colegio de México, 1950.
Vicens Vives, Jaime. *Historia de España y de América,* 4 vols. Barcelona: Editorial Teide, 1957–59.
Villoro, Luis. *La revolución de independencia: Ensayo de interpretación histórica.* Mexico: 1953.
Wolf, Eric R. "The Mexican Bajío in the Eighteenth Century: An Analysis of Cultural Integration." In M. S. Edmonson, *Synoptic Studies of Mexican Culture.* New Orleans: Middle American Research Institute, 1957.
Zamacois, Niceto de. *Historia de Méjico,* 18 vols. Barcelona, 1876–82.

INDEX

Abad y Queipo, Manuel, 296, 297
Abercrombi, Juan de, 42
Acapulco, 3
Acayucan, 9, 28, 94, 96-97, 99
Acordada. *See* law enforcement
Acosta, José María, 131, 132
Aculco, 299
Adams, John, 84
Aguascalientes, 211
Aguirre, Francisco Miguel, 213
Aguirre, Guillermo de, 115, 287, 291
Aguirre, José de, 259, 276
Aguirre, Teodoro Francisco de, 103, 104
Ajofrín, Francisco, 42-43
Alamán, Lucas, 75, 283
Alava, José Manuel, 194, 195
Alberni, Pedro, 196
Alcalá Galiano, Dionisio, 55
alcaldes mayores: corruption of, 18; opposition to militias, 17
Alcaraz, Conde de: formation of militias, 158; marriage and career, 257-58; opponent of Iturrigaray, 282; wealth, 142-43; mentioned, 113, 195, 217
Alcudía, Duque de. *See* Godoy, Manuel
Aljajayucán, 143
Allende, Ignacio de, 222
Almaráz, Carlos, 232
Almoloya, 257
Alonso, Pedro de: career, 196, 203-4; commander at Arroyo Moreno, 266; financial difficulties, 206; military governor of Veracruz, 72, 73-74; mentioned, 54, 279, 296
Altotonga, 127
Alvarado, 9, 97
Alvarez de Sotomayor, Gaspar, 144, 258

Alzate, José Antonio, 149-50, 225
Alzuvide, Jaime, 196
American Revolution, 5, 86, 203
Amiens, Peace of, 59
Andalusia, 30, 295, 296
Angamacutiro, 163
Angulo Guardamino, Lorenzo, 167, 213
Anteparaluzeta, Tomás, 127, 128
Antigua, 48, 267
Anza, Marcelo de, 211
Aranda, Conde de, 29, 32, 157
Aranjuez, 279
Araujo, Juan Antonio de, 253
Arce, Manuel Francisco de, 131
Archudía, José María, 252
Areche, José Antonio, 17-19
Arellano, Juan de, 230
Ario, 240
army. *See* army of operations; defense; desertion; disease; fortifications; *fuero militar;* horses; hospitals; provincial militia brigades; provincial militia officers; provincial militias; recruitment; regular army; regular army officers; regular army soldiers; Urban Regiment of Commerce; weapons
army administration. *See* Audiencia of Mexico; cabildos; census; Consulado of Mexico; intendants; subdelegates; subinspector general
army of operations: cantonments, 44, 153-55; mobility, 39-40, 51-52, 68; pay, 123
Arriaga, Julián de, 13, 16
Arroyo Moreno, 53-54, 63, 69, 240, 266, 267, 275
Asuchitlán, 241
Atongo, 143

357

Atotonilco, 248
Audiencia of Mexico: duties of the *Auditor de Guerra*, 114–16; military role, 107
Azanza, Miguel José de: *afrancesado*, 73; Conspiracy of the Machetes, 103–4; defense policy at Veracruz, 53, 55; mentioned, 50–51, 92, 101, 110, 112, 113, 115, 144, 152, 167, 187, 204, 207, 209, 210, 214–15, 230, 239, 248, 266, 267
Azcárate, Juan Francisco de, 281

Badillo, Mateo, 154
Bailén, 278
Barragán, José Florencio, 289
Barreiro, José, 196
Barrios, Antonio, 200–201
Barrios, Juan María, 200–201
Barros de Alemparte, Vicente, 209, 216
Basle, Treaty of, 6
Bassoco, Antonio de, 186
Bataller y Vasco, Miguel, 114, 115–16
Bejarno y Frías, José María, 82
Benítez Gálvez, Francisco, 102, 103
Berenguer de Marquina, Félix. *See* Marquina, Félix Berenguer de
Bermudo, Rafael, 134
Bernal, Francisco, 291
Beven, Agustín, 195, 200, 201, 221
Beye y Cisneros, Ignacio, 246
Blanco, Francisco, 289
Blanco, Rafael, 258
Blanco, Valdovinos, 250
Bligh, John, 65
Bonaparte, Joseph, 72
Bonaparte, Napoleon, 72, 76, 86, 90, 279, 281, 287, 294, 296
Bonavía, Bernardino, 92–93, 111, 122, 183
Bonifacio, Ignacio, 154
Bonilla, Antonio: career, 195; contraband, 219–20; debts, 207; secretary of New Spain, 108–9; mentioned, 162, 201, 202
Bonilla, Juan Manuel, 196, 202, 220
Borica, Diego, 195
Brading, David, 5, 178, 210
Branciforte, Marqués de: ability to satisfy criollos, 156–57, 158, 183–85; campaign against French residents, 83–84; charged with corruption, 165; commander at Orizaba, 45; militia deferment to mineworkers, 245; opposition to Gorostiza, 108; personality and politics, 34–37; mentioned, 39, 44, 45, 46–47, 48–49, 50, 54, 58–59, 62, 65, 70, 82, 83, 84, 91, 92, 109–10, 112, 115, 120, 122–23, 144, 145, 146, 149, 150, 156, 158, 160, 161, 163, 164–65, 180, 182–84, 198, 203, 205, 207, 210, 232, 240, 241, 243, 258, 264, 272, 274, 276
Britain: military strategy, 3, 67; plans to invade New Spain, 67, 68, 72; mentioned, 4, 6, 34, 37, 44, 45, 62, 77, 80–81, 89, 198, 278
Bucareli, Antonio María: against intendant system, 116; theories on militias, 17; mentioned, 17, 20, 90, 91, 116, 170
Buenos Aires, 6, 67, 72
Burr, Aaron, 86–87
Bustamante, Carlos María de, 252, 282, 285, 292, 293
Bustamante, Juan de, 133
Bustillo, Juan Ignacio, 57

Caballero, José Antonio, 69
Cabezas, Leandro, 248
cabildos: controls over militias, 16–17, 139–40, 158–67; opposition to militias, 145–47, 151–52, 161, 163; relations with other authorities, 136, 141–42, 153–56. *See also* Veracruz
Cabrera, Lorenzo José, 172
Cacho Calderón, Hemeterio: views on the *fuero militar*, 184; mentioned, 115, 183
Cadena, Conde de la. *See* Flon, Manuel
Cádiz, 10, 84, 94, 229, 230, 281, 284, 288, 295, 298
Calapis, José, 216
Calera, Juan Francisco, 213
Calleja, Félix: career, 194, 196, 202–3; commander of the Tenth Brigade, 85, 111; critical of clergy, 219; ordered to Veracruz, 76–77; views on *fuero* disputes, 128; views on militia officers, 165–66, 215–16; mentioned, 79, 100, 110, 191, 192, 198, 214, 236, 286, 296, 299
Campeche, 3, 45, 65–66, 88
Campo de Alange, Marqués del, 32, 34, 81
Canal, Narciso de la, 191, 209, 212, 222
Cano y Moctezuma, Dionisio, 297
Caracas, 116, 296
Carbonel, Julián, 288–89
Carbonera, 143
Carraras, Juan Antonio, 154, 155
Cartagena, 3
Casa Alta, Marqués de, 284, 285
Casa Irujo, Marqués de, 67, 84, 86, 87
Casades, Joaquín, 173
Casa Rul, Conde de. *See* Rul, Diego
Castañeda, José Antonio, 233
Castaneira, Ildefonso, 134
Casteras, Rosalio, 295
Castillejos, Julián, 287–88
Castillo, Antonio, 129

INDEX

Castro, Gregorio Joaquín de, 250, 251
Castro, José de, 245–46
Castro, Mariano, 250
Catalonia, 64
Catholic Church: asylum, 272, 273; danger to society, 18; dominance of plebeians, 93; opposition to militias, 249–50
census: inaccuracy of, 141, 152, 225–26; use by military, 27, 233
Cevallos, Ciriaco: described as traitor, 88; involved in the *Vaillant* incident, 73–76; problems with naval defense, 64–65; resident of New Orleans, 88–89
Cevallos, José Manuel de, 212, 215, 264
Charles III, 3, 4, 29, 106, 204
Charles IV, 6, 32, 72, 279
Chocándiro, 163
Ciría, Marqués de, 167
Cisneros, Pascual de, 17–19, 20, 139, 172, 173–74, 175
civil disorders: caused by poor harvests, 293–94; riots, 1, 12, 73–77, 90; unemployment, 93. *See also* insurrection; criollo versus peninsular
Clavijo, Manuel Antonio, 249
Colla, Joaquín, 187–90, 283
Collado, Juan, 290
Collado, Martín del, 294
Colotlán, 202, 254
commerce: muleteers in, 223; naval blockades of, 56–57, 65; neutrals involved in, 6, 75; suspension of by Iturrigaray, 62–66. *See also* contraband; Consulado of Mexico; Consulado of Veracruz; merchants; repartimientos; Urban Regiment of Commerce
Conejo, José, 150
Consolidation Decree, 280, 289
Conspiracy of the Machetes, 103–4
Consul, Angel, 241
Consulado of Mexico: controls over the Urban Regiment, 174–76, 186–89; *fuero* conflicts with the Urban Regiment, 171–75, 179–81. *See also* Urban Regiment of Commerce
Consulado of Veracruz: critical of naval defense, 49–50, 57; opposition to Iturrigaray, 63, 65, 69–71, 76; origins of members, 50; views on militias, 53, 55–56
contraband: army officers involved in, 219–20; charge against Marquina, 102; traffic at the coasts, 6, 32, 41, 58, 59, 64, 75
Contramina, Conde de, 167, 212
Contreras, José Joaquín, 276
Contreras, Tomás, 132
Córdoba, 26, 40, 44, 116, 124, 152, 263, 275
Cork, Ireland, 72
Corral, Miguel del, 97, 98

Corral Velasco, Antonio del, 249
Cortés, Luis, 256
Cortina, Conde de la, 180
Cosamaloapan, 9, 97
Costansó, Miguel: career, 196, 221; quartermaster general, 123, 153, 156; road engineer, 39; surveys, 44, 51; mentioned, 58, 222, 296
Council of the Indies, 104, 117
Coyoacán, 247
Crespo, Francisco: defense plan, 21–25; ideas on recruitment, 227; proposals to reform Urban Regiment, 176; views on Mexicans, 224
crime: banditry, 91–92; in Guadalajara, 91–92; in Oaxaca, 121; in Puebla, 120. *See also* civil disorders; insurrection
criollo versus peninsular: conspiracies and plots, 102–5, 280–82, 291, 295; divisions, 7, 12–13, 29, 30, 34, 146, 229; in the army, 17, 27, 31, 191–98, 200–201, 227–29; municipal control, 136; overthrow of Iturrigaray, 283–85, 286–87; suspension of animosity in 1810, 299; theory of European dominance, 143; views of viceroys on, 30–31, 36, 156–57, 289
Cristalinas, Manuel, 150
Cristo y Conde, José Antonio del, 116, 130, 281
Croix, Carlos Francisco de, 12, 13
Cruillas, Marqués de, 9, 10–11
Cuautla Amilpas, 247
Cuba, 29, 33, 45, 60, 269–70, 271, 272
Cuernavaca, 247, 251
Cuervo, José María, 220
Cuvillas, Manuel, 209
Cuzamala, 241

D'Alvimart, Gaëten, 78, 290
Dávila, García, 57, 58, 59–60, 61, 70, 76, 77, 78, 195, 199, 222, 281, 282, 284
defense: costs, 9; dangers of colonial armies, 4, 12; imperial strategy, 3–4; plans, 21–24, 29, 32–60
desertion: causes, 46, 233, 267–68; impact of on regular army, 61, 113; by militiamen, 274–75; punishment, 20, 36, 255, 268–74
Díaz de Celía, Francisco, 248
Díaz de Ortega, Felipe, 119, 293
Diez de Bonilla, Mariano, 213
disease: chronic conditions, 14, 150–51, 233, 262; epidemic at Valladolid, 43–44; factor in defense, 2, 48, 51, 55; mineworkers' ailments, 245–46; resistance of pardos to, 54; venereal, 152, 262, 265. *See also* Arroyo Moreno; hospitals; smallpox; Veracruz; yellow fever

Domínguez, Cristóbal, 68
Domínguez, Miguel, 293
Dorantes, Agustín, 131
Douché, Francisco, 12, 15
Durango, 117, 119

Ecala, Tomás, 140
Echarrí, Juan Francisco de, 121–22, 145, 212
El Desengaño del hombre, 84
Eliza, Francisco de, 98–99
Emparán, Miguel de, 156, 196, 202, 221, 287, 291, 296
epidemics. *See* disease; smallpox; yellow fever
Escovedo, Francisco de, 92
Estrada, José María, 254–55
Ezpeleta, José de, 28, 30, 109

Ferdinand VII, 72, 73, 278, 279, 282, 287, 289, 292, 296
Fernández, José Antonio, 129
Fernández Abascal, José, 98–99, 113
Fernández Munilla, Juan, 212, 215
Fernández Solano, Manuel, 213, 281
Fidalgo, Salvador, 99
Figueroa, Cayetano, 242–43
Flon, Manuel de, 59, 110, 119, 123, 196, 232, 286, 296, 299
Florescano, Enrique, 294
Flórez, Manuel Antonio, 21, 24, 25, 26, 27–28, 36, 94, 95, 114, 117, 119, 194, 198, 221, 227, 270
Floridablanca, Conde de, 29, 81
Foncerrada, José Bernardo, 162, 163
Foncerrada, Melchor, 116
fortifications: at Perote, 39; at Veracruz, 39–40, 59, 66–67, 68–69, 72, 78. *See also* Perote; San Juan de Ulúa
France, 5–6, 33, 37, 64, 72, 73, 82, 83–84, 86, 278, 279, 286, 292
French Revolution, 5, 33, 36, 81–82, 83, 198, 226, 278. *See also* revolution
fuero militar: abuses of, 126–27, 220; conflicts with other jurisdictions, 10, 16, 23, 125–26, 127–35, 145–46, 170–75, 179–80, 181–82, 276; controls over, 116; delays judicial process, 218; problems with deserters, 272; rigor of military law, 275–76; role of brigade commanders, 112; used to encourage donations and candidates, 164–65, 183–85, 210, 300

gachupines. *See* criollo versus peninsular
Galicia, 30
Gallegos, Bernardo, 197
Gallo, Juan, 185
Gálvez, Bernardo de, 20, 27, 208
Gálvez, José de: replacement of criollos, 17, 139–40; system of intendants, 116–117;
mentioned, 1, 12, 18, 19, 20, 21, 90, 106, 109, 128, 145, 157, 176, 258
Gálvez, Matías de, 21, 24, 26, 174–75, 180, 181
Gamiz, José, 196
García, Andrés Antonio, 96
García, Juan José, 100–101
García, Manuel de, 202
García Amoroso, Juan, 96
García Conde, Diego, 197, 202
García Panes, Diego: historian, 221–22; interim governor at Veracruz, 47–48, 49; mentioned, 42, 51, 126, 195
García Quintana, Manuel, 213
García Revollo, Ignacio, 111, 144, 196, 209, 222, 256–57
Garibay, Pedro de: career, 204–6; concern about the United States, 89; debts, 113; efforts to pacify Mexico, 289–90; problems with Veracruz, 77–78; viceroy, 281–92; mentioned, 79, 88, 189, 195, 208, 215, 218, 263, 296, 300
Gazeta de México, 43, 68, 69, 72, 279
Godoy, Manuel: scapegoat for Spain's weakness, 6; supports Veracruz merchants, 66; suspension of commerce, 64–65; mentioned, 32–33, 67, 68, 70
Gómez, Guadalupe, 132
González, Francisco, 220–21
González, Manuel, 240
González, Marcos, 213
González Carvajal, Ciriaco, 291
González Retana, José, 243
González Roxo, José, 138
Gordon, J. D. R., 72
Gorostiza, Pedro de: conflicts with Branciforte, 36; death, 36; friend of Revillagigedo, 30; governor-intendant of Veracruz, 108; illness, 34; reform of the army, 177, 180–81, 201–2; plans for defense, 19–20; mentioned, 148, 149, 178, 179, 194, 270–71
Goy, Manuel Ramón de, 211
Grajales, José, 216
Guadalajara, 12, 26, 31, 91, 92, 117, 119, 294
Guanajuato, 12, 18, 26, 30, 90, 92, 117, 119, 120, 138, 140, 158–60, 191, 214, 292, 294, 299
Guango, 163
Guatemala, 270
Güemes y Sierra, Manuel, 252
Gutiérrez de los Ríos, Joaquín, 206, 207, 212, 286

haciendas: horse production in Querétaro, 140–43, 144
Haiti, 67, 81, 301

Havana, 3–4, 16, 20, 27, 33, 45, 52–53, 55, 57, 60, 81, 84, 94, 113, 204, 205, 219, 233, 255, 258, 272, 300
Hernández, Antonio, 197
Hernández, Josefa, 132
Hernández, Nicolás, 132
Hernández, Patricio, 132
Hernández, Rafaela Manuela, 130
Herrera, José María, 295
Hidalgo, Francisco, 263, 279
Hidalgo y Costilla, Miguel, 298, 300
Hierro López, Francisco, 252
Hilano, Juan, 101
horses: for cavalry use, 24, 138, 140–43, 144
hospitals: at cantonments, 263; poor treatment of soldier patients, 261–67; staff, 262; treatment of venereal diseases, 262; at Veracruz, 41–42, 46, 54, 55–56, 265–66
Huamantla, 9
Huexutla, 252
Huichapán, 287
Humboldt, Alexander von, 38, 42, 94, 165, 191, 225–26

Iguala, 249
Indians: head tax, 292, 296–97; molested by soldiers, 257; repartimiento abuses, 18; uprisings, 28, 94–101; use of alcohol, 95–96
insurrection: at Acayucan and Papantla, 28, 94–98; against Iturrigaray, 281, 287–89; fear of, 80, 90, 278, 280; Francisco Benítez Gálvez affair, 102–4; of 1692, 168; Rising of Mariano of Tepic, 98–101; the Valladolid conspiracy, 292–93. *See also* civil disorders; revolution
intendants: army officers as, 118–19; conflicts with the army, 119–22; census duties, 225; intendancy of the army, 123–24, 264; introduction of, 5, 106, 116–19; superintendent, 117–18. *See also* army of operations; repartimiento; subdelegates
Isla del Carmen, 88
Iturbide, Agustín de, 299
Iturrigaray, José de: conflict with Veracruz interests, 64, 67, 69, 70, 76; conspiracy of the gachupines, 77, 189, 281–82, 284; favors criollo interests, 280, 284–85; military strategy, 68, 248–49; opinions about Garibay, 205; mentioned, 61, 62–63, 66, 68, 71, 73, 74, 87, 94, 105, 113–14, 116, 123, 129, 130, 156, 189, 205, 208, 217, 221, 248, 250, 251, 259, 264, 266, 276, 300
Ixtapalapa, 251
Izquierdo, Antonio María, 122
Izúcar, 94, 252

Jabat, Juan, 280
Jacob, William, 67
Jalapa, 37, 39, 40, 43, 44, 45, 58, 59, 78, 90, 116, 123, 124, 152, 154–55, 156, 204, 257, 263, 267, 284, 298
Jamaica, 3, 41, 46, 58, 88, 93, 219
Jáuregui, Manuel Francisco de, 280, 284
Jáuregui, Ramón, 242–43
Junco, Antonio, 119
Junta de Seguridad y Buen Orden, 74–75, 290

Kingston, 41, 219

Labra, Fernando, 242
Laguna, Pedro de: comments on *fuero* disputes, 125–26; opposition to Iturrigaray, 70; problems with Oaxaca militias, 145–47; mentioned, 49, 51, 77
Landa y Garcés, Antonio de la, 247
Landero, Pedro Telmo, 76
Lanuza, José María de, 160
Lanzagorta, Juan de, 213
Las Animas, 143
Lascano, José Antonio, 243
Lasso, José Mariano, 163
Lausel, Jean, 82
Lavin, Antonio, 131–32, 134
law enforcement: Acordada, 90–92; abuses by subdelegates, 128–35; cabildos in, 137–38; tobacco monopoly guard, 94; urban policing, 91–92, 94, 147. *See also fuero militar*
Ledesma, Agustín, 255
León, Estéban, 250
León, Manuel Velázquez de, 285, 291
Lerdo de Tejada, Miguel, 44
Leyra, Ana María de, 156
Lezama, Francisco, 130, 131
Linares, Duque de, 168
Lisa, Francisco, 196
Lizana, Francisco Javier de: plots, 294–96; Valladolid conspiracy, 293; viceroy, 290–91; mentioned, 79, 114, 204, 279
Llano y Villaurrutia, Joaquín de, 16
López de Angulo, Ramón, 86
Louis XVI, 6
Louisiana, 16, 33, 60, 81, 84, 86, 109, 272, 279, 300
Lozano, Pedro, 159, 288
Luna, Francisco de, 167
Luyando, José, 79
Luz, Mariano Ignacio de la, 251

Macali, Juan, 198
Machín, Manuel, 131, 132, 133
Madeira, 67
Madera, José, 120
Madison, James, 88
Málaga, 295

Malaspina, Alejandro, 29, 34, 157
Maling, John, 65
Maneiro, Ignacio, 196
Mangino, Fernando José, 117
Maravatío, 163, 239
Mariano of Tepic, 98–101
Marín, Pedro Andrés, 153, 154
Marquina, Félix Berenguer de: charged with contraband, 102; Conspiracy of the Machetes, 103–4; difficulties with Veracruz, 58; fear of the army, 102; overwork, 112; rising of Mariano of Tepic, 98–101; mentioned, 55, 57, 59, 60, 61, 62, 85, 109, 113, 152, 155, 188, 199, 203–4, 209, 210, 219, 255, 256, 266, 275
Martín, José, 134
Martínez de Irujo, Carlos. *See* Casa Irujo, Marqués de
Martínez de la Lastra, Manuel, 163
Martínez de Lejarza, Manuel, 213, 214, 217, 239
Mateos, Manuel, 133
Maureta de la Barrera, Santiago, 43–44
Mayorga, Martín de, 20, 94, 139
Mazatán, José Luz, 127
Medellín, José Basilio, 127
Medina, Agustín Bernardo de, 210
Medina, Martín de, 247
Medina y Torres, Joaquín Benito de, 150, 212
Méndez, Francisco, 133
Mendinueta, Pedro, 25–26, 27, 109, 140, 227, 270
Mendivil, Antonio, 197
Mendoza, Felipe, 185–86
Mendoza, Fernando de, 244
Menocal, Francisco, 162, 163, 212, 262
Mercado, Antonio, 134
merchants: competition with army for buildings, 156; demands for improved defenses, 47–48, 49–50; fears of invasion, 46; involved in repartimiento, 18; political power of, 53; transport of goods, 40. *See also* commerce; Consulado of Mexico; Consulado of Veracruz; contraband; provincial militias; repartimiento; Urban Regiment of Commerce
Merino, Manuel, 274
Merino, Martín, 18
Merino Moreno, Manuel, 291
Mexico City: difficulties with soldiers in, 269, 275; high cost of living, 252, 260; hospitals, 261–62; police, 59, 93, 139, 253, 255–56, 276; population, 18, 26, 29, 229–30; recruitment in, 147–49, 150, 166, 183, 225–26, 232–33; unrest in, 78, 94, 102, 105, 281–83, 284, 285, 286–87, 288; mentioned, 11, 12, 21, 24, 32, 35, 85, 115, 128, 140, 175, 203, 205, 214, 255, 261–62, 275, 280, 299. *See also* Consulado of Mexico; Urban Regiment of Commerce
Mextitlán, 129–30, 131, 134
Michaus, Angel, 188–89, 221, 283
Michelena, José María de, 292–93
Michoacán, 26, 30, 161
military. *See* army administration; army of operations; defense; desertion; disease; fortifications; *fuero militar;* horses; hospitals; provincial militia brigades; provincial militia officers; provincial militias; recruitment; regular army; regular army officers; regular army soldiers; Urban Regiment of Commerce; weapons
mining industry, 93, 94
mining tribunal: deputation of Oaxaca, 121; militia deferment for mineworkers, 245; opposition to enlistment, 244–45, 248–49
Miramón, Joaquín, 130, 132–33
Miranda, Francisco, 45, 67, 72
miscegenation, 18
Monte de Lobo, 143
Monteagudo, Nicolás de, 54, 194, 197
Montero, Casimiro, 196, 201
Montevideo, 6
Mora, Alexo de la, 163
Mora, José María Luis, 280
Mora, Manuel Antonio, 259, 275
Mora y Peysal, Antonio de, 121–22, 147, 191, 253, 300
Morales, Mariano, 131
Morcillo, José María, 94
Moreno, Vicente, 119
Mosquera, Joaquín: as *auditor de guerra,* 115; Conspiracy of the Machetes, 103; investigates Benítez Gálvez, 102–3; transferred to Caracas, 116
Muesas, Vicente, 203
Muñoz, Ignacio, 129, 130, 131, 132
Muñoz, José, 196, 202
Muñoz, Juan Manuel, 74
Muñoz, Mariano, 242
Músquiz, 85
Murphy, Thomas, 74, 75
Mutiny of Aranjuez, 279

Nacogdoches, 290
Natchitoches, 86
Nava, Vicente, 254
Navarro Caziño, Ignacio, 160
navy: cannon launches at Veracruz, 54, 65, 66; deterioration of warships, 41, 57; weakness, 2, 64–66
Nayarit, 202
New Orleans, 2, 60, 74, 84, 87
Nieto, Vicente, 195, 202, 204, 255, 260
Nolan, Philip, 85–86
Nootka Sound controversy, 81

Noriega, Juan de, 208-9
Norma, Francisco, 196
Nueva Galicia, 203
Nuevo León, 1
Nuevo Santander, 1, 85, 88
Nuñez de Haro, José, 194

Oaxaca, 12, 26, 30, 65, 90-91, 92, 93, 117, 119, 121-22, 145-47, 191, 236, 238
Obeso, José María, 292
Obregón, Ignacio, 160, 191, 211, 212, 215, 281
Oca, Bernardo de, 289
Ojanguren, Antonio, 120
Olivares, Paula Gertrudis, 133
Olla, Félix, 277
Ometepec, 237
Onía, Luis de, 89
Ordenanzas de intendentes, 121-22, 124
Orizaba, 26, 38, 40, 44, 45, 46, 115, 122, 124, 152, 153, 257, 263
Oroz, Diego de, 196
O'Sullivan, Daniel, 262

Pachuca, 244
Paiseron, Justo Patricio, 287, 288
Palacio, Manuel, 287
Pánuco, 12
Papantla, 28, 94, 95-96, 97, 237
Parodi, Manuel, 131-32
Pasten, José Domingo, 243
Pastor, Manuel, 109
Patiño, Ignacio, 237
Pátzcuaro, 12, 138, 163
Peimbert, Juan Nazario, 297
Peñasco, Conde del, 165, 166, 212
peninsulares. *See* criollo versus peninsular
Pérez de Haro, Francisco, 218
Pérez de Lema, Ignacio, 89
Pérez de Tagle, Mariano, 143
Pérez Fernández, Manuel, 172
Pérez Galvez, Antonio, 102, 103, 120-21, 160, 191, 210-11, 212, 222
Pérezcano, Juan José, 171, 173, 176
Perote, 39, 40, 46, 152, 159, 189, 233, 269
Peru, 94
Philippines, 16
Piedras, Andrés de, 220
Pitt, William, 84
Ponce, Pedro, 195
Posada, Joaquín, 195
presidarios, 63-64
Prieto de la Maza, Angel, 213
Prince of the Peace. *See* Godoy, Manuel
provincial militia brigades: conflicts with intendants, 122; functions, 112; organization, 110-11; origins, 108-9
provincial militia officers: absentee commanders, 214-16; donations for rank, 158, 163; ignorance of, 125, 137; relations with regulars, 216
provincial militias: costs of raising, 157; criollo domination of, 16; danger of arming Mexicans, 12, 192; hardships of service, 26, 217, 239-40; incompetence, 94-98; marriage age, 14; misdemeanors, 122; opposition to in 1819, 26, 31, 50, 162, 165, 224, 247; police duty, 147; regular army cadre in, 15, 17, 19, 26, 32, 138, 216; reserve companies, 19, 32; resistance to service with regular units, 52, 53, 240-44; taxes to support, 63-64, 93, 137-38, 140-43, 147, 164; training, 252-53; uniforms, 44, 141. *See also* Urban Regiment of Commerce
Puebla, 12, 18, 24, 29, 39, 102, 117, 119, 140, 152, 232, 233, 258, 285
Puerta, Juan de la, 266
Puerto Rico, 45
purga de jalapa, 131-34
Puruándiro, 163
Puy y Ochea, Francisco del, 154

Querétaro, 12, 137-39, 140-41, 142, 143, 144, 215, 232, 256, 276, 293, 294
Quevedo y Bustamante, Manuel de, 69
Quijada, Pedro, 250

Rancho de la Vega, 143
Ravago, Antonio, 180, 181, 182
Rayas, Marqués de, 287, 289
Real Academia de San Carlos, 21, 221
Real Ordenanza de Milicias Provinciales, 178
rebellion. *See* insurrection
recruitment: abuses, 6, 129-35, 149-50, 152, 241-45, 250-51; anti-Mexican attitudes, 223-24; conflicts with intendants, 119-22; confusions over race, 120-21; of criminals, 227; damages to society and economy, 15, 23, 55-56, 77, 223, 237-38; enlistment bonuses, 227-28; exemptions, 26, 223, 235-36, 245-46, 248-49; of illegal immigrants, 229-30; of Indians and *castas,* 224, 237, 248-49; of militiamen into regular units, 152, 233; of militias, 12, 17, 234-35, 236, 241-44; opposition to, 145-47, 161, 244-45, 247, 248-49, 250; *quintas,* 226; riots against, 90; role of cabildos in, 137; of vagabonds, 232-33. *See also* desertion; disease; yellow fever
regular army: artillery companies, 199; barracks, 47-48, 153-56, 260; commissary, 51; conflicts with civil authorities, 125-26; courts-martial, 114-16, 220-21; negligence in inspections, 113; overseas duty, 33, 45, 53; police functions, 90-93; promotions,

regular army (*continued*),
194, 197; resistance of militiamen to regular army duty, 152, 240–44; Spanish units in New Spain, 10, 15, 22, 27, 227; troop shortages, 52–53. *See also* army administration; *fuero militar*

regular army officers: anti-Mexican attitudes, 4, 14, 223; courts-martial, 276–77; dislike of colonial service, 199; dominance of peninsulares, 192–98; immorality, 218–19, 220; as intendants, 118–19; marriage, 206–10; promotions, 198–99, 200–201; response to the overthrow of Iturrigaray, 283; retirement, 199–201; salary, 206; sale of commissions to, 194, 197–98. *See also fuero militar*

regular army soldiers: crime, 255–58; discipline and punishment, 259–60, 271–72; education, 259; immorality, 254; origins, 228–29, 255; pay, 129; sale of uniforms and weapons, 260–61. *See also* desertion; disease; hospitals; recruitment; yellow fever

Rendón, Francisco, 51, 123–24, 153, 263, 264

Rengel, José. *See* Alcaraz, Conde de

repartimiento: abuses, 18, 122; described, 124; Indian rising against, 94; *purga de jalapa,* 131–34

Revillagigedo, Conde de: attitudes toward Mexicans, 28–29, 229; defense plans, 29; dislike of pardos, 32, 192; ideas on revolution, 29–30, 156–57; on intendant system, 118–19; relations with the cabildo of Mexico City, 148–49; views on criollos in offices, 34; mentioned, 8, 34, 37, 41–42, 81, 82, 91, 107–8, 114, 115, 120, 145, 158, 166, 176–78, 179, 180–81, 182, 184, 186, 192, 194, 200, 201, 202–3, 204, 208, 222, 223, 225–26, 227–29, 240, 262, 271, 273

revolution: concern about in New Spain, 5–6, 29, 81–82, 82–83, 84; propaganda favoring, 81, 84, 88. *See also* French Revolution; insurrection

Reyes, José de los, 200
Riaño, Antonio, 120, 196, 294
Ricardos, Antonio, 14
Richards, Mordecai, 85
Rincón Gallardo, Manuel, 212
Río, Juan del, 161
Ríos, Gaspar de los, 96, 97, 98
Rivascacho, Marqués de, 212
Rivero, Julián, 288–89
Roca, Antonio de la, 218
Rodríguez de Biedma, Tomás, 150–51, 229
Rojas, Manuel, 201
Rollín, Roberto, 197, 202

Romero de Caamaño, Joaquín, 247
Romo, Joaquín, 201
Rubí, Marqués de, 137
Ruiz, Baltasar, 126
Ruiz Calado, José Ignacio, 144
Ruiz Dávalos, Pedro, 139, 140–41, 144, 195, 205, 215, 231
Rul, Diego: donations for militia command, 160, 211, 214; hardships of duty, 217; interests, 214; mentioned, 191, 221, 222

Sabón de Oliveros, Manuel, 96, 97
Sagazurieta, Ambrosio de, 71
Sahagún, Bernardino de, 221
Sainz de Alfaro, Isidro, 287
Salazar, José, 150
Salcedo, Nemesio, 195, 259
Salinas, José, 257
Salinas Medilla, Pedro, 160–61
Salvatierra, 137
San Diego, 267
San José Muro, Antonio, 147
San Juan de Díos, 247
San Juan de Ulúa, 2, 39, 40, 41, 42, 45, 47, 48, 53, 56, 59, 62, 67, 68, 69, 72, 73, 74, 78, 203, 220. *See also* fortifications
San Juan del Río, 12, 139
San Luis Potosí, 12, 16, 26, 77, 85, 90, 92, 94, 100, 110, 117, 138, 142, 165, 166, 236, 285, 288, 293
San Miguel de Perote. *See* Perote; fortifications
San Rafael, 143
Sánchez, José Mariano, 232
Sánchez, Pablo, 195
Santa Bárbara Coapa, 247
Santa María, Manuel de, 91, 128, 181
Santa Rosalita, 143
Santander, 229, 230
Santiago, Conde de, 216
Santiestevan, José, 258
Santo Domingo, 20, 33, 203, 255, 272, 300
Sarmiento, Pedro, 243–44
Sefarino, Cayetano, 257
Segura, Estanislao, 250
Selma, Manuel, 255
Septién, Francisco de, 159, 213
Septién, Pedro Antonio de, 139
Sessé, Martín de, 44
Seven Years' War, 3, 8–9
Seville, 295
Silao, 294
situados, 16
smallpox: epidemic of 1797, 152, 247, 264; in the Provincial Regiment of Mexico, 150; at Veracruz, 46. *See also* disease; hospitals
Solar Iglesias, Antonio del, 141

Someruelos, Marqués de, 60
Sonora, 117, 119
Soto, Juan María, 196
subdelegates: abuses of, 6, 124–25, 128–35; command of reserve companies, 240–44; conflicts with intendants, 122; opposition to militias, 241–45, 249, 250–51; use of Indians for public works, 39. *See also* intendants; repartimiento
Sub-Inspector General, 107, 112, 113, 114. *See also* army administration

Tabasco, 45
Tacuba, 251
Talamantes, Melchor de, 281
Tampico, 12, 88, 203, 218–19
Tangancícuaro, 163
Tarímbaro, 163
Taxco, 244, 248, 249
Tecpan, 297
Tehuacán, 297
Tepa, Conde de, 116–17
Tepantitlán, 241–42
Tepeaca, 288
Tepecuacuilco, 249
Tepic, 98, 99
Tetela del Río, 241
Texcoco, 285
Tizón, Esteban, 95–96
Tlacotalpan, 96, 97
Tlaxcala, 9, 100, 167, 288
Tlazazalca, 163
Toluca, 26, 257, 276
Tomás, José, 243
Tonalá, 295
Torre, Marqués de la, 12, 14, 24–25, 127
Torres, José, 163
Torres, Manuela de, 207
transportation: muleteers, 40, 223; roads, 39, 41
Trasviño, Santiago, 218
Tres Villas, 236
Tribunal del Protomedicato, 44
Trinidad, 6, 45
Troncoso, Bernardo de, 95, 96, 97
Tuchitlán el Grande, 143
Tulancingo, 243, 248
Tupac Amaru Revolt: parallels in Mexico, 94
Tuxtla, 9

United States, 5, 84, 89, 278–79, 286, 293
Urban Regiment of Commerce: duties, 169–70; financing of, 169; opposition of merchants to, 175, 178–79, 185–87; origins of, 168–69; plans to disband, 177, 188–89; use of mercenary replacements in, 170, 175, 177, 179, 180, 186–87, 246–47

Urizar, Tomás, 180, 186
Urrutía, Carlos de, 110, 114, 195, 204, 205, 221, 222, 257–58, 296

Vaamonde Villamil, Manuel, 207
Valcarcel, Domingo, 216–17
Valdés, Antonio, 194
Valenciana, Conde de, 210, 211
Valladolid, 12, 43–44, 91, 117, 119, 140, 160, 161, 292, 293
Valladolid Conspiracy, 292–93
Valle, José Luis, 251
Valle, Rosalía María del, 92
Valle de Santiago, 137
Varela, Pedro de, 184
Vasco, Rafael, 269–70
Vázquez Fernández, Francisco Antonio. *See* Benítez Gálvez, Francisco
Velasco, Francisco, 171, 182
Velázquez, Juan, 161–63, 195, 199, 200, 219, 259
Venegas, Francisco Javier de, 298, 299
Venezuela, 296
Ventura de Taranco, Antonio, 273
Veracruz: assaults against, 8; civilian militias, 53, 63–64, 71; climate, 40–41; fear of by militiamen, 152, 240, 265, 275; garrison, 35, 46–47; opposition to Iturrigaray, 62–66, 77–78; sanitation, 41, 44; shipping, 54–55; *Vaillant* incident, 73–77; mentioned, 2, 3, 10, 11, 12, 14, 35, 38–60, 65, 66, 67, 68–70, 81, 87, 95, 97, 102, 108, 113, 117, 119, 126, 139, 145, 203, 204, 231, 233, 236, 237, 255, 260, 264–66, 267–68, 277, 278, 280, 281, 284, 285, 292, 298, 300, 301. *See also* Consulado of Veracruz; hospitals; yellow fever
Verdía, José, 100
Viana, Francisco de, 229
Vidal, José, 88
Vilamil, Antonio, 197
Villa de la Vega, 229
Villalba, Francisco, 195
Villalba y Angulo, Juan de, 10–12, 14, 118, 137, 225, 259
Villanueva, Fernando, 254
Villar, Pablo del, 182
Volunteers of Ferdinand VII, 285–86, 289
vómito negro. *See* yellow fever

weapons: for civilian militias, 47, 63, 64, 66; poor quality of muskets, 24, 54, 70–71, 96–97, 253; purchase of arms in Jamaica, 88; shortages of, 9
Wellesley, Arthur, Duke of Wellington, 38, 67–68, 72, 301
Wilkinson, James, 87, 88

women: hardships for army wives, 252; involvements with soldiers, 258, 269; marriage to officers, 206-7, 210

Xacona, 163
Xalacingo, 126-27
Xamapa, 267
Xamiltepec, 237
Xilotepec, 274
Ximénez, Eusebio Lúcas, 257
Xochimilco, 246, 247
Xonacatepec, 243

Yberri, Nicolás de, 197, 222
yellow fever: destroys the Arroyo Moreno cantonment, 55, 266-67; epidemics at Veracruz, 9, 39, 41, 44, 46, 59, 61, 78-79, 265; fear of by highlanders, 63-64; mortality at Veracruz, 267; theories about, 44; treatment of, 42-43; mentioned, 53, 268, 300. *See also* disease; hospitals
Yermo, Gabriel de, 190, 251-52, 282, 284, 287
Ynguanzo, Antonio, 127
Yucatán, 117, 119

Zacatecas, 117, 124, 214, 295
Zacualtipán, 133-34
Zamgrano, 143
Zamora, 162-63
Zaragoza, 278
Zárate, Luis de, 146, 277
Zimapán, 92, 242, 243, 244, 245-46, 248
Zitácuaro, 239

LIBRARY OF DAVIDSON COLLEGE